GU01019405

To Dearest Jean

with much love, always

Ros and Michael

xx

1,001
Questions
—— *and* ——
Answers
on Rosh Hashanah
and Yom Kippur

Jeffrey M. Cohen

JASON ARONSON INC.
Northvale, New Jersey
Jerusalem

This book was set in 10 pt. Times Roman by Alabama Book Composition of Deatsville, Alabama.

Library of Congress Cataloging-in-Publication Data

Cohen, Jeffrey M.
  1001 questions and answers on Rosh Hashanah and Yom Kippur / by
Jeffrey M. Cohen.
       p.   cm.
  Includes bibliographical references and indes.
  ISBN 0-7657-9973-1 (alk. paper)
  1. High Holidays—Miscellanea.   I. Title.
BM693.H5C56   1997
296.4'31—dc21   97-13022
                                                            r97

Manufactured in the United States of America. Jason Aronson Inc. offers books and cassettes. For information and catalog write to Jason Aronson Inc., 230 Livingston Street, Northvale, NJ 07647.

To Gloria
with love and gratitude

And to our dear children,
Harvey and Lorraine,
Suzanne and Keith,
Judith and Bobby, Lewis,
and our darling grandchildren:
Joel, Phil, Alexander, Elliot, Abigail,
and Charlotte

Contents

Part II   YOM KIPPUR

Foreword

'Seek God where He is to be found. Call Him when He is close' (Isaiah 55:6). But where is God to be found? When is He close? Judaism's early sages gave a simple answer. The verse, they said, refers to the Ten Days of Penitence between Rosh Hashanah and Yom Kippur.

At no other time of the year are we so conscious of standing personally and directly in the presence of God. The other festivals—Pesach, Shavuot, and Sukkot—speak to us of the history of our people, the exodus from Egypt, the revelation at Sinai, and the long years of wandering through the desert. Celebrating them we become one with our past, our future, and our ideals. We join the great journey of the Jewish people through the centuries. We encounter God in the events of history, a history of which we are a part.

On Rosh Hashanah and Yom Kippur, though, we are caught up in a different kind of drama, at once more personal and more cosmic. For these are days of self-reckoning. God is enthroned in the seat of judgement. From the first notes of the shofar on the New Year through to the 'closing of the gates' at Neilah on the Day of Atonement, the Ten Days describe a vast courtroom drama. A trial is in session. The books of life and death lie open. We are called on to give an account of our deeds. If Pesach begins with questions asked by a child, the Ten Days constitute a series of questions asked by Heaven itself. Where are you? How have you lived? What have you done with the single greatest gift of God, the span of years allocated to each of us on earth? No other questions could be more penetrating, and they give this time of the year its gravity and depth. Truly these are the 'days of awe.'

Behind them lies a view of the universe as revolutionary today as it was millennia ago. It can be summed up in a single sentence: There is justice because there is a judge. The world is more than the endless slow collision of random forces. The events which make up the human experience are something other than 'a tale told by an idiot, full of sound and fury, signifying nothing' (Macbeth, V, v. 26–28). Beneath its distracting surface, the universe is governed by a moral rule. What happens to us is in some way related to what we do. Good is rewarded and evil has no ultimate dominion. It is this idea, even more than monotheism itself, that is Judaism's greatest contribution to human civilization, and its most inspiring challenge. It is this that lies behind Judaism's holiest days.

Humanity has never lacked the idea that we are surrounded by forces larger than ourselves, personified literally or metaphorically as 'gods.' Wind and rain, fertility and death, technology and the environment, the market and the genetic stream: these and others have been seen as impersonal powers, shaping our fate yet indifferent to our intentions. One generation after another has constructed its own version of a deterministic universe governed by chance and necessity. We can seek to escape its decrees by luck or guile, or we can reconcile ourselves to them in world-denying resignation. Such a view of life is ultimately and inescapably tragic.

Against this Judaism stakes its very existence on a view of the world which defies tragedy in the name of morality. The human personality is more than the sum of forces acting upon it. Made as we are in the image of God, we can sense the difference between the world which is and the world which ought to be. Between them lie two things: The human will, expressed in responsibility and choice, and the Divine will, expressed in Torah and mitzvah, teaching and command. The Divine will charts the society we are called on to make; the human will gives us the strength to make it. Since we are free, we can master our inclinations. We can set duty above desire. We will sometimes fail. We err. In the language of Judaism, we sin. But because we are responsible, we can recognize our mistakes, express remorse, make good the harm we may have done, and redirect our lives for the future. And because, at the core of existence, there is not a blind nexus of cause and effect, but God-who-is-a-person and who relates to us as persons, we know that our remorse is accepted, our wrongs forgiven, and our capacity to change and grow affirmed.

These are the beliefs by which Jews have lived and for which, at times, they have been prepared to die. They frame the drama of Rosh Hashanah, Yom Kippur, and the days between. They are summed up in a single word, *teshuvah*, which means both 'repentance,' in the sense of regretting our wrongs and committing ourselves not to repeat them, and 'return,' in the sense of coming back to our proper place in the universe and realigning ourselves with the moral law. *Teshuvah* encapsulates Judaism's radical faith in the freedom and responsibility of mankind under the sovereignty and justice of God. Only a being who is free can repent. Only in a world ruled by God can repentance be accepted. That is why Rosh Hashanah and Yom Kippur, though they are days of judgement, are also days of celebration. For if Judaism is true, we are not the playthings of blind, impersonal forces, nor are our hopes destined to be dashed against the rocks of necessity. From repentance flows forgiveness and the possibility of new beginnings.

Judaism does not teach these truths abstractly. It invites us to live them, entering them annually for ten days through a succession of prayers and rituals and customs, symphonic in their structure, beginning with the warning note of the shofar and culminating in the majestic final movement of Yom Kippur itself, a day on which we divest ourselves of all earthly enjoyments and come as close as we dare to heaven itself. Somehow, most Jews at most times have intuitively sensed that on these days we approach the mystery at the core of Judaism, and throughout the world synagogues are full and laden with an atmosphere of solemnity and introspection.

Neither the prayers nor the rituals emerged all at once. In biblical times the rites of the Day of Atonement were focused on a single individual, the High Priest, who performed them on behalf of all Israel. With the destruction of the Second Temple and the dispersion of the Jewish people, prayer took the place of sacrifice and repentance became democratized, undertaken by each on behalf of all. Successive generations added new layers of detail to the observances, so that in the liturgy and customs of the High Holy Days one can almost trace the history of the Jewish spirit.

That is what Rabbi Jeffrey Cohen has undertaken in this masterful compendium of insights and explanations. As with his previous work, *1001 Questions and Answers on Pesach*, his grasp of the many facets of his subject—law, custom, historical background, and commentary—is awesome, his style erudite but always accessible, his natural gifts as a teacher and communicator displayed on every page. No one, however well versed in the literature, will come away from this work without having learned something new, and without appreciating more fully the intricate detail of these great festivals of the spirit.

At the heart of the Ten Days of Penitence is a simple prayer, 'Write us in the book of life.' Rabbi Cohen has written a book which invites us to understand more fully the life of Judaism as expressed in its holiest days. It is a large work on a large theme. It will enhance our experience of the High Holy Days for many years to come.

Rabbi Jonathan Sacks
Chief Rabbi of the United Hebrew Congregations
of the Commonwealth

Preface

Following in the wake of my *1001 Questions and Answers on Pesach* (1996), I must first express my gratitude to the Almighty for granting me the stamina, persistence, and inspiration to produce this even longer companion volume on Rosh Hashanah and Yom Kippur.

In my Preface to the former work, I indicated that my purpose in writing was "to provide, in one volume, as much information as possible on every aspect of the festival . . . in short, a veritable encyclopedia of Pesach." My purpose in writing this book is identical. The spare time available to the non-student is becoming more and more circumscribed in the rat-race of modern living; and, notwithstanding all the good intentions to read up and prepare oneself fully for the festivals, yet, in reality, those holy days have a habit of arriving more suddenly than anticipated. The result is that people do not grow in knowledge and insight as the cycle of festivals comes around each year, and the Rabbinic maxim, "Whoever does not increase, decreases," is fully confirmed. Hence the necessity for a one-volume distillation of the essentials of every aspect of each festival, which is the objective of this series.

In the Preface to *1001 Questions and Answers on Pesach*, I acknowledged that there were "thousands of books on the background history of the festival, on its talmudic and halackic sources and prescriptions, on its liturgy and commentaries on the Haggadah, on the practicalities of preparing for the festival, on the do's and don'ts of *Yom Tov* observance, and on the unique customs of exotic Jewish communities around the world." Yet, I continued, "it would require a lifetime to wade through them!"

Compared with Pesach, there is only a minute proportion of books on Rosh Hashanah and Yom Kippur. But it would also require a lifetime to wade through them! My hope is that the present volume will provide more than a flavor of their contents, and that it will inspire my readers to further and wider study. Indeed, Rita Berman Frischer, reviewing my Pesach book, states that it "provides much more than everything you've ever wanted to know about the holiday" (*The Jewish Journal*, March 1996, p. 37). I hope that readers of that volume will have had their curiosity so heightened that, in anticipation of the present work, it would be an impossibility to provide more than they would like to know about Rosh Hashanah and Yom Kippur, and that their levels of religious sophistication and expectation will already have grown immeasurably, and will continue to do so with each succeeding volume.

It is important for me to reiterate the ideological approach that I take. I write from the standpoint of an Orthodox rabbi, and I make the assumption that my readers are interested in, and concerned for, the minutiae of the halakhic process. I, nevertheless, do not assume any prior knowledge, and my avowed, and unashamed, purpose is to inspire all my readers, of whatever religious ilk, to greater observance by reawakening their interest in the fascinating, richly textured, colourful and multifaceted panorama of their religious heritage and culture. My purpose is also to de-mystify all the laws and customs by providing a rationale for them and an explanation of their contemporary relevance.

Whereas, in the case of Pesach, there is a preponderance of practical and ritualistic information that is required, the treatment of Rosh Hashanah and Yom Kippur will be weighted more toward the theological and the liturgical. There are complex areas of man's relation to God, as well as to his fellow man, that lie at the basis of these festivals, and which call for definition and elucidation. These cannot be treated clinically, and the inspirational concepts that underlie them are meant to move our hearts toward a closer and deeper relationship with our Father in heaven and our brethren on earth. This must also constitute one of the main objectives of any religious writer. In this context, for the selection on the liturgy of these festivals I have to admit drawing on many of the ideas contained in one of my previous books, *Prayer and Penitence: A Commentary on the High Holy Day Machzor* (Northvale, NJ: Jason Aronson Inc., 1994).

The present age is characterized by a disturbing religious polarization. The religiously-sensitive are becoming bound to their heritage with ever stronger cords, studying their Torah and Talmud with increased assiduity and taking on board more and more observances, while the rest are divesting themselves of any form of religious affiliation or identification. Some, ironically, view this as a favourable development, preferable to the tokenism of an empty "lip-service" to a few meaningless rituals.

I believe that to be a defeatist approach. As long as the religious pulse is beating, however faintly, there is scope for stimulation and resuscitation. And knowledge is one of the main instruments of revival and renewal. Indeed, renewal is the main objective of the festivals of Rosh Hashanah and Yom Kippur with their preoccupation with *teshuvah*, repentance, return. To return means to go back to the state of faith, trust, innocence, and purity with which we all commenced life. In calling us back to repentance each year, these festivals make the point that we must never give up on man, that he is never beyond redemption, and that, in the words of the daily liturgy:

> "O my God, the soul which You gave me is pure; You created it, You formed it, You breathed it into me. You preserve it within me; and You will take it from me, but will restore it to me in the Hereafter. So long as the soul is within me, I will give thanks unto You, O Lord my God and God of my fathers . . ."

The capacity of every soul is infinite. The religious outreach workers in Jewish communities around the world have realized in recent decades just how easy it is to activate those Jewish souls, thirsting for knowledge, spirituality, meaning and direction in life. Even the totally assimilated Jews living in the Former Soviet Union are embracing their spiritual roots once again with joy and enthusiasm, and glorying in the sense of renewal and purpose that this has restored to their lives. The purpose of this book is to provide the knowledge and the insights to speed that voyage of discovery that so many of our co-religionists have already embarked upon, and to aid them in their return and their quest for renewal.

Although the question-and-answer format is tailor made for the treatment of the festival of Pesach, the significance of which, already in the Torah source, is presented in that form, yet we have adopted this genre for the present work, and indeed for the projected remaining volumes on the rest of the festivals. It has been well received, and is appreciated especially because it offers the opportunity to "dip in" to as many or as few questions that one has the time for at any given session. One does not have to wade through pages of information for what one is seeking, and one can easily skip over areas that are not of immediate concern or interest.

While there is a plethora of current works written from the single-dimensional perspective of *drush* (rabbinic exposition), this book seeks to make available the broadest possible range of insights, taking account of the quintessential fruits of modern Jewish scholarship. It traces the origins and development of the two festivals, describing their essential spirit, both as generated in the home as well as the synagogue. It provides a full analysis of the concepts of *teshuvah* (repentance), *tefillah* (prayer), and *tzedakah* (charity), and grapples with the issue of "the three books," or ledgers, that tradition depicts God as inscribing at this time. A special chapter is devoted to man's place in the universe, as perceived by Jewish philosophy. At the practical level, chapters are devoted to a description of Elul, the month of preparation for the High Holy Days, the requisite preparations for the festivals, the do's and don'ts and the home rituals. The structure of each and every service is explained, and a veritable commentary on the entire Rosh Hashanah and Yom Kippur *machzor* is provided. The Rosh Hashanah section concludes with chapters on the ceremony of *Tashlikh*, Hasidic festival practices, and a fascinating account of exotic Rosh Hashanah customs from around the world. Before proceeding to Yom Kippur, there is a chapter on the Fast of Gedaliah, revealing its historical background and contemporary relevance, followed by a section on *Shabbat Shuvah*, the intermediate Sabbath of the Ten Days of Penitence.

Yom Kippur is similarly treated, from the historical, theological, philosophical, existential, and halakhic perspectives. There is a special chapter devoted to the "five abstentions," penetrating to basic principles, and explaining them and all the other laws and customs within the context of their historical and sociological development. The book of Jonah is given special treatment for the important issues of Jewish-gentile relations which it raises. Again, Yom Kippur customs and practices from around the world are recorded, many in the form of first-hand testimony from emigrants from those countries, and two chapters are devoted to the practical laws governing bereavement observances throughout the High Holy Day period. It is a book for college students and their teachers, rabbis, and laymen, and for all who seek to heighten the experience of celebrating these spiritual highlights of the Jewish year.

Acknowledgments

I would like to express my appreciation to several people who have rendered valuable assistance in the research for this book. As always, to my wife, Gloria, for her love and indulgence, and for her encouragement of my rabbinic, pastoral, and literary endeavors; and to my darling children and grandchildren for providing that special measure of pride, joy, and love, which help make every burden light and every challenge attainable.

I thank friends and members of my Stanmore and Canons Park Synagogue in London, and other colleagues who provided reminiscences for the chapter on Rosh Hashanah and Yom Kippur customs around the world, notably Mr. Edward Ezra, Mr. Zaki Dweck, Mrs. Parry Faigenblum, Mr. Percy Gourgey, M.B.E., Rabbi Abraham Levy, Mr. David Moradoff, Mr. Mendel Sudak, and my *mechutanim*: Mr. Ralph Levy and Mr. Max Moryoussef. I also thank the following holders of copyright for their permission to quote: The editors of *Daf Hashavua* (United Synagogue, London); Dvir Publishing House, Tel Aviv; *The Jerusalem Post;* *Judaism* (New York); *The Jewish Chronicle* (London); and Dr. Meir Tamari and the Jewish Association for Business Ethics, London.

I would also like to place on record my appreciation to my son, Harvey, and Mrs. Tamara Selig of Stanmore, for having read the proofs, to Mr. Ezra Kahn and his helpful staff of librarians at my *alma mater*, Jews' College, London, and—*acharon acharon chaviv*—to the Chief Rabbi Jonathan Sacks, for his great encouragement and for once again gracing and enhancing another of my books with a penetrating and illuminating Foreword.

To all the above: *Tavo aleihem berakhah,* thanks and blessings.

I

ROSH HASHANAH

I

The Origin and Development
of the Festival

THE BIBLICAL SOURCE FOR ROSH HASHANAH

1. What is the biblical source for the festival of Rosh Hashanah?

There are three verses that describe the nature of this festival:

And the Lord spoke to Moses, saying: Speak unto the children of Israel, saying: In the seventh month, in the first day of the month, shall be a solemn rest unto you, a memorial proclaimed with the blast of the ram's horn, a holy convocation. You shall do no manner of servile work; and you shall bring an offering made by fire unto the Lord. [Leviticus 23:23-25]

2. But nowhere in the above verses does the term Rosh Hashanah (New Year) occur! Is it not found in the Torah?

No, it is not. It is a later term, found for the first time in the Mishnah (first through third centuries c.e.). In any case, the biblical "New Year" is identified with the month of Nisan, wherein the festival of Pesach is celebrated, and which is referred to in the Torah as "the beginning of months . . . the first month of the year" (Exodus 12:2).

3. Is it not a bit of an anachronism, then, for Judaism to have a second new year in "the seventh month" of the calendar?

It is if one insists on calling it by the popular term "new" year. There is nothing in the Hebrew word *Rosh*, however, to connote "newness"! The Hebrew word *Rosh* (literally, "head") occurs frequently in the Bible in the sense of a "peak."[1] One can have twin peaks! And that is how we might view Nisan and Tishri and their respective festivals of Pesach and Rosh Hashanah.

Another answer to our problem is provided by taking the literal sense of the word *Rosh*, "head," in the sense of "heading," as in a document. The "heading" serves to highlight a new and significant area of attention and discussion. Obviously, one can

---

1. *Numbers* 23:9; *Song of Songs* 4:8, and the place name, *Rosh ha-Nikra.*

have more than one heading in any document. So, one can have more than one
highlight of a year.

If we think about it further, we will realize that the very term "New Year"—
irrespective of when it is celebrated—is an anachronism. After all, how can we
apply the concept of "beginning" to what is, from the point of view of time, nature
and agriculture, an interminable and unbroken *cycle* of seasons? And even if we do
insist on retaining the term, it is obvious that, viewed in the context of man's
partnership with nature, it is also most difficult to define. For, while from the
perspective of man's agricultural expectations and material needs, the spring month
of Nisan would seem to be the obvious candidate for the title of "New Year," being
the time when nature awakens from its slumber to yield its buds and blossoms as the
harbinger of a rich harvest ahead yet an equally strong case could be made for
starting to count nature's year from Tishri (the seventh month). For, after all, the
fields are nourished and ultimately yield their climactic harvest, only as a result of
the blessed autumnal and winter rains that commence from that month!

So we see that the term "New Year" is both inaccurate and imprecise. By
translating it as "peak of the year," we have no difficulty with it being in the seventh
month and with it sharing its crown with Nisan in the first month.

4. Is this problem only a question of semantics then, due to our inaccurate use of the term "New Year," or was it a matter that engaged the attention of our commentators?

It was, indeed, a matter that troubled our commentators. In fact, the great
Talmudist and Bible commentator Nachmanides (Rabbi Moses ben Nachman,
1194–1270) chose to elucidate this precise problem in a famous discourse that he
gave in the city of Acco, on Rosh Hashanah of the year 1268, not long after he had
arrived to take up residence in the holy land.[2]

He points out that until Israel was redeemed from Egypt, the months of the year
were all calculated from the month (later to be called Tishri) in which the sowing
for the following year's harvest begins. That, indeed, is nature's "new year," the
point at which, in accordance with Rabbi Eliezer's teaching, the world was created.[3]
Now, when the Torah subsequently stated, in reference to the month of Nisan, that
"it shall be *unto you* as the beginning of months," this clearly implies that it is not
in reality the first month, but that Israel should henceforth regard it—in addition to
Tishri—as such, in commemoration of the fact that it was in that month that her
redemption from Egyptian bondage was being secured.

Nachmanides then elucidates the Talmudic statement that "the names of the
months came up with us from Babylon,"[4] which suggests that until the return from
Babylon (537 B.C.E.), we simply used the ordinal numbers, "first," "second," "third,"

2. Chavel, C. B., ed. (1978). *Ramban: Writings & Discourses*. New York: Shilo Publishing House,
Vol. I, pp. 246–248.
3. Talmud *Rosh Hashanah* 27a.
4. Talmud Yerushalmi, *Rosh Hashanah* 1:2.

etc., when referring to the months as counted from Nisan. From the period of the return, however, the Babylonian names were employed in order to remind ourselves that we were once exiled in Babylon and God performed a great redemption for us from there. So, the system that employs the Nisan, Iyar, Sivan order is, in effect, a later form of Jewish historical recollection, enshrining within it a dual commemoration of the two great acts of national redemption, from Egyptian and Babylonian exile.

5. We have already referred to the name Rosh Hashanah. By what other names is this festival known?

In our prayers, the term *Yom Ha-Zikaron* ("Day of Memorial") is the one most commonly employed. This is because our prayers are couched in biblical language, and this is the term used in the biblical source: "A *memorial* (*zikhron [teruah]*) proclaimed with the blast of the ram's horn" (Leviticus 23:24).

It also shares with Yom Kippur the title *Yom Ha-Din*, "Day of Judgment." This term is used, for example, in the special *Miy Shebeirakh* blessing for people who have just been called to the Torah.

There is another name for the entire period, covering the "Ten Days of Penitence" and taking in also Yom Kippur. This is referred to as *Yamim Noraim*, the "Days of Awe." In English-speaking countries, the term "High Holy Days" is also popularly employed to describe that entire season.

6. We mentioned above (Question 5) the biblical name *Yom Ha-Zikaron* ("Day of Memorial"). To what does the term "memorial" refer?

In truth, we are unsure of its origin or precise significance. Theodor H. Gaster states that, "A prevalent opinion among scholars is that it refers to a public *commemoration of the dead*; for . . . it is standard belief of primitive peoples that the dead return to rejoin their descendants at the beginning of the year, or are especially called to mind on that occasion. Moreover, the Hebrew word rendered 'memorial' is actually employed in other Semitic languages to denote such a commemoration."[5]

It is of significance in this context that in the weeks immediately preceding Rosh Hashanah it is, in fact, a time-hallowed custom to make a special visit to the graves of parents (*kever avot*). The key liturgical motifs of God "remembering" the covenant with the departed patriarchs of our nation (*Zikhronot*), and "remembering" Israel's deeds to grant reward or punishment, may well have been the logical developments from a (pre-*Sinaitic*) festival of remembrance.

7. So why, then, was the month of Tishri chosen as the time for a Rosh Hashanah festival of repentance and introspection?

We may conjecture that it was chosen because the year's harvest has by then been ingathered and the farmer's preoccupation is now with the uncertainty of whether or

---

5. Gaster, T. H. (1953). *Festivals of the Jewish Year*. New York: William Morrow & Co., p. 108.

not the required rainfall will come to secure next year's prosperity. That sober frame of mind would have been a far more appropriate time for such an introspective festival than the first month of Nisan when sight of his blossoming estates might engender a rather self-satisfied state of mind.

The approach of autumn is also a symbolically appropriate period for introspection, when nature's lush and green foliage begins to wither and die. The reflective man's thoughts—especially those of the ancient Israelite farmers who lived so close to nature—would then turn to consideration of our human destiny and the ultimate fate of all men. The backcloth of nature at that period was ideal, then, for this annual exercise of spiritual stock-taking and repentance.

Another explanation for why Tishri was chosen for a festival of atonement is that, if the world received its final form on Rosh Hashanah, then that was also the day when Adam was created.

Now, according to the Midrash, Adam sinned by eating of the forbidden fruit on the very first day of his life. He also repented and was forgiven on that very day.[6] Hence, the very first Rosh Hashanah of Creation provided a paradigm for repentance, to be taken up on all its subsequent anniversaries.

8. How do we explain the fact that the Torah does not make the slightest mention of this festival as a day of judgment?

Moses Nachmanides views the absence of any biblical explanation of the significance and character of Rosh Hashanah as explicable in terms of both its proximity in time to the Day of Atonement as well as in the fact that the details of the latter follow immediately after the biblical passage that designates the first day of the month (i.e., Rosh Hashanah) as a "holy convocation" (Leviticus 23:24). It was self-evident, therefore, that the Torah intended that convocation to serve as a spiritual preparation for the climactic exercise of atonement 10 days later.[7]

9. Do we have any biblical evidence that Rosh Hashanah was, indeed, from the outset a festival of repentance associated with the divine judgment of man?

Modern research has, indeed, uncovered many elements of early Israelite tradition that formed an intrinsic part of its ritual and theology without necessarily having received any explicit mention in the Bible. Such elements survived for centuries as oral traditions, but only came to be analyzed and recorded in the pages of the Talmud (first through sixth centuries), thus creating the erroneous impression that they were recent innovations of that period.

Now, critical investigation of the book of Psalms has shown that among the various types of psalms composed for special occasions during the period of the monarchy, there is a group called "enthronement psalms,"[8] so called because they

---

6. Talmud *Sanhedrin* 38b; Midrash *Vayikra Rabba* 29:1.

7. Chavel, C. B., ed. (1959–1960). Commentary of *Ramban* on Leviticus 23:24. *Peirushei Ha-Torah LeRabbeinu Moshe ben Nachman*. Jerusalem: Mosad Ha-Rav Kuk.

8. Mowinckel, S. (1962). In *The Psalms in Israel's Worship*. Oxford: Basil Blackwell, pp. 106–192.

were clearly composed as hymns of praise for an annual festival celebrating the enthronement of God as king of all mankind. An analysis of those psalms reveals several references that indubitably foreshadow the key elements of Rosh Hashanah as we know it.

10. Can this be demonstrated beyond any doubt?

Indeed. To do so, we will select three Psalms and isolate the key themes of Rosh Hashanah to which they allude.

Psalm 95:3–7 emphasizes God's attribute as king and Lord of Creation:

> He is a king, greater than
> all other gods.
> In his hand are the depths of the
> earth;
> the heights of the mountains are
> his also.
> The sea is his, for he made it;
> for his hands formed the dry land.
> O come let us worship and bow
> down,
> let us kneel before the Lord, our
> Maker!
> For he is our God,
> and we are the people of his pasture,
> and the sheep of his hand.
> O that today you would hearken to
> his voice.

Psalm 98:4–6, 9, another enthronement Psalm, serves to convey the ecstatic spirit that prevailed at those annual enthronement festivals:

> Make a joyful sound to the Lord,
> all the earth;
> break forth into joyous song and
> sing praises!
> Sing praises to the Lord with the
> lyre,
> with the lyre and the sound of
> melody!
> With trumpets and the sound of the
> horn
> make a joyful noise before the
> King, the Lord!
> . . . before the Lord, for he comes to
> judge the earth.

> He will judge the world with right-
> eousness,
> and the peoples with equity.

Psalm 99:1–4 describes the awe that greets the divine king as he ascends his throne:

> The Lord reigns; let the peoples tremble!
> He sits enthroned upon the cherubim; let
> the earth quake!
> The Lord is great in Zion;
> he is exalted over all peoples.
> Let them praise thy great and terrible
> name!
> Holy is he!
> Mighty king, lover of justice,
> thou hast established equity;
> thou hast executed justice
> and righteousness in Jacob.

A close look at the above Psalms, reflective of the mood and significance of that ancient annual enthronement festival, demonstrates that it was nothing less than the forerunner of our Rosh Hashanah festival. Note the common denominators:

(i) God is described here as Lord of Creation (Psalm 95:4–5), and Rosh Hashanah commemorates the anniversary of the creation of the world.

(ii) It is an occasion that involves worship (95:6).

(iii) God is hailed as "king" (95:3; 98:6; 99:1,4)—a dominant motif of our Rosh Hashanah liturgy.

(iv) It is an occasion that blends both a festive and an awesome mood (95:6; 98:4–6; 99:1).

(v) Kneeling and prostrations are the order of the day (95:6).

(vi) An act of judgment, encompassing not only Israel, but the entire earth, accompanies his accession to the throne (98:9; 99:4). This is a basic concept of Rosh Hashanah.

(vii) The shofar is to be introduced among the regular musical instruments (98:6).

(viii) It is an occasion to declare the sanctity and might of God (95:3; 98:5; 99:2–3).

(ix) God is depicted as Israel's shepherd who exhibits loving care for his flock (95:7). This is a motif that recurs in the liturgy of this period.

(x) Not only Israel, but the entire earth, will acclaim God (99:2–3). This is a dominant liturgical motif, especially in the verses of the *Malkhuyyot* section of the Rosh Hashanah *Musaf Amidah*.

Thus, we see quite clearly that although the Torah does not provide a description of the nature and significance of this festival, it was observed, in all its majesty and with its symbolism well developed, already in the period of King David, the traditional author of the Psalms, but a few hundred years after the giving of the Torah at Mount Sinai.

11. Do we have any other biblical sources that shed light on the celebration of Rosh Hashanah?

In the book of Nehemiah (8:1–8), we have a description of the religious reforms initiated by Ezra the Scribe. Fifty years into the Babylonian captivity, in the year 539 B.C.E., Cyrus the Persian, on having defeated the Babylonians, grants the Jews permission to return to their land and rebuild their Temple.

The "Second Commonwealth" does not get off to a good start, however, neither economically nor spiritually. The Temple is still in ruins, the Sabbath is widely profaned, and intermarriage is rife. In the year 458 B.C.E., Ezra obtains permission to leave Babylon as an official emissary of the Persian King Artaxerxes, with full authority to reorganize religious life in Judaea (See Ezra 7:1–7).

He inaugurates his wide-ranging reforms with a national convention held in front of the Water Gate in Jerusalem. He reads from the Torah to the entire population, "giving the sense and making them understand" (Nehemiah 8:9) how far they had strayed from the law of God. This national convention was held "on the first day of the seventh month" (verse 2), that is on Rosh Hashanah, a festival that was clearly already traditionally designated for repentance, both personal and national. This is reinforced by Ezra's words to the people:

'Today is a sacred day to the Lord your God. Therefore, do not mourn or cry.' For all the people had been weeping while they listened to the words of the law. Then he said to them: 'You may go now; refresh yourselves with rich food and sweet drinks, and send portions of food to all who cannot provide for themselves; for this day is holy to our Lord. Let there be no sadness, for joy in the Lord is your strength.' [Nehemiah 8:9–10]

12. We analyzed above (Question 8) three enthronement Psalms that share many of the characteristics of Rosh Hashanah. Is there any other reference in the Psalms that points unequivocally to the rituals of this festival?

Our sages believed that Psalm 81:4 alludes specifically to Rosh Hashanah. It states, "Sound the shofar for the new month, when the moon is obscured, for the day of our festivity. For it is a statute for Israel, (heralding) judgment by the God of Jacob."

The opening reference is to the shofar of the Rosh Hashanah festival, which occurs on the first of the month of Tishri, being the only "festivity" of Israel's religious calendar to occur on such a date in the month. The moon is, naturally, "obscured" on the first of the month, its horns only just becoming visible, with its size and brightness increasing toward the full moon on the fifteenth of the month.

The reference to "judgment by the God of Israel" points clearly to the main significance of this festival. The need for Israel to prepare for this judgment through acts of contrition is also alluded to in this Psalm: "If only my people would hearken to me, if Israel would walk in my ways . . ." (verse 14).

So confident were the sages that the above psalm-verse "Sound the shofar (*Tik'u bachodesh* shofar . .) . . ." refers to Rosh Hashanah that they prescribed this verse as the daytime *kiddush* (sanctification over wine) on this festival.

A ONE- OR TWO-DAY FESTIVAL?

13. But that Psalm refers to "the _day_ of our festivity," which suggests that originally Rosh Hashanah was but a one-day festival, not two days as universally observed, even in the State of Israel. Has there been a change in the number of days observed?

There is indeed evidence that Rosh Hashanah was observed in ancient Israel on some years as a one-day festival, and on other years over two days. The Talmud[9] expressly refers to this difference between the respective practices of Babylon and Israel on this matter, with the former always celebrating two days and the latter frequently celebrating only one.

Originally, the number of days of Rosh Hashanah was determined in the land of Israel on the usual basis of whether or not witnesses appeared before the court in Jerusalem to testify that they had seen the appearance of the new moon the previous evening. The court at Jerusalem, charged with fixing and consecrating the new moon (and, in the case of Rosh Hashanah, the festival itself, since it corresponded with the appearance of the new moon of Tishri), always sat on the thirtieth day of the month. The court would, in the case of Rosh Hashanah, always declare that day (the thirtieth of Elul) as holy, and the sanctity of Rosh Hashanah would commence from the previous evening. This was done as a precautionary measure, in case witnesses appeared late on that thirtieth day, to testify that they had seen the first appearance of the moon the previous night. The court would then confirm and sanctify that very day as the first day of Tishri and Rosh Hashanah. The following day would then be an ordinary working day, so that there would be only one day of Rosh Hashanah that year. If the court had not declared the thirtieth day as Rosh Hashanah, and the witnesses were delayed, and only appeared late in the day, after the time for offering festival offerings had passed, then it would have meant that the festival day would have passed without being consecrated by the special and proper offerings.

However, if the witnesses failed to appear that day, then the court would declare the previous month a "pregnant month" (*me'ubar*), that is an extended month of 30 days, and they would consequently consecrate the following day as the first of Tishri and Rosh Hashanah. In that situation, the Jerusalemites would have had to

9. Talmud *Beitzah* 5a.

observe two days as Rosh Hashanah, with the precautionary day turning out to have been, with hindsight, unnecessary.

Thus, it is clear that originally there were times when Jerusalem celebrated only one day of Rosh Hashanah, and other times—when witnesses did not appear in time—when they celebrated two days.

The Talmud states that it was with the destruction of the Temple, and the suspension of the sacrificial system, that Rabban Yochanan ben Zaccai decreed that, as there was now no longer any worry about offering the wrong late afternoon sacrifice, the court could sit until nightfall to receive the testimony of witnesses to the appearance of the new moon, and there was no longer any need, therefore, to observe two festival days as a precaution. From that time onward, the land of Israel reverted to its original practice of observing but one day of Rosh Hashanah. Thus, even if the witnesses arrived late that day, the court would declare that day as the first day of Elul, that is, Rosh Hashanah. If no witnesses appeared, then they would declare the following day (only) as the holy day.

14. That arrangement, of witnesses testifying in Jerusalem, was clearly satisfactory as a method of informing the inhabitants of the capital, but how did the rest of Israel and the diaspora communities know which day to celebrate as the festival day?

The Mishnah tells us precisely how that information was communicated further afield, by means of a series of fire stations that swiftly passed the signal across Israel and eastward to the Babylonian diaspora:

> What was the arrangement for the torch lighting? They would bring long cedar wood poles, reeds and oily wood, together with strands of flax, and tie them together with a cord. Someone would then be deputed to carry them to the designated mountain top. He would set them alight, and wave the torch to and fro, up and down, until he saw his fellow torch bearer doing likewise on the summit of the second mountain top. That method of signalling was continued across subsequent mountains.[10]

15. Do we have any idea where those fire stations were situated?

The Mishnah is very thorough. Having been produced by Rabbi Judah the Prince over a century after the destruction of the Temple (70 c.e.), the need to preserve those traditions was keenly realized:

> And from where did they light the torches? From the Mount of Olives to Sarteva; from Sarteva to Grofina; from Grofina to Chavran; from Chavran to Beit Biltin. The chain of fire stations ended there, and they would not move

---

10. Mishnah *Rosh Hashanah* 2:3.

from there, but would wave the torch to and fro, up and down, until the entire diaspora was spread out like a mass of fire.[11]

16. But could the entire diaspora communities possibly be linked up in this way?

Definitely not. The Jewish diaspora at the time of the second Temple encompassed large communities in Egypt and Syria, in the important cities of Asia Minor, in Cyprus and Crete, in Greece and Macedonia. Jews began arriving in Rome in the second century B.C.E., from where they spread to other cities of Italy, and even to Rome's western provinces of Gaul, Spain, and Africa.[12]

Thus, the reference in the Mishnah to "the entire diaspora" being lit up refers exclusively to the Babylonian communities, about 600 miles east of the Holy Land. Babylon was unique, after Palestine, for its autonomy and strong organization, under the supreme authority of a hereditary *Resh Galuta* or *Exilarch* who claimed descent from the royal house of David. Hence, the calendrical information flashed to Babylon by means of the fire signals would be utilized promptly in order to regulate religious life there. This was not the situation, however, in the other far-flung communities of the dispersion. Hence, the restricted direction in which notice of the particular day of the new moon, or Rosh Hashanah, was communicated.

17. For how long was the practice of fire signals continued?

The Mishnah is unclear, stating merely that, "At first they would light torches, but from the time when the Cutheans ruined (this system of communication), they instituted the sending out of messengers (to inform the wider communities)."[13]

18. Who were the Cutheans, and why should they have wished to interfere with Jewish religious practice?

Cutheans is another name for the Samaritans, who occupied the northern region around Mount Gerizim and Shechem. For a full description of the community and their practices, the reader is referred to my companion volume, *1001 Questions and Answers on Pesach.*[14]

They regarded themselves as descendants of the Joseph tribes (Ephraim and *Menasseh*) of original Israel, and alleged that the Jews originated as a result of a defection of the rest of the Israelite tribes, establishing a monarchy in defiance of the divine wish, revering Jerusalem as holy, and building a temple there, instead of the true holy site, namely their "Mountain of blessing, Mount Gerizim."

---

11. Mishnah *Rosh Hashanah* 2:4.
12. Ben-Sasson, H. H., ed. (1976). *A History of the Jewish People.* Cambridge, Massachusetts: Harvard University Press, pp. 277–281.
13. Mishnah *Rosh Hashanah* 2:2.
14. Cohen, J. M. (1966). In *1001 Questions and Answers on Pesach.* Northvale, NJ: Jason Aronson Inc., pp. 283–287.

The Jews hotly dispute the Samaritan version of their origins and point to the biblical account of II Kings 17:24, which states that the Assyrian conqueror, Sargon, after having removed the Jews into captivity in Assyria, rather than leave the land depopulated, imported heathen settlers from Cutha in Babylonia. Hence, the name *Cuthim* (Cuthians) applied to the Samaritans in Talmudic literature.

There was constant friction between Jews and Samaritans, and the above Mishnah is preserving a tradition that the latter lit beacons on the wrong night in order to confuse the fire stations into transmitting the wrong information regarding the new moon and the day officially fixed and sanctified as Rosh Hashanah.

19. Were not the Samaritans—who, after all, shared much of their religious tradition with the Jews—stooping rather low by attempting to sow confusion within Judaism?

If the Mishnaic tradition is taken at face value, then they were indeed guilty of an unpardonable offense. However, the present writer is not convinced that the alleged Samaritan practice was motivated by any such mischievous intention. During my doctoral researches into the Samaritan community of antiquity,[15] I discovered various references to fire practices of the community and Samaritan belief in the concept of atonement and purification by fire. The monthly religious festival of the new moon (Rosh Chodesh) is, in both traditions, a time for atonement; and, as the Samaritans did not follow the same method of determining the new moon as the Jews, they may well have lit their own beacons as part of their purification rites on the day before or after that fixed by the Jerusalem court. The signal stations would inevitably have been confused, but not necessarily as a result of any malicious intent of the Samaritan authorities.

20. So, what method was employed of informing the diaspora of the precise day consecrated as the new moon or Rosh Hashanah once the lighting of beacons had to be abandoned?

The authorities had to resort to sending out messengers to carry the information in person. It took them approximately 14 days to reach most of the cities in Babylonia. This information was only essential, however, when a festival occurred during that month, so as to be sure that it was observed on the day that had been properly sanctified according to the reckoning of the religious authorities back in Jerusalem. Hence the Mishnah states:

> For each of six months in the year the messengers of the court go out. For Nisan, for determining the occurrence of Pesach; for *Av*, for the fast (of the ninth of *Av*); for Elul, for determining Rosh Hashanah; for Tishri, for the

---

15. Cohen, J. M. (1977). *A Critical Edition of the Baba Rabbah Section of the Samaritan Chronicle No. II: With Translation and Commentary.* Ph.D. thesis, University of Glasgow, pp. 337–347.

festivals (of Yom Kippur and Succot); for Kislev, for determining the festival of Chanukah, and for Adar for Purim.[16]

21. But it is still unclear what the Mishnah means when it says that they sent out messengers "for Elul" in order to inform the diaspora when Rosh Hashanah occurs. Surely, Rosh Hashanah is on the first day of Tishri, so how could the messenger—or the Jerusalem authorities for that matter—know which day would be fixed, by the witnesses' testimony as Rosh Chodesh Tishri (and therefore Rosh Hashanah)?

Tosafot states that the diaspora communities got around this problem by universally observing Rosh Hashanah for two days: on the thirtieth day of Elul (in case that month was "defective," that is, comprising only 29 days) and on the thirty-first day (in case it was a "pregnant" (*me'ubar*) month of 30 days). They, nevertheless, were still required to send out the messengers, in order to establish the precise date of the previous Rosh Chodesh, Elul, so as to know from which day to count to the two days at the end of the month that had to be observed out of doubt.[17]

22. Why was that method abandoned of fixing the new moon and Rosh Hashanah on the basis of witnesses' visual testimony?

It was abandoned in the period of the Patriarch Hillel II (330–365 C.E.), when conditions deteriorated in Palestine, as a result of the harsh measures imposed by the Romans, severely limiting the freedom and authority of the Sanhedrin, the supreme ecclesiastical court, which, at that period, was based in Tiberias. It was no longer possible, therefore, for it to administer the fixing of the calendar and to guarantee safe passage for its officers, and it was no longer possible to find experts in the field of calendrical intercalation, whose calculations served as a vital control to the visual evidence supplied by the witnesses.

Hillel took the dramatic step, therefore, of surrendering that great privilege of the Sanhedrin to determine the calendar of the Jewish world, and he published two tracts—*Sod Ha-Ibbur* ("The secret of Intercalation") and *Kevi'uta de-Yarcha* ("The fixing of the new month"), which disclosed fully the formulae for, and methods of regulating, a fixed calendar.

Hillel made one proviso: that although the land of Israel might continue its practice of observing but one festival day (the first and seventh of Pesach and Sukkot, and the first day of Shavuot) as holy days, yet the diaspora communities, which had traditionally observed two days as holy, out of doubt as to which precise day Jerusalem had fixed as the first of the month (Rosh Chodesh and Rosh Hashanah), must continue its practice of observing two days as festival days. Hillel established that as a decree on the diaspora communities. Indeed, that was his precondition for allowing the diaspora to sever its umbilical cord from the authority

16. Mishnah *Rosh Hashanah* 1:3.
17. *Tosafot* on Talmud *Rosh Hashanah* 18a.

of the mother land and to gain calendrical independence. And it is for that reason that Orthodox rabbis find themselves unable to countenance the observance of one day only, even in the face of the great pressure that is brought to bear and the otherwise persuasive argument for bringing the diaspora into line with the State of Israel and creating a unity of observance throughout the Jewish world.

23. Surely, then, in the light of Hillel's fixed calendar and the exception he made in the case of the land of Israel, that it should observe only one holy day at a time (the first and the seventh days of Pesach and Sukkot, and the first only of _Shavuot_), why does Israel still, to this day, observe two days of Rosh Hashanah?

Rabbi Zerachiah Ha-levi of Gerondi (1125-1186) sheds light on this in his commentary on the _Rif._[18] He reports that, "a novel situation has arisen in the land of Israel, with an influx of scholars from the Provence, who have introduced their practice of observing two days of Rosh Hashanah."

24. But how was it possible for this in-comer group of rabbinic sages to have had such an influence as to overturn the long-standing native tradition of one-day Rosh Hashanah observance?

We are able to answer this question on the basis of a full account that we have of the conditions that were obtained in the holy land at that time. The famous traveler Rabbi Benjamin of Tudela visited Palestine around the year 1170, which was the period that Rabbi Zerachiah is writing about, when the Provencal sages arrived in Palestine.

Benjamin wrote a full account of the way of life of the various Jewish communities that he visited. We learn from his diary that Jewish settlement in the holy land was sparse at that time, numbering only 2,000 families. Inevitably, therefore, the arrival of a group of rabbinic scholars would have made a profound impact on the community, and their influence and authority would have been far-reaching and profound.

---

18. _Ha-Maor Ha-katan_ to commentary of _Rif_ on Talmud _Beitzah_ 5a.

II

The Spirit of Rosh Hashanah

25. We have described Rosh Hashanah as a festive occasion. How do we equate that with its solemnity as a period of introspection and penitence?

Notwithstanding its sober spirit, the rabbis insist that Rosh Hashanah is definitely a *Yom Tov*, a festive occasion. Indeed, like the other main festivals, it is prepared for with the joyful anticipation of a family occasion and with meticulous gastronomic attention. And the new Rosh Hashanah attire is almost *de rigueur!*

However, although the satisfying privilege of ringing out the old and ringing in the new year is keenly felt, yet, compared with that of other festivals, the *simchah* (joyful spirit) of Rosh Hashanah is manifestly more reserved. It may be compared with the celebration of birthdays by the elderly. It is a happy milestone, but one that, at the same time, constitutes a sober reminder of the approach of the winter of life. Rosh Hashanah, likewise, is a festive occasion, but also one on which some serious concerns have to be addressed.

26. Is there any special way in which our tradition indicates that restricted joy?

Maimonides sees it reflected in the fact that we do not recite Hallel, the liturgically prescribed festive psalms, on this particular festival. He observes that "this is because these are days of repentance, not of special joy (*simchah yeteirah*)."[1] This is based on the Talmudic view that "it is inconceivable, at a time when the books of life and death are being opened, and the king occupies the throne of strict justice, that Israel should sing such praises."[2] To recite Hallel, one requires a wholehearted joy. Where this is diluted somewhat by our consciousness of sin, or by feelings of apprehension or guilt, Hallel is inappropriate. Thus, on Rosh Hashanah, our quiet confidence in our ability to secure forgiveness enables us to home in to the *simchat ha-regel*, the joy of the festival, but the ingredient of special joy, the *simchah yeteirah*, is certainly missing.

A pointer to the requisite mood might be gained from an analogy with the famous 1985 Live Aid Concert, which raised millions of pounds for the famine-stricken Ethiopians. While there was profound pleasure at the success of the venture, it was

---

1. Maimonides *Mishneh Torah, Hilkhot Chanukah* 3:6.
2. *Arakhin* 10b.

tempered by our intense concern for the lives of those starving millions. There was *simchah*, but not *simchah yeteirah*. Whether we can feel the same concern for our own lives, which hang in the balance at this time, is the challenge of Rosh Hashanah.

REPENTANCE AND SYNAGOGUE ATTENDANCE

27. Is there not something rather contrived in fixing three specific days for confession and penitence?

This is a mistaken premise. Judaism does not fix just three days for penitence. Penitence is a daily exercise; and our prayers urgently acknowledge consciousness of our sin and our desire for repentance. In the *Hashivenu* (the fifth) blessing of the *Amidah*, the central prayer recited three times a day, we utter the prayer for divine guidance for our efforts to return to the path of penitence: "Bring us back, O our Father, to Your Torah; draw us near, O our King, to Your service; and cause us to return to You in perfect repentance. Blessed are You, O Lord, who desires repentance." And in the following blessing, *Selach lanu*, we have a veritable formula of confession: "Forgive us, O our Father, for we have sinned; pardon us, O our King, for we have transgressed."

Again, in the extended version of the *Tachanun* prayer, recited on Mondays and Thursdays, we include several pleas to God to accept our heartfelt repentance:

"O Lord, in You lies our hope, O god of forgiveness. We beg You to forgive, O good and forgiving God."

You open a hand for repentance, ready to receive transgressors and sinners. Our soul is overwhelmed by our great sorrow. Do not forget us for ever. Arise and save us, for we trust in You. Our Father, our King, though we are without righteousness and good deeds, remember for us the covenant of our fathers, and our daily proclamation: 'The Lord is One.'

28. So, if we pray for forgiveness every day, why designate three special days in the year for the performance of the same exercise?

It is like asking why football or basketball teams should hold big league and championship games. Why not rather restrict themselves merely to training sessions and practice matches?

The answer is surely that it is only the challenge of the big games that generates the tension that ensures that the players maintain the momentum of giving of their utmost at all times, of keeping themselves in peak condition, maximizing their abilities and perfecting their skills and tactics. It is the awesome excitement and challenge of "the big day" that they carry over within their emotions and that, in turn, generates the adrenalin to power their ongoing determination to give of their best both in practice and in competition.

Without the "big days" of Rosh Hashanah and Yom Kippur, days of specially focused prayer and repentance, we would hardly take repentance seriously throughout the year, and the impetus to lead righteous lives—which those High Holy Days generate—would hardly survive. So both are vital: the ongoing awareness of the need for repentance every day of our lives and the High Holy Days, which serve as the dynamo to power that repentance.

29. But is it the wish to repent that motivates most people to attend synagogue on the High Holy Days?

There is clearly no one single reason why the "three-times-a-year" folk continue to attend synagogue on these occasions. They probably could not even explain their own motivation. They just know that synagogue is the place that they have to be, seeking out their co-religionists and marking at least a few days in the year as sacred and spiritually significant.

Where people have been taught and shown religious values and have enjoyed the spirit of religious ritual in their early childhood, their sensitivity to it all rarely dies out. The religious impulse survives deep within their subconscious, no matter how little stimulation it receives by way of ongoing and formal commitment and observance. It is not difficult, therefore, to understand their perceived need, or at least their willingness, to seek an outlet for the expression of that impulse at such a spiritually supercharged time.

The desire for an exercise of repentance may not be uppermost in their minds, but that dominant liturgical motif, which impresses itself upon the whole spirit of the festival, cannot totally fail to leave its imprint.

30. Is there any other reason why Jews the world over flock to their synagogues at this time?

We cannot ignore the magnet of nationalism. The High Holy Days afford our people the opportunity to join in what is very definitely a national review and to draw strength and a continued sense of identity from the solidarity exuded by the large assemblage.

Jewish life is rarely dull; and each passing year inevitably brings in its wake a variety of national agonies and ecstasies, especially as they relate to the State of Israel. Rosh Hashanah and Yom Kippur afford an opportunity for national stock-taking, for locating our bearings, for the cathartic exercise of putting behind us the failures of the past and committing ourselves to try much harder to remedy them in the future.

31. But for those who are not particularly observant, what possible relevance can a festival of repentance have for them?

Teshuvah (repentance) should not be perceived exclusively as a religious exercise. The motivation to regret one's unworthy actions should spring instinctively from the conscience. That is an essential component of our emotional and moral response mechanism. Children are fairly universally taught to say "sorry" when they have misbehaved or upset another. That is, effectively, a gesture of repentance.

It is obvious that, if people did not express regret for offenses against their neighbors, there would be no chance of any reconciliation. Unintentional hurts would fester and become inflated into major vendettas, and society would soon degenerate into an agglomeration of warring factions. So repentance and the acknowledgment of our wrong-doing are vital components of interpersonal relationships and the smooth-running of any civilized society. As such, even those who are not religiously observant will appreciate the value of a few days being set aside each year for a close analysis of the nature of their relationships and their treatment of their fellow man.

Of course, the religiously committed will also undertake at this time a close assessment of their attitude and devotion toward their religious duties and responsibilities and the quality of their dialogue with God. If, on the other hand, the less religiously inclined were to utilize Rosh Hashanah exclusively for a survey of their *bein adam lechavero* (man-to-man) interaction, that should not be underestimated. There is always the hope and chance that the atmosphere of spirituality and prayer that the festival generates might also move them to give consideration, albeit subconsciously, to their relationship *bein adam la-Makom* (between man and God) and to reflect upon what their Judaism means to them.

32. But surely man's relationship with his neighbor, good or bad, is a matter purely for his own conscience. How can it possibly be equated with his religious responsibilities, as clearly delineated in the Torah?

When the Torah states that man was created "in the image of God" (Genesis 1:26), it did not mean that our physical form approximated that of our Maker, but that we were endowed with a higher intelligence and with powers of perception and creativity that are unique among the created species. The purpose of that God-given uniqueness was that we should become partners with God in the development of His world and bring to perfection all the still unfulfilled inherent potential.

That unique task with which man was entrusted and the exalted status with which man was accordingly endowed as co-partner with God in the creative process is highlighted in Psalm 8:1–6:

> When I look at thy heavens, the work of thy fingers,
> the moon and the stars set in their place by thee,
> (I ask in amazement:) What is man that thou shouldst remember him,
> mortal man that thou shouldst care for him?
> Yet thou hast made him little less than the *angels*,
> crowning him with glory and honour.
> Thou makest him master over all thy creatures;
> thou hast put everything under his feet . . .

Now it stands to reason that God, who has placed such responsibility into the hands of man, has a vested interest in the way men conduct themselves on earth. We cannot perfect the world before perfecting ourselves.

The psalmist describes our status a "little less than the angels." That is, in fact, a free translation of a far more daring Hebrew phrase: *Vatechasrehu me'at me'Elokim,* which means, "You have made him just a little less *than God!*" We may now understand why Judaism does not believe that man's relationship with his fellow man is a matter purely for his own conscience. Man's conscience has to be conditioned by his sensitivity to his role as co-partner with God. Hence, when man performs deeds of kindness and charity toward his fellow man, he earns *mitzvot* thereby, namely religious merit, on a par with the fulfilment of other purely religious duties. He is, in essence, fulfilling the biblical prescription of loving one's neighbor as oneself. It follows that when he offends against his neighbor, he perpetrates *aveirot,* spiritual debit. This means, in essence, that, on account of his having been created in God's image and entrusted with a special mission on earth, his interaction with his fellow man can only be construed as a sacred relationship governed by religious, moral, and ethical criteria. We are all fellow priests in God's earthly temple; and we have to conduct ourselves, at all times, in a manner that is in keeping with that special status.

33. Where do we find it written that the rabbis regarded it as equally important to make peace with our fellow man at this period as it is to make our peace with God?

There is an explicit statement to this effect in the Mishnah:

Sins committed by man against God are atoned for by the Day of Atonement; sins committed by man against his fellow cannot be atoned for by the Day of Atonement unless he first intercedes for his neighbor's pardon. Rabbi Eleazar ben Azariah derived this from the verse: 'For on this day shall atonement be made for you . . . From all your sins before the Lord shall ye be cleansed.' [Leviticus 16:30][3]

The implication of Rabbi Eleazar's inference is that only for sins "before the Lord" is forgiveness secured automatically, not for sins against fellow man. The latter may be seen, therefore, to involve a much greater act of appeasement than those against God. Those against God only require remorse and a plea for atonement, whereas those against one's fellow require remorse, an act of appeasement followed by a plea to God that He should also forgive the sin perpetrated against fellow man—one of God's co-partners. Thus, a sin against man carries the double burden of being at the same time a sin against God, from which perspective it is, of course, all the more serious.

---

3. Mishnah *Yoma* 8:9.

34. But is it not a fact that a high proportion of Israelis do not mark Rosh Hashanah as a religious occasion?

It is truly a sad fact that many Israeli secularists do not mark the festival of Rosh Hashanah or the Fast of Yom Kippur, other than by utilizing those days as national holidays and opportunities to spend the day with their families at the beach!

Perhaps naively, we expect our Jewish secularists to be more traditional than their Christian counterparts. We cannot compare the situation to that which exists in the United States and Europe, where Orthodoxy, Reform, and Liberal Judaism provide an entire spectrum of choice for religious expression and theological orientation, and an environment wherein people of every shade of faith and observance may find a whole range of benefits in belonging to a synagogue. High on the list of benefits will be the sense of Jewish kinship, belonging, and communal identity that the synagogue, with its social ambiance and activities, cements. To such an extent is this the case that one may almost define a Diaspora Jew in terms of his synagogue affiliation. Most secularly inclined Jews who maintain synagogue membership and attend on the High Holy Days do so exclusively for these reasons.

Israeli secularists, however, do not require to define their Jewishness in terms of the synagogue and do not require its facilities. In any case, the facilities offered by the Israeli synagogues, which are, almost exclusively, houses of prayer, are hardly enticing. They bear no comparison with their Diaspora counterparts, which strive to be veritable community centers, offering a whole range of facilities: crèches, nurseries, Hebrew schools, youth fellowships, sporting activities, silver and golden age clubs, adult cultural groups, learning *chavrutot*, and so on. In Israel, on the other hand, these are all at hand at school, the local youth club, or within the general orbit of *iriyah* (city council) provision. So secularists do not look to the synagogue to provide anything the state cannot provide for them on a much more professional level. It is not surprising, therefore, that Israeli secularists are totally divorced from the synagogue and that even such sacred days in the lives of the Diaspora synagogue-affiliates as Rosh Hashanah and Yom Kippur exert absolutely no emotional, spiritual, or social influence over them or their children.

35. Are there any prospects for hoping that there might be a bridging of the great divide between secularists and religious in Israel?

Until Saturday, November 4, 1995, one may have been inclined to express some optimism on that score. With the assassination of Premier Yitzchak Rabin by a young man who professed membership of the religious community and the ensuing bitter recriminations that have tragically and dramatically widened the gap even further, as secularists make the entire "religious camp" scapegoats for what occurred, one can hardly be optimistic of any rapprochment taking place for many decades to come. The bridge-building will be very slow; but it is a process that both sides must make an absolute priority if internal peace is ever to be achieved. Ironically, it may prove easier for Israelis to make peace with the Arabs than with themselves.

36. Why does God have to judge us at all?

Because we ourselves are judgmental. We spend our days and lives making judgments and assessments of the people around us—their views, their behavior, their vices and their virtues, their strengths and their weaknesses, their talents and their shortcomings, their successes and their failures. We judge others in order to measure ourselves. It is only just, therefore, that we should all be subject, in turn, to the judicial scrutiny of "the judge of all the earth."

In business and the professions "annual reviews" are now generally recognized as valuable means of keeping the workforce constantly attentive to their duties and of monitoring and rewarding the achievements of the assiduous while exposing the underachievers. Rosh Hashanah and Yom Kippur is the annual review that God undertakes. It is intended to focus the mind, so that we are motivated to pre-empt God in undertaking this exercise of self-scrutiny, and in correcting any shortcomings before the judgment day. We are thus enabled to correct the record and present ourselves as worthy, loyal, and true subjects of God, optimistic of being confirmed in our life's situation, and, indeed, of being the recipients of even greater reward and blessing.

It is a measure of God's love and concern for us, and His view about the importance of our role on earth, as His co-partner, that He undertakes this annual review of our progress. We believe that it is undertaken primarily in order to reward our achievements rather than to punish our waywardness.

III

The Mechanics of Repentance:
Teshuvah Tefillah Utzedakah

PROPER REPENTANCE

37. How can we be sure that we have properly repented?

In truth, we cannot be sure until we are confronted by the identical enticement, in similarly conducive circumstances and conditions to those that stimulated the sin's commission in the first place. Only then, when we no longer experience those original uncontrollable urges, and when we can look dispassionately at the situation and respond with an instinctive and resounding "no!"—only then can we say that we are ready to become rehabilitated regarding repentance.

But that is only the first stage. Real repentance is determined by an instinctive recoiling from sin. Only when sin stops us in our tracks, when it disturbs and embarrasses us, when it gives us sleepless nights and makes us feel totally unworthy, only when we cry out like Cain, "My sin is too great to bear"—only then can we be sure that we have become *ba'alei teshuvah*, true penitents. Viewed from this perspective, it may be doubted that many do attain full repentance. Defined in these terms, it will be understood why we need a recurring, annual summons to put aside our sin and waywardness. In truth, however, if we have to wait until Rosh Hashanah to review the sins of the past year, then it is doubtful whether Rosh Hashanah will be particularly efficacious.

And perhaps this is why Rosh Hashanah is designated as a *mo'ed*, "a festive day," rather than, as we might have expected, a day of lament at human frailty and the weakness of the flesh. It is precisely *because* it does not—or should not—come upon us unawares, confronting us with our compacted wrong-doing. Rosh Hashanah, if anything, is merely the act of putting the final stamp on the profound inner resolve that we have been making and perfecting since the moment our consciences were smitten by the particular sin. It is but the formal affirmation of our determination to wipe the slate clean and begin afresh, living our lives on a higher and purer plain, from this Rosh Hashanah on, buoyed up by the expectation of God's exclamation: *salachtiy*, "I have forgiven you!"

38. Do the sages give any practical illustration of what constitutes proper repentance?

The Talmudic sages preempted Freud by some 2,000 years in their recognition that it is the sex urge that is the most powerful determinant of human behavior and, consequently, the motivation to sin. Hence, their depiction of a situation of immoral temptation as an exemplification of a typical scenario.

The Talmud states in the name of Rabbi Judah that "True repentance is measured by a person, having once succumbed, finding himself on a subsequent occasion with the same woman in the same location [as the gratification of the original temptation] and in the identical circumstances."[1]

39. What is the precise point of that particular illustration?

It is clearly to indicate the nature of proper *teshuvah* (repentance). There is an old joke about the Catholic who went to a priest for absolution and was told to recite fifty "Hail Marys" and put ten dollars into the charity plate. The sinner found that he only had a twenty dollar bill and there was no one in the chapel to supply him with change. "OK," said the priest, "Put the twenty dollar bill on the plate, and sin just one more time!" This rather "uncharitable" joke nevertheless illustrates just how perfunctory the act of penitence can become. Just going through the motions of acknowledging that one has sinned, especially when one can hide comfortably behind the plural formulation in which the prayer book confessions are couched, does not constitute a proper act of *teshuvah*.

Teshuvah means, literally, "going back," that is undertaking a wide-ranging and thorough-going review of one's sin and the circumstances that prompted it, consciously working at constructing a mental block to the pleasurable sensations that attended its original commission, and filling the emotional vacuum created thereby in one's imagination with a sense of shame and regret. Only then will one be morally strengthened in a way that it will be possible to resist any subsequent enticements.

40. While we recognize the necessity for sincere repentance, what is the status of one who recites the confessions in synagogue together with the congregation but who has no repentant thoughts in his heart?

Maimonides does not mince his words in this context, but employs a Talmudic analogy of such a self-contradictory situation to one who, wishing to purify himself, immerses himself in a *mikveh* while still clutching an unclean reptile![2]

Although from Maimonides' spiritually elevated position he would naturally view it as a bogus confession, we would, nevertheless, caution against reading too much into the pejorative Talmudic analogy. The intention is certainly not to brand such a person as "unclean," but simply to draw attention to the indubitable contradiction in mouthing insincere sentiments in the context of a solemn confession.

---

1. *Yoma* 86b.
2. Maimonides *Mishneh Torah, Hilkhot Teshuvah* 2:3; *Ta'anit* 16a.

We would take a slightly different view and recognize that there is some positive benefit and value in a sinner attending synagogue and reciting such formulae of confession. While atonement *at this moment* can obviously not be expected—nor, by the nature of the situation, is it being sought!—the influence of the praying and confessing community around him and the awe of the occasion is very likely to leave its imprint on his soul and make him far more sensitive to repentance at some future time.

41. What is the status of a person who, year after year, goes through all the motions of *teshuvah*, *tefillah*, and *tzedakah* and is really sincere about his repentance, determining not to repeat his sin, and yet, before long, slips back into the old routine?

If he is truly sincere at the time and he does everything within his power to prevent its recurrence, then his repentance is nevertheless accepted, and the slate is wiped clean of that offense during the interim. If, however, he consciously proceeds, subsequently, to put himself into a situation where its recurrence is inevitable then he frustrates his *teshuvah* retrospectively.

42. Does the act of repentance count in any way in the case of a person who intends to sin during the coming year, but is quite prepared to go through all the motions of repentance?

No, it does not. This is the classic Talmudic definition of a totally sham act: "Whoever says 'I shall sin and then repent; I shall sin again and then repent,' heaven will afford him no opportunity in the future to effect a sincere repentance. Whoever says, 'I shall sin and Yom Kippur will atone,' for such a person Yom Kippur does not effect atonement."[3]

God cannot be hoodwinked. Religious practice cannot be exploited for personal advantage. Repentance involves a state of mind and a change of heart. Without sincerity, it has to be meaningless.

43. Do the sages counsel us regarding an appropriate time for penitence?

They do. Basing themselves upon the verse, "Seek ye the Lord when He may be found, call upon Him when He is near" (Isaiah 55:6), the sages explain that the prophet was referring to the Ten Days of Penitence when God is especially "near" and accessible to our penitence.

But they certainly did not mean that we have to put our feelings of remorse and our desire for atonement on hold until the propitious moment comes around each year. Hence the Talmudic comment on the teaching of Rabbi Eliezer that one should repent on the day before one's death.[4] "His disciples asked Rabbi Eliezer, 'But does a man know then when he is going to die?' Rabbi Eliezer replied: How much more

---

3. *Yoma* 85b.
4. Mishnah *Avot* 2:10.

then should a man repent each day in case tomorrow he dies? The consequence of that will be that all his days will be spent in repentance."

44. We have referred above, albeit jocularly, to the Catholic mode of penance. Do we Jews have any parallel to that, in the form of some required practical demonstration of regret?

In biblical times, there was a prescribed ritual whereby an individual or community manifested its contrition. This consisted of rending one's garments, praying, fasting, putting on sackcloth, and sitting in the ashes. The penance of the people of Nineveh, as described in the book of Jonah,[5] was so demonstrative that even their beasts were made to share in its expression. Like their owners, they were also draped in sackcloth and deprived of food and drink.

In the sacrificial system, there was a specific sin-offering—the *chattat*—prescribed for individual sins. This involved the laying of the hands on the head of the beast and the public acknowledgment of guilt by specifying the particular sin committed.[6] Human pride being what it is, it is difficult to imagine that anyone emerged from such an ordeal with anything other than a deflated ego and a very real sense of humility. The sacrifice was secondary in importance to the cry of confession; and it may be said to have existed only in order to evoke such an emotional response. When David was severely censured by the prophet Nathan for his sin with Bathsheba, his first words were "I have sinned."[7] There is no mention of any subsequent sacrifice brought by David. His spontaneous confession sufficed to obtain forgiveness.

For the rabbis of the Talmud, repentance was entirely a state of mind. The Temple having been destroyed, prayer and study replaced the sacrificial cult as a means of communication with the deity. It was natural, therefore, that they should have redefined repentance as a psychological state and played down any external forms of penance other than private fasting, which was often employed as a means of atonement.[8]

CONFESSING OUR SINS

45. Even though our prayer book confessionals are couched in the plural, is it necessary or preferable to specify any particular sin that one knows one is guilty of?

This is the subject of a difference of opinion in the Talmud[9] between Rabbi Judah ben Bava, who believed that it is necessary to acknowledge the specific sin, and

5. Jonah 3:7–8.
6. Leviticus 26:40.
7. II Samuel 12:13.
8. *Mo'ed Katan* 25a; *Hagigah* 22b; *Sanhedrin* 100a; *Baba Metzia* 33a.
9. *Yoma* 86b.

Rabbi Akivah, who believed that it is not necessary, as God in any case knows what we have done.

Rabbi Judah bases his opinion on the biblical precedent of Moses' plea for God to forgive Israel for the heinous sin of worshiping the Golden Calf. In spite of the fact that God knows what Israel has done, Moses includes mention of the specific sin in his confession: "This people have sinned a great sin and have made for themselves a god of gold. Now, therefore forgive them their sin . . ." (Exodus 32:31–32). Rabbi Judah viewed this formulation as a paradigm for all confessions, which, similarly, must include mention of the sin committed.

Rabbi Akivah based his view on the biblical maxim: "Happy is he whose transgression is pardoned, whose sin is concealed" (Psalm 32:1). As to the objection that Moses did see fit to refer specifically to Israel's sin, Rabbi Akivah explains that this was not because Moses regarded it as a precondition of confession to do so, but because he wished to defend Israel's action by hinting that God Himself had to bear the responsibility for it. Moses reminds God that the "god of gold" only came about on account of the vast amount of silver and gold that God insisted Israel take away from Egypt. They just had to channel that gold into some enterprise and thus was born the notion of making a representation of deity in the form of the Golden Calf.

46. But if there is a difference of opinion between those two great Talmudists, where does that leave us regarding a practical course of action? Do we specify the sins we have been guilty of or not?

Although there is another view in the Talmud[10] that a distinction exists between sins against God, which do not require specifying, and sins against fellow men, which do, Maimonides does not take up that distinction, but codifies the law in general terms in accordance with the view of Rabbi Judah ben Bava that it is necessary to specify the sin.[11]

47. Is it enough then merely to confess our sin to God?

No, it is not. As we say in our High Holy Day prayers, "Repentance, prayer and charity avert the severe decree." We have to accompany our confession with fervent prayer to God to forgive our sins against Him and against our fellow man. And we have to donate to charity as a practical demonstration of our resolve to lead a life based on giving, rather than taking. For "taking" is generally the underlying basis of sin: taking what belongs to others or taking unfair advantage of others. Charity is intended to restore the balance.

Just as prayer has to be entirely sincere and appropriate to the remorseful feelings that are being expressed, so must one's charity be meaningful and the apology one

---

10. *Ibid.*
11. Maimonides *Mishneh Torah, Hilkhot Teshuvah* 1:1.

makes to one's neighbor be wholehearted and generous. Adin Steinsaltz puts it succinctly:

> There are things on this lowly earth of which we are particularly fond, but each of us has his own peculiarities in this regard. To give money, for instance, is for some of us a molehill, whereas to apologize for having offended someone is a mountain. Now beware! If you offer a sacrifice to God, make sure that you offer what really costs you dear, for God would not appreciate a fool's deal.[12]

48. Fine. So we have to indulge in a three-fold exercise of intense penitence, incorporating confession, prayer, and charity. Now, regarding the first two exercises, confession has, by its very nature, to be spontaneous and unambiguous; prayer is fully determined and circumscribed by our official liturgy. This leaves charity. What guidance is offered by our sources as to an appropriate penitential act of charity?

Jewish tradition stood firmly by the principle of not closing the door before would-be penitents, that is of not imposing such rigorous preconditions for absolution that sinners would be deterred from the outset from commencing on the road to repentance. The prescription of a punitive financial penance would certainly have that effect.

By the same token, our tradition did not believe that people had to impoverish themselves in the performance of their faith. While recognizing the determination of the faithful to give as much as possible to charity and to spend more than they could afford on the performance of *mitzvot* and the purchase of ritual objects, such as on a beautiful and rare *etrog* for use on the festival of Sukkot, yet the halakhah lays down the clear principle that "One who dispenses money to charity [or for a religious purpose] should not feel obliged to outlay more than one fifth [of his income]."[13]

It should be said, however, that this guidance is for lower or average earners. In relation to people who are more comfortably off and who could easily donate a larger percentage of their annual salary without it making any inroads into their savings or difference to their lifestyle, then obviously a more meaningful donation is expected—hence, Maimonides' advice that "one should donate to charity in accordance with one's ability."[14] Nevertheless, according to one authority, even people in this category are not required to outlay more than one-third of their income.[15] We may infer from the above the level of charitable donation that our tradition regards as "meaningful" and that would therefore be appropriate in the context of an act of penance.

---

12. Steinsaltz, A. (1988). *The Strife of the Spirit*. Northvale, NJ: Jason Aronson Inc., p. 99.
13. *Ketubot* 50a.
14. Maimonides *Mishneh Torah, Hilkhot Teshuvah* 2:4.
15. *Magen Avraham* on *Shulchan Arukh Orach Chayyim* 656:1 (6).

SEEKING THE FORGIVENESS OF OUR FELLOW MEN

49. If one has stolen from another, assaulted or insulted him, or spread malicious reports about him, what procedures of penance are required?

As mentioned above (Question 33), the High Holy Day spiritual exercises and tokens of penance are only effective when it comes to sins against God. For offenses against our fellows, on the other hand, direct and full restitution is demanded as a precondition for penitence.

And neither is it merely a matter of restoring the object stolen or paying full compensation. Rather, one has to accompany that with a direct, sincere, and abject petition for forgiveness, and, where one has spread lies about another, with a public apology. In the words of Maimonides:

> It is praiseworthy for the penitent to confess in public, and publicize the precise nature of his transgressions, revealing to all the nature of his offence against his neighbor. He should say: 'In truth I have sinned against so-and-so, having done this or that act. This day do I repent and express my sincere regret.'[16]

50. Why is it necessary for the person to obtain a verbal pardon from the wronged party?

It is vital for the person to obtain a verbal pardon for the simple reason that if the wronged party withholds that, then it is a sign that he or she is still harboring a grudge against the wrong-doer. This means that the latter's slate cannot be wiped clean, nor can reconciliation between the two parties be properly effected. It means also that the offended party is now guilty of transgressing such biblical laws as "hating one's brother in one's heart" (Leviticus 19:17) and "bearing a grudge or taking revenge" (verse 18).

51. Granted that one must petition one's neighbor in a direct manner and obtain a verbal pardon, but if one is embarrassed to do that, may one petition for forgiveness in a letter?

This question is dealt with in a responsum of Rabbi Chaim David Ha-Levi[17] who inclines to the view that where the wrong that was committed was just between the two parties, as opposed to where one went about publicly speaking ill of the other, then a letter of apology might possibly fulfill the halakhic requirement.

The issue here is that there is a view in the Talmud, that of Rav Chisda, that at the very outset one must take along "three rows of three men before whom to intercede with the person he has wronged,"[18] in order to publicize his desire for

---

16. Maimonides *op. cit.* 2:5.
17. *Asei Lekha Rav* (1981), vol. 4, Tel Aviv, Committee for the Publication of the Works of Rabbi Chaim David Ha-Levi, pp. 206–209.
18. *Yoma* 87b.

reconciliation. This is interpreted to mean that he is obliged to take with him three men to witness his first petition. If that is rebuffed, he must take another three, and if that is also rebuffed a further three people. Since this is the procedure codified by the *Shulchan Arukh*,[19] it follows that a private letter would not satisfy that requirement of a public display of remorse at the very outset.

The position is not so cut-and-dried, however, since Maimonides rules that it is only where the person refuses to accept the initial gesture of apology that the petitioner is required to bring groups of three people with him, but in the first instance a private appeal would suffice.[20] Indeed, in practice, it is this view that has been followed over the ages, where a private appeal for reconciliation has always been regarded as sufficient.

Thus, as an initial overture, a private letter would seem to be in order. If the appeal is rebuffed, then one would require a more public act of intercession.

52. Is it halakhically acceptable to send an agent to beg pardon and seek reconciliation on one's behalf?

Once again, the same considerations pertain. In Jewish law, there is a principle that *Shelucho shel adam kemoto*, "A person's agent is as himself,"[21] according to which a petition through a representative should be construed as an improvement on a letter in that it effects a direct appeal, while at the same time introducing, through the participation of another, the desired element of publicity. Nevertheless, most authorities do not accept this as a proper mode of seeking forgiveness if the appeal is made entirely by an agent. Where his services are employed merely in the initial stage, however, to "sound out" the other party, enabling the offender to follow that up with a direct appeal, then that would be acceptable, certainly according to the view of Maimonides.

Clearly, if the offended party states, on the basis of a petitionary letter or an appeal of a representative, that he accepts the plea and grants forgiveness, then that is regarded as a full and acceptable state of reconciliation, irrespective of the doubt as to the halakhic propriety of such methods of appeal.

53. What course of action is open to one if the wronged party consistently refuses to grant forgiveness after the petitioner has complied with all the halakhic preconditions?

Maimonides states that if forgiveness is still refused after the three appeals have been made, with at least two of the appeals having been made in the company of three people, then the petitioner need do nothing further, but rather is the sin transferred to the offended party for his sin in not granting forgiveness.[22]

19. *Shulchan Arukh Orach Chayyim* 606:119.
20. Maimonides *Mishneh Torah, Hilkhot Teshuvah* 2:9.
21. Mishnah *Berakhot* 5:5.
22. Maimonides *op. cit.* 2:9.

54. Is there any situation when the halakhah would condone refusal to grant forgiveness?

In general, the principle, as quoted by Rabbi Moses Isserles in his gloss to the *Shulchan Arukh*[23] is that "the offended party shall not exhibit cruelty by refusing forgiveness and reconciliation." However, an exception is made in a case where one had been publicly slandered. In such a case, the slandered person may justifiably fear that, because people tend to gossip about other people's wrong-doings, not everyone who heard the calumny will get to know that the one who originally spread it admitted his crime and petitioned the wronged party for forgiveness. Thus, nothing can really be done by the petitioner to totally and effectively expiate his wrong-doing. The crime thus remains on the slate, and the suffering of the wronged person is never assuaged.

That is not to say that one wronged in this way is not at liberty to grant full forgiveness if he desires; but he has halakhic support if he refuses to do so.

55. Are there any other situations where a refusal to grant forgiveness may be justified?

Moses Isserles[24] refers to the situation where the wronged party honestly believes that it is in the petitioner's best interest for him to withhold forgiveness from him. He refers to a case in the Talmud where Rabbi Chaninah refused to be reconciled to his colleague, Rav, because he saw in a dream that Rav was destined to succeed to a position of communal leadership. Rabbi Chaninah feared that if such a brilliant scholar became preoccupied with communal affairs he would find no time for his studies. He therefore refused reconciliation, knowing that Rav would then feel that his position in the rabbinic hierarchy in Israel was untenable. His only course would be to leave and move to Babylon, where he would undoubtedly make a unique contribution to Torah scholarship in that country of future cultural promise.

Magen Avraham infers from this rather unusual and bizarre situation that where, for example, there is a need to make the offender more sensitive to the seriousness of his offense, it is permitted to withhold forgiveness if it is believed that this will serve that constructive end.[25]

56. Why is it only necessary to make three such formal petitions for forgiveness?

The Talmud, on which Maimonides' formulation is based, states quite clearly that, "Whoever petitions his fellow's pardon should do so no more than three times."[26] The Talmud goes on to infer this from the Torah's account of the three

---

23. *Rema* on *Shulchan Arukh Orach Chayyim* 607:114.
24. *Ibid.*
25. *Magen Avraham ad loc.*
26. *Yoma* 87a.

terms of pleading for forgiveness addressed to Joseph by his brothers: *Anna sa na* ("We pray thee, forgive, we pray thee . . .") *Ve'atta sa na* ("And now, we pray thee, forgive,") (Genesis 50:17). As *Rashi* explains, "The expression *na* denotes a special act of petition."[27]

57. Are there any exceptions to this procedure?

Maimonides states that in the case of one's Torah teacher, if, for reasons best known to him, he obdurately refuses to grant pardon to his student, then the above procedures are not appropriate, but one must be prepared to keep up the petitioning "even a thousand times until the teacher is prepared to become reconciled."[28]

58. Does the Talmud make any suggestions as to how one might approach the wronged person and break down any barriers?

Indeed, the Talmud records the lengths to which some of the great sages of the Talmudic era went in order to secure forgiveness. There is one account of Rabbi Yirmiah who had wronged Rav Abba, and who wished to express his abject regret. He sat outside Rav Abba's home in the place where the latter's maid usually threw out the slops. When she emerged and performed her chore, some of the water splashed upon Rabbi Yirmiah's head, at which he cried out in a loud voice: "They have made me like a trash can!" He went on to apply to himself the verse, "From the trash heap he raises up the destitute" (Psalm 113:7). Rav Abba, overhearing all that, came out to Rabbi Yirmiah and, seeing the lengths the latter had gone to in order to abase himself and to attract the attention of the man he had wronged, Rav Abba immediately became reconciled to him.[29]

59. What if the person wronged has passed away before forgiveness can be obtained from him?

Again the Talmud gives advice here, recommending that one assemble a group of ten men at the graveside, where one should make the required confession: "I have sinned against the Lord God of Israel and I have harmed so-and-so in such-and-such a way."[30]

Maimonides adds that, "If he still owed the deceased compensation, then if there are heirs he should make restitution to them, but if he is unsure whether there are heirs (or of their whereabouts), then he should deposit it with the Bet Din."[31]

27. *Rashi ad loc.*
28. Maimonides *op. cit.* 2:9.
29. *Yoma* 87a.
30. *Yoma* 85b.
31. Maimonides *op. cit.* 2:11.

MORTIFICATION PRACTICES

60. Does Judaism know of any exercise of physical mortification or flagellation in order to atone for and erase every single trace of sin?

Mainstream Judaism keeps strictly to the three categories of *teshuvah*, *tefillah*, and *tzedakah*, and there are no special penances referred to either in Bible or Talmud for any particular kinds of sins. However, there were pietistic groups, as well as individual pietists, in the Middle Ages who submitted themselves to bodily mortification in order to become thoroughly cleansed of sin. The chief exponents of this doctrine were the so-called *Chasidei Ashkenaz*, the German pietists who flourished in the Rhineland during the twelfth and thirteenth centuries. They found a scriptural basis for their concept of a mortifying penance in the account of the Prophet Isaiah's "call": "And one of the Serafim flew to me, having in his hand a burning coal which he had taken with tongs from the altar. And he touched my mouth and said: 'Behold this has touched your lips, your guilt is taken away and your sin forgiven'" (Isaiah 6:6–7).

These pietists distinguished four types of penance. The first, and mildest, is the Talmudic "repentance of opportunity," whereby one displays one's sincere resolve in a situation where the opportunity to repeat the sin presents itself, but the penitent does not succumb. The second type is "the preventive form of penitence," whereby the penitent strives to avoid like the plague any experience or situation that might present him with the temptation to repeat the sin. The third in order of severity is "the penance of correspondence," wherein the penitent is expected to endure that intensity of physical pain that corresponds to the amount of pleasure he derived from the commission of the sin. Finally comes "the biblically prescribed repentance," whereby the truly penitent has to inflict upon himself tortures corresponding to the pain that would have accompanied the imposition of the penalties prescribed by the Bible for his particular sin. Where the Pentateuch prescribed flogging, the penitent must submit to forty lashes, and where the penalty was death he was expected to undergo "tortures as bitter as death." Penitents belonging to that sect were known to lie in the snow for hours in the winter and to expose their bodies to ants and bees in the summer in order to fulfill this last category of repentance.[32]

61. How long did such pietistic groups and their mortification practices survive?

For quite some time. Indeed, we hear of very similar practices among the pietists who settled in Safed in the sixteenth century and made that town the leading center of Jewish scholarship in Palestine. Their activities are described by Solomon Schechter, who refers to one Safed fraternity called *Sukkat Shalom* ("Tent of Peace"), who would hold weekly meetings at which they would be expected to give a complete account of how they filled their time over the past week and make a full

---

32. Cohen, J. M. (1994). *Prayer and Penitence.* Northvale, NJ: Jason Aronson Inc., pp. 121–122.

and frank confession of any time they wasted on activities outside Torah study and the practice of *mitzvot*, or, God forbid, on sinful or vain pursuits.

There are records of another "Society of Penitents," who indulged in the most arduous ascetic practices.[33]

Now, although the majority of the Safed community comprised exiles from Spain and Portugal, Schechter states that "there is reason to believe that at this time also a German Jewish community was established in Safed, perhaps presided over by the father-in-law of [Joseph] Caro."[34] It is not beyond the realm of possibility, therefore, that it was those German immigrants who transplanted into Safed the ascetic traditions and mortification practices of the *Chasidei Ashkenaz*. Safed and its Sephardi exiles were, of course, ripe for such practices as the punishment of exile and martyrdom that had been visited upon them gave them an overwhelming sense of sin and a burning desire to effect a total spiritual regeneration and purification of heart and soul.[35] The exercise of self-chastisement and physical purgation would have been welcomed as a most appropriate means of atonement.

62. What kinds of bodily mortification were practiced by those Safed pietists?

In the words of Schechter:

Some of its members, we are told, refrained from food and drink during the day, performed their afternoon devotions in tears, and put on sackcloth and ashes. Others, again, observed every week a fast extending over two or three days and nights in succession. . . . Some among them used to observe a fast extending over three or four days and nights, at the change of the four seasons of the year. . . . Many pious scholars refrained from wine and meat during week days.[36]

63. Leaving aside those special pietistic fraternities, were any penances imposed by religious authorities on individuals who were found guilty of sinful conduct?

They were indeed. For the following examples we are indebted to Rabbi Louis Jacobs' excellent study, *Theology in the Responsa*.

Rabbi Jacob Weil (fifteenth century) was called upon to prescribe an appropriate penance for a young married woman who had been unfaithful. He decided that the woman had to publicly confess her sin from the ladies gallery of the synagogue. For an entire year, she was to wear only black garments and wear none of her jewelry. She had to sleep on the ground and to fast every single day, except for Sabbaths and

---

33. Schechter, S. (1908). *Studies in Judaism*, Second series. Philadelphia: The Jewish Publication Society of America, pp. 244–246.

34. Schechter, S. *op. cit.*, p. 229.

35. Schechter, S. *op. cit.*, p. 204.

36. Schechter, S. *op. cit.*, p. 245–246.

festivals. In addition to that, during the winter, she was to sit twice a week in snow for a quarter of an hour, and in summer she was to sit where there were bees, so that she would be stung. She was to eschew the company of men and spend the rest of her life in prayer, repentance, and mortification.[37]

The sixteenth century authority, Rabbi Meir ben Gedaliah of Lublin (*Maharam*), imposed similar penances on a scholar who had an affair with a married woman while he was under the influence of drink. In addition to the above penances, the scholar was to receive thirty-nine lashes each day for 1 year, after which he was to continue fasting every Monday and Thursday for a further 3 years.[38]

For a man who had taken a false oath, Rabbi Weil imposed public confession and three sessions of flogging. In addition, the man was to observe 40 consecutive days of fasting, after which he was to observe every Monday and Thursday as fast days for an entire year. If he lacked the strength to continue with these penances, he was to compensate fully by giving liberally to the poor.[39]

Rabbi Moses Isserles deals with the issue of penance to be observed by someone who inadvertently shot his servant. He ruled that the man should leave his home for 1 year and wander from place to place, staying nowhere for longer than a single day and night. He should fast during each daytime and confess his sin every night, and should observe the anniversary of the tragedy each year as a day of fasting and mourning.[40] In a similar situation, where a cripple accidentally shot someone, *Maharam* ruled that, instead of the customary punishment of exile from place to place, this cripple "should undertake a token exile to a neighboring community each Monday and Thursday, there to be flogged, and he should prostrate himself at the threshold of the synagogue. This he should do for half a year and he should eat no meat and drink no wine during this period."[41]

What emerges from these examples is that there are a few, generally accepted, forms of penance prescribed for serious sins, in addition to which some authorities recommend that repentant sinners set aside one day a year, in addition to Yom Kippur, to be observed as an awesome occasion for fasting and penance for the particularly heinous sins that weigh heavily upon their consciences.[42]

64. Presumably, then, apart from those guilty of serious crimes, the mainstream Jewish community knew nothing of such practical penances?

No, this is not a correct assumption. If we consult our standard code of law, Joseph Karo's *Shulchan Arukh*, in his section on "The order of confession at Minchah time on the eve of Yom Kippur," we find the following prescription:

---

37. Jacobs, L. (1975). *Theology in the Responsa*. London and Boston: Routledge & Kegan Paul, pp. 101–102.
38. Jacobs, L. *op. cit.*, p. 153.
39. Jacobs, L. *op. cit.*, p. 102.
40. Jacobs, L. *op. cit.*, p. 142.
41. Jacobs, L. *op. cit.*, p. 152.
42. Jacobs, L. *op. cit.*, p. 216.

"All members of the community subject themselves to forty lashes following the Afternoon Service, by means of which people are moved to repent of their sins."[43]

65. But surely Jewish courts no longer have the authority or power to impose any of the biblical penalties, including that of forty lashes?

That is quite correct. Indeed, the Vilna Gaon, in his comment on the above statement of the *Shulchan Arukh,* refers us to the clear statement of Maimonides to that effect.[44] For that reason, the *Shulchan Arukh* does not state that the lashes constitute an atonement in themselves, which was the case in biblical times, but that "by means of [those lashes] people are moved to repent of their sins."

66. So those lashes were only symbolic?

Precisely. And this is made abundantly clear in the gloss of the *Remah* (Moses Isserles), which immediately follows Karo's statement:

And it is customary to administer the lashes with any kind of (soft) strap, since it is only as a symbolic commemoration of the forty lashes. But he should use a strap made of calf's hide since this is reminiscent of the verse, 'Even the ox knoweth his owner . . . But Israel doth not know, my people doth not consider.' [Isaiah 1:3][45]

The *Magen Avraham* states that the great Rabbi Isaac Luria (who, as a member of the Safed school of Kabbalists, might have been expected to promote proper flagellation) would only administer four symbolic lashes corresponding to the four-letter divine name.[46]

DIVINE RESPONSES TO PENITENCE

67. What is the divine response to human sin and atonement? Does the God of justice administer judgment according to the strict letter of the law or does the "quality of mercy drop as the gentle rain from heaven"?

The whole basis of the prophetic ministry rested firmly on the assumption that the God of Israel was a forgiving and merciful father. "Have I any pleasure in the death of the wicked, says the Lord God, and not that he should turn from his evil way and live?" (Ezekiel 18:23). The prophet here expresses a conviction shared by

---

43. *Shulchan Arukh Orach Chayyim* 607:6.
44. *Biurei Ha-Gaon Rabbi Eliyahu* on *Shulchan Arukh Orach Chayyim* 607:6 [13]. Also, Maimonides *Mishneh Torah Hilkhot Sanhedrin* 16:1.
45. Isserles, M. Gloss of *Remah* on *Shulchan Arukh ad loc.*
46. *Magen Avraham* on *Shulchan Arukh ad loc.*

all his colleagues. It was, in fact, more than a conviction; it was their whole raison d'etre. The prophet could never accept—nor was he intended to accept—the role of passive "foreteller" of the nation's fate. He saw himself rather as a "forthteller," whose message of doom—if the heavenly communication insisted that it had to be articulated—was always expressed as a last resort, a concomitant of the nation's obdurate refusal to heed the call to repentance.

The inevitability of doom was alien to his whole thinking. Its announcement is, in reality, merely the pronouncement of the penalty that is compatible with the nation's crimes. The prophet's moment of supreme fulfillment and achievement comes precisely when his threats are negated, and his promise of doom invalidated, by the nation's repentance and the divine decree of forgiveness.[47]

68. But surely the prophet Jonah didn't feel that way about the nation he was called upon to denounce?

Good point. And that is precisely the purpose of that book: to demonstrate the unenviable role of the prophet.

His victory as a prophet lies in his defeat as an individual. He can never claim the affection of men, for even in the moment of their salvation his threat of doom must appear to have been misguided. If the prophet is counsel for the prosecution, God is counsel for the defense. . . . Jonah wished to be a foreteller rather than a forthteller. Compassion had no place in his conception of divine judgment. If God had proclaimed doom, then surely He had foreseen the ultimate repentance, and rejected it. Otherwise why compromise His elected prophet by putting into his mouth a false prediction?[48]

69. But is that not a real dilemma?

It may be a thankless mission to have to undertake, but it is not really a dilemma, because the basic qualification of the prophet has to be his readiness to accept unpopularity and to bear even the mockery of the multitude. Hoseah bears eloquent testimony to that situation when he reports the snide comments that were directed at him:

> "The prophet is a fool, the man of
> the spirit is mad. . .
> As for the prophet, a fowler's
> snare is in all his ways,
> And enmity in the house of his God."
> —(Ezekiel 9:7–8)

---

47. Cohen, J. M. *op. cit.*, pp. 122–123.
48. *Ibid.*

70. So why, indeed, does God not prepare and cushion the prophet by disclosing to him that ultimately his sentence of doom will be frustrated by the nation's repentance?

God's ways are truly inscrutable. They do not conform to our own preconceived notion of logic, neither do they show deference to the reputation of a prophet, priest, or saint. Indeed, we may conjecture that their harsh treatment at the hands of the nation may constitute their personal punishment in this world for their own shortcomings, leaving them totally free of sin to enjoy the rewards of the Hereafter.

God will not disclose the fact or time of the repentance of an individual or nation even to His prophets—and certainly not to a Jonah. The moment of repentance is sacred and intimate. For God to have granted foreknowledge of it to a third party would have been an act of betrayal. The true prophet should rejoice with God that His mercy has been given the opportunity to vanquish His anger.[49]

71. But does this not beg the question of why God chose to use a patently flawed prophet to carry His message to Nineveh?

The answer may well be that Jonah was not really flawed, but rather that he was a nationalistic Jew who, perhaps understandably in the context of his times, had no wish to extend God's grace to the Assyrian gentiles, the arch enemy of his people, that ultimately took away into captivity ten of the northern tribes of Israel.

Another answer may be to demonstrate that penitents are even more precious in the eyes of God than prophets. The rabbis themselves maintained that "even the perfectly and consistently righteous cannot stand on the level where sincere penitents stand."[50] Thus, the book of Jonah, wherein the sincere Assyrian penitents are cast in a good light, responding instantly to the call of the prophet of God while that very prophet is preoccupied with energetically challenging His will, is a powerful exemplification of that very principle.

72. If, as suggested, Jonah was not in fact flawed, then surely as a prophet we should be able to learn something worthwhile from his words. What is there to learn?

One teaching emerges most forcefully from his response to the torrent of questions that poured forth from the mariners after they had cast lots and discovered that Jonah was responsible for the storm that threatened their boat. They asked: "For what cause has this evil befallen us? What is thine occupation? Whence comest thou? What is thy country? Of what people art thou?" (Jonah 1:8). To all of these questions, Jonah made one simple, yet profound, answer: "I am a Hebrew, and I fear the Lord, the God of heaven who hath made the sea and the dry land" (verse 9).

As far as Jonah was concerned, there is only one way to define oneself. It is

49. *Ibid.*
50. *Berakhot* 34b.

immaterial what one's occupation is: whether one is a professional, a manual worker, or, indeed, unemployed. It matters little where one comes from: whether one hails from a prosperous or a poor country. It matters little "of what people" one hails: whether influential or powerless, strong or weak, cultured or primitive. What matters is one's faith and conviction. The only meaningful identity is the one conferred by the God we affirm, not the location we inhabit. Our faith makes us rich and powerful in spiritual terms, however much we lack in things material.

Jonah's simple answer contains a veritable philosophy of faith. For all his apparent shortcomings, he has left us a message of great and enduring worth. He has provided the clearest and most direct definition of what it is that has to condition our every action: our Jewishness and our God-given mission. Jonah remains a great teacher. His profound spirituality was recognized instinctively by the people of Nineveh. His Jewishness impressed them. It is also a model for us.

73. Are there any laws governing appropriate attitudes toward penitents?

Indeed. The Talmud regards as biblically mandated the prohibition against causing embarrassment or pain to a penitent or convert by reminding them of their previous condition of sinfulness or impurity:

> Ye shall not wrong one another (Leviticus 19:17)—The Torah refers here to wronging by means of speech. How so? If he is a penitent, do not say to him, 'Remember what you used to do!' If he is the offspring of converts, do not say to him, 'Remember how your ancestors used to behave!' If he was a convert who was coming to study the religion, never say to him 'How can the mouth that devoured carrion, forbidden foods, reptiles and other detestable creatures, now presume to repeat words of the Torah given from the mouth of the Most High?' . . . Whoever publicly shames his neighbor is guilty of bloodshed . . . as can be seen visually when the blood vanishes from the face and it turns pale [with humiliation].[51]

The rabbis viewed the facial loss of blood as tantamount to an act of bloodshed. *Tosafot* points out that the prior reddening of the face is "merely the compression of [cranial] blood in one place as a prelude to it being discharged."[52]

The sages were acutely sensitive to the guilt feelings that gripped penitents and converts, and to how easily their feelings could be hurt on that score. Whoever is responsible for that infringes a biblical prohibition.

74. Where in the Bible do we have the first example of someone repenting and being granted absolution from sin?

The Midrash attributes this occurrence to Cain after he killed his brother, Abel. God did not impose the death penalty upon him even though he was guilty of a capital crime. Instead God commuted it to exile, and the reason for this, the sages

---

51. *Bava Metzia* 58b.
52. *Tosafot ad loc.*

suggest, was because of his sincere repentance and horror at what he had done. This is implied in the phrase "my sin is too great to pardon" (Genesis 4:13).[53]

That Midrash states that Adam met Cain immediately after he received the divine judgment on his slaying of his brother, and Adam asked him how he fared. Cain answered that he had repented and, as a result, had his sentence of death commuted. Adam thereupon began to beat his [own] head and cried out, "How could I have been so blissfully ignorant of the great power of repentance? Thereupon Adam composed the psalm for the Sabbath day [Psalm 92, commencing with the words *Tov lehodot le-Hashem*—"It is a good thing *to confess* to the Lord."].[54]

75. The above example being a trifle "Midrashic," which is the first clear, textual example of someone repenting and being forgiven?

It is the case of Avimelech, the Philistine king who seized Sarah, wife of Abraham, and who was accordingly told by God, in a dream, that he would die for his behavior. Avimelech declared that it was in all innocence that he had seized Sarah, not realizing that she was a married woman, at which God told him that if he restored Abraham's wife, Abraham would pray for him and his life would be saved.[55]

76. In which biblical situation is forgiveness for sin granted almost immediately after confession?

In the case of King David, after his sin with Bathsheba. The prophet Nathan castigates David in the harshest of terms, foretelling the most fearful punishment on him and his household. No sooner has the prophet finished his last word, when David says, simply, "I have sinned against the Lord." Nathan answers just as readily, "The Lord also has removed your sin. You shall not die."[56]

77. Did the sages introduce any measures that were calculated specifically to facilitate repentance?

The sages did all in their power to encourage and to help penitents. There was one special enactment, called *takkanat ha-shavim* ("The enactment for the penitents"), which was especially intended to encourage thieves to repent.[57]

People who had stolen raw materials and fashioned or converted them into some object, or who had stolen beams and built them into their houses, had a particular difficulty that was calculated to obstruct their path to repentance. The problem is that the biblical law, which states "And he shall restore that which he took by

---

53. Midrash *Bereishit Rabbah* 22:28; *Pirkei D'Rabbi Eliezer* Chapter 21. However, this verse is also construed by other sages in the Midrash (as quoted by *Rashi*) in the very opposite sense of an angry rhetorical question: "Is my sin so heinous that it cannot be pardoned?"

54. The literal translation of *lehodot* is "to give thanks."

55. Genesis Chapter 20.

56. II Samuel 12:1–13.

57. *Bava Kamma* 94b.

robbery" (Leviticus 5:23), implies that repentance can only be secured where it is possible to restore the actual object in its original condition. Someone who had already built stolen beams into a house was hardly going to be able to demolish the entire house in order to retrieve the beams.

The sages, therefore, instituted that special enactment that essentially established the thief as owner of the original raw materials as a result of his having changed their state. His obligation to make restitution was confined, therefore, to monetary compensation for their value (plus the usual fine of the full value once over). This removed a very great obstruction to repentance.

78. At the psychological level, does not the essentially weak nature of man militate against the possibility of his making a perfect repentance?

If by that question we mean that because "there is no righteous man on earth who doeth only good and sinneth not" (Ecclesiastes 7:20), it must follow inevitably that the odds are considerably increased of people repeating the sin for which they currently repent, then we must answer in the affirmative. Indeed, it has to be admitted that although the thrill and novelty of the experience of sinning for a first time inevitably become diluted as the practice becomes habitual, yet, sadly, this is compensated for by the ease with which we find ourselves able to repeat the sin on subsequent occasions, due to the psychological barrier having been removed.

Indeed, this is the meaning of the otherwise curious Talmudic maxim that "Once a person has sinned it becomes permitted to him."[58] The Talmud understandably queries such a strange theology and elucidates that its meaning is that on subsequent occasions people find it so easy to repeat the sin that it is as if they were performing a permitted act.

So, at the psychological level, complete repentance is a most difficult and unpredictable exercise. But the fact that we might fall into the trap of repeating our sin should not deter us from repenting, any less than the fear that a physical illness might return should prevent us from attempting to cure it with medicaments. It is generally only when sin comes upon us unaware that it gains the upper hand. If we are in a constant state of readiness for its appearance, by keeping up the exercise of *teshuvah*, by constantly reminding ourselves of the shame and humiliation we once brought upon ourselves by the commission of that sin and the abject repentance we had to undergo, the odds are that, under such conditions, its repetition is most unlikely.

79. But if man's *yetzer ha'ra* (evil inclination) is responsible for his sinning, then are we not still beating our head against a brick wall when it comes to defeating what is, after all, an innate element of our psyche?

There is a charming Chasidic account of an exchange between the famous Rebbe, Rabbi Naftali of Rupschitz and his little boy, Eliezer, later to become the saintly

---

58. *Yoma* 87a.

Rebbe of Dzikov. Reb Naftali once caught his son doing something wrong. He brought him into his study and for an hour reproved him on his behavior.

'What could I have done, daddy?' said the child. 'It was the *yetzer ha'ra* who is constantly standing by me to trip me up. And on this occasion he really enticed me to misbehave even more!'

'On the contrary,' replied Rabbi Naftali. 'You should have been able to learn an important lesson from the *yetzer ha'ra* itself. Just observe how faithfully and unwaveringly that evil inclination fulfills his alloted task of enticing us humans. You should have learnt single-mindedness from it!'

'What a comparison!' retorted the brilliant, if rather precocious, young Eliezer. 'The *yetzer ha'ra* starts with a unique advantage, for it has no *yetzer ha'ra* of its own to deflect it from its mission, whereas man has to contend with an overwhelming inclination which prompts sin to lie in wait at the "door"' (Genesis 4:7).[59]

80. Is any particular group of people especially susceptible to the onslaught of the evil inclination?

Strange as it may seem, although the study of Torah is the greatest antidote to sin, the Talmudic sages believed firmly that members of their own fraternity were most susceptible to the influence of the evil inclination, since, the greater the man, the stronger the temptation. There is a telling illustration of this in the Talmud:

Abbaye once heard a man say to a woman, 'Let us go off together!' He said this because their destination was in the same direction. Abbaye thought, 'I shall follow them in order to prevent them from sinning.' He followed them for three parasangs across a lonely meadow. As they separated to go their separate ways, they each said, 'Thank you for your pleasant company along such a lengthy way.'

Abbaye, reflecting on their innocence, said to himself, 'If the one who hates me (the evil inclination) had tempted me in that same way, I could not have resisted it.' He then went and leant against the doorpost of his house in a distressed state. An old man came and said: 'Do not be upset, for he who is greater than his neighbor, his *yetzer ha'ra* is also greater.'[60]

81. So does the Talmud abound then with accounts of the "fall" of great men?

No, it does not. In spite of the principle just enunciated, the sages of the Talmudic period were, truly, uniquely morally and ethically principled men. Rabbi Joseph Soloveitchik notes what he calls "an interesting phenomenon," namely that "when reading the lives of the Christian saints, we discover that their lives were plagued by

---

59. Becker, M. (1983). *Parperaot La-Torah*. Jerusalem: Omen Publications, I, p. 32.
60. *Sukkah* 52a.

a continuous struggle between conflicting drives, particularly the sex drive. Many stories of their lives and exploits revolve around this theme."[61]

Rabbi Soloveitchik believes that the story in the Talmud about the fire in Rabbi Amram's house (See Question 82) is "an untypical example." He maintains that although the sages recognized the presence and even the devastating potential of the evil inclination, they were, in the main, totally disciplined masters of their emotions who led their lives and filled their waking hours in such a way that such a tendency was totally sublimated by their total preoccupation with pious living.

Perhaps Rabbi Peli, the editor of this statement of Rav Soloveitchik's thoughts on repentance, should have developed the master's theme a little more fully here, because it has to be admitted that even a cursory study of any Talmudic treatise does, in fact, reveal that the sages do have a great deal to say about sex and human passions. This might, indeed, suggest that they were similarly "plagued by a continuous struggle between conflicting drives." Rav Soloveitchik's view on this would be that the fact that those sages were keen to fathom and address the nature and behavior of man and offer guidance to him as to how best to control the "conflicting drives," they themselves gave an inspiring lead in this direction by the objectivity and sensitivity with which their own disciplined natures enabled them to discuss such matters.

There are some, however, who would think that Rav Soloveitchik had overstated the situation, as there are several recorded examples—even on the very page of the Talmud where that story of Rav Amram's temptation occurs—of sages who clearly did have to struggle with their desires.

In this context, Claude Montefiore (1858–1938) observes that "the Rabbis were prevailingly chaste . . . but this chastity was obtained at a certain cost. The lack of healthy, simple companionship and friendship caused a constant dwelling upon sexual relations and details."[62]

82. What was the story of the fire in Rav Amram's house?

The Talmud relates that a group of young Jewish girls had been taken captive and held up for ransom by the Romans and were subsequently redeemed by the community. They were provided with accommodations in the large garret of the home of Rav Amram chasida (the pious). The ladder, which required ten people to move, was then removed.

One night, as Rav Amram was studying, his lamp caught the reflection of one of the girls' faces looking down at him. He became so transfixed with her beauty, and his passions were aroused to such an extent, that he went and single-handedly raised the garret ladder into its position and began to ascend it. He got half way when he

---

61. Peli, P. H. (1980). *On Repentance—in the Thought and Oral Discourses of Rabbi Joseph B. Soloveitchik*. Jerusalem: Oroth Publishing House, p. 189.

62. Montefiore, C. G., and Loewe, H. (1938). *A Rabbinic Anthology*. New York: Meridian Books, p. xix.

suddenly froze in his tracks at the realization of what he was doing. Whereupon he screamed out, at the top of his voice: "Fire at Rav Amram's house!"

In an instant, scores of his disciples and colleagues rushed into his house. When they saw that there was no fire, and assessed the reality of Rav Amram's position, they reproved him, saying, "You have brought great shame on us all!" Rav Amram retorted: "Better you be ashamed of the house of Amram in this world rather than in the next!"[63]

83. Are there any examples quoted in the Talmud of wives of Talmudic sages succumbing to temptation?

There are examples, the most notable of which is the oblique reference to the fall of Beruriah, wife of Rabbi Meir.

Beruriah was a sage in her own right; and there are several references to her having corrected her husband's theological ideas, as well as her having rebuked and guided her husband's disciples. The Talmud refers to the fact that her husband fled to Babylon, and it offers two explanations, one of which is "because of the episode of Beruriah."[64]

The Talmud does not spell out the "episode," but *Rashi* quotes a tradition that once Beruriah scoffed at the fact that her husband's Talmudic colleagues regarded it as axiomatic that "Women are capricious." Rabbi Meir determined to prove that the truth of that assessment applied to Beruriah herself, so he induced one of his handsome disciples to attempt to seduce his wife. Whether or not she finally succumbed or merely agreed to do so is unclear, but when she discovered that it had been a ruse all along she was so ashamed that she committed suicide, and Rabbi Meir fled to Babylon, overwhelmed with remorse.

84. So would her suicide be regarded as a token of remorse, and consequently as a means of securing repentance?

This is an interesting question. Normally, there is a Talmudic principle that "death atones"; but where death is neither an act of God nor of a Jewish court, but of suicide, it would be unthinkable that it could bring with it any positive religious benefit. Thus, while we may conclude that the balance of Beruriah's mind was disturbed, to the extent that she would not be held guilty of any sin in having taken her own life, it could hardly "atone" for any act of adultery that might have been committed.

In medieval times, there are many cases recorded of communities and individuals committing suicide—and even murdering their own children—to avoid the inevitable fate of apostasy. This is not to be compared with Beruriah's action that was taken merely out of shame for what she had done. Shame is not necessarily a bad thing. It is the essential first stage of remorse and penance. It is something to

---

63. *Kiddushin* 81a.
64. *Avodah Zarah* 18b.

live with and face up to, not to escape from by taking one's life. Forced apostasy, on the other hand, is one of the cardinal sins for which one must be prepared to surrender one's life.

85. When the Temple was standing, we had a ready means of obtaining absolution through the bringing of sacrifices. Since its destruction, is full atonement still available?

The Temple was never regarded as indispensable to obtaining divine pardon for sin. While it stood, there was an obligation to mark one's repentance by a final act of the bringing of a sin-offering, but that was merely the climax to a change of heart and an outpouring of remorse that constituted the essential *teshuvah*.

Hence, the Talmudic statement: "How do we know that it is accounted to the credit of a penitent as if he had gone up to Jerusalem, built the Temple and the altar, and offered all the sacrifices enumerated in the Torah? Since it states: "The sacrifices of the Lord are a broken heart" (Psalm 51:19).[65]

86. We have referred to the three-fold prerequisite for the removal of any trace of sin: repentance, prayer, and charity. Do they come in any order of respective importance?

They do. They are always quoted in that form—*teshuvah, tefillah, utzedakah*—conforming to a descending order of importance. The Talmud states that repentance and prayer are greater than charity since "sometimes charity is dispensed to people who do not deserve it."[66] Repentance is, in turn, greater than prayer, since with reference to the former it states that "The world will be filled with knowledge of the Lord as the waters cover the sea-bed" (Isaiah 11:9). The Midrash observes that "Just as the sea is never shut, and whoever wishes to bathe at any time may come and do so, so it is with repentance, that whenever a person is disposed to repent he may do so and God will accept it. Prayer, on the other hand, is far more restricted since there are specially prescribed times allocated for its recitation."[67]

87. Bearing in mind that Judaism believes in human free will, does God remain completely aloof, then, from man's struggle toward repentance and righteousness?

No. Judaism has a concept—albeit not too well-developed—of God, as it were, picking up the faintest vibes of human remorse, even before it has surfaced fully into our consciousness. Thus, at the earliest fluttering of a human pang of conscience or a sensitivity to self-improvement, God activates the process to enable us to facilitate our desire. This is expressed pithily in the Talmudic maxim: "Whoever comes with the intention of purifying himself, heaven opens for him the gate of

---

65. Midrash *Yalkut* on Psalms, section 766.
66. Midrash *Shochar Tov* on Proverbs, Chapter 6.
67. *Op. cit.* on Psalm 25.

purification; whoever comes to defile himself, heaven helps him to achieve his evil objective."[68]

The classical example of this is, of course, the case of God "Hardening Pharaoh's heart." It is not until the sixth plague that this formulation is employed. In the case of the first five plagues, it states that "Pharaoh's heart became hard" or that "Pharaoh hardened his [own] heart." This precise phraseology is to teach that God initially gave Pharaoh plenty of leeway, allowing him fully to exercise his own free will. But there is a limit to God's patience, and the gift of free will is not infinite. After hardening his own heart on five occasions, God is entitled to intervene and to assume that this is Pharaoh's entrenched philosophy. Once that stage has been reached, God is entitled to "help man to achieve his evil objective," an objective exercised initially and consistently through the agency of free will. God then takes over the initiative, and He actively hardens that heart in order to compact the crimes of the sinner and justify the ultimate imposition of the heaviest of sentences.

That the gate of encouragement that God opens for those who seek out purity is unbounded, and man's path to repentance strewn with roses, is stated in a most beautiful teaching of the sages: "Make for me," says God, "an opening [for your return] as narrow as the point of a needle, and I shall open for you gates through which wagons and coaches may pass."[69]

88. Why is there a need for reward and punishment? Would it not have been far less complicated for humans if God had created us exclusively with a good inclination and without any propensity to do evil?

It would certainly have been less complicated, but we would have been reduced thereby to a mere robotic existence—puppets on a divine string. Being created in the divine image means being in charge of our moral and spiritual destiny while on earth. And just as God is possessed of choice, so is man.

Again, reward and punishment is also a vital component for the nurturing of character traits and the stimulation of human ambition. Without reward for effort and achievement, it is doubtful whether most humans would ever submit to the discipline of education, training, and constructive endeavor. Without punishment, it is doubtful whether most people would be law abiding. So reward and punishment is the natural element in which humans survive, develop, and progress. It is only natural, therefore, that God should employ it as His response to human conduct.

89. Does a person's motive for repenting have a bearing upon the divine reaction to it?

Our tradition believes that it does. The Talmud distinguishes three motivations: one who repents out of conviction based upon *love of God*; one who repents out of

---

68. *Avodah Zarah* 18b.
69. Midrash *Shir Ha-Shirim Rabba* on 5:2.

simple fear of the consequences of sin; and, the lowest category of repentance, that which is prompted by suffering and affliction.[70]

The rabbis were cautious in their statements about the comparative effect of these three motives for repentance. According to one view,[71] repentance occasioned by love of God has the effect of totally effacing any trace of the individual's sin, whereas repentance out of fear prompts the Almighty merely to disregard the record of that particular sin. Penitents in both of these categories are regarded as "sons" of God, whereas those whose penitence was only brought about as a result of suffering are relegated to a servant–master relationship with Him.[72]

90. Is it conceivable that one might repent for one particular sin while consciously ignoring another that one is aware of, but which one cannot summon the strength of will to confront?

It is, of course, conceivable, though it is by no means proper conduct. Repentance cannot be confined to the nonrepetition of a particular sin. The consciousness of sin and the positive and sincere desire to remove its taint impose upon a penitent a duty of striving for a total regeneration, whereby his whole way of life becomes reconsecrated. An oft-repeated phrase in rabbinic literature is *teshuvah uma'asim tovim* ("repentance and good deeds").[73] Good deeds are considered as the logical corollary of the act of repentance. The implication is that it is inconceivable for a true penitent to regret and desist from one act of sin while perpetuating another. Repentance must be unconditional and unrestricted to qualify for acceptance.

91. So does this mean that a person who truly wishes to repent is expected to swing to the very opposite pole and become a *Ba'al teshuvah*, taking on board an entire regimen of the most exacting spiritual demands?

Any such dramatic and overnight swing, from nonobservance to total observance, is not to be recommended. Judaism believes in the gradual approach, moving forward and upward steadily and firmly, on the basis of the conviction and the new vistas that study and increased observance open out before the true searcher for truth.

Rabbi E. Dessler (1891–1954) warns us against attempting an overambitious and unrealistic level of repentance and resolve:

We have been taught that only the most dramatic arousal of our soul from its slumber will be effective for repentance. Nevertheless, when the penitent makes his resolution for the future, he must ensure that it is appropriate to the spiritual level he has attained. For if he attempts to overreach himself, he will

---

70. *Yoma* 86a.

71. *Ibid.* See *Rashi*'s comment *ad loc.*

72. On the distinction between "father–son" and "servant–master" relationships with God, see Cohen, J. M. (1994). *Prayer and Penitence.* Northvale, NJ: Jason Aronson Inc., p. 49.

73. Cf. Mishnah *Avot* 4:11, 4:17; Talmud *Shabbat* 32a; *Yoma* 87a; *Nedarim* 32b; *Sanhedrin* 87b, etc.

fail, God forbid, and his repentance will be nullified. Thus, although his desire for repentance and his remorse has to be at the most intensive level, yet, if it is to be sustained, he must restrain his temptation to take upon himself too much at the outset, and realize that even such (spiritual) longings have to be controlled.[74]

92. Speaking of the _Ba'alei teshuvah_, the born-again Jews who put behind them a life of sin and return to whole-hearted faith, do our sages make any comment on who ranks higher on the ladder of spiritual achievement: the latter or those who have remained consistently religious from birth.

Over the last few decades, since the evolution of the _Ba'alei teshuvah_ "movement" with its network of yeshivot and seminaries in Israel, those two respective categories are the subject of much discussion and are conveniently referred to as either B.T.'s (_Ba'alei teshuvah_) or F.F.B's (_Frum_ [religious] from birth).

It has to be admitted that a measure of rivalry frequently surfaces between the adherents of the respective groups, with the latter speaking rather disparagingly about the former's meteoric catapulsion into faith, and often into extreme forms of observance. Suspicion is regularly expressed regarding both the motives and the durability of their commitment.

But that rivalry is not, in fact, a phenomenon of the twentieth century. Already in the first century c.e. the political and religious turmoil of Palestine begat a host of Messianic, nationalistic, and other sectarian groups, which succeeded in capturing the hearts and souls of previously irreligious Jews, many of whom "saw the light" as a result of contact with one of the itinerant charismatic Torah teachers who preached either in the synagogues or marketplaces of their towns. And hence the ancient Talmudic debate began regarding which group stands higher in God's estimation: the _Ba'alei teshuvah_ or the righteous from birth:

Rabbi Yochanan said, "Although all the great prophets who foretold Israel's national salvation gave credit for that to the merit of the _Ba'alei teshuvah_, yet, as regards the righteous [from birth], the prophet stated: 'No one's eye can glimpse God as clearly as you'" (Isaiah 64:3).

Rabbi Abbahu contested this view, stating that "even the perfectly righteous cannot aspire to the spiritual level of attainment which the newcomer penitent enjoys."[75]

And it is the opinion of Rabbi Abbahu that won the consensus support of rabbinic authorities, a view to which Maimonides inclines in his _Mishneh Torah_, in the section on the Laws of Penitence.[76]

---

74. Dessler, E. L. (1955). In _Mikhtav Me-Eliyahu_, ed. S. A. Halpern and A. Carmell. London: Chaim Friedlander, p. 88.

75. _Berakhot_ 34b.

76. Maimonides _Mishneh Torah, Hilkhot Teshuvah_ 7:4.

93. But is not Rabbi Abbahu's view rather illogical, for surely people who have never been enticed into sin and who have maintained loyalty and righteousness from birth deserve, if only as a reward for that loyalty, to be placed on a higher pedestal than those who once espoused a life of sin and impurity?

The consensus view, as we have said, does not see the situation in that way. It rather takes account of the superhuman effort and courage required of a person to extricate himself from the persuasively alluring clutches of a sinful and immoral lifestyle. It recognizes the hardships and psychological adjustments such a person has to make in order to eradicate the addiction of sin and temptation. Heroic faith is required to exchange the real and potent thrill of today for the mere promise of some vague state of future divine grace. Heroic sacrifice is required to jeopardize one's livelihood by closing one's business on Sabbaths and festivals for the far less tangible promise of a divine dividend.

The one who is righteous by upbringing, on the other hand, is not called upon to effect any such a dramatic transformation of the self. He has few temptations to resist or crises of faith to resolve. Observance comes to him as a second nature, almost as a reflex action. Such people often relate to their faith and observances mechanically, without engaging their inner selves—and frequently without even engaging their Maker.

94. Is there any message to take away from that vote in favor of the newcomer penitents?

The message is surely to raise the banner of hope to those who have not been reared in an observant home. It tells them that their religious efforts, however elementary, are charged with significance in the eyes of Judaism. It tells them that every small step that they take along the path of observance is, in reality, a giant leap. It tells them not to lose heart if the going is tough, if their Hebrew reading is halting, if they are not sure how to follow the synagogue service properly, or whether what they are doing is quite right or not. It tells them that they are truly beloved of God, because they have voted for Him of their own free will, not because of the pervasive influence of home background, parental pressure, or the lethargy of breaking away from a cozy tradition.

95. Is there any other reason that can be offered to account for the superiority of the *Ba'alei teshuvah* over the righteous from birth?

There is another rationale that takes account of the fact that the righteous from birth are likely to be totally unprepared for the temptations of the real world. There is no guarantee, therefore, that, subjected to an unexpected temptation, they might not be overwhelmed and succumb.

The *Ba'al teshuvah*, on the other hand, has reached his decision to change his lifestyle after a critical appraisal of its hollowness. He has tasted the forbidden fruit. He knows how ephemeral is the pleasure it offers, compared with the all-embracing inner joy and spiritual warmth of the consecrated life. He has made, therefore, a well-considered decision to resist sin in the future; and the strength he gains from that will ensure his future commitment.

The future of the one nurtured in an observant home, on the other hand, is in no way guaranteed. He is only human, after all. He may crave just one taste of the forbidden fruit. And there is no saying that his righteous upbringing will protect him from its consequences.

96. Is repentance necessary only when a crime or sinful act has been perpetrated?

No, its application is much broader. Maimonides expresses it very clearly:

Do not imagine that repentance only applies to acts committed, such as immorality or theft. For, just as a person must repent for them, so must he identify his evil character traits, and repent of anger, jealousy, enmity, a readiness to mock others, a pursuit of materialism and honour, or a tendency to gluttony. Indeed, once one is prone to these sins, it is more difficult to liberate oneself from them than from any one-off act of commission.[77]

97. Is divine forgiveness ever withheld?

The rabbinic concept of divine mercy allowed for even the most inveterate sinner to obtain immediate forgiveness. The rabbis took their lead from the case of Manasseh, King of Judah (696–641 B.C.E.) whose reign stands out as one of the darkest periods in the religious history of Israel. Idolatry, apostasy, murder, and immorality are all included in the list of charges made against him. Yet, according to the testimony of 2 Chronicles 33:12-13," When he was in distress, he entreated the favor of the Lord his God and humbled himself greatly before the God of his fathers. He prayed to Him, and God received his entreaty and heard his supplication. . . . Then Manasseh knew that the Lord was God."

However, in one situation—leading a multitude into sin—divine forgiveness is withheld. Such a sinner, declare the rabbis, is not even given the opportunity to repent. For profanation of God's name, there can be no forgiveness during the lifetime of the offender, but the combined efforts of his penitence, the Day of Atonement, his suffering, and, ultimately, his death, will succeed in securing for him eventual redemption. Within the definition of profanation of God's name, the rabbis particularize the case of a religious leader who by his conduct brings religion into disrepute.[78]

98. What should be the attitude of God-fearing people toward evil-doers?

There is a basic *mitzvah*—described by Rabbi Akivah as a fundamental principle of the Torah[79]—to "love one's fellow man as oneself" (Leviticus 19:18). However, it would seem that there is also a *mitzvah* to hate evil-doers. This is inferred from

---

77. *Op. cit.* 7:3.

78. *Yoma* 87a; Maimonides *Hilkhot Teshuvah* 1:4.

79. *Sifra* to Leviticus 19:18.

the verse, "Thou shalt not hate thy brother in thy heart; thou shalt surely rebuke thy brother, and not bear sin because of him" (Leviticus 19:17). This verse insists that we rebuke a sinful person in order to eradicate his sinfulness; for, should he persist with his sin, we would have to maintain an attitude of antipathy ("hatred") toward him, which would, in turn, cause us to sin through infringement of the prohibition of hating one's brother in our heart! However, our halakhic authorities have stated that this command to hate evil-doers is restricted to those who have received the biblically mandated "rebuke," but who have totally disregarded all such efforts to dissuade them from their sinful way.

Now, the Talmud[80] states that by its time it was accepted that there was no one sufficiently capable of administering the prescribed rebuke in a manner that would guarantee success. Most of us would tend either to humiliate or at least embarrass the sinner, which would have the opposite result of that intended. On that basis, we must regard all evil-doers as those who have not yet received proper, sensitive, and loving rebuke; and, as such, one may not treat them as transgressors or hate them.

Maimonides[81] offers another reason why the Karaites of his day should, likewise, be regarded as those who were coerced into sin, and, are therefore not responsible for their actions they should consequently be befriended and encouraged to re-enter the Orthodox fold. Maimonides categorized them as a *tinnok shenishbah lebein ha-goyyim*, "one who was captured [in infancy, and brought up] among heathens." They cannot be held responsible or bear guilt for sins of omission or commission wrought through their ignorance of Jewish prohibitions and practices. And, on the basis of the two principles we have mentioned, this remains our attitude toward evil-doers in our day.

It may be objected, however, that the very opening verse of the book of Psalms commences with the statement, "Happy is the man who has not joined the counsel of the wicked, nor walked the road that sinners tread, not taken his seat among scoffers."[82] The implication is clearly that people who wish to lead a religious life should maintain no close ties with those whose lifestyle is inimical to the way of Torah. The psalmist's three categories—the wicked, sinners, and scoffers—clearly refer, however, to people who have resisted many opportunities for *teshuvah* and whose attitudes have hardened over a long period to the extent that they justify their evil ways and even scoff at those who pursue a life of piety.

While it can only be dangerous to fraternize with such people, yet others, who have adopted an evil course of action as a result of enslavement to their passions through a particular set of circumstances, but in most other ways lead good and honorable lives, these should be befriended, counseled, and encouraged toward moral and spiritual regeneration.

Rav Kook employs this approach in order to exonerate those who abandon their Jewish practice as a result of assimilation to the all-pervasive secular culture of the age:

---

80. *Arakhin* 16b.
81. Maimonides *Mishneh Torah, Hilkhot Mamrim* 3:3.
82. Psalm 1:1.

Just as the Tosafists remark in *Sanhedrin* 26b that someone who is suspected of an act of sexual immorality because he was seized by passion is not disqualified as a witness because 'his passions coerced him,' and, by the same token, the Tosafists in *Gittin* 41b write that seduction by a maid servant is considered a form of coercion, so we may regard the modern age as an evil temptress who entices the young with her charm and her spells. They are truly 'coerced,' and God forbid that we judge them as willful heretics.[83]

It should be borne in mind that it is not always easy to determine accurately the motives and attitudes of others. This is exemplified in the following Talmudic report:

In the neighborhood of Rabbi Zera there lived some lawless men. He nevertheless showed them friendship in order to lead them to repentance. The Rabbis were annoyed at his action.

When Rabbi Zera died, the wicked men said: 'Until now, we had the Rabbi to implore Divine mercy for us. Who will do so now?' Thereupon they felt remorse in their hearts, and repented.[84]

99. But why were Rabbi Zera's colleagues against his fraternization with them?

Rabbi Zera's colleagues were unhappy because they had concluded that those "lawless men" were beyond the stage of redemption. This is hinted at by the term the Talmud uses to describe them: *biryoni*, which elsewhere in the Talmud has the common meaning of "highwaymen, rebels, outlaws." The sages clearly, and understandably, kept their distance from such men and viewed them with the greatest fear and suspicion. Rabbi Zera, on the other hand, who shared a neighborhood with them, saw another side to them and realized that they could be won back to lawful, even righteous, living.

Rabbi Zera consequently prayed for those men—a fact known, and appreciated by them. The rabbi's example of pious and constructive living, his positive attitude and concern for them, his proximity and his words to them were all clearly having an influence on them and subconsciously eroding the barriers they had set up to spirituality.

100. But is it not curious that as long as Rabbi Zera was alive they leaned on his redemptive powers and did not bother, therefore, to repent? Surely, then, Rabbi Zera was having the very opposite of the desired effect and was actually obstructing their repentance as long as he was alive?

It was not that Rabbi Zera was obstructing their *teshuvah*, but simply that their capitulation to repentance coincided with, and was clearly triggered by, his death.

83. R. Abraham Isaac ha-Kohen Kook, (1965). *Iggrot Ha-Re'iyyah*, Jerusalem: Mosad Ha-Rav Kuk, I, p. 171.
84. *Sanhedrin* 37a.

Their repentance was their token of reverence and gratitude to him for having shown them the way and prayed for their souls.

The point of that episode is to teach that one should never categorize anyone as an inveterate sinner and assume that he has gone beyond the point of return; one should never condemn from afar; and one should never despair of the positive, though imperceptible, influence one might well be having on another. Indeed, a statement to that effect is quoted in the name of Rabbi Zera as a preamble to the above story of his relationship with the lawless men in his neighborhood:

> Rabbi Zera quoted the verse, "And he [Isaac] savoured the smell of *begadav* (Esau's clothes)" (Genesis 27:27). Do not read *begadav*—said Rabbi Zera—but *bogdav* (those who deal treacherously with Him).

Rabbi Zera applies this verse to God who savors even those who behave wickedly and contrary to His will. "God is good to all, and His mercy extends to all His creatures" (Psalm 145:9). If God can love the evil-doers, how much more should we?

This is especially emphasized in the Talmud, in a comment on the verse: "Let *chata'im* (evil deeds) cease from the earth" (Psalm 104:35). The Talmud asks, "Is it written *chot'im* (that "*sinners* shall cease from the earth")? No, it states *chata'im*—that it is only their sinful deeds that should be eradicated.[85]

101. How important a role does repentance fulfill in Judaism?

A pivotal role. All the private and public sacrifices that are offered on account of sins presuppose a corresponding act of private or public contrition. Furthermore, a recurring theme in the prophetic literature is that the future redemption of Israel and the fulfillment of the vision for the "end of days" is made conditional upon Israel returning to her God and hearkening to His voice. Repentance is the primary spiritual objective to which society, and especially Israel, must devote itself.

102. That being so, presumably repentance is listed as one of the 613 biblical commandments?

Surprising as it may seem, the command to repent is not listed as a biblical law by Maimonides, who wrote an important work, called *Sefer Ha-Mitzvot*, enumerating all the positive and negative biblical laws of the Torah! The reason for this omission is that Maimonides viewed repentance from the perspective of a philosopher and concluded that repentance is not something that can be internalized or expressed in purely conceptual terms.

Sacrifices were prescribed because one had transgressed a particular biblical presciption by way of an act of omission or commission. Repentance consists, therefore, in the abandonment of that particular sin by returning to the proper

---

85. *Berakhot* 10a. On this subject of the appropriate attitude to be adopted toward sinners, see N. Lamm, "Loving and Hating Jews as Halakhic Categories," *Tradition*, vol. 24, No. 2 (Winter 1989), pp. 98–122.

fulfillment of the command that the sin negated. Thus, the feeling of remorse is only the first stage of a process of repentance that can only be said to have been achieved when proper observance of the prescription of the law is once again complied with, and the proper rhythm of religious life restored.

Repentance does not exist in a vacuum, therefore, as a separate *mitzvah*. It is inseparable from the other 613 commands of the Torah. It is, in fact, the state of mind that is the precondition for proper observance of any command.

103. So, does the Torah totally ignore the entire exercise of repentance?

No, it does not. It refers to it in the context of the confession (*Viddui*) that the penitent is called upon to make. In Maimonides' *Sefer Ha-Mitzvot*, this is listed as *Mitzvah* number 73:

> The Torah here commands us to confess all our sins and transgressions against God, and to recite them at the time of our repentance. Its intention is that we should recite the formula: 'I beseech You, O Lord, I have sinned, transgressed, behaved contrary to Your will in having done such-and-such. . . .' He should recite the confessional in full, and beg forgiveness in as clear and direct a way as possible. . . . This is derived from the verse: 'When any man or woman shall commit any sin . . . to commit a trespass against the Lord, and that soul be guilty; then *they shall confess their sin* which they have done. . . .' [Numbers 5:6–7]

The Torah is clearly exercising economy here by referring to the required confession that must accompany repentance, rather than by allocating a separate *mitzvah* to the duty of repenting one's sins.

104. But is it not still rather surprising that the Torah should have omitted such an important *mitzvah* as repentance?

It is, though we may conjecture that this is because repentance is in a totally different category to other *mitzvot*. It is merely a restoration of the *status quo*, an exercise in the removal of the negative rather than the assertion of the positive. It is an act of *tikkun*, of repairing the breach in the person's relationship with God that was created as a result of his sin. For this to be truly effective, it has to be spontaneous on the part of man. And only when man has, of his own volition, felt the stirring of remorse and is clearly searching for a means of channeling it effectively does the Torah guide him as to the required concretization of that state of mind in the form of a verbal confession.

105. Granted that repentance is not allocated a separate *mitzvah* in the Torah. It nevertheless is clearly a *mitzvah* (under the umbrella of the *mitzvah* of confession). Why then is there no blessing prescribed for the penitent?

We suggest that it is precisely because it is what we have described as "an exercise in the removal of the negative rather than the assertion of the positive."

Repentance is a dawning realization of the existence of the divine admonition that what we are doing is negative and prohibited. In Judaism, we do not recite blessings over negative *mitzvot* or that refer to prohibited acts. The only blessing that contains a reference to prohibition is the marriage blessing: "Blessed art thou. . . . Who has prohibited unto us those that are (merely) betrothed and permitted unto us those that are married unto us by means of the canopy and sanctification." This exception to the rule is because the negative serves merely as the foil for emphasizing the positive and overarching state of marriage, by which the sanction of the relationship is achieved. Thus, the main thrust of that blessing is also over a positive *mitzvah*. Repentance, on the other hand, although it has to lead to a life of positive action, is primarily a state of remorse and a negation of one's former lifestyle.

106. Is there any other reason why no blessing is prescribed?

We may also suggest an analogy with the biblical *mitzvah* of reciting the Haggadah, over which no blessing is made. We have suggested elsewhere[86] that this is because it is a blessing that has no prescribed or precise time frame, since some people allocate only a short time to it, while others (like the five sages) spend the entire night. Similarly, it is a *mitzvah* that is constantly interrupted, for the performance of ritual acts and the eating of ritual foods, as well as for eating the meal, hiding the *Afikoman*, and family chat and reminiscences. We do not recite a blessing over such a *mitzvah* that is so protracted and interrupted since it is impossible to keep one's mind exclusively on the *mitzvah* in that situation. (Such interruptions may, indeed, explain why we recite a separate blessing each night when we count the Omer, even though it is, basically, one biblical *mitzvah*.)

107. But why is repentance construed as a protracted and interrupted act? Surely it is an ongoing state of mind.

From a halakhic as well as a psychological point of view, it is not. We can do no better than quote Rav J. B. Soloveitchik's description of the repentance process:

> Repentance is not a function of a single, decisive act, but grows and gains in size, slowly and gradually, until the penitent undergoes a complete metamorphosis, and then, after becoming a new person, and only then, does repentance take place. And what is the concluding act of repentance? It is confession.[87]

On the graph of repentance, there is no single, uninterrupted, vertical line from the first stirring of remorse or recognition that one's life is going in the wrong direction, to the peak of complete repentance. It is invariably punctuated by interludes of regression. One starts with good intentions to repent, and then one is overwhelmed by the blandishments of habit. There are times when great energy is

---

86. Cohen, J. M. (1996). *1001 Questions and Answers on Pesach*. Northvale, NJ: Jason Aronson Inc., pp. 105–106.

87. Peli, P. H. (1980). *On Repentance*. Jerusalem: Oroth Publishing House, pp. 84–85.

expended in the battle against the evil inclination and in the tortuous uphill climb toward moral cleansing. And there are other times—which can be most protracted—when the exercise of repentance is put on hold while the person gets on with other aspects of his life. Blessings are pithy and compact ways of consecrating equally compact *mitzvot*. Where the time scale is outspread, interrupted, and intermittent, the blessing is dispensed with.

By the same token, we do not recite blessings over *mitzvot* that are ill-defined and left to individual motivation. Thus, there is no blessing over the giving of charity. We can never be certain that the amount we contribute at any given time or to any given cause is totally appropriate to our financial situation and the worth of the particular cause. It is ill-defined. We can never be sure whether we have really fulfilled a *mitzvah* by having given significantly, or whether we have merely gone through the motions and salved our consciences by what is merely a token donation, given our financial circumstance.

It is the same with repentance. We cannot make a blessing over an exercise that is truly impossible to quantify. We cannot know when, and whether, we have truly reached a level of repentance that constitutes the optimum of our potential. Most of us choose a point of remorse at which we, subjectively, make the assessment that we have effectively put the past behind us. But that may well be an incomplete repentance. We may well have curtailed the exercise of repentance before we have actually gained the requisite moral strength to resist subsequent temptations. Repentance is too illusory and subjective an exercise over which to recite a confident blessing.

108. Is there any acknowledgment in the Torah to the fact that repentance is a stage-by-stage process?

It may indeed be inferred from a verse in the book of Lamentations: "Let us examine our ways, let us put them to the test and return to the Lord" (3:40). This verse plots the three stages through which the penitent must proceed. The first involves examination of one's ways, that is stepping back to take a general and objective look at the direction of one's life. If one is shocked at the results of that initial assessment and is determined to change direction, then one must proceed to the next stage, which is putting our ways to the test.

This involves a more thorough-going process of introspection, of examining every aspect of one's life, both in relation to one's fellow and in relation to God. Included in the former is a detailed analysis of one's ethical and moral values: one's integrity, relationships with family, spouses, parents, children, siblings, teachers, business associates, employers, employees, clients and creditors, as well as one's character traits (Am I quick to pick quarrels? Do I impose my own will on others, without taking any account of their views? Am I vain? Do I spend my spare time exclusively on selfish social and leisure activities, without allocating any of my time, or devoting any of my energy, talent, and resources to worthy and charitable causes?).

Included in an examination of our relationship to God is the religious orientation of our lives. Do we make room for Him in our lives? Do we devote time each day to the study of His Torah and the practice of His *mitzvot*? Are we bringing up our children in homes that are religiously inspirational? Are we satisfying them by providing the very best religious education, or are we satisfying ourselves that we have gone through the motions of identifying with our tradition? Does the relationship with our wife betoken a spiritual, as well as a physical, dimension? Are our homes totally *kasher*? Does the spirit of Shabbat and festivals permeate them and transform them into focuses of spiritual light?

The list is endless, but only when both of those major stages have been reached and completed can we be said to have attained the final stage of returning to the Lord, in absolute repentance and reconciliation. Repentance is certainly a stage-by-stage, delicate, and traumatic exercise.

IV

Rosh Hashanah's Three Ledgers

109. What are those three ledgers that are supposed to be opened by God on Rosh Hashanah?

The Talmud states as follows:

Rabbi Yochanan said: 'Three books are opened on Rosh Hashanah: One containing the names of the totally wicked; one containing the names of the totally righteous; and the third containing the names of those who rank between them both. The totally righteous are immediately inscribed and sealed for life; the totally wicked are immediately inscribed and sealed for death, and those who rank midway have their judgment suspended from Rosh Hashanah until Yom Kippur. If they merit it, they are inscribed for life; if they do not, they are inscribed for death.'[1]

110. How could the Talmud possibly affirm something like that when our most cursory observation of the fate of righteous and wicked people contradicts it so palpably?

Indeed, if understood literally, it cannot be corroborated, for there are many righteous people who suffer a sad fate or even meet their death, while there are also many rogues who see out the ensuing year amid good health and prosperity.

Moses Nachmanides devotes a special discourse to this very difficulty[2]. He begins by quoting a diametrically opposite Talmudic statement that reads as follows: "He whose meritorious deeds exceed his sins will have evil done to him . . . He whose sins exceed his meritorious deeds will have good done to him."[3]

Rashi explains that the reference is to the rewards and punishments meted out in this world. The righteous have evil visited upon them here so that they will enter the Hereafter completely purged of all their sins and ready to enjoy the reward for perfect righteousness. Conversely, the wicked will be granted the reward for

---

1. *Rosh Hashanah* 16b.
2. Chavel, C. B. (1978). *Ramban: Writings and Discourses*, vol. I. New York: Shilo Publishing House, Inc., pp. 272–277.
3. *Kiddushin* 39b.

whatever good deeds they might have done in life so that they will enter the Hereafter laden only with the stigma of their wickedness and with no merit to mitigate their punishment.

Nachmanides' purpose in quoting this exposition is to indicate that, in the words of the Mishnah, "It is not in our power to explain either the security of the wicked or the suffering of the righteous."[4] One thing is sure, however, and that is that the respective fate of the wicked and the righteous, as we perceive it, gives no clue as to their ultimate fate in the world of eternity. Hence, when the Talmud refers to the righteous and the wicked being respectively inscribed immediately for life and death, this is not necessarily contradicted by the fate they appear to be experiencing in this world. It is their ultimate fate that is "immediately" sealed. Indeed, their respective prosperity or adversity in this world is the essential preparatory stage in the shaping of their ultimate and deserved destiny.

111. Is there any other way of explaining the apparent contradiction between the Midrash of the three ledgers and our own perception of the apparently contrary fate of both the righteous and the wicked?

Nachmanides offers another intriguing insight. He refers to the verse in the Torah that deals with the judicial process: "And they [the judges] shall acquit the righteous, and they shall condemn the wicked" (Deuteronomy 25:1). The Torah refers here to a single and specific charge being brought against someone. The terms "righteous" and "wicked" are employed, therefore, in the very narrow sense of their respective innocence or guilt of that specific charge. It does not refer to their broader degree of religious commitment, and attainment.

Similarly, says Nachmanides, the Talmudic reference—to "the righteous" being inscribed immediately for life and "the wicked" for death—has to be understood in that judicial sense. "The righteous" are those who have been acquitted in the judgment of this particular Rosh Hashanah on account of some merit that they may have gained during the past year. There is no suggestion, then, that they are objectively and comprehensively "righteous," and there is no contradiction, therefore, between the life they are granted on this Rosh Hashanah and the suffering they may otherwise endure.

Similarly, "the wicked" are those who are destined to die during the coming year. They are "wicked," that is "condemned," only regarding the judgment of this particular year. In all other respects, however, they may well have lived good and reputable lives. There is again no contradiction, therefore, between the deserved pleasures they have hitherto enjoyed, as righteous people, and their death this coming year.[5]

---

4. Mishnah *Avot* 4:19.
5. Chavel, C. B. (1978). *Ramban: Writings and Discourses*, vol. I. New York: Shilo Publishing House, Inc., p. 276.

112. Is there any other way of interpreting the Talmudic reference?

Indeed, Nachmanides adds another original interpretation. He suggests that the terms "life" and "death" were not being employed here by the sages in their usual, narrow, and specific sense: "They seized upon life as the epitome of all benefits, and death as the principal of all evils. Thus, they subsumed all the punishments of the world—plagues, death of children, poverty, and all physiological mishaps—under the term death. And they included all the benefits—riches, property, honor, children, peace and health—under the term life."[6]

According to this interpretation, the contradictions between the Talmudic statement and our general observation of life and fate no longer exist. When it states that the righteous are immediately granted "life," it can refer to one or more of a whole range of benefits. The righteous may well suffer in other respects, but be blessed—as a specific reward for goodness—with one of those benefits. Conversely, the punishment of "death" that is visited on the wicked person as a punishment for his deeds does not necessarily mean loss of life, but may be one particular punishment that is classified under that category.

113. Do any other commentators offer explanations of this difficulty in the Talmudic reference to the three ledgers?

Rabbi Avraham ben David of Posquieres (1125–1198), author of (*Rabad*) glosses to Maimonides' Mishneh Torah, interprets the Talmudic reference to the three ledgers rather differently. He refers us to a Talmudic interpretation of the verse: "The number of your days I shall complete" (Exodus 23:26).

This refers to the years of life that are prescribed for a person from birth. If he merits it, he completes their number; if he does not merit it, heaven reduces the number. That is the view of Rabbi Akivah. The Sages said that if he merits it, heaven adds to that number; if he does not merit it, heaven reduces it.[7]

Now, according to this statement, when the Talmud states (in the passage of the three ledgers) that "the totally righteous are immediately inscribed for life," this means that the number of years originally allotted to them is either confirmed (in accordance with the view of Rabbi Akivah) or extended (according to the view of the sages). Similarly, when it states that "the totally wicked are immediately inscribed for death," it means that an immediate and detrimental adjustment to their originally allotted life span is inscribed.

According to this interpretation, there is no longer any problem in the Talmudic reference to the three ledgers, since the "life" that the righteous earn has to do with quantity, and not with quality. We may, indeed, see righteous people suffering, but that does not mean that they have not earned reward for their righteousness. Again,

6. *Op. cit.*, p. 277.
7. *Yevamot* 49a–50b.

we may well see wicked people prospering, but that does not mean that they have not suffered—by having their life span reduced.

114. Are there any problems with this interpretation of Rabbi Avraham ben David?

There are. For, while the reduction of their life span is clearly a punishment for the wicked, notwithstanding any pleasures they seem to be enjoying, it is difficult to appreciate the benefit of the reward to the righteous of an extension of "life" which is not accompanied by an enjoyment of other blessings. For the righteous to have their life span confirmed, or even extended, but for it to be characterized by ill health or other adversity, is hardly a blessing. Indeed, it might even be construed as the very opposite! So, the conflict between the Talmudic reward and the situation we see all around us, of the righteous suffering, remains problematic.

115. But is there not still a difficulty in the Talmudic formulation, for we are not told exactly how the assessment of "the totally righteous," "the totally wicked," and "those who rank midway" (See Question 109) is made and how their respective good deeds and sins are measured?

Maimonides helps to clarify this point. He states that

Every single person performs both good as well as evil deeds. One whose good deeds exceed his evil deeds is designated 'righteous,' one whose evil deeds exceed his good deeds is designated 'wicked' and one whose respective deeds are equal is designated as of 'midway rank.'

This assessment is not made according to the quantity of the good or evil deeds performed by a person, but according to their nature. There are some individual good deeds that are so meritorious that they neutralize the effect of many sins, and there are some individual sins that are so heinous that they neutralize the reward for many good deeds. And those relative assessments can only be made by the All-knowing God who weighs justly and precisely the good and evil deeds.[8]

116. Are there any particular lessons to be derived from this statement of Maimonides?

There is, indeed, a most salutary lesson here for all, and particularly for those who presume to assess and comment on the religious standards of others. In this age of religious polarization, with the gulf widening between the religious and the non-religious, the Ultra-Orthodox and the Centrist (or Modern) Orthodox, and between the Orthodox and the Progressives, with each camp setting itself up as the ideal religious model, and tending to de-legitimize the others, it is vital to note Maimonides' caution that only the All-knowing God can possibly assess the quality

---

8. Maimonides *Mishneh Torah, Hilkhot Teshuvah* 3:1–2.

of a person's piety. We may think that the *mitzvot* to which we accord priority give us the spiritual advantage and secure for us an honored place in the World to Come, but we may get for ourselves a terrible shock one day when the true comparative assessments are revealed to us by God. The people we demean on account of their non-observance of ritual practices may well have chalked up immeasurable merit on account of concealed deeds of kindness and charity that may totally outweigh all their other religious shortcomings, leaving them, veritably, as "totally righteous."

Similarly, many who seem on the surface to be performing all the rituals with great zeal may, in their business or private lives, be perpetrating unethical or immoral acts that totally negate all the merit for their high profile piety. It is safer to get on with raising one's own standards and to avoid making any comparative religious assessments of others. Quite apart from our total incompetence to make such assessments, as Maimonides makes clear, such an exercise will assuredly compound our guilt as we inevitably resort to disparagement of others, involving the cardinal sins of evil speech (*leshon ha-ra*) and defamation (*motzi shem ra*).

117. But if, according to Maimonides, the concealed deeds of kindness and charity of an outwardly unobservant person may outweigh the merit obtained by another's commitment to ongoing religious observances, does that not lead to the strange conclusion that relationships with one's fellow man may actually be regarded as more significant than one's relationship with God?

Precisely! Rabbi Chaim David Ha-Levi explains this point most lucidly:

If a man commits a sin against God, his repentance is quite easy and straightforward, since the repercussions of his sin rebound upon him alone. God then punishes the sinner not because he has harmed God (heaven forfend!), but as a father who wishes to train his son to behave properly, or as a doctor who chides a patient who disregards his instructions out of his desire that he should be properly healed.

This is not the case, however, with offences committed against one's fellow man, where one inflicts physical wounds or financial damage on him, or defames him or hurts him in any other way. In this situation, where he wishes to repent, his repentance will not be accepted without a true and heartfelt intercession with his neighbor. Can it be so easy to intercede with a person that one has hurt when even the halakah declares that one is not always obliged to forgive?[9]

118. Do we have any proof that our relationships with fellow man are more significant in God's eyes than our relationship with Him?

An analysis of the causes suggested for the destruction of our two Temples is revealing in this context. The destruction of the first Temple is attributed by the

9. Ha-Levi, D. C. (1976). *Asei Lekha Rav*, vol 3. Tel Aviv: Committee for the Publication of the Works of HaGaon Rabbi Chaim David Halevi, p. 55.

Talmud[10] to the fact that most of the population were unobservant and steeped in the most heinous cardinal crimes of idolatry, immorality, and murder, whereas the people who lived at the time of the destruction of the second Temple were, in the main, totally observant of God's law. The crime that caused the destruction of their Temple lay more in the realm of ethics, namely their quarrelsomeness and causeless hatred of their fellow man.

Now, from the fact that the first Temple was speedily rebuilt whereas the second has lain in ruins for centuries, the Talmud infers that there is ready and prompt forgiveness from God for religious crimes, as specified in His Torah, whereas for sins against fellow man no heavenly forgiveness is extended.[11] Indeed, there is a view that no value is attributed to one's religious observances if one does not fulfill the *mitzvot* that govern our relationship with our fellow man.[12]

119. But how can the Talmud refer to them as *totally* righteous and *totally* wicked if, in fact, it is really only a question of a comparative assessment and of determining whether their good or their evil deeds are in the majority?

This is because once the majority situation has been determined, God effaces any trace of the minority record. Thus, for those whose good deeds outweigh their evil, God erases the debit side of His ledger, leaving the distinct impression that the person has only performed good deeds and is, consequently, "totally righteous." And the same procedure is applied in the case of those whose evil outweighs their good deeds.

This concept has its origin in the Talmud,[13] which is quoted in the recurring Penitential (*Selichot*) refrain: *ma'avir rishon rishon*, "You remove them [all trace of our sins] one by one."

Rashi explains this rather abstruse statement to mean that, rather than placing all the good and evil deeds in the scales together, and risk having to condemn man, God places them in in small clusters. If, in the first cluster, they are equal in number, or if the good deeds outweigh the bad, God then 'removes the sins' from the cluster, and pardons them, leaving only the good deeds in the scale, to augment the good deeds of the subsequent clusters.[14]

---

10. *Yoma* 9b.
11. *Ibid.*
12. See Chaim David Ha-Levi, *op. cit.*, pp. 58–60.
13. *Rosh Hashanah* 17a and *Rashi ad loc.* 81.80.
14. Cohen, J. M. (1994). *Prayer and Penitence*, Northvale, NJ: Jason Aronson Inc., p. 150.

V

Man's Place in the Universe

120. What is man's standing within the hierarchy of Creation?

This is a most difficult question to answer, because there is no objective means of assessing man's position within the divine scheme of things. Man has the potential to be "just a little less than the angels, a being whom God has crowned with glory and honour" (Psalm 8:6), and yet, on the other hand, his moral vulnerability can prompt the psalmist to despair of man and ask "Lord, what is man that Thou relatest to him or the son of man that Thou takest account of him? Man is like a breath; his days are as a shadow that passeth away" (Psalm 144:3–4).

This polarity is well summed up by the Midrash when it states that if man merits it, God tells him, "You are the crown of my Creation. I created everything in anticipation of your arrival; and you found everything ready for you like a laid table awaiting a guest." If, however, man is found wanting, God mocks him, saying, "You are so insignificant that even the gnat and the flea were created before you!"[1]

The Hebrew name given to the first man was *adam*. This may be derived either from the word *adamah*, "earth," or from the word *demut*, "likeness." Man's physical origins lie in the earth from which he was created; but his creative potential is absolutely unlimited—a gift with which he was endowed at Creation when God determined to create him "in our image and after Our likeness." Man is, therefore, potentially, of infinite value.

121. What exactly does man's creation "in the image of God" actually mean?

Again, it is a concept that is impossible to define with any degree of certainty, and several explanations are offered by the commentators. What is clear is that it is an accolade calculated to set man apart from the animals as something morally and spiritually elevated. Bearing in mind that many contemporary civilizations of the ancient Near East deified animals, the Torah seems to be intent upon neutralizing that obscenity by emphasizing, in the same verse,[2] man's dominion over all the animal world, on the one hand, and his exalted and special relationship with God, on the other.

Rashi, on the verse "Let us make man in our image (*betzalmeinu*)" (Genesis 1:26)

---

1. Midrash *Bereishit Rabbah* 4:2. See also Talmud *Sanhedrin* 38a.
2. Genesis 1:26.

states that it means, simply, "in the image we have determined for him."[3] *Rashi's* purpose here is clearly to negate any suggestion that man bears any resemblance to His Maker, either in attribute or form. The continuation of the verse—"after our likeness (*kidmuteinu*)"—he understands as "possessing understanding and wisdom."

Maimonides deals at length, in his monumental *Guide for the Perplexed* (composed between 1185 and 1190), with this phrase: *betzalmeinu kidmuteinu*. He interprets the noun *tzelem* ("image [of God]," as in the phrase *betzalmeinu*) in the same sense that *Rashi* understood the term *kidmuteinu*, namely as a reference to the divine intellect with which man has been endowed:

> As a man's distinction consists in a property which no other creature on earth possesses, namely intellectual perception, in the exercise of which he does not employ his senses, nor move his hand or his foot, it has been compared— though only apparently, not in reality—to the divine excellency which requires no instrument whatsoever.[4]

Maimonides quotes various biblical examples of the term *demut* being employed to denote, not a tangible shape or form but rather, an abstract idea associated with, or quality inherent in, the accompanying proper noun. For example: "I am like (*dimitiy*)[5] a pelican of the wilderness" (Psalm 102:7). Says Maimonides: "The author does not compare himself to the pelican in regard to wings and feathers, but in point of sadness."[6]

Thus, for Maimonides, the couplet, *betzalmeinu kidmuteinu*, denotes simply an attribute, associated with God, with which man has been endowed. And that attribute is man's intellectual capacity to transcend his senses and the instinctive desires that they generate, in order to reason and plan creatively, not just for his own benefit, but also, as a socially responsible creature, for the benefit of his fellow man and society. Thus, man's creation "in the image of God" suggests, in addition to intellectual intuition, an element of co-partnership in the wise direction and supervision of God's world.

122. Maimonides represents a medieval way of viewing the relationship between God and man. Do we have any earlier, classical, rabbinic formulations of this concept of man as co-partner with God in the act of Creation?

We do, indeed. The Midrash already illustrates this concept in a graphic manner:

> The wicked Roman general, Tornosrufus, once asked Rabbi Akivah, 'Whose products are better, God's or man's?' Rabbi Akivah responded: 'Man's!'

---

3. *Rashi* on Genesis 1:26.

4. Maimonides. (1881). *Guide for the Perplexed* (ed. M. Friedlander). New York: Hebrew Publishing Co., p. 32.

5. The word *demut* ("likeness") is a noun derived from the verb *damah*, 'to be like, resemble' (cf. Numbers 33:56; Isaiah 1:9).

6. Maimonides *Ibid.*

Tornosrufus countered and said: 'But can man possibly make heaven or earth?' Rabbi Akivah objected, saying, 'Do not confuse the debate with elements that are totally outside of man's capacity, and over which he has no control. Let us rather operate with elements which concern man.' Akivah then went and produced some ears of corn and a cake. 'These,' said Akivah, pointing to the ears of corn, 'are God's products, whereas that,' said he, pointing to the cake, 'is man's. Is not the cake superior to the ears of corn?'[7]

Akivah did not, of course, intend to imply that man was superior in any way to God. He wished only to stress the uniqeness of man and the Jewish concept of the latter's co-partnership with God in the work of Creation. God provides the raw materials and the potential that is inherent in the earth's vegetable and mineral resources. It is man's task to take those raw materials and mold them into the form that best serves man's needs and objectives. God is the primary Creator, but He leaves for man the task of selection, adaptation, construction, and presentation.

123. So what relevance does that concept of man having been created in the image of God have in the context of a discussion about Rosh Hashanah?

It is particularly relevant. For no reward or punishment of man could possibly be contemplated in the absence of that concept. It connects man to God, imposing upon man the awesome responsibility of living out his life and regulating his behavior in a manner that reflects that divine image. It gives man a reason for following after the good and rejecting the evil. It gives him a sense of his own worth and his unbounded spiritual potential. And it serves as a constant reminder to him that one day he will be called to account by the One in whose image he was created for having tarnished that image in any way, through sin or through failure to exercise the qualities of goodness and mercy that are of the essence of God's beneficent relationship with His world.

124. If man is created in God's image, does the fact that man is often motivated to repent suggest that God, likewise, can have that same inclination?

Yes and no. God, like man, does occasionally feel impelled to change His predetermined course of action. But whereas human repentance means abandoning a sinful or unworthy activity, that obviously cannot be attributed to God.

It is axiomatic (See Questions 87–88, 127) that man has total free will to act righteously or wickedly. God's foreknowledge of how man will act in no way affects or influences man's actions in that respect. God, therefore, proceeds and prepares plans for man, on the basis that man will steer a righteous course. God does that because He is righteous and merciful. He follows that course even in the knowledge that man will assuredly sin and not repent! The bestowal of free will upon man means that God must supress His knowledge of man's ultimate sin—even wipe it

---

7. Midrash *Tanchuma* on *Tazriah*, Chapter 5.

out of His mind—and await events. How this process works and why God feels the need to go along with it is open to speculation.

The fact that God does so is clear from several biblical passages. We may quote just two examples. When the generation of the flood perpetrated their unprecedented evil and violence, the Torah states: "And it repented the Lord that He had made man on earth, and it grieved Him at His heart" (Genesis 6:6). Again, when the Israelites worshiped the Golden Calf, God told Moses that He had decided to destroy Israel and form a new nation from Moses (Exodus 32:10). After Moses' earnest pleading with God, the Torah states, "And the Lord repented of the evil that He said He would do unto His people" (verse 14).

So Creation in the image of God really does mean that man shares a number of thought-processes with God and that we are, to an extent, on His wavelength. Indeed, if that were not the case, we could hardly be expected to comprehend His word and His expectations of us, as revealed at Sinai and as recorded in His Torah.

125. Do all Jewish thinkers view the concept of Creation in the image of God as spiritually challenging?

Most do. An exception to the rule is the provocative treatment of this concept provided by the contemporary Israeli thinker, Yeshayahu Leibowitz:

Moreover, it is not even possible to say that having been created in the image indicates something about the value of man. Man is only the image of God, without intrinsic essence, much as the picture hanging on the wall is only a surface treated with paint and meaningful only as representing something else. If what that picture represents is something I don't recognize, or that, in my opinion, doesn't exist or has no value for me—then the painted surface has no value. In other words, the very fact that man is created in the image of God deprives man of intrinsic value. Man is not divine, but only an image of God. He is not valued as an end-in-himself, and his significance consists only in his position before God. This is in extreme contrast to the view of Kant, for whom man replaces God, and the human individual becomes the highest value.[8]

126. What objection may one take to Leibowitz's negative assessment of the concept of Creation in the image of God?

Simply that it uses man's acknowledged inferior position in relation to God—as a created being, placed in the world to serve God's purpose—as a rod with which to beat man. This is quite illogical. Of course, compared with God, man is only an "image," a pale reflection. But even to acknowledge that, is, itself, to endow man with a unique spiritual quality that totally transcends the biological form and composition that he otherwise shares with other animal species.

---

8. Leibowitz, Y. (1992). *Judaism, Human Values and the Jewish State*, ed. E. Goldman. Cambridge, Massachusetts; London: Harvard University Press.

Let us take the analogy of the light of the moon. The fact that its light is a mere refraction of that of the sun in no way negates its purpose and benefit or the exalted and prominent position that the moon occupies within the stellar system. Man may only be an image, but it is an image that is directly associated with, and powered by, the primary Being that is reflected. Man reflects His light, radiates His spirituality, and attests to His presence in the world. Even to dub him a mere "image" of God is to set man apart as unique in Creation. To say that man is consequently "without intrinsic essence" is a *non sequitur*. Man's essence lies precisely in what he makes of himself and how he rises to the spiritual challenge of reflecting that image. And that speaks volumes for the value of man.

Leibowitz seeks to demean man by comparing him to a picture hanging on a wall, which is "only a surface treated with paint and meaningful only as representing something else." The analogy is flawed, for, while the surface treated with paint may serve to stimulate the visual senses or the power of recollection, inspire with beauty or excite emotion, that is only true in the subjective sense. Its appeal is limited to the extent with which the viewer identifies with it. To achieve its purpose, there has to be an interplay between the subject of the picture and the esthetic and imaginative faculties of the viewer. People stand for hours admiring such paintings as the Mona Lisa; for others, it is a plain and rather sober painting.

In the case of man, however, the divine image in which he was created is not merely recollective; it is real, objective, and dynamic. The rabbis regarded man as a *chelek Eloah mimaal*, "a veritable part of God above"—not a pale reflection, not a "surface treated with paint," but the real thing, a co-partner in the creative process, a being that carries His imprint deep within man's soul.

The painting cannot materially change either itself or the world outside its frame, and its value is limited by commercial considerations. Man's divine image, on the other hand, gives him the free will, the energy, and the wisdom to shape and completely transform his world, for better or worse. To that extent, he is, truly, "an end-in-himself," and his value is infinite. And viewed in that light, we are not all that far from the Kantian position. Man does, to an extent, "replace" God, as His (free) agent and disseminator of His word and will within the world; and within that world, God willingly vacates His seat to enable "the human individual" to attain to "the highest value."

127. Where is such an exalted assessment of man enunciated?

It is found in many of our medieval philosophic writings, such as, for example, in this quotation from Maimonides:

Man has total freedom to incline either to the good way, and to become totally righteous, or to incline to the evil way and to become wicked. That is what the Torah meant when it stated, "Behold man has become like one of us, knowing good and evil" (Genesis 3:22). This means to say that man is a species unique in the world, with no other comparable species that, of his own volition, and through the exercise of his own reason and intellect, knows what is good and what is evil, and there is none that can prevent him from exercizing that choice of good or evil.

Do not entertain the view, expressed both by some foolish gentiles and most of the naive among the Jews, that God decrees for a person at the beginning of his life whether he will be righteous or wicked. That is not the case: any man has the potential to become as righteous as Moses or as wicked as Jeroboam; he can [develop himself to] become wise or [allow his faculties to atrophy, rendering him] foolish; he can determine to become merciful or cruel, niggardly or generous, and similarly with all other qualities. There is no one who can coerce him or decree what he should do.[9]

This is certainly not a description of man as a mere painting on the wall, but rather of man as the very artist himself, glorious, independent, and dynamic, touching and shaping the lives of all he comes into contact with, and constantly altering and embellishing the canvas of God's world.

128. What is the purpose of the Creation?

We cannot answer this with any degree of certainty, since we cannot possibly fathom the mind of God. As the prophet Isaiah reminds us: "For My thoughts are not your thoughts, neither are your ways My ways, saith the Lord. For as the heavens are higher than the earth, so are My ways higher than your ways, and My thoughts than your thoughts" (Isaiah 55:8–9).

The medieval Jewish philosophers discuss this subject at length, and a popular view is that, because one of the overriding attributes of God is His goodness and bountiful generosity, this translated itself into a need to create a world and with it a species that was best suited to be the recipient of that bounty, and that would have the requisite intelligence to husband it effectively and to develop and expand it, in order to share it with fellow creatures. This would, in turn, make His creatures happy and grateful, and would, in consequence, move them to love and serve God.

129. But, philosophically, can we really speak of God having a "need" to create, for whatever reason?

Indeed, it does create problems. And it is for that reason that Saadiah Gaon states another view, reflecting the Muslim *Asharia* school of thought, that God created the world for no reason. That does not mean, however, that He created it in vain. According to the exponents of this doctrine, only humans act vainly if they perform some act without any purpose, since they are, at the same time, neglecting some other activity that could be beneficial to them or others. It is philosophically impossible to impute that to God.

---

9. Maimonides *Mishneh Torah, Hilkhot Teshuvah* 5:1–2.

130. But surely, even if we accept that God was not neglecting any other activity, is it really creditable that the Creator should bring anything into being for no purpose at all?

It certainly does not commend itself to our minds as particularly logical. Indeed, it would make nonsense of the assumption that man and God can hold discourse and dialogue, and understand each other's requirements and objectives. It begs the question that if God has no "reason" for what He commands, then why should man take His commands so seriously?

It is on account of such considerations that some thinkers adjust that theory of Creation without purpose and interpret it to mean that God had no *personal* purpose or benefit. He could truly have contained His "goodness" within Him, without seeking any outlet for it in Creation. He also did not need man's gratitude or prayers. His act of Creation, however, was not, as we assumed on a literal reading of that theory, without any purpose at all. Its purpose was to benefit man. He did not "need" to create man and his world, but He chose to do so exclusively as an act of grace to man.

131. So is man, therefore, the sole purpose and center of the universe?

This is also a highly debated issue. Saadia Gaon believed that man was, indeed, the exclusive focus of Creation. He stressed the harmony and design implicit in all existing things, all of which was purely to facilitate the existence and happiness of man. He regards it as axiomatic that the pivotal and most important aspect of Creation is always situated in the center, like the yolk of an egg or the heart of man. Since (according to medieval cosmology) the earth is in the center of all the spheres, it follows, for Saadia, that it is the most important planet, and its design must have been shaped by the requirements of its primary and most developed inhabitant, man.[10] This view is in line with the mainstream Talmudic perception, as reflected in the statement of Rabbi Eleazar that, "The Holy One, blessed be He, declared the whole world, in its entirety, to have been created only on behalf of man."[11]

Maimonides, on the other hand, rejected that anthropocentric view of man, as well as the suggestion that Creation was determined by human needs. His view—akin to that of the Muslim *Asharia* (See Question 129)—was that all existing things were brought into being purely by the divine will; and we cannot, therefore, seek reason or purpose for it.

Another point made by Maimonides, to disprove the theory that man was the sole purpose of Creation, is that man has, in fact, no need for the greater part of the universe.[12]

---

10. Gaon, S. (1945). *Emunot Vede'ot* (See Altmann, A. Saadya Gaon, Oxford, East and West Library) Treatise IV, Introduction.

11. *Berakhot* 6b.

12. Maimonides (1981). *Guide for the Perplexed, Book III* (ed. M. Friedlander). New York: Hebrew Publishing Co.

132. Does modern scientific theory of cosmology shed any light on this particular matter?

According to our present-day knowledge, hydrogen and helium were the only elements that were present seconds after the beginning of the universe. All the other elements essential for human life were generated subsequently, as by-products of the blazing interiors of large stars that existed before the appearance of the sun and planets. Through those stellar explosions, all the atoms necessary for human life were brought into being. Thus, it may be said that even the distant stars that comprise "the greater part of the universe" had their function as facilitators of human life. So man may, indeed, be viewed as the primary objective of Creation.

133. But does not their vast distance from man's abode disprove the latter assertion?

Quite the contrary. Even that vast distance may be viewed as being in the best interest of man, because those stellar explosions, in addition to the beneficial chemical elements they brought into being, also emitted deadly cosmic radiation. It is the very distance of those stars from the earth that reduces the intensity of that radiation so that it does not harm us. We may plausibly infer that the nature of Creation, the location of all its building blocks, and the principles and laws of physics and astronomy, all seem to have as their primary purpose the survival and happiness of the human species!

134. So if God created the universe with man in mind, what expectations does God have of man?

That he keeps God's commandments, maximizes on his God-given potential, and furthers the best interests of God's world and His creatures. The prophet Micah expresses it in this way: "It hath been told unto thee, O man, what is good and what the Lord requires of thee: only to do justice and love mercy, and to walk humbly with thy God" (Micah 6:8).

The Talmud adds to that the duty of emulating the ways of God—*imitatio dei*. This is explained in the Talmud:

Why does the Torah state 'One should walk after God' (Deuteronomy 13:5)? Is it really possible to walk after the Divine Presence? Is He not like a consuming fire (Deuteronomy 4:24)?

What it means is that we must imitate His ways. Just as God clothed Adam and Eve,[13] so should we clothe the naked. Just as He visited the sick,[14] so

---

13. Genesis 3:21.
14. *Rashi* on Genesis 18:1.

must we. Just as He comforted the bereaved,[15] so must we. Just as He attended to the burial of Moses,[16] so must we care for the dignity of the dead.[17]

135. But is the Talmud's answer really satisfactory? Surely man has a need for a more intimate relationship with his God than that achieved by the performance of some ethical acts?

Perhaps the Talmud is stating the level of relationship that ordinary folk must realistically expect to achieve. The mystic will, naturally, not be satisfied with that fairly superficial relationship and will condition himself and regulate his life so that it is totally consecrated to, and sacrificed on the altar of, oneness with God. He will necessarily have to divorce himself to a great degree from God's world to achieve for his soul the very first level of that blessed state of mystic union and the intimacy with God that is the goal of mysticism.

But for the rest of us, all we can expect is a piety-induced feeling of being "blessed by God" as a result of our goodness, the kindness we dispense, and the image of God, which becomes more focused through lives lived out in the consciousness of "what the Lord requires."

136. But can God really care for puny man, especially when He allows such terrors as the Holocaust to be inflicted upon us?

This is not a question that we can answer, even superficially, in the context of a book like this, which allows but a paragraph or two to each question. Indeed, we detract from the awesomeness of the subject by even raising the issue here.

An entire Holocaust literature has developed over the past few decades, with Holocaust Studies offered as an option in most colleges where Jewish Studies are taught. The interested reader should seek the advice of an expert as to the book best suited to his or her level of understanding.

Having raised the issue, we are obliged to offer just one comment. God never ceases, for even an instant, to care for His creatures. If He did so, the world would be reduced to primeval chaos. He has given man free will, which inevitably involves the capacity to act in defiance of God's will and to perpetrate the most unspeakable crimes upon his fellow. But it is that heaven-bestowed free will that makes our lives so exciting, unpredictable, creative, challenging, and fulfilling. It is only through the exercise of that free will that we can become "like God, knowing good from evil" (Genesis 3:22); and it is because of our free will that the moral choices we make register as significant, making us take full responsibility for our actions and legitimately enabling God to hold us to account some day for our choice of evil and to render reward for the good.

---

15. The reference is to God comforting Isaac after the death of his father Abraham. See *Rashi* on Genesis 25:11.

16. Deuteronomy 34:6.

17. *Sotah* 14a.

137. But can God really exist in the face of so much evil in the world?

If by that we mean that surely the very proximity of the divine presence should make the perpetration of evil impossible, then we are thrown back to our previous answer. God would not be granting us free will if He frustrated it by His presence.

God is still there, even in the face of the suffering of His children. But there are times and situations when God is Himself forced—as a result of having granted man free will—to hide His face and let evil triumph. This doctrine is based upon a biblical statement dealing with this very question: "And they will say on that day: 'Are not these evils come upon us because the Lord is not in our midst?' But I have surely hidden my face (*astir panai*) on that day because of all the evil which they have wrought . . ." (Deuteronomy 31:17–18).

The implication is that man, by his actions, can send God into a mode of *hester panim* concealment. God is still there, just as, during an eclipse, the sun is still there, just as large and bright, but is concealed by an opaque body, so that the light and warmth cannot reach us.

Enough. Let us get back to less perplexing issues![18]

138. What relationship is man expected to cultivate with his environment?

We have already indicated that man's main purpose is to be a co-partner with God in the development of His world and to enable all those created in His image to fulfill their God-given task. The Midrash states that when God created the first man, He took him on a guided tour of all the trees in the Garden of Eden, and told him: "See how beautiful and praiseworthy is what I have created. And all of it has been created only for you to enjoy. Take great care, therefore, not to spoil or destroy my world; for if you do, there will be no one to come and rectify it after you."[19]

Twentieth century man, who has plundered, polluted, and ravaged his environment, must find this Midrash rather chilling. The earth is for man to *enjoy*, not *exploit*; to tend and preserve, not to exhaust. Its rain forests are to be respected, not devastated; and when a tree has to be felled, a new sapling must be planted in its stead. Man has to be both master and servant of his environment, never its rival. His task is to cultivate it, and in so doing to cultivate himself. That is his privilege and his purpose.

---

18. As an introduction to this issue, see chapter on "Theological responses to the Holocaust" in my *Moments of Insight* (1989). London: Vallentine, Mitchell & Co., pp. 185–201.

19. Midrash *Kohelet Rabbah*, Chapter 9.

VI

The Month of Elul

THE SIGNIFICANCE OF THE MONTH

139. Why is the month of Elul significant?

It is traditionally the time for beginning the process of heart-searching and *teshuvah*, "repentance," and for conditioning ourselves psychologically for the arrival of the Days of Awe.

Rabbi Jonah of Gerondi states in his *Sha'arei Teshuvah* that the sin of not repenting at this time is more heinous than the commission of the sin itself. The sin was committed, after all, in the heat of the moment, when the person was a slave to his passion and not able to assess the situation objectively, whereas the opportunity for repentance comes at a later time when the person ought to be able to put his action into a proper perspective and realize its ramifications for alienating him from God and man.[1]

140. But why do we only designate one annual period for calling people to repentance? Surely people should not have sins hanging over their heads throughout the year?

Indeed not. And for that reason, we actually pray for forgiveness three times a day in the *Hashivenu* blessing of our *Amidah*, our central prayer.

The blessing reads "Cause us to return, O our Father, unto thy Law; draw us near, O our king, unto thy service, and bring us back in perfect repentance unto thy presence. Blessed art thou, O Lord, who delightest in repentance."

So, the opportunity and stimulus to repentance is paramount in Judaism. However, it was recognized that the recitation of such a blessing, particularly as part of a catalogue of nineteen blessings dealing with a variety of themes and petitions, can easily lose the power to actually activate a thorough-going process of soul-searching and repentance. It was recognized that a special period in the year was required in order to highlight repentance as the overarching priority. And the

---

1. Rabbeinu Yonah. (1976). *Sha'arei Teshuvah.* New York: Feldheim Publishers, Gate 1 sec. 2.

month of Elul was designated for that purpose, its days being already earmarked by tradition as *yemei ratzon*, "days of goodwill," and divine favor.

141. Why was the month of Elul regarded as especially auspicious for repentance?

Because already when Israel was in the desert, on their way out of Egypt, God displayed special indulgence to Israel and pardoned their most grievous sin of worshiping the Golden Calf.

After the revelation of the Torah to Israel on Mount Sinai, on the sixth of Sivan,[2] Moses was invited to ascend the mountain in order to be with God, and receive the rest of the Torah and the Ten Commandments engraved upon the two Tablets of Stone. On the seventeenth of Tammuz, 40 days later, he descended. However, on seeing the Israelites dancing around the Golden Calf, he shattered the Tablets.[3] He then subsequently ascended Sinai a second time, to pray for forgiveness for Israel, and he stayed a further 40 days, descending on the twenty-ninth of *Av*, but still uncertain as to God's final decision in the matter. The following day, on Rosh Chodesh, the first day of the month of Elul, God announced to him that he could come back up and receive replacement Tablets, since Moses' plea had been accepted. Moses returned for a third time to Sinai and descended 40 days later on the tenth day of Tishri, with God's words *salachti kidvarekha* ("I have forgiven in response to your plea") ringing musically in his ears. That tenth day of Tishri was subsequently designated, therefore, as Yom Kippur, the most effective day for achieving at-one-ment with God.

Thus, the 40 days from the beginning of Elul, when Moses went up to receive the second set of Tablets until the final reconciliation on the tenth of Tishri, became "days of good will" for all subsequent generations of our people, days when God is in the closest of proximity to us, and yearning to grant us His forgiveness.

THE NAME ELUL

142. Does the word Elul have a meaning?

Significantly, in Aramaic, there is a verb *le'allela*, meaning "to search out." It occurs in the *Targum*, the official Aramaic translation of the Torah. When the spies returned to Moses, they declared that they had "traversed the land *to search it out*" (Numbers 13:32). The *Targum* renders the latter phrase as *le'allela*. Thus, the very name of the month heightens its spiritual purpose as a time for soul-searching.

---

2. This is, in reality, anachronistic, since the Babylonian names were not yet employed by Israel. The Torah merely refers to the months by employing their ordinal numbers: the first month, the second month, etc. Our rabbinic sources employ the later Babylonian names of the months, however, for convenience, even in describing the chronology of the early biblical period.

3. Exodus 32:19.

143. Is there any other significance in the name Elul?

The sages linked the name with the theme of the period by viewing it as representing an acronym of various biblical phrases, each representing another aspect of repentance.

The most well-known acronym is the verse from Song of Songs, *Ani Ledodi Vedodi Li*, "I am for my (heavenly) Beloved, and my Beloved is for me" (Song of Songs 6:3). This suggests the reconciliation at the heart of this period.

Another acronym suggested is taken from the unlikely book of Esther and referring to the obligation, on the festival of Purim, of "sending presents to our friends and gifts to the poor" (Esther 9:22): *Ish Lere'ehu Umatanot La'evyonim*. This is clearly an allusion to the *mitzvah* of *tzedakah* (charity), which is an essential exercise in order to secure repentance at this period.

The final one we will refer to is a quotation from Deuteronomy, which refers to "God circumcizing (that is, melting) Israel's stubborn heart and that of her children" (30:6): *Et Levakha Ve'et Levav (zar'akha)*.

ELUL OBSERVANCES

144. Does the month of Elul have a special quality in Orthodox circles?

In the world of the Orthodox yeshivahs and seminaries, Rosh Chodesh Elul marks the end of the summer recess and the beginning of a new term characterized by indescribably heightened spiritual activity. The rabbis and teachers take *teshuvah* as their main theme and direct the minds and hearts of their disciples to undertake a total spiritual renewal and to attain a special intensity in their love and service of God and in their relationship with their fellows.

In some circles of *Chabad* Hasidim, it is the practice to observe a *fahrbrengen*, a fellowship meeting on the two first nights (Rosh Chodesh) of Elul:

> They discuss particularly the religious practices and rituals of the months of Elul and Tishri, the relevant Hasidic texts and the prayers, ways of improving one's character and behaviour, not only by eradicating bad qualities, but by cultivating new and good ones, and intensifying one's *yir'at shamayim* (fear of heaven).[4]

145. Are there any special prayers prescribed for the month of Elul?

It is the custom to recite Psalm 27, *LeDavid Ha-shem Oriy Veyishiy* ("The Lord is my Light and my salvation"), at the end of the morning and evening services. The reason for this is found in the Midrash:

> The Rabbis expound this psalm with reference to Rosh Hashanah and Yom Kippur: *The Lord is my light*—on Rosh Hashanah, the day of judgment, as it

---

4. Mondscheim, Y. *Otzar Minhagei Chabad (Elul VeTishri)*. (1995). Jerusalem, *Heikhal Menachem*, p. 4.

is written 'He will make your righteousness shine clear *like a light*, and the justice of your cause like the noonday sun' (Psalm 37:6). And my salvation—on Yom Kippur, when He grants us salvation and pardons all our sins.[5]

The recitation of this psalm each day in synagogue extends until after the seventh day of the festival of Tabernacles, *Hoshana Rabbah*, which also partakes of the nature of a "Day of Judgment." The psalm also contains a reference to God hiding the psalmist "in His *sukkah*," and this ensured that its recitation was declared appropriate for the duration of the Tabernacles festival.[6]

During the final week of the month of Elul, in the lead-in to Rosh Hashanah, we recite the special *Selichot*, prayers and petitions for repentance (See Questions 160–180).

146. Is it only on account of that Midrashic interpretation, then, that this psalm was prescribed at this period?

No, it goes much deeper. I have written elsewhere that

There can be few psalms that breathe such faith and confidence in the guiding hand of God. It is an expanded counterpart of perhaps the most famous in that entire inspired collection, Psalm 23.

God's presence—felt so overwhelmingly by the psalmist—creates for him a sense of reassurance beyond the capability of even his parents to provide. The source of that confidence is twofold: the house of God and the ways of God.

First, the house of God:

One thing I ask of the Lord, only this do I seek: to dwell in the house of the Lord all the days of my life, to gaze upon the beauty of the Lord and to worship in His temple.

The house of the Lord for King David was not the glorious physical reality into which his son, King Solomon, transformed it. Furthermore, as Samson Raphael Hirsch notes, not even the priests dwelt in the house of the Lord all the days of their life. So King David could only have been speaking figuratively, alluding to the life of holiness and of constant awareness of God's presence which transformed everywhere he went into a veritable 'house of God,' in the spirit of the verse, 'For the Lord thy God walks in the midst of thy camp' (Deuteronomy 23:15).

Second, the ways of God:

Teach me Your ways, O Lord, and lead me on a level path, because of my insidious foes.

The psalmist views physical and spiritual salvation as inextricable. He wishes God to inspire him to holiness, because he recognizes that only then will he deserve to be 'led on a level path' and granted relief from his

---

5. *Midrash Tillim* on Psalm 27.
6. Cohen, J. M. (1994). *Prayer and Penitence*. Northvale, NJ: Jason Aronson Inc., p. 18.

enemies . . . With truth, holiness, faith and justice on his side, the psalmist senses his invincibility.

Throughout the period of the High Holy Days and Sukkot, when this psalm is recited, although predominantly a period of repentance and remorse, it is the confident sentiments of this psalm that give us the temerity to face the bar of heavenly justice and beg for health, happiness and prosperity."[7]

147. Are there any other observances prescribed for the month of Elul?

The shofar is sounded in synagogue every morning, toward the end of the morning service, with the exception of Shabbat and the morning preceding Rosh Hashanah. It is also customary, when writing a letter during this month, to sign off with the Hebrew greeting for a good year ahead: *Ketivah vachatimah tovah* ("May you be written and inscribed for good").

Since one should have one's *tefillin* and *mezuzot* checked approximately every 3 years, it became the practice to arrange for such an inspection to coincide with the month of Elul. While this practice cannot be faulted as a way of reinforcing the message of punctilious attention to the performance of our ritual *mitzvot* in the strictly prescribed manner, it cannot have been the favorite custom for the poor *soferim* (scribes), overwhelmed as they would have been with a sudden avalanche of work, all concentrated and having to be completed in that self-same month.

Some authorities have recommended Elul as a particularly auspicious month for the celebration of marriages.[8] There were some authorities who refused to allow weddings during the second half of the month, when the moon was in decline, this being regarded as a highly inauspicious period. During Elul, however, an exception was made, since the entire month is regarded as *Yemei ratzon*, being comprised of "days of good will."

148. What is the origin of sending New Year cards?

It was inspired by the practice, referred to above (see Question 147), of extending special wishes for the new year whenever writing to one's friend or associate during the month of Elul. It was only a short step from this to the sending of a special letter of greeting for the new year; and from that the market developed for special greetings cards, which obviated the need to pen lengthy letters to all one's acquaintances. The parallel practice in the Christian world of sending Christmas cards has certainly helped to make this a universal practice.

Some have the practice of employing the New Year cards as decoration for the walls of their sukkah. A collage of these cards certainly brightens up the walls and helps to create a cozy atmosphere.

---

7. *Op. cit.*, pp. 19–20.
8. *Darkhei Teshuvah* on *Yoreh De'ah* 179:18.

149. Is it not also customary to visit the graves of parents (*kever avot*) during the month of Elul?

There is no law that prescribes such a visit during this particular period, though it has become almost a universal practice:

> Propitious times to visit the grave are on days of calamity or of decisive moments in life: on the concluding days of *shiva* and sheloshim, and on yahrzeit; on fast days, such as Tisha B'Av, or before the High Holy Days; on erev Rosh Chodesh, the day prior to the first days of the months of Nissan and Elul. One or another of these days seems proper for families to visit their beloved dead. There is no rule of thumb as to the annual frequency of such visitation, excepting that people should avoid the extremes of constant visitation on the one hand, and of complete disregard on the other.[9]

(See also Questions 201–208.)

SOUNDING THE SHOFAR DURING ELUL

150. Why is the shofar blown during the month of Elul?

The late Midrash, *Pirkei D'Rabbi Eliezer*, states that when Moses ascended Mount Sinai for the third time, to obtain the second set of Tablets (See Question 141), the shofar was sounded around the camp to alert everyone as to the precise moment of his departure. This was on account of the fact that the making of the Golden Calf during his first absence was because many people had mistakenly assumed that the day he left was "day one" of the 40 days he had indicated he would be away. When he did not arrive on the fortieth day according to their calculation they assumed the worst and sought a replacement manifestation of God's presence in their camp.

Since this sounding of the shofar by the Israelites on Rosh Chodesh Elul served the purpose of preventing Israel repeating their sin, it became customary to sound it on that day and throughout the month, to serve as a warning to our people not to continue to sin.[10]

151. Why is it blown only in the morning and not at the evening services?

While it is the present practice only to blow in the morning, the *Tur* (of Jacob ben Asher, born in Germany in 1270) relates that "It is customary in Germany to blow every morning and evening after the service." The more common practice of restricting the blowing to the morning service was on account of the fact that Moses

---

9. Lamm, M. (1969). *The Jewish Way in Death and Mourning*. New York: Jonathan David, p. 192.
10. Friedlander, G. ed. (1965). Midrash *Pirkei D'Rabbi Eliezer*, Chapter xlvi. New York: Hermon Press, pp. 359–360. Quoted in *Tur Orach Chayyim* 581.

ascended the mountain in the morning, in accordance with God's instructions: "Be ready by the morning, and come up in the morning unto Mount Sinai and present thyself there to Me" (Exodus 34:2).[11]

152. Are there any other reasons offered for blowing the shofar during Elul?

Some authorities[12] view the blowing practically, rather than historically, and quote to the prophet Amos's reference to the dread, which the sound of the shofar instills within the heart: "Can the shofar sound in a city and the people not tremble?" Thus, the sounding of the shofar during Elul is simply to make us tremble in order to quicken the pace of our soul-searching and repentance.

Other sources[13] view its purpose as a medium of sowing confusion in the mind of Satan who is poised at Rosh Hashanah time to accuse Israel. By blowing the shofar every day, he is confused as to which day is Rosh Hashanah. Thus, when he hears it for the first time, he runs to condemn sinful Israel, thinking it is already Rosh Hashanah and hoping to trap those whose evil deeds outweigh their good deeds (See Question 109). But God can stop him in his tracks and tell him that there is still time for the sinners of Israel to do *teshuvah*. As this process is repeated day after day, Satan becomes more and more confused and crestfallen, ultimately losing all his zest to condemn.

153. On which particular day of the month of Elul do we commence the blowing of the shofar?

Since Rosh Chodesh Elul is always two days (the first day being the thirtieth day of *Av*), authorities were divided as to which day of Rosh Chodesh to commence blowing. *Mishnah Berurah* and several other distinguished authorities,[14] taking account of the fact that Elul is always a "defective" month, of only 29 days, maintained that the blowing should commence from the first day of Rosh Chodesh (i.e., the thirtieth of *Av*) in order that the total of 40 days blowing, corresponding to the time Moses was on Mount Sinai, may be completed.

Other authorities, basing themselves upon the *Midrash Tanchuma*, assert that in the year the Israelites came out of Egypt and Moses ascended Mount Sinai, the month of Elul had a full 30 days, unlike our calendar wherein it has only 29. Moses's ascent, on the first day of the month, corresponded, therefore, with our second day of Rosh Chodesh: "Therefore we should not depart from the original situation, but should blow on the second day of Rosh Chodesh."[15]

---

11. *Bach* on *Tur Orach Chayyim* 581:1.

12. *Tur ad loc.*

13. *Tur* and *Bach ad loc.*

14. *Tur ad loc.*, *Maharshal* (on tractate *Shabbat* 89b); *Magen Avraham* on *Shulchan Arukh Orach Chayyim* 581:1, *et al.*

15. *Magen Avraham ad loc.*

154. Are there any other customs in this respect?

The *Chabad* Hasidic practice represents an interesting compromise between the two views. They recommend[16] that "we should blow the shofar in order to practice (for Rosh Hashanah) during the course of the first day of Rosh Chodesh Elul, but commence blowing in synagogue on the second day. Quite ingenious!

155. Is the blowing of the shofar during Elul a universal practice?

Not quite. Significantly, Joseph Karo, Sephardi author of the *Shulchan Arukh*, does not refer to the practice, and although some Sephardim adopted it, other communities, such as the Syrian, did not. The *Sefer Ha-Manhig* refers to the custom in one community of blowing it on the first day of Elul only and not during the rest of the month.[17] This is based on a reading of the Midrash *Pirkei D'Rabbi Eliezer*, which, after describing how the Israelites blew the shofar when Moses left, for the third time, to ascend Sinai (See Question 141), states "And for this reason it was instituted to blow the shofar on Rosh Chodesh Elul every year." Thus, according to this reading, the shofar is blown only once, at the outset of the month of Elul.

The Ashkenazi practice to blow it throughout the month of Elul is based on an expanded version of the above Midrash, as quoted in the halakhic Codes of *Rosh* and *Tur*, which states: "And for this reason it was instituted to blow the shofar on Rosh Chodesh Elul every year, and *throughout the month*."

Oriental Sephardim blow the shofar twice during the morning service: once during the recitation of the special *Selichot* and once toward the end of the service. The Sephardim of London and Amsterdam blow the shofar only during the Ten Days of Penitence, at the end of the *Selichot* service.

156. Which notes are blown each morning?

In Ashkenazi communities it is customary to blow a single *teki'ah shevarim teru'ah teki'ah* (On the sounds and combinations of these notes, see Questions 488–501). In many Sephardic and Hasidic communities, it is the practice to foreshadow the Rosh Hashanah combinations by blowing *teki'ah shevarim teru'ah teki'ah—teki'ah shevarim teki'ah—teki'ah teru'ah teki'ah*.

157. At what stage in the service are they blown?

We sound the shofar after the special psalm for the particular day of the week, and we follow the blowing with the recitation of *LeDavid Ha-shem oriy veyishiy* (See Question 145).

---

16. Mondscheim, Y. *Otzar Minhagei Chabad* (*Elul VeTishri*). (1995). Jerusalem Heikhal Menachem, p. 7.
17. (1855). *Sefer Hamanhig, Hilkhot Rosh Hashanah*. Berlin: J. M. Goldberg.

158. Why do we not blow on the morning preceding Rosh Hashanah?

In order to make a separation between the shofar sounding that is rooted merely in *minhag* (custom)—namely, the blowing throughout the month of Elul—and the blowing that is biblically mandated for Rosh Hashanah.

YOM KIPPUR KATAN

159. But if Elul is meant to be a penitential month, surely there must have been some special services or prayers composed in order to nurture the inclination toward repentance?

Indeed, authorities recommend that we recite all our prayers during this month with extra concentration and religious fervor. We are meant to focus our minds upon our conduct and to make our peace with God and our fellow man.

To this end, the month itself was launched, in pietistic circles, with the observance of a fast day on the twenty-ninth of *Av*, which is the day before Rosh Chodesh Elul. The great sixteenth-century mystic, Rabbi Moses Cordovero of Safed, called that day *Yom Kippur Katan* ("the minor Day of Atonement"), in order to bring home to his community the importance of initiating the process of repentance in as solemn and meaningful a way as possible. If Rosh Chodesh fell on Shabbat, then, to avoid fasting on a Friday, *Yom Kippur Katan* was brought forward to the Thursday before.

The choice of the twenty-ninth of *Av* is based upon the fact that, when Moses returned to Sinai for the second period of 40 days, to intercede for the sin of the Golden Calf, the fortieth day coincided with the twenty-ninth of *Av*, on which day God became reconciled to Israel. From this context, every eve of Rosh Chodesh became known as *Yom Kippur Katan*, and was utilized, in pietistic circles, as an opportunity for petitioning with extra urgency for repentance and for the recitation (during the afternoon service) of special penitential prayers (*Selichot*).

ORIGIN OF THE *SELICHOT*

160. When were *Selichot* prayers first composed?

Selichot, prayers for forgiveness as part of petitions for special communal needs, were introduced already in biblical times as an accompaniment to the special fast days that were declared by the authorities for such purposes.

Drought was the most common reason for the introduction of such emergency measures and for calling upon the collective voice of Israel to wrest compassion and grace from on high, and in the biblical book of Joel we have a most poignant reference to such an occasion:

> Mourn, you priests, ministers of the Lord,
> the fields are ruined, the parched earth mourns;

for the corn is ruined, the new wine is desperate,
the oil has failed. . . .
Priests, put on sackcloth and beat your breasts;
lament, you ministers of the altar; come, lie in sackcloth
all night long, you ministers of my God. . . .
Blow the trumpet in Zion, sound the alarm upon my holy
hill; let all that live in the land tremble. . . . Great is
the day of the Lord and terrible. Who can endure it?
And yet the Lord says, even now, turn back to me with
your whole heart, fast and weep, and beat your breasts.
Rend your hearts and not your garments; turn back to the
Lord your God; for he is gracious and compassionate, long-
suffering and ever constant, and always ready to repent
of the threatened evil. . . .
Blow the trumpet in Zion, proclaim a solemn fast,
appoint a day of abstinence; gather the people together,
proclaim a solemn assembly; summon the elders, gather the
children, yes, babes at the breast; bid the bridegroom
leave his chamber and the bride her bower. Let the
priests, the ministers of the Lord, stand weeping between
the porch and the altar and say, 'Spare thy people, O
Lord, thy own people, expose them not to reproach, lest
other nations make them a byword, and everywhere men ask,
"Where is their God?" '[18]

We see reflected in this quotation not only the origin of our *Selichot* petitions but also the spirit of this period with its call for a collective exercise of soul-searching, repentance, acknowledgment of sin, abstinence, fasting, petition, and, above all, trepidation before the bar of divine judgment. The last-quoted verse represents the kernel of a petitionary liturgy. Although this was the recommended composition of the prophet himself, there is no doubt that other formulae would have existed at that time, which, alas, have not been preserved.

161. At what point, then, do we have evidence of the existence of an official genre of *Selichot* compositions?

It is difficult to say. Some of the biblical psalms express acknowledgement of sin and a petition for forgiveness and may well have been employed, during the second Temple period, as prescribed hymns for fast days and times of national crisis. The post-biblical Prayer of Manasseh (*circa* late second century B.C.E.) has been described as

One of the most beautiful and eloquent utterances of the human heart . . .
[articulating a] need for divine forgiveness and acceptance. . . . Two main

18. Joel Chapters 1–2.

ideas permeate the verses: God's infinite mercy and grace, and the assurance that authentic repentance is efficacious. Other significant concepts are the power of God's name, the idea that righteousness is through God alone, the concept that the patriarchs did not sin, and the idea that chastisements are good and atone for sin.[19]

All these elements, present in such an early work and sharing so much of the spirit and sentiment of the *Selichah* genre, suggest that it was already an accepted liturgical form at least by Maccabean times.

When we come down to the Mishnaic period (first and second centuries C.E.) we already have in place *Selichah* compositions that were so popular that they were officially prescribed for recitation on fast days. Thus the Mishnaic[20] order of service for fast days (particularly those instituted for periods of drought) prescribes for the expansion of the *Amidah* by another six blessings. It also preserves a special concluding formula for each blessing:

> Over the first blessing he says: *Miy she'anah et avraham behar ha-moriah hu ya'aneh etkhem* . . . ("He who answered Abraham on Mount Moriah, may He answer you and hearken unto your cry on this day. Blessed art thou, O Lord who redeems Israel.").
>
> Over the second blessing he says: *Miy she'anah et avoteinu al yam suf hu ya'aneh etkhem* ("He who answered our forefathers by the Red Sea, may He answer you and hearken unto your cry on this day. Blessed art thou, O Lord who remembers the things that are forgotten by us.").
>
> Over the third blessing he says: *Miy she'anah et yehoshua bagilgal hu ya'aneh etkhem* . . . ("He who answered Joshua at Gilgal, may He answer you. . . .").

This genre, invoking the past kindnesses of God to our patriarchs, and throughout history to leaders and saints of our people, is a hallmark of one of the most well-known of our present *Selichot* and is employed as a climax to the entire *Selichot* service. Thus, although the majority of the compositions we recite are by the later medieval poets, yet the genre itself was clearly well-established by Mishnaic times (first and second centuries C.E.), and may well go back even two centuries earlier.

162. So does our recitation of *Selichot* at this period go back to Talmudic times?

No, it does not. The Talmud only refers to the ten days between Rosh Hashanah and Yom Kippur (inclusive) as a period of special penitence when God is in closest proximity to Israel.

Quoting the verse from Isaiah, "Seek the Lord while He may be found, call on

---

19. Charlesworth, J. H. (1985). "Prayer of Manasseh" in *The Old Testament: Pseudepigrapha*, ed. J. H. Charlesworth. New York: Doubleday, p. 629.

20. Mishnah *Ta'anit* 2:1-4.

Him while He is near" (Isaiah 55:6), the Talmud says, "This refers to the ten days between Rosh Hashanah and Yom Kippur."[21] As far as the Talmud is concerned, it is only certain liturgical changes and additions that are required during this period, not the recitation of *Selichot*.

The main liturgical adjustments that are prescribed by the Talmud[22] are the replacement of the reference to "God" in the concluding formula of the eleventh blessing of the *Amidah* blessings by a reference to Him as "King." Thus, instead of describing Him as *ha-El ha-kadosh* ("the holy God"), we substitute with *ha-melekh ha-kadosh* ("the holy King"). Another change recommended by the Talmud is to replace *melekh oheiv tzedakah umishpat* ("a king who loves righteousness and justice") with a specific reference to God as *ha-melekh ha-mishpat*, "the King of justice." While in this instance the reference to God as "King" was already in the original formula, the Talmudic prescription has the effect of bringing that kingship into much sharper focus by defining it exclusively with reference to His adminis-tration of justice in the world, which is, of course, the main theme of these ten days.

FASTING DURING THE *SELICHOT* PERIOD

163. When do we first hear of special *Selichot* services being held?

Around the eighth century, additional brief insertions into the *Amidah*, such as *Zokhreinu lachayim* and *Mi khamokha*, were added during the Ten Days of Penitence, and in the Geonic period (ninth century) we hear of the custom, in the two great Babylonian academies of Sura and Pumbedita, for people to rise early, before dawn, on each of the ten days to recite *tachanunim*, "supplications."[23] This was the origin of our *Selichot* services.

At the same time, the custom developed to observe those ten *Selichot* (or *Tachanunim*) days as full-blown fast days. And that went not only for Rosh Hashanah and the day before Yom Kippur, but also for *Shabbat Shuvah*, the intermediate Sabbath of the period! They would also read from the Torah each day the specific (*Va-yechal*) portion prescribed for fast days, and, on *Shabbat Shuvah*, would also recite the statutory *Tachanun* (petitionary) prayer that was customarily never recited on Sabbaths, festivals, or even minor festival days.

164. But surely it is not in keeping with the spirit of Shabbat or *Yom Tov* to observe them as fast days?

Indeed it is not; and one wonders whether perhaps this strange practice might have been introduced originally merely as an emergency measure in the face of some persecution facing the community in Palestine and was never officially

---

21. *Ta'anit* 15a.
22. *Rosh Hashanah* 18a.
23. *Otzar Ha-Geonim* on Talmud *Rosh Hashanah* (1931). Haifa, Jerusalem: Otzar Ha-Geonim Publications, p. 31.

abrogated, but taken by the expatriate refugees to be transplanted and continued in the countries of their exile.

Be that as it may, we know that major halakhic authorities strongly opposed this practice from the outset. Thus, in the middle of the eighth century, the blind Babylonian Gaon, Yehudai, objects to this Palestinian custom. He complains that it has no basis in Scripture or Talmud, but was a private custom that may not, therefore, override the Shabbat. He emphasizes that these are called "days of repentance," not "days of fasting."[24]

This is reiterated in the fourteenth century by Jacob ben Asher in his authoritative code, the *Tur*:

> And one must eat, drink and be joyful on these days, and not indulge in fasting. Rav Natronai Gaon has written, however, that while one may not fast on the first day (of Rosh Hashanah), since it is a biblically prescribed festival day, yet there is no objection to doing so on the second day and on *Shabbat* (*Shuvah*). It was because these ten days were unique from all the other days of the year that our Sages permitted fasting both on weekdays and Sabbath.[25]

165. But how can the *Tur* possibly declare it as more acceptable to fast on Shabbat than on *Yom Tov*. Is not the Sabbath a far more important and sacred day than *Yom Tov*?

The *Bach* [26] explains that it is not a matter of comparative importance here, but of the maintenance or impairment of the festive spirit. As regards *Yom Tov*, the Torah states "And you shall rejoice on your festivals." Thus, fasting is prohibited because it impairs the spirit of "rejoicing." As regards the Sabbath, however, it is nowhere referred to as a festive day, and there is no biblical prescription to "rejoice." Yes, there is a later prophetic recommendation that we "should proclaim the Sabbath a delight" (Isaiah 58:13), but that is a subjective feeling; and for many people, the observance of that Sabbath—*Shabbat Shuvah*—as a fast day, which serves to heighten their spiritual senses and give them the good feeling that their repentance is being most authentically expressed—that, for them, truly constitutes "a delight." It certainly does not impair the sanctity of the Sabbath. Quite the contrary: it invests it with added spiritual significance.

Bach goes on to quote the *Maharil* (1365–1427) who, for that reason, permits people to observe on the Sabbath a personal fast in order to purge themselves of the effects of a recurring bad dream, yet he prohibits observing such a fast on a *Yom Tov*. *Bach* might have added, according to Midrashic tradition, that it was on the first Sabbath of Creation that Adam was granted forgiveness for his sin of partaking of the forbidden fruit. Hence, the Sabbath is a singularly appropriate day for seeking atonement by the traditionally most effective method, that of fasting.

---

24. Quoted in Pirkoi ben Baboi's letter to North African communities, written around 800. Schechter, S. (1928). *Ginzei Schechter*, II. New York: Jewish Theological Seminary, p. 564.

25. *Tur Orach Chayyim 597.*

26. *Bach ad loc.*

166. Bearing in mind those objectors, do we know how medieval communities observed those Ten Days of Penitence?

We do have references to their observance in some of our halakhic works and codes. Thus, we learn from the *Machzor Vitri* (twelfth century), which codifies the Northern-French traditions of the school of *Rashi*, that in Franco-German (Ashkenazi) communities they discounted the objections and observed them as fullblown fast days, accompanied by the recitation of the fast day liturgy. In some other Ashkenazi communities, they made an exception in the case of the day before Yom Kippur, when it is a *mitzvah* to eat.[27]

The *Tur*, reflecting the Spanish practice, states that "it is the practice of individuals (*yechidim*) to fast on those days." By that term, he probably refers to rabbis, disciples, and groups of pietists.

167. For what other occasions were *Selichot* composed?

Such compositions were also composed for the five historical fasts of the Jewish calendar: those of the seventeenth of Tammuz, ninth of *Av*, third of Tishri (Fast of Gedaliah), tenth of *Tevet*, and the thirteenth of Adar (Fast of Esther). If we add to them the distinctive *Gezerot*, martyrological laments and elegies that were composed from the thirteenth century onward by Franco-German communities lamenting the devastations of the Crusades, which were recited especially on the commemorative fast days of *BeHaB* (the succeeding Monday, Thursday, and Monday of the weeks following the festivals of Pesach and *Sukkot*), we have all the ingredients of a special *Selichot* genre of liturgy.

THE EXTENSION OF THE *SELICHOT* PERIOD

168. How did our custom arise of commencing the *Selichot* period a few days before, and in some years more than a week before, Rosh Hashanah?

In the light of what we have said above regarding the halakhic furor over the observance of the two days of Rosh Hashanah, as well as the intermediary Sabbath (*Shabbat Shuvah*), as fast days, we are in a position to understand clearly why the extension of the *Selichot* period was introduced.

Because of the halakhic opposition, more and more ordinary people abandoned the practice of fasting and reciting the *Selichot* and fast day liturgy on those four disputed days: the two days of Rosh Hashanah, *Shabbat Shuvah*, and the day before Yom Kippur. Since we do not totally abandon the solemn commitment of rituals hallowed by age, it was preferred to simply transfer those four days of *Selichot* and fasting to the period before Rosh Hashanah.

Now, since we always commence the *Selichot* on a *Motzei Shabbat* and since we have to introduce four compensatory days before the onset of Rosh Hashanah, our

---

27. Hurwitz, S. ed. (1923). *Machzor Vitri*. Nuremberg: J. Bulka, p. 345.

practice is, therefore, that in any year when there are not four clear days in the week before the incidence of Rosh Hashanah (which means, unless Rosh Hashanah occurs as late as Thursday in that week [Rosh Hashanah cannot commence on a Wednesday]), we commence reciting the *Selichot* from the *Motzei Shabbat* of the previous week.

169. Why do we commence the *Selichot* on a *Motzei Shabbat*?

This is because the spiritual state that we have attained on the Sabbath facilitates our appeal and petitions for forgiveness. It is also because Adam was granted absolution on the Sabbath day (See Question 165). This tradition of commencing the *Selichot* on *Motzei Shabbat* is alluded to in the first main composition, which commences with the words *Bemotzei menuchah kidamnukha techilah*—"At the termination of the day of rest we approach Thee for the first time."

170. We have referred to *Selichot* as at first being recited during the entire Ten Days of Penitence (See Question 163) and subsequently to an adjustment having been made, and their recitation brought forward to some days before Rosh Hashanah (See Question 168). What is the origin of the further extension of the *Selichot* services to include the entire month of Elul?

The earliest reference to these particular penitential services is found in a responsum of Hai Gaon (939–1038), head of the Babylonian academy of Pumbedita, who states that although it is the custom of the Babylonian academies to restrict the recitation of those special petitionary *Selichot* to the Ten Days of Penitence, he had heard of some communities who already introduced them from the beginning of the month of Elul.[28] This was on account of the fact that Moses went up Mount Sinai for the third time on the first day (Rosh Chodesh) of Elul to receive the replacement Tablets of the Law. This practice indeed became popularized in many Sephardic communities.

THE *SELICHOT* GENRE

171. Have the *Selichot* compositions always been in their present form?

No, considerable development has taken place over the centuries. Originally, the *Selichot* consisted merely of biblical verses and passages suitable for the particular occasion for which they were employed (fast days, prayers for drought, national calamity, etc.). To these were added, already in Talmudic times,[29] the liturgical plea *Miy she'anah Le'Avraham*, ("May He who answered our father, Abraham on Mount

---

28. Quoted in *Otzar Ha-Geonim, loc. cit.*
29. *Berakhot* 12b.

Moriah, answer us." See Question 161). Another example of an early invocation is the plea *Anneinu Ha-Shem Anneinu* ("Answer us O Lord, answer us!"), which alphabetically describes God's various attributes with each succeeding phrase.

The Geonic period (eighth through twelfth century) witnessed the expansion of the daily prayer book and the *Selichot* with an outpouring of poetic and liturgical compositions. The early poets composed their *piyyutim* ("sacred poetry," from the Latin: *poetas*) to be inserted between the biblical verses that formed the core of the *Selichot* and to be subsidiary to them. However, in the course of time, it was the poetic compositions that came to be regarded as the essential element of the *Selichot*, displacing, in many instances, even the original biblical verses.

172. For which part of the morning service were these *Selichot* prescribed?

As we have seen (See Question 160), any national calamity was associated with the sinfulness of the nation, and consequently prayers for forgiveness were the dominant motif of the fast days instituted to pray for its cessation. Because of this, the special petitions became designated as *Selichot*, which means "prayers for forgiveness," and it was accordingly felt appropriate for such *Selichot* to be inserted into the sixth (*Selach lanu*) blessing of the *Amidah*, which is a petition for forgiveness.

This is certainly the case for the *Selichot* recited on the historical fast days. There is evidence, however, that for specially-instituted emergency fast days, when the prayers and petitions, punctuated by expositions and moral exhortations, would be extended for most of the day, it was felt unacceptable to interrupt and drag out the repetition of the morning *Amidah*. The *Selichot* were consequently deferred until the end of the service. Joseph Karo tells us that, in general, this was the long-established tradition in Palestine, adding that "this is the authentic practice.[30]

As regards present-day practice, some communities continue to insert the *Selichot* into the *Selach lanu* blessing, while others recite them before the commencement of the service. This latter custom takes account of the necessity of demonstrating the urgency of those prayers, by giving them priority in this way, while at the same time expressing a wish to avoid any interruption at all of the *Amidah*.

173. The recitation of the "Thirteen Divine Attributes" (Exodus 34:6–7) recurs with unusual frequency throughout the *Selichot*. What is the reason for this?

This is based on a well-known Talmudic statement that, when disclosing to Moses His attributes, "God enwrapped Himself in a *tallit* like a Reader and indicated to Moses that when Israel sins, if they recite these attributes in prayer, God would

---

30. *Shulchan Arukh Orach Chayyim* 666:4.

protect them."[31] This is also the sense of the verse *El horeita lanu lomar shelosh esrei,* "God, who did instruct us to recite the Thirteen Divine Attributes."

The composers of our liturgy were most sensitive to such Talmudic statements, which they took as guides and principles for their compositions. Hence, the "Thirteen Divine Attributes" became a veritable refrain after each major composition. In different prayer rites, however, the frequency of its recitation varies, and when time is short it is frequently omitted.

174. The "Thirteen Divine Attributes" are introduced, whenever they are recited in the *Selichot,* by a composition beginning *El melekh yosheiv.* This contains the sentiment *mitnaheig ba-chasidut,* that God "governs with piety." What exactly is the sense of that concept?

The phrase is, indeed, unclear, and the application of the attribute of piety to God is particularly strange, if not unbecoming. Some commentators connect it with the biblical phrase, "with the pious (*chasid*) you show Yourself as pious (*titchasad*),"[32] which the *Targum* relates to the three patriarchs, each of whom received a full measure of reward for their piety. This does not explain, however, the particular nuance of the word *chasidut,* which suggests a reward in excess of what was deserved.

Gersonides[33] comes closest to a satisfactory explanation. He relates the expression to the experience of King David who composed the verse. David was reflecting here on the fact that, whereas his own heinous sin with Bathsheba was, nevertheless, instantly pardoned,[34] his predecessor, King Saul, lost his kingdom for a comparatively minor offense![35] David's rationale of this is expressed here. Because he strove to be a pious man (*Chasid*) throughout his life and only once was vanquished by the onslaught of his passion for Bathsheba, God, in return, also displayed *chasidut,* a unique degree of loving indulgence. Saul, on the other hand, who showed indifference to God all his life, was punished with a commensurate absence of such divine *chasidut.* In this introduction to the Thirteen Divine Attributes, the author asserts that the quality of *chasidut* governs God's entire relationship with his people.

175. But does this not leave unresolved the question of the anachronism and impropriety of referring to God as governing "with piety?"

No, it does not. It simply means that, according to Gersonides' explanation, the translation "piety" is incorrect. What the phrase *mitnaheig bachasidut* really means is, "you govern with [a superabundance of] mercy." *Chasidut* is, in this context, to be related to the word *chesed,* mercy, kindness.

---

31. *Rosh Hashanah* 17a.
32. II Samuel 22:26.
33. Levi ben Gershom, 1288–1344. French Bible commentator and philosopher. See commentary of *RalBag* in standard rabbinic editions of the Prophets.
34. II Samuel Chapters 11–12.
35. I Samuel 13:14.

176. In each of the *Selichot* services there is one composition that is designated as a *pizmon*. What does this word mean and what is its significance?

The word *pizmon* is a most obscure word. According to Ismar Elbogen,[36] it occurs once or twice in some fragmentary Palestinian Targumim as a translation of the Hebrew verb *anah*, "to respond." It is probably from the Greek word *psalmos*, and originally referred to any writing composed in a poetic mode. It was later applied specifically to poems that were endowed with a recurring refrain; and the term *pizmon* was applied either to the poem as a whole or specifically to the refrain.

Because of its special literary embellishment and the fact that this allowed for the interaction of *Chazan* and congregation, the *pizmon* was regarded as a superior type of poem. And for this reason, some rites prescribe that the Ark be opened for this composition.

WEARING THE *TALLIT* FOR *SELICHOT*

177. Why is it customary for the reader, leading the *Selichot*, to don a *tallit*, even though at the time before dawn when they are recited there is no halakhic requirement to wear tzitzit?

While it is quite true that the halakhic requirement to wear *tzitzit* is only operative in daylight, since the Torah states, "And you shall see them" (Numbers 16:39), nevertheless an exception is made in the case of the recitation of *Selichot* before dawn. This is because the above-quoted Midrash (See Question 173), from which the very significance of the "Thirteen Divine Attributes"—the crux of the *Selichot*—is derived, refers to God having "enwrapped Himself in a *tallit* like a Reader" in order to disclose those attributes to Israel, so that they might employ them in order to secure divine indulgence.

178. Are there any other prescriptions regarding the wearing of this *tallit* for *Selichot*?

It is recommended that the Reader leading the *Selichot* not use his own *tallit*, but borrow one from another worshiper. The reason for this is that there is some doubt about whether or not he needs to recite a blessing over a *tallit* that is worn while it is still night. While most authorities would not require it, the *Rosh* maintains that a blessing is still required over a daytime garment (the *tallit*) even when worn at night. In order to side-step this halakhic issue, it is better to borrow someone else's *tallit*, since most authorities maintain that one does not recite a blessing over someone else's *tallit*, and all would agree that in this situation a blessing is not required since

---

36. Elbogen, I. (1913). *Ha-tefillah beyisrael behitpatchutah ha-historit* (translation of the German: *Der judische Gottesdienst in Seiner Geschichtlichen Entwicklung*, ed. J. Heineman. Tel Aviv: Devir, pp. 154–155.

he is clearly not borrowing it in order to fulfill the *mitzvah* of *tzitzit*, but only to comply with the dress code for *Selichot*.

THE *SELICHOT* PERIOD IN YIDDISH LITERATURE

179. The *Selichot* period, from the week before Rosh Hashanah until Yom Kippur, is obviously a religiously supercharged time. Was this exploited in any way by writers on Jewish life and religious themes?

It was, indeed. We shall have to content ourselves here with a précis of perhaps the most well-known and best-loved story to be set in and inspired by this period. Entitled, "If not higher," it was written by Isaac Leib Peretz (1852–1915), one of pre-World War I Jewry's most distinguished Hebrew writers and regarded, at the same time, together with Mendele Mokher Seforim and Shalom Aleichem, as one of the founders of modern Yiddish literature:

> One of the most remarkable features of Peretz's creative ability was his deep penetration into the human soul. A writer of contrasts, he could portray the shoemaker and the coachman, the tailor and the water carrier with the same sympathy as he portrayed the world of the learned Jew. His Hasidic and folkish tales were superb. As a poet he appreciated the warmth of feeling, the emotional upsurge and the joyful philosophy of life fostered by Hasidism.[37]

The story begins by referring to the mysterious disappearance from his home, and subsequent absence from synagogue, every single morning during the *Selichot* period, of the rabbi of the Hasidic community of Nemirov. He would return home later in the morning; and, although the townsmen were desperate to know what their rabbi had been doing, no one had the temerity to question their saintly leader on his personal affairs. It was soon universally assumed that there was only one thing the rabbi could be doing, and that was ascending to heaven in order to add his most persuasive plea for repentance, before the very bar of the heavenly court, to that of his townsmen and women.

But once there was passing through Nemirov a Litvak, a cold-blooded skeptical Lithuanian Jew, who had neither the sympathy nor the faith of Hasidim. He determines that he will get to the bottom of this matter, once and for all. So one evening, while the rabbi is in synagogue, the Litvak slips into his home, goes up to the rabbi's bedroom, and hides himself under the bed.

Long before dawn the next morning, all the rabbi's family bestir themselves, rise quickly, wash and dress, and leave the house for the synagogue to recite the *Selichot*. The rabbi has been awake for hours, sitting up in his bed and praying for all the sick and afflicted of his people and for those weighted down with iniquity. But he waits and does not rise from his bed until all have left the house.

Then the rabbi dresses himself, goes to the clothes-closet and takes out a bundle.

---

37. Kravitz, N. (1973). *3000 Years of Hebrew Literature*. London and New York: W. H. Allen, p. 491.

Out of the bundle tumbles a heap of peasants' clothes, a smock, a huge pair of boots, a big fur cap with a leather strap studded with brass buttons.

The rabbi puts these on, too, and, from one of the pockets in the smock, there sticks out the end of a thick peasant's rope.

The rabbi leaves the room. The Litvak follows. Going through the kitchen, the rabbi stoops, picks up a hatchet, hides it under his smock, and leaves the house.

The Litvak trembles—but persists!

The dread of those days of judgment reverberates throughout the town. Here and there you can hear the desperate cry of Jews attempting to storm the very gates of heaven with their prayers. Or, through some open window, may be heard bitter moaning from a sickbed close by it. The rabbi sticks to the shadows, flitting from house to house, with the Litvak, who can hear the beating of his own heart keeping pace with the heavy footsteps of the rabbi, following, with a light tread, some 20 paces or so behind.

A little forest comes into view at the end of the town, and the rabbi proceeds into the forest. The Litvak watches in amazement as the rabbi stops near a young tree, takes out his hatchet, and begins to chop the tree. He watches as the rabbi musters all his strength to fell the tree and then chop it up, first into logs and then into chips. He gathers up the chips into a bundle, binds it round with the rope, which he takes from his pocket, throws the bundle over his shoulder, shoves the hatchet back under his smock, and begins to walk back to the town. He stops in one of the poorest alleys at that end of town, at a broken-down hut, and knocks on the window.

A frightened voice asks, in Russian, from within: "Who's there?" The Litvak, straining his ears, recognizes the voice of a sick woman.

"Vassil," answers the rabbi.

"Which Vassil," cries the frightened voice within. "I don't know you. What do you want with me? I'm cold and sick. Go away."

"You do know me. I'm Vassil the woodcutter. I've got wood to sell—very cheap. For you, next to nothing. . . ."

With that, the rabbi, not waiting for an answer, makes his way into the hut.

The Litvak steals after him, and, in the grey light of the dawn, peers in through a crack in the wooden door. He sees inside a woman wrapped in rags, lying in bed. He then hears her address the rabbi in a weak voice, a voice full of care and sorrow: "Buy? What shall I buy? I'm a sick, old widow, with no money at all to buy food, let alone wood!"

"I'll give it you on credit," says the rabbi, "six groschen in all."

"But I've already told you, Vassil," moaned the sick woman. "Where am I going to get the money from to pay you back?"

"Foolish woman," the rabbi rebuked her. "See, you are a sick woman, old and widowed, and yet I am willing to lend you this wood. I will trust you, as I am certain that you will be able to pay for it some day. And you have a great and mighty God in heaven, and you are not even prepared to trust Him to the extent of six groschen!"

"But who will light the fire for me?" she moaned again. "I am sick and do not have the strength to rise."

"I will, of course," said the rabbi. "That's part of the service I offer." And with that, he bent down to the fireplace, and began to light the fire. And, as he arranged the wood, he recited in a low voice the first part of the *Selichot* prayers; and when the fire was well lit, he prayed the second. And when the fire had died down, and he had covered the oven, he recited the final part of the *Selichot*.

The Litvak, who had seen everything, decided, there and then, to settle permanently in Nemirov. And he became one of the most passionate followers of the rabbi.

And later, when the admirers of the Rabbi of Nemirov told how, every year, during the dread *Selichot* days before New Year, it was the custom of their rabbi to leave earth and to ascend upward as high as heaven, the Litvak would add quietly, "And maybe even higher still!"[38]

180. Are the *Selichot* services well attended?

In truth, in most large Orthodox synagogues these days, there is little difference between the attendance during these days leading up to Rosh Hashanah and any other weekday of the year. This was not the case in the communities of Eastern Europe (*der heim*) before the First World War. There, the *shamash* (sexton) would make the rounds of the hamlets before dawn and knock on the door of each home, rousing the slumberers to get up and come early to the *Selichot*. This was a period of great awe, when the entire community felt the spiritual urgency of the hour.

The only exception these days is the special *Motzei Shabbat* midnight *Selichot* services that are "staged" by some large congregations, who frequently invite an internationally renowned *chazan* to lead their choral service. In New York and London, officionados of *chazanut* will travel the length of the city to attend such services. They will testify to the unique spirit that characterizes these occasions, generated by the combination of the crowded synagogue, the bewitching hour of midnight, the awareness that the *Yamim Noraim* (days of awe) are approaching, and the beauty of the service with its stirring compositions and melodies. They are a desideratum for anyone whose soul thirsts for true nourishment and who wishes to prepare himself in some meaningful way for the approaching period of spiritual regeneration.

---

38. This précis is by the present writer, and is based on the translation of Peretz's Yiddish story, which originally appeared in Edmond Fleg's *Jewish Anthology* (1925). New York: Behrman's Jewish Book House.

VII

Shabbat and *Yom Tov* Prohibitions:
Cooking on Rosh Hashanah;
Eiruv Tavshilin

181. May one not cook on Rosh Hashanah?

One may cook, unless of course Rosh Hashanah coincides with *Shabbat*. But it is certainly preferable to be able to enjoy the day relaxing with one's family after a long morning in synagogue and after partaking of one's *Yom Tov* lunch. It is hardly in the spirit of *oneg Yom Tov* ("making the festival a delight") to have to spend it in the kitchen!

182. Why may one cook on *Yom Tov* and not on *Shabbat*?

As regards *Shabbat*, the Torah states, "You shall kindle no fire in all your habitations on the Sabbath day" (Exodus 35:3). This prohibition includes switching on a light or a cooker, or activating a car ignition, even though they are non-exertive.

Such highly creative acts, designated as *nolad*, "bringing something into being," are prohibited in order to demonstrate on the Sabbath that there is only one ultimate and primary source of creative energy, and that is God. He rested on the first Sabbath of Creation; and we must do likewise, as a demonstration of deference and awe before the creative Spirit that keeps our universe in existence and that invests and generates man's own limitless progress and creative energy.

Shabbat ensures that we put our genius into perspective. By not striking a match, generating heat, or changing the composition of raw materials through cooking on the Sabbath, we demonstrate that we have no mastery over matter, that we are privileged tenants on God's estate, not its masters, and that we have to acknowledge God's absolute title on a weekly basis.

As regards *Yom Tov*, however, the Torah itself made a concession in order to enable us to enjoy the festival days to the full. It states that, "No manner of work shall be done on them, except that which is necessary for what man must eat, that alone may be done by you" (Exodus 12:16). Thus, any act, such as cooking or baking, required to provide food for that particular festival holy day, may be undertaken.

Rabbinic oral law and tradition disclosed that this concession to the food requirement was always interpreted in the very broadest sense, to include any other activity required for human enjoyment and convenience, such as lighting, heating, pushing a baby carriage, washing dishes, or (not recommended!) smoking. Thus, while carrying out of doors is prohibited on the Sabbath, on *Yom Tov* it is permitted to carry, with the proviso that they were objects permitted to be touched and used on that day. Hence, one may carry books, clothes, food, *tallit*, and similar objects, but not money, since business transactions are not permitted on *Yom Tov*.

PERMITTED ACTIVITIES

183. Are absolutely all activities permitted, then, if they are in the cause of the preparation of food or for other forms of human enjoyment?

No, they are not. The halakah prohibited certain activities, such as reaping, grinding, squeezing, hunting, even if it was intended to employ them in the preparation of a meal. This was a preventive measure, since people are accustomed to performing these activities on a daily basis—reaping their fields, grinding and milling the corn, squeezing the grapes of the vintage, hunting animals and fish—and the rabbis felt that if they permitted these activities, albeit strictly for the purpose of food on *Yom Tov*, people would be tempted to go into their fields and spend the holy day at work. (This was especially so in the centuries before our festival liturgy was created, when people did not have their entire morning taken up with prayer and synagogue attendance.)

184. Why is the cooking concession only extended to food required for that particular day?

Whereas in the Diaspora we observe two days of *Yom Tov*, the Torah only states that "the first day is a holy convocation unto you . . . and the seventh day is a holy convocation" (Leviticus 23:7-8). Thus, to spend time and effort on the first day of the festival preparing food for the second day, or to prepare on the seventh day for the last day (or on *Sheminiy Atzeret* for *Simchat Torah*)—notwithstanding the fact that in the Diaspora the next day is also holy—was nevertheless regarded as a diminution of the sanctity of the biblical holy day.

185. Are there any exceptions to that rule?

Yes. The halakah prescribes that, providing one requires to eat some of the food one cooked on the first day of *Yom Tov*, a larger volume of food than is required for that day may be cooked in order to have sufficient for the next day also. The principle is that the first intention is regarded as his primary intention.

186. But if exceptions like that can be accommodated, why should it not be allowed to cook on *Yom Tov* for a Shabbat that follows immediately after it?

The objection here is also a precautionary one, for if we permit people to cook on *Yom Tov* for the following day, they might easily jump to the conclusion that it is always permitted to do such cooking for the following day, even if it is a weekday. However, by insisting that cooking on *Yom Tov* even for Shabbat is prohibited, the clear inference will be drawn that obviously one may not cook and prepare on *Yom Tov* for an ordinary weekday that follows it.

187. So how do we get around the problem of enabling people to eat appropriate Shabbat meals?

While we have just explained that one may not cook or prepare on one day of *Yom Tov* for the next, even if be a *Shabbat*, nevertheless, having regard to the paramount sanctity of *Shabbat* and the prophetic challenge of calling it "a delight," the halakah took account of the great inconsistency in having well-cooked food over the two days of the *Yom Tov* (Thursday and Friday) and then having to eat frugally on the Sabbath because of the prohibition of preparing food on *Yom Tov* for the day after.

In that spirit, tradition introduced a method of circumventing the strict law for those prepared to make a tangible statement, by thought, word, and action, affirming their total commitment to the sanctity of *Yom Tov* and their awareness that by cooking on *Yom Tov* for *Shabbat* they are not allowing themselves any concessions that may be extended to other situations, such as cooking on any future *Yom Tov* for a following weekday.

EIRUV TAVSHILIN

188. What is the nature of that affirmation?

It is referred to as *Eiruv Tavshilin*, which means, literally, "mixture of cooked dishes." This involves a symbolic act of reducing the volume of cooking required to be done on the second day of *Yom Tov* for the *Shabbat*, by setting aside some food for *Shabbat* even before the festival has commenced. Conceptually, one is already giving priority of thought to that *Shabbat* day and setting in motion its preparation, not on *Yom Tov*, but even before it has commenced.

189. How is the *Eiruv Tavshilin* prepared?

The head of the household sets aside a small piece of cooked or roasted food (about the size of half an egg) that is normally eaten with bread, such as meat, fish, or a boiled egg, and places it on a dish together with a small bread roll (or, on Pesach, a piece of *matzah*). After the formal declaration (See Question 190), the food is placed in a carefully designated place until all the cooking and preparations for *Shabbat* have been completed on the Friday. If it becomes eaten or is lost, no further preparations may be made for the *Shabbat*. It is customary, however, to use the bread roll, or *matzah*, as one of the two loaves required for *Seudah Shelishit*, the "third meal," eaten late *Shabbat* afternoon.

190. What is the *Eiruv Tavshilin* declaration?

The blessing is recited: *Barukh attah . . . asher kidshanu bemitzvotav vetzivanu al mitzvat Eiruv*—"Blessed are You . . . who has sanctified us by His commandments, and commanded us concerning the *mitzvah* (sacred prescription) of making an *eiruv*."

This is followed by the declaration: "By means of this *eiruv* it shall be permitted for us to bake, cook, heat dishes, light the Sabbath lights and prepare during the festival all we need for the Sabbath—for us and for all Jews who live in this town."

191. What if someone forgot to make an *Eiruv Tavshilin*?

It is the tradition for the rabbi of the community to have in mind when he makes his *Eiruv Tavshilin* that he is also making it, not merely for himself and his own family, but on behalf of any people of his town who might have been ignorant of the law requiring an *eiruv* to be made or for any who genuinely forgot to attend to it or who were prevented by circumstances beyond their control. They may rely on the rabbi's *eiruv* and proceed to do all their cooking for the Sabbath on *Yom Tov*.

The rabbi's *eiruv* does not, however, cover those who, through laziness or indifference, just did not bother to attend to it in time. Nor does it cover religious and learned people who, knowing that, under certain circumstances, the rabbi's *eiruv* may be relied upon, decide not to bother and to rely on him.

STRIKING A MATCH AND SWITCHING LIGHTS ON AND OFF ON *YOM TOV*

192. So may one strike a match on *Yom Tov*?

No, one may not. Some distinction between the ordinary working day and the holy festival day had to be made, and it was in that area of *nolad*, or primary creativity, that this was demonstrated. While all cooking, baking, boiling, and so forth are permitted on *Yom Tov* (as long as the food is required primarily for that particular day), nevertheless the medium or instrument of ignition of the fire or cooker has to be an indirect or secondary source—symbolic of man's creativity in relation to that of God. In other words, we may not create fire anew by striking a match, but, if we have an existing source, in the form of a gas burner, pilot light, or candle that was kindled before *Yom Tov* and kept burning throughout, we may take a taper and utilize that existing source for *extending* the flame to create further sources of heat.

193. Could the switching on of an electric light not also be construed as merely activating a secondary source?

This is actually a hotly debated issue in modern halakhic literature. From a technical point of view, the action of switching on the switch merely joins two wires together. It is only indirectly, therefore, that this creates a conduit for the current to pass from the generator in the power station that powers the light. No new electric charge is created merely by activating the switch. All that happens by that action is that electric charges are moved from one point to another. The electric current so created is not the same, therefore, as creating sparks from the friction of rubbing wood or stones, as prohibited in the Mishnah,[1] because in the case of electricity one is not creating something totally new.

194. So if it is an indirect act, why is it "a hotly debated issue?"

Because some distinguished authorities, notably Rav Isaac Judah Schmelkes (1828–1906) and Rav Chaim Ozer Grodzinsky (1863–1940),[2] have maintained that other prohibitive halakhic principles have to be applied to the act of creating light from electricity.

One of the principles they invoked was that of lighting incense on a festival, which was permitted by Rabban Gamaliel in the Mishnah.[3] Commenting on this Mishnah, R. Assi states that while a permissive ruling could be justified in the case of scenting a room in that way (that is, by using fire) on *Yom Tov*, yet impregnating a garment with scent is forbidden under the category of *molid*, generating something new, a chemical composition that did not previously exist within that fabric. Similarly, the authorities who prohibit using electricity on *Yom Tov* relate it to the act of impregnating a garment with scent, which is tantamount to an act of creating something new as a result of chemical composition, or, as expressed by Rav Schmelkes, an "electric construction."

195. So what counter principles are invoked by the authorities who permit the use of electricity?

They discount the parallel with scenting a garment, referring instead to that of the placing of a match next to a piece of hot coal or metal, with a view to the match becoming ignited. This is permitted, even though the "fire" in the coal or metal is not a visible flame, but rather merely a "source" of heat.[4] In the view of many authorities, the latter situation is the proper precedent for the situation of the light being created in the bulb as a result of the switch creating a contact with a "source" of energy.

---

1. Mishnah *Beitzah* 4:7.
2. For a full analysis of this subject, See Lev, Z. (1988). "Electricity and Shabbat." In *Crossroads: Halacha and the Modern World*. Gush Etzion: Zomet Institute, pp. 7–28. Also, Klass, R. S. "Is it permitted to turn lights on and off on *Yom Tov*?" *The Jewish Press*, Friday, March 29, 1996, p. 40.
3. *Beitzah* 22b.
4. *Mishnah Berurah* 502:1(4) and *Arukh Ha-Shulchan* on *Orach Chayyim* 502:6.

196. So much for switching on the electric light, but surely the act of switching it *off* must be characterized, halakhically, as "extinguishing fire," which is prohibited on *Yom Tov*?

Not necessarily, for it is not clear that the light or fire generated by electricity is classified halakhically as proper, biblical fire. Hence the view of Shemuel in the Talmud[5] that "One may extinguish a piece of hot metal that had been thrown into a public thoroughfare [on the Sabbath], in order that the public should not suffer harm; but this does not apply in the case of burning wood."

The burning of wood is what the Torah meant by its prohibition of "kindling fire on the Sabbath day." To that medium, the biblical prohibition of both kindling and extinguishing applies. Wood is a combustible material that ignites and also consumes itself in the provision of fire, heat, and light. Metal does not follow that process and is therefore prohibited not by biblical law, but only rabbinically. Hence the doubt regarding the light or fire generated along metal coils by electrical current.

Because, unlike wood, the hot, metal conductors of electricity are not consumed in the process, many authorities take the view that the prohibition of *kibbuy,* "extinguishing," cannot apply. Thus, because (i) there is no biblical prohibition of electrical "fire," (ii) the act of "extinguishing" does not apply to metal fuel sources of fire, heat, and light, and (iii) there is the constructive benefit of *simchat Yom Tov,* furthering our enjoyment of the festival, many distinguished authorities permit switching off the electric light on *Yom Tov.*

197. Did any world halakhic authority ever issue a permissive ruling regarding the switching on and off of an electric light on *Yom Tov*?

Indeed. Rabbi Yechiel Epstein (1829–1908), the author of the *Arukh Ha-Shulchan,* makes his view on this issue abundantly clear:[6]

It is permitted to switch on an electric light on *Yom Tov.* This is not to be prohibited as *nolad,* creating a totally new fire in the same way as striking a match is prohibited, for the essential, live fire does not reside in the match, only the ingredients with the potential to create fire. [It is the act of striking the match, therefore, which actually initiates, *ab initio,* the process of ignition.] In electricity, on the other hand, the actual power of fire is dormant within the wires.

When the positive and negative wires are joined together, the fire [or light] is produced. This is similar to blowing on a dormant coal and making it flame, which is permitted. This is not regarded as *nolad,* even though the act of blowing constitutes the generation of "power," which is responsible for making the fire shoot forth from the seemingly dead coal.

---

5. *Shabbat* 42a.

6. This responsum was first published in *Bet Va'ad La'chakhamim,* London, (1902); reprinted in *Sarei Ha-Me'ah* (Mosad Ha-Rav kuk, 1955), vol. 3, p. 14.

It is the same with electricity. When we activate the switch, we only release the preexistent "fire," and when we close it, we simply "push it back."

And even if one might object and say that, nevertheless, we are *gorem*, "causing," an act of *nolad*—this is no objection, for nowhere do we find that a *gorem* is prohibited. It is only the actual and immediate act of creating the fire (such as by rubbing two sticks together to create a spark) that is forbidden. The Talmud states this quite clearly, when it says that "*Asi'ah*, actual work, is prohibited, but causation (*gorem*) is permitted" (*Shabbat* 120b). In electricity, it is as if we were merely opening [and closing] a door. This is my view based on what I know of electricity.

> Signed,
> Yechiel Michel Epstein
> Rabbi of Novogrudok

198. So may we accept the lenient ruling for switching on and off lights on *Yom Tov* without hesitation?

One must always be guided by one's own rabbi in matters of practical halakah, especially when it involves a departure from one's traditional practice. Suffice it to say that a considerable body of halakhic opinion now inclines toward a permissive ruling. Rabbi David Slush, Sephardi Chief Rabbi of Netanya, in his *Chemdah Genuzah*, adds his name to a host of other authorities who permit the turning on and off of electricity on *Yom Tov*.[7]

199. Does the same lenient ruling apply to Shabbat?

Decidedly not. It only applies to *Yom Tov*, when we are already permitted to use fire, for heating, cooking, and providing light. On Shabbat, however, we may not switch on and off any electric lights.

---

7. Slush, R. D. (1973). *Chemdah Genuzah*. Jerusalem: D. Slush, pp. 67–84.

VIII

Preparing for the Festival

SPIRITUAL PREPARATIONS

200. What specific preparations should one make for the arrival of Rosh Hashanah?

The most important preparations are, of course, the spiritual ones. This cannot be overemphasized, given the inordinate attention that is devoted by so many to the culinary and domestic aspects of our festivals. As for those many homemakers who spend so much time in sending out scores of New Year cards, making detailed lists of the invitees to their table, of the many things they will need to buy and cook in time for the festival and of the new clothes that each member of their family will require, it would be far preferable if they invested at least as much time and effort in making some spiritual lists. These would itemize the sins and offenses they knew they had succumbed to during the past year, the people they had hurt or slighted, the specific areas of their religious and communal lives wherein they had been less committed over this past year, and any support of, and attention to, worthy charitable causes that had been allowed to wane from its previous years' levels of commitment.

Our spiritual checklist would also review personal relationships and the elderly or less fortunate members of our family and circle to whom we had not paid the requisite attention, visited sufficiently, and dispensed kindness and consideration.

Following on from this comes the responsibility to take practical steps toward fulfilling the halakhic requirement of interceding personally with anyone whom we know we have offended. However difficult, we have to pick up the phone and ask if we might come over or meet at a mutually convenient place so that we might resolve and put behind us our issue of grievance.

KEVER AVOT—VISITING THE GRAVES OF THE DEPARTED

201. What other important preparations should we make in time for Rosh Hashanah?

It is customary to visit *kever avot*, the graves of parents and family, in time for the festival. Judaism discourages excessive preoccupation with the dead. We are meant to put our losses into perspective and to affirm life. We are not permitted to pray to the dead, and we are discouraged, therefore, from making too many visits or pilgrimages to the cemetery. For this reason, our tradition allocated some specific occasions when it is acceptable to visit (such as on the concluding days of *shivah* and *sheloshim*, on a *Yahrzeit*, at times of personal or family calamity, or at decisive moments of life), and before Rosh Hashanah has become the most popular time for at least an annual visitation.

202. What form should such a visit take?

It should be remembered that the purpose of such a visit at this time is twofold: First, it is to show the respect due to parents even after they have departed. An example of this deference is the requirement that, when mentioning a departed parent in conversation, one should add the term *alav ha-shalom* (for a male) or *aleiha ha-shalom* ("peace be upon her"), or *hareini kapparat mishkavo* (for a woman: *mishkavah*), ("May I serve as an atonement for him/her"). Since such a visit is intended as a token of love and respect for their memory, and to afford an unhurried opportunity for nostalgic and loving recollection, or, sometimes, for the outpouring of remorse for a strained relationship that might have been avoided or for aggravation caused to parents, it is important, therefore, to arrange one's commitments in such a way that one can allocate more than sufficient time to take full advantage of the visit. There is nothing worse than a hurried and merely perfunctory visit just "to do one's duty" and satisfy the religious convention.

Secondly, the visit before Rosh Hashanah is intended to concentrate the mind and emotions upon the brevity of life and to humble us into a proper evaluation of our own values and shortcomings. We, or at least the synagogue cantor, will don the *kittel*—the shroud of the dead—for the forthcoming Rosh Hashanah services. In our oft-repeated prayers for life at this season, we will be reminded—and it will be reinforced by this visit we have just made—just how brief life is and how, if we utilize it wisely, honorably, and spiritually, it will pave the way for us into life eternal. Again, therefore, we should allow ourselves plenty of time during this visit for reflection and resolution.

203. What prayers do we recite when visiting *kever avot*?

Special prayer cards should be available. It is worthy of noting that, if one has not visited the cemetery for 30 days, the following special blessing should be recited:

Barukh attah Adonai Blessed be the Lord
Eloheinu melekh ha-olam asher our God, king of the universe,
yatzar etkhem ba-din vezan who formed you in judgment,
vekhilkeil etkhem badin, who nourished and sustained
veheimit etkhem badin you in judgment, and brought
veyode'a mispar kulkhem death on you in judgment, who
badin; ve'atid lehachazir knows the number of you all in
ulehachayotkhem badin. judgment, and will hereafter
Barukh attah Adonai, mechayei restore you to life in judgment.
ha-meitim. Blessed art Thou, O Lord, who
brings the dead back to life.

Several Psalms are also recommended to be recited, especially Psalm 119, which takes the form of an alphabetical acrostic psalm, which allocates eight verses to each succeeding letter of the *alef bet*. It is customary to read, in turn, the succeeding eight verses of the letters that make up the name of the departed. Other significant Psalms are Psalm 1, 15, 16, 23, 24, 49, 91, 103. For a woman, the famous *Eishet Chayyil* (Proverbs 31:10–31) is recited.

For the more learned, it is considered appropriate to study a short section of the Mishnah by the graveside. Mishnah was regarded as particularly significant, because its letters also make up the word *neshamah*, which means "the soul!"

204. Besides the traditional texts, is there anything a little more personal and specific that may be recommended for recital when visiting *kever avot*?

The present writer has composed a series of personal English meditations, recalling each specific departed member of the family, to be recited as an accompaniment to the *Yizkor* service.[1] These are also eminently suited to recitation by the graveside. We reproduce below some of these meditations.

There is nothing wrong with composing one's own message or tribute to the departed, either in Hebrew or English, in poetry or prose. It should, however, be appropriate and reverential and should not contain anything risqué or of dubious taste, even if the departed, during his or her lifetime, may have had a penchant for that form of expression!

We should also be mindful of the words of Rabbi Maurice Lamm in his book, *The Jewish Way in Death and Mourning*, that

> Much care must be taken to direct one's personal prayers at graveside to God. To pray to the deceased, or to speak directly to him in the form of prayer, borders on blasphemy. . . . Not all the good intentions in the world can justify praying to the dead as intermediaries. . . . Better no visitation to the cemetery at all than one which induces 'inquiring of the dead.'[2]

MEDITATIONS FOR THE DEPARTED

205. What form of meditation may be recited for a parent?

We suggest the following:

> Father of mercy, look down upon me as I stand here at this time paying my fond and reverent tribute to the memory of my beloved (father/ mother/parents) (insert their Hebrew and/or English names).

1. Cohen, J. M. (1994). *A Yizkor Memorial Booklet.* 2nd revised edition. London: Gnesia Publications, pp. 18–19.
2. Lamm, M. (1969). *The Jewish Way in Death and Mourning.* New York: Jonathan David Publishers, p. 194.

Each soul that You have created is unique and unbounded in its capacity to give love and to radiate joy. When that soul is removed from among us, the quality of our lives is sorely diminished.

The nature of man is to take for granted the love that is shown to him and the sacrifices made for us by our parents. Frequently it is only in retrospect that the magnitude of their gifts to us is appreciated. And then it is too late to say, "thank you!"

But if the soul you have created is immortal, and if death cannot wound it nor the grave suppress its vitality, then my thanks and appreciation are yet heard and my prayers are not in vain. If the soul yet lives with Almighty God, then my debt can still be repaid by my leading an exemplary life, by studying Your sacred Torah and by rearing my children to be loyal to Your sacred name.

May my beloved (father/mother/parents) rest in peace, content in the knowledge that (his/her/their) memory is still revered and precious in my heart and vivid in my memory and in that of all the family. Amen.

206. What form of meditation may be recited for a sister or brother?

Father of mercy, look down upon me as I stand here at this time, paying a fond and reverent tribute to the memory of my beloved (sister/brother) (insert their Hebrew and/or English names).

I recall with gratitude the years of our childhood and the bond that linked us as we shared confidences and hopes, as we helped each other to develop and mature, and as we inherited together the valued traditions of our parental home.

And even in later years, when we were separately preoccupied with the task of establishing a career and building our own family life, that bond of love and esteem remained strong.

May my beloved (sister/brother) rest in peace, content in the knowledge that (her/his) memory is still revered and precious in my heart, and vivid in my memory forever. Amen.

207. What form of meditation may be recited for a husband or wife?

Father of mercy, look down upon me as I stand here at this time, paying fond and reverent tribute to the memory of my beloved (husband/wife).

Oh, how I miss my twin soul and partner who shared with me all my dreams and confidences, and who walked lovingly and proudly at all times by by side, making the joys we shared so much sweeter and the sorrows so much easier to bear. Oh how I miss the companionship, the love, the kindness, generosity, and support that (he/she) gave and that I gratefully recall at this sacred moment.

Almighty God, only You really know how much light has been removed from my life since (his/her) passing. Send me, therefore, Your soothing comfort and compensate me with Your protection, Your love and Your blessing until the moment of blessed reunion arrives.

Send me the gift of health and strength so that I will not become a burden to others, especially to those I love. Give me good reason, Lord, to be content and fulfilled, and to bless Your name. Amen.

208. What form of meditation may be recited for a child?

Father of mercy, look down upon me as I stand here at this time, to recall, lovingly and tearfully, my beloved child (insert their Hebrew or English names) who was taken away from us so tragically before (his/her) life had run its normal course.

I do not presume to understand the mystery of life and death, nor to call into question the righteousness of Your will. Man's pilgrimage on earth is, after all, to serve Your sovereign and unfathomable purpose. Indeed, from that do I draw strength and courage, in the knowledge that the period of my beloved child's existence on earth was pre-determined by you according to a sacred plan. All that You do is for the best; and in my grief I humbly acknowledge Your righteousness.

Help me, Lord, to bear my burden without complaint, without giving in to self-pity or despair, without spreading gloom. Renew within me the will to smile, to look forward to the future with hope, joy, and confidence.

My child's soul is committed to Your loving care. It lives on with You, enjoying the rewards that are treasured up for the innocent and the righteous. That, I do believe, and for that I shall hope until the day of reunion arrives.

God bless (his/her) immortal soul forever. Amen.

HATARAT NEDARIM—ANNULMENT OF VOWS

209. What other spiritual preparations do we make for Rosh Hashanah?

Already from before Rosh Hashanah we anticipate *Kol Nidre*, by performing in synagogue the formal and solemn ritual of *Hatarat nedarim*, the annulment of vows taken and not fulfilled.

Because the Torah binds us to "fulfill the utterance of your lips" (Deuteronomy 23:24), Judaism regarded the mere expression of an intention to perform a particular religious act—such as a vow of abstinence or nazaritehood, or the making of a charitable pledge—as a binding obligation. Failure to carry out such an expressed intention, for whatever reason, was regarded, therefore, not just as a most serious character flaw but also as the breaking of a covenant sealed with one's lips.

Where the person has made a promise to, or entered into a business undertaking with, another person, such a binding agreement cannot be annulled by this ritual. It refers exclusively to personal vows that govern one's own behavior in the sphere of religious law, charity, or moral conduct.

It was recognized that circumstances beyond their control frequently prevent people from carrying out their best intentions and also that often people make verbal or mental promises to themselves to pursue some noble course of action, and subsequently, as a result of distractions or other pressures, completely forget about those "commitments." For this reason, the ability to annul such "vows" was regarded as justifiable and acceptable. Thus, as a prelude to this period, when we will be naturally disposed to make all sorts of resolutions—many bordering on vows—it was felt appropriate, at the outset, to impress upon people, in a solemn and awesome manner, the importance of abiding by their word and of begging God and the community to be indulgent if they find themselves unable to do so.

210. Is there any precedent for the annulment of expressly made commitments and undertakings?

There is a biblical precedent allowing for a father to annul the vows of his unmarried daughter and for a husband to annul the vows of his wife.[3] The relationship between a father and his unmarried daughter and between a husband and his wife was construed as that of single-entity bonding. Thus, they cannot act independently of their partner's wishes, especially in this context where the commitment to a vow might well impair the domestic harmony of the home or the nature of their previous relationship in a way they may never have envisaged when they first committed themselves to that vow or commitment. Hence, the father or husband has every right to veto it in his own interest.

211. But does the Torah go as far as to extend that right of cancellation to any person who had made a vow?

This was a debatable point even in Talmudic times. One view in the Mishnah acknowledges that the concession of approaching a *Bet Din* (court of three) or an individual sage to seek annulment or absolution of vows is an institution that "floats in the air, with no firm Scriptural basis."[4] A succession of other sages, however, such as Rabbis Eliezer, Joshua, Isaac, Chananiah, and Rav Judah, contested this and expressed the view that there was, indeed, a Scriptural basis for *hatarat nedarim*. Significantly, however, they each quote a different verse as the basic proof-text!

Maimonides[5] and other *Rishonim* (pre-sixteenth century authorities; that is, those who lived up until the appearance of Joseph Karo's *Shulchan Arukh*) acknowledge that the absolution of vows was not, in fact, given its place in the Torah, but that it does go back, through oral transmission, to Moses on Sinai. They detect an implied reference to it, however, in the verse, "If a man shall make a vow unto the Lord, or swear an oath to bind himself in some way—*lo yacheil devaro*—he shall not [be able to] break his word" (Numbers 30:3). Those authorities interpreted the phrase *lo yacheil devaro* to mean that he, *himself*, cannot, just on a whim, break his vow, but

---

3. Numbers Chapter 30.
4. Mishnah *Chagigah* 10:1.
5. Maimonides *Mishneh Torah, Hilkhot Shevuot* 7:2.

that, in a situation where he had proper grounds for regretting having made the vow, or did not fully appreciate its implications, others may annul it for him.

212. Are there any examples of biblical personalities taking vows?

There are, indeed. It may even be said that vows hold a respectable position in the context of man's relationship both to his fellow man as well as to God.

As regards fellow man, Abraham sought to bind his servant, Eliezer, by an oath to fulfill to the letter all the details of his mission to him to return to Abraham's family in Mesopotamia in order to find a wife for Isaac. So solemn was the oath Abraham imposed that he first made his servant "place his hand under his thigh" before adjuring him "by the Lord, the God of heaven and the God of earth."[6]

As regards man's relationship with God, Jacob, on awakening from his famous dream of the angels ascending and descending the ladder spanning heaven and earth, resorted to a vow in order to enlist God's protection:

> And Jacob vowed a vow, saying: 'If God will be with me and will protect me in this way that I go, and will give me bread to eat and garments to wear, and bring me back safely to my father's home, then shall the Lord be my God, and this stone that I have set up for a pillar shall be God's house; and of all that Thou shalt give me I will surely return a tenth of it to You.'[7]

There are two episodes in the early books of the Bible that demonstrate most clearly the irrevocable status of a vow. The first is that of the Gibeonites, a tribe who inhabited an area close to Canaan. When they heard how Israel had captured Jericho and Ai, and that they were intent upon putting Canaanite tribes to the sword, the Gibeonites feared that they would be the next to be overrun. They therefore devised a plan to trick Joshua into making a solemn treaty with them by pretending that they were a far-off tribe. They achieved this by sending their peace emissaries to Joshua with worn out coverings on their asses and worn out and holed clothing and shoes on the emissaries, as well as making them carry stale and moldy bread and worn out wine-skins. Joshua believed their story that they had come from a distant land to enter into a treaty, and he "sealed a covenant with them to preserve them alive, sworn by the princes of the [Israelite] congregation."[8]

Now, even when it was subsequently discovered that the Gibeonites had hoodwinked Joshua, and they were, after all, a local tribe, Joshua still felt bound to adhere to the terms of his vow to them and to spare their lives. What mattered was that one's word had to be one's bond, irrespective of the fact that one's vow had been extracted from one under a false impression.

The second case was that of the daughter of the Judge Jephtha. He took a solemn vow that if God gave him victory over the Ammonites, then "Whatever emerges

---

6. Genesis 28:20.
7. Genesis 24:3.
8. Joshua 9:15.

from the doors of my house, and comes out towards me on my safe return from the Ammonites, shall be for the Lord, and I shall offer it up as a sacrifice."[9]

Tragically, it was his own daughter who came out to greet him, with the result that Jephtha felt constrained to apply to her the conditions of his vow.

Again, from the phraseology of that vow it seems obvious that Jephtha had originally assumed that it would be an animal that would amble out toward him, and he would therefore choose it as a thanksgiving offering. But because he had phrased it so generally, and because the scrupulous fulfillment of the terms of a vow was regarded as so important in those times, Jephtha feared the consequences of not carrying it out to the letter.[10]

213. But have we not said that Judaism's oral tradition permitted such vows to be annulled, especially where one was ignorant of their tragic consequences?

Indeed. The rabbis were equally perplexed by Jephtha's conduct. They have some harsh words for him on this score, as well as for the religious leaders who should have taken the initiative and instituted the procedure of annulment.

The Midrash condemns Jephtha as an ignoramus who deserved his fate. "What would have happened," asks the Talmud, "if a dog, pig or camel would have emerged from his estate? Could he possibly have offered such unacceptable animals as a sacrifice? Obviously not. Similarly, when his daughter came out, he should have realised that this was an exception to the rule requiring strict adherence."[11]

Another Midrashic tradition condemns both Jephtha and the religious authority of the day, Pinchas, for failing to resolve the problem together by a formal act of annulment:

Pinchas said, 'I am the High Priest, son of a High Priest. Should I abase myself by taking the initiative and going to that ignoramus?' Jephtha, in turn, said, 'I am the head of the Israelite tribes, the Commander-in-Chief of the army. Should I abase myself and take the initiative to visit someone of lower status than me?' Because of such foolish and misplaced pride, that poor girl lost her life![12]

---

9. Judges 11:31.

10. Commentators are divided as to precisely how Jephtha carried out his vow; whether he offered her as a human sacrifice or merely "offered her to the Lord," that is, made her devote her life to spiritual meditation and abandon all normal social and marital experience. The latter interpretation is supported by the end of the episode, which states that "She said to her father, 'Give me two months' grace that I may go up into the mountains and weep for my virginity together with my girlfriends' (Judges 11:37) . . . Each year, four times a year, the daughters of Israel would go to lament for the daughter of Jephtha the Gileadite (verse 40)." The Hebrew could also be rendered "to lament *to* the daughter of Jephtha," which might suggest that she lived out her life in some solitary retreat and that her friends were permitted just four visits a year. The Talmudic sources, on the other hand, do suggest that she actually lost her life.

11. Midrash *Tanchuma* on Sidra *Bechukotai*.

12. *Ibid.*

214. Are there any specific statements found in the Bible regarding the propriety or otherwise of taking vows or of expressing one's intentions in terms of oaths or vows to do, or to refrain from doing, something?

The only value-judgment on the taking of vows is found in the book of Kohelet: "When you make a vow to God, do not delay to fulfil it . . . Better that you should not vow than that you vow and do not fulfil it" (Kohelet 5:3–4).

Kohelet is clearly speaking here of the optional and conditional vows that people make, as in the case of the person who promises God that if he wins the lottery, he will devote a large percentage to charity; or the gravely ill person who vows to God that if He enables him to recover, he will consecrate all his time and wealth to good causes.

215. Are there any examples in the Bible of people making such a "deal" in the context of a vow to God?

The example that springs readily to mind is the case of the barren Hannah who took a vow, saying: "O Lord of hosts, if You will indeed look on the affliction of Your handmaid, and remember me, and not forget Your handmaid, but will give unto Your handmaid a male child, then I will give him unto the Lord['s service] all the days of his life, and there shall no razor come upon his head" (I Samuel 1:11).

216. What other types of vows were common in ancient Israel?

The Torah already refers to the category of vows that are calculated "to impose a prohibition upon oneself" (Numbers 30:3). Thus, it was common for people to take a vow of self-denial, for example by binding themselves to refrain from enjoyment of particular foods, either for a specific period of time or even forever. Such a vow may have been taken as a demonstration of remorse, either for gluttony or some other kindred sin.

Another popular category of vows was related to Temple donations. These are referred to specifically in the Torah: "You may not eat within your own gates the tithe of your corn, or of your wine . . . *nor any of your vows which you vow*, nor your free-will offerings, nor the donations of your hand" (Deuteronomy 12:17). It was common for people to utter the promissory formula, *harei alai* . . . ("I am henceforth obligated to donate . . ."), and to designate a particular form of sacrifice as their donation: a burnt offering (*olah*), a peace offering (*shelamim*), or a meal offering (*minchah*).

A most unfortunate aspect of vowing was the exercise of denying another any benefit (*madirin hana'ah*) from oneself or, conversely, vowing not to enjoy any benefit at the hands of the other. This was a binding vow that effectively severed all social and commercial relations between the parties and was too easy to resort to in the heat of the moment of dispute.

217. What do the later, rabbinic sources have to say about taking vows?

By Talmudic times, attitudes toward the taking of vows unnecessarily had hardened. The Temple had been destroyed by the Romans in the year 70 C.E., and its sacrificial system had been brought to an end. There was thus no necessity for people to express their joy and generosity in the form of the traditional vow to the Temple. Hence, we find sages expressing very strong opposition to the employment of vows. The second century Talmudist, Shemuel, states, for example, that "One who takes a vow, even if he fulfils it, is regarded as a sinner."[13]

There may well have been two reasons for this. Talmudic civil law had invested the oath (*shevu'a*) with a most important and awesome judicial status. It was imposed by the court as a means of ascertaining the trustworthiness of testimony in certain categories of claims or denials of money owing or property deposited. A special tractate of the Talmud, *Shevuot*, is devoted to the administration of oaths, and there is much discussion of the subject in other tractates also, notably *Bava Metziah*, which deals with the use of the oath in cases of theft and dereliction of duty of care on the part of those charged with looking after the property of others. Now, in order to uphold and maintain the efficacy of the oath within the judicial system, it was necessary to wean people away from treating it lightly by using it indiscriminately in their everyday affairs.

Secondly, the important status that vows had achieved within early sectarian initiation rites, as well as the vows of celibacy, poverty, obedience, and other forms of self-denial in Roman Catholicism, and, in particular, in its religious orders and congregations, was very likely a major factor in the rabbinic opposition to the taking of vows. This reached such a pace that the rabbis even recommended that people should append the disclaimer *bli neder* ("this does not imply a vow") whenever expressing an intention to perform any undertaking in the future!

218. Are absolutely no types of vows condoned then?

In general, the answer is no. Jewish practice has eschewed the vow. The only exception, curious as it may seem, is the vow to contribute to the synagogue or to charity that is made after a person has been called up to the Reading of the Law. This act of donating is actually called *shnoddering*, which is a contraction of the word *[ba'avur] shenadar* ("inasmuch as he has vowed"), found in the special *Miy shebeirakh* blessing made for the person called up.

This exception to the rule was probably permitted because it was a monitored vow, to the extent that the person would be highly unlikely to default on, or forget about, since the synagogue treasurers would assuredly follow it up and ensure that the pledge was redeemed.

219. So, if Jews are testifying before a gentile court, should they refuse to take a vow on a Bible?

Wherever possible they should, indeed, avoid any formula that is in the nature of a vow. In many countries, there exists the option of making an "affirmation" that the evidence one will give will be the truth. Some take the view, however, that because

13. *Nedarim* 22a.

the formulae of vows in Judaism are so circumscribed, with the Hebrew technical terms employed being of the essence of the commitment, and establishing its precise status as a vow or otherwise, the form of vow generally taken in the English language ("I swear . . .") would not present any problems.

As regards swearing on a Bible, some authorities have suggested that this practice should be discouraged, if only because it signifies that the word of a Jew cannot be relied upon on its own merit, but requires his awe for his Bible in order to be coerced into telling the truth.[14]

It is interesting that the first Jewish member of the British Parliament, Baron Lionel de Rothschild, was prevented from taking his seat in 1847, and for a further 11 years until a new Relief Bill was passed, because he refused to take the prescribed Oaths of Allegiance and Supremacy. He actually had no personal objection to the first two oaths, which he was allowed to swear, with his head covered, on an Old Testament. It was the third one, the Oath of Abjuration of the temporal authority of the Pope, which stuck in his gullet. Not, of course, because he felt any allegiance to the Pope, but because the formula contained the words "on the true faith of a Christian."

Sir David Salomons, later to become the first Jewish Lord Mayor of London, was heavily fined when he entered Parliament in 1851, for arbitrarily altering the wording of the three oaths to suit his conscience.[15]

220. To return to our pre-Rosh Hashanah ceremony of annulment of vows: What form does it take?

After the morning service on the eve of Rosh Hashanah, or at any time during the Ten Days of Penitence, a lay *Bet Din* of three men is constituted from among members of the congregation to serve as the first set of judges who will grant absolution to the petitioners before it.

People stand, in small groups, before the "court," and recite a standard though urgent petition that

> in relation to both vows that are known to me and those that I have already forgotten, I regret them retroactively, and I ask and seek of your eminences an annulment of them. For I fear that otherwise I might stumble and become entrapped, Heaven forbid, in the sin of vows, oaths, naziritehood, bans, prohibitions, abstentions and violation of agreements.
>
> I do not regret, Heaven forbid, the performance of the good deeds I have undertaken, rather I regret having accepted them upon myself with the formal and binding expression of a vow or an oath or nazirism or ban. . . .
>
> Therefore I request annulment for them all. I regret all the aforementioned, whether they were matters relating to money, or to physical acts or to spiritual matters. . . . Now, behold, according to the law, one who regrets and seeks

14. Jacobs, L. *op. cit.*, p. 208.
15. Roth, C. (1962). *Essays and Portraits in Anglo-Jewish History*. Philadelphia: The Jewish Publication Society of America, pp. 277–281.

annulment must specify the vow. But, you should know, my masters, that it is impossible to specify them because they are so numerous. . . ."

The three "judges" then pronounce:

May everything be permitted you; may everything be forgiven you; may everything be allowed to you. There is no longer any vow, oath, naziritehood, ban, prohibition, abstention, violation of agreement. There is no liability to ostracism, excommunication or curse; there is only pardon, forgiveness and atonement. And just as the earthly court grants absolution for them, so may it be granted in the court on high.

Three of the petitioners will then stay behind and serve as "judges" for the next group of petitioners, and so on, until all those present in synagogue have participated in the *Hatarat nedarim* ritual.

221. What is the origin of the *Hatarat nedarim* ritual?

It is rooted in the same Talmudic passage that was the inspiration for the *Kol Nidre* declaration, recited at the outset of Yom Kippur, which petitions for any vows made "from this Yom Kippur until next Yom Kippur" to be null and void. The Talmud states: "Whoever desires that his [unfulfilled] vows throughout the year should not be counted against him, should stand on Rosh Hashanah and declare, 'All vows that I am destined to make should be [retroactively] null and void.' "[16]

The first reference to the *Hatarat nedarim* ritual occurs in the *Shnei Luchot Ha-Berit* of R. Isaiah Horowitz (seventeenth century). He refers to it as "a custom of the land of Israel, practised by a holy congregation of Sages and God-fearers." He also describes the declarations and adds that, in addition to petitioning for annulment of past vows, there is a further declaration that any vows made in the future should be regarded retroactively as null and void. This declaration is also included in some modern editions of the siddur.[17]

Rabbi Horowitz, who settled in Palestine in 1621, was much influenced by the Kabbalistic traditions of the Safed school, especially those of Isaac Luria, Moses Cordovero, and Joseph Karo, and we may conjecture, therefore, that the practice of *Hatarat nedarim*—like those of *Kabbalat Shabbat*, *Tikkun Leil Shavuot*, and *Tikkun Leil Hosha'na Rabba*, among others—was an offshoot of that mystical tradition.

We conclude our discussion of the *Hatarat nedarim* ritual by quoting the words of Rabbi Jacob Emden in his *Siddur Bet Ya'akov*: "In general, we annul only vows and oaths which a person has taken in matters relating exclusively to himself, but not to matters which affect others. If he has taken an oath to his fellow, the ritual of *Hatarat nedarim* is of no avail."[18]

---

16. *Nedarim* 23b.

17. (1984). *The Complete Art Scroll Siddur*. Eds. Nasson Scherman and Meir Zlotowity. New York: Mesorah Publications, p. 764.

18. Emden, R. J. (1904). *Siddur Bet Ya'akov*. Lemberg: D. Balaban, p. 316.

222. Are there any other spiritual preparations that should be made for Rosh Hashanah?

Hasidim have the practice of immersing themselves in a *mikveh* throughout the year before the morning prayers. This is not halakhically prescribed, but is a pietistic exercise of spiritual cleansing, a symbolic "washing away" of all the dross of everyday life's enticements, and a demonstration of their sincere wish to pray to God in a state of absolute purity, of body and mind, to aid the efficacy of their prayers and petitions.

Before Rosh Hashanah and Yom Kippur, it became customary for many non-Hasidim, especially of the younger, yeshiva fraternity, to follow suit, and pay a visit to the *Mikveh* at this time, as a special demonstration of their wish for all their sins to be washed away and atonement granted.

SYNAGOGUE PREPARATIONS

223. What preparations for the festival have to be made by the synagogues?

There are far too many to list here! One could devote an entire book to the subject, and any synagogue warden or secretary will tell you that already for a few months in advance their preoccupation is with Rosh Hashanah and the lengthy festival period that it inaugurates.

Many synagogues sell seats specifically for the High Holy Days; others have an annual membership account, which members are expected to have settled before the festival. Inevitably, there are queries, or downright slanging matches, over disputed accounts!

Then there is the seats' allocation. Which person is ever satisfied with the temporary seat that is allocated to him or her? It is either too near the door, so that they are disturbed by people coming in and out. Or it is too far back, so that they allege they cannot hear the service. Or it is too near the front, so that they are deafened by the voice of the *Chazan* and choir! Another frequently heard complaint is that they do not wish to sit near Mr. or Mrs. so-and-so, because they do not get on with them, or because they talk too much during the service. Some younger people are upset if they are not placed next to their parents. Others are upset if they *are*! Synagogue wardens need the patience of Job as they embark on the task of seat allocation! Perhaps that is why Job preferred to sit in the ashes, in the open air, rather than in synagogue!

Then, there are the allocation of *mitzvot*, synagogue honors, such as being called up to the Reading of the Law, opening the Ark, etc. Naturally, the reading of the *Haftarah* (section from the Prophets, read as the conclusion to the Torah reading) calls for someone who has a passable voice and who can master the *trop*, or musical notation. It also requires someone who enjoys some status within the congregation, to justify the award of such a prize honor. This, again, could well be a mine-field (What's he done to deserve such a *mitzvah*?) unless organized with discretion and authority!

In larger congregations, which have to stage overflow or—a preferred terminology—parallel services, there is the task of employing officiants to lead those services. Again, the wardens have to contend with members' personal preferences. Some like a *Ba'al tefillah*, a reader without frills, who will get through the service at an acceptable pace. Others will maintain that their congregation—by that they invariably mean they, themselves—deserves a distinguished cantor, commensurate with its fashionable status. In addition, people have to be designated to read from the Torah each day and on Yom Kippur twice. There is a special melody for the Reading on the High Holy Days, so not everyone can volunteer for this honor.

Of course, an extra preacher might well have to be engaged. Leaving aside the congregation's own rabbi (which many would like to do!), one may well ask which temporary preacher has the learning, oratorical skills, wit, and authority to command the attention and interest of the congregation? And if the preferred candidate has all that, then why, it will be asked, is he looking for temporary employment?

Naturally, the subject-matter of his sermons will also be critically scrutinized. Members will not like it if an outsider castigates them for sins of omission or commission, nor if he is too *frum*, and certainly not if he is not *frum* enough. Again, if he is unmarried, it will be felt that he could not possibly bring the requisite spiritual *gravitas* to the occasion. If he is both good looking as well as unmarried, he may also distract the young women of the congregation. Of course, if the warden has an eligible daughter, it is a totally different matter! We jest, but anyone who has served as a warden will know that a host of considerations, not too remote from the above, has to be juggled.

In addition to the above, there is the time-tabling and allocation of duties to the officiants. In the present writer's congregation, which has 2,500 members, we run five very large parallel services, including a vast marquee in the car park. Naturally, time-tabling of officiants is a very difficult task. The wardens have to ensure that all the services are made to feel that they are "parallel" and not "overflow." By that, we mean that the main synagogue has to be seen to have no special advantage as regards the officiants. The rabbi and *Chazan* cannot relax on their padded synagogue thrones. They have to circulate and interchange between all the services during the entire period of Rosh Hashanah and Yom Kippur.

Because we run five parallel services, five separate groups of temporary wardens are also required! Naturally, the main synagogue wardens will have to liaise with those groups in good time before Rosh Hashanah to determine policy and procedures. Meetings of officiants will also be held in many such large congregations. Truly, there aren't enough days in the run-up weeks to the High Holy Days!

One can imagine, in a large congregation like mine, just what a burden is imposed upon the caretaking and cleaning staff, with lists of prior instructions given out to ensure that every venue is cleaned and the chairs properly reset for each and every service. Obviously, overtime work also has to be agreed before-hand.

I hope my very general overview has not deterred any of my readers from offering themselves as a candidate for synagogue wardenship!

224. In this context of the appointment of temporary officiants, what is their halakhic status in relation to acquiring *chazakah*, annual "tenure"?

This question clearly relates to the situation of the permanent synagogue employee who, halakhically, enjoys not only tenure, but also a measure of authority, to the extent that he cannot be removed from his post unless he is guilty of serious misconduct.[19] Moses Isserles[20] states that a *Chazan* also has the right, when he gets old and needs assistance on occasions, to ask his son to deputize before any one else. Also, on retirement, he has the right to insist that his son succeed him. *Magen Avraham* states, however, that this only applies in the case of an incumbent who is appointed for life. He adds that it was "the accepted custom that sons succeeded their fathers."[21]

As regards a part-time or one-off appointment, the *Shulchan Arukh* states that

A community that is accustomed to make appointments for a specified period, and when that period is over others are appointed to replace them, whether in the case of a Chazan, or charity officers or any other appointee, and whether or not they are paid for their services—even if no definite period was specified, the community reserves the right to determine the conditions of that appointment.

Thus, it is clear that although many authorities accord *chazakah* to a *Chazan* even after his first occupancy of the *Bimah*, while others require him to have led the service at least three times, yet, in the case of one-off annual appointments, it is clear that the community reserves the right to change its officiants each year.[22]

HOME PREPARATIONS

225. Is not the sending out of Rosh Hashanah cards just a chore that should now be abandoned?

I hope no one will think that I have a share in a card business when I say that, while many do regard this exercise as a chore, it is also accepted by many as a useful opportunity of "maintaining the contact" with far-flung family, friends, and associates who once figured significantly in our lives and toward whom we still have warm feelings and possibly also a residual debt of gratitude. If those people are elderly, infirm, or housebound, it will certainly brighten up their festival to know that they are not forgotten. It may also stimulate happy memories on their part of past relationships and of the days when they were in their prime.

19. *Shulchan Arukh Orach Chayyim* 53:25.
20. *Remah ad loc.*
21. *Magen Avraham ad loc.*, note 33.
22. Druck, R. Z. (1989). *"Ta'anat chazakah bisheliach tzibbur."* In *Shanah BeShanah*. Jerusalem: Heichal Shlomo Publications, p. 180.

A case could be made out, however, for not sending to people who live in the same town, who attend the same synagogue, or who meet each other fairly regularly.

226. What home preparations are required for Rosh Hashanah?

Naturally, as for all festivals, the home should be cleaned in honor of the festival. One should ensure, in good time before the festival, that one's shabbat/festival clothing (including one's *tallit* and *kipah*, and one's *kittel* if one wears one for synagogue on Rosh Hashanah and Yom Kippur) is clean and pressed. One should have a haircut and a shave (if one customarily shaves) in honor of the festival.

The dining table should be covered with a white cloth and set with one's finest tableware, and the *bechah* (silver goblet), the wine, and the two *challot* (loaves)—covered with the special challah cloth—should be set out in front of the senior member of the family. The festival meals should, where possible, have been prepared in advance, and, for the evening meals, an apple and honey should be provided. At the second night's meal, a new fruit is eaten or a new garment worn (See Questions 230–242).

If the first day of Rosh Hashanah is a Thursday, the *Eiruv Tavshilin* should be made (See Questions 187–191).

IX

The Eve of the Festival:
At Synagogue and at Home

LIGHTING THE *YOM TOV* LIGHTS

227. What blessings are recited over the festival candles?

On both evenings, two blessings are recited: The first is the usual *Yom Tov* blessing: *Barukh attah Ha-Shem Elokeinu melekh ha-olam, asher kidshanu bemitzvotav vetzivanu lehadlik ner shel Yom Tov.* If Rosh Hashanah coincides with *Shabbat,* the conclusion of the blessing is . . . *lehadlik ner shel shabbat veshel Yom Tov.*

This is followed by: *Barukh attah . . . shehecheyanu vekiymanu vehigiyanu lazman ha-zeh.* This is the traditional blessing prescribed for inaugurating every festival, when performing a *mitzvah* for the first time and on buying new clothes or acquiring some significant possession.

228. Why is it the custom, when lighting the *Shabbat* and *Yom Tov* candles, to cover one's eyes while reciting the blessing, and then to look at the candles?

In the case of all *mitzvot,* one has to recite the blessing before performing the act. The problem is, however, that as soon as the blessing "to kindle the Sabbath lights" has been made, it becomes *Shabbat* for the person who has lit them. Once it is *Shabbat,* one can no longer strike the match and light the candle! We overcome this by lighting the candle at the outset without any sacred intention in our minds. We then cover our eyes, shutting out the light. We recite the blessing, and then uncover our eyes, and the light suddenly flooding in before our eyes is regarded as tantamount to its being created at that instant. Hence, it is as if the blessing had indeed been recited before the flame was created.

The necessity to cover the eyes really only applies when lighting the *Shabbat,* and not the *Yom Tov* candles. One may, of course, handle fire on *Yom Tov,* so that it is technically quite possible to recite the blessing first, and then to bring a taper and light the *Yom Tov* candles, thereby complying with the requirement of reciting the blessing before the act, with none of the complications that are created by doing so on *Shabbat.*

229. Why do women extend and retract their arms three times in front of their eyes before covering them to recite the blessing?

The origin of this custom is not certain. The present writer believes that it was introduced in the same spirit as some other rituals whose basic validity was denied by sectarians. The common rabbinic tendency was to respond polemically and to demonstrate their belief in the validity of the ritual by insisting that it be performed in a most flamboyant manner.

The obvious example is the cutting of the Omer in Temple times on the evening of the sixteenth of Nisan, which is the first *Yom Tov* day of Pesach. The Saducean sect denied that this was the day the Torah intended for that ritual when it referred to "the morrow of the Sabbath" (Leviticus 23:15). (The Pharisees maintained that "Sabbath" was a general term, meaning "day of rest," which included *Yom Tov*, rather than exclusively referring to the Sabbath.) The Sadducees claimed that "the morrow of the Sabbath" means Sunday; and they therefore began the cutting and offering of the Omer sheaf of barley on the first Sunday into Pesach.

Now, the Mishnah[1] preserves a most flamboyant ceremony, accompanied by declarations and declamations, to accompany the cutting of the Omer immediately at nightfall after the first day of Pesach. This pomp and ceremony was introduced "in order to demonstrate the folly of the Sadducean view."[2]

I believe that it may well be for a similar reason that we exaggerate the ritual of lighting the Sabbath candles, because the Sadducees (third century B.C.E. through first century C.E.), as well as their sectarian descendants, the eighth century Karaites, maintained that it was forbidden to have any lights or fire burning on the Sabbath day. They interpreted the biblical verse *Lo teva'aru eish bekhol moshvoteikhem* (Exodus 35:3) to mean "You shall not *have* fire burning in all your habitations on the Sabbath day." They consequently extinguished all fires in their hearths and all lanterns, sitting in the dark and eating cold food on Friday night and Shabbat.

The Pharisees, on the other hand, in the spirit of Isaiah's clarion call to "proclaim the Sabbath a delight" interpreted the phrase *lo teva'aru* far less restrictively, to mean "You shall not *kindle* any fire." Thus, fire already kindled before the onset of Sabbath was quite permitted—indeed encouraged—to be kept burning, giving light and heat to the household and warm food to put everyone in a happy frame of mind.

It was in the face of that Karaite view that the practice of lighting special Sabbath lights in the home was introduced in order to make a deliberate demonstration of the fallacy of the Karaite interpretation of the biblical verse. To reinforce the rabbinic confidence that their permissive tradition was the authentic one, they even prescribed a blessing, testifying to the fact that "God [Himself] has commanded us to light the Sabbath lights" (*Vetzivanu lehadlik ner shel shabbat*).

It would be in keeping, therefore, with the normal rabbinic tendency to exaggerate controversial rituals, for the candles to be prescribed to be lit in that

---

1. Mishnah *Menachot* 10:3.
2. For fuller discussion of this subject, see Cohen, J. M. (1996). *1001 Questions and Answers on Pesach*. Northvale, NJ: Jason Aronson Inc., pp. 176–188.

dramatic manner by extending the arms three times in front of the face to publicize the ritual one is embarking upon, and to demonstrate our confidence, thereby, that the sectarians have it wrong, and that having Sabbath lights is not only permitted, but is even invested with the greatest significance as marking the very inauguration of the Sabbath day.

It is significant that in the exaggerated Omer ritual, as described in the Mishnah,[3] the repetition of each instruction and declaration is also made three times. *Three* is clearly the significant number when it comes to making a rabbinic protestation of the validity of their view. And it is not surprising, therefore, that before lighting the Sabbath lights the arms are extended and retracted precisely that number of times.

A NEW FRUIT OR GARMENT

230. Why, on the second evening of Rosh Hashanah, is it customary to eat a new fruit or put on a newly bought garment?

This is recommended in order to justify the recitation of the *Shehecheyanu* blessing when lighting the candles on the second evening or when making *kiddush*.

The problem here is that we do not permit the recitation of a blessing unless it is absolutely required. Now, unlike the second festival days of the other main festivals, in the case of the second day of Rosh Hashanah it is not required. Whereas the former are a mere duplication of the first and seventh days, because of doubts in Diaspora communities as to which day Jerusalem had declared the first day of the month (See Question 13), in the case of Rosh Hashanah, there were actually occasions when even in Jerusalem they observed it as a two-day festival (*ibid.*). Thus, the rabbis regarded the second day of Rosh Hashanah, not as a carbon copy, but as *yoma arikhta*, "an extended [first] day." This being the case, there was considerable doubt as to whether or not the *Shehecheyanu* blessing ought to be recited, since the second day could not be construed as a "re-run" of the first, with the attendant requirement of that blessing.

To overcome the problem, the rabbis ingeniously suggested that one should have a new fruit on the table for the second night, and the doubtful *Shehecheyanu* recited over the lights will be converted into a certain and obligatory blessing by looking at the new fruit at that moment and determining that this *Shehecheyanu* should also cover that fruit when it is eaten later at the meal. Another suggestion is that the woman lighting the lights should wear a new dress for the second evening and that the blessing of *Shehecheyanu* should also be intended for that. (Who says Judaism isn't on the side of women?)

That arrangement covers the *Shehecheyanu* recited over the *Yom Tov* lights on the second evening. The person making *kiddush* is also called upon to recite *Shehecheyanu*. He should also have in mind, therefore, that this blessing should cover the new fruit, or, if he is wearing a new item of clothing for the second evening, that the

---

3. *Berakhot* 57a; *Eiruvin* 19a; *Sanhedrin* 37a.

Shehecheyanu he is reciting in *kiddush* should also be for that. This double insurance means that if, strictly speaking, we should not be reciting this blessing on the second evening, we have not infringed thereby the principle of not uttering a *berakha she'eina tzerikha*, "an unnecessary blessing."

231. But doesn't the one blowing the shofar also recite what must therefore be a doubtful *Shehecheyanu* on the second day?

He does. And for that reason it is recommended that he should also wear a new item of clothing on the second day, to cover his recitation of *Shehecheyanu*. This will not be necessary, however, if the first day of Rosh Hashanah fell on *Shabbat*, since he will not yet have recited *Shehecheyanu* over the shofar on the second day.

232. What is meant by a "new" fruit?

By this, we mean a fruit that is at the very beginning of its season and that we have not eaten since the end of its previous season the year before. It is customary to use pomegranates for this purpose. The pomegranate has numerous pips or seeds, and seeds are the source of the life we are praying for at this season. Furthermore, the Talmud observes that even the least observant Jew is really filled with [the urge to perform] *mitzvot* just like the pomegranate is filled with seeds.

233. If we are so particular about not reciting unnecessary blessings, why do we make *kiddush* in synagogue when we are going to recite it not long after, on arriving home?

It is true that, nowadays, the recitation of *kiddush* in synagogue is not strictly required. However, in ages past, the synagogue also served as a refuge for the homeless and for travelers passing through communities. Adjoining the synagogue chamber, there would be the communal soup kitchen and dining room. Thus, *kiddush* was recited at the end of the service primarily for their benefit, so that they could repair directly after the service to their meal.

Since our synagogues, in the main, no longer have to supply that provision, and we would, in any case, certainly extend hospitality in our homes to occasional visitors to our synagogues, the continued recitation of the *kiddush* is justified as a formal act of "testimony" to the sanctity of the Sabbath.

Since the *Chazan* will later be making *kiddush* at home for his family, he should consciously have in mind at that time that he is not fulfilling thereby the actual *mitzvah* of *kiddush*. For this reason, he does not himself drink the wine, but, instead, hands it to the young children present. He has not made an unnecessary blessing in this way, since he is actually merely reciting the blessing on their behalf.

Ashenazi synagogues, in particular, have continued the practice of reciting *kiddush* in synagogue, not wishing to abandon a long-standing tradition. As we have said, it is converted into a liturgical act of testimony to the sanctity of the Sabbath day, rather than a ritual or ceremonial act; and for this reason no objection was raised to its recitation both in synagogue and later in the home.

THE PROHIBITION OF EATING NUTS

234. There is a common belief that one should not eat nuts on Rosh Hashanah. Is this true?

It is, indeed, mentioned in our halakhic sources, where the reason given is that the numerical value (*gematria*) of the Hebrew word for "nut,"—*egoz*—is seventeen (*alef*=1, *gimmel*=3, *vav*=6, and *zayin*=7), which is the identical numerical equivalent of the Hebrew word for "sin"—*chet*![4] Another explanation is that the prohibition is, in fact, merely by way of practical and sound advice, in that nuts tend to increase saliva, which will interfere with the proper recitation of one's prayers.[5]

235. But surely, if you add up the numerical value of *chet*, you will find that it does not add up to seventeen, but to eighteen (*chet*=8, *tet*=9, and *alef*=1)!

Oops! No, the rabbis haven't made a blunder. According to the traditional method of working out *gematriot*, where a final letter is silent, as in the case of the *alef* at the end of the word *chet*, it was regarded as quite legitimate to discount it from the calculation. In fact, in quite a number of medieval manuscripts, as well as in the early Hebrew poetry of Yannai, the word *chet* is spelt without the final *alef*.

236. But, doesn't the *gematria* of *egoz* also equal that of the word *tov*, "good" (*tet*=9, *vav*=6, and *vet*=2)?

Don't complicate matters! Who allowed this question in, anyway? It is clear that once we start with *gematria*, we can prove absolutely anything we like! We must assume that the rabbis who offered this *gematrial* explanation for the prohibition were also aware that it could be construed in a beneficial light, as the numerical equivalent of *tov*, but that the force of evil was perceived as more potent than that of good.

237. But does not the first reason above (*gematria*) for not eating nuts appear extremely flimsy, and the second reason (increased saliva) hardly so acute, or even persuasive, for rabbinic authorities to have taken the step of issuing a prohibition?

It does rather sound as if the rabbis who thought up this prohibition were taking a sledge hammer to crack a walnut! And once we get into the realm of numerical values, one could probably find many more things to prohibit on that score!

Furthermore, one may ask why those same authorities did not prohibit the eating of nuts throughout the year for the identical reason that it interferes with the proper recitation of one's prayers? It is for these reasons that we have to look further and deeper to explain why they issued this prohibition, and we have to assume that the

4. R. Moses Isserles. *Darkei Mosheh* on *Tur Shulchan Arukh Orach Chayyim* 583:1; *Rema* on *Shulchan Arukh Orach Chayyim* 583:2.

5. *Darkei Mosheh Ha'Arukh ad loc.*

reasons offered by later authorities were merely rationalizations of an old tradition that they could not explain to their total satisfaction.

Light has been shed on the true reason by Chaim Leshem, who investigated the folkloristic background of this tradition and who attributes its origin to the ancient identification of the nut as a symbol of destruction. The germ of this lay in the tendency of the nut tree's sap and shadow to damage and destroy other trees growing in proximity to it. This underlies the Latin name for the nut, *nux*, which is derived from the verb *nocere*, "to damage, destroy," a fact revealed already by the seventh century Bishop Isidore of Seville.[6] It now makes greater sense why the rabbinic authorities should have wished to avoid such a blatant symbol of danger and destruction on the very festival when we pray so fervently for our life and security from harm.

238. But do we not first need to prove that our rabbinic authorities were actually aware of that classical piece of folklore identifying the nut with destruction?

No problem. Leshem reminds us that Rabbi Joseph Kimchi (1105–1170), in his commentary on the verse, "I went down to the nut garden" (Song of Songs 6:11), states, "The arrogant kingdom (Rome) is compared here to the nut. Just as the nut tree kills whatever is planted under its shade, so the arrogant kingdom despoils and destroys Israel that is compared to the vine and pomegranate."

Thus, the two popular "explanations" why nuts were prohibited were probably no more than a brave hypothesis of rabbis who were unaware of the classical association of nuts with destructive forces.[7]

EATING THE *CHALLAH*, THE APPLE IN HONEY, AND THE NEW FRUIT

239. What is the origin of the practice to dip an apple in honey after eating of the *challah*?

This is but one of a number of symbolic foods that the sages recommend to be eaten at the table. The choice of these particular foods was conditioned by the fact that their names are reminiscent of one of the cherished objectives of this festival.

The Talmud states, with special reference to Rosh Hashanah, that *simana milta*, "omens are significant."[8] Thus, the apple in honey symbolizes the sweet year; and by eating it we reinforce our need for that blessing, which will, in turn, invest our prayers for it with extra urgency. In the modern age of psychological advertising, we know the benefit of visual reinforcement.

---

6. Leshem, C. (1969). *Shabbat U-moadei Yisrael*. Tel Aviv: Niv, pp. 111–114.

7. Sperber, D. (1995). *Minhagei Yisrael*. Jerusalem: Mosad HaRav Kuk, pp. 41–49.

8. *Horayot* 12a; *Keritut* 6a. See *Shulchan Arukh Orach Chayyim* 583:1.

240. How is the *challah* and the apple and honey eaten?

The piece of *challah* over which we recite the *ha-motziy* is dipped in honey, instead of salt. After eating it, we dip the apple into the honey, recite the blessing *Borei periy ha-eitz*, eat the piece of apple, and then recite the plea *Yehiy ratzon milfanekha Ha-Shem Elokeinu ve-Elokei avoteinu shetechadesh aleinu shanah tovah umetukah*—"May it be thy will, O Lord our God and God of our fathers to renew unto us a good and sweet year."

241. Are there any variant practices in this regard?

The Lubavitch Hasidim have a tradition to recite the *Borei periy ha-eitz* and to recite the *Yehiy ratzon* plea before eating the fruit.

The usual practice, to recite the *Yehiy ratzon* after eating the fruit, is based on the consideration that nothing should interrupt between the recitation of a blessing and the eating of the fruit (or, in general, the fulfillment of the *mitzvah*). The Lubavitch view assumes that the *Yehiy ratzon* cannot be regarded as an interruption since it merely gives expression to the objective of the ritual and may therefore be construed as a part of the blessing itself. There are, of course, many examples of composite blessings containing several themes, such as the final blessing of the marriage, *Sheva Berakhot*.

242. What is the procedure on the second night, when we eat the new fruit?

Precisely along the lines of the first day's procedure. After dipping the *challah* into honey, reciting the *Ha-motziy*, and eating it, we take the new fruit, recite over it the blessing *Borei periy ha-eitz*, take a bite and then recite the same *Yehiy ratzon* as on the first day. Although it is a new fruit, over which we would normally recite *Shehecheyanu*, we do not need to do so on this night of Rosh Hashanah because, as we have explained (See Question 230), the *Shehecheyanu* we recite during *kiddush* also covers the new fruit we eat at this time.

OTHER SYMBOLIC FOODS

243. We mentioned above that several other symbolic foods were recommended, since their names suggested good omens. What are those foods?

Pomegranate is the favorite choice as new fruit since it contains many seeds. On eating it, we tailor the conclusion of the *Yehiy ratzon* plea to read *shenirbeh zekhuyyot kerimon*, "May it be Your will that our merit should be multiplied like [the seeds of] the pomegranate."

Fenugreek is recommended, because its Hebrew name is *rubya*, meaning "increase." On eating it, we tailor the conclusion of the *Yehiy ratzon* to read *sheyirbu zekhuyyoteinu*—"May it be Your will . . . to *increase* our merit."

The choice of carrots is fascinating in that it invests the Yiddish language with a significance normally, in the context of our ritual, only reserved for Hebrew. The choice of carrot is based on its Yiddish name, *mehren*, which also means "many." The same *Yehiy ratzon* is recited over it as for fenugreek.

Dates are also recommended, in that the Hebrew *temarim* is associated with the word *tam*, "to bring to an end." This lent itself to a special *Yehiy ratzon* petition, concluding with *sheyitamu son' einu*—"May it be Your will . . . that our enemies be brought to an end."

Perhaps the strangest recommendation as symbolic food is the head of a sheep (some substitute the head of a fish, which is a little more esthetic on the table!). The special *Yehiy ratzon* concludes *sheniheyeh lerosh velo lezanav*—"May it be Your will . . . that we become the head and not the tail."

244. On which night are those symbolic foods meant to be eaten?

Primarily on the first night, though the *Sha'arei teshuvah*[9] and some other authorities recommend that it should be repeated on the second night, together with their accompanying *Yehiy ratzon* petition.

245. Is there any reason why just honey was chosen as the symbol of a sweet year?

There is a tradition[10] that it is associated with God's provision of sustenance for the Israelites throughout their 40 years of wandering in the desert. This was in the form of *manna*, which the Torah tells us was "like honey wafers" (Exodus 16:31). Thus, on Rosh Hashanah, when our sustenance and livelihood for the coming year is being determined, we remind ourselves of the honey that God provided and recall that whatever protection, sustenance, or material benefits come our way are solely dependent upon God's grace and favor.

A weaker explanation is that the *gematria* (numerical value) of the word for honey, *devash* (306), is the equivalent of that of the words *Av Harachamim* ("Father of mercy"), and it constitutes an omen, therefore, for the evoking of God's mercy.[11]

A homiletical interpretation has been offered, to the effect that while bees are feared because of their sting, they are also the dispensers of the sweetness we enjoy. So it is with God. He is feared for His harsh decrees, but, if we are deserving, we can also enjoy the sweetness of His mercy.[12]

246. Is there any additional reason why we eat honey cake on Rosh Hashanah?

The popular explanation is that, because honey cake is traditionally called *lekach*, which means "portion," it is evocative of our wish for a "goodly portion" in the year ahead.

The only problem with this explanation is the "chicken and egg" situation (By

---

9. *Sha'arei Teshuvah* to *Shulchan Arukh Orach Chayyim* 583:2.
10. The source of this explanation is not known.
11. Shapira, Z. E. (1806). *Benei Yissaschar*. Lvov (*Chodesh Tishri, maamar* 2:13).
12. Isserlein, I. (1903). *Leket Yosher*. Berlin, p. 124.

this, we are not suggesting that chicken is an ingredient of honey cake!). Most probably honey cake got the name *lekach* because it was traditionally eaten on Rosh Hashanah in order to extend the use of honey. It is illogical, therefore, to turn that on its head and claim that because it is called *lekach*, it was chosen for consumption on Rosh Hashanah!

WHERE HAVE ALL THE *PIYYUTIM* GONE?

247. Normally, on the eve of festivals, special *piyyutim*, poetic compositions on the themes of the festival, are inserted into the blessings before and after the *Shema*. Why are these omitted from the evening service of Rosh Hashanah?

It is not that we lacked sacred poetry on the themes of sin and atonement, the *Akedah*, or the shofar.. We recite plenty of these during the course of the daytime services on both days of Rosh Hashanah, and there are plenty of other compositions that have been preserved and that could have been drawn upon to supplement the evening services.

So it was not for the lack of poetic material that it is omitted from the evening services. It was rather a conscious decision to make the evening services shorter, dating back to the time when the whole of the Ten Days of Penitence, including the festival days, were observed as fast days (See Questions 163–166). Because people were hungry after fasting during the daytime, the authorities did not wish to prolong their fast with additional compositions after nightfall (See also Question 628).

SPECIAL INSERTIONS INTO THE *AMIDAH*

248. What are the special insertions that we make into the *Amidah* on Rosh Hashanah?

It has to be said at the outset that these liturgical insertions are not restricted to Rosh Hashanah, but are recited throughout the Ten Days of Penitence.

The idea of introducing slight modifications into the statutory blessings of this season goes back to Talmudic times, and is attributed to *Rav* (third century),[13] who had a formative influence on the development of our liturgy. It was he who stated that instead of concluding the third blessing with the words *Ha-El Ha-Kadosh* ("the holy God") we should highlight God's special role as judge at this period by saying *ha-melekh ha-kadosh* ("the holy king"). Similarly, said Rav, we should conclude the eleventh blessing with *ha-melekh ha-mishpat* ("king of justice"), instead of *melekh oheiv tzedakah umishpat* ("A king who loves justice and mercy").

---

13. Talmud *Berakhot* 12b.

249. Do we introduce the phrase *ha-melekh ha-kadosh* anywhere else, outside the context of the *Amidah*, during the Ten Days of Penitence?

We do. The *Magen Avot* prayer, recited after the *Amidah* on Friday evenings, is a composite of the key words and *chatimot* ("conclusions of benedictions") of the Sabbath *Amidah*. The phrase *ha-El ha-kadosh* occurs as an allusion to the ending of the third blessing of the *Amidah*. During the Ten Days of Penitence, this is replaced with *ha-melekh ha-kadosh*.

If the *Chazan* inadvertently recited the year-round formula, *ha-El ha-kadosh*, instead of *ha-melekh ha-kadosh*, the rule is as follows: If he realizes it immediately, then he merely corrects himself. If he realizes only after a few moments (the space of time it takes to speak three or four words), then there is no need to do anything at all.

250. Does not the phrase *ha-melekh ha-mishpat* offend against the laws of Hebrew grammar, which dictate that a construct noun ("king of") cannot take the definite article, *ha*?

It is quite true. "King of justice" has to be rendered, simply, *melekh ha-mishpat* (just like "king of the world" is *melekh ha-olam*, not *ha-melekh ha-olam!*).

Rashi[14] already spotted the difficulty, and he quotes three parallel examples in the Bible where we find the construct noun endowed with a definite article.[15] These are, however, anomalous and rare literary examples. It is most strange, however, that such an anomaly should have been prescribed for regular liturgical usage.

Rabbi David Abudarham, in his commentary on the prayers,[16] states that "this form is employed to enhance God's eminence, and to indicate that He is the very essence of the justice that infuses the world at this season."

Abudarham wishes to indicate that God's justice does not derive from anything outside of Him. He is the ultimate embodiment and source of all justice in the world. If the grammatical construct form, without the definite article ("king of justice") had been employed, it might have suggested that God, the king, controls justice, but that it is not necessarily of His essence. Instead, *Rav* recommended that both nouns— *ha-melekh* ("the king") and *ha-mishpat* ("justice")—be in apposition to each other, as dual epithets of deity—He is the king; He is justice.

251. What are the other insertions into the *Amidah*?

In the very first blessing of the *Amidah*, which refers to God "remembering (*zokher*) the lovingkindness of the Patriarch," the theme of rememberance is taken up with the insertion *Zokhreinu lachayyim melekh chafeitz bachayyim*—

14. *Rashi* on Talmud *Berakhot* 12b.

15. Cf. *ha-aron ha-berit* (Joshua 3:14); *ha-misgerot ha-mekhonot* (Kings 16:17); and *ha-emek ha-pegarim* (Jeremiah 31:39).

16. Rabbi Avudarham, D. (1963). *Avudarham Ha-shalem*. Jerusalem: Usha Publishing House, p. 111.

"Remember us unto life, O king who delightest in life, and write us in the book of life, for thine own sake, O living God."

In the second blessing, which deals with the theme of God as the preserver of life in this world and the restorer of life in the Hereafter, an extra plea for life is inserted at this time. Because the statutory blessing contains the rhetorical question, "Who is like unto thee (*Miy khamokha*), Lord of the mighty ones?" the identical formula is deliberately employed to create the link: *Miy khamokha av ha-rachamim, zokheir yetzurav lachayyim berachamim*—"Who is like unto thee, Father of mercy, who in mercy rememberest thy creatures unto life?"

The next insertion is made in the *Modim* blessing, which contains a reference to *chayyeinu ha-mesurim beyadekha*—"Our lives that are committed unto thy hand." This was regarded as an appropriate context, therefore, for a reinforcement of the plea for life: *Ukhetov lachayyim tovim kol benei veritekha*—"O inscribe all the children of thy covenant for a happy life." The word *tovim* in this insertion is also meant to link up with the phrase *Ha-tov [kiy lo khalu rachamekha]* in the *Modim* prayer.

The final, and lengthiest, insertion—*Beseifer chayyim*—is placed just before the *chatimah*, "concluding benediction (*Barukh attah Ha-Shem*)," of *Sim shalom*, the final blessing of the *Amidah*.

Toward the end of *Sim shalom*, there contains the phrase *vechayyim veshalom vetov*. The insertion links up with this phrase, reading *lechayyim tovim uleshalom*.

Although *Sim shalom* is primarily a blessing for peace and contains no reference to prosperity, the *Beseifer chayyim* insertion includes the plea for *parnasah tovah* ("a good livelihood"). This is, however, not an extraneous theme, because peace is not single-dimensional. It brings in its wake a host of attendant benefits, including the opportunity for economic stability, growth, and prosperity, which, in turn, filters down to enhance the livelihood (*parnasah tovah*) of the individual citizens.

252. Why does the *Beseifer chayyim* insertion create a variant *chatimah* (concluding benediction) from the usual one employed for *Sim shalom* throughout the year?

The usual *chatimah* is *Barukh . . . hamevarekh et ammo yisrael ba-shalom* ("Who blessest thy people Israel with peace"), whereas the *Beseifer chayyim* insertion ends with *Barukh . . . oseh ha-shalom* ("Who makest peace").

The latter is more appropriate to the High Holy Days, when we acclaim God as judge, not only of Israel but of all mankind. The year-round *chatimah* is more restrictive, invoking peace merely for Israel, whereas the more general formula of the High Holy Day insertion can be construed to refer to God as the dispenser of peace to all mankind.

It is not the case, however, that *Oseh ha-shalom* represents a conclusion especially composed for the High Holy Days. It and the *ha-mevarekh et ammo yisrael ba-shalom* version actually represent the two variant versions used *throughout the year* in Israel and Babylon respectively. The original liturgy was taken to Babylon where it underwent development and revision in accordance with the liturgical and halakhic principles and preferences as developed in the Babylonian Talmud. So, although the Babylonian formula (*ha-mevarekh* . . .) became statutory, nevertheless, the version as used in Israel was allowed, for nostalgic reasons, to regain its place, and to be employed on festivals.[17]

253. What does one do if one inadvertently omits any of these insertions while praying?

If, during the Ten Days of Penitence, he said *Ha-El ha-kadosh*, instead of *ha-melekh ha-kadosh* or he is in doubt which formula he recited, if he remembered the instant he had uttered the wrong one, he may immediately correct himself. The same goes for the conclusion *ha-melekh ha-mishpat*.

If, however, he only realizes after he has completed the respective blessings, then, in the case of *ha-melekh hakadosh*, he has to return to the beginning of the *Amidah*. This also applies to the *Chazan* in his repetititon of the *Amidah*, even though this will necessitate repeating the *Kedushah*! This is because the first three blessings are regarded as a thematic unity, directed to praise of God. In the case of *ha-melekh ha-mishpat*, however, nothing requires to be done to counter the error, because the term *melekh* is expressed even by using the usual, year-round formula: *melekh oheiv tzedakah umishpat*.

254. What if he omitted the other special insertions (*Zokhreinu, Miy khamokha, Ukhetov* and *Beseifer chayyim*)?

As long as he has not yet uttered God's name in the conclusion of that particular blessing, he may go back and make the insertion. Once he has recited God's name, he should conclude the blessing, and he is not required to make up for his omission. This is because these other insertions are not mentioned in the Talmud, and so we do not need to interrupt our prayers for the sake of correcting their omission.

255. Are there any other recurring variations that we make during this period?

During every *kaddish* recited from Rosh Hashanah to Yom Kippur, we double the word *le'eyla (min kol birkhata)*. This phrase praises God as being "exalted" above all the blessings and praises that mortal man can frame. During the Ten Days of Penitence, it is the tradition to repeat the word *le'eyla*, in order to convey the heightened sense of God's exaltedness that grips us at this season.

We have already referred to *gematria*, the significance attached to the numerical value of certain words and phrases. Similar significance was attached to the precise number of words in certain compositions, especially when these compositions were regarded as central to our liturgy, or when they were invested with mystical significance. Thus, the number of words in the *Shema* was regarded as sacrosanct, to the extent that, in synagogue, when the introductory line, *El melekh ne'eman*,

17. Cohen, J. M. (1994). *Prayer and Penitence*. Northvale, NJ: Jason Aronson Inc., pp. 42, 46–47, 100.

is omitted, it was regarded as essential to compensate for those three words in some other way, in order to preserve the original number of words; and this is done by having the *Chazan* repeat the phrase *Ha-Shem Elokeikhem emet.*

Another example of the choice of compositions being based on significant numerology is the recitation of Psalm 67 for recitation after counting the Omer. Its contents bear no relation at all to the Omer ritual, but its forty-nine words (with the omission of the four opening words that form the Psalm heading), which correspond to the forty-nine days of the Omer period, were sufficient to establish its relevance to this context.

This wish, to preserve intact the original number of words in a major composition, underlies a slight adjustment that is prescribed to be made in the *kaddish* to compensate for the added word *le'eyla*. Instead of the usual reading, *min kol [birkhata]*, we reduce the number of words by one, and read *mikkol.*

256. Normally on *Yom Tov* we include in the *Amidah* the reference *moadim lesimchah chagim uzemanim lesason*—"[You have given us] festivals for joy, and festive seasons for rejoicing." Why is this omitted on Rosh Hashanah (and Yom Kippur)?

The *Levush Mordechai* explains that this particular passage is only relevant to the three foot festivals (*shalosh regalim*) of Pesach, *Shavuot*, and Sukkot, which merit the name of *moed*, since the root of this word is *va'ad*, "assembling" (at the Temple). On those three occasions each year, the ancient Israelites were summoned to "appear before the Lord." On Rosh Hashanah (and Yom Kippur), no such "assembling" is prescribed, and they cannot be referred to, therefore, by that usual festival liturgical reference.

SEASONAL GREETINGS

257. What traditional greetings should one address to one's neighbors in synagogue and one's family on returning home?

The traditional greetings are as follows:

(i) When addressing an individual male, one says, *Leshanah tovah tikateiv veteikhateim*—"May you be inscribed and sealed for a good year." Some abbreviate this to *Ketivah vachatimah tova*—"To a favorable inscription and sealing!"

(ii) When addressing an individual female, the grammar has to be adjusted to *Leshanah tovah tikatviy veteichateimiy.* If using the abbreviated form (above), no adjustment is required.

(iii) When addressing a group of males or a mixed group, one says, *Leshanah tovah tikatvu veteichateimu.* Again, if using the abbreviated form, no adjustment is required.

(iv) When addressing a group of women, one says, *Leshanah tovah tikatavnah veteichatamnah*. Again, one may use the abbreviated form as it stands.

Some add the phrase *le'alter lechayyim tovim uleshalom* at the end of the full greeting.

X

The First and Second Days' *Shachrit* Services

THE *MACHZOR*

258. What is the origin of the term *machzor* to denote the festival prayer book?

It is derived from a post-biblical Hebrew root *chazar*, meaning "to do something again," "to come around," in the sense of a "cycle." Hence its application to the prayer manuals for the annual cycle of festivals.

An encounter with the *machzor* is what all Jews share in common when they attend synagogue services. The majority of Jews in Western countries attend rather infrequently. We should not think, however, that this is a facet of our modern age. The first century Alexandrian Jewish philosopher, Philo, records that many Jews in that city would only come to synagogue on three days in the year, and some only on Yom Kippur. Little has changed in 2,000 years!

259. Have the prayers changed much over the past two millenia?

They have changed and developed beyond all recognition. Indeed, the nonobservant Jews of Philo's day may have been forgiven for their lack of enthusiasm. In their day, the liturgy was in a very underdeveloped state, with even the blessings of the central *Amidah* prayer in a state of flux. The Talmudic period was not yet in top gear, and no serious efforts had yet been made to develop a liturgy that was relevant to the needs, emotions, and aspirations of Jewry—especially the Diaspora Jewry of Egypt, which, though large and important, was quite assimilated.

The real development and poetic expansion of our liturgy grew as a result of the post-Temple need to provide an inspirational replacement for the sacrificial focus of Temple Judaism. As prayer, poetry, meditation, study, and exposition became the hallmark of the burgeoning Talmudic academies of the early centuries C.E., each of those genres found its expression represented within the evolving liturgical output that changed the entire spirit and complexion of the synagogue experience.

The prayer book grew as a living organism over many centuries and in many countries, although the earliest and greatest contribution to its formation and evolution was made in Palestine and Babylon during the Talmudic period (first through fifth centuries), with inspired religious poets adding their distinctive embellishments to the statutory liturgy during the succeeding five or six centuries. Later differences between Ashkenazi and Sephardi traditions, reflecting their respective poetic preferences as well as certain distinct halakhic principles, set in motion the trend toward the creation of other prayer rites in various countries of Jewish domicile.

The rise of a school of mysticism in Safed in the sixteenth century, emphasizing meditation and prayer as its central concern, had a profound influence, both directly and indirectly, even on mainstream communities. It was the Safed school, for example, that introduced our *Kabbalat Shabbat* service for Friday evening. One of the leading *Kabbalists* of that school, Rabbi Yitzchak Luria (the *Ari*), even produced his own version of the prayers, *Nusach Ari*, which was taken up in the following century by the nascent hasidic movement. The modern day Sephardi prayer rite, common in the State of Israel, is based upon the Lurianic traditions.

260. We referred above to expensive handwritten *machzorim* produced before the age of printing (fifteenth century). What was the nature and quality of those *machzorim*?

Great efforts were made and large sums expended to create as beautiful and artistic a work as possible. The skilled artists and scribes who were commissioned to produce the illuminated *machzorim* were frequently accommodated together with their families at the home of their patron, with their entire board and lodging constituting the lion's share of their fee.

Sometimes, the tasks of writing the body of the text and the production of artistic embellishments were shared by two different craftsmen. It was not unknown for a third person to be employed to insert the punctuation and vocalization of the text.

Nikkud ("pointing") was regarded as a specialist skill, calling for a thorough knowledge of the rules of Hebrew grammar. Not surprisingly, therefore, it was not uncommon to find many errors in spelling and vocalization in those medieval manuscripts. Some scribes omitted important compositions, put them in the wrong order, and confused the accompanying rubrics. This was compounded by later copyists, with the result that the printed editions, based upon those faulty manuscripts, regularly passed those variants down for posterity.

Had it not been for the pioneering efforts of Wolf Heidenheim (1757–1832), who collected, analyzed, and compared a vast number of liturgical manuscripts and printed versions, as a prelude to his own nine-volume critical edition of the *machzor* (Roedelheim, 1800–1802), we would have inherited a chaotic liturgical tradition. His standardized version of the Ashkenazi *nusach* soon became accepted as authoritative, and it had the effect of displacing most of the localized differences and the faulty versions that had hitherto existed.

DIFFERENT PRAYER RITES

261. Do all communities throughout the Jewish world recite the identical Rosh Hashanah prayers?

The basic structure of the services is the same for all Orthodox congregations, as is the tripartite division of the *Musaf Amidah* into *Malkhuyyot, Zikhronot,* and *Shofarot* verses (See Questions 548–554), with each section culminating in the sounding of the shofar. There are differences, however, between Ashkenazi and Sephardi traditions, with each culling poetic compositions (*piyyutim*) of their own respective provenance. Both Franco-Germany and Spain had rich poetic traditions, so they were able to exercise personal choice in this area of the liturgy where great flexibility exists.

262. So were there no guidelines regarding the choice of poetic compositions?

There were guidelines. The major consideration was to adorn the service with the religious poetry of acknowledged and popular sages of their respective Ashkenazi and Sephardi traditions. These poems had to complement the particular parts of the service that allowed for such expansion. Thus, special genres of poetry arose, based upon those specific parts of the service for which they were written.

Poems written for inclusion in the *Nishmat* prayer (just before the phrase *Ilu fiynu malei shirah ka-yam*) were called by the general term *Nishmat*. Many such poems of this genre were composed, with each strophe commencing with the word *Nishmat*. The blessings before the *Shema* were called either *Ofan* (if it was to be included in the section commencing *Veha-ofanim vechayyot ha-kodesh*) or *Yotzer* (if it was intended for the *Shema* blessing, *Yotzer Ha-me'orot*. The term *Me'ora* is also employed for poetry written for this blessing.)

Poetry written for the second of the *Shema* blessings (*Ahavah rabbah*) was designated *Ahavah* poetry, and that written for insertion into the blessing after the *Shema* was called *Zulat*, after the phrase *ein Elokim zulatekha* in that blessing. Poetry inserted into the final paragraph of that long blessing after the *Shema* is referred to as *Ge'ulah* ("redemption") since the blessing describes God's redemptive acts on behalf of Israel and ends with the words *ga'al yisrael*.

The insertions into the festival evening services (though, as we have said, these were omitted from the Rosh Hashanah *Ma'ariv* service. See Question 247) were called *Ma'aravot* (or *Ma'arivim*); those composed for insertion into the *Chazan's* repetition of the *Amidah* were called *Kerovot*, and the poems composed specifically for the *Chazan*, as an introduction to the poetic section (or sections) of the service, enabling him formally to seek the authority of the congregation to lead them in prayer, are called *Reshut* ("permission").

The long introductory poems, written for insertion before the *Kedushah*, were called *Silluk*, meaning, "finale," probably because they concluded the first three blessings of the *Amidah*, which constitute a separate unit whose theme is praise of God.

263. What is the meaning of the term *Kerovot*?

Since the *Amidah* was, at first, the only prayer to be led by a *Chazan*, the earliest *piyyutim* were designed for insertion into that prayer. Because of their position in the *Chazan*'s prayer, they came to be called *Kerovot*, after the name given to the *Chazan* himself at that early period. He was known as the *Karovah*, the one who "brings near" the prayers of Israel to the heavenly throne.

In Franco-German communities the term *Kerovot* was generally pronounced as *Kerovetz*. This inspired a popular, though quite erroneous, interpretation of the term as an acronym (*notarikon*) for the phrase in *Hallel*—*Kol rinah viyeshua be'oholei tzaddikim*, "The sound of joyful singing in the tents of the righteous" (Psalm 118:15).

264. How vocal ought we be in praying along with the *Chazan* on these days?

The *Shulchan Arukh* is quite explicit on this point and states that, "Although during the rest of the year we should pray silently, yet on Rosh Hashanah and Yom Kippur it is the custom to raise one's voice. We are no longer concerned that this will distract other worshipers, since they will all have *machzorim* in their hands."[1]

The desire of worshipers to raise their voices in prayer and, in joining in with the *Chazan*, to respond to a feeling of spiritual arousal is fully recognized in this halakhic concession. Before the age of printing, very few congregants, other than the wealthy, would have been able to afford a hand-written daily prayer book. This did not matter, since most would have known the regular daily prayers by heart. For those who were not regular worshipers, the *Chazan*'s repetition of the *Amidah* would have afforded them the opportunity of saying it with him, word for word. It was with that group in mind that the halakah cautions against joining in loudly together with the *Chazan*, since they might easily distract the other non-regular worshipers trying to catch the words of the *Amidah* that the *Chazan* is repeating.

On Rosh Hashanah and Yom Kippur, when most of the words of the compositions interpolated into the *Amidah* are unfamiliar to everyone, it was imperative for both regular and not-so-regular worshipers to obtain texts of the prayers. They would all endeavor to purchase *machzorim*, however expensive this was. Hence, there was no fear about distracting people, since it was not necessary to be attentive to the *Chazan*'s every word. Praying the silent *Amidah* from their High Holy Day *machzorim* meant that all congregants fulfilled their own prayer obligation. If they missed part of the *Chazan*'s repetition, it was not serious.

265. Is there any difference between the early part of the morning service on Rosh Hashanah and that of ordinary Sabbaths and festivals?

The first part of the service, until *Yishtabach*, is almost identical. The only differences are that we commence the service with the chanting of *Adon Olam* and *Yigdal*—two of the most popular hymns in our liturgy—and continue with *Shir*

---

1. *Shulchan Arukh Orach Chayyim* 582:9.

Ha-Kavod ("Hymn of Glory," popularly referred to as *Anim Zemirot*, after its opening words), the psalm for the (particular) day of the week, followed by Psalm 27 (*Le-David Ha-Shem oriy*). It was customary to begin with *Shir Ha-Yichud* ("Hymn of Unity"), though few communities have preserved this tradition.

The place of these compositions is usually at the end of the service. I conjecture that they were moved to the beginning in order that the congregation might leave the synagogue with the sound of the final notes of the shofar still ringing in their ears. This effect would be weakened if those regular concluding hymns had still to be recited. For the sake of consistency, this arrangement would then have been preserved on Yom Kippur.

NO *TEFILLIN* ON SABBATHS AND FESTIVALS

266. Why do we not wear *tefillin* on Sabbaths and festivals?

The Talmud[2] provides the explanation, in the name of Rabbi Akivah, that it is because the Torah states, in relation to *tefillin*, that "they shall be for you as a *sign* upon your hand" (Exodus 13:9). Thus, the *tefillin* reinforce for us the awareness of our special relationship with God, and the requirement of holiness that this mandates. Since the Sabbaths and festivals constitute in themselves a most high profile "sign" of that covenant with God, it does not require any additional, external reinforcement on those days.

The *Shulchan Arukh* states that it is actually forbidden to wear *tefillin* on Sabbaths and festivals, since the employment of that extra "sign" would in fact serve to cast doubt on the effectiveness of the holy day itself, by implying that it required further augmentation.[3]

YIGDAL AND *ADON OLAM*

267. Is there any special reason why *Yigdal* and *Adon Olam* are placed at the very beginning of the service?

Those who prescribed this order seem to have been motivated by the feeling that it was highly inappropriate that we should commence our prayers by appearing as selfish petitioners, launching into a catalogue of pleas and petitions for personal needs, which is what the early blessings essentially are. They may appear to be merely praises of God, but to read them as such is to miss the point. For when we bless God, in the *asher yatzar* blessing, as the One "who wondrously heals all flesh," we would do a disservice to the framers of that blessing to imagine that they did not intend it also as an implied plea to God to keep our bodies healthy and heal any of

2. *Eiruvin* 96a.
3. *Shulchan Arukh Orach Chayyim* 31:1.

our physical defects. Similarly, when praising Him for having given us His Torah, it would be a hollow blessing if it was not infused by the hope and plea that He should continue to regard us as worthy to be its custodians. And so on, with all the subsequent fifteen *Birkot Ha-Shachar* blessings.

To avoid giving the impression, therefore, that our prime concern was that of praying for the satisfaction of personal needs, these two hymns of praise were intoduced into our prayer book at the outset—and, at times, at the conclusion—of our services. We thereby put God before ourselves; we acknowledge His attributes. We submit ourselves to Him as subjects and sing joyful songs of praise to Him. Only then do we express our needs.

This also explains the presence of the six, disparate biblical verses that are placed at the very outset of the Morning Service, commencing *Mah tovu*. They share a common spirit of joyfulness and gratitude to be part of "the throng" of Jewry, privileged to worship in the house of God. Thus, taken together with *Yigdal* and *Adon Olam*, they may be seen as serving to preempt the self-centered elements of the liturgy that follow, by expressing, through both biblical verses and medieval poetry, a pure praise of, and joy in, the God of Israel.

268. *Yigdal* appears to be setting forth a catechism, or a credal list of beliefs that Jews have to affirm. Is this, indeed, its purpose?

Yes and no. It does set forth some of our basic beliefs, but there is no "authorized" creed that any professing Jew has to affirm. That having been said, the Mishnah already denies a place in the world to come to heretics (*epikoros*), as well as to those who reject the reality of the Resurrection or the divinity of the Torah. The list was added to by two other Mishnaic sages. Rabbi Akivah includes in the anathema one who reads "external books" and one who utters a (mystical) charm over a wound, to which Abba Saul adds, one who expressly pronounces the Ineffable Divine Name.

We can see that this is quite a half-hearted attempt at establishing the fundamental Jewish beliefs. Akivah and Abba Saul were clearly referring to *actions* they wished to prohibit, rather than *beliefs* to eradicate.

It is only in the Middle Ages, when Judaism had to contend with the challenge of Christianity, Islam, and Greek philosophy, as well as the Karaite heresy, that Judaism was constrained to formulate its basic credal beliefs in order to counter the critical views of those competing systems.

Such formulations were never native to Judaism. Had they been, we would have expected such a credal list to have appeared in the Torah. Jews were urged, rather, to "love the Lord Your God with all your heart, and all your soul and all your might." We were also enjoined to fulfill all the *mitzvot* that the Lord commanded, that is to immerse ourselves in a holy way-of-life wherein we walk constantly and joyously "in the light of the Lord," rather than to philosophize on the nature and attributes of God.

Thus, it was only in the medieval period that people like Saadiah Gaon (882–942), Moses Maimonides (1135–1204), Hasdai Crescas (1340–1410), and his disciple, Joseph Albo (1380–1445), delved into, and disputed, the matter of Judaism's basic beliefs, with Maimonides establishing "thirteen principles of faith" and the others adopting a variant number and a different criteria of categorization.

269. What is the meaning of the term *epikoros*?

Maimonides regards it as an aramaic word, derived from the verb *lehafkir*, "to be free, unrestrained, ownerless," from which it came to mean, a "freethinker, who does not believe in the fundamentals of the Torah, or one who despizes the Sages or any particular Sage or his Torah teacher."[4]

Others take the view that the term is derived from the Greek philosophical system promoted by the philosopher Epicurus (341–270 B.C.E.) that the highest principle in life is the pursuit of human happiness. Anticipating modern psychology, he sought to dispel mental turbulence, particularly that caused by the fear of death and fear of the gods. His views that the gods did not interfere with the government of our world or possess benign or malevolent feelings toward man and that there is no life, and therefore retribution, after death, because the soul is immediately dissolved at that point, helped to reinforce his therapeutic objectives.

Epicurus was given bad press in Judaism, and his philosophy was identified as the epitome of godlessness and the rejection of morality. The fact that he did not, in reality, reject religion, that he did actually support piety and that he did not preach that all pleasure was good, did not deflect the sages from identifying *epikoros* as a term of opprobrium for those lacking in faith and others guilty of rejecting some cardinal Jewish beliefs.

270. What specific beliefs does the *epikoros* deny?

Maimonides, in his *Mishneh Torah*, specifies three categories of *epikoros*: "Whoever denies the existence of prophecy or that divine communication ever reaches the heart of man; whoever denies the prophetic status of Moses; and whoever denies that the Creator has foreknowledge of man's actions."[5]

Joseph Karo, in his *Kesef Mishneh*,[6] expresses surprise that Maimonides selects just those three categories of rejection from the Talmudic source,[7] which also includes those who despise scholars as well as those who slight others in front of scholars. It is clear from this flexible attribution of the term *epikoros*, as well as from the circumscribed menu of rejected beliefs referred to, that the sages were not intent upon creating a comprehensive list of dogmas that every Jew has to affirm, but were merely expressing, in as strong a manner as possible, their expectations—both theological and ethical—of those who would aspire to commitment to Orthodox belief, coupled with a special emphasis on certain character traits that needed particular correction.

---

4. *Peirush Ha-Mishnaiot LeHa-Rambam* to *Sanhedrin* 10:1 (various editions).
5. *Mishneh Torah, Hilkhot Teshuvah* 3:8.
6. *Kesef Mishneh ad loc.*
7. *Sanhedrin* 99b.

271. So if there is such flexibility on the subject of Judaism's basic creed, on which particular authority did the author of *Yigdal* rely for his particular list?

He based himself upon the list provided by Maimonides in his early work, the *Peirush Ha-Mishnaiot* (Commentary on the Mishnah).[8] The list is popularly referred to as the *Shelosh Esrei Ikkarim*, the "Thirteen Principles of the Jewish Faith." This is a far more accurate translation, which removes the dogmatic overtone from the list.

Maimonides would have the Jew affirm his belief (i) in the existence of God, (ii) in His unity, (iii) in His incorporeality, (iv) in His eternity, (v) in His exclusive right to our adoration and worship, (vi) in the validity of the prophetic communication, (vii) in the primacy of Moses's prophetic powers, (viii) that the Torah was given by God to Moses, (ix) that the Torah is immutable, (x) that God knows our innermost thoughts and foresees all our deeds, (xi) that there will be reward for good deeds and punishment for evil, (xii) that the Messiah-Redeemer will come at the end of days, and (xiii) that this will be followed by the resurrection of the dead.

272. But what prompted Maimonides to create such a comprehensive list of beliefs that the Jew is committed to affirm, when even the Talmudic sages did not make such a great demand?

Rabbi Norman Lamm addresses this question, and concludes that it is perfectly consistent with Maimonides' philosophical approach:

> Systems which hold that the acme of Judaism is attained in formulating correct ideas and true notions about God, as opposed to proper conduct, will consider any divergence from such correct opinions to be severe violations of the integrity of the faith. Since Maimonides is the supreme rationalist, who holds that metaphysics is beyond halakhah and that the loftiest goal is the forming of correct concepts about the Deity, it is in the area of ideas and theory that the test of faith takes place. It is in that realm, rather than in behavior, that one stands or falls as a Jew.[9]

273. But did Maimonides not do a disservice by this exercise, excluding thereby from membership of *klal Yisrael* countless Jews who cannnot, in all honesty, make such a comprehensive affirmation of faith?

It does rather seem as if this might be the natural ramification of this exercise. However, bearing in mind just how zealous Maimonides was, on a number of occasions, to exonerate those who were forced, by circumstances beyond their control, to affirm "wrong beliefs"—such as those whom he addresses in his *Iggeret Ha-shemad*,[10] who were forced to take the oath of allegiance to Islam on pain of

---

8. *Peirush Ha-Mishnaiot LeHa-Rambam* to *Sanhedrin* 10:1.

9. Lamm, N. (1989). "Loving and Hating Jews as Halakhic Categories." *Tradition*, 24:109.

10. Halkin, A., and Hartman, D. (1985). *Crisis and Leadership: Epistles of Maimonides*. Philadelphia: The Jewish Publication Society of America, pp. 13–90.

death—it would hardly be consistent for him to deny membership of *klal Yisrael* to those whose minds denied them the absolute faith to affirm each and every one of those credal beliefs.

Rabbi Abraham Isaac ha-Kohen Kook articulated this view when he stated that

> Just as the *Tosafists* remark in Sanhedrin 26b (s.v. *he-chashud*) that someone who is suspected of an act of sexual immorality because he was seized by passion is not disqualified as a witness because 'his passion coerced him' and, by the same token, the *Tosafists* in *Gittin* 41b (s.v. *kofin*) write that seduction by a maid-servant is considered a form of coercion, so we may say that the *zeitgeist* acts as an evil intellectual temptress who seduces the young people of the (modern) age with her charm and her sorcery. They are truly 'coerced,' and God forbid that we judge them as willful heretics.[11]

Because of the progressive age in which we live, with people from a tender age being exposed to so many persuasive arguments that purport to prove that the axioms of religion are untenable, those who succumb to such ideas may truly be categorized as "coerced" into denial, with the consequence that they do not bear the stigma or punishment of the Talmudic *epikoros*.

274. Who wrote the *Adon Olam*?

Its authorship is uncertain. Some have attributed it to the tenth century Babylonian Gaon, Sherirah, although it is more popularly attributed to the distinguished eleventh century Spanish poet and philosopher Solomon ibn Gabirol.

The Kitzur Shelah quotes the early German pietist Rabbi Judah He-Chasid (See Question 278) as affirming that "whoever has the requisite intentions when reciting *Adon Olam*—that beautiful and praiseworthy hymn—I stand surety that his prayers will be heard, and no Satanic power will be able to neutralize them, particularly on Rosh Hashanah and Yom Kippur." The *Shelah* adds that this may explain why the custom developed to recite it at the beginning of our daily service, before the recitation of all our blessings and praises, as well as at the end of the service.[12]

275. What does the subject-matter of *Adon Olam* deal with?

Unlike *Yigdal*, which deals with a variety of theological concepts and basic beliefs, *Adon Olam* is exclusively concerned with the nature of God (as expounded in the first six lines) and with Israel's total reliance upon Him in the face of life's unremitting crises, as well as in the Hereafter when we have shed our mortal coil and awakened to a new and unique existence. It is, therefore, a most appropriate hymn to recite as a prelude to prayer. We have first to affirm with clarity the nature of the God we worship, and His paramount place in our lives and emotions, before we proceed to engage Him in prayer and petition.

---

11. Rabbi Abraham I. Kook, *Iggerot Ha-Re'iyyah*, vol. 1, p. 171, quoted in N. Lamm (note 9) above.
12. Sperling, A. (1957). *Taamei Ha-Minhagim*. Jerusalem, p. 20.

Some believe that *Adon Olam* may well have been composed originally, however, for recitation before retiring to sleep, as suggested by the penultimate line: "Into His hands I entrust my spirit when I shall be asleep and when I awake." From that context, because of its popularity, it was probably taken up into the prayers of the statutory services. In Morocco, it was customary to recite it at weddings, before the bride was brought under the *chupah*.

276. There seems to be a definite and regular rhythm underlying *Yigdal* and *Adon Olam*. Does Hebrew poetry conform to a metric system?

It certainly does. Medieval Hebrew poetry patterned itself upon Arabic meter and evolved four or five metric variations, or patterns, for its poetry. Hebrew meter is characterized by the particular number and type of stresses in a line. Hebrew words are stressed according to the way they are extended from their original and basic form. Thus, *melekh* ("king") has the stress on the initial (open) syllable, *me*; whereas, when the plural form, *melakhim* is created, the stress, or tone, is thrown forward onto the final syllable: *khim*.

Now, Hebrew meter consists in the creation of poetry wherein every line has the identical number of syllables with the identical pattern of corresponding stresses (and half-stresses). Thus, in the opening two lines of *Yigdal*:

$$\overline{Yig\text{-}dal}\ \overline{\breve{E}\text{-}lo}\ /\ \overline{kim}\ \overline{chai}\ \overline{\breve{ve}\text{-}yish}/\ \overline{ta\text{-}bach}$$
$$\overline{Nim\text{-}tza}\ \overline{\breve{ve}\text{-}eyn}\ /\ \overline{et}\ \overline{el}\ \overline{\breve{me}\text{-}tzi}\ /\ \overline{u\text{-}to}$$

It will be seen that each of these half-lines contains three units. The first two comprise two stresses (— —) leading into a subsidiary stress (*sheva* or composite *sheva*) linked to a main stress (˘ —). These are rounded off with a short unit comprising just two main stresses. This pattern is sustained throughout the hymn.

In *Adon Olam*, there is a different metric pattern:

$$\overline{\breve{A}\text{-}don}\ \overline{o\text{-}lam}\ /\ \overline{\breve{a}\text{-}sher}\ \overline{ma\text{-}lakh}$$
$$\overline{\breve{be}\text{-}te}\ \overline{rem\text{-}kol}\ /\ \overline{\breve{ye}\text{-}tzir}\ \overline{niv\text{-}ra};$$
$$\overline{\breve{Le}\text{-}eit}\ \overline{na\text{-}sah}\ /\ \overline{\breve{ve}\text{-}chef}\ \overline{tzo\text{-}kol}$$
$$\overline{\breve{a}\text{-}zai}\ \overline{me\text{-}lekh}\ /\ \overline{\breve{she}\text{-}mo}\ \overline{nik\text{-}ra}$$

It will be seen here that, in both the first and second half of each line, the pattern is a subsidiary stress (*sheva* or composite *sheva*) followed by three main stresses.

ANIM ZEMIROT

277. Although we popularly refer to this majestic praise of God as *Anim Zemirot*, after its opening words, our prayer books designate it as *Shir Ha-Kavod*, "Hymn of Glory." In what sense is this term used?

This hymn was invested with the greatest significance by many authorities, since it was believed that its passionate and forthright description of God could only have emanated from a poet vouchsafed with a unique mystic revelation. He succeeds in investing his lyrical poetry with both an awe and an intimacy, which, though normally regarded as conflicting emotions, yet, in the context of sacred passion, are elevated into a majestic synthesis.

The term *Shir Ha-Kavod* derives from the fact that, although the poet speaks of many attributes of God and describes them in a most daring manner, using, in many instances, grossly anthropomorphic language (speaking of God as possessing human parts and attributes), his purpose in employing this vocabulary is only to enhance the "glory" of God and to bring His reality closer and not to demean it in any way by such familiarity. This he makes clear in the third line: "As I speak of Your *kavod* (glory), my heart craves for Your love."

The term *kavod* in relation to God was probably inspired by Psalm 24 wherein the expression *melekh ha-kavod* ("King of Glory") appears no fewer than five times.

278. What do we know about the author of the *Shir Ha-Kavod*?

It is generally attributed to Rabbi Judah He-Chasid of Regensburgh (1150–1217), founder of a twelfth century German pietistic movement and author of the celebrated *Sefer Chasidim.*

Little contemporary information has survived regarding Judah's life and activities, but later sources attribute to him mystical and wonder-working achievements, and especially the performance of miracles in order to deliver fellow Jews from the hands of gentiles. He wrote a number of kabbalistic works that have not survived, probably on account of his extreme humility, which prevented him from promoting or even selling his writings. Significantly, his major work was entitled *Sefer Ha-Kavod* ("The Book of Glory"). Although this also did not survive, quotations from it are preserved in later works.

The circle of pietists that he attracted were referred to as *Hasidei Ashkenaz* (the pietists of Germany), and their practices were characterized by extreme asceticism and intensity of religious devotions, especially as regards prayer, fasting, and repentance. The study and practice of mysticism were their main preoccupation, and Judah himself wrote a mystic commentary to the prayer book.

279. Are there any poetic characteristics worthy of highlighting?

Anim Zemirot is an alphabetical acrostic—that is with the exception of the introductory four and the final three lines. These seem to have been added in order to make up a specific and significant number of lines. The *Hasidei Ashkenaz* did attach mystical significance to the number of lines and words in compositions, and we may conjecture that this was the objective here.

The total number of lines is thirty-two. This is actually contrived not only by the additional seven lines (to the twenty-two alphabetical ones), but also by doubling the lines commencing with the letters *reish* and *tav*. The final line—*Ye'erav-na*—was meant to be recited twice, once by the *Chazan* and again by the congregation, thus making a total of thirty-two lines, which happens to be the *gematria* (numerical value) of the key theme of this composition: *kavod* ("glory").

It commences by addressing God in the second person until, and including, the letter *vav*. It then reverts to the third person for most of the poem, picking up the second person, direct mode of address at the second *reish* line. This is based on the structure of our blessings, which commence by addressing God directly (*Barukh attah*) before moving into the third person mode of address (*asher kidshanu bemitzvotav*—"[He who] has sanctified us with His commandments").

280. For those of our readers who do not have immediate access to a prayer book, what sort of attributes are used in *Anim Zemirot* to describe God's "glory"?

The attributes of God are of the genre found in the Song of Songs—passionate, anthropomorphic superlatives, descriptive of God's absolute perfection. The influence of Song of Songs, which, in rabbinic tradition, is essentially a metaphor on the nature of Israel's love of God and relationship with Him, seems very clear, with six lines of the poem being direct quotations from that book.

The author of *Anim Zemirot* speaks of his yearning for God, his desire to fathom all God's mysteries and to sing love songs to Him. He acknowledges that, never having seen or truly known God, his love is predicated exclusively on the potency of the "countless visions" of the prophetic descriptions of God's splendor and power. The manifold aspects of God's exploits, as the God of Creation and history, are reflected in His description as a youthful warrior, wearing a helmet over his long black curls and wielding the sword of battle; and in His other role, as judge of mankind, He is portrayed as aged and grey of hair.

The poet seems to be describing the coronation of God. His head is "like fine gold," and his people adorn it with a royal crown, prior to His taking up residence in His most glorious palace, the Temple in Jerusalem. He, in turn, crowns Israel (as His bride?)—"Because they were precious to Him, He so honoured them." Toward the end of the poem, this imagery of the crowning of God is concretized as occurring through the act of prayer: "May my praises be a crown for Your head; may my prayers rise like incense before You.[13]

281. There is one reference to God that seems to transcend the boundary of propriety. How do we explain the reference to God "showing the knot of His *tefillin* to Moses"?

This is based upon the Talmudic interpretation of the verse in Exodus 33:23 where God, having rejected Moses' plea to have vouchsafed to him a physical manifestation of the divine presence, tells him that He would place Moses in the cleft of a rock where God would pass by and grant him sight of His "back." It is difficult to understand what is meant, if not some celestial jet stream!

The sages explained God's "back" in the mystical sense of the knot of His

---

13. For incense as a symbol of (divine) monarchy, see Cohen, J. M. (1989). *Moments of Insight.* London: Vallentine, Mitchell, pp. 95–96.

tefillin,[14] since those are wound around the heads of the morning worshipers, with the knot at the "back," lying next to the nape of the neck.

The Talmud[15] states that God wears *tefillin* in which is inscribed the verse, "Who is like unto Your people, Israel, a unique nation on earth?" (I Chronicles 17:21).

How to "explain" such references, that are of the warp and woof of the mystical tradition, is truly difficult, especially if we approach them in the cold light of reason. They are meant to be experienced, not analyzed. They have meaning only for those so in love with God that they have totally liberated themselves from such cold considerations as textual meaning and propriety. For such mystics, as for the Talmudic sages, it was axiomatic that there is a real measure of spiritual correspondence between heaven and earth.[16] Thus, it may be assumed that God would not have revealed a ritual, or ritual object, to Israel that did not have its counterpart in the heavenly store. God's *tefillin* were regarded, therefore, as a metaphor for the eternal faith that He keeps with Israel.

282. What is the sense of the abstruse reference in *Anim Zemirot* to God's "clothes [being] as red as when He came down from treading the winepress in Edom"?

This description is derived from Isaiah 63:1–3 where the prophet has a vision of the final destruction of the Edomite forces after a most bloody battle. The land of Edom was the country inhabited by the descendants of Esau; and Israel's victory provides the ultimate vindication of Jacob in his age-old struggle against the brother whose enmity surfaces, in one form or another, throughout the ages. "Treading the winepress" suggests the total letting of the blood of the enemy, as well as the wine that will be toasted in the cup of final salvation.

This imagery has also to be viewed against the backcloth of the place and period in which the poem was written. In the aftermath of the First (1096) and Second (1147) Crusades, when Rhineland Jewry was at its lowest ebb, there is no question but that the reference to Edom here is an implied *cri de coeur* for speedy retribution for the devastation of the Jewish communities and the massacres of Jewry wrought by the Crusading knights of Christendom.

283. What is the meaning of the line (beginning with the letter *reish*) that states that "The opening of Your word is *emet* (truth)"?

It is a reference to the Talmudic statement that "the seal of the Almighty is *emet.*"[17] By the method of *remez* (hidden allusion within the text), it will be seen that God has, indeed, impressed his seal into the opening of His word, that is into the first three words of His Torah (*Bereishit bara' Elokim*), whose final letters, albeit in a different order, make up the word *emet*!

---

14. *Berakhot* 7a.
15. *Berakhot* 6a.
16. *Berakhot* 58a.
17. *Shabbat* 55a.

284. We have referred above to the many attributes of God contained in *Anim Zemirot*. But, how can we possibly justify speaking in these grossly physical terms of a God who Maimonides (in his "Thirteen Principles"), as well as the author of *Yigdal* and all the medieval Jewish philosophers, emphasizes is totally incorporeal?

This is a variation of the basic question of Islamic as well as Medieval Jewish philosophy, namely how could God, who by His nature must be "One," possess attributes? The problem was already grappled with by the Cynics of Greek philosophy who asked how one subject could be composed of many predicates—a consideration that prompted the Neoplatonists to conclude that God was, indeed, devoid of attributes, and therefore totally beyond the grasp of human reason. In Islam, there was much support for the view that God did, indeed, possess corporeal attributes (There is evidence that the Saducean sect [third century B.C.E. through first century C.E.] within Judaism held the same view), a concept strenuously rejected by the school of Mutazilites.

Maimonides, in his rejection of that gross conception of God, evolved the doctrine of "negative attributes," namely, that the only sensible thing that human reason can say in relation to God is what He is not! Such an exercise may not add up to any purposeful image of God, or make our understanding of Him any clearer, but it does serve the purpose of refining the concept of deity of any gross misconceptions that could well obstruct our path to spiritual enlightenment and development.

285. But how do we overcome the fact that the Bible does, in fact, enumerate positive attributes of God?

One of the most distinguished medieval Jewish philosophers, Saadia Gaon, author of *Emunot Ve-De'ot*, devoted much attention to the question of God's attributes, and especially to the way we have to understand the biblical anthropomorphisms that speak of parts of God's "body."

Saadia enumerates ten parts or organs of the body attributed to God in the Bible, and he sets out systematically to rid those terms of the meaning we naturally attribute to them and to neutralize the association we instinctively make with them. He begins by demonstrating that even in relation to man, those organs are, on occasion, biblically applied in a metaphoric sense and in a way that cannot possibly be taken literally. He then quotes the relevant passages where the nouns "head" can only refer to man's elevation, "ear" to the notion of acceptance, "eye" to supervision, "heart" to wisdom, "leg" to coercion, "knee" to submission, etc. Saadia then infers, *a fortiori*, that in relation to God these terms must certainly convey nonbodily meanings; and he proceeds to set out the precise sense in which these attributes are to be interpreted.

Saadia reinforces his view by noting that the Bible actually ascribes human parts to the earth and to water, speaking of their "head, eye, ear, belly, womb, heart, etc. As far as earth and water are concerned, our sense of perception is sufficient to convince us that those attributes cannot be understood in their literal sense. As far as God is concerned, while we have no equivalent sense of perception, our rational thought (*aql*) must lead us to the identical conclusion."

286. So, granted that we reinterpret metaphorically the anthropomorphic references, but does that mean then that all Jewish thinkers went along with Maimonides' view that we cannot postulate any positive attributes to God?

No, that is not the case. Saadia himself did believe that the notion of God meant that He had to be possessed of existence, power and wisdom. Specifically, Saadia states (i) that He is, (ii) that He is able, (iii) that He is wise, (iv) that He is one, (v) that nothing can compare with Him.

As to the problem of how God could be a true unity if He possessed several of those aspects or attributes, Saadia (to some scholars, unconvincingly) followed the Islamic Mutazilite explanation that the attributes were, in fact, inherent in His essence, not separate distinguishable elements. Saadia believed that the so-called "attributes" were, in reality, merely the essential facets of the Creator, illuminating Him from different angles. Saadia maintained that it was the inherent weakness of language that prevented us from framing the notion of His three attributes—life, power, and wisdom—as a unity.

287. Why was *Anim Zemirot* introduced into the liturgy?

The Talmud states:

> From the day the Temple was destroyed
> there is no day which is not accursed. If that is so, what
> is it that keeps the world in existence? It is the
> recitation of *Kedushah De-sidra* (that is the *Kedushah*
> verses that are included, and rendered into Targumic
> Aramaic, as part of the *U-va letziyyon* prayer at the end
> of the daily morning service) and the *Amen yehei shmei
> rabba* recited after *Aggadic* (Midrashic) quotations.[18]

Rabbi Yoel Sirkis (*Bach*) states[19] that he had received a tradition that *Anim Zemirot* was introduced in order to neutralize that curse by providing the element of *Aggadah* in the context of the Midrashic allusion it provides to God having shown the knot of His *tefillin* to Moses. The recitation of *kaddish* after *Anim Zemirot* provides the second neutralizing agent referred to, the *Amen yehei shmei rabba* recited over *Aggadah*.

288. But if *Anim Zemirot* was originally prescribed for daily recitation, why do most communities reserve it exclusively for Sabbaths and festivals?

This probably arose as a result of the strong opposition to its daily recitation on the part of Rabbi Mordechai Jaffe (1530–1612).

In his *Levush Ha-tekhelet* he states:

---

18. *Sota* 49a.
19. See *Bach* on *Tur Orach Chayyim* 132.

I have been most surprised at the practice of reciting the Song of Glory, *Anim Zemirot*, every day . . . for it seems to me that it should not be recited every day, not on account of any shortcomings, but rather on account of its excellence. Because it is regarded as such a sublime praise it should be reserved exclusively for special occasions like Sabbaths and festivals. . . . If they do persist in their desire to recite it daily, they should not open the Ark. . . .

Had it not been for my concern for the loss to charity—since the honor [of opening the Ark each day] is sold, with the proceeds being given to charity—and that my action would cause great surprise to the masses, I would, wherever I had the power, abolish the practice of opening the Ark, except on Sabbaths and festivals.[20]

289. When was *Anim Zemirot* officially introduced into the liturgy?

According to Ismar Elbogen, it was first printed in the Venice edition of the prayer book, published in 1549, and was subsequently reprinted in all *siddurim* of the German-Polish rite.[21] It was not incorporated into the Sephardi, *Yemenite*, Italian, or *Nusach Ari* rites.

290. Why is it common practice for children to lead the congregation in the recitation of *Anim Zemirot*?

It was presumably regarded as most appropriate that those without the taint of sin and with the purest love and awe of God in their hearts should offer up this purest expression of man's desire to experience God's presence and extol His praise. It was for a similar reason that it was traditional in Talmudic and later times for children to commence studying the *Chumash* with the book of Leviticus, "since the children are pure and the sacrifices are pure; let the pure ones come and occupy themselves at the outset with matters of purity."[22]

BIRKOT HA-SHACHAR—THE MORNING BLESSINGS

Blessings for Hygiene and Health

291. The first blessing of the morning service is the one recited over the washing of the hands (*Al netilat yadayim*). Is not the proper time for this blessing on awaking from sleep?

Technically it is. It is placed in the siddur, however, because the washing of the hands (*kiddush yadayim*) was the first act performed at the Temple by the priests each morning before entering upon their duties. Because our services and prayers

---

20. Jaffe, R. M. *Levush Ha-tekhelet*, Chapter 133.
21. Elbogen, I. (1972). *Ha-tefillah Be-yisrael*. Tel Aviv: Dvir, p. 89.
22. Midrash *Vayikra Rabba* 7:3.

replace the daily sacrifices in the Temple, we do not recite this blessing when washing our hands immediately upon awaking. Instead, it is deferred until the beginning of the service where it symbolizes the ancient priestly routine, while, at the same time, serving as an act of consecration, symbolic cleansing, and preparation for the exercise of prayer.

In Temple times, when people had to maintain high levels of purity, and especially priests in their handling of the tithes, washing of the hands assumed a ritual significance, hence its place as the very first blessing recited each day.

292. What is the purpose of the second of the morning blessings, the *Asher yatzar*?

It is essentially a blessing over attending to the needs of nature.
The blessing states as follows:

> Blessed art thou, O Lord our God, King of the universe,
> who hast formed man in wisdom, and created in him many
> orifices and hollow passages. It is revealed and known
> before the throne of Thy glory, that if one of those
> [that should be closed] is opened, or one of those [that
> should be opened] is closed, it would be impossible to
> exist and stand before Thee. Blessed art thou, O
> Lord, who healest all flesh and performest wonders.

Rabbi Ellie Munk explains the purpose of reciting a blessing over attending to the needs of nature:

> The physical act of excretion, without which "it would be impossible to exist and stand before thee," is divested of all that is vulgar and repulsive in it by this *berakhah*. In this way the religious precepts elevate all the organs of man, the very lowest which serve purely physical ends, as well as the noblest and most highly developed ones, to the rank of moral and ethical agents.[23]

The actual ritual of washing the hands after attending to the needs of nature also serves the very practical and hygienic purpose of ensuring the non-transmission of germs. Indeed, the comparatively low incidence of Jewish fatality during the Black Death has been explained on the basis of Judaism's insistence on the washing of hands before partaking of food, as well as its various rituals of purification, cleaning the body, and changing bed linen and undergarments after menstruation.

293. But surely the proper time for the recitation of the *Asher yatzar* blessing is on awaking from sleep and attending to the needs of nature? Why recite it again in synagogue?

As a prelude to prayer, it extends the context of nature's needs. In the latter situation, the blessing constitutes a straightforward token of thanksgiving for our

---

23. Munk, R. E. (1961). *The World of Prayer*. New York: Philipp Feldheim, p. 20.

good health and the proper functioning of our bodies. When recited in synagogue, however, it becomes invested with spiritual significance.

It is an axiom of rabbinic philosophy that we can only know God through His works. We glimpse a reflection of His power and wisdom by contemplating the beauty, wonder, and power of nature. And we glimpse a reflection of God's wisdom through our contemplation of the genius of the complex and interacting laws that undergird nature. Everything has its place and purpose, and every piece of nature's multifarious jigsaw slots harmoniously into the next and is constructed to facilitate a chain of development and survival making for the unique interrelationship of each species and ultimately of all existence.

This awe for the Creator is a prerequisite for prayer; and the *Asher yatzar* blessing draws our attention at the outset to the God "Who created man with wisdom." Man is the pinnacle of Creation; and by reflecting on the majesty and beauty of our physical attributes, our unbounded intellectual and creative capacity, and our unique sensitivity to matters of the spirit, we are placed in the appropriate frame of mind to offer praise and thanksgiving to the divine source and inspiration of all Creation.

The specific allusion to prayer within this blessing is found in the passage that states that if the bodily orifices were not functioning properly "it would be impossible to exist and stand before thee (*vela'amod lefanekha*)." The choice of the verb *la'amod* ("to stand") is in order to trigger off an association with its noun *Amidah*, the "Standing Prayer," which is the name of the central and most important part of our daily service. Thus, that phrase means, in essence, that it would be impossible to stand in prayer before God were it not for the wondrous attributes with which man is endowed.

Blessings over the Torah

294. Why do we proceed to recite three blessings over the Torah: *La'asok bedivrei Torah*, followed by *Veha'arev na*, followed by *Asher bachar banu*?

Believe it or not, this was the solution of the editors of the liturgy to the dilemma of having three different and illustrious sages of the Talmud each suggesting his own preferred and/or inherited version of this blessing.

The Talmud[24] states that R. Judah said in the name of Samuel that we should say *Barukh . . . la'asok bedivrei Torah*. R. Jochanan suggested a second blessing: *Veha'arev na*; and Rav Hamnuna strenuously recommended *asher bachar banu*. The later rabbinic sages preferred not to decide between the opinions, but instead to incorporate (and sometimes to synthesize) them all. Hence, we have three blessings over the Torah!

---

24. *Berakhot* 11b.

The Priestly Blessing

295. Why do we follow with the Priestly Blessing?

We have mentioned above (See Question 291) that our prayers are rooted in Temple precedents and associations. Because the priests were the officiants at the Temple and it was they who offered the sin, thanksgiving, and freewill offerings on behalf of the individual donors, while blessing the entire community of Israel each day through the recitation of the Priestly Blessing (Numbers 6:24–26), it was regarded as most appropriate, therefore, to introduce an allusion to them in this way.

The juncture at which the Priestly Blessing is introduced is also significant. We have just recited blessings over the Torah. Given that we do not recite blessings in a vacuum, it was felt necessary at this point to follow with some words from the Torah itself. Hence, the biblical quotation, and the specific choice for the reason we have mentioned.

Mishnah Peah

296. Why do we follow with a quotation from the Mishnah?

Jewish tradition maintains the indivisibility of the written and the oral laws. Moses gave to Israel a full oral elucidation of all the laws in the Torah, most of which are sketched in very broad outline. We are told, for example, to "do no manner of work on the Sabbath day," but nowhere in the written Torah is "work" defined. It is the oral law, discussed in the Mishnah and Talmud and codified in the later law books (such as Moses Maimonides' *Mishneh Torah* and Joseph Karo's *Shulchan Arukh*), which provides the background explanations, as well as supplementary laws and customs, attending all the biblical institutions.

It was in order to reinforce this message of the unity of the biblical and oral traditions—particularly in the light of those sects (such as Sadducees and Karaites) who denied the validity of the latter—that we follow the blessings of the Torah with quotations from both the written law (that is, the Priestly Blessing) and the oral law, in the form of Mishnah.

297. But why was that particular Mishnah, from *Peah*, selected to exemplify that principle?

There are several reasons. First, there is no other single Mishnah to contain within it so many references to different religious and ethical institutions. Secondly, it concludes with the statement that "the study of the Torah surpasses them all," which links up so perfectly with the theme of the blessings over the Torah and the reading of passages from both the written and oral law that we are, at this very moment, engaged in. Thirdly, if we count the number of institutions enumerated in this Mishnah, we will see that they amount to fifteen, which is the precise number of blessings that we recite in the cluster that follows (beginning *Barukh . . . asher natan lasekhviy viynah . . .* , and ending with *Barukh . . . ha-ma'avir sheinah mey' einay*). Fourthly, this Mishnah contains the most apposite reference to devotion in prayer (*iyyun tefillah*). Fifthly, it speaks of "appearing before God" (*ra'ayon*), which, although referring specifically to the pilgrim festival visitations at the Temple, has its counterpart in our "appearing before Him" in synagogue. It has also been observed that this Mishnah, unlike most, does not contain any differing or conflicting statements of different sages. In its very formulation, therefore, this particular Mishnah contains a powerful message and challenge: That we should aim to conduct ourselves throughout the day in a spirit of harmony with our fellow man, as well as by embracing all the worthy ideals, causes, and pursuits outlined therein.

298. Is there any underlying association between the blessings over the Torah, the Priestly Blessing, and the Mishnah *Peah*?

There is. We have first to refer to the statement in Ethics of the Fathers: Simeon the righteous was one of the last surviving members of the Great Assembly. He used to say, "Upon three things the world stands: upon Torah, Temple Service (*avodah*) and acts of kindness (*gemilut chasadim*)."

If we examine those first three components of our daily prayers, we will see that they exemplify precisely those three principles of Simeon the righteous. The blessings over the Torah, of course, highlight the Torah as the first and foremost principle of our spiritual life. Next follows the Priestly Blessing, recited by the priests in the Temple each day as the climax of the *avodah*, the Temple service. And, finally, if we read the Mishnah *Peah*, we see that it contains more references to acts of kindness than any other in the entire collection of the Mishnah. Not only does the very phrase *gemilut chasadim* appear twice, but there are also references to hospitality to strangers, visiting the sick, accompanying the dead to the grave, and providing for a poor bride.

Thus, at the outset of our prayers, we give expression to Simeon the righteous's blueprint for leading a full Jewish life.

Elokai Neshamah

299. The next prayer—*Elokai neshamah*—speaks of the purity of the soul and ends with a blessing of God "who restores the soul to the dead." What is the relevance of this theme to morning prayer?

The Talmud states that this should be recited immediately upon awakening from sleep,[25] which suggests that, in the perception of the rabbis, sleep is akin to death, and the act of awakening involves the restoration to us of our soul. Indeed, the Talmud states that "sleep constitutes one-sixtieth of death."[26] There is also the implication here that we may infer the future resurrection from the precedence of having our souls restored to us each morning.

---

25. *Berakhot* 60a.
26. *Berakhot* 57b.

Jewish prayer involves not only praise, thanksgiving, and petition, but also an affirmation of our fundamental theological beliefs. We have already referred to this in our comments on *Yigdal* and *Adon Olam* (See Questions 267–274). Bearing in mind that the Sadducees denied the resurrection, it may well be that *Elokai neshama*'s unequivocal affirmation of the doctrine was inserted near the very beginning of our daily prayers in order to establish our Orthodox credentials and aim a polemical broadside against those who would reject or dilute our basic beliefs.

The reason this blessing was moved from its recommended place, on awakening, to being recited as part of the service proper was because of those who were lax as regards the washing of the hands immediately on awakening, and who consequently recited God's name at the very beginning of *Elokai neshamah*, in a state of impurity. It was replaced, therefore, by a simple sentence that does not contain the divine name, but that expresses the identical reference to the soul: *Modeh ani lefanekha melekh chai vekayyam, shehechezarta biy nishmatiy bechemlah, rabbah emunatekha*— "I thank thee, O living and eternal king, for having restored my soul to me in Your mercy. Abundant is Your faithfulness."

The Fifteen Birkot Ha-Shachar *(Morning Blessings)*

300. The fifteen blessings that follow seem rather disconnected. Is there any coherent connection and relevance to the particular time of the day they are being recited?

Most definitely. For convenience, we will list the themes of these blessings. They constitute praise of God for the following:

   (i) Giving the cock intelligence to discern between night and day.

  (ii) Not making us a gentile.

 (iii) Not making us a slave.

  (iv) Not making us a woman (recited by men), or making us "according to His will" (recited by women).

   (v) Giving sight to the blind.

  (vi) Clothing the naked.

 (vii) Loosening (the chains of) the bound.

(viii) Straightening the bent.

  (ix) Spreading out the earth above the water.

   (x) Providing all our needs.

  (xi) Making firm man's steps.

 (xii) Girding Israel with might.

(xiii) Crowning Israel with glory.

 (xiv) Giving strength to the weary.

  (xv) Removing sleep from our eyes.

Now, although we recite them all in synagogue, the Talmud[27] states that these blessings—most of which are couched in symbolic language—are functional and are essentially connected with the various actions involved in getting out of bed in the morning. Thus, they were originally composed for recitation as one performs each successive movement of one's limbs. It will be seen that there is a slight variation in the order that we recite them from that of the Talmudic source.

The Talmud states that the first blessing (i) is to be recited, literally, on hearing the crowing of the cock, and is a praise of nature awakening to a new day. The second, third, and fourth blessings form a separate and independent category (See Questions 302–305). The fifth blessing (v) is to be recited on opening one's eyes. The sixth (vii above) is recited on stretching (an act that resembles that of a person trying to loosen himself from his bonds) and sitting up. The seventh blessing (vi above) is recited when putting on one's robe. The eighth blessing (viii) is recited when one lifts oneself up (to get out of bed). The ninth blessing (ix) is recited when placing one's feet on the firm ground. The tenth blessing (xi) is recited when one takes one's first few steps. The eleventh blessing (x) is recited while one ties one's shoes. The twelfth blessing (xii) is reciting while one fastens his belt. The thirteenth blessing (xiii) is recited while tying on one's head scarf. The fourteenth blessing (xv) is recited while washing one's face.

It will be seen that the blessing of God for giving "strength to the weary" (xiv) is not mentioned in the Talmud. The eclectic commentary, *Iyyun tefillah*, suggests that it might have been introduced in Medieval Germany as a blessing of encouragement and faith to a Jewish community that was "weary" as a result of successive Crusades and persecutions.[28]

301. So why were these blessings removed from their natural context to become synagogue blessings?

For the reason mentioned above, namely that people were remiss about keeping some water next to their beds (*neigel wasser*) in order to wash their hands on awakening (and in particular their nails, to which the evil spirits of the night were believed to adhere). In order to prevent them from reciting these blessings in an impure state, their recitation was delayed and incorporated into the synagogue prayers.

It is also possible that the change was introduced in Medieval Europe at a time when the wearing of head covering for prayer became common practice. There was conern, therefore, that people would recite these blessings in bed with a bare head. The Talmud took no account of this, since in Talmudic times it was only the sages who wore head gear to enhance the dignity of their position.

---

27. *Berakhot* 60b.
28. Commentary of *Iyyun tefillah*. See (1966) *Siddur Otzar Ha-tefillot*. New York: Hebraica Press, pp. 130–131.

Thanks for not making me a gentile, servant, or woman

302. To return to the second blessing in the list, which (together with the third and fourth) is not couched in symbolic, but rather in concrete, language. Is it not rather xenophobic to pray to God for "not making me a gentile (*shelo asani goy*)"?

First, let it be said that the original Talmudic formulation was far more refined, and couched as *Barukh attah . . . she'asani yisrael*—"Blessed art thou . . . who has made me a Jew."[29] This could hardly cause offense and is the natural emotion of a nation that believed itself to be the chosen recipient of a divine Torah.

Before determining the precise meaning of the variant form, *shelo asani goy*, that superseded the Talmudic formulation, we have to be aware that two other variants are found in different prayer rites: *shelo asani nokhriy* ("who has not made me a heathen") and *shelo asani akum* ("who has not made me an idolator"). So there was clearly no consensual disparagement of "gentiles," that is those who possess another religious faith, in the formulation of this blessing.

Indeed, because in some Ashkenazi circles the term *goy* has taken on a slightly pejorative overtone—largely as an understandable response to the centuries of unremitting antisemitic persecution—it is tempting, though historically anachronistic, to assume that it had that nuance when first incorporated into our prayer book. Indeed, the term is used in the Bible in the exclusive sense of "a nation," without any qualitative connotation. It should not be forgotten that Abraham, the founding father of our people, is promised (Genesis 18:18) that "he will surely become a great nation (*goy gadol*). Again, Israel is referred to by God as "a holy *goy*" (Exodus 18:6), as well as by Moses: "And consider that this *goy* is Thy people" (Exodus 33:13). Thus, the translation "gentile" is clearly inaccurate and has no place in today's climate of sensitivity to racism.[30]

303. What is the relevance of the third of this succession of blessings: *Barukh . . . shelo asani aved* ("who has not made me a slave")?

There were two original purposes underlying this blessing. First, to enable a nation that had suffered enslavement (in Egypt) at the dawn of its history, followed by three conquests of its land (by the Assyrians in 721 B.C.E., the Babylonians in 586 B.C.E. and the Romans in 66 C.E.) with conditions, in each case, akin to enslavement, to express the conviction that this has still "not made me a slave." Jews never developed a slave mentality. They retained their independent spirit, buoyed up by their certainty that, one day, redemption would assuredly come, and that "though he (the Messiah) tarry, yet will I wait patiently for him."[31]

The second purpose was to express thanksgiving for the fact that, unlike slaves whose time is regulated by their master's work schedule, our time is regulated by

29. *Menachot* 43b.
30. See R. Barukh Ha-Levi Epstein (1979). *Tosefet Berakhah*. Tel Aviv: Am Olam, p. 28.
31. Maimonides' *Ani Ma'amin* formulation.

our schedule of three-times daily prayer, study, and performance of *mitzvot* (good deeds).

304. Is not the fourth blessing, *Barukh . . . shelo asani ishah* ("who has not made me a woman"), an unpardonable indictment of Judaism's attitude toward women?

It has to be understood that we are referring to a 2,000-year-old blessing. We cannot possibly measure the ancient world and its perceptions by the criteria and perspectives of our modern, and in many respects revolutionary, world.

Unlike the Graeco-Roman tradition, women in Judaism were always accorded the greatest respect. The biblical acclaim of woman, for her wisdom and business acumen as much as for her role as homemaker, as expressed in the famous final passage (*Eishet chayyil*) of the book of Proverbs, recited every Friday night by Jewish husbands, represents Judaism's overarching attitude of respect and gratitude toward women.

That having been said, it has to be admitted that women did have a marginal role when it came to the performance of ritual *mitzvot*, and synagogue prayer in particular. While this is justified exegetically in our sources, it probably had more to do with the imposition by the Graeco-Roman world of its political and commercial conventions upon its conquered peoples. Hence, the Jewish women of ancient Palestine were simply excluded from participating in socioeconomic life and were relegated to fulfilling a domestic role. The rabbis did their utmost to pacify their womenfolk by regularly quoting the verse, "All glorious is the daughter of the king within" (Psalm 45:14)—though it is doubtful that their words offered much balm.

It may have been indelicately expressed, but the blessing "who has not made me a woman" was the way Jewish males expressed their sense of privilege that, not only were they spared the difficulties of menstruation, the travail of childbirth, and the inexorable routine of the domestic treadmill, but, on the positive side, they were also able to spend time in prayer and in the tranquility of meditation and study in the synagogue.

305. What is the origin and sense of the alternative blessing, *Barukh . . . she'asani kirtzono* ("who has made me according to His will"), recited by women?

The first thing to note is that this alternative is not found in either the Babylonian or Palestinian Talmud, and its origin is unknown. The *Tur* states that "Women have adopted the practice of reciting this blessing, perhaps in order to express their acceptance of their sorry fate!"[32]

We may conjecture, however, that it was not a "tit for tat" innovation, but rather that the impetus for a corresponding blessing for women arose as a result of the concern of some rabbinic authorities that the original and liturgically significant

---

32. *Tur Orach Chayyim* Chapter 47.

number of fifteen blessings recited here should not be reduced by women through their omission of the special "men's blessing."

It has been suggested—some might think, apologetically—that the women's blessing is not, as *Tur* suggests, an expression of resignation to their fate, but, quite the contrary, a thanksgiving by women for the extra measure of grace and beauty with which they are endowed. The noun *ratzon* has the overtone of "good will, favor." Hence, the blessing *she' asani kirtzono* could well mean "who has created me His most favoured form."

R. Barukh Ha-Levi Epstein[33] states that, on account of the principle that over blessings not referred to in the Talmud we do not recite God's name, women should merely recite the words *Barukh attah she' asani kirtzono*.

THE NUMBER FIFTEEN IN JEWISH LITURGY

306. We have referred to the number fifteen as being liturgically significant. Where else in our prayers do we find that particular number employed?

In addition to the fifteen *Birkot Ha-Shachar* blessings, there are (ii) fifteen words in the Priestly Blessing, (iii) fifteen *Shir Ha-ma'alot* psalms, (iv) fifteen expressions of praise in the *Yishtabach* composition, (v) fifteen epithets in the *Emet ve-yatziv* composition following the *Shema*, (vi) fifteen expressions of praise in the *kaddish*, (vii) fifteen designations of God (including *melekh ha-olam*) in the fourth benediction of the Grace After Meals, (viii) fifteen *ma'alot tovot* ("goodly benefits") words in the *Dayyeinu* composition of the Passover Haggadah, and (ix) fifteen occurrences of the word *barukh* in the original form of the *Barukh She'amar* composition. (Our prayer books have only thirteen expressions, but if we consult the *Machzor Vitri*, for example, representing the Franco-German tradition, we find two extra expressions, making a total of fifteen.[34])

307. So why is the number fifteen so significant?

For two reasons. First, because of the fact that there were fifteen steps in the Temple, leading up from the women's enclosure to the men's court, and, as we have observed, a place was found in our liturgy for as many aspects and reminiscences of Temple worship as possible.

Secondly, it is significant on account of the fact that the Priestly Blessing contains fifteen words. The implication of this is that, just as the priests were commanded to bless Israel with a formula containing fifteen words, so we praise God with formulae containing that particular number.

---

33. R. Barukh Ha-Levi Epstein, *op. cit.*, p. 30.
34. Hurwitz, S. ed. (1923). *Machzor Vitri*. Nurenberg: I. Bulka, p. 61.

KORBANOT—THE SACRIFICIAL PASSAGES

308. The next major section of our prayers is the *Korbanot*, the recitation of Mishnah *Zevachim* (chapter 5), dealing with the details and laws of the sacrificial system. How does this "learning" fit in with the exercise of prayer?

Very well! We have to understand that although the English term "prayer" has the connotation of "entreaty" (from the Latin, *precare*; Old French, *preier*), this is but one aspect of the Jewish experience. For us, prayer involves devotion, in its widest sense, to all aspects of the divine revelation and the God–Israel dialogue.

God chose to reveal Himself at Sinai in the course of the bestowal of His Torah on Israel; and the main dialogue between God and Israel, mediated through Moses, was in relation to the revelation and clarification of His will, as enshrined in the written and oral laws. Prayer's main objective, quite apart from petition, is to recapture the mystic immediacy and sanctity of that moment of Sinaitic revelation. It is inconceivable, therefore, that prayer should not also be expressed through the study of written and oral Torah.

If we wed this consideration to the liturgical desire to keep the memory of the Temple and its ritual fresh in our minds and hearts, we will appreciate why we now proceed to study—as an act of "prayer"—the written (biblical) reference to the offering of the daily Temple sacrifices (Numbers 28:11–15), followed by the oral references in the form of the Mishnah *Zevachim* chapter 5. Since the destruction of the Temple and the cessation of animal sacrifices, the sages believed that reciting the passages dealing with aspects of those sacrifices was tantamount, in the eyes of God, to actually offering them.

309. But is there really any point, in our modern age when few people really look forward to the restoration of the sacrificial system, in including such references in our prayers?

We have to understand that if our prayer book only contained relevant material, or things of contemporary significance, then we would have to rewrite it in every generation. Indeed, Jews in Israel, in the former Soviet Union, and elsewhere would all be looking for specific compositions and formulations that reflected their own agonies and ecstasies, as well as their particular objectives. Even if it were possible to revise prayers in this way every few years, such prayer book revision would become a most controversial and divisive matter, and the *siddur* would cease to be the unifying force for *klal yisrael*, which is its prime significance and proudest boast. Jews the world over pray the same prayers, and even the variants between Ashkenazim, Sephardim, Hasidim, etc., are comparatively small and few. The *siddur*, as much as the Sabbaths and festivals that world Jewry observe in common, creates that sense of a shared fellowship that is at the root of the concept of nationhood.

We have mentioned above that when the Jew "prays," he does more than that. He also studies. And one of the most common subjects of study are the details of the sacrificial cult. The *Korbanot* section concludes with a prayer for "the rebuilding of the Temple speedily in our days, where we will serve Thee in awe, as in days of old." Such a prayer was introduced shortly after the Temple was destroyed, at a time when Jews certainly did look forward to the reintroduction of animal sacrifices. And it has been retained in our prayers, even by those who do not relish the reintroduction of sacrifices, because of an unwillingness to excise anything from our spiritual and historical scrapbook, which is what the *siddur*, in some respects, has become.

Reciting and studying the details of the sacrificial system take us back nostalgically into antiquity and provide us with a historical backcloth against which to view the long, loyal, and proud covenant that we Jews have had with both the land of Israel, the city of Jerusalem, and the Temple Mount. That sense of covenanted history has provided us with the strength and determination to put behind us the adversity of two millenia and never to be deflected from our passionate desire to return to our ancestral land.

The Bible constitutes our main title to that land, chronicling the millenia during which we once lived in that holy and promised land as a proud nation under our own kings and with our priests, prophets, sages, and heroes. At that time, the ancestors of most of the "developed" countries of today—if they yet existed—were still primitive, war-mongering tribes. The *siddur*, with its nostalgic historical reminiscences of a vibrant and colorful Temple Judaism, and its numerous prayers for its restoration "speedily in our day," has been a most effective way of preserving and fostering the Zionist ideal within the emotions of our people, leading to the return of our people to Israel in the twentieth century.

RABBI ISHMAEL'S THIRTEEN PRINCIPLES

310. What is the purpose of reciting the next section, Rabbi Ishmael's "thirteen hermeneutical principles"?

The rather frightening Greek word "hermeneutics" means, simply, "the art or science of interpretation" and is especially applied to the Bible. In this context, it refers to the method of applying certain hermeneutical principles to the biblical text with a view to expanding Jewish law far beyond the parameters of the written word. These principles are employed, primarily, to justify the validity of the expanded laws, principles, or regulations—all of which were already part of our oral heritage—by demonstrating that they, all along, constituted a biblical subtext of attendant legislation.

Orthodox Jewish tradition, as handed down from Moses on Sinai to its successive bearers down the ages (the chain of tradition is enumerated in *Ethics of the Fathers* chapter 1), was committed to one basic axiom, and that was that the divine law-giver consciously drafted every letter and word of His Torah in a particular form, so that they created an integrated hermeneutical circuit. This means that when the proper "key" is applied to establish the legislative linkage, it activates points of contact that illuminate the appropriate parallel or related biblical laws and principles, so that the laws applying in one context may be extended to the other. The principles outlined by Rabbi Ishmael constitute the "key" to link the various biblical contexts.

311. Just in case this "definition" of the hermeneutical laws makes our reader more perplexed than he or she was before, can we please have an example of how a particular hermeneutical principle is applied?

With pleasure! Let us take the law of marriage wherein Jewish law requires that, in order to "acquire" a wife, a man has to present her with some money or an object of value, such as a wedding ring. What is the authority for this procedure? It is not expressly stated in the Bible, and yet our sages insist that this has always been biblically mandated.

The Talmud[35] demonstrates to us that by applying hermeneutical principle number two, the *gezerah shavah* (an inference drawn from the identical words or terms in two passages), we may infer this regulation. Thus, in connection with the purchase of a field as a burial place for Sarah, the Torah states *kesef ha-sadeh kach mimmeni* which literally means "The money for the field *take* from me" (Genesis 23:13). Thus, the Hebrew verb *lakach* ("to take") is used in the sense of one person paying money to acquire something.

Now, in connection with acquiring a wife, the Torah uses the identical phraseology: *Kiy yikach ish ishah*, "When a man shall *take* a wife" (Deuteronomy 22:13). Yet nowhere are we told explicitly in the Torah what means are to be employed to achieve that acquisition. The *gezerah shavah* principle allows us, therefore, to make a link between those identical usages of the verb *lakach* in the respective contexts and to state that its meaning in the one, clear context (that is, the payment of money to Ephron) also applies in the second context. Consequently, we may conclude that one of the biblically mandated ways of acquiring a wife is by paying over some money to her.

KADDISH DERABBANAN

312. The *Korbanot* section is followed by *kaddish Derabbanan*. What is the purpose of this prayer?

This is an expansion of the ordinary kaddish *Yatom* (mourner's kaddish). The added paragraph, commencing with the words, *Al yisrael ve'al rabbanan*, is a blessing of the sages of the Torah and their disciples all over the world.

This particular kaddish is recited whenever we introduce into our prayers any passages from our oral law. These can easily be identified by their source-heading, which will refer to either *Mishnah, Beraita,* or *Talmud* and will contain references to Rabbi so-and-so. This *kaddish* is also recited by mourners at the conclusion of the Rabbi's *shiur* (discourse) in synagogue.

---

35. *Kiddushin* 2b.

313. We have referred above to Judaism's attitude to women. May women recite the mourner's *kaddish* or the *kaddish Derabbanan* in synagogue?

The question is dealt with by some present day halakhists,[36] most of whom are disinclined to grant permission to a daughter to recite *kaddish* in synagogue for a departed father. Where the departed left also a son, it clearly devolves upon him to attend synagogue and to recite the *kaddish*.

What has militated strongly against any halakhic concession on this matter is the fear that a woman in such a high profile situation might draw lascivious male attention to herself. A rather small concession is offered by one authority[37] who maintains that during *Shivah* (only), if she is surrounded exclusively by members of her immediate family, she may recite the *kaddish*.

This problem, of women drawing attention to themselves, might well be regarded as existing only from the perspective of right-wing communities, where the sexes never mingle and the women either rarely come to synagogue or are totally out of sight. In Centrist Orthodox communities, however, where there is a natural socializing between the sexes, with coeducational schools, mixing at universities, and even dating, it seems unwarranted to deprive a woman of a deeply-felt need to recite the mourner's *kaddish*, especially as, even in our synagogues, the women are either separated by a *mechitzah* (partition) or by the great distance between the ladies' gallery and the men's section.

One would have thought that a more cogent reason for adopting a strict view on this matter is the fact that *kaddish* involves a summons to the congregation to join in one's praise of God, hence, the phrase *ve'imru amen*, "And say, Amen." Since, in Orthodox tradition, women do not form part of the praying community, as exemplified by the fact that they cannot be counted to the *minyan* (quorum of ten required to hold public worship), it stands to reason that they cannot instruct the remaining male congregation to join in with their prayer. This would apply only to a situation where she recites *kaddish* alone. There should be no objection, however, to her reciting the prayer together with other male mourners in a tone that is fairly muted and heard only by the women. Obviously, one's own rabbi should be consulted in such a situation.

MIZMOR SHIR CHANUKAT HA-BAYIT

314. What is the origin of the recitation of *Mizmor shir chanukat ha-bayit* (Psalm 30)?

Other than the Prayer for the State of Israel, which, in any case, is optional, the inclusion of this psalm is the latest addition into our statutory liturgy, having been introduced only in the seventeenth century.

---

36. See, for example, Ha-levi, C. D. (1983). *Asei Lekha Rav*. Tel Aviv, pp. 230–236.
37. Ha-levi, C. D. *op. cit.*, pp. 233, 236.

It seems to have originated in the Spanish rite, where it was prescribed exclusively for recitation on Chanukah, because of the obvious link between both the name and the significance of that festival and the words *chanukat ha-bayit* ("dedication of the house [that is, the Temple]") in the heading of this psalm. According to Ismar Elbogen,[38] its subsequent elevation to daily recitation was based on an error. Apparently, some printed prayer books omitted the psalm heading, with its specific use of the word *chanukat*, while others omitted the original rubric, "On Chanukah say the following psalm." On both counts, communities assumed that it was to be recited every day.

315. But if the daily recitation of Psalm 30 is based on error, why did the authorities not object and clarify the matter?

There was no need to object. Quite the contrary; there was every justification to include this psalm on the basis of the liturgical principle that a place has to be found somewhere in our prayers for those psalms or biblical passages that were part of the ancient Temple ritual. Now we know from the Mishnah that this particular psalm was sung while the *bikkurim* (first fruits) were being presented at the Temple on the festival of *Shavuot*.[39]

316. But if it was originally prescribed to be sung on the festival of *Shavuot*, how do we explain the reference to the "dedication of the Temple" in the psalm heading?

We have to be aware that the psalm heading ("A psalm of David. A song for the dedication of the Temple.") bears no relation to the actual contents of the psalm! This is not unusual with the psalm headings, which were clearly appended to the psalms long after they were composed. Indeed, there is not a single reference within the psalm to any dedication of the Temple, quite apart from the fact that King David, the psalm's putative author, did not live to see its dedication by his son, Solomon! This being the case, the contents of the psalm were available for any other identification to be read into it.

317. But this begs the question, for surely its original significance as a *Shavuot* psalm is hardly a reason for its daily recitation throughout the year?

Our answer to this question brings us onto a collision course with Elbogen's view that this psalm came into the liturgy as a result of an oversight. Bearing in mind that it was in the Sephardi rite that this psalm was first extended to daily usage, we suggest that it was most probably introduced quite consciously by the descendants of the exiles from Spain (1492) and Portugal (1497) once they had put down new

---

38. Elbogen, I. *op. cit.*, p. 65.
39. Mishnah *Bikkurim* 3:4.

roots and established new and flourishing communities in the lands of their dispersal: Turkey, Holland, North Africa, the Balkans, Asia Minor, Syria, and Palestine.

The sentiments of Psalm 30 are truly well suited to those who have suffered adversity and exile, but have been newly redeemed. And, viewed in this light, we may detect special significance in such phrases as "When I was carefree, I thought, 'I shall never be displaced (*bal emot*)' . . . Weeping may linger at nightfall, but joy comes in the morning . . . You have turned my lament into dancing; You undid my sackcloth and girded me with joy."

PESUKEI DE-ZIMRA

318. What is the purpose of the next composition, *Barukh She'amar*?

It is generally considered as a prologue to the morning prayers in general, rather than just to the section that follows: the *Pesukei De-zimra*, psalms of praise. It essentially sets out to provide an answer to the maxim that appears as the inscription over the Ark in many synagogues: "Know before Whom you are standing."

It constitutes a list of designations of God as found in rabbinic literature and blesses Him by appending the word *barukh* to each definition. God is the *amar vehayah ha-olam*, "the One Who spoke, and (by His mere word) the universe came into being." He is "the One Who relates mercifully to His creatures (*meracheim al ha-beriot*)"; and He is "the One Who repays a goodly reward to those that fear Him (*meshaleim sachar tov liyrei'av*)."

319. But *Barukh She'amar* also ends with a blessing. What is the point of a lone blessing at this point in the service?

The reason is that this is the blessing over all the psalms that follow and that are referred to as the *Pesukei De-zimra*, Songs of Praise. This purpose is clearly enunciated within the composition, which states that "With the psalms of Your servant, David, we will acclaim You."

A reason for reciting joyful psalms as a prelude to the statutory service is offered by one Talmudic sage, Rabbi Simlai, who stated that "A man must always arrange his praise of God before proceeding to offer prayer and petition."[40]

320. Now, on weekdays we recite the last six psalms of the Book of Psalms, to which, on Sabbaths and festivals, we add a further nine psalms. Why, on weekdays, do we recite just the final psalms of the Book?

It goes back to a pietistic practice in Talmudic times: "Rabbi Jose stated, 'May my portion be among those who complete the praises (*gomrei ha-Hallel*) each

---

40. *Berakhot* 32a.

day . . . in the *Pesukei De-zimra.'*"[41] Now, we have another reference in the Mishnah to some "early pietists who would come to synagogue an hour early each morning."[42] We are not told what they occupied themselves with, but, on the basis of Rabbi Jose's exclamation, we may assume that he was referring to that same group. The use of the term "complete the praises" suggests that they would recite the entire Book of Psalms before the ordinary congregants arrived. When the latter did arrive, they would probably join in with the pietists who were just completing the final few psalms of the Book of Psalms. And this is how those last six psalms—from *Ashrei* (Psalm 145) until the verse *Kol ha-neshamah tehallel Yah* (Psalm 150) ultimately made their way into the statutory service. It is not the only element of our tradition that began as the private predilection of an individual pietist or a fraternity and ended up being adopted as official practice.

321. So why were the *Pesukei De-zimra* expanded for Sabbaths and festivals?

For the answer to this question, we must look to the Talmud, which states that "We should not commence prayer in a state of mind that is sad . . . frivolous or preoccupied with vain things, but only with a sense of joy in the privilege of performing the *mitzvah* (of prayer)."[43] The *Tur*[44] employs this as the source for the original custom of reciting *Pesukei De-zimra* (verses of praise) as a prelude to the service proper, which commences (as does the *Ma'ariv* service) with *Borakhu*. The singing of psalms of praise is intended to heighten that joyful spirit.

Now, during the weekdays, people have to rush to work, for which reason the psalms of praise were restricted to the last six. On Sabbaths and festivals, however, when people have plenty of time to devote to their spiritual pursuits, the psalms of praise were augmented with others that breathe especially joyful and optimistic sentiments.

322. Which particular psalms are added on Sabbaths and festivals?

There was considerable variety in the different prayer rites in their choice of psalms with which to augment the Sabbath and festival *Pesukei De-zimra*. The Ashkenazi prayer rite adds an extra nine psalms (19, 34, 90, 91, 135, 136, 33, 92, and 93); the Sephardi prayer rite adds fourteen psalms, plus the alphabetical *Ha-Aderet Ve-ha'emunah* hymn, which Ashkenazim reserve for the morning service on Yom Kippur.

The fourteen Sephardi psalms include all the nine Ashkenazi psalms, as well as Psalm 98 (recited by Ashkenazim as part of the Friday night *Kabbalat Shabbat* psalms) and four of the *Shir Ha-Ma'alot* psalms (121–124). The Yemenite rite also has these *Shir Ha-Ma'alot* psalms.

---

41. *Shabbat* 118b.
42. Mishnah *Berakhot* 5:1.
43. *Berakhot* 31a.
44. *Tur Orach Chayyim*, Section 93.

323. In what way do "joyful and optimistic sentiments" infuse the additional Sabbath and festival psalms?

We only have to take a cursory glance at each of those psalms to see how they are underpinned by these sentiments. We shall demonstrate this by selecting just one sentence from each of the psalms recited:

He has pitched a tent for the sun, which comes out like a groom from his wedding canopy, rejoicing like a champion to run his race. [Psalm 19]

Those who look to Him shine with joy; their faces never blush with shame. [Psalm 34]

Satisfy us in the morning with Your lovingkindness, that we may exult and rejoice all our days. [Psalm 90]

No harm shall befall you, no calamity shall come near your tent. For He will charge His angels concerning you, to guard you in all your ways. [Psalm 91]

Sing praises to His name, for it is pleasant. For the Lord has chosen Jacob for Himself, and Israel as His treasured possession. [Psalm 135]

Give thanks to the Lord, for He is good; For His lovingkindness is for ever! [Psalm 136]

For in Him our hearts rejoice, for we trust in His holy name. [Psalm 33]

For You have made me glad by Your deeds, O Lord. I sing for joy at Your handiwork. [Psalm 92]

The world is firmly established, it cannot be shaken. Your testimonies are very true. [Psalm 93]

ASHREI

324. Among the *Pesukei De-zimra* that psalms are recited both on weekdays as well as on Sabbaths and festivals is *Ashrei* (Psalm 144). Why is this psalm repeated so frequently?

It is, indeed, repeated frequently. On weekdays, it is repeated once again toward the end of the service and then again at the beginning of *Minchah*, the afternoon service. Similarly, on Sabbaths and festivals, it is recited in the *Pesukei De-zimra*, then again before the *Musaf Amidah*, and, finally, in *Minchah*.

The custom of reciting it three times each day goes back to a statement in the Talmud: "Rabbi Eleazar said in the name of Rabbi Abina, 'Whoever recites *Tehillah leDavid* three times each day is assured of a place in the World to Come.'"[45] In fact,

---

45. *Berakhot* 4b.

the practice of reciting it so frequently accords with a liturgical principle that "parts of the Bible, especially psalms and psalm verses to which great importance was attached in the Talmud, are recited in our liturgy more than once."

Ashrei was regarded as a most significant psalm because it contains the most fervent, concise, and direct expression of thanksgiving to God for providing all that the human race requires for its existence and prosperity: "You open Your hand and satisfy the desires of all living things." At the utterance of this single verse, we extend the Judaic parameters of our praise to express our concern that the entire human race should continue to be recipients of God's bounty. To underscore its importance, when we reach this verse we kiss our head and hand *tefillin*.

THE *SHIRAH*

325. Why do we include the *Shirah* (Song of the Red Sea) in our daily prayers?

Because of the liturgical principle mentioned above, that a place had to be found in our prayers for portions of the Bible that were connected with the Temple service. Now, the Talmud[46] tells us that during the offering of the daily sacrifice, the Levites in the Temple would sing ordinary psalms of praise (that is psalms of David, that did not have a special sanctity[47]), whereas on the Sabbath they would sing praises from the Torah itself, such as the *Shirat Ha-yam*, Song of the Red Sea.

326. Why do we repeat the verse *Ha-Shem yimlokh le'olam va'ed*?

Simply to indicate that this is the end of the Pentateuchal text of the *Shirah*. It was felt that this should be highlighted, bearing in mind that some extra verses have been tacked on to it. The same device of repeating a verse to mark it off from the next section is found in the practice of repeating the line *Kol ha-neshamah tehallel Yah Halleluyah*, at the end of Psalm 150, to indicate that this marks the end of the *Pesukei De-zimra* psalms.

327. Why are some extra verses tacked on to the end of the *Shirah* that are not found in the Torah?

We tack on to the end of the *Shirah* three verses: (i) *Kiy la-Hashem ha-melukhah* (Psalm 22:29), (ii) *Ve-alu moshi'im* (Obadiah verse 1), and (iii) *Vehayah Ha-Shem lemelekh* (Zechariah 14:9). These verses were added in order to reinforce the idea of God's kingship, contained in the climactic verse of the *Shirah*—*Hashem yimlokh le'olam va'ed* ("The Lord shall reign for ever and ever"). It was a rabbinic tendency—introduced in order to emphasize the unity of the entire Bible—to bring proof texts from the books of the *Neviim* (Prophets) and *Ketuvim* (Sacred Writings)

---

46. *Rosh Hashanah* 31a.
47. *Maharsha* on *Rosh Hashanah* 31a.

for teachings contained in the Five Books of Moses. Thus, the first verse recited is taken from the Sacred Writings (the Book of Psalms), and the second and third verses are from the Prophets. The reason why the biblical chronological order is reversed and the Sacred Writings are placed before the Prophets is simply because the Psalms were composed by King David, who lived before the period of the classical prophets.

328. Do not some prayer books add a further verse: *Uvetoratkha katuv leimor Shema Yisrael . . . ?*

The *Vilna Gaon* took the view that this addition of the first verse of the *Shema* (Deuteronomy 6:4) was a scribal error that became perpetuated in some printed editions of the prayer book. The scribe was influenced by the verses of the *Malkhuyyot* (affirmation of God's kingship) contained in the *Musaf* prayer of Rosh Hashanah. In the latter composition, the *Shema* verse does, indeed, follow that same verse from Zechariah 14:9, which we recite at the end of the *Shirah*. The scribe was so accustomed to the linking of these two verses from the Rosh Hashanah liturgy that he also appended it when writing out the *Shirah*.

NISHMAT KOL CHAI

329. Why do we recite the *Nishmat* prayer?

Its Mishnaic name provides a clue as to its purpose. It is referred to in the Mishnah[48] as *Birkat Ha-Shir*, "Blessing over the Song," which suggests that it was introduced as a concluding blessing over the *Shirah*, the *Song* of the Red Sea.

The main theme of the latter is the uniqueness of God, as exemplified in the phrase, *Miy khamokha ba'eilim Ha-Shem* ("Who is like unto You, O Lord among the mighty? Who is like You, glorious in holiness?"). And this is precisely the theme that is taken up in *Nishmat* blessing: "All my bones shall say, 'Lord who is like You?' . . . Who then is like You? Who is equal to You? Who can be compared to You?" Again, the *Shirah* describes God's miraculous redemption of Israel from Egypt, and *Nishmat* takes up this theme in the words "You redeemed us from Egypt, O Lord our God, and freed us from the house of bondage."

Nishmat may also contain a rather subtle allusion to the theme of the Song of the Red Sea, and, indeed, to its Hebrew title, *Shirat Ha-Yam*, in the verse "Even if our mouths were filled with song (*shirah*) like the sea (*ka-yam*) [is filled with water]."

330. Who wrote the *Nishmat* blessing?

Sadly, we have no idea who composed this most beautiful and majestic piece. Some have conjectured that the author's first name was Yitzchak and that of his

---

48. Mishnah *Pesachim* 10:7.

wife, Rivka. This is based on the fact that both of these names may be mined from
the four lines, each containing three words, commencing *Befiy yesharim tithallal.*
Thus, if we read downward, we have **Y(i)TZCH(a)K** and **R(i)BK(a)H**:

> *Befiy Yesharim titRomam*
> *Uvedivrei Tzadikkim titBarakh*
> *Uvilshon CHasidim titKaddash*
> *Uvekerev Kedoshim titHallal*

Other scholars have rejected this allusion as just coincidence, on the basis that such
early Talmudic compositions did not employ name acrostics. Furthermore, the order
of the last word of each line does not conform to the above in many prayer rites, and
there is, therefore, the slightest suspicion that some clever scribe might have just
interchanged the final words in order to highlight the names and support his hunch
that the names of the author and his wife were nestled within the lines.

YISHTABACH

331. What is the purpose of *Yishtabach*?

Just as *Barukh She'amar* constituted the blessing before the *Pesukei De-zimra*
psalms, so *Yishtabach* is their concluding blessing. This is evident from its sentiment
that "to You . . . song and praise are appropriate, hymns and psalms," as well as
to the conclusion of the blessing, extolling God as "exalted in praises."

SHIR HA-MA'ALOT MIMA'AMAKIM (PSALM 130)

332. Why do some communities insert Psalm 130 at this point, reserving it exclusively for the High Holy Days?

Recent editions, such as *Birnbaum* and *ArtScroll*, have revived the custom of
reciting this psalm, *Mima'amakim* ("Out of the depths I call unto Thee"), which was
always optional. In Hasidic synagogues, it enjoys a respected status and is recited
aloud with great feeling by *Chazan* and congregation. Its petitionary force,
suggestive of our truly calling "out of the depths"—of despair, self-doubt, and
existential perplexity—coupled with its several references to forgiveness of sin,
rendered it most appropriate to Rosh Hashanah and Yom Kippur.

The Midrashic comment on the verse "Out of the depths" also made it an
appropriate insertion at this juncture when the *Chazan* proper takes over the leading
of the service. The Midrash on this verse states, "A man should never pray on an
elevated place, but rather from a low level, as it is written, 'Out of the depths I call

unto Thee, O Lord.' "[49] Thus, this psalm, at another level, was a timely caution to the *Chazan* to maintain a posture of great humility at this awesome moment, notwithstanding that he was occupying a most privileged position as carrier of the prayers of Israel to their Father in heaven.[50]

BORAKHU

333. What is the point of this responsive call by the *Chazan* to the congregation to "Bless the Lord who is to be blessed"?

The point is to highlight the fact that from this point commences the statutory part of the service. We have already mentioned that the recitation of the *Pesukei De-zimra* psalms came about as a result of the practice of some early pietists who came early to synagogue to recite the entire Book of Psalms. Thus, although the recitation of the last six psalms by the arriving members of the general congregation became common practice, it never had the imprimatur of the Talmudic or later authorities. Indeed, Saadia Gaon states quite categorically that "our people have volunteered to recite these psalms," and we know from liturgical fragments found in the Cairo Genizah that there was great flexibility as regards the recitation of those morning psalms. Some communities recited up to thirty psalms, whereas others recited no complete psalms, but only selected verses of a wide variety of psalms.

To indicate, however, that what follows are not voluntary, but statutory, blessings, the *Chazan* formally summons the congregation to "bless the Lord," and the congregation makes an immediate response, indicative of their readiness to do so.

From *Borakhu* onward, we are not supposed to speak until the end of the silent *Amidah*. This is not only on account of the paramount importance of this section of the service, but also because what follows constitutes one unified section. *Borakhu* introduces the two blessings recited over the *Shema*—and, as we know, we may not speak once blessings have been recited until the particular *mitzvah* they refer to is completed. But the *mitzvah* of reciting the *Shema* is not complete until we have recited its concluding blessing (*Emet veyatziv*, ending *Barukh attah . . . ga'al yisrael*). However, the Talmud requires that we connect the *Amidah* seamlessly to the end of the *Shema*'s concluding blessing, for which reason the *Chazan* recites in an undertone the final words of the blessing (*ga'al yisrael*). So, notionally, we have one long unit of blessing, commencing with *Borakhu* and ending after the conclusion of the *Amidah*, thus allowing for no interruption from beginning to end.

---

49. Midrash *Shochar Tov, ad loc.*; *Berakhot* 7a.
50. For further commentary on the *Mima'amakim* psalm, see Cohen, J. M. (1994). *Prayer and Penitence.* Northvale, NJ: Jason Aronson Inc., pp. 22–23.

BARUKH . . . YOTZEIR OR

334. What is the significance of this blessing?

First, it should be noted that this blessing comprises a verse from Isaiah 45:7. It is highly unusual, however, to take a biblical verse in its entirety and use it as the formula for a blessing.

It serves as the opening of the first of the two *Shema* blessings whose theme is praise of the Creator for the gifts of light and darkness, day and night; the former in which to pursue ennobling work; the latter in which to enjoy bodily rest and refreshment.

The sages never tampered with biblical verses, hence, the anomaly that our blessing employs an amended form of the end of that Isaiah verse. The original has *oseh shalom uvorei ra* (". . . and creates *evil*"), whereas our blessing has *oseh shalom uvorei et ha-kol* (". . . and creates *all things.*"). The reason for this emendation was probably that retention of the original might have provided fuel for the adherents of the dualist Persian (Zoroastrian) religion, who believed that the world was created and preserved by two opposing forces, a god of light and a god of darkness, who manifest their will through good and evil, respectively. The reference to God as the Creator of evil was accordingly replaced.

OR OLAM BE'OTZAR CHAYYIM

335. What is the meaning of this abstruse phrase, "The eternal light is in the treasury of life"?

It can only be understood in the light of Talmudic mysticism, according to which the primordial light enjoyed by Adam was possessed of supernatural properties that enabled him to take in the whole panorama of Creation at one glance. This light was clearly quite unique, having been brought into being at the very outset of Creation when God said, "Let there be light!" It was not of the same ilk as nature's light, which came into being at a later time with the creation of the luminaries on the fourth day.

The Midrash states that God refused to bestow the gift of that primordial light upon the wicked generations of the flood and the Tower of Babel, so He stored it away for the exclusive enjoyment of the righteous in the Hereafter. And this explains the first part of the line, "The light (*or*), by means of which the whole world (*olam*) could be surveyed (by Adam), is stored away in the treasury of eternal life (*be-otzar chayyim*)."

Thus, according to this mystical idea, the light of the sun and moon (*orot*) that we enjoy is of a far inferior quality to that original, unique source of illumination. Our light only merits its name when it is contrasted with darkness (*orot me-o-fel*). And it was our circumscribed light that God commanded (*amar*) and that came into being (*vayehi*).

PETICHACH—OPENING THE ARK

336. Many congregations open the Ark for the latter and several other compositions. What is the purpose of opening the Ark?

Some authorities view it as the symbolic opening of the Holy of Holies in the Temple. That inner sanctum also contained an Ark, housing the Tablets of the Testimony, which represented the entirety of Israel's Torah. Originally, the Ark was opened during the course of a service only in order to take out the Torah scrolls. This has remained the practice in most other rites except for that of the Ashkenazim who, at a very early period, opened the Ark for particularly favored compositions, in order to stress their importance and to stimulate a greater degree of concentration during their recitation. It was also a useful source of revenue for congregations that auctioned the various honors.

In Franco-Germany, in the thirteenth century, some communities opened the Ark for the whole of the repetition of the *Shacharit* and *Musaf Amidahs*, closing it only for *Kedushah* and the Priestly Benediction. This did not win universal acceptance. Firstly, it necessitated people remaining on their feet for most of the service, and, secondly, it restricted the number of honors that could be distributed and the amount of revenue ingathered!

PIYYUTIM—POETIC COMPOSITIONS

337. Various poetic compositions, which clearly enjoyed great popularity, are inserted at this point into our High Holy Day services. Was that popularity universal?

It was not. Saadia Gaon (ninth to tenth century), though a distinguished writer of sacred poetry himself, was uncompromising in rejecting a large number of *piyyutim* that, in his opinion, departed from or impaired the original structure of the prayer they were embellishing or that injected ideas that were not directly related to the basic theme of the passage.

The impropriety of so much of the sacred poetry of his day prompted Moses Maimonides to the following scathing criticism:

> We cannot approve of what those foolish persons do . . . describing God in attributes that would be an offence if applied to a human being . . . letting their eloquence run away with them . . . composing things that are either pure heresy or which contain such absurdities that the reader is prompted to laugh, but also to grieve that anyone could have the temerity to apply such references to God. . . . I declare that they are guilty not only of ordinary sin, but also of profanity and blasphemy! This applies also to the multitude that listens to the prayers of such a foolish person.[51]

---

51. Maimonides, *Guide for the Perplexed*, ed. M. Friedlander, p. 218.

From such strictures, we may infer that those *piyyutim* that did pass the highly critical eye of such illustrious scholars were of a special quality. And it is those that ultimately won a place in our liturgy.

EL ADON AL KOL HA-MA'ASIM

338. What is the significance of this poem that is sung every Sabbath morning by the congregation, as well as on Rosh Hashanah if it coincides with the Sabbath?

This is an alphabetical acrostic poem, which has its counterpart in the alphabetic poem *El Barukh Gedol Deah*, recited on weekdays at the same stage of the service. It is quoted, with variant phraseology, in the *Zohar*, the textbook of Jewish mysticism, where its structure is regarded as possessing mystical significance. Thus, the opening sentence has ten words, corresponding to the Ten Commandments; the last sentence has twelve words, corresponding to the twelve signs of the Zodiac; and the middle nine verses each contain eight words, making a total of seventy-two words, corresponding to the most sacred, seventy-two letter name of God.

Its relevance to this particular part of the service lies in its reference to God's praise being recounted not only in the mouths of mortals, but also in those of the heavenly hosts. It also refers to the grandeur of the luminaries, "filled with lustre and radiating brightness," which represents the overall theme of this blessing of the Shema—the *Yotzer (ha-me'orot)* blessing—which sets out to thank God for the light of the sun and the moon.

Its very closing words detail three main categories of angels: fiery angels (*serafim*), angels of the heavenly chariot (*ofanim*), and the holy beasts that draw the heavenly chariot (*veChayyot ha-kodesh*). This reference is contextually suited to the passages that follow, which continue the theme of the heavenly court and the praise to God uttered by the angelic hosts. The same categories of angels are mentioned, among others, in the composition *Veha-Chayyot yeshoreiru*, which follows shortly afterwards.

THE *SHEMA*

339. What is the relationship between the subject matter of the two blessings prescribed for recitation before the *Shema* and the *Shema* itself?

In the *Shema*, we are told that the Lord is our only God and that we must love Him with all our heart, soul, and might. The blessings beforehand constitute the rationale of our allegiance to Him and gratitude toward Him.

The first blessing, commencing *Le'El barukh ne'imot yiteinu*, affirms that

He alone performs mighty deeds and creates new things; He is the Lord of battles. He sows righteousness, and causes salvation to flourish; He creates remedies . . . and, in His goodness, renews the creation continually every day. . . . Blessed are You, the Lord, Creator of the heavenly lights.

It was recognized that we humans could not possibly affirm God as an abstract concept or express our love of Him in a vacuum. We have to be able to point to tangible boons that prove His existence to us and move us to personal or at least human gratitude. Hence, we commence with a blessing of God as the source of all creativity, goodness, salvation, and healing. We refer to the renewal of Creation each day, with its manifold new discoveries and opportunities; and the closing *berakhah* uses the creation of the sun, moon, and stars, which appear to be recreated anew each day and night, as a metaphor for that creative spirit that infuses all existence.

The second blessing moves from universal to Jewish national boons and offers thanksgiving to God for having shared His wisdom, in the form of the Torah, with our people. It petitions for God to continue to implant within us the great desire to "understand, discern, learn and teach, observe and fulfill *with love* all the teachings of Your Torah." Note how the author consciously inserts here the idea of observing God's Torah and His will "with love." Serving God with love is far more precious to Him than serving Him out of fear of punishment for sin and defiance.

The gift of the Torah is the essence of Israel's election. The "chosen people" means nothing more than that to Israel was entrusted the Torah and with it an exacting spiritual mission. And the second blessing proves—if proof were necessary—that our idea of chosenness is not racial superiority, but custodianship of the divine law, by its linking here of the theme of Torah with the concluding reference to God having "chosen his people Israel in love."

Significantly, the closing *berakhah* picks up that key word "with love" (*be'ahavah*), preparing us thereby for the opening word of the first paragraph of the *Shema*—"And you shall love (*Ve'ahavta*) the Lord your God."

340. What is the meaning of the opening verse, "Hear O Israel, the Lord our God, the Lord is One"?

A 6-year-old child in my Hebrew School once told me that he knew how old God was. Intrigued, I invited him to tell me. "Two," came back the reply. "How do you know?" I queried. "Because last year you told us that 'God is *one!*'"

To that little boy, God must have been very tangible, and the concept of His being "One" presented few difficulties. To the rest of us, however, the phrase is rather more abstruse.

We understand "One" in this context as suggesting three main ideas: (i) He is totally unique in all His attributes, (ii) He is an absolute unity, (iii) He is the one and only Being to Whom we attribute divinity.

Rashi[52] explains the phrase "the Lord our God, the Lord is One" to mean that the Lord who is currently only "our God" will, in the future, be acknowledged as the "one (and only) God"—of all mankind.

---

52. Commentary of *Rashi* on Deuteronomy 6:4.

341. What do we mean by saying that God is "an absolute unity"?

Moses Nachmanides[53] views this concept as the antithesis of that espoused by other religions. The Persian Dualists believed that good and evil, reward and punishment, could not possibly emanate from one and the same Source. There had to be two rival Powers, therefore, each dealing with mankind in a contrariwise way. Similarly, Christianity, with its doctrine of the Trinity, one element of which could become embodied into the person of Jesus, was viewed by Judaism as false and heretical.

In Judaism, God is the source of both reward and punishment. Nothing evil comes from Him. What may appear to us as adverse is, if we only knew it, in our best interest. Sometimes it may be in the interest of our immortal soul, though apparently not of our transient body. We acknowledge at all times that God, in His infinite wisdom, guides our personal and national destiny, and that there are no variant aspects of His being or competing forces working against Him.

342. What does the Torah mean by loving God with all our "heart, soul, and might"?

The Talmud[54] defines "*all* your heart" as "with your good inclination (*yetzer tov*) as well as with your evil inclination (*yetzer ra*)."

Perhaps "evil inclination" is an inaccurate definition in this context, where the sense is, rather, "with your physical instincts and passions." These can also be consecrated into the service and love of God. Thus, sex outside of marriage is regarded as the mere satisfaction of one's lust. In the context of marriage, however, it becomes a veritable *mitzvah*, a religious act, a counterpart of the love, gratitude, and oneness that are also essential ingredients of our spiritual life and our relationship with God. Again, eating serves our physical needs. Making a blessing over the food, however, overlays that physical act with a spiritual significance. In both cases, our *yetzer hara* is made a vehicle for serving God "with all our heart."

The Talmud[55] elucidates the meaning of "with all your soul"—"Even if He takes away your soul, love Him!"

This is a call to accept the approach of death with loving resignation. It is referred especially to the context of martyrdom, the most supreme demonstration of refusal to compromise on God's will, and the most powerful expression of "love of God."

The Talmud[56] exemplifies this with the famous story of Rabbi Akivah. When the Romans were executing him, by tearing his flesh with iron combs, he occupied himself with the recitation of the *Shema* with a serene and contented look on his face. When his disciples asked how he could display such courage, he replied, "All my life I was concerned as to how I might fulfill the divine command to love God

---

53. Commentary of *Ramban* on Deuteronomy 6:4.
54. *Yoma* 86a.
55. *Berakhot* 54a.
56. *Ibid.*

'with all your soul.' Now that the opportunity has at last presented itself, shall I not welcome it?'"

The final summons, to love God "with all your might," presents problems of definition. *Me'od* occurs in the Bible in the sense of "muchness, abundance"; so the basic sense would then be to demonstrate love of God by showering upon Him one's wealth and substance.[57] This would be expressed through thanksgiving offerings in Temple times, and charitable donations and gifts to synagogues and Torah institutions in the present day.

But the sages also dug out from the phrase *bekhol me'odekha* a moralistic interpretation, connecting the word *me'od* with the like-sounding word *midah*, meaning "measure." Hence, their alternative interpretation: *Bekhol midah umidah shehu moded lekha*—"Love Him, irrespective of whatever fate He *measures out* to you."[58]

These are the various and overwhelmingly difficult challenges that those six simple words—*Bekhol levavkha uvekhol nafshekha uvekhol me'odekha*—hold out to every Jew!

343. But how can the Torah possibly command us to love? Love is an instinctive emotion, which either is, or is not, ignited. How can the Torah possibly legislate for this emotion?

Indeed. This was recognized by our sages and accounts for the rather loose definition that they gave to this particular command. On the words "You shall love the Lord your God," the Talmud states:

"Perform deeds whereby, through you, the name of heaven will *be beloved*. If you study Torah assiduously, minister to Sages, conduct your business affairs with integrity and speak respectfully with others, what will people say?— 'Happy that man who has studied Torah . . . see how ethical are his ways.'"[59]

The sages were clearly accepting the difficulty we have posed and offering the suggestion that the Torah was not, in fact, legislating for emotions. It was telling us rather to cause God's name to "be beloved" and the religious way of life to be admired.

344. Why is the *Shema* so significant in Judaism?

Its significance lies in the fact that it was perceived as encapsulating some of Judaism's most fundamental religious principles: The idea of the personal God who craves Israel's love; the doctrine of reward and punishment, which forms the theme of the second paragraph; and, in the third paragraph, the idea that Israel should publicize her faith, as exemplified in the *mitzvah* of *tzitzit*, the outward sign of adherence to the Jewish faith. The third paragraph also contains the instruction "and

---

57. *Berakhot* 61b.
58. *Berakhot* 54a.
59. *Yoma* 56a.

thou shalt be holy unto thy God," as well as a re-statement of the opening of the Ten Commandments: "I am the Lord thy God who brought thee out of the land of Egypt, to be for you as your God."

The *Shema* is also significant in that it formed, together with the Ten Commandments, the kernel of Jewish prayer already in the Temple, long before the introduction of an *Amidah* and the evolution of an independent synagogue liturgy.

Its significance was reinforced by the fact that the *Shema* became the very first prayer that Jewish parents taught to their tender children, the prayer they recited with them each night as they went off to sleep; and it was the last prayer that people recited with their dying breath, as they surrendered up their soul to God. The first two paragraphs of the *Shema* are also contained in the *Mezuzah*, attached to every Jewish door—a sign that all those therein affirm their commitment to the Jewish way of life and accept the yoke of the kingdom of heaven.

345. Since there is a positive biblical *mitzvah* (duty) to recite the *Shema* each day—"when you lie down and when you rise up" (Deuteronomy 6:7)—why was no specific blessing (*Barukh . . . vetzivanu al keriat Shema*) prescribed for recitation before performing this *mitzvah*?

The reason is that the recitation of these, and all other, biblical passages are covered by the blessing *la'asok bedivrei Torah* (". . . who has commanded us to occupy ourselves with words of Torah") recited at the very outset of our daily prayers (See Question 293).

THE REPETITION OF THE *AMIDAH*

Mi-sod Chakhamim unevonim

346. What is the purpose of this recurring introduction to the *Chazan*'s repetition of the *Amidah*?

We mentioned earlier the opposition of the religious authorities to any *piyyutim* that did not meet the most exacting standards, from the point of view of style, as well as the appropriateness of the epithets of praise employed and the sources relied upon.

Because of this, as well as on account of the opposition of other authorities to the interrupting of the statutory services for the recitation of *piyyut*, the *Chazanim* who at first introduced, or composed, these compositions felt the need to utter an introductory *reshut* ("permission"), seeking the indulgence of the congregation for the particular poem, and affirming that it is rooted in Orthodox tradition, emanating "from the company of wise men and sages" (*mi-sod chakhamim unevonim*), and not the author's independent imagination. In an age when people were also most sensitive to the inroads of sectarianism, such as the Karaite heresy, it was also felt necessary to allay the fears of the community—especially in an age when texts were unavailable for examination and control—and to assure them that any poetic innovations were strictly in line with Orthodox ideology.

ZOKHREINU LA-CHAYYIM

347. Is it really appropriate to plead to God to "Remember us for life" when we know that it is the nature of things that man must at some time pass away? Is it not a vain prayer?

No, it is not. A prayer for God's blessing cannot possibly be vain. The classical definition of a vain prayer (*tefillat shav*) is praying that something that has already occurred should be as if it had not occurred. The Mishnaic example is of a man approaching the street where he lives and, hearing the sound of a tumult (an ambulance or police siren), prays to God, saying, "May the crisis not be in *my* home!"[60] The truth is that the crisis has already occurred and cannot be reversed. If it is not in his home, he does not need to pray; if it is in his home, then his prayer cannot reverse a reality. As regards our prayer for life, however, the sages believed that no divine decision was irrevocable and the power of prayer is strong enough to move God to revise His plan.

While the notion of God having to revise His plans may pose its own problems, there is a biblical precedence in the reprieve granted to those who worshiped the Golden Calf: "And the Lord repented of the evil which He said He would do unto His people" (Exodus 32:14).

A way out of that philosophical dilemma, of having to posit a change of mind on God's part, is to assume that, as He is not restricted to the chronology of time, the plea in mitigation for Israel, though uttered by Moses after the sin was committed, was yet actually witnessed and received by God contiguously with the commission of the sin. Thus, at the very outset, when God responded to Israel's act of faithlessness, He was already persuaded, on the basis of Moses' fervent plea, to forgive His people. And this might also explain the value of petitionary prayer, such as this one for life. This is, indeed, affirmed in the words of another High Holy Day composition: "Prayer, penitence and charity *avert* the evil decree."

348. How is it that we ask merely to be remembered for "life," but we do not define the nature and quality of the life we would like?

The Hebrew word for life, *chayyim*, is a plural word. For the Jew, the totality of life is not the restricted period we spend in this world, but must also encompass the other "life" that lasts for all eternity. Like an investment policy, to which we contribute for years in order eventually to realize a happy and secure future, so in the spiritual realm we likewise have to contribute and build up a substantial capital while on earth in order to secure the eternal benefits in the Hereafter.

Thus, the plea "Remember us unto life" may also be construed as referring to the "life eternal" that our repentance secures for us. And viewed in this light, not only is the immediate question answered, but our previous problem is also removed, in

---

60. Mishnah *Berakhot* 9:3.

that the *Zokhreinu* plea becomes even more relevant during that fateful year when God terminates our existence on earth.

HA-SHEM MELEKH, HA-SHEM MALAKH

349. Who wrote this popular alphabetical composition, and for which particular prayer of the statutory service did he compose it?

It was written by one of our earliest and most prolific Hebrew poets, Eleazar Kallir, author of some sixteen poems recited during Rosh Hashanah and Yom Kippur in the Ashkenazi liturgy. There is considerable doubt as to precisely when Kallir lived, though the seventh century is the most probable period.

Kallir composed most of his poetry for insertion into the blessings before (and also after) the *Shema*, for which reason they are referred to as *Yotzerot*, that is insertions into the blessing that ends with the words *[Barukh attah . . .] yotzer [ha-me'orot]*. The composition *Ha-Shem melekh* was written, however, in order to provide a poetic and mystical setting for the *Kedushah* in the repetition of the *Amidah*.

350. How does this poem relate to the *Kedushah*?

The *Kedushah* opens with the statement that "We [Israel] will sanctify God's name on earth just as they [the angels] sanctify it in the highest heavens." Kallir is inspired by this vision of Israel as the angelic counterpart; and in this composition he fuses together the attributes of both, making it difficult, in fact, at times, to ascertain whether he is referring to the angels or to Israel.

The core of the *Kedushah* is the triple-evocation, *kadosh kadosh kadosh*. Kallir keeps this threefold emphasis in the forefront, and hence his major refrain—*Ha-Shem melekh . . . malakh . . . yimlokh*—is also in triplicate.

Another link with the *Kedushah* is the word *ve-kol* ("with a loud voice"), which climaxes each phrase. This connects with the second word of the *Kedushah*—*[Az] be-kol*. Again, the opening word of this composition, *Adirei [ayumah]*, links up with the *Kedushah* phrase *adir [vechazak]*.

LE'EL OREIKH DIN

351. Why did the practice develop to recite this composition during the *Amidah* of the Morning Service on the first day, but to defer it until *Musaf* on the second day?

This may have arisen in order to do justice to both opinions in a Talmudic dispute[61] as to the exact time of the day when God judges the world on Rosh

---

61. *Avodah Zarah* 4b.

Hashanah: whether early, at *Shachrit* time, or a little later in the day, at *Musaf*. This composition, refers, in each alternate phrase, to "the day of judgment" (*beyom din*) and "the judicial process" (*ba-din*), respectively. By varying the time of its recitation, we ensure that our minds are solemnly attuned to the awesome process of judgment at the precise time at which it is being enacted.

THE *KEDUSHAH*

352. What is the significance of the *Kedushah*?

The third blessing of the *Amidah—Attah kadosh*—refers to the absolute holiness of God. It also contains a reference to "the [angelic] holy ones who praise Thee each day" (*ukedoshim bekhol yom yehallelukha*). In the corresponding blessing of the repetition of the *Amidah*, this interface between Israel's praise and that of the angels is graphically portrayed through quotations from Isaiah's and Ezekiel's visions of the heavenly congregation in praise of God. The *Kedushah* emphasizes that Israel's praise of God is patterned upon that of the angelic choir.

The *Attah Kadosh* blessing of the *Amidah* refers to God as "a great and holy king." The *Kedushah* seizes upon the latter epithet, and, with a tincture of irony, asks, "When will You reign in Zion (*mattai timlokh betziyyon*)?" This prompts the fervent prayer: "May You be exalted and sanctified within Jerusalem Your city," and the final, supportive quotation from the psalms, "May the Lord your God reign forever, O Zion, throughout all generations" (Psalm 146:10).

By employing the responsive mode, between *Chazan* and congregation, the *Kedushah* seeks to echo the heavenly choir, which, on its own evidence, from Isaiah, praises God in that identical mode: "And each [category of angel] called to the other [category] saying, 'Holy holy holy is the Lord of Hosts'" (Isaiah 6:3).

UVEKHEIN TEIN PACHDEKHA . . . UVEKHEIN TEIN KAVOD . . . UVEKHEIN TZADDIKIM . . . VETIMLOKH ATTAH

353. We noted earlier that the *piyyutim* were intended to provide a poetic amplification of the theme of the blessing for which they were composed. Why is it, then, that these three compositions make no reference to the "holiness of God," which is the central theme of this third blessing of the *Amidah*, and which the Talmudic sages refer to as *Kedushat Ha-Shem* ("Sanctification of the Name")?

The origin of this prayer is, indeed, a matter of dispute. Its universalistic theme, looking forward to the time when God will be acknowledged as the one and only "ruler over all His works" (*Vetimlokh attah Ha-Shem levadekha al kol ma'asekha*), has suggested to some scholars that it was originally composed not for here, but as an introduction to the *Malkhuyyot* section of the *Musaf Amidah*, which deals with that specific theme.

Although our *Malkhuyyot* section is introduced into the fourth blessing of the (repetition of the) *Amidah*, the Mishnah[62] refers to the view of Rabbi Yochanan ben Nuri that its proper place is in the third blessing. The four paragraphs, commencing *Uvekhein tein pachdekha*, which deal with God's "kingship," may well have been Rabbi Yochanan's original introductory prayer to the *Malkhuyyot* section, which was retained in the third blessing—in the place where he recited it—even though the *Malkhuyyot* verses themselves were universally assigned, by his colleagues, to the fourth blessing.

354. What is the connection between these four paragraphs of the *Uvekhein tein pachdekha* composition?

They will actually be seen to constitute an integrated thematic development. The first paragraph looks forward to the Messianic era when "all God's creatures will form a single society to do Your will wholeheartedly."

The second paragraph (*Uvekhein tein kavod*) refers to the glory, the gladness, and the joy that will pervade the land of Israel and the city of Jerusalem when, in the future, they are reconstituted as the place of residence for "the offspring of Jesse, Your annointed (Messiah)."

The third paragraph (*Uvekhein Tzaddikim*) continues that theme of the Hereafter, when "the righteous will rejoice and the pious will exult" in their spiritual vindication, and "wickedness will evaporate like smoke."

The fourth paragraph amplifies that longed-for situation, referring to God ruling over the entire world from Mount Zion and from Jerusalem His holy city. Indeed, the epithet "holy," applied here to the city of Jerusalem (*kodshekha*), provides the link, however loose, with the overall theme of this third blessing, which is *Kedushat Ha-Shem*, the *holiness* of God's name. Indeed, this key-word (*kaddosh*) immediately follows in the final paragraph (*Kaddosh attah*), which was the original version of the daily third blessing of the *Amidah*.

ATTAH VECHARTANU

355. Does not *Attah Vechartanu* ("You have chosen us from all the peoples") smack of racial superiority?

God forbid that Israel should ever have regarded itself as racially superior to any other people! The prophet Amos already strongly disabused his people from entertaining any such thoughts when he equated the origins of other nations with having been of equal significance to Israel's Exodus from Egypt: "Are ye not as the children of the Ethiopians unto Me, O children of Israel?" saith the Lord. "Have I

---

62. Mishnah *Rosh Hashanah* 4:5.

not brought up Israel out of the land of Egypt, and [in the same way] the Philistines from Caphtor and the Syrians from Kir?"

Racial superiority is a concept identified in the twentieth century with Nazism and, to a lesser extent, with the caste system of India. It connotes purity of blood, innate superiority of national stock. Judaism never knew of that odious concept. Hence, anyone who ever wished to join the ranks of the Jewish people as a convert was welcomed into the fold. Some of the greatest sages of the Talmudic period proudly traced their ancestry to converts, and the royal line of King David is traced back in the Bible (Ruth 4:22) to Ruth the Moabitess who converted to Judaism.

The exclusive aspect wherein Israel's historical "choice" is manifest lies in her having been the recipient of the Torah and accordingly summoned to God's service and to disseminating His word and will to the nations. And it is precisely this aspect of *chosenness* that is identified in this composition: "And You sanctified us with Your commandments and drew us close to Your service."

This was never an exclusive club. Anyone could join. And it certainly did not bring with it privilege or license. For, if ever anyone thought that Israel believed herself to be, or indeed was, singled out for privilege and grace, then they should re-read their Jewish history. For to become the "chosen people" was the most invidious and dangerous mission that was ever imposed upon any nation. Israel was resented by, and became a pariah among, the family of nations. It was the latter who confused "chosenness" with "superiority." For Israel, it connoted only service, sacrifice, selflessness, and suffering.

356. But why should Israel have been singled out for suffering, especially when she was only performing her God-given mission of being a light unto the nations?

Raphael Jospe has answered this with an analogy drawn from standards that parents apply to their children.

This perspective on chosenness can perhaps be understood in terms of the standard that parents apply to their children. When the child comes home from school or play, and the parent sees the child has done something wrong, they ask, 'You know that's wrong; why did you do it?' To which, if the child doesn't say, 'I don't know,' he or she often responds, 'But everyone was doing it.' Typically, then, the parent will reply, 'It doesn't matter what everyone else was doing. You are our child, and—having taught you what is correct—we expect more of you.'

The point here is not that the child is, in fact, better than the other children. The parents are telling the child that, because they love him or her, and care especially about him or her, they, therefore, expect more; whatever others may do, they expect their child not to betray their love and trust, but to do what they know is right.[63]

---

63. Jospe, R. (1994). "The Concept of the Chosen People: An Interpretation." *Judaism* 43:139.

YA'ALEH VEYAVO

357. What is the special significance attached to this blessing, to the extent that it is recited on every festival?

It is referred to in the Talmud[64] as the blessing of *me'ein ham'orah*, literally, "conveying the essence of the occasion."

On all the major festivals, a *Musaf Amidah* is recited. This contains references to the additional festival sacrifices offered in the Temple on those occasions and highlights the festival by name. In the Morning Service of the Temple, it was the regular daily sacrifice that was offered; and hence, in our corresponding *Shachrit Amidah*, there would normally be no opportunity for a specific reference to the festival. It was to remedy this that the *Ya'aleh Veyavo* was composed, providing an opportunity to name the specific festival we are celebrating. The same applies to the Grace After Meals, where the *Ya'aleh Veyavo* provides the only reference to the specific festival being celebrated.

358. There are repeated references in the *Ya'aleh Veyavo* to "remembrance" (*zikhron*). What is the connection between this concept and that of festival celebration?

Ya'aleh Veyavo employs a succession of eight verbs to express the basic theme of "remembrance," asking God to remember Israel, the merit of her forefathers, the promise to bring the Messiah, son of David, as well as Jerusalem, the holy city. "Remembrance" is a necessary prerequisite to national deliverance, as the Torah itself makes clear in its promise of redemption: "And I shall *remember* My covenant with Jacob, and also My covenant with Isaac, and also My covenant with Abraham will I *remember*; and I will *remember* the land" (Leviticus 26:42).

Some commentators believe that the fivefold reference to (Israel's) "remembrance" in the *Ya'aleh Veyavo* is intended to correspond with the five times that the term *Israel* is mentioned in Numbers 8:19, in order to signify the warmest degree of endearment. They adduce, by way of illustration, the analogy of a king who, in seeking information of the royal nanny regarding his only infant son, asks proudly, "Did my son sleep, well? Did my son eat his breakfast? Did my son go to school?" and so on. Israel is similarly proud of God's several promises to "remember" her and to redeem her, and from that she has drawn great comfort and faith that the long night of exile would soon come to an end, and God would "remember" his land and reunite His people with it.

The eighth century Gaon, Paltoi, believed that *Ya'aleh Veyavo* was originally composed for the *Zikhronot*, the special "Remembrance" section of the Rosh Hashanah *Musaf* service, which would naturally account for the constant repetition of the word *zikhron* in this composition.

---

64. *Shabbat* 24a.

MODIM ANACHNU LAKH—"WE GIVE THANKS UNTO YOU"

359. What is so significant about this thanksgiving blessing that we bow while reciting both its opening and closing words—*Modim anachnu lakh* and *Barukh attah Ha-shem [ha-tov shimkha . . .]?*

Thanksgiving was considered by our sages as the most important genre of prayer. We commence our *Amidah* with three blessings of praise. But our praise can mean nothing to God, for we cannot have the minutest notion of God's true nature, power, and wisdom, so that our praise is, at best, irrelevant, and at worst a veritable limitation of His true attributes.

We continue our *Amidah* throughout the year with thirteen petitionary blessings. Our great need to petition for so many things merely shows our powerlessness and overwhelming dependence on God.

It is only the *Hoda'ah*, the thanksgiving blessing that introduces the last section of the *Amidah*, that is properly appealing to God. When we offer thanks for benefits received, we hold our heads high. We know and mean what we say. Those are the only blessings that truly *are* blessings, not hollow praise or pathetic pleadings. Our hearts are full when we say "Thank you." No wonder the sages believed that "in the Hereafter all the prayers will be abolished, but the Thanksgiving Blessing will never be abolished."[65]

360. Why, of all the repetition of the *Amidah* blessings, is *Modim* the only one for which a special form of the blessing is prescribed for recitation by the congregation while the *Chazan* is reciting the ordinary *Modim*?

Precisely on account of the significance attributed to the act of thanksgiving by our sages (See Question 359). It was in this way that they demonstrated its paramount importance. It was also regarded as singularly inappropriate for the *Chazan* to be offering thanksgiving on behalf of his congregation while they sat mute. Or, in the words of David Abudarham, "A servant does not customarily give thanks to his master through the agency of an intermediary. Petitions and requests, on the other hand, are frequently entrusted to agents who might have greater influence."[66]

361. Why is the congregation's version referred to as *Modim De-rabbanan*, the "Rabbis' *Modim*"?

Believe it or not, it is simply because it is a composite blessing, a patchwork of various phrases of thanksgiving that different sages of the Talmud each volunteered as significant and as essential to be included in an appropriate thanksgiving prayer.[67]

---

65. Midrash *Vayikra Rabba* 9(7).
66. *Abudarham Ha-Shalem* (1963), p. 115.
67. *Sota* 9b.

The editor, Rav Pappa, not wishing to upset any of his colleagues, simply compromised by weaving all their suggestions into one lengthy blessing!

BIRKAT KOHANIM—THE PRIESTLY BLESSING

362. Why is the Priestly Blessing not endowed with the usual *berakhah* formula, neither at the beginning nor at the end?

Because it is not an independent *Amidah* blessing, but rather a biblical formula. It is not recited in the silent version of the *Amidah* because it is meant to recall the Priestly Blessing of the people, uttered each day in the Temple, which could only be administered in the presence of ten people (a *minyan*).

It is recited at this juncture, just before the *Sim shalom* blessing for peace, because the final word of the Priestly Blessing is, similarly, *shalom*. Another point of textual contact between the two is that the phrase *Ya'er [Ha-Shem] panav* ("May the Lord cause His face to shine"), in the Priestly Blessing, is almost identical with the phrase *[kiy] be'or panekha* in the *Sim Shalom* blessing.

363. What is the precise meaning of the formula of the Priestly Blessing?

Rashi explains it as follows:

May the Lord bless you—"May you be endowed with material prosperity."

And keep you—"And keep your possessions safe from thieves."

May the Lord cause His face to shine upon you—"May He always appear kindly and generous to you."

And be gracious unto you—"May He endow you with grace."

The Lord turn His countenance toward you—"May He supress any anger He might feel toward you."

And grant you peace—*Rashi* does not comment on this final phrase, assuming that Jews know precisely what peace means. Indeed, it is the most cherished objective of Jewish life and the most frequently prayed-for blessing. The *kaddish* prayer, the *Amidah*, and the Grace after Meals all conclude with the line *Oseh shalom bimromav hu ya'aseh shalom aleinu . . .* , "He who makes peace in His celestial regions (that is, the harmonious interaction and motion of the planets), may He bestow peace upon us and upon all Israel."

Shalom (peace) is our age-old, traditonal greeting. We employ it in modern Hebrew to mean both "hello" and "good-bye." It is the special greeting for the Sabbath: *Shabbat shalom*; and, in our mystical tradition, it is even one of the names of God.

364. Is there anything significant about the structure of the Priestly Blessing?

It is interesting to note that the number of words in the three lines of the blessing proceed from three in the first line, to five in the second, and seven in the final line. All three numbers are, of course, significant numbers in Jewish tradition, and the total number of fifteen words is especially so (See Question 306). The divine name occurs in the identical position—the second word—in each line.

365. Why is it that in Israel the priests perform their duty of blessing the people during the *Shachrit* repetition as well as *Musaf*, whereas in the Diaspora this is not performed at *Shachrit*?

This is because in Israel the Priestly Blessing is performed every single day during the repetition of the *Shachrit Amidah*. It is consistent, therefore, that they should also perform it at that point on festivals, even though they will do so again to *Musaf*. It was not considered an unnecessary repetition of a blessing since it was accepted that many people, potential recipients of that blessing, and especially women and children, would arrive late at the service, having missed the Priestly Blessing at *Shachrit*, thereby justifying its repetition at *Musaf*.

As regards the Diaspora communities, who do not recite the Priestly Blessing daily at the *Shachrit* service, there was no reason to do so on festivals, but rather to delay it until *Musaf*, by which time all worshipers would have arrived.

366. At this point, the conclusion of the repetition of the *Shachrit Amidah*, we recite *Hallel* on all other festivals (except Purim). Why is it omitted on Rosh Hashanah and Yom Kippur?

The reason given in the Talmud is that "it is inconceivable, at a time when the books of life and death are open, and the king occupies the throne of strict justice, that Israel should sing such praises."[68]

Underlying that statement is a significant distinction between the High Holy Days and the other festivals. The latter are predominantly historical and, therefore, commemorative. The spirit of such festivals is generated by means of the act of reliving the past and celebrating the history of our people at that early biblical stage of their national evolution. We look back with pride, and celebrate the redemptive process that brought us out of Egypt (on *Pesach*) to Sinai (on *Shavuot*), and on, through the desert (on Sukkot), to the Promised Land. We celebrate all that by reciting joyous and vigorous *Hallel* psalms, which lyrically recall that glorious chapter in our history—*Betzeit Yisrael mi-Mitzrayim*—"When Israel came up out of Egypt."

While those "*Hallel* festivals" look *backward*, Rosh Hashanah and Yom Kippur are primarily concerned with looking forward, to our acceptance of a future set of values that will be spiritualized and refined through the soul-transforming experience that these special days of awe engender and the resolve that they inspire.

---

68. *Arakhin* 10b.

Realistically speaking, however, our ability to achieve such a permanent self-transformation in the future must remain uncertain, and we are troubled by the possibility that we will not be able to translate into practice all the spiritual challenges of these days. It follows, therefore, that any such *Hallel* celebration is, at this time, rather premature and overconfident.

Hence, although Rosh Hashanah and Yom Kippur are certainly days for quiet confidence, what Maimonides calls *simchah yeteirah*, "extraordinary celebration,"[69] the likes of which *Hallel* symbolizes and expresses, is decidedly inappropriate.

AVINU MALKEINU

367. What is the origin of the *Avinu Malkeinu* prayer?

The kernel of it goes back to Talmudic times when the formula was first employed by Rabbi Akivah while officiating as *Chazan* at a special service of intercession for rain during a period of prolonged drought. The immediate heavenly response convinced the people that it was his particular mode of appeal that was the key to unlocking the gates of mercy. The result was that, while R. Akivah's *Avinu Malkeinu* contained but five lines, subsequent authorities and *Chazanim* expanded the prayer to suit their particular needs and emotions. Hence, while the Sephardi version has twenty-nine lines, the Ashkenazi rite has thirty-eight, and the Polish rite has forty-four. The great nineteenth-century liturgist, Seligman Isaac Baer, in his famous commentary on the siddur, *Yakhin Lashon*,[70] testifies to having seen as many as fifty-three variants in the prayer books and manuscripts he consulted!

368. Why do we not recite *Avinu Malkeinu* if Rosh Hashanah falls on *Shabbat*?

Basically, because it is patterned not on the Rosh Hashanah *Amidah* but on the intermediate petitionary blessings of the weekday *Amidah*, with a direct correspondence of phraseology between the two. A few examples will suffice:

Avinu Malkeinu	*Weekday Amidah*
Choneinu va'aneinu	*Chonein ha-da'at*
Hachazireinu bitshuvah sheleima	*Ha-rotzeh bitshuvah*
Selach umechal lekhol avonoteinu	*Selach lanu*
Kotveinu besefer ge'ulah	*Go'eil yisrael*
Shelach refuah sheleimah	*Veha'alei refuah sheleimah*
Chadesh aleinu shanah tovah	*Bareikh aleinu et ha-shanah hazot . . . letovah*

---

69. Maimonides, *Mishneh Torah, Hilkhot Chanukah* 3:6.
70. Baer, S. I. (1937). *Siddur Avodat Yisrael*, p. 109, and commentary, *Yakhin Lashon ad loc.*

369. But why should the fact that there is this correspondence of phraseology constitute such a barrier to its recitation?

Because we have a principle that we do not petition for personal needs on Sabbaths and festivals, and for this reason the entire middle section of thirteen petitionary blessings recited on weekdays is replaced on Sabbaths and festivals by one blessing (*Kedushat Ha-Yom*) dealing with the sanctity of the day. On these occasions, we are supposed to focus on the spiritual blessings that we have had bestowed upon us—such as the holy rest days—and not on the things that we lack and need to petition for.

There is also another objection to its recitation on a *Shabbat*, raised by the *Orchot Chayyim*, and that is that this prayer was originally introduced by Rabbi Akivah for recitation on public fast days, and no public fasting is permitted on the Sabbath.[71]

370. Is the *Avinu Malkeinu* not unusual in that it constitutes a confession, and our Rosh Hashanah prayers do not seem to contain any other such confession?

It is, indeed, unique in this respect. We do not wish to draw God's attention at this time to all the sins we have perpetrated. We credit Him with knowing them all too well! And for this reason, we do not recite the *Al Chet* catalogue of sins on Rosh Hashanah.

The *Avinu Malkeinu* opens up with a confessionary statement: "Our father, our King, we have sinned before Thee." This is certainly not in harmony with the atmosphere of *Yom Tov*, of contented and humble confidence that God will indeed forgive all our sins, which should be the overriding emotion of this day. And this is a further reason why Ashkenazim, based upon the ruling of R. Moses Isserles,[72] do not recite the *Avinu Malkeinu* if Rosh Hashanah falls on a Sabbath. To recite confessions of sin on a Sabbath would convert a day of spiritual joy into one of existential *angst*.

71. Yoseph, O. (1977). *Yechaveh Daat*. Jerusalem: Porat Yosef and Makhon Yemshalayim Academies, pp. 155–161; also, Cohen, J. M. *Prayer and Penitence*, p. 270, note 88.

72. *Remah* on *Shulchan Arukh Orach Chayyim* 584:1.

XI

Reading of the Torah
and *Haftarah* for the First Day

371. What is the theme of the reading of the Torah for the first day of Rosh Hashanah?

The reading is taken from Genesis chapter 21, which describes the birth of Isaac, a child of his parents' old age. It describes the unsurpassed joy in the household of Abraham and Sarah, and the great feast that Abraham made to mark the weaning of his son. Weaning in the ancient Near East was usually delayed until at least 2 years after birth. There is a reference in the Talmud[1] to weaning after 4 or 5 years, though in Egypt and Mesopotamia 3 years was quite normal.

It goes on to relate the evil influence that Ishmael—offspring of Abraham and his handmaid, Hagar—exerted on Isaac, and Sarah's determination that Ishmael be banished from their home. Abraham is, naturally, most reluctant to banish his son, but God appears to him and bids him carry out Sarah's wishes, assuring him that Ishmael will survive to become a great nation.

Hagar and Ishmael leave and make a lonely and hazardous journey into the desert. Their water is used up, and Ishmael faints. Hagar weeps as she lays her son under some bushes and prepares to leave, not wishing to witness his death. At that, an angel appears and, promising divine protection and guidance, shows Hagar a well of water, at which she is able to refill her water flask and revive her son. Ishmael grows up to become an archer and settles down with his Egyptian wife to realize the divine promise.

The reading goes on to describe Abraham's growing confidence now that his posterity is assured. This is clearly exemplified in the fact that he does not shrink from chiding the Philistine king, Avimelech, whose servants had seized a well of water belonging to Abraham. Abraham is possessed of such great wealth and such a vast tribal entourage that this neighboring monarch is eager to conclude a peace treaty with him. The ritual that accompanies the forging of this alliance includes the presentation by Abraham of a gift of seven lambs to the king. Abraham accordingly (re)names the site of their treaty *Be'er Sheva* (Beer-sheba), "well of seven," or "well

---
1. *Ketubot* 60a.

187

of the oath." Abraham settles in Philistia for many years, thus underscoring the strength of their alliance.

372. What is the relevance of this reading for Rosh Hashanah?

There is no overt association between the reading for the first day and any of the major themes of the festival. Indeed, it would seem that this portion is read on the first day purely as a contextual prelude to the main reading, the story of the binding of Isaac (*Akedah*), which follows on from it in the Torah and which is one of the most prominent themes of Rosh Hashanah.

Nevertheless, the Talmud[2] provides the point of contact when it tells us that the conception of Isaac, with which the reading commences, took place on Rosh Hashanah. This was the day when "God remembered Sarah."

373. Is there any other association between the reading for the first day and the theme of Rosh Hashanah?

We may detect another hidden message, as contained in the opening verse: the message of faith that God always fulfills His promises and that the moment He chooses is the right moment in the context of Israel's unfolding destiny. Abraham and Sarah had to wait for their child until they were, respectively, 100 years old and 90 years old. They must have long given up hope; but God knew when the time was right. He "remembered" Sarah and performed what for her was the impossible—a pregnancy at that age.

But God demonstrated to them—and to us—that nothing is impossible for God, that man's destiny is in His hands, and, in the words of Maimonides' article of faith, *Ani Ma'amin*, "Even though it may tarry, nevertheless I shall wait patiently for it." This is also the purpose of Rosh Hashanah: to reinforce that faith in God, to emphasize that we are all in His hands, and to affirm that, if we are deserving, God will "remember" it to our merit and our reward. Faith, prayer, righteous living, and patience ultimately wrest blessing from the divine grip. Despair and loss of faith put it even further from our reach.

374. Is there any association between the episode of Hagar and an aspect of Rosh Hashanah?

There is the message of never despairing of God's redemptive power. Hagar had given up hope of her child's survival. She was in a desert, and the flask was empty. She could be forgiven, of course, for having lost her faith in that situation. But the message is that she was foolish to have done so. She trusted implicitly in her own limited sight and unsafe instinct; and hence she despaired. She failed, however, to realize that, if God chooses, He can "open our eyes," enabling us to find salvation close to hand where we least expected it. It is that conviction that Rosh Hashanah comes to engender and inspire.

---

2. *Rosh Hashanah* 10b–11a.

375. Are there any thematic links between the reading for the first day and that of the second?

Indeed. We detect seven main parallels between our reading for the first day and that for the second. First, in both chapters we are told that, *Vayashkeim Avraham baboker*, "Abraham rose up early in the morning" (Genesis 21:14; 22:3)—to respond readily and zealously to God's instruction. In the first day's reading, it is to provide the provisions for Hagar and to see her off on her way; in the second day's reading, it is to saddle his ass and prepare the requirements for his own three-day journey to sacrifice his son. So both days' readings convey the message of dutiful and ready responsiveness to whatever religious mission we feel called to perform or duties our tradition requires of us. This is assuredly one of the aims of the Rosh Hashanah experience.

A second, close parallel between the two readings is that, in both, two young people escape death by a divine intervention. Ishmael escapes death, in the first day's reading, when the angel appears to his mother; Isaac escapes execution in the reading for the second day when an angel intervenes with his father.

Thirdly, in both passages, God makes a promise regarding the future expansion and greatness of the nations of which Ishmael and Isaac, respectively, are to be the progenitors. Ishmael, Hagar is told, "will become a great nation" (Genesis 21:18); Isaac's line, Abraham is told, will "become as numerous as the stars of the heaven and like sand on the seashore; and . . . shall inherit the gate of its enemy." Abraham is told further that "all the nations of the earth shall bless themselves by your offspring" (Genesis 22:17).

A fourth parallel is that, in both instances, God reveals something that the respective parents had not previously noticed. Hagar is vouchsafed the vision of a well of water, and Abraham notices "a ram caught in the thickets by its horns."

Fifthly, in both passages, Abraham gives a special name to the place that had become significant for him. In the first day's reading he names it *Be'er Sheva*; in the second day's episode, he calls the scene of the *Akedah* experience *Ha-Shem Yireh*.

A sixth parallel is that, in both passages, *Be'er Sheva* figures as the place where the final act of the event is played out. In the first day's reading, we are told that, after the treaty with Avimelech, Abraham plants a tamarisk tree in *Be'er Sheva* (21:33); and, on returning to his lads at the conclusion of the *Akedah*, we are told that "they arose and went together to *Be'er Sheva*" (Genesis 22:19).

Finally, both episodes conclude by describing where Abraham took up residence. In the first day's reading, we are told, "And Abraham sojourned in the land of the Philistines many days" (21:34). In the second day's reading, it is stated that "Abraham dwelt at *Be'er Sheva*" (22:19).

376. Is there any moral link between the two episodes?

One cannot help but wonder whether it is more than a matter of coincidence or even chronology that the two episodes—the banishment of Ishmael and the binding of Isaac—should have been juxtaposed to each other. Perhaps the anguish that Abraham, albeit unwillingly, caused Hagar and Ishmael during their banishment had to be atoned for in a similar way—"measure for measure" (*midah keneged midah*)—by Abraham and his beloved son.

Just as Hagar and Ishmael roamed in the desert, so Abraham and Isaac had to travel for 3 days to an unknown destination. God simply told Abraham that he should travel "to the land of Moriah and offer him there upon one of the mountains that I shall tell you of" (Genesis 22:2). And just as the journey for Hagar and Ishmael was physically overwhelming, so for Abraham and Isaac it must have been emotionally so. After all, the unspoken question—that Isaac only summoned the courage to ask after 3 days had elapsed—must have hung like a pall over father and son: "I see the fire and the wood; but where is the lamb for the burnt offering?" (verse 7). Isaac was no fool. He must have detected the fear and anxiety in his father's eyes. He must have known that the neighboring tribes practiced child sacrifice, and there was no reason for him to think, or know, that his father's God did not demand the same! Those three days must have been the longest and the most turbulent in the lives and relationship of Abraham and Isaac. No wonder that Isaac appears as a shadowy figure throughout the few episodes that are recorded about his subsequent life, and his father, on his return, feels that he cannot survive for much longer. His preoccupation is hitherto with burying his wife and ensuring that his son is provided with a worthy wife to continue the dynasty and fulfill God's promise.

So, the events of those three days of the *Akedah* clearly traumatized both Abraham and Isaac; and the conclusion seems inescapable that those two events that we read about on the two days of Rosh Hashanah are, in fact, cause and effect. No more graphic illustration of reward and punishment—one of the key themes of this festival—could be found than the one suggested by the relationship between the Torah readings for the two days.

377. But why should Abraham have been punished when we are told that God actually instructed him to listen to Sarah's voice and banish Ishmael (Genesis 21:12)?

It is not for us to theorize about what sin our father Abraham might have been guilty of, or to try and fathom God's mode of reward and punishment. We are entitled, however, to utilize the information the Torah actually provides for us and to build a theory on that basis. It might have been that Abraham was being made to suffer for Sarah's ill-treatment of Hagar years before, during the latter's pregnancy.

We are told (Genesis chapter 16) that Sarah (at that time still called Sarai), on realizing that she was barren, gave her handmaid, Hagar, as a wife to Abraham (as yet called Abram), so that any children born from that union would be able to be brought up by her and nourish thereby her maternal yearnings. However, when Hagar saw that she was pregnant, she adopted an attitude of contempt for, and superiority over, her barren mistress. Sarah complained bitterly to Abraham who effectively gave his wife *carte blanche* to do whatever she wanted to Hagar. "And Sarai so afflicted her that she fled from before her" (verse 6).

One of our classical commentators, Moses Nachmanides, states categorically that "Sarah, our mother, sinned thereby." He could have added that guilt must also have attached to Abraham—the one who gave permission for such physical violence to be administered. So, if we are looking for a reason why Abraham should have had the trial of the *Akedah* inflicted upon him, we need look no further. (For more on the *Akedah*, see Questions 388–437.)

378. What is the sense of the rather vague statement, in our first day's reading, that Sarah gave birth "at the season (*la-mo'ed*) which God had forecast" (Genesis 21:2)?

The word *la-mo'ed* harks back to the visit of the three angels to Abraham (Genesis chapter 18), when Abraham was told by one of them that he would return "at the appropriate time (*la-mo'ed*) and Sarah would have a child" (verse 14). *Rashi* states that this identical word is employed again, to record Isaac's birth, in order to demonstrate that Sarah went full term, that is 9 months from the date of the angels' visit. This was in order to stifle mischief-spreaders who, knowing that Sarah could never previously conceive from Abraham, and knowing also that, recently, and subsequent to the visit of the angels, she had been detained by the King Avimelech (Genesis chapter 20), put two and two together and spread abroad the malicious report that Sarah had been made pregnant by the king.[3]

379. Is it not strange that Sarah, after having been reprimanded by God for having laughed derisively at the angel who brought the news of her pregnancy (Genesis 18:12–15), should behave in the identical way after she actually gives birth?

It is indeed true that the Torah employs the identical phraseology in both contexts. On receiving news of her pregnancy we are told that "Sarah laughed within her (*Vatitzchak Sarah*)." God then asks Abraham, "Why has Sarah laughed (*tzachakah*) in this way?" (18:12–13).

Now, on the birth of Isaac, we are told that "Sarah said God has made me a *tzechok*; all who hear will *yitzchak* at me."

It does look rather suspiciously as if Sarah has fallen into the same trap and is expressing her embarrassment at having a baby at such an advanced age of 90 years. It does rather look as if we should translate the word *tzechok* as "a laughing stock," and the second phrase as, "all who hear will laugh at me."

This is not, however, how the traditional commentators render it. Thus *Targum Onkelos*, the official Aramaic translation of the Talmudic sages, renders the verse, "And Sarah said: 'God has *bestowed* joy upon me; all who hear *will rejoice* with me.'"[4] This interpretation might well have been based on the view that Sarah, knowing how her original skepticism was received by God and how she was forced to cover it up by denying to her husband that she had laughed (Genesis 18:15), would hardly have been foolish enough to fall into the same trap.

---

3. *Rashi* on Genesis 21:2.
4. *Targum Onkelos* on Genesis 20:6.

Be that as it may, it begs the question of why the Torah proceeded to employ that identical verb *yitzachak* and its noun *tzechok*, with their clear nuance and their ready association with the previous context where their meaning is unequivocal.

For those who feel that this verbal linkage cannot be denied, and with it the conclusion that Sarah was indeed repeating her mixed feelings of happiness and embarrassment, support may be obtained from another Targumic tradition, the *Targum Yonatan*, which translates the verse, "And Sarah said, 'God has made me an object of astonishment; all who hear will be astonished by me.' "[5]

So, the textual evidence would seem to support the view that Sarah was, indeed, laughing ruefully at her predicament. This is further supported by the use of the identical verb, *metzachek*, only three verses on (Genesis 21:9), to describe the mocking demeanor of Ishmael, which was the reason why it met with the decision to banish him from Abraham's home.

As to why Sarah was apparently so foolhardy as to repeat her previously censured behavior, we may but speculate that she had no choice. She reacted instinctively. Perhaps it was the effect of giving birth at such an age that sent her hormones into turmoil so that she was not in control of her emotions. This might also explain why, significantly this time, no censure is forthcoming.

380. According to *Targum Onkelos* and the many commentators who understand the phrase *kol hashome'a yitzachak liy* as "all who hear will rejoice with me," why, we may ask, should Sarah have been so certain that everyone would be so happy for her?

The Midrash asks the same question, rather pithily—"If Reuven is happy, what does Shimon care?"[6]

The answer that it gives is to quote the tradition that when Sarah became pregnant, scores of other barren women were blessed through her merit. In addition, scores of sick people were healed, scores of deaf people regained their hearing, scores of blind people their sight, scores of mentally unstable people their sanity. A veritable amnesty for the sick of the world was declared."[7] Hence Sarah's certainty that absolutely everyone would share in the joy of her pregnancy.

381. We mentioned above (Question 379) that the decision to banish Ishmael was on account of the fact that Sarah saw him *metzachek*, "mocking" Isaac. How exactly do our sages understand Ishmael's crime?

They certainly understand the word *metzachek* as a euphemism for something far more heinous than mere mockery, which would hardly have justified such a strong measure as banishment.

Rabbi Akivah understood it as referring to the fact that Ishmael was indulging in the practice of idolatry in Abraham's home. This was rejected vehemently by his

---

5. *Targum Yonatan* on Genesis 20:6.
6. *Rashi* on Genesis 21:9. See also the critique of *Ramban* in his comment on this verse.
7. Midrash *Bereshit Rabba* Chapter 53; Midrash *Tanchuma* on *Toldot*.

colleague R. Shimon bar Yochai—"Heaven forfend that Abraham would have tolerated that!"

R. Levi's answer is provided Midrashically—"Ishmael said to Isaac: 'Let us go out to father's estates and survey our future inheritance.' Once there, Ishmael took a bow and arrow, and shot it at Isaac, though making out that he was only playing. When Sarah saw that, she told Abraham [of her fears for the safety of her son]."[8]

382. The latter are, of course, Midrashic traditions. Is there any other literal sense of the participle *metzachek* that might offer a fresh insight into Ishmael's heinous crime?

The Torah occasionally uses the participle *metzachek* ("playing") as a euphemism for sexual foreplay. Hence, on their arrival at the Philistine capital city of Gerar, Isaac had made out that his wife, Rebecca, was, in fact, his sister. This was a precautionary deception that his father, Abraham, had used before him and was in order to save his life if the monarch should decide to seize his wife. After some time, the King Avimelech was looking out of his window, "and he saw Isaac *metzachek* with Rebecca his wife" (Genesis 26:8).

The identical verb is used again by the wife of Potiphar to frame Joseph after he had spurned her sexual overtures: "The Hebrew servant whom you brought to us came in to me *letzachek* with me" (Genesis 39:14). So there are strong grounds to assume that the crime of Ishmael lay in the area of immoral behavior.

The Torah does not actually state that Ishmael was *metzachek* "with Isaac," so there are no strong grounds for assuming that he was seen by Sarah interfering sexually with his much younger half-brother. She may well have come across him in uncompromising situations with the maid servants on Abraham's estates.

383. What is the sense of the rather vague assurance to Hagar that "God has listened to the voice of the lad where he is now (*ba'asher hu sham*)"?

The Talmud explains this to mean that, although God foresees the future and knew, therefore, just how wicked Ishmael would turn out to be in later life, at that particular moment, at the youthful stage where he was (*ba'asher hu sham*), he had not yet chalked up such a volume of sin as to forfeit God's redemption.

The Talmud expresses it rather graphically:

Ba'asher hu sham—According to his present deeds, not what he will do in the future. For the Ministering Angels denounced him, saying, 'Master of the Universe, are You going to raise a well for the very one whose seed is destined to destroy Your (Israelite) children by thirst?'[9] But God answered: 'Now, what

---

8. Midrash *Bereshit Rabba* Chapter 53.

9. The attempt of Ishmael to destroy Israel by thirst was when Israel was being led into exile by the Babylonians. The Ishmaelites came out and offered the Israelites meat and salted fish. They also provided them with blown-up skin bottles that the Israelites thought were filled with water, with which to slake their thirst. When they put it to their mouths and sucked in, the air entered their lungs and killed them.

is he? Righteous or wicked?' 'Righteous,' they replied. 'Then I shall judge him according to his present deeds—*ba'sher hu sham*,' said God.[10]

384. Is there any other general message that may be derived from the Reading of the Law for the first day?

There is the overall message of God's universal concern for all His creatures. Man may cast out his fellow—in the same way as Ishmael was banished from his home—but God will never abandon His creatures. He may have selected Isaac as the repository of His spiritual message to the world, but Ishmael is still an object of His loving concern. This message is reinforced in the story of Jonah, read on Yom Kippur, where God demonstrates to the prophet that *all* men are worthy of salvation and that God hears the cries of *all* men when they issue forth from a truly contrite heart.

THE *HAFTARAH* FOR THE FIRST DAY

385. What is the connection between the *Haftarah* and the Torah portion for the first day?

The *Haftarah* describes the domestic life of the family of Elkanah, which parallels in a number of aspects the situation in the household of Abraham.

First, just as Abraham had two rival wives whose relationship was marked by acrimony, so did Elkanah's wives, Hannah and Peninah, bicker continuously with each other. Just as Sarah was barren for years and desperately longed for a child, so did Hannah. Just as Hagar, when she became pregnant, mocked at her mistress's barrenness, so did Peninah "provoke her rival wife [Hannah] to anger."

The Talmudic sages offer another link between the episodes of Sarah and Hannah by stating that both women conceived on Rosh Hashanah.[11]

386. During which period in Israelite history is the story of Hannah set?

It is set toward the end of the period of the judges (*circa* 1050 B.C.E.). The child that Hannah was blessed with was Samuel, who was the last of the judges of Israel before the monarchy was established. Indeed, Samuel was the one commanded by God to annoint Saul as the first king of Israel.

To place this period into a historical context, it might be helpful to provide some chronological data:[12]

This is inferred by the Midrash (*Tanchuma* on *Yitro* sec. 5) from a rather vague and concise reference in Isaiah 21:13–14.

10. *Rosh Hashanah* 16b.

11. *Megillah* 31a.

12. With some minor adjustment, we follow here the chronological table contained in Bright, J. (1964). *A History of Israel*. London: SCM Press Ltd., pp. 463–465.

1900–1750 B.C.E.:   The period of the Patriarchs
1650–1300 B.C.E.:   The Hebrews in Egypt
circa 1280 B.C.E.:   The Exodus from Egypt
1240–1200 B.C.E.:   The conquest of Palestine under Joshua
1200–1020 B.C.E.:   The period of the judges
1020–1000 B.C.E.:   The reign of King Saul

387. How do the events described in the *Haftarah* unfold?

We are told that Hannah and Peninah's husband, Elkanah, would make an annual pilgrimage to the central sanctuary, which, at that early period before the building of the Temple at Jerusalem, was located at Shilo. On that special occasion, he would bestow gifts on his two wives. To Peninah and her sons and daughters he would gift special "portions"—probably of food delicacies; but to his favored wife, Hannah, he would give "a double portion." This was probably to assuage her anguish at seeing her rival, Peninah, celebrating the festival surrounded by all her offspring, while she, Hannah, had no one. This was aggravated by the fact that Peninah would utilize this occasion each year to slight Hannah and mock her barrenness. Elkanah's assurance that his love for her was surely worth that of ten children was insufficient to stem the flow of her tears.

One year, she decided to visit the sanctuary and to offer there a special and fervent prayer to God. She entered, though without noticing that the High Priest, Eli, was sitting there in the shadows in silent meditation. Hannah wept and prayed, and took a vow that if God favored her with a male child, she would devote him to the service of God all the days of his life.

Eli observed Hannah who, because she was so choked up with her overwhelming grief, was not able to invest her pleading with any sound—"only her lips moved but her voice could not be heard." Eli became aware of her presence, and, because it was highly unusual for people—and especially unaccompanied women—to come there and offer private prayers, he mistakenly took her for a drunkard and chided her on that account.

Hannah told Eli that he had seriously misjudged her and explained that "it is on account of my bitterness of spirit and my anguish that I have been praying in that [strange] way." Eli, rather shame-faced, tells her to go in peace and adds the prayer that "the God of Israel should grant you your petition." By the time Elkanah went to Shilo the following year, Hannah's prayer had been answered. She called the son born to her, *Shemuel* (Samuel), which is a contraction of the words *sha'ul me'El*, "requested of the Lord."

The next time the festival came around, Hannah did not accompany her husband, telling him that she preferred to wait until she had weaned her son. Two years later, she makes the pilgrimage, introduces her son to Eli, and formally presents him to the sanctuary to be brought up, educated, and trained as a future prophet, judge, and leader of Israel.

This time, Hannah more than compensates for the loss of voice on her previous visit. She breaks forth into a majestic song of praise, faith, and hope in God, whose main theme is the greatness of God, His ultimate vindication of the cause of the righteous, and how faith can succeed in making barren women fruitful and in "raising the needy from the dungheaps to sit among princes."

XII

Reading of the Torah (The *Akedah*) and the *Haftarah* for the Second Day; *Yekum Purkan*; Prayer for the Government

388. What is the outline story of the *Akedah*, which we read on the second day of Rosh Hashanah?

It is the story of God's command to Abraham to take Isaac and offer him up as a sacrifice at a place God would disclose, some three days' journey from his home.

Abraham responds without complaint and sets out on his mission, together with Isaac and two of his servants. On the third day, he leaves the servants behind and takes Isaac up into the hills, arriving at the place where God directs him. He binds Isaac on the altar, and, as he takes his knife and raises it to kill his son, an angel calls out to him and bids him stay his hand: "For now I know that you are a God-fearing man, since you have not withheld your son, your only one, from me" (Genesis 22:12).

At that point, Abraham notices a ram caught in the thickets by its horns, and he offers that as a sacrifice instead of his son. He then receives a second heavenly message that, on account of his merit in having been prepared to sacrifice his son, God will make Abraham's offspring as numerous as the stars of the heaven and the sand grains on the shores, and, through them, all the nations of the earth will be blessed.

389. Why do we read the *Akedah* on Rosh Hashanah?

We have already referred to the fact that, according to tradition, Sarah conceived on Rosh Hashanah (See Question 372). Another reason is that the "third day" (Genesis 22:4) of Abraham's journey to the *Akedah* coincided with the first day of Tishri, which is Rosh Hashanah (*Avudraham*). Naturally, there is also the dramatic association of the ram used by Abraham as a substitute for Isaac with the shofar blown on this festival. The shofar serves, therefore, not only as a summons to penitence, but also as a call to God to find some substitute for us if we are similarly found to be deserving of forfeiture of our lives.

390. What could have been God's purpose in making such a demand of Abraham?

The *Akedah* imposed upon Abraham the greatest of dilemmas: the choice between his God and his son. No situation could probe more thoroughly the extent of a person's belief in a God whose existence is beyond doubt and whose moral will is beyond question.

Of course, Abraham had been the recipient of several divine revelations and communications. God had bidden him leave his parental home in Mesopotamia and journey to Canaan where he would make him into a great nation (Genesis 12:1). He had appeared to him at the "Covenant between the pieces" (Genesis chapter 15) and confirmed that promise. He had disclosed to him the new significance with which circumcision would hitherto be invested, as "an eternal covenant" between God and Israel (Genesis 17:7). He had also sent angels to heal Abraham and to foretell the birth of a child to him (Genesis chapter 18).

On all these occasions, Abraham was the recipient of benefits, actual or promised. He could well have assumed, therefore, that there is an immediate correlation between righteousness and reward. The *Akedah* was the very first real "trial," in the sense that the righteous man was being taught that cause and effect is not applied so manifestly in the context of God's dealings with man. Abraham was being shown that suffering is frequently the essential anvil upon which true faith is forged. In order to fully appreciate, empathize with, and pray for the relief of the suffering of others, the righteous man has to experience it himself.

At the last moment, Abraham's anguish was relieved; but his experience of nearly having lost his son and, worse still, at having been selected to be the instrument of his son's sacrifice, was to remain with him for the rest of his life. No longer was Abraham merely the man who offered token hospitality to others. No longer was he merely the exemplar of *chesed*, of charity and benevolence to others. He—and the son who had shared that faith and sacrifice with him—represented, forever after, the Jewish people's primary characteristic of being "merciful children of merciful parents."

The test of Abraham and the sacrifice of Isaac foreshadowed the fate of the Israelites and the Jewish people down the ages. The cry, "My God, my God, why have you slain me?" has resonated down the ages and pages of Jewish history. And the enigmatic prophecy of Ezekiel, "You will live by your blood," has remained the haunting and unfathomable dilemma of the Jewish people. It is a fate that Abraham had himself to undergo if ever he was to lay claim to being the founding father of the Jewish people. And it was a trial that he had to come through in order to mediate to his offspring the faith, courage, and determination to survive trials six million fold that of his own.

391. But why does the Torah describe it, at the outset, as God "testing Abraham"? Surely it was as much a test of Isaac, who, an adult, could well have resisted what his old father was doing to him, and escaped, but who, instead, displayed a unique degree of resignation to God's will?

Rabbi Isaac Arama (fifteenth century) in his *Akedat Yitzchak*, answers by means of a parable:

A thief was once apprehended, but refused to admit to the crime. The judges commanded that he be whipped until he confessed, but he resisted the most intense whipping. The judges then commanded that the thief's son be brought in, and they started whipping the son. The child cried out in terrible pain: 'Daddy, stop them; I can't take any more!' Whereupon the thief immediately confessed.

When asked subsequently about it, the thief disclosed that he had made up his mind, before committing the crime, that even if they subsequently apprehended him and beat him to death, he was never going to own up to having committed the crime. But he never ever bargained, he said, for the judges bringing in his beloved son and afflicting such agony on him. That he just could not bear to watch. And that prompted him to confess.

It was the same with the *Akedah*. Abraham was so imbued with faith that he was prepared to accept whatever God inflicted upon him, even death itself should that be demanded. But it never occurred to Abraham that God would demand the life of his son! His own life, yes; but never that of his son! And surely not that he, Abraham, should have to be the one to take that life!

Nevertheless, he was still able to summon the deepest reserves of courage and faith, to put his feelings aside, and obey the summons. That, indeed, was 'the test' of Abraham, the test of a father who has to witness in silence the shock and pain of his son, and the look of incredulity, horror and silent condemnation in his son's eyes as he watched his father surrendering him to execution. That was God's test of Abraham, more than that of Isaac.[1]

392. So was it, in any way, a test of Isaac?

As we have observed, Isaac was not a child at the time of the *Akedah*. The chronology of events suggests that he was already a man of 37. He could well have forcefully resisted. He was young and much stronger than his father. He could have escaped. He could have pleaded with his father that the God who had revealed Himself to him was so morally perfect that, unlike the idolatries of the Middle East, He would surely never have demanded the sacrifice of a human being. He could put doubts into Abraham's mind in that way as to whether or not the instruction to him was the authentic voice of God.

The fact that he did not resist his father, but submitted to the *Akedah*, notwithstanding the many doubts he may well have entertained, speaks volumes for

---

1. Arama, I. *Akedat Yitzchak* on Genesis 22:1.

his awe for, and total trust in, his father's judgment. A son who could throw himself so totally on the mercy of his father is also a worthy progenitor and patriarch of a nation called upon throughout their history to throw themselves so unreservedly upon the mercy of their Father in heaven.

It was, indeed, therefore, a great test of Isaac, albeit not quite as traumatic as for his father, Abraham.

393. How do we answer the basic question of why the All-Knowing God had to subject Abraham to a "test" when He surely knew that the righteous man, with whom He had already forged an "eternal covenant," would come through the test with his faith intact?

This is a question addressed by our classical commentators. Ibn Ezra,[2] after analyzing and rejecting a number of explanations, concludes that the test was, simply, in order that Abraham should merit to acquire reward for his righteousness. This is amplified by Nachmanides who states that the reward for "applied righteousness" of necessity far exceeds that for "potential righteousness." As long as Abraham had not been put to the test, his reward was that offered to one with "a good heart," that is, with the potential to display great faith and sacrifice. But once he had been put through a traumatic trial of his faith, he then earned the infinitely greater reward offered for the actuality of "a good deed."[3]

394. How do we explain the fact that the God Who abjured human sacrifice nevertheless chose to utilize that abomination as a means of testing Abraham?

Ibn Ezra quotes a view[4] that when God told Abraham "*ha'aleihu* there on one of the mountains" (Genesis 22:2), it does not mean "offer him up," as generally rendered, but simply, "take him up." In other words, God never gave any instruction at all to sacrifice Isaac, merely to take him up; and the obedience to that instruction, as far as God was concerned, would be tantamount to Abraham's having offered him up. Abraham, however, did not appreciate the subtlety of that symbolic instruction and assumed that the *ha'aleihu* instruction implied the command to "offer him up." Thus, when Abraham took out his knife, God was constrained to intervene and assure him that this was not His intention.

Another answer to our question, and a popular way of interpreting the *Akedah*, is that its primary objective was to teach Abraham the precise message that the religion he was embracing differed from all the other religions of the Near East in its abomination of child sacrifice. Because human sacrifice was such an ingrained institution, God had to make such a major issue of it and demonstrate in as dramatic a way as possible its unacceptability.

---

2. Ibn Ezra on Genesis 22:1.

3. *Peirush Ha-Ramban* on Genesis 22:1.

4. This view is found in the Midrash and is actually quoted by Rashi in his comment on 22:12.

395. We have referred to the *Akedah* as a test of either Abraham or Isaac. Is there any other way of viewing it?

Sidney Breitbart[5] has suggested that, in the final analysis, it represents a test of God! Abraham is shown as having developed, with each subsequent encounter with God, not only a growing religious confidence, but also a more mature and perceptive religious outlook. Indeed, the divine plan is for him to assume an active participation in the man–God dialogue, and hence his presumption in chiding God with the words, "Will you sweep away the innocent with the guilty?" (Genesis 18:23), "Shall the judge of the whole earth not deal justly?" (18:25). The *Akedah* could not have been a test of Abraham's faith because Abraham had passed that test, notably when he complied with God's first command to leave his father's home and country and journey into the unknown.

Now, Breitbart suggests, Abraham felt himself caught on the horns of a dilemma when God commanded him to sacrifice his son. He knew instinctively that this was not a straightforward command, one that he was expected to comply with by God, but rather a moral obstacle that was being thrown in his path in order for him to tackle in a way that would deepen and develop further his understanding of God's ways. Indeed, the three days' journey may well have been an opportunity provided by God for Abraham to agonize over how he should respond.

Abraham's dilemma was straightforward: He had come to know God as a God of justice and mercy. This certainly excluded any possibility that He would want Abraham to take literally His command to him to sacrifice an innocent child. And yet, God had, indeed, expressed such an instruction! So how could he ignore it and undermine God's authority? Furthermore, God had promised him that this son would become a great nation. But, if Abraham sacrificed his son, he would be negating God's promise! In brief: If Abraham did not obey, he was rejecting God's authority. If he did obey, he was negating God's promise!

396. So in what way was it a test of God?

It was a test of God in the sense of a challenge to Abraham to see if his religious maturity was so developed that he would be able, in the context of such a dilemma, to determine which course of action His God would prefer him to adopt. Abraham had to prove that he was capable of teaching and initiating religious values, and harmonizing the contradictions of faith. And the fact that after the *Akedah* he had no further encounters with God suggests that he well passed that test. He was able "to walk *before* his God" (Genesis 17:1)—to go on ahead and blaze new spiritual trails for him.

Abraham came to the conclusion that human sacrifice offended God far more than the disregarding of His command. But he still had to put his conclusion to "the

5. Breitbart, S. (1986). "The Akedah—A Test of God." *Dor Le Dor* XV. The World Jewish Bible Center, No. 1 (Fall 1986), pp. 19–28.

test," to prove that he had read His God and his new religion correctly. So he had to go through the motion of submitting to the *Akedah*, knowing full well that His God would never allow the sacrifice to be carried out, but that if He did, then he, Abraham, would pull away at the last moment.

397. Why did Abraham not tell his wife, Sarah, before he left, of the divine command to take Isaac to the *Akedah*?

Breitbart is not satisfied with the Midrashic answer that it was to spare her pain, since the shock and pain that she would suffer after they had gone, wondering where they were and what they were up to, compounded by her resentment at having been excluded from their confidence, would have been much worse for Sarah.

His answer is, simply, because Abraham had not yet been able to rationalize the command to his own satisfaction. He had to spend the next 3 days working it out, working through his own shock and religious turmoil, attempting to resolve the fundamental dilemma—without the pressure of a fearful mother's overwhelming emotions, which could only but interfere with what was, basically, a moral and theological conundrum.

398. Does our tradition make any comment on Abraham's apparent indifference to the feelings of his wife?

According to Lippman Bodoff,[6] there is a reference to this in a most unexpected place, namely the *Zikhronot* section of the Rosh Hashanah *Musaf Amidah* (See Question 553), where we find the following: "Let there appear before You [the remembrance of] the *Akedah*, when Abraham our father bound Isaac his son upon the altar, and he *suppressed his mercy* to do Your will wholeheartedly. So may You suppress Your anger at us and deal compassionately with us."

Bodoff asks the pertinent question why God should deal compassionately with us if Abraham did precisely the opposite, and "suppressed his mercy"! His answer is that Abraham knew that God had to be allowed to make a dramatic demonstration to mankind—by way of the *Akedah*—that murder, even when it took the form of sacrifice, was abhorrent. To enable God to proceed with His demonstration, Abraham had to "suppress his mercy" for Sarah and Isaac and his natural desire to spare them agonies. Toward that noble end, he had to keep the *Akedah* a secret from Sarah and slip away "early in the morning." Similarly, he had to keep his intention a secret from Isaac and brush aside his searching questions.

Thus, we pray, may God suppress His anger against us, as a reward for Abraham's co-partnership with God in enabling His moral will to become manifest in the world.

---

6. Bodoff, L. (1993). "The Real Test of the *Akedah*: Blind Obedience Versus Moral Choice." *Judaism* Vol 42. The American Jewish Congress, pp. 84–85.

399. Do we have any textual evidence that Abraham was convinced that, come what may, he would not be sacrificing his son?

Breitbart believes that there are several pointers in the text that prove this. First, the fact that he told his servants to stay with the ass while he and Isaac went up the mountain, and "we will worship and *we* will return to you" (22:5). Abraham was stating confidently from the outset that Isaac would be accompanying him back from the *Akedah*.

Secondly, when Isaac questioned his father as to why he had not brought with him a lamb for the sacrifice, Abraham answers that "God will provide the lamb for his burnt offering, my son" (22:8). Now, according to Breitbart's theory that Abraham had no intention at all of sacrificing Isaac, we can now appreciate that he was, indeed, telling the whole truth, out of his firm conviction. He was not, as popularly explained, putting Isaac off with some lame answer. As far as Abraham was concerned, Isaac just had to survive because of God's promise that he would become a great nation. God's promise must win out when in competition with a command that could in no way be justified on moral grounds. God would, indeed, have to provide a lamb, because human sacrifice was out of the question.

400. Is it conceivable that the *Akedah* ordeal may have been some sort of punishment for Abraham, perhaps in order to atone for his sins before he discovered God?

It is inconceivable that the Torah would not have told us if Abraham had led a sinful life before his discovery of God. Indeed, it would have made his subsequent conversion to righteousness even more significant and dramatic. In any case, it was only a heinous crime, such as Cain's slaying of his brother, that would have attracted to it such a high profile punishment in that period before the giving of the Torah.

There is a theory, though hardly convincing, that the *Akedah* came to atone for Abraham's expulsion of Ishmael.[7] This cannot be justified textually, for God is clearly represented as having given His support to Sarah's instruction to Abraham to banish Ishmael, and Abraham is promised that no evil will befall Ishmael and that he will grow into a great nation.

401. How do we explain the fact that, when pleading for the Sodomites, Abraham is prepared vigorously to challenge God's apparent abdication of morality ("Shall the judge of the whole earth not execute justice?" Genesis 18:25), and yet, in the episode of the *Akedah*, he does not utter a word of complaint at the grossly immoral directive to kill his son?

It is a thorny question addressed by many commentators. Michael J. Harris addresses this question, and seeks to account for it on the basis of Abraham's

---

7. Polish, D. (1957). "The Binding of Isaac." *Judaism* Vol 6. No. 1, pp. 17–21.

third-party objectivity in his assessment of the plight of the Sodomites, as opposed to his personal involvement and conflict of interests in the *Akedah* situation:

> In Genesis 18 . . . he is an onlooker, a spectator. The structure of the *Akedah* episode is obviously different. Here Abraham himself is commanded by the Almighty to perform an immoral action. And for Abraham to dispute a divine revelation directed at him personally, even if the content of that revelation is apparently immoral, may not be legitimate. Within the context of an encounter between a human individual and the Supreme King of Kings, utter submission is arguably the only acceptable response. . . . Abraham is assertive in Genesis 18 and submissive in Genesis 22 because, while moral challenge to God is religiously legitimate, the religious believer can never disobey a direct command from the Almighty. To do so would be to no longer recognize him as God.[8]

402. Does the Torah make any specific reference to the prohibition of child sacrifice, or is it only to be inferred from the *Akedah*?

The Torah does, indeed, denounce the practice in the very strongest of terms:

> Moreover, thou shalt say unto the the Children of Israel: Whosoever he be, of the Children of Israel or of the strangers that sojourn in Israel, that gives of his offspring unto Moloch, shall surely be put to death . . . I will also set My face against that man, and will cut him off from among his people, because he has given of his offspring unto Moloch, to defile My sanctuary. [Leviticus 20:2-3]

403. Are there any references in the Bible to child sacrifice having been performed?

There is a reference in II Chronicles to the evils perpetrated by King Ahaz of Judah (743-727 B.C.E.): "Moreover he offered in the valley of the son of Hinnom, and burnt his children in the fire, according to the abominations of the heathen, whom the Lord cast out from before the Children of Israel" (28:3).

The reference here is to the ancient Canaanite cult of Moloch worship, which involved "passing one's son or daughter through fire."

There is also a reference to Mesha, king of Moab, who, in extreme distress at the devastation of his land by Israel, "took his eldest son, that should have reigned in his stead, and offered him for a burnt offering upon the wall" (II Kings 3:27).

Whether or not Jephtha actually offered up his daughter as a child-sacrifice or merely separated her from society to devote her life in monastic seclusion to God remains a moot point (See Judges 11:30-40 and Questions 212-213).

---

8. Harris, M. J. (1992). "The Shared Moral Universe of God and Man: A Re-Reading of the *Akedah*." *L'Eylah, Rosh Hashanah* 5733, 34:19.

404. Are there any indications that the Jews themselves indulged in such heinous practices?

There are, indeed. The prophet Jeremiah (ministered 627–586 B.C.E.) specifically denounces the inhabitants of Judah and Jerusalem for their evildoing:

> Because they have forsaken Me, and have estranged this place, and have offered in it unto other gods . . . and have filled this place with the blood of innocents; and have built the high places of Baal to burn their sons in the fire for burnt offerings unto Baal; which I commanded not, nor spoke it, neither came it into My mind." [Jeremiah 19:4–5]

The prophet Micah, who ministered a century earlier, provides a more oblique reference to child-sacrifice, suggestive of a situation where such things were practiced, though perhaps not on such a scale as in Jeremiah's day:

> O My people, what have I done unto thee?
> And wherein have I wearied thee?
> Testify against Me . . .
> Wherewith shall I come before the Lord,
> And bow myself before God on high?
> Shall I come before Him with burnt-offerings,
> With calves of a year old?
> Will the Lord be pleased with thousands of rams,
> With ten thousand rivers of oil?
> Shall I give my first-born for my transgression,
> The fruit of my body for the sin of my soul?
>
>   [Micah 6:3–8]

THE *AKEDAH* IN MIDRASH

405. Does the Midrash address the question of why Isaac also had to undergo the ordeal of being "tested" at the *Akedah*?

It deals with this question, suggesting that Isaac himself prompted the test to be carried out upon himself.

The Midrash, on the verse "And Sarah saw the son of Hagar, the Egyptian . . . mocking" (Genesis 21:98), states that Ishmael was vaunting his piety over that of Isaac. Ishmael said to Isaac, "I was thirteen years old when God commanded my father to circumcize me, and yet I put up no resistance, but submitted to it!" Isaac thereupon responded, "Why do you boast of that little bit of flesh which you gave from your body? If the God of my father, Abraham, should say to him, 'Take your son and offer him up as a sacrifice,' I would not resist, but would joyfully agree."[9]

---

9. Midrash *Bereshit Rabba* 55(4).

In this way, the Midrash neatly exonerates God and Abraham from any charge that they made Isaac an unwilling victim of a trial that really had nothing to do with him.

406. Did God attempt in any way to soften the shock of His command to Abraham to sacrifice his son?

The Midrash regards the phraseology of God's disclosure to Abraham of the trial of the *Akedah* as particularly significant: "Take, please, your son, your only one, whom you love, Isaac, and offer him up . . ." (Genesis 22:2). The Midrash understands this as a delicate, psychological unfolding by God of His will, to give its import time to sink in gradually, in preference to a direct and blunt command: "Take Isaac, and offer him up."

The Midrash views the text as the contraction of a dialogue between God and Abraham: "God said: 'Take please your son.' Abraham responded, 'But I have two sons!' Whereupon God continued: 'Your only one.' 'But,' said Abraham, 'both of them are only ones to their respective mothers!' 'The one whom you love,' countered God. 'But I love them both!' insisted Abraham. 'Take Isaac,' commanded God."[10]

407. We are not told anywhere in the Torah whether anyone ever disclosed to Sarah, either before or after the event, what her husband had done. Did she die in ignorance?

For the rabbis, it is significant that the episode recorded immediately following on from the *Akedah* is the death of Sarah (Genesis chapter 23), and the rabbis interpret this juxtaposition as representing cause and effect. Sarah must have known of the *Akedah*, they aver, and it was the shock of that which caused her death.

408. But she clearly did not know before Abraham left for the *Akedah* or she would have objected; and by the time Abraham returned, Sarah had already died. So who could possibly have told her?

Midrashic tradition comes into play here to answer this question. The rabbis state that:

At the time of the *Akedah*, Satan appeared to Sarah in the guise of Isaac. When she saw him, she said: 'My son, what did your father do with you?' Isaac answered, 'He took me up hills and down valleys, until we reached the summit of a lofty mountain, where he arranged an altar, and bound me on it. He then took a knife to slay me, and had it not been that God cried out to him, "Do not stretch forth your hand!" I would already have been slaughtered.' No sooner had Satan/Isaac uttered that last word, when Sarah expired [from the shock].[11]

---

10. *Sanhedrin* 89b.
11. Midrash *Tanchuma Sidra Va-yeira*, sec. 23.

Satan clearly did not represent Abraham's actions as a response to the divine command, which might have gone some way toward explaining her husband's actions. According to his account, it was purely a murderous initiative of Abraham. No wonder Sarah's heart gave out!

409. But is it at all conceivable that Abraham could have slipped away from his home, together with Isaac and his two lads, as well as with the provisions of food, water, and wood (for the sacrifice), without Sarah being aware of it and demanding an explanation?

One Midrashic tradition seems to be addressing this very question when it suggests that Abraham did take steps to apprise Sarah that he would be taking Isaac on a journey—though of a different kind:

> One day he asked Sarah to prepare special delicacies and drink. 'What is the special occasion?' asked Sarah, in surprise. 'Well,' said Abraham, 'when I was thirteen years of age I already had a special relationship with my God, and yet our own son has not yet been spiritually initiated. Furthermore, I know a place some distance from here where they prepare young men for the spiritual life, and I wish to take him there.' 'With pleasure, do so,' said Sarah.[12]

410. Why does the Torah bother to tell us such a mundane fact that Abraham rose early on the morning of the *Akedah* (22:3)?

Its purpose is to demonstrate Abraham's eagerness to respond to a divine instruction—even one as unpalatable as this. The Torah surely intends us to learn the message that, in the performance of all *mitzvot*, we should hasten to perform them at the earliest opportunity and with the utmost enthusiasm.

This approach to the performance of *mitzvot* is regarded as so important that it is formulated at the very beginning of the *Shulchan Arukh*: "A man should strengthen himself like a lion to rise early in the morning for the service of his Creator, to the extent that he himself rouses the dawn."[13]

The meaning of the latter phrase is that he should be self-motivating. He shouldn't sleep in until the dawn sunlight wakes him up and he can no longer sleep, but rather he should be up, ready and eager to serve his Maker as soon as it is dawn and the time for morning prayer arrives. This is the lesson we learn from Abraham.

411. But why do we need to be informed of the mundane act that Abraham performed in "saddling his ass" (22:3)?

Because, says the Midrash,[14] this verse wishes to draw our attention to the significance of this particular ass. For this was no ordinary ass that Abraham

---

12. *Yalkut Shim'oni Va-yeira*, sec. 22.
13. *Shulchan Arukh Orach Chayyim* 1:1.
14. Midrash *Pirkei D'Rabbi Eliezer*, Chapter 31, ed. G. Friedlander, pp. 224–225.

selected. It was the offspring of that special ass that was created during the twilight of the first Sabbath of Creation,[15] the same ass that was later ridden upon by Moses when he came down to Egypt,[16] and the ass that the Messianic King will one day ride upon as he enters Jerusalem.[17]

The intention is also to display Abraham's great zeal to be involved with every aspect of the performance of the *mitzvah*, however menial and mundane.

412. Do we know the identity of the two lads who accompanied Abraham and Isaac to the *Akedah*?

The Midrash states that they were Eliezer, the steward of Abraham's estates, and his son, Ishmael, who had returned to his father's home a few years after he was banished.

413. Why did Abraham take Eliezer and Ishmael with him to the *Akedah*, since they clearly had absolutely no part to play in the events described?

A man of rank would always be accompanied in antiquity on any journey by at least two attendants. Furthermore, the journey to the *Akedah* was along unfamiliar terrain, which may well have been frequented by bandits. Both Ishmael and Eliezer were fearless warriors; the former is described as "a wild ass of a man whose hand will be against everyone, and everyone's hand will be against him" (Genesis 16:12), and Eliezer, according to the Midrash,[18] was the one who accompanied Abraham in his battle against the confederacy of the four kings (Genesis chapter 14). It is logical, therefore, that Abraham would have taken them with him for protection.

414. What, then, made Abraham tell them, after three days' journey, to "stay behind together with the ass" (Genesis 22:5), while he and the lad journeyed on alone to the *Akedah*?

The Midrash[19] explains that it had been Abraham's original intention to have them accompany and protect Isaac and him up to the place of the *Akedah* itself; however, it was soon demonstrated to him that they were unworthy to witness what was going to happen:

On the third day they reached Tzofim, where Abraham and Isaac saw the glory of the *Shechinah* (Divine Presence) resting on the top of the mountain. What did they see? A pillar of fire spanning heaven and earth. Abraham said to Ishmael and Eliezer, 'Do you see anything on that mountain ahead?' 'No, nothing,' was their response. He then realised that they were as (spiritually)

---

15. Mishnah *Avot* 5:9.
16. Exodus 4:20.
17. Zechariah 9:9.
18. *Rashi* on Genesis 14:14.
19. *Pirkei D'Rabbi Eliezer*, Chapter 31, pp. 225–226.

dull as an ass, and so he said to them, '[Since you don't see anything,] stay behind together with the ass—that is where your place clearly belongs!'

415. Why did the angel have to say twice to Abraham, "Do not stretch forth your hand against the lad," as well as "nor do him any harm?" (22:12). Surely, the former command includes the latter?

The Midrash[20] explains that when Abraham heard the angel say, "Do not stretch forth your hand," Abraham felt a sense of deep frustration. "If so," he told the angel, "then I have come here for nothing. Let me, at least, make a wound and draw a little blood, so that I can be said to have partially fulfilled my mission." Hence, the necessity for the angel to respond and add, "nor do him any harm."

416. Although Abraham came through his "test" with flying colors, is it not still legitimate to ask how God could have justified inflicting such emotional turmoil on the perfectly righteous Abraham?

The explanation of the *Zohar*[21] is that in one matter, and on one occasion only, Abraham dropped his usually impeccable level of sensitivity, kindness, and hospitality to the less fortunate.

On the very day that Abraham made his great feast to celebrate the birth of Isaac, to which were invited all the princes and distinguished people of the time, Satan disguised himself as a poor beggar. Abraham and Sarah were so excited and preoccupied with the birth and with their important guests that they forgot to invite the poor to enjoy a fine meal and share their joy. They also took no notice of the beggar at the door. Having found a chink in Abraham's religious armor, Satan exploited it by denouncing Abraham before the heavenly tribunal. The decree was that Abraham should, indeed, suffer some mental torment for his uncharacteristic oversight.

417. We have referred to Satan as having callously disclosed to Sarah what her husband had done to their son. Did Satan interfere in any other way in the events of the *Akedah*?

The Midrash states that Satan tried desperately to thwart Abraham and Isaac's progress toward the *Akedah*. At first, Satan appeared to Abraham in the disguise of a very old and wise man, and attempted to sow doubts in Abraham's mind by telling him that he must have been misled into thinking that it was God who had isssued the summons to him. "Surely," said the old man, "God who gave you such a precious gift of a son would never demand his execution!" Abraham was not deflected from his purpose, however, for he suspected that this was Satan speaking.

Satan then attempted to dissuade Isaac, but failed. Whereupon he transformed

---

20. See *Rashi* on Genesis 22:12.
21. Zohar, *Bereishit* 10a–11b.

himself into a deep brook that blocked their way. Undeterred, Abraham led his party into the water, until it reached up to their necks. While terror gripped the others, Abraham knew for sure that this was Satan's work, for he remembered that spot and knew that there had never previously been any brook there. So Abraham invoked the name of God to rebuke and banish Satan. In terror, Satan fled, and the place became dry land again, enabling the group to complete their journey.[22]

SELECTED COMMENTARIES
AND EXPOSITIONS ON THE *AKEDAH*

418. When God first gives Abraham his instructions, he tells him to take Isaac to "the land of Moriah" (22:2). What precise place is being referred to here by the name *Moriah*?

Rashi[23] equates "the land of Moriah" with Jerusalem, based on the verse, "to build the house of the Lord in Jerusalem on Mount Moriah" (II Chronicles 3:1). *Rashi* quotes the Talmudic explanation of the term *Moriah* as derived from the noun *hora'ah*, "(religious) instruction," because from that place (Jerusalem) religious guidance and instruction goes out to the world.[24]

In support of this identification, *Rashi* quotes *Targum Onkelos* who renders *Moriah* as "the land of service," which *Rashi* supposes is derived from the spice *mor* (myrrh), which was one of the ingredients of the fragrant incense used in the Temple service.

Nachmanides[25] takes issue, however, with *Rashi*'s understanding of *Targum Onkelos*. He states that *Targum* could not possibly have maintained that Jerusalem would have acquired its name *Moriah* merely on account of one ingredient (myrrh) of one of the sacrifices offered in Jerusalem. Nachmanides construes *Targum*'s rendering far more comprehensively, therefore, as "the land of the service of God."

419. But if the reference is to Jerusalem as the chosen site of the *Akedah*, then why did God tell him to go to "the *land* of Moriah," and not to "the *city* of Moriah"?

Nachmanides[26] offers two suggestions: Either the land as a whole was called after the city within it, which, in turn, was named after the Temple Mount whereupon all that "service of God" was destined to be focused; or, God knew that Abraham was familiar with the land, but not with the particular mount, so He merely directed him, in general terms to "the land [where Mount] Moriah [is located]."

22. *Sanhedrin* 89b; Midrash *Bereishit Rabba* 56(4); *Sefer Ha-Yashar* on *Va-yeira*, pp. 44b–45a.
23. *Rashi* on Genesis 22:2.
24. *Ta'anit* 16a.
25. *Peirush Ha-Ramban* on 22:2.
26. *Ibid.*

420. Why does the Torah state, "And Abraham took his two lads with him, as well as Isaac his son?" (22:3). Does it not look as if Isaac was secondary in importance to the lads?

R. Samson Raphael Hirsch[27] regards the order as particularly significant. It suggests to him that Abraham first woke up the lads and told them to prepare for a long journey, before he woke up Isaac and disclosed to him what they were about to do. He wanted to spare Isaac's feelings for as long as possible, so that he would have almost no time to deliberate on what was being asked of him, or to cross-examine his father.

421. Why did Abraham need to bring wood with him? Surely he would not have found any difficulty finding some at his destination?

Nachmanides[28] suggests that Abraham, who, according to tradition, kept all the minutiae of the *mitzvot* later to be given at Sinai, was concerned that he might not find suitable wood that had no worms or maggots, since no wormy wood could be offered on the altar (Mishnah *Middot* 2:5), and hence he preferred to bring with him the best quality wood, in keeping with the great *mitzvah* he was to perform.

422. What does it mean that Abraham took "fire in his hand" (verse 6)? How can one transport a flame for 3 days?

E. A. Speiser[29] translates the Hebrew *ha-eish* as "the firestone," which would seem more likely. Nahum Sarna[30] suggests that it might also refer to a brazier.

423. The Torah employs a strange formulation when recording Isaac's question to his father as to why he has brought no lamb with him: "And Isaac spoke to Abraham, his father, saying, 'My father.' And he replied: 'Here am I, my son.' And Isaac said, 'Behold there is wood and fire, but where is the lamb for the burnt offering?'" (22:7). Why was Isaac's question broken into two parts, instead of being combined into one question: "My father, behold there is wood, etc . . . ?"

Against the backcloth of the Midrashic tradition that people were all whispering that Sarah must have become pregnant from King Avimelech (See Question 378), R. Jacob Culi (1685–1732)[31] explains the interrupted dialogue here. He suggests that

---

27. Levy, I. ed. (1959). *The Pentateuch, Genesis*. London: I. Levy Publisher, p. 369.

28. *Op. cit.* Commentary on 22:3.

29. Speiser, E. A. (1964). *Genesis*. Garden City, NY: Doubleday & Co., p. 163.

30. Sarna, N. (1989). *The JPS Torah Commentary, Genesis*. Philadelphia: The Jewish Publication Society, p. 152.

31. Culi, J. (1967). *Yalkut Me'am Lo'ez* (Original in Ladino). Hebrew edition, Ed. Shmuel Yerushalmi. Jerusalem: *Ohr Chadash* Publications, Bereshit, vol. 1, p. 437.

when Isaac says, "My father," he is alluding to that malicious allegation: "How could you really be 'my father'—people will rightly charge—if you were prepared so readily to slaughter me? You are confirming their allegation!"

Abraham answered, "On the contrary. If you were the seed of Avimelech then you would have been disqualified as a holy sacrifice on God's altar, for any sacrifice which has a bodily blemish, however minute, cannot be offered. So 'Here am I,' ready to fulfill this unique *mitzvah* on you 'my son' my pure seed."

424. We referred above (See Question 414) to the Midrashic explanation of why Abraham excluded his two lads from accompanying him further to the place of the *Akedah*. Is there any other, practical explanation that could be offered?

R. Samson Raphael Hirsch[32] suggests that Abraham was worried that they would intercede and prevent him from carrying out God's decree, because it was totally out of character for Abraham. Also knowing his great love for Isaac, they might well have misconstrued his actions as the mental aberration of a man in his declining years, and might forcefully restrain him, for his own, as well as for Isaac's, sake.

425. How could the angel, who called out to Abraham not to touch Isaac, say, on behalf of God, "For *now* I know that you are God-fearing, in that you have not withheld your son . . . from me"? Surely God knew all along that Abraham feared him and would demonstrate that when called upon to do so?

R. Jacob Culi[33] quotes the view that angels cannot read the hearts of men and know only what God programs them to know. Hence, the angel who first visited Abraham had to ask, "Where is Sarah, your wife?" because, even though he was a superior being, he did not know her whereabouts. Hence, in our situation, it is the angel speaking for himself—not for God—when he says "for now I know that you are God-fearing."

426. Is there any other, more literal, way in which to explain the angel's words, "for now I know?"

R. Jacob Culi himself offers such an explanation,[34] though without stating from whom he heard it. He interprets the verse elyptically: "For now I know—that I have to show mercy to you—because [of the fact that] you are a God-fearing man; and even though you did not slaughter your son, I must account it to you as if you had done so."

---

32. *Op. cit.*, p. 370.
33. R. Jacob Culi, *op. cit.*, p. 442.
34. *Ibid.*

427. Is there any significance in the fact that, whereas the original command to take Isaac to the *Akedah* was issued by God, yet the command to stop was given by an angel?

R. Samson Raphael Hirsch addresses this point. He states that:

To tell him to stop, an angel was quite sufficient. Herein too, we are shown the depth of the struggle which Abraham had to overcome. Had an angel brought him the message to kill his son, he would simply not have believed it. It was so much out of any connection with, so directly contrary to, everything he knew of God in general, and in particular to what God had revealed to him concerning Isaac. But to tell him *not* to sacrifice his son, a message through an angel sufficed. . . . For that there was no necessity for an extraordinary revelation. That fitted in harmoniously with everything else that Abraham learnt to know of God.[35]

428. What does the Torah mean by stating that "they both went together" (22:8)?

This refers to the last leg of their journey when just Abraham and Isaac walked alone, seeking out the place to which God was directing them. The phrase "they both went together" betokens a unity of purpose and joyful anticipation of their shared mission. However, some have cast doubt on that sense, since both father and son must have entertained great forboding of what lay ahead. The *Yefei Eynayim,*[36] therefore, ingeniously explains it simply as a statement of the way in which they walked along. He points out that Abraham was a very old man, whereas Isaac was in the full bloom of his youth. To ensure that they did not become separated as Isaac—as was his wont—romped ahead, exploring the surroundings and distant vistas, Abraham weighed him down by placing upon his shoulders the heavy "wood for the sacrifice" (verse 8). Thus encumbered, "they both went together"—at the same pace.

429. Which mountain is more important in our tradition, Moriah or Sinai?

The Hasidic Rebbe, R. Chayim of Zanz[37] used to say that, surprising as it may seem, of these two unique mountains—Moriah, where Abraham sacrificed his son, and Sinai, whereon the Torah was given–it was not Sinai that was chosen as the site of the Temple, but Moriah. The reason is that without self-sacrifice Torah observance will not survive.

---

35. *Op. cit.,* p. 373.

36. *Yefei Eynayim* on Genesis 22:6.

37. Quoted in *Parperaot La-Torah* (Ed. M. Beker, Jerusalem, Omen Publications, 1983), *Bereishit,* p. 76.

430. At the end of the *Akedah,* **we are told that "Abraham returned to his lads" (verse 19). Why did the Torah need to include such an insignificant fact, especially as it may be assumed from the fact that, when taking leave of them, Abraham promised that, "we shall return to you" (verse 5)?**

R. Menachem Mendel of Vorka reads into that phrase a moral lesson. One might have supposed that, after having successfully come through that incomparable trial of a human being, Abraham would have been filled with self-congratulation. To indicate that there was not a grain of such pride in his heart, the Torah states that "Abraham returned to his lads, and they arose *and went together.*" In other words, they walked in the identical frame of mind. Just as the lads had absolutely no idea of what had transpired in their absence and of the spiritual heights to which their master had soared that day, so Abraham returned without a tincture of pride in his heart.

THE *AKEDAH* IN OUR LITURGY

431. Is the *Akedah* **a dominant theme in our liturgy?**

It is not a dominant theme, to the extent that it was not incorporated into the daily liturgy. There is evidence from the Mishnah[38] that on public fast days a special prayer of intercession was recited that included the plea, *Miy she'anah et Avraham behar ha-Moriah hu ya'aneh etkhem*—"He who answered Abraham on Mount Moriah, may He so answer you and hearken to the sound of your cries on this day." It also appears in the *Zikhronot* section of the Rosh Hashanah *Musaf Amidah* (See Question 554). The blowing of the shofar is, most popularly, explained as commemorative of the ram offered by Abraham instead of Isaac at the *Akedah*. It also gave its name to an entire genre of medieval penitential poems that made the *Akedah* the symbol of Israel's self-surrender for *kiddush Ha-Shem* (martyrdom).

432. So are there no references at all to the *Akedah* **in our daily prayers?**

There is just one specific reference, early in the morning service. In the composition commencing *Ribbon Kol Ha-Olamim* (following the *Birkot Ha-Shachar*): "But we are Your people, sons of Your covenant, the children of Abraham, Your friend, to whom You made a promise at Mount Moriah; the offspring of his only son, Isaac, who was bound (*shene'ekad*) on the altar. . . ."

Significantly, the concluding blessing of the section containing this reference to the *Akedah* is *Barukh . . . mekaddesh et shimkha ba-rabim* ("Blessed are You . . . who causes Your name to be sanctified in public"). This formula is a direct reference to *kiddush Ha-Shem*, martyrdom, as symbolized by the *Akedah*. The inclusion, in this section of the liturgy, of the first verse of the *Shema*, the last

38. Mishnah *Ta'anit* 2:4.

declaration of faith uttered by the Jew as he surrenders his soul, is especially relevant to this *Akedah* context.

433. But is not the entire section of the *Akedah* printed in several editions of the daily prayer book? Surely, then, it is truly a dominant theme of our daily liturgy?

No, its appearance in those editions is merely in conformity with a pietistic practice *recommended* by the *Tur*, Rabbi Jacob ben Asher (1270–1340). He states, "It is a good thing to recite the *Akedah* portion (and the portion of the Manna, and the Ten Commandments, and the portion of the daily sacrifices . . .)."[39]

Clearly, congregants would not have to be in a hurry to get to work in order to have time to recite all those biblical sections. It is only the last mentioned, the *Korbanot*, that became incorporated with something approaching statutory status.

The Art Scroll edition of the prayer book includes the *Akedah* as an introduction to the section where the reference to it appears.[40] Surprisingly, however, it does not present it as an optional reading. Most other editions of the prayer book relegate it to an appendix at the end of the morning service. The standard, *Authorized Daily Prayer Book* (popularly called the "Singer's"), of Anglo-Jewry included it in the latter position until the Centenary Edition of 1990 when it was removed entirely.

434. Would we not have expected the *Akedah* to have become a more dominant theme in our liturgy?

We certainly would; and we may assume, therefore, that its low-key status was a reaction to the emphasis that was placed on the *Akedah* in early Christianity, wherein the sacrifice of Isaac is depicted as foreshadowing the Crucifixion of Jesus, the "lamb of God."

In the Koran, the *Akedah* is also hailed as a great demonstration of faith in God, though Islamic tradition tended to substitute Ishmael—the founder of the Muslim faith—for Isaac, and credit Ishmael with having readily responded to the call for self-sacrifice.

It was the consistent rabbinic approach to play down any elements of Jewish tradition that Christianity invested with its own theological significance, and we may be fairly certain that this is why the *Akedah* does not enjoy the prominence that it otherwise would.

THE *AKEDAH* IN SYNAGOGUE ART

435. To what extent was the *Akedah* represented in artistic or dramatic form?

Archaeology uncovered an ancient synagogue at Bet-Alfa, near Mount Gilboa, dating back to the sixth century. It was discovered by Professor E. L. Sukenik in

---

39. *Tur Orach Chayyim* 1:1.
40. *The Complete Art Scroll Siddur* (1986). New York: Masorah Publications, pp. 22–24.

1929 and contains a mosaic flooring and inscription. It also contains wall panels, richly embellished with artistic scenes from the Bible. On the first panel, next to the entrance, the *Akedah* is represented by four drawings, each bearing the respective titles: "Isaac," "Abraham," "Do not stretch forth (your hand)," and "Behold a ram!"

The third-century C.E. synagogue, discovered in 1932 at Dura-Europos, on the Euphrates, also contained wall paintings and geometric designs. On a panel above a niche, in the western wall, which was probably for housing a Torah scroll, is decpicted the scene in the *Akedah* of a hand stretching forth from heaven to restrain Abraham. This is not in conformity with the biblical account wherein it is an angel that calls out from heaven to stop Abraham proceeding.

THE *AKEDAH* IN THE CREATIVE ARTS

436. To what extent did the *Akedah* theme infiltrate the creative arts?

Because it was appropriated as a symbol of the Crucifixion, the *Akedah* became a popular theme among Christian writers and artists and was used in the medieval miracle cycles and mystery plays, as well as by secular dramatists. It was drawn on by several painters in the early Renaissance period, and, in 1635, Rembrandt produced a painting entitled "The Sacrifice of Isaac," followed by an etching on the same theme in 1655, currently housed in the Israel Museum of Jerusalem. Shortly before his death in 1669, he produced his "The Return of the Prodigal Son."

> In the two paintings, the sons are naked as a child is when he is born, thus indicating that they were born again. In both pictures the sons' faces cannot be seen. They are blotted out; in the first case by the father's hand and in the second by his clothing. The fathers' faces in both pictures are shown with an expression as shining in supernatural joy. . . . It is also seen in a painting by a follower of Toriti in the Chiesa Superiori di S. Francesco, at Assisi.[41]

In many paintings of the *Akedah*, Abraham wields a large sword. This is not quite true to the biblical text, which refers to him taking with a *ma'akhelet*, from the root *akhal*, "to eat," which suggests a small knife, usually used to carve meat. In several paintings, the angel is female and is depicted as grasping the blade of that large sword.

Early tapestries, such as the one at Halberstadt in Germany, woven in the twelfth century, or the one in Hampton Court Palace, England, woven about 1540,[42] depicted the *Akedah* scene: "Abraham is depicted as a Lord and priest, wearing flowing white draperies and having a halo."[43] It was also commonly represented in stained-glass window design, such as the one in Canterbury Cathedral, behind St.

41. Yassif, E. (1978). *The Sacrifice of Isaac*. Jerusalem: Makor Publishing.
42. Wellisch, E. (1954). *Isaac and Oedipus*. London: Routledge & Kegan Paul, facing p. 80.
43. Yassif, *ad loc.*

Augustin's Chair, dating back to *circa* 1230,[44] and on pulpit reliefs, such as at Volterra, sculpted around 1200.[45]

Akedah was also a popular theme for illustrators of Bibles and Haggadot in the thirteenth and fourteenth centuries. It is depicted on Roman catacombs of the third century, in Vatican grottos, and in cathedral and church murals.

The theme was also employed by wood-carvers, especially in their production of the engraved handles of circumcision knives, the covenant of circumcision being a symbolic act of bodily self-surrender.

THE *AKEDAH* IN LITERATURE

437. Yiddish literature borrowed heavily on native Jewish themes. Was the *Akedah* given any literary treatment?

It was a most popular theme in Yiddish literature for over 300 years, and its first appearance seems to have been in the form of a poem, entitled *Akedat Yitzchak*, attributed to a certain Pinchas ben Yehudah Shalit, who relied heavily on Midrashic literature for his sources. The original has been lost, though copies still exist in several libraries, the earliest of which dates back to 1570 and is housed in the library of the Jewish Theological Seminary of New York.

The *Akedah* also featured prominently in Yiddish Purim plays, and in 1902, Abraham Goldfaden (1840–1908), the Yiddish poet, dramatist, and composer, composed a biblical operetta in four acts around that theme. Ishmael is cast as the "fall-guy" of the piece, a foolish character who cannot fathom what is going on around him, whose only objective is to inherit Isaac's possessions after he is slaughtered by Abraham, and who can communicate with no one except the donkey.[46] "In European music there are at least fifty works on the sacrifice of Isaac, mostly oratorios."[47]

THE *HAFTARAH* FOR THE SECOND DAY

438. What is the theme of the special *Haftarah* for the second day of Rosh Hashanah?

It is taken from chapter 31 of the book of Jeremiah, and it expresses the reciprocal divine response to Israel's faith, loyalty, and self-sacrifice. Its message exudes encouragement and love, promising Israel that her dark night of exile and suffering will ultimately give way to a dawn of national restoration.

44. Yassif, *ad loc.*
45. Wellisch, E. *op. cit.*, facing p. 81.
46. Matenko, P. (1975). "The Sacrifice of Isaac Theme in Yiddish Literature." *Dor LeDor* IV: 1–7.
47. Roth, C. (1971). "*Akedah*" in *Encyclopaedia Judaica*. Jerusalem: Keter Publishing House, p. 486.

439. What is the link between the *Haftarah* and Rosh Hashanah?

The link appears in several passages of the *Haftarah*, most notably in the two images employed to describe God's relationship with Israel: "I am as a *father* to Israel, and Ephraim is My firstborn" (31:9), and "He that scattered Israel will gather him, and watch over him as a *shepherd* watches his flock" (31:10). Both of those images figure prominently in our Rosh Hashanah liturgy.

A further link with Rosh Hashanah is forged by the reference to the matriarch Rachel, who is depicted as lamenting and weeping for her children in exile (verse 15). This echoes the reference, in both the Torah and *Haftarah* readings for the first day, to the longings for maternity expressed by Sarah and Hannah. Whereas they both longed for the personal fulfillment that motherhood confers, Rachel longed for the national fulfillment that can only be secured by the rebirth of her children and their restoration to the ancestral homeland.

A particularly strong thematic link with Rosh Hashanah is forged at the conclusion of the *Haftarah* when the prophet asserts that because the nation's repentance is sincere, her plea for divine mercy must be accepted: "Turn to me, and let me return; for You are the Lord my God. For after I repented I was filled with remorse, and after I realized my errors I beat my thigh in agitation. I was ashamed and confounded" (31:18–19).

The *Haftarah* ends with the climactic promise of divine reconciliation: *Rachem arachamenu ne'um Ha-Shem*—"I shall surely have pity on him, says the Lord" (verse 20).

THE *HAFTARAH* AND ITS BLESSINGS

440. What is the meaning of the term *Haftarah*?

It means "conclusion." There is some scholarly dispute, however, as to the precise sense in which this term is to be understood. One explanation is that the *Haftarah* originally constituted the finale of the entire service, though we have no evidence of that from our ancient sources. The most popular explanation is that it is the "conclusion" of the reading from the Torah.

441. Why was the reading from the Prophets, in the form of the *Haftarah*, first introduced?

It seems to have been introduced during a period of persecution, when Jewish practices were outlawed and it was certainly impossible to hold a public service and to bring bulky scrolls of the Torah to a prayer meeting (before the age of fixed places of worship) and past the watchful eyes of the conqueror's soldiers. As a substitute, they smuggled in small rolls or pieces of parchment on which was written a short selection from the Prophets, carefully chosen to correspond thematically with elements in the weekly *Sidrah* that would otherwise have been read.

Following the age-old, conservative Jewish approach, once the crisis had passed, the tradition was not abandoned, but retained its honored place in the synagogue tradition.

442. Do we know exactly when the practice of substituting a *Haftarah* was first introduced?

We cannot be sure when it was first introduced. The fourteenth-century Spanish liturgist, Rabbi David Abudraham, followed by Elijah Bachur (sixteenth century),[48] placed its introduction quite early, in the period of the Syrian repressions that resulted in the Maccabean revolt (168–165 B.C.E.), though this is pure conjecture, unsubstantiated by historical evidence.

Another view has it that the *Haftarah* reading from the Prophets was introduced as an anti-Samaritan measure. This sect only accepted the authority and canonicity of the Pentateuch and the book of Joshua. They denied sanctity, however, to the later books, which, according to their reading of their history, were composed after the schism between them (the true Israel) and the rest of the (renegade) Israelites, and the abandonment by the latter of the true tradition. The theory has it that, in order to rebut that diminution of the status of the Prophetic books by the Samaritans, the Pharisaic sages invested it with special importance by prescribing that it be read in synagogue following the Reading of the Law.

All we can say is that it certainly antedated the Common Era, since the New Testament refers to it as an established institution.[49]

443. We referred above (See Question 441) to special *Haftarah* rolls. How long did the practice survive of reading the *Haftarah* from a special parchment roll?

The Talmud refers already to the existence of *Sefer Aftarta*, "*Haftarah* scrolls,"[50] each containing the entire selection of *Haftarot* read in synagogue, though there is mention of opposition to their production. We may conjecture that this was either because it seemed to be investing the particular *Haftarah* chapter(s) with extra sanctity, over and above the other parts of that prophetic book, or for fear of sectarian tampering with the text.

Evidence suggests that in Muslim countries the custom of reading the *Haftarah* from a scroll survived much longer than in Western countries, which, on the introduction of the printed and bound book, chose that format for the *Haftarot* in order to indicate their secondary status to that of the Torah scroll of the Pentateuch. The one notable exception, in Ashkenazi communities, were those who followed the traditions of the Vilna Gaon who insisted on the reading of the *Haftarot* from a scroll.

---

48. Elbogen, I. M. (1988). *Ha-Tefillah BeYisrael*. Tel Aviv: Dvir, p. 132.
49. Luke 4:17; Acts of the Apostles 13:15.
50. *Gittin* 60a.

444. Why is it that the person reading the *Haftarah* is also called up to the Torah for a *Maftir* portion, wherein the last few verses of the *Sidrah* are repeated for him—or, on a festival, a special Torah section is read from a different scroll—even though we have already called up the required number of people?

The Talmud tells us that this was instituted, *mishum kevod ha-Torah*, "to preserve the honour of the Torah."[51] In other words, to ensure that, in the popular imagination, the Prophetic readings were not placed on a par with those from the Torah. Hence, the one called up to read the *Haftarah* still has to read in (or have read to him from) the Torah—the indispensable reading.

445. Are there any other ways in which the lesser status of the *Haftarah* is demonstrated?

Indeed. The half-*kaddish* is recited after the main Torah reading has been completed, and before the commencement of the *Haftarah*, in order to demarcate the latter as secondary to the main reading of the Torah.

Its lesser status was also demonstrated through the practice of giving the reading of the *Haftarah* to minors or Barmitzvah boys to perform, other than on certain special Sabbaths when it was reserved for distinguished members of the congregation, such as on *Shabbat Shuvah* and *Shabbat Ha-Gadol*, when it was customary for the rabbi to recite it.

446. Why do we take out an additional scroll for the *Maftir* portion, instead of rolling the first scroll to the required *Maftir* location?

Because of the principle of avoiding *tircha de-tzibbura*, making the service irksome for the community. If they are kept waiting while the scroll is rolled to the festival *Maftir* location—which could take as long as 10 minutes—people become impatient and bored, and start to chatter to their neighbors, which inevitably impaires the decorum, dignity, and religious effect of the service.

447. What is the theme of the blessing recited before the *Haftarah*?

There is one blessing recited as a prelude to the *Haftarah* and four recited after it. Together with the two blessings recited over the reading of the Torah, this makes a total of seven blessings, corresponding to the maximum number of prescribed call-ups, that is the seven people called up on a Shabbat morning.

The blessing before the *Haftarah* highlights the divine choice of the "good prophets" whose words are all faithful. The conclusion of the blessing (*chatimah*), however, puts the prophets last in the order when it emphasizes God's choice of the Torah, Moses, the lawgiver, Israel His people, and, finally, the true and righteous prophets. In this way, a link is forged between the Torah (of Moses), just read, and the words of the prophets to follow.

---

51. *Megillah* 23a.

448. What is the theme of the blessings recited after the *Haftarah*?

The first blessing asserts the truth and faithfulness of all God's words and promises.

The second blessing petitions for the restoration of Zion and the redemption of those who are "grieved in spirit."

The third blessing looks forward to the Messianic era and the coming of the prophet Elijah to herald the arrival of the Davidic king and Messiah. The phrase, "upon his throne let no stranger sit, nor let others inherit his glory," suggests an anti-Maccabean sentiment on the part of those who felt that, being a priestly fraternity, the Maccabees had no right to inherit royalty, which, according to the Torah, is the sole privilege and prerogative of royalty, as it says, "The ruler's staff shall not depart from Judah" (Genesis 49:10).

The fourth blessing takes the form of a thanksgiving for the Torah, for divine worship, for the prophets, and for the Sabbath or the relevant festival day (the name of which is inserted into the blessing).

449. Is there a minimum or maximum number of verses prescribed for each *Haftarah*?

There is no maximum number of verses prescribed. The length of the *Haftarah* is usually determined by the natural size of the Prophetic passage employed and the end of the chosen prophecy or episode.

There is, however, a prescribed minimum number of verses, and that is twenty-one. This corresponds with the sum total of prescribed call-ups on a Sabbath (seven) multiplied by the minimum number of verses to be read to each call-up (three). An exception to this regulation is made, however, in the case of a self-contained prophetic unit that the Bible brings to a natural close (*salik inyana*) in less than the prescribed number of twenty-one verses. This is the case, for example, with the *Haftarot* for the Sidra *Va-yeitzei* (for Sephardim), *Va-yishlach* (for Ashkenazim), *Bo*, *Terumah*, and others.

YEKUM PURKAN

450. Why is *Yekum Purkan* written in Aramaic, and not in Hebrew like the rest of our prayers?

The reason is because it was composed in Babylon where the *lingua franca* was Aramaic. Babylon was particularly proud of its long tradition as the most illustrious center of Talmudic scholarship in the Jewish world. This blessing for the health and welfare of the Torah community, both in Babylon and also in Israel—its scholars and students, heads of the academies, judges, and, most important of all, the *Exilarch* (head of Babylonian Jewry)—was clearly so practical and direct that they wished the laymen to understand perfectly every word they were uttering, so that their prayers would be recited with the utmost sincerity and fervor.

451. So when would the *Yekum Purkan* have been written?

On the basis of the foregoing, we would have to place it in the Geonic period (seventh to eleventh centuries). Stefan C. Reif[52] casts doubt on this attribution, however, "since it is preserved only in the Ashkenazi prayer rite, inherited from its North French predecessor, which cannot be traced before the twelfth century." Reif places its origin, therefore, a little later and views it as having been introduced as an expression of support for the Torah community at a time when its scholarship was already in decline.

452. But surely the Ashkenazi community of Northern France would hardly have been interested in creating a prayer for the heads of a declining Babylonian community?

I think this is a valid point. Indeed, it has been suggested[53] that the fact that *Yekum Purkan* is not found in the standard Babylonian prayer books of Amram and Saadia is no proof that it was not instituted in the Geonic period, but simply that this blessing was instituted for recitation by communities in Babylon other than the main Torah centers of Sura and Pumbedita, over which those Geonim presided.

The blessing reflected the pride of the wider Babylonian community in their main centers of learning and their illustrious leaders and scholars. It was hardly appropriate for the latter to invoke a blessing upon themselves!

453. Why do we recite two, almost identical, *Yekum Purkan* blessings?

Although the vocabulary appears the same, it will be seen that there is no reference, in the second *Yekum Purkan*, to any of the Torah leaders of Babylon. It refers exclusively to "this holy congregation, great and small, children and women." Indeed, it is the following composition, commencing *Miy Shebeirakh*—a prayer for the general congregation—which may be viewed as something of a repetition of the second *Yekum Purkan*! A cursory glance at the various categories of public spirited people who are singled out in it for praise and blessing, will, however, demonstrate that this is not the case.

454. Why is it not recited on festivals, unless they coincide with the Sabbath?

This is a very difficult question to answer, since hardly any rabbinic sources venture an explanation. One, very far-fetched suggestion is that of the *Eliyahu Rabbah* who attempts to explain it on the basis of the belief in the existence of demonic forces, offspring of Cain, who are banished to the distant regions throughout the week, but enabled to return to civilization for the Sabbath. On this day, therefore, humans are in danger of their pernicious influences and their envy,

---

52. Reif, S. C. (1993). *Judaism and Hebrew Prayer*. Cambridge: Cambridge University Press, p. 217.
53. Eisenstein, J. D. (1917). *Otzar Dinim Uminhagim*. New York: Hebrew Publishing Company, p. 170.

and for this reason *Yekum Purkan*, with its prayer for "healing of body" (*varyut gufa*), was regarded as a useful prophylactic against any demonic physical assault. On festivals, however, unless they happened to coincide with the Sabbath, the demons were kept away in their distant habitat![54]

Another, less than satisfactory, explanation has it that its omission on weekday festivals—when cooking is permitted—is in order to shorten the service so that people can get home earlier and prepare their meal. On Shabbat, however, cooking is not allowed, so there are no lengthy preparations to make. Hence, *Yekum Purkan* is reserved exclusively for Sabbaths and festivals occurring on Sabbath.[55]

This explanation founders on consideration of the fact that *Yekum Purkan* is really such a short composition that the saving of perhaps 3 minutes is hardly likely to be noticed or to register as facilitating the joyous celebration of *Yom Tov* (for more on *Yekum Purkan*, see Questions 813–817).

PRAYER FOR THE GOVERNMENT

455. Why do we recite a prayer for the welfare of the government?

This is based upon the advice given in the Ethics of the Fathers: "Pray for the welfare of the ruling power, for, were it not for the fear of it, people would swallow each other up alive."[56]

The underlying idea is that, however hostile a government may be toward its Jewish subjects—as, indeed, the Roman government was at the time this maxim was created—a bad government is still better than anarchy. Governments are subject to constraints; and influence can often be brought to bear on them or political deals struck with them, or with individual ministers, departments, opposition parties, or civil servants. When government breaks down, however, latent anti-Semitism generally comes to the fore, and the Jews are generally cast in the role of convenient scapegoat.

Because medieval Jewry felt so vulnerable, this particular prayer was invested with special importance. The names of the king, queen, and principle members of the royal family or Head of State is specified, the Torah is held for its recitation, and a special atmosphere of reverence and decorum invariably settles over the congregation at this time. Ironically, infinitely more reverence is accorded to prayers for earthly monarchy than to the King of Kings!

456. Is there any biblical precedent for offering up a prayer for the ruling power?

There is. The prophet Jeremiah lived at the time of the invasion of Judaea by the Babylonians and the wholesale deportation of its citizens to captivity in Babylon. He

---

54. Shapira, E. (1757). *Eliyahu Rabbah*, Sec. 284:11.
55. S. Z. Schick, ed. (1894). *Siddur Rashban*. Vienna: p. 206.
56. *Avot* 3:2.

sent a message of hope to the captives from Jerusalem, promising them that their captivity would be short-lived and that before 70 years had elapsed God would bring them back to their land (Jeremiah 29:19). In addition, he advised them to settle down dutifully in their new environment and "seek the welfare of the city to which you have been taken captive, and pray on its behalf to the Lord, for within its prosperity lies your own" (verse 7).

457. Have we any evidence that such prayers for their welfare were appreciated by the foreign monarchs?

The monarchs of antiquity certainly regarded the prayers and good wishes of their subject peoples and religions as efficacious. This explains why King Darius I of Persia (521–486 B.C.E.) gave permission for the Jews to rebuild their Temple, on the proviso that they brought sacrifices and offered up prayers there for the life of the king and his sons (Ezra 6:10).

458. With what frequency was the prayer for the king and government recited?

It has been the common practice for several centuries to recite this prayer once a week on the Sabbath and on festivals. Some Sephardic rites also recite it at the end of the *Kol Nidre* service. R. David Avudarham[57] refers to the custom of blessing the king in the context of his comments on laws governing the Reading of the Law on Mondays and Thursdays. This suggests that in fourteenth-century Spain this prayer was recited whenever the Torah was read.

459. Can we suggest any reason why fourteenth-century Spanish Jewry should have been more zealous in this regard than any other?

Our knowledge of the history of Spanish Jewry during this century explains precisely why they should have felt so terribly vulnerable and why they should have felt constrained to exaggerate their loyalty to the crown in this way.

Hatred of the Jews knew no bounds at that time, especially fomented by fanatical converts to Christianity who not only initiated anti-Jewish legislation, but also called for the destruction of Jewry. The arch-persecutor was one Abner of Burgos, a Jewish kabbalist and scholar who converted around 1321, and who devoted his life and energies to the writing of viciously anti-Semitic tracts and defamatory allegations that the whole of Talmudic law was a distortion of ethical and moral principles. He called for Jews to be deprived of their livelihood until they accepted conversion. Abner was followed by a succession of apostates who sought to outdo each other in their vitriolic charges against their perfidious former faith and people.

---

57. Avudarham, Rabbi D. *Sefer Avudarham Ha-shalem.* Jerusalem: Wertheimer, S. A. (1959), p. 136.

460. But surely they did not concern themselves with what Jews were reciting in their synagogues?

They most certainly did. In 1380, King John of Castile prohibited Jews from reciting the *Velamalshinim* prayer against apostates and heretics in the weekday *Amidah*:

> And if anyone shall recite this prayer or affirm it [by reciting Amen], he shall be publicly flogged with one hundred lashes; and if it be written down in any prayer book, the copier shall be fined three thousand gold pieces . . . in order that they shall know that, henceforth, we shall treat very harshly anyone who demeans the Christian faith.[58]

The Christian authorities were clearly extremely zealous when it came to observing and controlling what Jews said and did in their synagogues. It was more than politic, therefore, for the Jews not to be found wanting in their expressions of loyalty to the sovereign and his family.

461. Did medieval Muslim rulers expect similar demonstrations of loyalty to be made as part of public worship in synagogue?

They did, indeed. An Arabic "Prayer for the Welfare of Muslims," dating back to the twelfth century, was recently discovered in the Cairo Genizah:

> We also pray for all Muslims, males and females, who dwell in our country, their sons and daughters, male and female believers. May God hasten the healing of their sick, gather in their dispersed ones, and let loose and liberate those who have been taken captive. May He spread over them the tabernacle of His peace. Amen.[59]

This prayer dates back to the twelfth century and was customarily recited on *Simchat Torah*, when Muslim dignitaries were probably present in synagogue.

462. But surely such a prayer, for Muslim compatriots, goes far beyond the religious requirement of praying for the welfare of the "ruling power." Is this not an example of capitulation to religious discrimination?

It is, indeed, a fact that Jews felt constrained to prove their loyalty at all times, especially to the Muslim authorities for whom no other religions were credited with legitimacy. However, we should not imagine that it was only Jews who were obliged to introduce such tokens of allegiance into their prayers. Because of the fact that medieval Muslims were notorious for their constant revolts against their own

---

58. Ben-Sasson, H. H. (1976). *A History of the Jewish People*. Cambridge, Mass.: George Weidenfeld and Nicolson, p. 584.

59. *Ms. Heb. f. 31* (Bodleian Library, Oxford), quoted by Paul Fenton (Yenon) in *"Tefillah be'ad ha-rashut u-reshut be'ad ha-tefillah: zutot min ha-Genizah,"* in *Mi-mizrach Umi-maarav*, vol. 4 (Ramat Gan: Bar-Ilan University, 1983) p. 15. We acknowledge permission to reprint, granted by Bodleian Library, Oxford.

leaders, it was made obligatory, at the Friday public services at the mosques, to deliver a kind of sermon declaring the congregation's allegiance to the incumbent ruler and his family.

463. We mentioned above that prayers for the government were already recited in fourteenth-century Spain. When is the earliest record of such prayers having been prescribed?

There is no mention of any such specific prayer in the earliest Babylonian *siddurim* of Amram and Saadia (ninth to tenth centuries), nor in the eleventh century *Machzor Vitri*, written by simcha ben Samuel, of Vitri in France, a disciple of *Rashi*. When the first official prayer of this genre became popularized and accepted in a prayer rite is still uncertain.

464. When was our *Ha-notein teshuah* ("He who gives salvation") formula introduced, and by whom?

It first made its appearance in a printed prayer book in 1658, though we may assume that it was introduced and standardized about a century before. By the mid-1660s, it was being recited throughout the Sephardic world, from England to Asia Minor. Since Franco-German Ashkenazi Jewry suffered from similar feelings of insecurity, this prayer was soon borrowed by them and came to enjoy universal popularity. It is invested with special significance by its being recited by the rabbi rather than the *Chazan* and is generally listened to in perfect silence and with a quiet reverence that few other parts of the service can claim.

XIII

The Blowing of the Shofar

465. We have already referred to the custom of blowing the shofar during the month of Elul (See Questions 147, 150–158). Is the blowing on Rosh Hashanah also merely custom?

Certainly not. It is a clear Biblical instruction: "In the seventh month, on the first day of the month, ye shall have a holy convocation; ye shall do no manner of servile work; *it is a day of sounding the horn (yom teru'ah)* for you" (Numbers 29:1).

In another passage, the Torah states: "In the seventh month, in the first day of the month, there shall be a solemn rest unto you, *a remembrance of the blast of horns (zikhron teru'ah)*, a holy convocation. Ye shall do no manner of servile work; and ye shall bring an offering made by fire unto the Lord" (Leviticus 23:24).

466. Why does the Torah use the word *teru'ah*, rather than shofar (ram's horn)?

Possibly because in biblical and Temple times, the blowing was not restricted to the ram's horn. Rosh Hashanah occurs on the first day of the month, which is also Rosh Chodesh. Now, for Rosh Chodesh (and other festive occasions) the Torah prescribes the blowing of silver trumpets (*chatzotzrot*).[1] Rosh Hashanah—being also Rosh Chodesh—was no exception; and hence, rather than specify the shofar, the Torah merely referred to the *teru'ah* sound that is common to both those wind instruments. The basic verb, *ru'a*, has the meaning of "to vibrate," and refers to the sound created by breath; and, hence, it is also used to denote the shout of a multitude of people.[2]

467. Do we know what form the blowing of the silver trumpet and the ram's horn took in ancient times on Rosh Hashanah?

The Mishnah[3] elucidates:

The shofar for Rosh Hashanah was from a wild goat, straight, and with a gold-covered mouthpiece. Two trumpets were stationed, one on either side

---

1. Numbers 10:10.
2. Exodus 32:17.
3. Mishnah *Rosh Hashanah* 3:3–4.

227

[and blown simultaneously with the shofar]. However, the blowing of the shofar was extended, while on the trumpets they blew a shorter note, because the basic commandment of the day is with the shofar.

468. We have quoted above (Question 465) the Torah's reference to Rosh Hashanah as *zikhron teru'ah* ("a remembrance of the trumpet sound"), while the festival itself is referred to as *Yom Ha-Zikkaron* ("a day of remembrance"). What is being remembered?

The famous Hasidic teacher Reb Levi Yitzchak of Berdichev answers by way of a parable.[4]

He describes a king who once went on an extended hunt on his own through neighboring lands. He entered a forest and lost his way. He kept on asking people who lived in the forest if they could direct him along the route that would lead him back to his own land and home. But not one of those simple folk could help, for they had never ventured out of their forest, and neither had they ever heard of the king or his country. Fortunately for him, he eventually asked a very wise and well-traveled man who recognized the king and knew where his palace was located. He personally accompanied him back to his palace.

On the journey back, the king had much time to recognize the man's unique wisdom and to cement a close relationship with him. On arrival at his palace, the king rewarded the man by appointing him to the highest position of state, over all his other ministers, and by investing him with splendid robes in place of his own clothes, which the king ordered to be stored away.

After several years, the chief minister did something that so offended his monarch that the latter commanded his other leading ministers to convene as a court to judge his chief minister for treason. The chief minister, realizing how desperate was his fate, fell on his face before the king, wept, and sorely petitioned that, before sentencing him, the king might grant him just one favor, namely to allow him to dress again in the garments he wore during those days when he led the king through the forest and brought him home.

The king agreed, and when he appeared before the king in those clothes, the king was suddenly and forcefully reminded of how this man had saved his life and of his other kindnesses to him on that journey, when he had taken such good care of him and brought him home safely to his palace. The king's mercy was aroused thereby, and he forgave him fully for what he had done and restored him to his former position.

Reb Levi Yitzchak compares this story to the God–Israel relationship before Sinai. God was wandering in the world, with no one to recognize His kingship and accept His authority. All the other nations had no interest in Him. None of them could locate His heavenly palace. Only Israel accepted His Torah, lovingly and willingly, and crowned Him as their God and monarch. Yet, there comes a time

---

4. Barukh, Y. L., ed. (1952). *Sefer Ha-moadim*. Tel Aviv: Dvir, p. 64.

when we succumb and rebel against His laws and authority, and so, on Rosh Hashanah, He sets up His court to judge us for our rebelliousness.

So what do we do to secure mercy? We take out the identical instrument—the shofar—that was blown at Sinai when we cemented that unique relationship with God, which no other nation was prepared to enter into. On that occasion, the Torah states, "And when the sound of the shofar grew louder and louder . . ." (Exodus 19:19).

The purpose of Rosh Hashanah is, therefore, to serve as a day of "remembrance" (*zikkaron*), whereon God will "remember" the loyalty we once displayed at Sinai, and, on its merit, will forgive us our rebelliousness and exonerate us in judgment.

CIRCUMCISION AS A PRELUDE TO THE SHOFAR

469. If a circumcision takes place on Rosh Hashanah, at which point in the service is it done?

It is performed just before the blowing of the shofar. This is a departure from the practice on Shabbat and festivals when it is done after the service, normally at home. The reason for this is because of the protracted nature of the Rosh Hashanah service, which continues until well after noon. Because of the principle *zerizim makdimin lemitzvot* ("Those who are zealous, perform *mitzvot* as early as possible"), such a great *mitzvah* as circumcision should certainly be performed while it is still morning.

It was prescribed to be recited just before the blowing of the shofar because, like shofar, circumcision is also a *zikkaron*, a "remembrance," as we say in the *Zikhronot* section of the *Musaf Amidah*: "Remember the covenant with Abraham (circumcision) and the binding of Isaac" (symbolized by the ram's horn). We follow the chronology of these two tokens of "remembrance" by first performing the ritual of the "covenant with Abraham" before proceeding with the blowing of the shofar.

470. If there is such a principle to perform a *mitzvah* as early as possible, then why do we delay blowing the shofar until just before *Musaf*?

The Talmud[5] raises this question and states that originally it was prescribed to be blown during the morning service, but that, on one occasion, the shofar's reveille was misconstrued by a Roman garrison as a signal for the Jews to rise up in rebellion, which prompted a cruel and bloody response. It was decreed that henceforth the shofar should not be sounded until late morning, during the *Musaf* service, by which time the occupying forces would have realized that there was no threat in this Jewish assembly, but that it was to observe a festival, and that the sounding of the shofar's alarm was an innocuous ritual.

---

5. *Rosh Hashanah* 32b.

471. But why, when that situation no longer obtained, was the sounding of the shofar not restored to its rightful place, in *Shachrit*, to demonstrate our eagerness to fulfill the *mitzvah* as early as possible?

This is not the way the evolution of Jewish custom and practice works. We are very conservative; and once a practice or an adaptation has taken root, even as an emergency measure, there is a tendency to leave it as it is or synthesize both the original and the adapted form of the practice.

And this is precisely what has happened in the case of the blowing of the shofar. Hence, we preserve a reminder of the original practice, of blowing *entirely* during *Shachrit*, by blowing the first thirty notes immediately after the Reading of the Torah; and we blow the rest during *Musaf* to recall the emergency measure adopted at a later period.

WOMEN'S OBLIGATION TO HEAR THE SHOFAR

472. Are women obliged to fulfill the *mitzvah* of hearing the shofar?

Technically they are not, since the blowing of the shofar is a positive *mitzvah* that is confined to a particular time, and women are absolved from rituals that fall under such a category. Nevertheless, women have accepted this *mitzvah* as an important stimulus to their repentance, and it has thus taken on obligatory status.

Because women are not as obligated as men to hear the shofar, *Maharil* states that it is better for young children, who may cause a distraction during the blowing of the shofar, to stand with their mothers in the ladies' gallery, rather than in the men's section.

473. May a woman blow the shofar, then, for herself, and is there any reward for the performance of the *mitzvah* in this way?

She may, indeed, blow for herself, but it is preferable for a male who is practiced in the skill of blowing the shofar to blow for her. The reason for this is that the woman may well be so preoccupied with trying to squeeze out the notes from the shofar (blowing is, after all, quite a skill) that she will be distracted from being able to muster that specially focused religious concentration that should enable the sounds of the shofar to effectively arouse us to repentance.

There is a reward for a woman who blows the shofar for herself, but it is the reward for a *mitzvah* that one is not obligated to fulfill (*mitzvah she'inah metzuvah ve-osah*), and the reward for this is not as great as for a *mitzvah* that we are obligated to perform.

474. May a woman blow, then, for another man or woman?

If absolutely necessary, she may blow for another woman, but she may not blow to enable a man to fulfill his duty of listening to the shofar. This is on account of the halakhic principle that anyone who is personally not obligated to perform a certain *mitzvah* may not perform it on behalf of another. As we have stated (See Question 472), women are not obligated to hear the shofar.

475. If a woman is required at home and cannot remain in shul for the entire service, which notes of the shofar should she endeavor to be in shul for?

It is preferable for her to be present for the blessings over the shofar and the first group of thirty notes, blown prior to the *Amidah*. These are regarded as fulfilling the *mitzvah* according to our biblical requirement (*mid'oraita*), while the remaining seventy notes are a rabbinic extension. For the same reason, when blowing for a housebound woman, it is sufficient to blow the first thirty notes.

476. When blowing for a housebound woman, who recites the blessing?

It is preferable for the woman to recite the blessings herself before the man blows for her. The reason for this is that, generally, the man would be blowing for her on his way home from synagogue, after he has already fulfilled his duty by listening to the blessings and the notes of the synagogue *toke'ah* (blower) who has blown on his (and the rest of the congregation's) behalf. Now, we are not allowed to recite blessings unnecessarily, so that man could not proceed, therefore, to recite shofar blessings on behalf of the housebound woman. If he had to do so, however, he would be required, while in synagogue, to make a conscious act of mental dissociation from being included among those for whom the *toke'ah* there was blowing. This is clearly not an advisable course of action, and hence, wherever possible, the woman should be encouraged (and helped) to recite the blessings.

If the man who has already heard the shofar is reciting the blessings for a woman who cannot herself recite them, he does not recite the *Shehecheyanu* blessing, since the sound of the shofar is not, in fact, novel for him.

477. Does the same principle apply if one is blowing for a housebound male, so that the latter should make the blessing?

No, it does not. A housebound male is biblically duty-bound to fulfill the *mitzvah*. In this situation, we apply the principle of *areivut*, "Jewish collective responsibility." According to this principle—which applies in the case of all *mitzvot*—even though a person has already fulfilled his religious obligation, he can perform that same *mitzvah* again, on behalf of another, purely in order to facilitate its performance by one unable to do so on his own. (In the case of a woman, who is not "responsible" for the performance of this particular [time-bound] *mitzvah*, the principle of *areivut* does not apply, and hence she has to recite the blessings herself.)

478. May a minor (that is, one under the age of bar mitzvah) blow the shofar for others?

No. A minor is, halakhically, in the same status as a woman, for whom there is no real obligation to hear the sounding of the shofar. There is, however, an obligation upon his father to train him in the way of observance of *mitzvot* when the child reaches the age of about 11 years. This does not, however, confer obligatory status upon the latter.

479. When listening to the blessings over the shofar, does the congregation make the usual responses, *Barukh hu uvarukh shemo* and Amen?

We do not respond with *Barukh hu uvarukh shemo* when someone is reciting a blessing on our behalf, since, in that situation, it is regarded as an interruption into the formula of the blessing. Obviously, if we were reciting a blessing for ourselves, we would not interrupt with the extraneous response ("Blessed is He, and blessed is His name"). That is prescribed only for when we hear someone else invoking the name of God as part of their blessing. The same consideration applies when someone is reciting the blessing on our behalf.

We do, however, recite Amen when someone is reciting a blessing on our behalf—as in the case here the blessings over the shofar—since such a short affirmation, after the blessing has already been concluded, was not regarded as an interruption.

THE SHOFAR ON SABBATH AND *YOM TOV*

480. Why do we not blow the shofar if Rosh Hashanah falls on the Sabbath?

The prohibition was introduced as a rabbinic precaution, in case a person might come to carry the shofar into a public place—either to synagogue or to the home of someone for whom he wishes to blow. Infringement of the Sabbath law in this way is a most serious, capital offense and outweighs consideration of the obligation of hearing the shofar. This obligation is not neglected, however, for the shofar will still be heard on the other day of Rosh Hashanah.

481. Is there any biblical basis for celebrating Rosh Hashanah in this way, without the blowing of the shofar?

There is, indeed. We referred above (See Question 465) to two separate biblical designations of this festival, one which refers to it as *yom teru'ah* ("a day of sounding the horn"), and the other as *zikhron teru'ah* ("a *reminder* of the sounding of the horn"). The Talmud attributes the first reference to the occurrence of Rosh Hashanah on a weekday and the second reference to its occurrence on a Sabbath—when we do not actually blow it, but have merely "a reminder" of it in the prayers that we recite.

482. May the shofar be handled on the Sabbath of Rosh Hashanah?

Without wishing to get into details of complex Sabbath laws, the simple answer to this question is that, because the shofar is forbidden to be blown on that Sabbath

day, it is designated as *muktzeh*, that is something divorced entirely from the
Sabbath context, and therefore forbidden even to be handled.

However, if the object was such that it could, technically, be put to some other
permitted use on the Sabbath, then, if one requires to use it for that (albeit unusual)
purpose, or if one requires to use the place that the *muktzeh* object is occupying, it
may be so moved or used. Hence, since the shofar could be used as a permitted
object, say to serve as a water container with which to feed a child, it may therefore
be handled either for such a purpose or moved off a table to make space for food.

483. May the shofar be handled or blown on a Rosh Hashanah that occurs on a weekday, after the service is over?

A shofar can clearly not be *muktzeh* on Rosh Hashanah, since it is specifically
designated for that day. By a halakhic quirk, however, there is one respect wherein
Yom Tov becomes more stringent than Shabbat. As we have said above, when Rosh
Hashanah falls on a Shabbat, the shofar can be used for a secular purpose (for
example as a bottle to feed babies), because it is not *muktzeh*, "specifically
designated," on that day for blowing, since we do not blow on the Sabbath. On the
weekday of Rosh Hashanah, however, the shofar cannot be put to such a secular and
everyday purpose, since on this day the shofar is blown, and becomes, therefore,
muktzeh, "specifically designated," for ritual blowing only, and not for any other
purpose.

As regards blowing the shofar for mere practice on Rosh Hashanah that occurs
on a weekday: there is a difference of opinion here between two of our main
codifiers. Maimonides takes the view[6] that there is no objection to minors practicing
with the shofar on *Yom Tov*, even if they have reached the age of training (11 years),
and that even an adult may supervise and demonstrate to them on that day. The *Tur*,
on the other hand, takes the view that even touching the shofar is prohibited and that
an adult or a child who has reached the age of "training" (11 years) may not blow
it, since he has already fulfilled his duty as regards that *mitzvah*.[7]

THE SHOFAR PRACTICES OF ANCIENT JERUSALEM

484. Was there any variety of practice between the blowing of the shofar in Jerusalem and the way it was blown in the rest of Israel?

There was a major difference as regards the blowing of the shofar on the Sabbath
day. Just as sacrifices were offered in the Temple on that day, so was the shofar also
blown there on the Sabbath, as long as it remained the seat of the supreme court (*Bet
Din Ha-gadol*). This did not only apply to the Temple, but also to the entire city of

---

6. Maimonides, *Mishneh Torah, Hilkhot Shofar* 2:7.
7. *Tur, Orach Chayyim* 588, and *Bach ad loc.*

Jerusalem; and not only to the city itself, but to any place within a radius of 2000 cubits of it and that had an unrestricted view and unrestricted access to Jerusalem, and that could hear the sound of a shofar blown in the holy city.[8]

485. Did any change take place after the destruction of the Temple as regards the blowing of the shofar on the Sabbath?

When the Temple was destroyed, Rabbi Yochanan ben Zaccai instituted that the Temple practice of blowing on the Sabbath should be continued in any place in proximity to Jerusalem where the High Court was in session. His reason was that, because of the awe of blowing in the presence of such an august body, no one would forget and carry his shofar there on the Sabbath. Maimonides adds that the *Bet Din* itself would issue warnings on that score to avoid such Sabbath desecration.[9]

486. Is this still the practice, to blow on the Sabbath in places near Jerusalem?

No. Rabbi Yochanan's ruling was not followed for very long. When he referred to blowing before a High Court (only), he understood that the court would convene to fix the new month and to regulate the calendar after hearing the evidence of witnesses who had seen the first signs of the new moon's crescent.[10] After the destruction of the Temple it was almost impossible for a High Court to meet in the proximity of Jerusalem, and by the year 358, Hillel II gave permission for a fixed calendar to be introduced, whereby mathematical means were employed to determine the calendar replacing thereby the reliance upon witnesses. Thus, there would have been no further justification for blowing the shofar on the Sabbath.

There were some sporadic attempts, however, to implement Rabbi Yochanan's ruling. The great Talmudist, Rabbi Isaac Alfasi (1012–1103) is said to have blown the shofar when Rosh Hashanah fell on a Shabbat; and, more recently, Rabbi Akivah Joseph Schlesinger attempted to reintroduce the practice in 1905, in the privacy of his own home, though this aroused a storm of protest in the Jerusalem *yishuv*. His book, *Bet Yosef Chadash*, wherein he justifies his opinion, was ordered to be burnt by the rabbis of Jerusalem.

487. But is not blowing the shofar a forbidden category of "work" on the Sabbath day?

Strangely, it was not so categorized. The Torah forbids *melekhet avodah* ("servile work") on the Sabbath. The blowing of the shofar was regarded by the sages as a *chokhmah*, a "skill," rather than a servile exercise.

---

8. *Rosh Hashanah* 30a; Maimonides, *Mishneh Torah, Hilkhot Shofar* 2:8.
9. Maimonides, *loc. cit.* 2:9.
10. See Question 13 and Maimonides, *loc. cit.*, 2:9.

THE DEVELOPMENT OF THE *TEKI'AH* SYSTEM

488. What are the three groups of notes that are blown on the shofar?

They are (i) the *teki'ah*, (ii) the *shevarim*, and (iii) the *teru'ah*.

489. What is the origin and meaning of the word *teki'ah*?

The actual noun *teki'ah* is not found in the Hebrew Bible, though the verb *taka'* is found, in the sense of "to strike, clap, deliver a blow, blast with a wind instrument." The prophet Amos states, *Ha-yitaka' shofar ba'iyr ve'am lo yecheradu*, "Can a horn be sounded in a city without the people trembling" (3:6). The noun used in the Bible to denote the blast of a horn is *teka'*, as in the phrase, *Halleluhu beteka' shofar*, "Praise Him with the blast of the horn" (Psalm 150:4). So *teki'ah* denotes, simply, one single blast of the horn.

490. What is the origin and meaning of the word *shevarim*?

The noun *shevarim* is derived from the root *shavar*, meaning "to break." It occurs in the Hebrew Bible, mainly in the singular, in the sense of "breaking, fracture, crushing, crashing." Hence, Jeremiah refers to *Kol milchamah ba'aretz veshever gadol*, "the sound of battle in the land, and a great crashing" (50:22).

Applied to our context, the *shevarim* refers, therefore, to a fractured note and takes the form of the standard *teki'ah* broken up into three separate blasts.

491. What is the origin and meaning of the word *teru'ah*?

We have already referred to the meaning of *ru'a*, the root of this word (See Questions 465–466, 481), namely, "to shake, vibrate." The phrase *yom* (or *zikhron*) *teru'ah* is the one employed by the Torah in its definition of this festival. Perhaps its choice of this particular noun was in order to create a *double entendre*, whereby it is not only the "vibration" of the shofar that is prescibed, but also a human "quaking" before the bar of divine justice.

The quaking or vibrating sound of the *teru'ah* is created by breaking the standard *teki'ah* into nine mini notes. These notes are formed by the rapid insertion of the tongue, into and out of the mouthpiece, nine times.

The length of each of the above three notes of the shofar is identical in duration, as the following diagram will demonstrate:

Teki'ah

Shevarim

_____ / _____ / _____

Teru'ah

____ ____ ____ ____ ____ ____ ____ ____ ____

492. Why do we blow a *teki'ah* before and after each *teru'ah*?

This is rooted in the biblical instruction with regard to the blowing. The Torah states *Veha'avarta shofar teru'ah*, "And you shall cause to be emitted a sound of the *teru'ah*" (Leviticus 25:9). The identical verb *Veha'avarta* is found again, in the phrase *Va-ya'aviru kol bamachaneh*, "And they transmitted the announcement around the camp" (Exodus 36:6). Hence, the phrase *Veha'avarta shofar teru'ah* was construed to mean that the shofar's *teru'ah* sound "should be announced" or "heralded" by another sound of the shofar.

We blow the *teki'ah* both before and after the main notes (*shevarim* or *teru'ah* or a combination of both) because of the apparently unnecessary repetition of this instruction to sound an accompanying note. In the same verse, the Torah states, *Veha'avarta shofar teru'ah*, and also *ta'aviru shofar* (Leviticus 25:9). This was construed, therefore, as a double requirement to accompany the shofar's sounds both before and after they are sounded.

493. Now the Torah makes reference exclusively to *teru'ah*. We have also explained why we have a *teki'ah* accompanying it. Why, though, do we add a third type of note, the *shevarim*?

Strange as it may seem, this was introduced on account of there being some doubt in Talmudic times as to the precise nature of the biblical *teru'ah*. Although its sense was clearly some expression of "vibration" or "quaking," it was unclear whether this should be expressed as a short, shrill wail or sob (*yillulei yelil*) or as a more protracted sigh (*genuchei genach*).

In their eagerness to reproduce the authentic biblical sound, the sages introduced the *shevarim* in addition to the *teru'ah*; the former (with its three medium-length blasts) representing drawn-out sighs, and the latter (with its nine rapid notes) representing the sounds of quick successive sobs. Rabbi Abbahu of Caesarea prescibed, therefore, that they should blow a *teki'ah*, followed by *shevarim-teru'ah*, followed by *teki'ah*, thereby ensuring against any doubt regarding the authentic biblical *teru'ah* sound.[11]

494. So why is our system of blowing so much more complex than that of Rabbi Abbahu?

Our system is, indeed, more complex, in that we blow a total of 100 notes. Our expanded pattern was necessitated by the desire to avoid the possibility of a (halakhic) interruption as a result of our uncertainty regarding the precise nature of the original biblical *teru'ah*.

The problem is this: If the authentic biblical *teru'ah* was identical to the way we blow it, then the *shevarim* that we blow with it (for the avoidance of doubt) may well constitute an interruption of the first *teki'ah*, which is supposed to precede the *teru'ah*. If, on the other hand, it is the *shevarim* that represents the authentic biblical

---

11. *Rosh Hashanah* 34a.

shofar blast, then the *teru'ah* that follows it may, in turn, constitute an interruption between it and the *teki'ah* that follows it.

For this reason, in addition to Rabbi Abbahu's simple combination of *teki'ah— shevarim—teru'ah—teki'ah,* the sages introduced the blowing of a *teki'ah— shevarim—teki'ah* (in case the *teru'ah* constituted an interruption) and also a *teki'ah—teru'ah—teki'ah* in case the *shevarim* constituted an interruption.

495. But, by covering both eventualities and avoiding halakhic interruption in that way, surely we do not require then Rabbi Abbahu's *teki'ah— shevarim/ teru'ah—teki'ah*?

The Talmud raises this question and replies that Rabbi Abbahu was apprehensive that the authentic biblical *teru'ah* may actually have been a composite note, reflective of a sigh followed by sobbing, since, when people are distraught, they often sigh deeply and then burst out into sobbing. Hence, to cover that possibility, we also include the *shevarim-teru'ah* combination (together with the statutory *teki'ahs* before and after).

496. But why do we associate the notes of the shofar with weeping and lament? Why also do we blow just 100 notes?

These are, indeed, related questions. The answer is that a tradition of the Geonic period has it that the 100 notes that we blow on Rosh Hashanah correspond to the 100 sobs that the mother of the Canaanite general, Sisera, gave out at the news of the death of her son at the hands of Yael (Judges 5:21).

The poetic account of the episode, contained in the Song of Deborah, states that "the mother of Sisera *sobbed (Va-teyabev)*." This unusual Aramaic word set off an association of ideas with the context of the shofar, since the Targum (official Aramaic translation of the Pentateuch) renders the phrase *Yom teru'ah* as *yom yebava*.[12]

497. But where does the tradition come from that the mother of Sisera sobbed just 100 sobs, since it is nowhere mentioned in the biblical account?

Numerology often underlies the creation of Midrashic associations. Here we have an example of this; for, if we count the number of letters in the two verses that describe the mother of Sisera's anguish (Judges 5:28–29), we will find that they total 100 letters. Hence, the idea that she wept with 100 sobs![13]

498. How are the 100 notes that we blow arranged?

They are divided up into three separate blowings. The first block, of thirty notes, is blown before the *Musaf Amidah*; the second block, of thirty notes, is blown during

---

12. *Rosh Hashanah* 33b.
13. Sperber, D. (1990). *Minhagei Yisrael*. Jerusalem: Mosad Ha-Rav kuk, Vol. 2, pp. 181–182.

the repetition of the *Musaf Amidah*; and the final forty notes are blown after the *Amidah*.

The thirty notes in each of those sections of the prayers are formed by creating a combination of the three notes: *shevarim, teru'ah,* and *shevarim-teru'ah,* together with the accompanying *teki'ahs*. Thus, the 100 notes are arranged as follows:

(i) Before the *Musaf Amidah*: *Teki'ah—shevarim/teru'ah—teki'ah (x3)*; *Teki'ah—shevarim—teki'ah (x3)*; *Teki'ah—teru'ah—teki'ah (x3)* (total: 30 notes).

(Instead of the final *teki'ah*, a lengthened *teki'ah gedolah* is blown at the end of this and the other two stages of blowing.)

(ii) After each of the three *Malkhuyyot, Zikhronot,* and *Shofarot* sections of the (repetition of the) *Musaf Amidah,* the above combination is blown just once, making a total of thirty notes blown during the *Amidah* (total thus far: 60 notes).

(iii) After the *Amidah*, the final forty notes are blown. These comprise the thirty notes, as blown in (i) above, followed by the same combination blown just once (which comprises ten notes).

The Sephardic tradition is to blow also during the recitation of the silent *Amidah*. The worshipers wait at the end of the *Malkhuyyot*, the *Zikhronot*, and the *Shofarot*, respectively, when the *toke'ah* sounds the shofar, though without any *makriy* (See Question 500) calling out the notes aloud for him, as this would constitute an interruption in his silent prayer.

499. Are there any special names for the thirty notes of the shofar blown before the *Musaf Amidah* and those blown during the *Amidah*?

Those blown before the *Amidah* are known in rabbinic literature as *teki'ot dimeyushav*, meaning "the sounds [blown] when seated." This means that, technically, the congregation (though not the person blowing) could sit while listening to these shofar sounds. The rest of the notes, blown during the *Amidah* ("standing prayer"), are known as *teki'ot dime'umad*, meaning "the sounds [blown] while standing," since standing is obligatory at this time.

500. Why does the one who blows the shofar require an aide on the opposite side of the *bimah* to call out the names of the notes to be blown?

This person is called the *makriy* ("caller"), and he is engaged in order to ensure that the *toke'ah* or *Baal toke'ah* ("blower") does not become confused regarding which note he is up to. Because one line of notes ends with a *teki'ah* and the following line commences with the same note, it is easy to become confused as to which *teki'ah* one is up to. Similarly, when one line of notes has to be repeated three times, his preoccupation with the blowing of the notes properly and loudly may well distract the *toke'ah* so that he is unsure whether he has repeated the line once or twice.

501. Can anyone be deputed to blow the shofar or act as *makriy*, and is it an honor awarded to a person of special religious merit?

These are honors that should be reserved for the rabbi of the congregation or another learned and pious elder. This is to ensure that holy thoughts and a fervent concentration on the matter of repentance accompany this biblically prescribed ritual.

A major difference in attitude toward this *mitzvah*, between Ashkenazim and Sephardim is, nevertheless, recorded by Rabbi Jacob ben Asher. He tells us that "there is a custom in Germany that the most important men of the community are zealous to be chosen to blow the shofar on Rosh Hashanah, while in Spain people flee from the *mitzvah*, so that it becomes necessary to hire a man from the street to blow for them."[14]

THE CONTROVERSIAL *YEHIY RATZON* SHOFAR PETITIONS

502. In some *machzorim*, there are some abstruse *Yehiy ratzon* petitions prescribed for recitation after each group of notes has been blown. Are these required to be recited, and if so, why do other editions omit them?

These compositions, popularized by the sixteenth-century mystics, have been the subject of much controversy over the centuries, especially on account of the personal names of angels that they appear to be invoking with the plea that they carry the merit of Israel before the heavenly throne. For many authorities, this was in flagrant breach of the basic principle of Jewish prayer, namely that we address God directly, without recourse to intermediaries. As a result of the criticism, many editors of *machzorim* printed more refined versions of the petitions, or omitted the angelic references.

The following is a version of the *Machzor Kol-bo* (with Yiddish translation and commentary): "May it be Your will . . . that the *teki'ah shevarim teru'ah* that we sound this day should be woven into the heavenly veil by the appointed angel Tartiel . . . and Jeshua, Minister of the Presence, and Metatron, Prince of the Countenance."

503. Were there any other grounds for objecting to these petitions?

One criticism of the above-quoted prayer will provide an example of the dangers inherent in such petitions. It was pointed out that there is absolutely no reference in our literature to any "Minister of the Presence" by the name of Jeshua. The only conclusion we can reach is that this is none other than a Christian reference to the

---

14. *Tur Orach Chayyim*, Chapter 585.

name of their founder, Jeshu, that has infiltrated the *machzor* through the guile of some missionary in the employ of the printers![15]

Others objected to their recitation on the grounds that they constituted an interruption in the *mitzvah* of this section's shofar blowing. This seems to be a rather lame objection here and may well have been a mere smoke-screen to obscure their more serious objections. The Routledge edition of the *Machzor* omits all these petitions. The Art Scroll edition includes them, but adds a rubric advising that "the angelic names . . . be scanned with the eyes, but not spoken." An interesting example of both having one's cake and eating it!

The great kabbalist, Isaac Luria, recommended that one should recite a short confession between each section of the blowing.

THE SIGNIFICANCE OF THE SHOFAR

504. What is the significance of the shofar?

The most popular explanation is that it recalls the ram sacrificed by Abraham instead of his son. This ram was "caught in the thickets *by its horns*" (Genesis 22:13).

Another explanation is that New Year, marking the beginning of Creation, also represents the moment when God became King of the universe. Just as trumpets are sounded at the coronation of earthly monarchs, so is the shofar sounded to mark the enthronement of God.

A further explanation relates the blowing to the revelation at Sinai, when "the sound of the shofar went stronger and stronger" (Exodus 18:19). On Rosh Hashanah, it is sounded, then, to summon us to renew that pledge made by our ancestors at Sinai.

Some authorities view the shofar as foreshadowing its role in the time to come, as herald to the day of judgment,[16] the in-gathering of the exiles[17] and the resurrection.

505. What exactly does the word shofar mean?

The precise meaning of its three core root letters is unknown. In Assyrian, the word *shappar(u)* means a wild goat, and, as this species may have been the favorite type of curved horn utilized in the ancient Near East, it may well have lent its name to all subsequent types of horns, whether obtained from a goat or any other animal.

Some homilists[18] relate the word shofar to another, totally independent, Hebrew and Aramaic root, *shafar*, meaning, "to be pleasant, beautiful, goodly." By a little

15. Braun, S. (1978). *She'arim Metzuyanim Be-halakhah*, published together with text of the *Kitzur Shulchan Arukh*. New York: Philip Feldheim, vol. 3, sec. 129:15, p. 163, note 16.
16. Zephaniah 1:14–16.
17. Isaiah 27:13.
18. Midrash *Shochar Tov* on Psalm 81:4, ed. S. Buber (Jerusalem 1966), sec. 5, p. 184.

stretch of the imagination, they view this as the ultimate objective of the shofar's summons, namely to make our actions more pleasant, beautiful, goodly—and Godly.[19]

506. Was the shofar blown at all on other occasions besides Rosh Hashanah?

It is also blown on Yom Kippur, to mark the conclusion of the fast. It was used in the coronation ceremony of kings. In Temple times, twenty-one blasts were sounded on the shofar each day. As the gates opened, three notes rang out, summoning the faithful to worship. Accompanying the public sacrifices, another nine notes were blown, and a further nine accompanied the afternoon offering.

Every Friday evening, six notes of the shofar were sounded to announce the approach of Shabbat. At the first sounding, the laborers in the field stopped work and made for home. At the second blast, the shops closed, and city life came to a halt. The third blast was a signal to light the lights in the homes in honor of the Sabbath. Then after a brief pause, three further notes were sounded, and the Sabbath began.

The shofar was also sounded when Israel went into battle. It inaugurated the Jubilee (fiftieth) year, to announce the year of release when all slaves were granted their freedom and all land was restored to its original tribal freehold-owners.

In the medieval period, it was also used in the solemn ceremony of excommunication, which imposed total isolation on any Jew who had rebelled against the ruling of the court or undermined the authority of the Torah or refused to be bound by the regulations of the community. It was also used each month to announce the appearance of the new moon. It was blown on fast days to rouse the people to repentance, and it was also employed in Sephardic communities, at funerals, and while performing the *taharah* ("purification rites"), when its plaintive notes set the mood of the occasion.[20]

LAMENATZE'ACH LIVNEI KORACH, MIZMOR

507. Why do we recite Psalm 47 before blowing the shofar?

The reason is that its two main themes are most relevant to the *mitzvah* about to be performed. It refers to God as ascending His throne of justice "to the accompaniment of the shofar's sound" (verse 6), and it refers to God as "King of the entire earth." These themes are particularly related to one aspect of the shofar's significance as a herald of God's coronation as ruler of the world (See Question 505).

---

19. Cohen, J. M. (1994). *Prayer and Penitence*. Northvale, NJ: Jason Aronson Inc., p. 63.

20. Zimmels, H. J. (1958). *Ashkenazim and Sephardim*. London: Jews' College Publications, Oxford University Press, p. 183.

508. But why is this psalm prescribed for recitation seven times before blowing the shofar?

The reason is that the name *Elokim*, which connotes the God of strict justice (as opposed to the four letter name or *Tetragrammaton*, which represents the God of mercy), appears seven times in this psalm. Thus, in total, God's name is recited forty-nine times.

Now, according to the mystical tradition, there exist forty-nine depths of impurity through which man may descend until reaching the fiftieth, and lowest, depth, at which redemption becomes impossible. Corresponding to these depths, there are also forty-nine gradations of purity through which man can rise. We recite these forty-nine expressions of divine strict justice, therefore, in order to indicate to God that, through the power of the shofar, we hope to rid ourselves of any taint of impurity, and we petition God to transport us from whatever negative level we occupy to a corresponding level of sanctity.

509. If King David was the author of the Psalms, what is the meaning of the heading, "A psalm of the sons of Korach?"

It is true that tradition attributes the authorship of the Psalms to King David, but this does not mean that the compilation of psalms that constitutes the biblical book contains only his psalms. Indeed, the Talmud states that David made use of the works of ten elders: Adam, Malki-Zedek, Abraham, Moses, Heman the Ezrachite, Yedutun, Asaf, and the three sons of Korach—authors of our psalm.[21]

Critical scholars do not accept this view that there actually existed psalms composed by Adam and the early biblical personages, that they survived until the time of David, and that they were of an advanced linguistic and poetic style as developed in the time of David. They treat the psalm headings with caution, especially since some of the early translations, such as the Greek Septuagint (third and second century B.C.E.) and the Syriac Peshitta (second century C.E.), have different headings for the same psalms, indicating that, even at that early period, there was doubt as to the authorship of the individual psalms. It is also difficult, unless one employs broad Midrashic license, to relate the content of those psalms that bear the name of a biblical personage with any episode or issue relating to his life.

It is possible that what the Talmudic sages meant was that David dedicated those specific psalms to the biblical ancestor whose name appears at the outset of the particular psalm.

510. What does the opening term, *Lamenatze'ach*, "For the leader," mean?

This title occurs fifty-five times in the Psalter, as well as at the beginning of the psalm, which constitutes chapter three of the book of *Habbakuk*. *Menatze'ach*

---

21. *Bava Batra* 14b.

means "director" or "choir master," and, since this term is only found elsewhere in the books of Chronicles, it suggests that the psalms that employ this term emanate from the period of the Chronicler, that is, from the middle Greek period (200–150 B.C.E.). As the great majority of the psalms that use this term are prayers, it seems likely that this collection was designed as a prayer book for use at the prayer-meetings of that period, out of which the institution of the synagogue developed.

Some have suggested that after the title *Lamenatze'ach*, "For the Director," the actual name of that choir master would originally have been inserted, in order to personalize his particular copy.

511. The term *selah* occurs in this psalm and in many others. What does it mean?

The term *selah* occurs seventy-one times and three times in the Habakkuk psalm. Its precise meaning is uncertain, as is its function in the psalms. The Greek Septuagint translates it as "interlude," indicating that at that point a pause should be made, perhaps for the insertion of a blessing. Each of the five books of psalms concludes with a doxology or final blessing. For example, Psalm 41 (end of the first book of psalms) concludes with the blessing *Barukh Ha-Shem Elokei yisrael meiha-olam ve'ad ha-olam amen ve'amen* ("Blessed be the Lord, God of Israel, from eternity to eternity, Amen and Amen"). It might be that this, or some other such prayer, was prescribed for insertion at the point indicated by the *selah* "interlude."

Another view has it that, particularly where *selah* appears in the middle of a psalm, as in the case of our Psalm 47, it is there to indicate the place where one might interrupt and abbreviate the psalm, perhaps, again, for a concluding benediction.

A further theory has it that, because the root of the word *selah* is *salal*, meaning "to ascend" (hence *sullam*, "a ladder"), the term is actually a musical instruction indicating that at this point the Temple choir should raise its voice *fortissimo*. Another view is that it comes to indicate the place where the congregation was to make a responsive affirmation.

512. Can we read any significance into the fact that we read a psalm of the sons of Korach at this point?

Indeed. Korach was the arch rebel against God and His annointed leaders.[22] He was swallowed up alive into the earth for his sin; yet, his sons remained untainted, having dissociated themselves from their father's wicked ways. It is most appropriate, therefore, that one of their psalms should have been honorably selected to serve as an introduction to the sounding of the shofar with its call to repentance.

---

22. Numbers, chap. 16.

THE *MIN HA-MEITZAR* VERSES

513. Why do we recite the collection of verses commencing *Min Ha-Meitzar?*

Psalm 47 is followed by a selection of verses, recited responsively, all but one of which (*Koliy shamata*, Lamentations 3:56) are taken from the psalms. Aside from the introductory verse (*Min Ha-Meitzar*), which was included to make up the liturgically significant number of seven verses, the initial letters of the last six verses form the acrostic K'r'a S'a't'a'n, "tear in pieces the accuser." This imprecation was regarded as particularly significant by the sixteenth century mystics of *Safed* who prescribed the recitation of these verses, and who, for the same reason, introduced into the Friday night liturgy the *Anna be-khoach* prayer. The second line of that prayer—*Kabbeil rinnat amkha; sagveinu tahareinu nora*—provides the same acrostic.

For the sounding of the shofar, the acrostic's sentiment is especially appropriate since the Talmud[23] explains the purpose of this ritual as "in order to confuse Satan." According to *Tosafot*,[24] his confusion arises from fear that this shofar might well be the messianic alarm that will herald Satan's own demise.

23. *Rosh Hashanah* 16b.
24. *Ibid.*

XIV

The *Musaf Amidah: Malkhuyyot, Zikhronot,* and *Shofarot*

HINNENIY

514. What is the function of the *Hinneniy* prayer recited by the *Chazan* before the silent *Amidah*?

The *Chazan* is essentially the *Sheli'ach tzibbur*, the "representative of the congregation." Originally the function of rabbi and *Chazan* were one and the same, so that, as the most learned man, expected to know the entire service by heart in an age when people did not yet have printed prayer books, he was relied upon accurately to frame the traditional prayers on their behalf, as well as to compose new compositions and chant new melodies in order to stimulate and augment the spiritual emotions.

The *Chazan* was acutely aware, therefore, of the awesome responsibility that he bore, to make the service attractive, meaningful, and original. He was also conscious of the fact that, as the spiritual representative of the community, the very highest standard of religious, moral, and ethical conduct was expected of him. He had to search his soul, therefore, to be sure that there was no impediment to his occupying that position and no sin that might obstruct him in his mission to carry the prayers of his community before the heavenly throne. This is the thrust of the *Hinneniy* petition.

He also confesses his feelings of unworthiness to perform that awesome task. He acknowledges his sinfulness and begs God not to condemn his people on that account, but to accept their prayers in love, and to convert all the adversity decreed upon them into joy, peace, and life.

WHY *MUSAF*?

515. Why do we have a *Musaf* service on Sabbath, Rosh Hashanah, and all other major festivals?

Because our synagogue prayers are patterned upon the sacrifices that used to be offered in the Temple of old, and the Torah already prescribed special *musafim*, "additional offerings," that were to be brought on these special occasions. We have, therefore, a corresponding "additional service."

While the *Musaf Amidah* for the Sabbath and other festivals focuses primarily on those additional sacrifices, with the addition of a paragraph referring to the sanctity and general significance of the particular occasion, the *Amidah* for Rosh Hashanah (and Yom Kippur) is far more expansive and includes many compositions and biblical passages dealing with a variety of themes.

WHY REPEAT THE *AMIDAH*?

516. But why do we need both a silent *Amidah* and a repetition?

Originally, only a silent *Amidah* was prescribed. However, in Talmudic times— even more so than today—there was a high proportion of people who had no basic education and who could not read. It was alright for those brought up and educated in the main cities, but the majority of Jews lived in outlying villages and on outspread farms or inaccessible hamlets in the hill country of Judaea. They had no access to teachers, nor could their parents afford to have them educated. Their services were needed, from an early age, to work on the land.

They nevertheless had a burning desire to communicate with their Maker and often felt embarrassed on the occasions when a service was held in their location or when they traveled to a local town or city and attended synagogue that they were unable to recite the prayers by heart. It must not be forgotten that we are referring to a period over 1,000 years before the age of printing and a situation wherein the average person could not even employ a scribe to copy out for him the *Amidah* prayer.

The solution was arrived at whereby those who knew the *Amidah* were given time to recite it silently, after which someone knowledgeable would go and stand before the *teivah* ("reader's desk") and repeat it slowly, so that the rest of the congregation could repeat it after him, word for word. In the course of time, the reader's repetition of the *Amidah* was expanded and embellished with additional passages and poetic compositions, as well as being endowed with an interactive *Kedushah*.

517. But, surely, if the *Chazan* was going to repeat the *Amidah* anyway, why was it deemed necessary for people who knew the prayers to recite it first silently? Why could they not also rely on the *Chazan*'s recitation?

This was, indeed, the view of one of the great sages of the Mishnah, Rabban Gamaliel.[1] His colleagues maintained, however, that there still remained an obligation on each individual to pray the *Amidah* if he was able to do so, in order

---

1. Mishnah *Rosh Hashanah* 4:9.

to maintain his own dialogue with God. Their debate was not restricted to Rosh Hashanah, but to the recitation of every *Amidah* throughout the year.

The Talmud's decision on the matter took the form of a compromise. It was decided to adopt Rabban Gamaliel's view for Rosh Hashanah, whose *Amidah* was inordinately expanded by the inclusion of the three extra unfamiliar *Malkhuyyot, Zikhronot,* and *Shofarot* blessings. On this occasion, even the educated could dispense with the silent *Amidah* and recite it together with the *Chazan*, word for word. Throughout the rest of the year, however, no such dispensation was permitted to the educated.

518. So did this become the regular practice?

Our evidence from the Geonic period is that in both of the famous Babylonian academies they did not totally avail themselves of the Talmudic concession to the educated individual worshiper to dispense with the silent *Amidah*. They did, in fact, recite it for themselves, but omitted the *Malkhuyyot, Zikhronot,* and *Shofarot* blessings, for which they relied on the *Chazan*'s repetition.[2] This was also the custom in Spain until the end of the tenth century, when Rabbi Chanokh (d. 1014) made the recitation of the extra blessings obligatory for the private worshiper.

The matter remained a bone of controversy for centuries. The great Nachmanides defended the practice of the private worshiper reciting only seven blessings (omitting the *Malkhuyyot, Zikhronot,* and *Shofarot*), whereas the codifier Asher ben Yechiel (*Rosh*) and other Franco-German authorities demanded the recitation of those extra blessings in the silent *Amidah*.[3] A consensus view was ultimately expressed in favor of this practice.

519. Were any other innovations introduced at any time affecting the recitation of the silent *Amidah* or the reader's repetition?

The boldest innovation was that of Maimonides who took the radical step of abolishing entirely the recitation of the silent *Amidah* on Sabbaths and festivals. From his responsum, we learn, *inter alia*, that there were communities in his day who adopted the Talmudic compromise of dispensing with it just on Rosh Hashanah (See Question 517).

Maimonides explains his action in a responsum:

> In the *Shachrit* and *Musaf* services on Sabbaths and festivals, when there are many worshipers, I have made the silent and the repeated *Amidah*s into one prayer—just as you do in your place at *Musaf* on Rosh Hashanah. I do the same if the *Minchah* service is greatly delayed and I am apprehensive that the sun may have set. I have instituted that the *Chazan* commences by reciting the *Amidah* in a loud voice, and also the *Kedushah*.
>
> What motivated me to institute this was that I noticed that no one was

---

2. *Otzar Ha-Geonim, Rosh Hashanah,* pp. 68–70; *Siddur Saadia,* p. 218.
3. Commentary of *Rosh*, end of *Rosh Hashanah*.

paying any attention to the *Chazan*'s repetition, but were, instead, chatting or even going outside, so that he was reciting what were tantamount to vain blessings since no one was listening. Furthermore, as regards those who were not *au fait* with the prayers, when they saw the scholars and their educated fraternity chatting and behaving disrespectfully during the repetition of the *Amidah* (having already recited it for themselves, and not requiring the *Chazan* to repeat it for them), they followed suit [and failed, thereby, to fulfill their duty of prayer by not having listened carefully to the words of the *Chazan* prompting them].

My innovation was intended to remove a profanantion of the Name of God, whereby the ignorant came to believe that public prayer, for the religious, is just a joke and a mockery, serving to help people avoid performing their own duty. However, when we pray during the weekdays, with fewer, but more informed, people, we maintain the original decree, and employ both the silent and the repeated *Amidahs*.[4]

THE HALF-*KADDISH*

520. What is the purpose of the half-*kaddish*?

It is a kind of liturgical punctuation mark that serves to demarcate certain parts of the service from other, more important, sections. Here it sets into sharper relief the *Amidah*, the most important prayer.

LE-EILA LE-EILA

521. Why do we double the word *le-eila* in every *kaddish* recited during Rosh Hashanah and throughout the Ten Days of Penitence?

This is an Ashkenazi tradition. The repetition of the word *le-eila* ("exalted") is to convey the idea that God is never more exalted than at this time of the year when the thoughts and prayers of all Israel are directed toward Him.

522. When was the practice of doubling *le-eila* first introduced?

It is a comparatively late innovation, there being no reference to it in any source before the fifteenth century, when it appears in the notes to the *Sefer Maharil* of R. Jacob ben Moses of Moellin. There was, in fact, a considerable variety of practice in this matter in Ashkenazi communities. In Posen, they only doubled the word in the first *kaddish* that preceded the *Selichot* services. In Frankfurt, the extra *le-eila* was only inserted on Rosh Hashanah and Yom Kippur—not during the rest of the

---

4. Responsa of Maimonides, No. 256.

Ten Days of Penitence—and only in the *kaddish* recited by the *Chazan*. Mourners did not include it.

523. Why do we alter the phrase *min kol birkhata* to *mikkol birkhata*?

This is because the number of words in certain prayers was regarded as mystically significant and not to be altered. Thus, because an additional *le-eila* was being inserted at this time, authorities suggested that we should compensate by taking out one word. The most convenient way was to make the regular contraction of the words *min kol* to *mikkol*, which does not in any way alter the meaning.

THE REPETITION OF THE *MUSAF AMIDAH*

[On *Mi-sod chakhamim unevonim*, See Question 346.]

UPPAD ME'AZ

524. Who wrote the first composition, *Uppad me'az*, and what is its structure and subject matter?

It was written by Eleazar Kallir, one of the pioneers of Hebrew poetry (early seventh century). It follows an alphabetical acrostic pattern in rhyming, four-lined stanzas.

The poet alludes to the fact that it was on the first day of his creation—the anniversary of which Rosh Hashanah celebrates—that Adam sinned and was judged. Because God spared him the full measure of retribution, "that day was established from then on (*Uppad me'az*) as a day of judgment" and divine indulgence.

525. Why was just this poetic composition chosen to embellish the first blessing of the *Amidah*?

The reason is that it alludes to the founding fathers of our nation—Adam and Eve, Abraham, Isaac, and Joseph, before concluding with an oblique reference to the *Akedah* in petitioning God to "remember the oaths to Your servants." This is a reference to the oath given at the *Akedah* that God would multiply Abraham's offspring" (Genesis 22:16–17). *Uppad me'az* is, accordingly, a most appropriate poetic embellishment for the first blessing of the *Amidah*, which opens with a reference to the three Patriarchs and calls upon God to "remember the kindness of the founding-fathers" (*vezokheir chasdei Avot*).

[On *Zokhreinu La-chayyim*, See Questions 347 and 348.]

TEIFEN BEMAKHON

526. Who wrote the second composition, *Teifen Bemakhon*, and what is its structure and subject matter?

It is also from the pen of Kallir and is a plea to God to leave His throne of judgment and to occupy instead the throne of mercy.

The poem conforms to the pattern of a reverse alphabetical acrostic. This is perhaps symbolic of the retreat of God from His remotest throne of judgment (represented by the letter *taf*, the last letter of the alphabet) to the throne of mercy at the closest proximity to man (represented by the first letter, *aleph*, the initial letter of the divine name *Elokim*, and of the word *Anokhi* with which God introduced and revealed His Ten Commandments).

The poem concludes with a plea for "a year of plenty, of dew, rains and warmth." This is based upon the prayer of the High Priest that he uttered on leaving the Holy of Holies, and which is quoted in full in the *Musaf Amidah* of Yom Kippur (See Questions 858–859).

MELEKH ELYON

527. Who wrote the third composition, *Melekh Elyon*, and what is its structure and subject matter?

Again, this is an alphabetical poem by Kallir, with each letter repeated three times in each stanza. In the form presented here, with only every alternate letter of the *Alef Bet* represented, it is clearly abridged from a longer composition in which all the letters were represented. The full version appears, in fact, in the Avignon *machzor* and in some fragments of the Cairo Genizah collection.

The poem, in its original form, juxtaposed one stanza, containing the theme of *Melekh Elyon* ("The supreme King"), to another that made reference to *Melekh evyon* ("an inconsequential king"), in order to highlight the yawning contrast between the glory of God and that of an earthly monarch in whom people naively put their trust. An editor has removed each alternate *Melekh evyon* stanza, perhaps at the instigation of the censor, so as not to offend the king of the host country to whom such references might have been regarded as offensive.

U-NETANNEH TOKEF

528. Who was the author of this most well-known composition?

This is truly one of the most well-known, cherished, and moving compositions of the High Holy Day liturgy and is recited by reader and congregation in a spirit of awe and with a concentration that is reserved for few other compositions.

It is popularly attributed to the tenth century Rabbi Amnon of Mainz (Germany). The bishop of that city was greatly impressed by the appearance, piety, and wisdom of Rabbi Amnon and decided that his place in heaven would be assured if he succeeded in converting him to Christianity. He sent his guards to convey to the rabbi his demand, and, in order to buy time, Amnon asked for 3 days grace in which to make up his mind. The reply came back that in 3 days he was to appear at the bishop's palace in order to be received into the church.

When the guards had left, Amnon fell into a state of deep remorse that he had given the impression that it was something he could even consider; and he spent the 3 days in fasting, prayer, and repentance. On the third day, when he did not appear, the bishop dispatched his soldiers once again to haul the rabbi before him. Rabbi Amnon cried out, "May my tongue, which sinned in asking for time to consider, be ripped out of my mouth." The archbishop readily complied and went even further in his brutality. He cut out his tongue, and he also chopped off Amnon's feet for not returning of his own volition. They severed also his hands, joint by joint, inquiring each time whether the rabbi wished to spare himself further agony by acceding to the bishop's request.

It was just before Rosh Hashanah, and, at his request, they carried what was left of Amnon's body into the synagogue. He asked to be placed before the holy Ark, and, just before the recitation of the *Kedushah* ("Prayer of Sanctification"), he stopped the *Chazan* and expressed his wish to be allowed to express his own personal sanctification in words, as he had with his body in the bishop's palace. He then uttered this *U-netanneh tokef* composition, and, at its conclusion, he expired.

Three days later, Rabbi Amnon appeared to the poet Kalonymos ben Meshullam (eleventh century) in a dream and taught him the poem. He instructed him to prescribe its recitation as part of the standard Rosh Hashanah service and to circulate it widely throughout Jewry.

529. To what may we attribute the unique appeal that this composition clearly has retained down to the present day?

In answer, allow me to quote from my book, *Prayer and Penitence: A Commentary on the High Holy Day Machzor*, from which I have drawn material for this chapter on the content of the services:

> *U-netanneh tokef* has never lost its emotional pull, neither has the relevance of its summons become dimmed even in our modern age. Indeed, in the light of . . . the many casualties of our too-frequent economic recessions, of the rootlessness that characterizes our age, and the overwhelming tensions and problems that the fragmentation of family life has brought in its wake, some of the references in this composition do strike highly responsive chords. Who shall go wandering? . . . who shall be harassed? . . . who shall be afflicted? . . . who shall become poor? . . . who shall be humbled? are all questions that, in an age of economic uncertainty, superficial relationships, and emotional turbulence, most of us will at some time be asking.

In the light of the typhoons, hurricanes, and earthquakes that, in recent years alone, have caused such widespread devastation in several countries and states, the reference to our apprehension of the consequences of such natural disasters is also truly relevant. And with the worldwide scourge of AIDS, the reference to those who will "die by plague" takes on a telling immediacy.[5]

530. But what is the modern day relevance of expressing apprehension of dying by strangling and stoning?

We cannot be too smug in this terribly violent world of ours that such references are not still relevant and that similar crimes are not being committed against innocent victims every day of the year. For "stoning," we might substitute the missile of the bullet and the bomb. The deadly effect is the same.

A modern edition of the *machzor* paraphrases these references as follows: "Who shall be strangled by insecurity, And who shall be stoned into submission."[6]

THE *KEDUSHAH*

531. We have already referred to the *Shachrit Kedushah* (See Questions 350, 352). In what way does the *Musaf Kedushah* differ?

They share a common opening theme, referring to the angelic praise of God. The *Musaf Kedushah*, however, continues with the theme of the *Shema*, quoting its opening verse and affirming that God is our father, our King, and our savior, and that He will redeem us "a second time" (*sheinit*) in the messianic era to prove His special relationship with Israel "in the presence of all mankind" (*Le'einey kol chay*).

532. Why was the theme of the *Shema* introduced into the *Kedushah*?

It is generally understood to have been introduced in reaction to the persecution initiated against the Jews by the Persian King, Jezdegaard II, around the year 455 C.E. Among his attempts to curb religious practice was the banning of the *Shema*, since its reference to only one God was construed as a denial of the dominant Persian, Zoroastrian belief in a dual deity of good and evil.

The rabbis of the day were forced to accede to its removal, but, in order to keep alive its recitation, they smuggled a reference to it into the *Kedushah* prayer at a point in the service when any visiting Persian inspectors were not listening for it. The reference took the form of the first line, and, at the end of the *Kedushah*, the concluding phrases, of the *Shema* (*Liheyot lakhem le-Elokim ani Ha-Shem Elokeikhem*). It was probably also recited rather rapidly and inaudibly.

5. Cohen, J. M. (1994). *Prayer and Penitence: A Commentary on the High Holy Day Machzor.* Northvale, NJ: Jason Aronson Inc., p. 81.

6. Rabinowitz, S., Kanter, S., and Riemer, J. (1992). "Reflections." In *Machzor for Rosh Hashanah and Yom Kippur*, ed. J. Harlow. New York: The Rabbinical Assembly.

Once the situation improved and the decree outlawing its recitation had been rescinded by Jezdegaard's successor, the custom of including that quotation from the *Shema* was dropped from every *Amidah* except that of *Musaf.* There being no *Shema* prescribed for that service, there was no unnecessary repetition involved in including it in the *Kedushah* of that service.

VEKHOL MA'AMINIM

533. Who wrote this composition, and what is its structure and subject matter?

Its authorship is not known for sure, but it is now generally attributed to Yannai, our earliest liturgical poet (sixth and seventh centuries c.e.).

Yannai's pioneering contribution to Hebrew poetry was only revealed during the twentieth century with the discovery of the Cairo *Genizah.* He was known hitherto only through some scattered references to him in early medieval sources. Through modern research, many anonymous poems and fragments of poetry have been discovered and attributed to him, and this important literary figure has been rescued from oblivion.

The poem proceeds alphabetically (following on after the word *shehu*) in a stair-like progression of ideas. An attribute or activity of God is presented in the first *stich* (introduced by the definite article *ha*), and the key word is then taken over to form the subject of the succeeding affirmation, introduced by the words *Vekhol ma'aminim.* Thus:

HA-BOCHEIN u-vodeik ginzei nistarot. . . . Vekhol ma'aminim shehu BOCHEIN kelayot.

534. Is it not disingenuous for us to sing aloud and affirm *Vekhol ma'aminim,* that "all believe," when there is such a high proportion of disbelief in the Jewish world?

Perhaps it is. But at the time the author composed this hymn, he was in no doubt that disbelief was akin to madness. God was an absolute and incontrovertible reality, for Darwin had not yet arrived on the scene to postulate an alternative to divine Creation. So when we sing that man of faith's poetic affirmation, we are, as it were, issuing a challenge to ourselves to work on our faith, to extend and deepen our dialogue with our Maker, and to stimulate the latent spirituality within us all.

This is what we mean, after all, by "all believe." It affirms that God has implanted within us all a reception apparatus for spirituality. We may never activate it. On the other hand, we never know when some crisis or dramatic experience in our lives may suddenly charge up those latent spiritual batteries and convince us that there is a God and that He cares for and guides our life and destiny.

UVEKHEIN TEIN PACHDEKHA

535. Is there any significance in the order of the three paragraphs commencing *Uvekhein tein pachdekha*, each of which commences with the word *Uvekhein*?

There is. These paragraphs move from the general to the particular. The first paragraph speaks universally, of God imposing his awe (*pachdekha*) upon all of mankind. This is followed by a narrowing of the focus, in which we petition for honor to be granted to God's people, Israel, and a realization of their national aspirations and Messianic expectations. The third paragraph narrows still further the focus and looks forward to the time when the righteous will rejoice in their well-earned reward and will be vindicated when "all wickedness will evaporate like smoke and when God will remove evil's domination from the earth." [For further comment on *Uvekhein tein pachdekha* and the succeeding paragraphs, See Questions 353 and 354]

VEYE'ETAYU

536. What is the subject matter and structure of this composition?

This is an alphabetical, unrhymed poem, with the succeeding letters of the alphabet appearing as the third letter of each *stich*, and with two *stiches* to each line, and three stresses in each *stich*.

It takes up the universalistic theme of the *Uvekhein tein pachdekha* and speaks of all mankind—those who inhabit "the distant islands" and "the ends of the earth"—abandoning their idolatry and coming to seek out and praise God and rejoice in His sovereignty.

Its overall theme serves as an appropriate introduction to the following section of the *Amidah*, commencing *Vetimlokh attah Ha-Shem levadkha* ("And You shall rule alone, O Lord"), and especially in the juxtaposition of its final word, *melukhah* ("kingdom") with the first word *Vetimlokh* of the next paragraph. [On *Attah Vechartanu*, See Questions 355 and 356]

KADOSH ATTAH VENORA SHEMEKHA . . .
BARUKH ATTAH HA-SHEM . . . HA-MELEKH HA-KADOSH

537. This conclusion to the third blessing of the *Amidah* differs from the one we usually employ throughout the year, namely *Attah kadosh veshimkha kadosh . . . Barukh attah Ha-Shem ha-El ha-kadosh*. Why do we employ a different conclusion for the High Holy Day liturgy?

The version we use throughout the year is the standard Babylonian version. The original liturgy of Israel was edited and expanded by the authorities in Babylon in accordance with the halakhic principles of their own Babylonian Talmud, as well as their preferred liturgical practices and poetic perceptions.

Now, the Babylonian authorities preferred the *Attah kadosh veshimkha kadosh* formula for daily, Sabbath, and festival use, as well as the concluding formula, *ha-El ha-kadosh*. The version we recite here on Rosh Hashanah (*Kadosh attah . . . ha-melekh ha-kadosh*) is actually the original version of the Holy Land. Because we utilize on the High Holy Days the poetry of the early Hebrew poets of Israel (Kallir, Yannai, etc.), as supplements to our *Amidah* blessings, the Babylonian authorities made a concession on these occasions and allowed the ancient Israeli version of the conclusion of those blessings to replace the usual formulae. The same applies also in the case of the formula *Oseh ha-shalom* (See Question 252).

UMIPNEI CHATA'EINU

538. What is the purpose of this composition?

It serves as an introduction to the recitation of the biblical verses that refer to the particular sacrifices prescribed to be offered on this festival. After the destruction of the Temple (70 C.E.), Jews were banished from Jerusalem, the Temple lay in ruins, and sacrifices ceased to be offered. The recitation of the biblically prescribed sacrifices induces, therefore, poignant feelings of nostalgia. This prayer articulates these feelings in its reference to "our inability to make good our obligations . . . because of the [crushing] hand that was stretched forth against Your sanctuary." The prayer petitions God to restore His glory to Israel, to gather in her exiles to Jerusalem so that we may, once again, perform our sacrificial obligations.

539. The opening words state that it was "on account of our sins that we were exiled from our land." Can we attribute the loss of Israel so glibly to our ancestors' sins when we know that, historically, it was due to the invasion of a superior Roman force?

In truth, we cannot fathom the way God guides our people's destiny, nor can we explain or make sense of our endurance of unremitting and unprecedented persecution down the ages. We were told in no uncertain terms, however, that God brought us out of Egypt "to be for you as your God." The gift of the land of Israel was clearly so that we might develop and heighten there our relationship with God, our observance of His Torah, and our perception of His Godliness, as well as to develop there a society that would personify the essence of the Torah's sensitivity to moral and ethical rectitude.

The Torah warns us that if we follow the ungodly ways of the previous inhabitants of the land, then we will suffer the same fate, and the land will "vomit us out as it vomited out those that came before us" (Leviticus 18:28). Then, we are warned, "You will be left few in number" (Deuteronomy 28:62) and "you will be scattered among the nations, from one end of the earth to the other end of the earth" (verse 64). The author of *Umipnei chata'einu* can be forgiven, therefore, if he interprets Israel's fate against the backcloth of that dire biblical warning.

The Talmud explains the loss of Jewish sovereignty over our land in terms of a widespread insensitivity to the feelings and needs of one's fellow man. Even the rabbis and leading men of Jerusalem, in the period leading up to the destruction of the Temple, had become self-centered and indifferent even to the public humiliation of decent ordinary citizens.[7]

Where there is an absence of fraternal feelings, national cohesion, and a sense of unity and common identity, a nation becomes vulnerable and morally and physically weak. The ease with which the Romans seized control of Palestine may be attributed to a combination of those factors, as warned and prophecied by the Torah.

ALEINU

540. As we recite *Aleinu* at the end of every service, why do we need to recite it again here in the *Musaf Amidah*?

The question is anachronistic, since this is the original and rightful place for this composition. It was originally composed, by the third century c.e. Babylonian Talmudist, Abba Arikha (called universally in the Talmud by the honorific title, *Rav*), to serve here as an introduction to the *Malkhuyyot* section of the *Amidah*. The three foregoing sections—*Malkhuyyot, Zikhronot*, and *Shofarot*—each comprise ten biblical verses dealing, respectively, with the themes of God's kingship, His remembrance of His people, and the power and significance of the shofar. It was felt that those ten biblical verses in each section should be augmented with compositions that expand upon the respective themes. Hence, the *Aleinu* is a prelude to the *Malkhuyyot*.

541. So why was *Aleinu* elevated to become the finale of every daily service throughout the year?

This was introduced as a tribute to the martyrs of Blois in southern France who were massacred in 1171 and who chose to utter in unison this Rosh Hashanah prayer as their dying affirmation of God's sovereignty and righteousness. Its recitation becomes, by association, a tribute to the martyrs of our people in every age.

Its choice was probably also determined by a particularly fierce reference in the prayer that originally referred to idolators, but that they clearly applied to their merciless Christian murderers: *Sheheim mishtachavim lehevel varik umishtachavim leEl lo yoshi'a*, "For they bow down to vanity and slabber and pray to a god who cannot save." This phrase was subsequently expunged by the censor, but it is still

7. *Gittin* 55b–56a.

recited in some prayer rites and has been incorporated into the popular ArtScroll editions of the daily and festival prayer books.

542. But how can we Jews, who are taught to be tolerant of other religions, justify such an insulting sentiment?

It is not for us, who are not about to be burnt alive—as they were—for no other reason than their professed faith, to condemn their bitter feelings. They must have been totally mystified as to how a religion of love, which taught the doctrine of turning the other cheek to one's persecutors, could initiate, foster, and perpetrate such atrocities upon those who had done them absolutely no harm, but lived peaceably among them. One is reminded of the comment of Elie Wiesel that the Holocaust is as much a problem for Christianity as it is for Jews.

543. Why do we close the Ark for the recitation of one of the verses of *Aleinu*?

For the reason we have just mentioned. The verse in question states, *Shelo sam chelkeinu ka-hem vegoraleinu kekhol ha-monam*, "For He has not made our portion like theirs, nor our fate like their multitude." Although, again, this was intended by its ancient author as a slighting reference to idolators, yet, because of the sensitivity of Christianity, it was felt that some gesture should be made to indicate that this is not a reference that has a contemporary application. This is done by closing the Ark for it and demoting it in that way.

544. But can we prove that the author did not have Christianity in mind?

We can, indeed. We have already stated that the author was the great third-century Babylonian Talmudist *Rav*. Unlike the scholars of Palestine in that period who had Christians in their midst and who had to contend with missionary activity, there were no Christian communities in Babylon. So *Rav* would never have had any reason to address that problem and to resort to the extreme measure of using the words of the liturgy as a polemical missile.

Indeed, even if *Aleinu* had been composed by someone living in the Holy Land, it was not until a century after *Rav* that Christianity became the official religion of the Roman Empire and commenced its persecution of Jews. So at such an early period as the third century there would have been no reason to use the liturgy for such anti-Christian purposes.

545. Why do some congregations have the practice of reciting *Aleinu* aloud, word for word, throughout the year?

This goes back to a decree of the Russian government in 1703, accompanied by the appointment of inspectors to visit synagogues in order to listen to its recitation so as to ensure that the offending phrase ("For they bow down to vanity and slabber . . .") was omitted.

546. Why is it that we only prostrate ourselves fully on Rosh Hashanah and Yom Kippur, when we recite the phrase *Va'anachnu kor'im umishtachavim umodim* ("And we bend our knees and prostrate ourselves and offer thanksgiving"), and not when we recite that phrase in the *Aleinu* at all other times?

Originally, prostrations formed a regular part of Jewish worship, which accounts for the fact that the same verb *shachah* occurs in the Hebrew Bible in the sense of "to bow down" and also "to worship." The frequency of the verb's occurrence—172 times—is also a measure of how common was the practice of prostration in biblical times.

It seems that Jews abandoned the practice of full prostration when this became a feature of other cults and religions. This is in conformity with the biblical prescription of "not walking in their ways." Especially in Christianity, prostrations were an essential element of worship from the outset.

It was a common reaction in Jewish practice that when others borrowed elements from our ritual, we tended to play down their significance or to totally abandon them. Only on the High Holy Days do we allow ourselves the concession of re-introducing the full prostration in order to express our abject submission and to symbolize our *falling* upon God's mercy.

547. Is the full prostration during *Aleinu* a universal practice?

No, it is not. For the reasons we have explained, there were still communities that felt uncomfortable, even on the High Holy Days, doing something that was such a dominant feature of Christian worship. In some communities, therefore, it became the practice that only the *Chazan* made a full prostration, and the congregation merely bows low.

MALKHUYYOT, ZIKHRONOT AND SHOFAROT

548. Why are there just ten verses in each of the *Malkhuyyot, Zikhronot,* and *Shofarot* sections?

The Talmud states that we must not have fewer than ten verses in each of the three sections. It explains that this corresponds to the ten times the word *hallelu(hu)* ("praise [Him]") occurs in Psalm 150—the three foregoing sections being the most superlative of praises. It also corresponds to the Ten Commandments, which were given to the accompaniment of the sound of the shofar, as well as to the *Asarah ma'amarot,* the ten times the phrase "And God said" occurs in the Genesis account—Rosh Hashanah constituting the anniversary of the Creation.[8]

---

8. *Rosh Hashanah* 32a.

549. Does the choice of verses in these three sections conform to any specific pattern?

There is a consistent pattern of (i) three verses chosen from the Pentateuch, followed by (ii) three verses from the third section of the Hebrew Bible, the *Ketuvim*, or "Sacred Writings," followed by (iii) three verses from the middle section, the *Neviim*, or prophetic literature. The tenth verse is taken, once again, from the Torah.

550. But why do the verses from the third section of the Hebrew Bible, albeit that they were invested with divine inspiration, take priority of position over those of the prophets whose spiritual standing is surely much higher than that of the authors of the Sacred Writings?

Among the explanations offered are that the arrangement of these verses was in order to follow the chronological order in which they were written. The verses from the third section are actually all from the book of Psalms, which was written by King David who lived before the period of the classical prophets. Another explanation offered is that the order conforms to the principle of *Ma'alin ba-kodesh ve'ein moridin*, that "We must ascend in holiness, and not decrease." Hence, after giving pride of place to the Torah, we then recite the lesser holy verses of the Sacred Writings before proceeding to the prophetic verses.

A more plausible explanation is, simply, that at the time of the composition of these three themes, the prophetic section of the Bible had not yet been invested with its higher status. This may have come about only after the Prophetic Writings were brought into the synagogue service to serve as the reservoir for the *Haftarah* at the time when the Romans prohibited the public reading from the Torah (See Question 441).

551. What is the purpose underlying the recitation of the ten *Malkhuyyot* verses?

Their purpose, according to the Talmud, is to symbolically crown God as king over us.[9] Reciting this each year constitutes an annual renewal of our allegiance to Him and a reminder of our indebtedness to Him for every blessing we enjoy.

It is a Talmudic axiom that "there is no king without a people."[10] This is tantamount to saying that God's kingship only exists because, and when, man acknowledges it. It is a daring concept, for it makes man indispensable to God's plan for the world. Dare we say it? God is shown thereby to need man more than man needs God; for man has the freedom to deny God (though he will suffer the consequences of that denial), whereas God is denied the freedom to give up on man, for that would run counter to His attribute as *El rachum vechanun*, "a God that is merciful and forgiving."

---

9. *Rosh Hashanah* 16a.
10. *Sanhedrin* 64a; *Midrash Eikha Rabbati* 5:19.

Hence, however presumptuous for us to recite these verses declaring God as our king, yet that is our unique privilege, and we must assume that is pleasing in God's sight.

552. How is it that the final verse of the *Malkhuyyot* is *Shema yisrael*, which, unlike all the previous verses, make no reference to God's "kingship"?

The answer is that the recitation of the opening verse of the *Shema* is described by our sages as *Kabbalat ol malkhut shamayim*, "accepting upon ourselves the yoke of the *kingdom* of heaven," hence, the insertion of the line, *Barukh shem kevod malkhuto le'olam va'ed*, "Blessed be the name of His glorious *kingdom* forever and ever."

When, in the *Shema*, we go on to describe God as "One" (*Ha-Shem echad*) and to declare our love for Him "with all our heart, soul, and might," we are, in effect, attributing to him far more than mere "kingship." We are tying ourselves to Him in an indissoluble bond of "oneness" that cannot be equated with any earthly relationship or experience. The verse from the *Shema* is the perfect choice, therefore, with which to climax the *Malkhuyyot*.

553. What is the purpose underlying the ten *Zikhronot* verses?

The Talmud explains that the purpose of these verses is "so that the memory of you should come before Me for good."[11] The first composition, *Attah Zokher*, speaks of the comprehensiveness of God's memory: "There is no forgetfulness before the throne of Your glory." This underscores our human accountability.

Our psyche may seek to camouflage and sublimate the memory of unworthy deeds, as a defense mechanism, in order to enable us to function without guilt, but the exercise of reciting these *Zikhronot* verses seeks to remind us that one day all will be revealed. This is intended as a stimulus to *teshuvah*, by helping us to face up squarely to what we have done, which will, in turn, help direct us along the path of therapeutic repentance.

Later in the passage, it proceeds to speak of God "lovingly remembering" Noah and saving him from the Flood: "Therefore his remembrance comes before You . . . to make his offspring as abundant as the dust of the earth. . . ." Memory is here equated with projected reward. In truth, the notion of God "remembering" is inapplicable, since "remembering" suggests recall of something that has been forgotten for a time, or that has at least receded into the recesses of the mind. But God cannot "remember," because He does not forget. When applied to God, therefore, "remembering" means, simply, rewarding, which, in turn, means causing past righteousness (or, for that matter, evil) to be "remembered" by those who benefit (or suffer) from its consequences.

"Remembering" means, essentially, "re-membering," or putting the "members,"

11. *Rosh Hashanah* 16a.

or separated fragments, back together to form an integrated whole. When righteousness remains unrewarded, or evil unpurged, they remain in suspension as unredeemed elements that have not yet been properly integrated into the total scheme of moral evolution. While this situation remains, *tikkun olam* ("the perfecting of the world") cannot proceed. Hence, God's "remembering" or, better still, "rewarding" has cosmic significance. And this constitutes the relationship of the *Zikhronot* to this festival that commemorates the Creation of the world and, at the same time, seeks to foster, through repentance, its perfection.

554. What is the purpose of the *Shofarot* verses?

According to the Talmud,[12] the shofar serves as a rousing accompaniment to the *Malkhuyyot* and the *Zikhronot*. It proclaims God's "Kingship," and it also heralds the "rememberance," or reward, that God bestows. The latter function is explained in the Talmud, as follows: "Why do we blow a shofar of a ram? Says the Holy One: Blow it before Me so that I will remember to your merit the binding of Isaac, and I will consider it as if you had offered yourselves to Me as an *Akeidah*."[13]

The *Akeidah* was an unrivaled act of total submission to God, which, on its own account, served to crown Him as King in the eyes of the world, hence, the link between the *Shofarot* and the *Malkhuyyot* verses. And that same act of selfless *Akeidah* secured an abundance of merit for the offspring of Abraham and Isaac, which, at the same time links the *Shofarot* and the *Zikhronot* verses. Hence, the unity of these three sections of the *Musaf Amidah*.

HA-YOM HARAT OLAM

555. What is the message underlying this short composition that is recited after the blowing of the shofar for each of the *Malkhuyyot, Zikhronot,* and *Shofarot* sections?

Its reference to our standing before God "either as children or as servants" reflects a rather fatalistic attitude toward human destiny. Just as a person has no control over whether he is born "a child (of a household)" or "a servant," but in either situation can merely hope to be the recipient of as much favor as is consonantal with his or her particular position, so man has no control over the determination of his own status in the eyes of God. God assigns a position to man in accordance with the nature of the relationship that God desires. We must hope and pray for a filial relationship, but we must also accept that, inevitably, there will be times when we are undeserving and are relegated to the subordinate status of servants.

---

12. *Ibid.*
13. *Ibid.*

Within the context of the sounding of the shofar, which, in biblical times, heralded the manumission of all slaves in the Jubilee year, these particular verses may be construed as a challenge to Israel to improve her relationship with God; and, if her status has hitherto been that of "servant," to regard the sounding of the shofar on Rosh Hashanah as heralding the opportunity for initiating a new relationship with God as children of a loving Father.

ARESHET SEFATEINU

556. What is the purpose of the *Areshet sefateinu* that follows?

This is a concluding plea to God to accept the petitions of Israel that invest the blowing of the shofar with meaning. The last word of the composition is altered each time it is employed. The first time it is recited, after the *Malkhuyyot*, we ask God, in the final phrase, to accept *seder malkhuyyoteinu*, "our specially-ordered verses of Kingship." The second time the shofar is blown, for the *Zikhronot* verses, we ask Him to accept *seder Zikhronoteinu*, "our order of the remembrance verses"; and the third time the shofar is sounded, after the *Shofarot* section, we petition for God to remember *seder shofroteinu*, "the order of the shofar verses."

It is not uncommon to have a prayer that petitions God to accept a ritual or the verses that pertain to it, especially if that ritual (such as the shofar) is biblical. The mystical school of Safed created many such prayers, which are retained in some editions after the recital of the morning *Korbanot* (sacrifices) section,[14] after a circumcision,[15] after the blessing over the counting of the Omer,[16] and after the final vacating of the Succah.[17]

THE PRIESTLY BLESSING: *BIRKAT KOHANIM*

557. Why is this ritual popularly referred to as *Dukhaning* or *Dukhanen* (with Yiddish or German ending)?

Probably because it is less of a mouthful! Also, because the *-ing* or *-en* ending helps to place it comfortably into the category of "actions" (like running, cycling, going, etc.).

The name derives from the word for the platform (*dukhan*) on which the priests stood in Temple times to perform this ritual.

---

14. Scheman, N. and Zlotowitz, M. eds. *The Complete ArtScroll Siddur*. New York: Mesorah Publications, pp. 32, 34, 40.
15. *Op. cit.*, p. 212.
16. *Op. cit.*, p. 284.
17. *Op. cit.*, p. 724.

558. At what stage do the priests leave the synagogue to wash their hands?

They leave early enough to give them time to remove their shoes, queue up to have their hands washed, and return to the Ark before the *Chazan* has commenced the *Retzei* blessing. The latter pleads for God to "restore the *Avodah* (Temple Service) to the habitation of Your house," and the Priestly Blessing was an important element of that Temple Service. Obviously, in a large congregation, with many priests, the preparations for *dukhaning* will take longer (Do not forget that the priests have to dry their hands in turn, usually using only one towel), so they will have to leave the synagogue earlier, to give themselves more time.

The Levites—members of the same ancestral tribe as the priests—leave the synagogue at the same time, or slightly earlier, as their task is to wash the priests' hands. This duty is derived from the divine instruction to Aaron the priest: "And your brethren also, of the tribe of Levi, bring near with you, that they may be joined unto you, and minister unto you" (Numbers 18:2).

The Levites draw the water into a large cup and pour an ample amount over the hands of each priest in turn. A basis for this washing is found in the verse, "Lift up your hands in holiness [i.e., in cleanliness] and bless the Lord" (Psalm 134:2). No blessing is recited over this washing.

559. Why do the priests remove their shoes?

Popular perception has it that it is to symbolize that they are standing on "holy ground," and so, like Moses, who was told to remove his shoes by the Burning Bush for that same reason, the priests do the same. This is, of course, quite erroneous, since we do not designate the place in front of the Ark as holy in that way, and in many congregations the *bimah* is placed on that spot, and the *Chazan* leads the service and people are called up to the Torah without having to remove their shoes! If an analogy was drawn with the Temple priests, who walked barefoot, we might be closer to a plausible explanation, but then again, the priests are not expected to walk barefoot on the synagogue *bima*.

Strange as it may seem, the removal of the shoes was merely a precautionary measure in case a priest's lace came untied in the middle of the blessing of the people, and he bent down to tie it. Worshipers noticing that might assume that he was actually a disqualified priest, and, in order not to embarrass himself in having to make public the nature of his disqualification, he was just going through the motions of ascending the *bimah*, but was not actually reciting the Priestly Blessing and was fiddling with his shoelaces instead.

560. Why do the priests conceal themselves under a large *tallit?*

This is another precaution, so that the worshipers will not become distracted if their attention is drawn to the priests' hands and the special and strange formation of the fingers that tradition bids them make. The worshipers, as recipients of the prescribed biblical blessing (See Numbers 6:23–27), have to give fervent concentration to every word being recited by the priests, and have to add their own mental petition that every word of that blessing should be fulfilled.

The priests have to make a total of five spaces between the fingers of both hands. This is achieved by having the thumb of the right hand hovering above that of the left hand, and spacing out the middle of the remaining four fingers of each hand. The mystics believed that these spaces were a kind of lattice window through which the Divine Spirit "peeps" to see whether Israel deserves the blessing.

561. Why do the priests first face the Ark and then, only in the middle of their blessing, turn around to face the congregation?

This is a compromise, introduced by Ashkenazi authorities, in order to satisfy two opposing views regarding when the priests should turn around. Maimonides took the view that they should recite the entire blessing over the act of *Dukhaning* while they are facing the Ark and away from the congregation, and only afterward turn to face them to deliver the biblical formula. This is in accordance with the usual procedure of reciting a blessing before performing any act whatsoever that is associated with the fulfillment of the *mitzvah* (A parallel with turning away from the congregation until after the blessing is the covering of one's eyes before reciting the blessing over the Shabbat candles. See Question 228). This practice is followed by Sephardim.

Joseph Karo took the opposite view, however, that one should face the people for the recitation of the blessing.[18] In order to satisfy both opinions, we recite half the blessing facing the Ark, and, at the word *vetzivanu*, the priests turn around to face the congregation.

562. Some congregants turn their backs in order not to gaze at the priests. Is this correct form?

It is not only not correct form, but is strictly forbidden. In order to be a recipient of a blessing, one must face toward the one administering it, so much so that those seated close to the Ark wall of the synagogue have to come forward so that they are not behind the priests while they are being blessed, since they would not then be included. One should face in the direction of the priests, but lower one's head, not to gaze at them.

563. What if a priest is feeling unwell, or, for personal reasons, does not wish to join in with the *Dukhaning*?

He should leave the synagogue and stay out for the entire duration of the Priestly Blessing. It should be said, however, that the halakah takes a very dim view of a

---

18. *Be'er Heitev* on *Shulchan Arukh Orach Chayyim* 128:11 (18).

priest who neglects his biblically prescribed duty and privilege. According to the *Shulchan Arukh*, "although he is abandoning but one Biblical *mitzvah*, it is as if he was transgressing three positive *mitzvot*."[19] This is because the three verses are construed as three separate *mitzvot*.

564. Is there anything significant about the wording of the blessing that the priests make over this ritual?

The formula of the blessing is "Blessed art thou . . . and commanded us to bless His people Israel *in love (be'ahavah)*." This is the only time that the required attitude of mind is articulated within the formula of a blessing. The reason for this is that to confer a blessing upon someone is a most intimate act, requiring the deepest feelings for that person or congregation. To bless someone and not to have loving feelings for him is a contradiction in terms. Hence, in the context of this *mitzvah*, the element of *ahavah* is a vital precondition. Any priest who is in contention with his congregation should not, therefore, presume to bless them.

565. At what stage do the priests turn around to conclude the *Dukhaning*?

They must wait until the *Chazan*, who leads them with each word of the Priestly Blessing, has commenced the next blessing, *Sim Shalom*, before they turn around to face the Ark again.

[For further questions on the Priestly Blessing, see our companion volume, *1001 Questions and Answers on Pesach*, Questions 581–604.]

THE FINAL NOTES OF THE SHOFAR

566. Why do some have the custom of inserting the final forty notes of the shofar into the *kaddish* that follows the *Amidah*?

This is the *Kaddish Titkabbal*, which not only signals the conclusion of the *Amidah*, the main section of the service, and compartmentalizes it from the non-statutory hymns and compositions that follow, but that also asks God that "our prayers and petitions should be accepted (*Titkabbal tzelotehon uva'utehon*) before our Father in heaven."

The final notes of the shofar are inserted just before that *Titkabbal* plea in order that the latter should refer not only to all our *Amidah* petitions—that they should be "accepted"—but also to our urgent desire for forgiveness as expressed through the notes of the shofar.

---

19. *Shulkhan Arukh Orach Chayyim* 128:2.

567. What is the origin of the Sephardi custom to blow a *teru'ah gedolah*, a lengthy *teru'ah*, as the climax to the entire blowing?

The *Tur* states, in the name of the authoritative Rav Amram Gaon, that "after the *Amidah* we sound a long *teru'ah*."[20] This is quoted by the *Shulchan Arukh*,[21] and reflects the Sephardic tradition. This also implies that this protracted *teru'ah* is the only note that is sounded after the *Amidah* and that all the 100 notes (apart from the first thirty) have to be contained within the *Amidah* itself.

The Ashkenazi authority, Moses Isserles,[22] writes in his gloss that "there are some places which have the custom to blow the (final) thirty notes at this stage (that is, after the *Amidah*), after which no notes should be blown unnecessarily." This last statement is interpreted to mean that after those final thirty, no protracted *teru'ah gedolah* should be blown.

568. So what is the origin of the Ashkenazi custom of blowing a *teki'ah gedolah*?

The custom is referred to for the first time by the *Maharil*, Rabbi Jacob Moellin (fourteenth century). He states that its purpose is to indicate to the congregation that the blowing of the shofar has now been completed. A biblical support for this practice is found in the verse: "When the ram's horn draws out a long note, they may ascend the mountain" (Exodus 19:13). This proves that the protracted sound of the shofar was the sign that God's presence on Sinai had been withdrawn and the people could therefore return to the mountain. Similarly, in the case of our ritual, the *teki'ah gedolah* is the sign that the shofar experience has been concluded.

Now the "drawing out" of a note is only possible with the *teki'ah*, which is one prolonged and uninterrupted sound. The original *teru'ah* note, on the other hand, cannot be prolonged or "drawn out." Its nine, short, independent notes can only be augmented by blowing many additional *teru'ah*s. Thus, to duplicate the practice at Sinai of "drawing out" the farewell note, Ashkenazi authorities insisted that it had to be a *teki'ah gedolah*, not a *teru'ah gedolah*.

569. So what was Amram Gaon's precedent for sounding a *teru'ah gedolah*?

Rabbi Tzvi Pesach Frank[23] quotes the suggestion of Rav Perla that Amram may have relied on the biblical story of the conquest of Jericho. After the seven days of walking around the city, Joshua commanded the people to "make a long blast with the ram's horn, and when you hear the sound of the horn, all the people shall shout with a prolonged shout (*teru'ah gedolah*), and the wall of the city shall fall down flat" (Joshua 6:5). Thus, just as that biblical *teru'ah gedolah* had the effect of

---

20. See *Tur*, sec. 596.
21. *Shulchan Arukh Orach Chayyim* 596:1.
22. See *Remah ad loc.*
23. Frank, T. P. (1979). *Mikra'ei Kodesh.* Jerusalem: Makhon HaRav Frank, p. 54.

initiating a favorable climactic response to the shofar blowing and the prayers of the Israelites, so the practice of sounding that note as the climax of the Rosh Hashanah blowing is intended to elicit that same divine grace, by demolishing the symbolic walls which separate us from God.

Rabbi Yosef Cohen, a grandson of Rabbi Frank, found, among one of Rav Perla's unpublished manuscripts in the Frank family's possession, another reason why the *teru'ah gedolah* may have been originally introduced.[24] This was because the Torah exclusively employs the term *teru'ah* in reference to Rosh Hashanah. The term *teki'ah* is never found and was only introduced by the Talmudic sages because of their doubt as to the precise sound of the *teru'ah* (See Question 493). Thus, it was regarded as most appropriate to climax the blowing with a dramatic blowing of the type of note that is biblically mandated.

570. But do not the Ashkenazim blow a *teki'ah gedolah* more than just as the final note?

As we have seen, there is no basis for this practice; but it is the case that the custom arose to sound a *teki'ah gedolah* at the end of the first set of thirty notes (the pre-*Amidah, teki'ot dimeyushav*), and some also sounded it at the end of the *Shofarot* section of the repetition of the *Amidah*. Customs vary on this matter.

EIN KELOHEINU

571. To what may the popularity of *Ein Keloheinu* be attributed?

Its appeal is probably on account of the fact that it creates a welcome change of mood from the solemnity of the lengthy *Amidah*, allowing the congregation to break into song and relax its concentration with a lively melody and most simple and direct lyrics. The simplicity of its meter, with four two-word *stiches* to each of its first four lines, has also facilitated a large number of musical compositions and arrangements.

572. But was this its original purpose?

Indeed not. Its concluding line gives the clue as to its original purpose in the liturgy. It reads, "It is You who are our Savior; it is You before Whom our forefathers burned the spice-incense." Thus, this hymn was employed as a lead-in to the *Pittum ha-ketoret* passage that follows, which enumerates the eleven spices that went into the compounding of the incense that was burnt in the Temple as part of the Sabbath and festival ritual.

The last line is not, in fact, part of the hymn proper (as will be noted from its meter), but was grafted on to create the link with the *Pittum ha-ketoret* that follows.

---

24. Cohen, R. Y. (1979). *Harerei Kodesh* commentary to *Mikra'ei Kodesh*. Jerusalem: Makhon HaRav Frank, p. 54.

573. Are any other reasons offered for its recitation?

The *Kol Bo* states that it comes to supplement the number of blessings recited on Sabbaths and festivals. We are required to recite 100 blessings each day. On weekdays, with the three-times recitation of an *Amidah* containing nineteen blessings, we are well on the way (add to that the washing for our meals and the blessings before and after, as well as the other blessings of our prayer book and the snacks or tid-bits and drinks that we take during the day).

On Sabbaths and festivals, however, the *Amidah* only contains seven blessings (nine on Rosh Hashanah). We are required, therefore, to considerable supplementation to make up the 100 blessings. The *Ein Keloheinu*, with its four expressions of *Barukh*, was regarded as fulfilling that particular purpose. And not only the *Barukh* lines, but even the other affirmations of faith were construed as satisfying the criteria for blessings, and thus serving to complement the existing blessings. This was reinforced by the fact that the initial letters of the first three lines make up the word, Amen, the traditional response for blessings. The *Kol Bo* maintains that *Ein Keloheinu* actually comprises twenty blessings!

574. So is it only prescribed for Sabbath and festival recitation?

No, in spite of the *Kol Bo*'s interpretation, it is also prescribed, by authorities such as Maimonides and the *Tur* (who quotes Amram Gaon as his source) for recitation each day at the end of the *Shachrit* service. On the basis of these authorities, Sephardim follow that practice. Moses Isserles states that the reason Ashkenazim do not recite it daily is because of time constraints and their wish to get to work without further delay. Traditionally, Sephardim have always recited their prayers at a more leisurely pace and invested greater time, effort, and concentration into them.

ALEINU

[See Questions 540–547.]

ADON OLAM

[See Questions 267, 274–276.]

XV

The Ceremony of *Tashlikh*

575. What does *Tashlikh* mean?

It means "casting out," and it refers to the ceremony of symbolically "casting out" one's sins into a river or running stream.

576. From where is the name derived?

It is derived from a verse in the book of Micah: "And You will cast (*Vetashlikh*) all their sins into the depths of the sea (7:19)." This verse forms the core of the formula recited at this ceremony. Other verses and psalms—notably Psalms 33 and 130—were added in the course of time.

577. When does *Tashlikh* take place?

It takes place during the afternoon of the first day of Rosh Hashanah, or if the first day is a Sabbath, on the second day.

578. Why, if the first day is a Sabbath, is it deferred to the second day?

This is because it was common practice to take some bread crumbs in order to throw into the water, and carrying is, of course, prohibited on the Sabbath.

579. Has this always been the practice, to defer it to the second day if the first day coincides with the Sabbath?

Apparently not. From our sources, it would appear that this deferment of *Tashlikh* was only introduced in the second half of the seventeenth century, by Rabbi Yechiel M. Epstein. In his work, *Kitzur Shenei Luchot Ha-berit*, he states that this decision is so that "people should not become involved in a profanation of the Sabbath."[1] He is clearly referring to the practice of carrying crumbs of bread and possibly also to another popular practice of shaking out the pockets and folds of one's garments into the water.

Before the seventeenth century, we must assume that most communities

---

1. Epstein, Y. M. (1864). *Kitzur Shenei Luchot Ha-berit*. Lemberg, p. 79.

performed *Tashlikh* even on the Sabbath, though they would have been reminded by their rabbis of the prohibition of carrying crumbs on that day.

580. Were there any other customs applied where the first day of Rosh Hashanah fell on a Sabbath?

There were some authorities who were of the opinion that the proper, and only, time for *Tashlikh* was on the opening day of judgment, and that when the incidence of the Sabbath prevented it from being performed on that day, it could not be deferred to the following day. This was the custom of the community of Fuerth in Bavaria in the eighteenth century, who simply omitted the *Tashlikh* altogether when the first day coincided with the Sabbath.[2]

This was in conformity with the view of some authorities who were in any case uneasy about this ceremony, maintaining that *Tashlikh* did not have its roots in pure monotheistic practice, and could, accordingly, with impunity, be dispensed with.

Since the seventeenth century, the consensus view has been that, as halakhically the two days of Rosh Hashanah are construed as one long day (See Question 13), it did not matter if *Tashlikh* was deferred to the second day in that situation.

581. Is this ceremony common to both Ashkenazim and Sephardim?

It is an example of an Ashkenazi practice being borrowed by the Sephardim. It commended itself particularly to Sephardic scholars who followed the mystical traditions of Rabbi Isaac Luria, and it was strongly recommended to the Sephardi world by two Italian sages, Rabbi Moses ben Mordechai Zacuto (d. 1697) and Rabbi Joseph Ergas (1685–1730), and from then it spread to the followers of the Spanish and Portuguese tradition and the entire Sephardic world as far as Kurdistan, North Africa, and Egypt.[3]

582. We mentioned above (See Question 575) that some authorities looked askance at the ritual. Did they meet with any degree of success in their opposition?

The main opponent of *Tashlikh* was the famous Vilna Gaon (1720–1797). He recognized "the heathen character of this ceremony even in the disguise of later interpretations; and for this reason, no doubt, he refused to observe it."[4] The Gaon's view met with few supporters, however, and certainly with none illustrious enough to undermine the practice. He remained a fairly lone voice, therefore, with the result that, from that time onward, it became entrenched as a charming and beloved Rosh Hashanah practice.

---

2. Lauterbach, J. Z. (1973). *Rabbinic Essays*. New York: Ktav Publishing House, Inc., p. 422. We acknowledge our reliance, in our treatment here of *Tashlikh*, upon Lauterbach's meticulously researched article, first published in the *Hebrew Union College Annual* (1936), pp. 207–340.

3. Lauterbach, *op. cit.*, p. 411, n. 139.

4. Lauterbach, *op. cit.*, p. 410.

583. But what particular heathen or superstitious beliefs were alleged to be at its basis?

The Gaon, as well as some modern scholars,[5] viewed the ritual as rooted in the ancient superstitious belief that malevolent spirits, including Satan and the fallen angels, have their residence in the depths of the sea. The ancient Babylonians had a belief in *Ea*, goddess of the deep; and the purpose of throwing the crumbs into the water was in order to propitiate the harmful spirits and win their friendship in return for these offerings of food, delivered to their home in the sea. It has to be understood that belief in demons was rife, across cultures, and including Jewry, in the ancient world.

584. But why then should this ceremony be restricted to Rosh Hashanah? Surely the demons were not only a danger on this festival?

Indeed. The ancients universally believed that the demons envied human happiness at any time, and wherever a loud and lively celebration attracted their attention, they were likely to pounce. The observance of a festival day, with everyone in a happy frame of mind, dressed in their finery and surrounded by their family, was most likely to arouse the jealousy of the demons and prompt them to attack. It does not surprise us, therefore, to learn that in some communities a ceremony akin to *Tashlikh* was practiced on *every* festival.

Thus, Rabbi Jacob Moellin (*Maharil*, 1365–1427) reports that his teacher, R. Shalom of Vienna, condemned those who went to the banks of rivers on festivals, carrying food to give to the fish, and remaining to observe until they had consumed it all.[6] The purpose of waiting in this way was clearly to be sure that the food would be transported by the fish to the spirits of the deep.

In the course of time, however, and especially after *Tashlikh* had been modified, invested with accompanying psalms and prayers, and become the recipient of a number of "acceptable" rabbinic reinterpretations of its significance, its original superstitious orientation was forgotten and, with one or two notable opponents, it was accepted as a worthy and beloved Rosh Hashanah ritual. It then ceased to be practiced on other festivals, primarily because the "harmless reinterpretations" were all directed exclusively to the Rosh Hashanah context.

585. What sort of "reinterpretations" of *Tashlikh*'s significance were given?

Perhaps the most popular interpretation links *Tashlikh* to the Midrash[7] which states that, in order to frustrate Abraham's journey to the *Akedah*, Satan transformed himself into a swollen river, blocking Abraham's way. Abraham walked through it, up to his neck, undaunted, crying out to God to save his life, whereupon God

---

5. Trachtenberg, J. (1939). *Jewish Magic and Superstition*. New York: Behrman's Jewish Book House, p. 165.

6. *Maharil, Hilkhot Yom Tov* (Lemberg 1860), p. 33a; Quoted in Lauterbach, *op. cit.*, p. 380, n. 107.

7. Midrash *Tanchuma, Va-yeira* (ed. Buber), p. 114.

rebuked Satan, and the river dried up. *Tashlikh*, according to this "reinterpretation," is merely intended to recall the unique commitment of father Abraham at the *Akedah* and to intercede for divine mercy on this day through his merit.

Moses Isserles, in his *Torat ha-Olah*,[8] provides a more rational and philosophical explanation of the custom. He states as follows:

> Jewish customs take on the binding character of Torah laws. Furthermore, when one goes to a river to recite *Tashlikh*, and observes there the great wonders of the Creator, who has made the sand as a boundary to the sea, so that its waters go so far and no further, one is moved to reflect on the greatness of the One who created the world at the beginning. . . . This is why we go to a river on Rosh Hashanah (the anniversary of the Creation of the world).

586. Were any other "harmless reinterpretations" offered to account for the origin and purpose of *Tashlikh* and to camouflage its superstitious origin?

We will content ourselves with quoting just two more reinterpretations.

Rabbi Mordechai Jaffe (1530–1612) states that the important thing is to go to that part of the river or stream where fish abound, in order to remind ourselves of the frailty and mortality of man who, like the fish, can so easily be caught in the net of judgment and death. Thus, for Rabbi Jaffe, the purpose of the ritual is to induce within us feelings of remorse, humility, and repentance.

Another popular interpretation of *Tashlikh* is that we go to a stream in order to recall, and symbolically reenact, the coronation of God on this day;[9] for it was customary to crown Jewish kings by a perennial stream, to symbolize that their reign should continue forever.[10]

587. So how early can we trace back the *Tashlikh* ritual?

Ch. M. Eliashow traces it back to the period of Ezra and Nehemiah (fifth to fourth century B.C.E.).[11] He sees it reflected in the great assembly that Ezra convened "before the Water Gate" in order to instruct the nation in Torah and extract a pledge of renewed loyalty to it (See Question 11). This sacred colloquium took place "on the first day of the seventh month," (Nehemiah 8:2), which is, of course, Rosh Hashanah. (The reference to "the second day" (verse 13) is an interesting corroboration of the view that Rosh Hashanah always was of two days' duration in ancient times!)[12]

588. How do we explain the popularity of this, essentially rather strange, ritual?

We believe that, intrinsically, it would have had little appeal, especially in recent centuries, to people who no longer felt that superstitious compulsion to pacify the

8. Isserles, M. (1848). *Torat ha-Olah* Lemberg, III, Chapter 56, p. 48b.
9. Epstein, B. H. (1979). *Barukh She'amar*. Tel Aviv: Am Olam Ltd., p. 362.
10. Talmud *Horayot* 11a.
11. Quoted by Jacob Z. Lauterbach, *op. cit.*, p. 430.
12. For another view, See Question 13.

spirits of the deep. It was preserved most probably on account of the fact that a walk to the local stream or river provided a pleasant and tranquil diversion from the very long and emotion-packed morning prayers in the invariably hot and stuffy atmosphere of the over-crowded synagogue. The afternoon stroll provided a very welcome breath of fresh air and some exercise after being hemmed-in in the narrow and hard synagogue pews.

It was probably the younger generation who were the custodians of this ritual. The stroll around the park or river bank, all dressed up in their new clothes, offered the youth an opportunity of fraternizing with their friends and showing-off a little; and, in a past age when dating was taboo, and social contact between the sexes kept to a minimum, *Tashlikh* also offered a not-to-be-missed opportunity of spotting the local talent!

TAKING A NAP

589. Is it true that it is forbidden to take a nap on Rosh Hashanah afternoon?

It is true that this is the commonly held view, though it is highly improbable that this tradition rests on any authoritative basis or should be taken at face value.

It is unclear where the idea originated, and it is referred to in halakhic sources only from the sixteenth century. Rabbi Moses Isserles (*Remah*) states that "there is a custom not to sleep on the day of Rosh Hashanah (Palestinian Talmud); and it is an appropriate custom."[13]

590. So is not Isserles a good enough source to rely upon for the prohibition of sleeping on Rosh Hashanah?

Of course he is. Isserles is one of Ashkenazi Jewry's most authoritative codifiers. However, there are certain aspects of this custom that have to be considered. First, Isserles is not "prohibiting" taking a nap; he is merely referring to it as "a custom" which has his approbation. Secondly, it is not an established custom that we can trace back as a practice hallowed by the ages before Isserles. Thirdly, there are serious difficulties in finding any proper source or reason for this prohibition.

591. But surely there is a most authoritative source, referred to by Isserles himself, namely the Palestinian Talmud?

It is significant that Isserles, uncharacteristically, contents himself with merely attributing the prohibition to the Palestinian Talmud, but without stating precisely where in that monumental work it is to be found and without even quoting the name of the tractate. Indeed, if such a reference was actually to be found in that source, we would have an open-and-shut case. But, it is not so straightforward.

R. David ben Samuel Halevi (*Taz*), commenting on Isserles' statement, attempts

---

13. *Remah* on *Shulchan Arukh Orach Chayyim* 583:2.

to identify the particular statement in the Palestinian Talmud, quoting the maxim: "Whoever rests (*man dedamikh*) on Rosh Hashanah, his good fortune will also rest (*damikh mazalei*)."[14]

R. Barukh Halevi Epstein notes that no such quotation occurs in any of our editions of that Talmud. He does concede, however, that "there are numerous examples of subjects covered in the versions of the Palestinian Talmud which were in the possession of the *Rishonim* (pre-sixteenth century halakhic authorities), but which were subsequently lost to later generations."

He proceeds to demonstrate, however, that even if such a quotation is authentic, it could not be used to justify any prohibition against sleeping on Rosh Hashanah, since the word *damikh* means exclusively "to die" in the Aramaic dialect of the Palestinian Talmud. The maxim quoted by *Taz* could only mean, therefore, "whoever *dies* on Rosh Hashanah, his good fortune has run its complete course (lit. 'died')." Whether or not we could make sense of such a maxim, one thing is clear: There is simply no Talmudic basis for any prohibition of taking a nap on this day.[15]

592. Point taken. But do any authorities actually state expressly that one may, in fact, take a nap on Rosh Hashanah?

Yes. The other main supercommentator to the *Shulchan Arukh*, Rabbi Avraham Abeli Gombiner (*Magen Avraham*), appositely observes that

Rabbi Judah [He-Chasid] states that after midday it is permissible to sleep, since the angel [of mercy] has already been aroused on our behalf by means of the prayers and the shofar sounds; and the *Bach* states that Rabbi Meir (of Rothenburg) used to take a nap on Rosh Hashanah. Indeed, he avers sitting around idly is no different to sleeping![16]

593. So what could have been the origin of that obscure prohibition of not taking a nap on Rosh Hashanah?

I have propounded the theory[17] that it owes its origin to the ancient primitive and widely held superstition that the forces of evil, in the guise of hostile demons, found their easiest prey among those who were asleep. This idea infiltrated mainstream Jewish belief and was responsible for the introduction of Psalm 91 into the prayers on retiring each night. This psalm is referred to as *Shir shel pega'im* (The hymn against evil mishap):

Do not be afraid of terror by night . . . of the pestilence that stalks the darkness . . . no evil shall befall you, neither shall the scourge approach your tent, for He will give His angels charge over you.

---

14. *Taz ad loc.*, n. 3.
15. Epstein, B. H. (1979). *Barukh She-amar*. Tel Aviv: Am Olam Publications, p. 362.
16. *Magen Avraham* on *Shulchan Arukh Orach Chayyim* 583:2 [6].
17. Cohen, J. M. (1994). *Prayer and Penitence*. Northvale, NJ: Jason Aronson Inc., p. 106.

We are told that many of the most distinguished rabbinic authorities—men of the calibre of R. Meir of Rothenburg and R. Jacob Weil—were also apprehensive of the power of the dark forces and would recite these verses even before taking a nap during the day.[18]

Hence, on Rosh Hashanah, when fear of Satan and his cohorts was particularly acute, as our sinfulness is exposed before the scrutiny of all the heavenly hosts, and the evil spirits are poised to assail those who are patently without merit, it was recommended that we do not sleep, since by doing so we would be making ourselves doubly vulnerable!

18. Trachtenberg, J. (1939). *Jewish Magic and Superstition*. New York: Behrman's Jewish Book House, p. 113.

XVI

A Selection of Bereavement Regulations

OBSERVANCE OF *SHIVAH* AND *SHELOSHIM*

594. If a near relative passes away a few days before Rosh Hashanah, what is the law regarding observance of mourning during the festival?

There is a principle that a festival cancels the specific period of mourning that is currently being observed. Thus, if a mourner has already commenced observing *shivah* (the first 7 days of home-based mourning), then the festival interrupts and cancels out the obligation to complete the remainder of the 7 days. This applies even if the burial takes place late afternoon on the eve of Rosh Hashanah, as long as the mourner has had time to take his seat afterwards and receive a greeting of consolation.

595. In this situation, what is the law regarding the rest of the 30-day period of mourning (*sheloshim*)?

We still regard the abbreviated *shivah* as a full 7 days, and the arrival of Yom Kippur cancels the next period of mourning, that is the *sheloshim*.

596. What are the ramifications of that cancellation?

It means that, for relatives other than parents (when a full year of mourning is prescribed), the official tokens of mourning are concluded. For those mourning parents, it also means that they are now in the post-*sheloshim* period when certain other restrictions may be relaxed.

597. So, in this situation where Yom Kippur cancels the *sheloshim*, can the mourners have a haircut and shave in time for Yom Kippur?

Yes, indeed; but this should be left until after *Minchah* on the eve of Yom Kippur, or as late as possible. This only applies, however, in the case of mourning for relatives other than parents. For parents, one may not shave or have one's hair cut until one is so unkempt that one's close friends comment adversely, after *sheloshim*, on one's appearance.

598. What if the near relative passes away on the eve of Rosh Hashanah, and there is no time to conduct the burial?

Then the burial takes place as early as possible after the festival, when the full *shivah* is observed in the usual way.

THE *ONEN*

599. What is the status of the mourners in this situation?

Normally, in the period between death and the conclusion of the arrangements for burial, the mourner is defined as an *Onen*, that is one who is expected to give his or her total attention to the required arrangements. During the period he is an *Onen*, he does not eat meat, drink wine, or have marital relations. Now, the basic halakhic principle is that one who is occupied with the performance of one *mitzvah* is absolved at that time from performing others. For this reason, the *Onen* is, *under* ordinary circumstances, absolved from prayer or any other positive religious duties.

But the situation we have described (in Question 598) is not "ordinary," since once the *Yom Tov* of Rosh Hashanah has entered, the mourners cannot attend to any practical arrangements for the burial. Accordingly, they do still have a duty to attend synagogue and recite home blessings (*kiddush*, grace after meals, etc.).

600. May he eat meat and drink wine in this situation?

Not only may he, but, according to some authorities, he has a duty to eat meat and drink wine in order not to neglect the positive *mitzvah* of *Oneg Yom Tov*, making the festival day pleasurable.

Now, eating and drinking are public acts, and the halakah relaxes such prohibitions on the festival, so that those around—family and friends—should not be saddened on the festival by being in the proximity of a friend displaying such tokens of bereavement. Private, intimate pleasures, on the other hand, such as marital relations, are still prohibited during this period, until after the conclusion of the *shivah*.

601. How can the mourner recite the festival *kiddush* when it contains the celebratory *Shehecheyanu* blessing, which a mourner during *shivah* is surely not meant to recite?

The halakhic authorities find no objection to the mourner reciting *Shehecheyanu* in a situation like this, where it cannot be deferred. As part of the *kiddush*, it is not a personal blessing, but a thanksgiving for the holy day, which the mourner is also obliged to mark and observe.

ROSH HASHANAH AND *SHELOSHIM*

602. What if Rosh Hashanah arrives after the mourner has already completed the full *shivah* (7 days of homebound mourning) and is in the middle of the next, 30-day, period of modified mourning (*sheloshim*)?

This is a similar situation to the one described in Question 597, where Yom Kippur cancels the existing period of *sheloshim*. Rosh Hashanah does likewise.

603. What if one's near relative was buried just before Rosh Hashanah, but the mourner did not receive notice of it until after the festival had begun?

The full *shivah* must be observed in the usual way after Rosh Hashanah is over, and the *keri'ah* (tearing of the garment) is performed in the usual way. The arrival of Yom Kippur would then cancel the *sheloshim* period.

YOM KIPPUR AND *SHIVAH*

604. What if one's near relative was buried a few days before Yom Kippur?

The arrival of Yom Kippur cancels the *shivah* observance. From Yom Kippur onward, the mourner enters the *sheloshim* period; and the arrival of the festival of Sukkot (4 days after Yom Kippur) cancels the *sheloshim*. Again, this has greater practical significance for those mourning other relatives, whose mourning comes to a complete end with the arrival of Sukkot, than for those mourning parents, whose mourning continues for the entire year. However, even for those mourning parents, this may also be significant where their rabbis permit them to attend certain functions after *sheloshim*.

605. What if one's near relative was buried just before Yom Kippur, but the mourner did not receive notice of it until the day after Yom Kippur?

He commences *shivah* (and makes *keri'ah*) immediately, and the arrival of the festival of Sukkot cancels the *shivah* in the usual way.

THE MEAL OF CONDOLENCE

606. Is the special meal of condolence (*Se'udat havra'ah*) served if one returns from the burial on the late afternoon before the onset of Rosh Hashanah or Yom Kippur?

No, it is not, because that is a time when there is no public observance of mourning, since the mourner would normally be permitted at that time to attend to his or her preparations for the approaching holy day. (For further information on the meal of condolence, See our companion volume: *1001 Questions and Answers on Pesach*, pp. 268–269.)

TIME FOR TERMINATION OF THE *SHIVAH*

607. So at what time is one permitted to get up from sitting *shivah* when the approach of Rosh Hashanah or Yom Kippur (or any other major festival) brings it to a premature end?

Strictly speaking, not before the time of *Minchah*, which is about 2½ hours before the onset of the festival.[1] The exact time varies with the seasons, so that in summer a little extra time may be allowed. If one requires a little longer time in order to prepare for the festival, this is also permitted.

SELICHOT IN THE *SHIVAH* HOUSE

608. Does someone sitting *shivah* during the *Selichot* period (in the run-up to Rosh Hashanah and through to Yom Kippur) attend morning services at synagogue, in order to recite the *Selichot* (penitential prayers) with the congregation, or are these recited at the morning service in the *shivah* house?

The mourner does not leave his house, even to recite *Selichot*. However, an exception is made for the morning before Rosh Hashanah, when there is a prolonged *Selichot* service. If he prefers, however, *Selichot* may even be recited in the *shivah* house, together with a minyan, on that day.

YIZKOR DURING THE FIRST YEAR?

609. Does one recite the *Yizkor* prayer for the departed during the first year of mourning?

Yizkor is recited on Yom Kippur, among other festivals. It is not recited, however, on Rosh Hashanah. Contrary to popular belief, there is a definite obligation to recite it during the first year. The authoritative *Kol Bo al Aveilut* states, "The custom not to recite it during the first year of mourning is a bad practice, without any halakhic foundation. . . . If one refrains from reciting it, one is classified as stealing from the dead [their right]."[2]

---

1. Greenwald, Y. (1947). *Kol Bo al Aveilut*. New York: Moriah, p. 404.
2. *Sha'ar Ha-Tziyyun* on *Mishnah Berurah* 548:39.

ACTING AS AN OFFICIANT OVER THE HIGH HOLY DAYS

610. May a mourner for parents act as an officiant during his year of mourning?

He may not serve as a *Chazan*, nor blow the shofar, unless no one as competent is available to take over. In a situation where a parent dies just before Rosh Hashanah, and the burial could not take place, so that he remains an *Onen* on the festival, the *Pri Megadim* decides that, where no other person is available to blow the shofar, he may do so, on the basis that the needs of the community override his own concerns.[3] Other authorities, likewise, permit a *Chazan* in that situation to lead the service, even when accompanied by a choir. The analogy is made between the *Chazan* and the High Priest, who, even as an *Onen*, was obliged to conduct the Temple service.[4]

611. May one who is in the middle of his *sheloshim* period of mourning for relatives other than parents act as an officiant on Rosh Hashanah or Yom Kippur?

If he has already served in that capacity for two or more years, he may continue to do so, since Rosh Hashanah and Yom Kippur in any case curtail the *sheloshim* observance. Where he has not established that precedence, however, and if there is someone available to stand in for him, then he should refrain from officiating. However, a mourner, even for parents, may lead the morning *Selichot* services, recited between Rosh Hashanah and Yom Kippur, once his *shivah* is over.

---

3. Braun, S. Z., ed. (1978). *Shearim Metzuyanim Behalakhah*. New York: Feldheim, vol. III, p. 151.
4. *Ibid.*

XVII

Hasidic Practices

612. In what way do Hasidim prepare, during the month of Elul, for the approaching High Holy Days?

In many Hasidic traditions, it is customary to pay special attention to the recitation of extra *tillim* (*tehillim*, psalms) during this month. In several Lubavitch communities, it was customary to recite ten psalms each day, at the end of the morning service, in order to complete the entire book of Psalms twice in time for Rosh Hashanah. Others recited eighteen psalms, because in Hebrew that is the numerical value of the word *chai*, "life."

Another common practice is to examine at this time the parchments of their *tefillin* and *mezuzahs*, and to have any errors in the script corrected. In general, they are meant to utilize this month in extra and closer attention to the performance of all their *mitzvot*, and to pray with even greater spiritual concentration.

Some rebbes encourage their disciples to intensify their study of Hasidic lore in groups of two or three, especially during the months of Elul and Tishri.

613. Are there any novel innovations that are exclusively reserved for this month?

We have already described the *fahrbrengen* of *Chabad* Hasidim on the first two nights of Elul (See Question 144). Another practice was to reserve exclusively for use at this time a special *nigun* (tune), composed by the first Lubavitcher rebbe and invested with the power to arouse even the most stubborn hearts to repentance and to sweeten the quality of divine justice and transform it into mercy.

In many Hasidic communities, they did not conduct marriages throughout the year in the second half of the month. The waning of the moon was regarded as inauspicious. The month of Elul, on the other hand, offering the opportunity for repentance and union with God, was an exception, and marriages were solemnized throughout the month.

614. What is the meaning of the *Pidyon nefesh* ritual?

This is a *Chabad* Hasidic practice.[1] The name derives from Exodus 21:30, and means "a ransom for his life." After morning prayers on the day before Rosh

---

1. Mondschein, Y. (1995). *Otzar Minhagei Chabad*. Jerusalem: Heikhal Menachem, pp. 41–47.

Hashanah, the followers queue up at the rebbe's door to present him with their envelopes containing their monetary donations, and their names and the names of their mothers, so that the rebbe may intercede for them for life in the coming year. The rebbe then blesses them and wishes them *shanah tovah umetukah*, "a sweet and good year!"

The last Lubavitcher rebbe would receive the *pidyon nefesh* with his right hand, and, after giving his greeting, transfer it to his left hand. He would gather all the envelopes until they grew into a pile in his arms, and he would then withdraw to his room and stay there a while until returning to continue receiving his Hasidim and their "ransoms."

615. What is the significance of the eighteenth (*chai*) of Elul for *Chabad* Hasidim?

The eighteenth of Elul is the birth date of both the *Ba'al Shem Tov*, the founder of Hasidism, as well as of the founder of the *Chabad* dynasty, R. Shneur Zalman of Lyady, author of the *Tanya* (Slavita, 1796). Among *Chabad* Hasidim, it became a day of special spiritual significance, and an opportunity to relate traditions regarding the lives and teachings of the illustrious rebbes, as well as to reinforce their own loyalty to the principles of Hasidism.

616. Why do Hasidim pay a special visit to their rebbes over the High Holy Day period?

They have borrowed an ancient Talmudic practice. The Talmud states that "a man is obliged to visit (and greet) his teacher on a festival." After the destruction of the Temple, these visits of students to their teachers might well have been viewed as symbolizing the appearance of the pilgrims at the Temple on the three foot festivals, to be blessed by the High Priest—the "rebbe" of all Israel.

617. Why, on these occasions, do the Hasidim bring to their rebbe *kvitlach*?

A *kvitel* is an intercessional note, containing the name or names of people for whom the Hasid wishes his rebbe to intercede with God. The Hasidim believe fervently that God accedes to the rebbe's every wish and demand.

Now there is a mystical belief that when the spirit of strict justice is abroad—such as on the High Holy Days—no person's name should be mentioned on its own, for intercession on his or her behalf, since this will focus the attention of the accuser on that person, hence, the idea of the collective *kvitels*—the "safety in numbers syndrome"—whereby the scores of visiting Hasidim bring with them the many names of sick and needy people, written on the various pieces of paper. Needless to say, the Hasidim do not come empty-handed; and the *kvitlach* are a major source of support for the rebbe and his "court."

618. Are there any special eve of Rosh Hashanah *Chabad* practices?

It is customary "for those who are healthy and strong enough" to fast on the day before Rosh Hashanah, as well as on the first day (the Sunday) of the *Selichot* period. It was considered as specially important not to indulge in any secular speech or pursuits, but to devote that day to prayer, recitation of *Tillim* and thoughts of repentance and holiness, so as to enter the day of judgment in a most appropriate frame of mind.

619. Is there any variant tradition regarding the formula of the blessing over the *Yom Tov* candles?

There is a very strange tradition, described in a responsum by the late Lubavitcher rebbe, of blessed memory, as practiced for generations exclusively within his family circle, of reciting the blessing *lehadlik ner shel yom ha-zikkaron* (instead of *lehadlik ner shel yom tov*). He is unaware of the origin of this departure from universal practice, but explains it as an attempt to achieve consistency with the references to *yom ha-zikkaron* recited in the *kiddush* and the *Haftarah* blessings.[2]

620. For how long do the Hasidim continue the practice of smearing honey on the *chalah* before making *ha-motziy*?

The Lubavitch practice is to continue this augury for a sweet year until after *Hosha'na Rabba*, the *terminus ad quem* for the final appeal for clemency before the heavenly throne. There is no hard and fast practice, however, regarding this matter.

621. Are there any special *Chabad* practices for Rosh Hashanah?

In some yeshivot, they would organize rotas to ensure that, at any time, throughout the day or night, there were always people (where possible, at least ten) reciting *Tillim*. Each rota would be on duty for about 2 or 3 hours.

During Rosh Hashanah, Hasidim are expected to make some firm spiritual resolutions, notably to intensify their commitment to *hiddur mitzvah*, the performance of *mitzvot* with greater degree of self-sacrifice and emotional and religious effort, and, where posssible, the investment of more money in the acquisition of the most beautiful ritual objects. They are also urged to work on themselves in order to remove the element of familiarity and routine from their performance of the recurring *mitzvot*.[3]

---

2. Schneerson, M. M. (1987). *Teshuvot Ubiurim BeShulchan Arukh*. New York: Kehat Publication Society, p. 57.

3. See Mondschein, p. 153. I am indebted to the above two publications for much of the material contained in this section on Hasidic practices. I thank my friend and congregant, Mr. Mendy Sudak, for bringing these sources to my attention.

622. Are there any additional *Chabad* prohibitions?

It was recommended that one should not engage in unnecessary conversation during the two days of Rosh Hashanah, one should reduce one's eating, drinking, and sleeping, and one should not smoke!

Enactments are found especially prohibiting the smoking of a pipe, even in private. The pipe was a most important spiritual accoutrement in some Hasidic circles. It was believed to aid some rebbes in having higher mysteries revealed to them. At the death of a rebbe, his pipe was regarded as a most prized inheritance, though many disciples were reportedly most disappointed that, when they lit the rebbe's pipe for the first time, all they saw was billowing smoke![4]

623. Do Hasidim all wear the *kittel* (white robe) during the High Holy Day services, as is the custom among pious men in some non-Hasidic communities?

It is not the practice for the ordinary worshipers to wear the *kittel* in most Hasidic communities on Rosh Hashanah—only the *Chazan*, the one blowing the shofar and the one calling the notes. In the Belz tradition, the rebbe wears a *kittel*, but other rebbes refrained from doing so on Rosh Hashanah. The reason given is that the *kittel* also recalls the garments of the ministering angels, and it was regarded as presumptuous on these days, when judgment is being considered, to display such a token of superconfidence.[5] On Yom Kippur, on the other hand, the rebbe and the entire congregation do so, secure in the belief that their prayers and repentance over Rosh Hashanah and the ensuing days of penitence will have secured divine grace.

624. Did Hasidim impose any restrictions on who may lead the services over the High Holy Days?

In general, they would not appoint a formal or professional *Chazan* to lead their services, preferring an ordinary Hasid who would pour out his heart before his Father in heaven. Hasidism did not go in for the formality of *Chazanut*, and some very caustic sentiments are recorded regarding the art of the *Chazan*, viewing it as an obstacle, rather than an impetus, to piety.[6]

Many Hasidic *shkibls* also excluded *Shochtim* (religious slaughterers) from leading the services over the High Holy Days. Because they were associated throughout the year with the taking of life, they were hardly the people to petition for life on behalf of their community.

625. What is their practice regarding having a drink and a snack before going to *shul*?

This is discouraged, as one is not supposed to eat or drink before hearing the shofar. However some permit themselves a drink of tea or coffee, but nothing else

4. Mondschein, pp. 52–54.
5. *Op. cit.*, p. 59.
6. *Op. cit.*, p. 62.

with it.[7] A weak or ill person is permitted, however, to eat some cake or fruit in order to sustain himself through the long service.

626. Do Hasidim differ in their perception of the *piyyutim* and in the amount they recite?

Indeed, they have much less regard for the poetic insertions into the prayers than do their non-Hasidic, Ashkenazi confrères.

They take their cue from Rabbi Shneur Zalman of Lyady who quoted R. Isaac Luria's view that "Only those prayers which the Men of the Great Assembly or the poet Kallir introduced are to be regarded as possessing the authentic structure, and serving as the heavenly-inspired conduit for the dissemination of the higher life-force. This is not the case with prayers that ordinary people have conjured up from their own minds."[8] The Hasidim also took as their maxim the principle of better say a little with proper concentration than a lot without.

Accordingly, they do not recite the *Yotzrot piyyutim* (those prescribed for insertion into the blessings of the *Shema*), which they would construe as interruptions of that part of the service, but confine themselves to those *piyyutim* inserted into the repetition of the *Amidah*.

627. Do the Hasidim have a different practice in relation to the recitation of *Avinu Malkeinu*?

The Hasidic authorities were uneasy about reciting *Avinu Malkeinu* on Rosh Hashanah because so many of its verses draw attention to the fact that "we have sinned before Thee." It was felt that this admission of compounded guilt would play into the accuser's hand.

Some authorities merely omitted the opening line of *Avinu Malkeinu*; others excised further lines, such as "Forgive and pardon all our iniquities" and "Blot out and cancel our transgressions from before Thine eyes." Others went further and prescribed the omission of the entire composition. Communities that do recite it on Rosh Hashanah do not have the *Chazan* and congregation reciting certain lines alternately, but recite the entire prayer together.[9]

628. Do the Hasidim perform the *Tashlikh* ceremony in the same way as the non-Hasidic community?

There are some slight variations of practice, and many Hasidim are not so particular to perform it while it is still day. It is reported that the Karliner Hasidim have the practice of going to *Tashlikh* when it is already dark, carrying lanterns.

The *Gur* tradition is to recite *Tashlikh*, but not to go to any river or stream.[10] The

---

7. *Op. cit.*, p. 90.
8. *Op. cit.*, p. 97.
9. *Op. cit.*, p. 101–102.
10. *Op. cit.*, p. 141.

followers of the Radzyn Hasidic tradition do not perform *Tashlikh* on Rosh Hashanah itself, but on the eighth of the Ten Days of Penitence, which has a special significance in Hasidic lore as the "Day of the Thirteen Divine Attributes," when God responds more readily than at any other time to Israel's petitions. This custom may have arisen originally because the Hasidic services on Rosh Hashanah were so protracted that there simply was no time left to fit in the recitation of *Tashlikh* as well as their *Yom Tov* meal and *Minchah*.

It is a standard Hasidic tradition that, after having recited the *Tashlikh*, they all shake out the edges of their *tzitzit*-garment, to rid themselves of the *klippot*, the residual kernels of uncleanliness that adhere to them.

629. Are there any other unique Hasidic practices?

There was a custom, practiced in some Hasidic traditions, to keep alight within the synagogues a specially prepared wax candle throughout *Shabbat Shuvah*, the intermediate Sabbath between Rosh Hashanah and Yom Kippur. This was called the "*teshuvah licht*" ("repentance light"), and the preparation of the wicks, which was done with great religious concentration, was regarded as a special *mitzvah*.[11]

---

11. *Op. cit.*, pp. 166–169.

XVIII

Rosh Hashanah Customs in Other Countries

AFGHANISTANI NEW YEAR PRACTICES

630. How did the Jews of Afghanistan observe the *Selichot* period?

To answer this and my other questions about this exotic Jewish community, I have the benefit of the firsthand experience of one of my congregants, Mr. David Moradoff, who lived in Herat, one of the larger cities of Afghanistan, from 1931 to 1957. In his own words:

> We started reciting the *Selichot* from the second night of the month of Elul, until the eve of Yom Kippur. The service started each morning at about 3:30 a.m., and three-quarters of the community attended. We did not have watches in those days, and I remember when I was a teenager, I used to wake up many times during the night and look to the stars. I had my own signs. When some bright stars were in certain places in the sky, I knew that it was time for *Selichot*, and I would then wake up my father and brothers for the service. My timing was always accurate.

631. How did the Jews of Afghanistan prepare their food for Rosh Hashanah?

Two or three days before Rosh Hashanah, those families who could afford it would buy a lamb from the market, and the *shochet* would come to each house in turn to slaughter it. This was regarded as a specially significant symbolic commemoration of the ram that father Abraham slaughtered instead of his son. The family would retain enough meat for its needs, with the rest being distributed to the poor.

632. Did they observe the ceremony of *Hatarat nedarim* ("Annulment of vows." See Questions 209–221)?

Not only did they, but they repeated the ceremony three times! The first time they performed it was forty days before Rosh Hashanah. They repeated it on the morning before Rosh Hashanah, after *Selichot*, and then again on the morning before Yom Kippur.

633. What home ritual did the Jews of Afghanistan perform of before eating their main festival eve meal?

On returning from synagogue, they would find the tablecloth laid out on the floor with all the special fruits and festival foods, and surrounded by mattresses. The father would then recite the last line of the well-known hymn *Achot ketanah*, recited across the Sephardi world: *Tikhleh shanah ukelaloteha, takhel shanah uvirkhoteha*, "Let the misfortunes of the last year be erased, paving the way for the blessings of the year to come." The family would then all exchange blessings.

They would then partake of apple dipped into sugar-water, after reciting the traditional formula: "May God renew unto us a good and sweet year." They would then take some leek. The Hebrew for this is *kareti*, which is also suggestive of the verb "to cut off" (*karet*), and is eaten, therefore, in order to reinforce the desire that "all God's enemies should be cut off."

They then eat some beetroot, dates, courgettes, black eye beans, pomegranates, head and lung of a lamb, and, finally, some fish. All of these have a Hebrew name that is symbolically applied to the needs and blessings of the coming year. Fish is eaten in order that we should be fruitful and multiply like fish; or, according to another explanation, because fish have no eyelids. This means that their eyes are always open, suggestive of God's constant and unwavering supervision of His people.

634. What did they have for their main course?

Believe it or not, they were not ready yet for the main meal! First, they had to eat their starters! They would have fried mince meat in a flat, oval case, called *Gontaveh*, or in a cylindrical shape, called *lule kebab*. With this they would serve round-shaped fried mashed potatoes mixed with egg, called *Kuku kartufi*, and some boiled chicken, called *yakhni*.

After all this, they were ready for their main course, which was generally a goulash cooked with tomato and aubergines, called *ghaime*. They did not eat anything sour, sharp, spicy, or hot on Rosh Hashanah, only sweet things to symbolize the sweet year ahead.

635. Did they have any ritual following the meal?

After the meal, but before grace, they read four chapters of the Mishnah of Rosh Hashanah, followed by a passage from the *Zohar* (*parashat Emor*) dealing with the theme of the shofar.

Following grace after meals, they would read half the book of Psalms, leaving the rest for the following morning, either at home before they went to synagogue, or in synagogue before the main service commenced. The entire book of (150) Psalms was then read again following lunch on the first day. The twice reading made a total of 300 psalms, which is the numerical value of the Hebrew word for "atone!"— *kapper*!

636. I put the following question to my good friend, Mr. Moradoff: What do you recall of the way the Rosh Hashanah synagogue services were conducted all that time ago?

He replied as follows:

The service in the synagogue commenced just after sunrise, and within five to ten minutes the synagogue was nearly full. We had four main synagogues in Herat, and a few special people were chosen to lead the services over the High Holy Days.

In our synagogue, called *Bet Kneset Mulah Yoav*, there was a most popular *Chazan*—Mulah Yoseph Ha-Cohen. He was my father's second cousin, and possessed all the necessary attributes: He was an elder, a sage of the Torah, possessed of a sweet voice and a fine appearance. On Rosh Hashanah and Yom Kippur, he wore white clothes, with a long white robe on top, called a *chuka*, and a white turban. He led the service with overwhelming religious fervor, and a voice that was quivering with emotion. During the entire service, no one dared to speak.

637. Was the form of the service any different from our own?

Again, let Mr. Moradoff reminisce:

There were two people deputed to stand on the *Bimah*, on either side of the *Chazan*, for the entire duration of the services. During the recitation of the unfamiliar Rosh Hashanah and Yom Kippur silent *Amidah*s, one of those aides would recite the silent *Amidah* aloud, to enable the whole congregation (most of whom would not have possessed printed prayer books) to recite it with him silently, word for word.

638. At the risk of being too interested in gastronomy (but I know my readers!), let me ask you again, my dear friend, David, what did you have for lunch on Rosh Hashanah and how did you spend the rest of the day?

Lunch was not as festive as the previous night. We had a special dish, called *pishkhurd*, comprising some of the starters from the previous evening, followed by the main course, called *chellow*, which was mostly rice with meat soup and small meatballs.

Most people did not sleep on the days of Rosh Hashanah. It was believed that if they did, their good fortune would also go to sleep for the entire year ahead.[1] After lunch, most people read psalms and the story of the binding of Isaac. Some people had a booklet, written in poetical style in the Persian language, and the ladies loved to hear it read, finding it very moving.

---

1. See above, Questions 589–593.

Later on, we would be served with coffee or tea, accompanied by dry and fresh fruits to enable us to complete the prescribed 100 daily blessings.

A NOVEL BARBARY AND KURDISTANI CUSTOM

639. How did the Jews of Barbary and Kurdistan observe *Tashlikh*?

We have a description of a quaint feature of the *Tashlikh* ceremony, as practiced by the Jews of Barbary, in a book written by L. Addison, Christian chaplain to the garrison of Tangier during the years 1662–1670.[2] They recited the various prayers in the usual way, but added one feature that was unique to their tradition, namely, that after concluding the *Tashlikh*, they did not shake out their garments, in the manner of the European tradition, but instead jumped into the water and started swimming around. He states that, "If . . . they have the good fortune to see a fish, they shake themselves lustily on purpose, to off-load it with their sins, so that it may swim away with them and be as the scape-goat of old which carried the people's sins into the desert."[3]

The Jews of Kurdistan had the identical practice. "They jumped into the water and swam around like fish. It was their belief that by so doing they would be effectively cleansed from their sins, for the water would wash away all their sins."[4]

A CUSTOM UNIQUE TO WORMS

640. Is the custom of omitting the *Ma'aravot* (special poetic insertions) in the evening services on Rosh Hashanah universally practiced?

There is an almost universal practice not to recite the usual eve of festival *Ma'aravot*, poetic insertions into the blessings before and after the *Shema*, on either evening of Rosh Hashanah (See Question 247). However there was one place that was out of line on this practice, and that was the Community of Worms, which recited them on both evenings.

The reason given was that R. Eleazar Rokeach, the great halakhist of Worms, took the view that one should fast on the eve of Rosh Hashanah until nightfall. They introduced the *Ma'aravot*, therefore, in order to extend the otherwise short evening service until nightfall, and, for the sake of consistency, recited them also on the second night.[5] No other authority demanded the extension of the fast until that time,

2. Addison, L. (1675). *The Present State of the Jews*. London, p. 192.
3. Lauterbach, J. Z. *op. cit.*, pp. 398–399.
4. Lauterbach, J. Z. *op. cit.*, p. 412, from Israel Joseph's *Sefer Masa'ei Yisrael* (Lyck, 1859), p. 30.
5. Zimmels, H. J. (1958). *Ashkenazim and Sephardim*. London: Jews' College Publications (New Series No. 2), pp. 106–107.

and therefore in all other communities they particularly omitted the *Ma'aravot* so that people could return home before nightfall and break their fast with their *Yom Tov* meal.

TASHLIKH IN SAFED

641. How did the inhabitants of Safed—an important center of mysticism from the sixteenth-century—observe *Tashlikh*, since the place had no rivers or streams?

Indeed, at that time it was a major problem for the adherents of that school who invested such rituals with the deepest significance. In subsequent centuries, with the development of inaccessible villages in northern Galilee, which possessed no perennial streams, the problem became quite widespread.

In Safed, and no doubt in other places where the unobstructed view facilitated it, the townsfolk would simply take themselves off to the highest vantage points, from which they could catch a glimpse of either Lake Tiberias or the Dead Sea, and would then recite the appropriate verses.

TASHLIKH IN JERUSALEM

642. Where did the Jews of Jerusalem recite *Tashlikh*?

In Jerusalem, the only natural spring is the Siloam Pool, at the base of the Kidron valley. There, or at the Silwan tunnel through which the Gihon spring flows, Jews from all over the city excitedly assembled to perform the colorful ritual. In the modern-day, much-expanded Jerusalem, there are sources of water much closer to hand for the inhabitants of many of the new districts.

YEMENITE TRADITIONS

643. How did Yemenite Jewry prepare for Rosh Hashanah in the days before their exodus to Israel in the famous "Operation Magic Carpet" airlift?

M. Geshuri[6] has left us a graphic account of the preparations for Rosh Hashanah on the part of the Jews of Yemen. It is especially important that these traditions be preserved and known, on account of the acculturation of the Yemenite community to the general Sephardic traditions of Modern Israel. It is for this reason that I have seen fit to include these and other vanishing, or indeed past, practices in this chapter.

The local Arab fruit and vegetable farmers knew well the dates of the Jewish

6. Geshuri, M. S. (1952). *"Rosh Hashanah eitzel yehudei Teiman."* In *Sefer Ha-Moadim*, ed. J. L. Baruch. Tel Aviv: *Agudat Oneg Shabbat*, pp. 151–155.

festivals and would come, laden with a very wide range of their products, to do a brisk trade with the Jews. The latter would also purchase nuts (they did not observe any prohibition of eating nuts on Rosh Hashanah), peas, and beans, which served as accompaniments to the strong brandy they consumed.

They observed the Talmudic practice of eating foods whose names evoked a good augury for the coming year, though in the far-flung areas the only thing available was the sweet *duba* fruit, over which they would petition for a sweet year. Those who could afford it would purchase a lamb; and the less well off at least tried to obtain the head, so that they could utter the prayer: "May we become the head, and not the tail." The poor would satisfy themselves with the head of a chicken, or, failing that, a garlic head! They discouraged the wearing of a new garment, since this generated a feeling of excitement, which they regarded as inappropriate to this day of introspection.

They placed great emphasis on the giving of charity and food, especially wheat, to the less well off. The children would be sent to leave money by the door of the poor in the middle of the night, so that the recipients would be unaware of the identity of their benefactor. There was, in addition, a communal collection, called *Kuppat Hekdesh.*

644. What spiritual preparations did Yemenite Jewry observe?

The more pious observed the custom of fasting the whole day before Rosh Hashanah. After morning prayers on the day before Rosh Hashanah, they would repair to the bath house, after which it was the custom to visit the graves of their near relatives or of acknowledged righteous people. In the early afternoon they would attend at the *Mikveh*, for a ritual immersion. Since the ritual baths were open to the elements, however, many refrained from immersing themselves on account of the cold.

The overall emotion that one was expected to elicit on Rosh Hashanah was that of true sadness at one's shortcomings. It was expected that one would shed real tears during the recitation of the prayers, and the inability to do so was viewed alarmingly as a sign that one was unworthy to be the recipient of divine grace.

645. What synagogal practices have the Yemenites developed since settling in Israel?

They have accepted upon themselves the practice of *Hatarat Nedarim,* the absolution of vows (See Questions 209–222), on the eve of Rosh Hashanah, though with some significant differences.

They first select the ten leading sages and leaders of the congregation, who repair, one by one, to the courtyard of the synagogue where they utter their confession of sins silently. As each one makes his confession, the rest of the congregation, indoors, recite the formula of absolution for that distinguished individual. Once all ten have completed their confessions, they proceed to utter the formal and collective absolution for the entire congregation. Following the ceremony, they recite the verses of the *Tashlikh* ceremony: *Miy El kamokha* ("What God is there like unto

Thee, forgiving of sin . . .") and *Vetashlikh* . . . ("And You will cast all their sins into the depths of the sea."). They use a new fruit for the second evening's meal, in order to be able to recite *Shehecheyanu* (See Question 230).

A practice that is most certainly imported from home is that of rising at midnight of the second day to go to synagogue in order to recite psalms in a supplicatory chant. This is followed by the reading of the *Akedah* and other prayers. At dawn, they sound thirty notes of the shofar and then proceed to pray the morning service.

They do not recite any *piyyutim* (poetic insertions) in the *Shachrit* or *Musaf Amidot*, regarding them as forbidden interruptions of the statutory service. They compensate by reciting many compositions before the blowing of the shofar—all on the theme of the *Akedah* and the merit they wish it to confer.

The one blowing the shofar does not wear the white *kittel* robe, nor are the Ark and Scrolls of the Law covered in white mantles. They do not provide a prompter (*makriy*) to announce each note, taking it for granted that the *toke'ah* will not get confused. It is the latter's prerogative to be called up to the fifth *aliyah* to the Torah on both days.

646. Why are the "Yemenite shofars" so different from the ordinary ones?

Because the Ethiopians were unable to obtain rams' horns, they used the very big, curly horns of antelopes or mountain goats. Their sound is much louder, deeper, and flatter than that of the high pitched and thin sound of the ram's horn.

Geshuri reports that in several places in Yemen the Jews had to obtain special permission to blow the shofar, since the local Arabs were most fearful of the sound emitted from it, attributing to it malevolent mystical powers. At certain times, the sounding of the shofar was banned altogether for that reason.

SYRIAN TRADITIONS

647. Are there any unique synagogue traditions among Syrian Jewry?

There is one tradition that is rare, but not quite unique, since we have already encountered it in the Afghanistani tradition (See Question 637), and which is also a Moroccan practice. We refer to the *Chazan* being supported on Rosh Hashanah by two associates (*seganim*), one on either side of him, aiding him in the recitation of the *piyyutim*. This is popularly explained with reference to Moses' battle against the Amalekites, when his two hands—uplifted in prayer to God—were supported "on either side" by Aaron and Hur. As long as they supported him, we are told, Israel maintained the upper hand in the battle, but as soon as he lowered his hands, Amalek prevailed. The two *seganim* represent that extra support that the *Chazan* needs in order to tip the scales in favor of Israel's merit.

Another, clearly superstitious, tradition they have is not to look at the person blowing the shofar at any time while it is being blown. This is also the custom of the Jews of Iraq.[7] I offer two theories to account for this: First, since one of the purposes of the shofar is to discomfit Satan, then better to keep one's eyes well away from looking in his direction, since even in his death-throes he can be malevolent. Secondly, it may have arisen out of confusion with the law that we may not look at the priests while they are blessing the congregation. Since, like the priests, the *toke'ah* also has his *tallit* over his head, it might have been supposed that whenever this occurs one must avert one's gaze.

648. Are there any other differences in the shofar practices of Syrian Jewry?

They blow the shofar during the silent *Amidah,* and the congregation actually sits down for the first group of notes, blown before the silent *Amidah.* Although the name of this group of notes is *Tekiyyot Dimeyushav* ("notes for which one may sit" as opposed to the rest of the notes, prescribed for insertion into the *Amidah,* which is a "standing" prayer), nevertheless most other traditions prescribe standing for all the notes of the shofar, out of deference to the biblical *mitzvah,* and the fear and trembling that its notes are meant to inspire. The Dutch practice, however, is identical to the Syrian in this respect.

The final group of notes is blown after reciting the *Borakhu,* which follows the repetition of the *Amidah* and precedes the *Aleinu.*

The final note is not a *teki'ah gedolah,* but a *teru'ah gedolah.* This is actually the 101st note. They add an extra note in order to make up the numerical value of the name of the Archangel Michael, the special protector of Israel from the Satanic forces bent upon condemning her before the bar of heavenly justice.[8]

649. Are there any variations in the way they recite the prayers?

Shema is recited in unison by the entire congregation, with the exception of the verse *Barukh shem kevod malkhuto.* This is curious, since one would have thought that a verse proclaiming God's *malkhut* (kingship) would have been singularly appropriate to loud recitation on this day, especially when one is already reciting the rest of the *Shema* aloud!

The priestly blessing of the people is inserted into the *Shachrit,* rather than the *Musaf Amidah.* This may be explained either in accordance with the principle of *Zerizim makdimin lemitzvot,* "Those who are zealous, perform mitzvot as early as possible," or because such an unconnected, independent ritual may have been construed as an interruption of the *mitzvah* of blowing the shofar.

Syrian tradition omits, in the *Avinu Malkeinu,* all those lines that draw attention to Israel's sins—even though it is in the context of an appeal for forgiveness of those sins.[9] It was probably in accordance with the rabbinic maxim, *Al tiftach peh leSatan,* "Do not give Satan as much as an opening"—by even admitting that we

7. Personal communication (November 1, 1995) from Mr. Percy S. Gourgey, MBE.

8. Dobrinsky, H. C. (1968). *A Treasury of Sephardic Laws and Customs.* New York: Yeshivah University Press, p. 320.

9. Gaguine, S. (1948). *Keter Shem Tov,* vol. VI. London: Author, pp. 114–115.

have sins that require forgiveness. This practice we have already noted as practiced by the Hasidim (See Question 627). Apart from these omissions, *Avinu Malkeinu* is recited even if Rosh Hashanah occurs on a Shabbat.

Some extra *piyyutim* are recited in the Syrian rite, notably the *Achot Ketanah* of Abraham Hazzan (sixteenth century), which opens the first evening service of the festival. This composition is also included in the Sephardic and Yemenite traditions and is sung to a special, traditional tune.

650. Is there any difference in their *Tashlikh* ceremony?

Syrian Jews no longer feel obliged to repair to streams or rivers, but, instead, make do with a symbolic pouring out of water, for which they use a hose-pipe in the rear yard of the synagogue![10] The ritual was originally practiced in the traditional way, but it clearly did not have the significance for them that it had within Ashkenazi communities.

MOROCCAN TRADITIONS

651. What Rosh Hashanah practices are observed by the Jews of Morocco?

They do not wear new clothes on Rosh Hashanah in order not to detract from the more appropriate mood of humility and solemn apprehension of the divine decree. The Jews of Rabat, however, did indulge themselves in the acquisition of new clothes for the "new" year.[11]

To the many traditional symbolic foods that they ate on the first evening of the festival, the Jews of Sefrou added lung, since the Hebrew word for lung is *re'ia*. In order to create an auspicious word-association, they would then recite the phrase from the weekday *Amidah*, "Look upon (*Re'ei*) our affliction, and plead our cause, and redeem us speedily for Your name's sake. . . ."

They did not use salt on Rosh Hashanah, but instead dipped their bread into sugar, as did the Jews of Syria. Whenever they would normally add salt to a dish, they substitute sugar on this festival. The foods eaten are, consequently, mostly very sweet.

My *mechutan*, Mr. Max Moryoussef, recalls that all the new fruits in season from August were saved in order to recite the *Shehecheyanu* blessing over them on Rosh Hashanah. The festival meals usually start with fish. Then follows the main course, usually of meat, accompanied by large helpings of raisins and plums. A special dessert is also eaten, made of different grains, sweetened with honey, sugar, and aniseed.

We have explained elsewhere[12] that salt was widely thought to be efficacious in

---

10. Dobrinsky, *op. cit.*, p. 320.

11. Gaguine, S. (1948). *Keter Shem Tov*, vol. VI. London: Author, p. 64.

12. Cohen, J. M. (1996). *1001 Questions and Answers on Pesach*. Northvale, NJ: Jason Aronson Inc., p. 151.

warding off the evil spirits who envied human enjoyment, especially at table. Not to use salt was a conscious demonstration that, on this day when Satan's condemnation is frustrated by our atonement, we have no reason to protect ourselves by such means.

As in other traditions (Afghanistan, Yemen, etc.), the recitation of psalms on Rosh Hashanah was regarded as very important. In order to ensure that people did not sleep on the afternoon of the festival—so that their *mazal* (good fortune) should not also sleep—they prescribed the reading of the book of Psalms. They were encouraged to read its 150 psalms twice over the festival, since the sum total, of 300, was the *gematria* (numerical value) of the word *kapper*, "atone."

652. Are there any traditions associated with the blowing of the shofar?

The timbre of the sound emitted by the Moroccan shofar differs from the norm, due to their practice of smoothing out its inside, as well as bending the shofar into an unusual shape.

As in the Syrian tradition (See Question 648), they blow an additional *teru'ah gedolah*, making up 101 notes, just before *Adon Olam*. The *toke'ah* is given the honor of being called up to the Torah for *chamishiy*, the fifth *aliyah*.

SPANISH AND PORTUGUESE TRADITIONS

653. What are the main characteristics of the Spanish and Portuguese Rosh Hashanah observances?

In Gibraltar, they still have the tradition of reciting many psalms on Rosh Hashanah, though the English Sephardim have largely abandoned this. Quite consistent with their more rational inclination, they do not go in for tasting the various symbolic foods whose names are auguries for a sweet year, contenting themselves with an apple and honey. They also have no qualms about using salt. Some add sugar and just a few grains of salt to their challah.

Before the commencement of the *Ma'ariv* (or, as they call it, using its original, Mishnaic name, *Arvit*), the *parnas* (warden) of the congregation announces the names of those who are to be honored with leading the *Zemirot* (or, as called in Ashkenazi tradition, *Pesukei DeZimra),* the *Haftarah* and the opening of the *heikhal* (Ark) the following morning.

As we have already encountered in other traditions, they also have two *seganim* standing on either side of, and assisting, the *Chazan*.

H. C. Dobrinsky[13] states that the Spanish and Portuguese practice is to have the Ark open for the entire *Shachrit* service on Rosh Hashanah. While this may have been the original practice, it is not the present-day custom of the Sephardim of England. They have the Ark open the entire day of Yom Kippur, but not on Rosh Hashanah.

---

13. Dobrinsky, *op. cit.*, p. 329.

My friend, Rabbi Abraham Levy, Senior Rabbi of the Sephardi communities of Great Britain, brings to my attention the fact that there was never any reference to the *Tashlikh* ceremony in the prayer book of the London Sephardim. Its omission is attributed to Haham Jacob Sasportas (1610–1698), a fierce opponent of the Shabbatean movement.

Because so many of Shabbetai Zevi heresies were rooted in (the misapplication of) kabbalistic doctrine, Sasportas sought to root out any rituals or ideas that were rooted in superstition or mystical lore. He regarded—with good reason—*Tashlikh* as falling within this category.

SUDANI CUSTOMS

654. What do we know about the Jews of the Sudan and their Rosh Hashanah customs?

I have invited a friend and member of my Stanmore synagogue, Mrs. Ruth Synett, to answer this question. She has, in turn, conferred with her father, Mr. Zaki Dwek, who grew up and spent most of his working life in the Sudan.

The Jews of the Sudan hailed mainly from Iraq, Syria, and Egypt, and only arrived there at the turn of the century. By World War I, there were about 100 families living there. There was only one synagogue, in Khartoum, and the community was close-knit, though not particularly observant. Kosher meat was available at the meat market, though the *shochet* would have to make a special visit to each home to slaughter chickens.

In the words of Mrs. Synett:

On the eve of Rosh Hashanah it was most important to place a lamb's head on the dinner table. Two varieties of *Kofta* (meatballs), one made with leeks and the other with spinach, were served to signify the new vegetables in season. Another traditional dish served was pumpkin pie. As pomegranates were not available, *lubia* (black eyed beans) were, and still are, served [since the name connotes the Hebrew *rubah, rabah*, ("many")], implying the wish that God should multiply our merits. It was regarded as important to serve at least five different dishes at that important meal.

655. How did Sudani Jewry observe Rosh Hashanah day?

Again, we allow Ruth Synett and Zaki Dwek to reminisce:

Everyone went to shul in the morning. The service started at 7:00 a.m. because of the heat and normally finished around noon. It was customary to go and visit the rabbi and all the elderly members of the community. Most visits lasted 5 to 10 minutes and started immediately after shul. During this short visit, at least ten kinds of sweets and pastries were served with lemonade (made with real lemon) or other cold drink. No coffee was served during the two days of *Yom Tov*, because of the color—so as not to have a "black year!"

After a big lunch, and, being unable to have the usual siesta, friends would gather to keep each other company. Then it was back to the synagogue, after which we would spend the evening with more guests, but on a smaller scale than the first night.

The second day was very much a repeat of the first, except that the people one visited on the first day returned the visit and had to be served with another ten different sweets and other goodies.

IRAQI-INDIAN PRACTICES

656. What do we know about the Rosh Hashanah practices of the Jews from Iraqi background who settled in India?

My informant here is another member of my congregation, Mr. Edward Ezra, whose grandparents moved from Basra and Baghdad to settle in Bombay at the turn of the century. The family prayed at the Knesset Eliyahu Synagogue, built in 1884 by Jacob Sassoon, one of two synagogues belonging to the Iraqi community in Bombay.

We shall let Mr. Ezra answer our question in his own words:

During the 30 days prior to Rosh Hashanah, and also during the Ten Days of Penitence, a community representative would stand outside the houses of known members of the community in the early hours of the morning and shout out at the top of his voice, '*Selichot, Selichot, Selichot*' —Our version of a town crier!"

On the morning of the eve of Rosh Hashanah, at 3:00 a.m., my father would go to synagogue for *Chatimah* (literally, "conclusion"), the recitation of psalms. During the day, my mother would prepare the evening meal, which always included a traditional dish called Apple Chamud, consisting of chicken cooked with apples in a sweet sauce. My sisters and I would help my mother arrange the table with the various vegetables and fruit whose names connoted happy augury (See Question 243). It was our custom to boil all the vegetables in sugar water. We did not have the custom of dipping the apple in honey, and we would dip our challah into sugar instead of salt.

During the shofar blowing, all the male congregants, without exception, would cover their heads with their *tallit*, and my father would cover my head with his. The *teki'ah* and *shevarim* notes were blown in much the same way as the Ashkenazim, however the *teru'ah*, instead of being a series of short staccato blasts, was sounded as much more of a continuous, though vibrating, sound.

Immediately following the *Shachrit* service, *Hatarah* (annulment of vows) would begin. This was interspersed with responsive passages from the *Zohar*, and it would last approximately 1 hour.

After the service, the community would be treated to a most wonderful *kiddush*, with a large variety of exotic fruit (as one would expect in India), including mangoes, papaya, sitafull (love apples), Jack fruit, perus, guavas, etc., so as to enable the congregants to recite the *Shehecheyanu* blessing.

For *Tashlikh,* my father would take the family to the Gateway of India, by the Ganges, and we would symbolically cast our sins in the water by shaking our handkerchieves.[14]

14. Written communication (October 31, 1996) from Mr. Edward Ezra.

XIX

The Fast of Gedaliah and the Intermediate Days of Penitence

GEDALIAH'S PLACE IN JEWISH HISTORY

657. Who was Gedaliah?

He was a Jewish governor of Judaea that the Babylonian king, Nebuchadnezzar, installed as a puppet leader over the country after his invasion of 586 B.C.E.. Gedaliah hailed from noble Judaean stock. His family had been very close to the prophet Jeremiah, and Gedaliah's father, Achikam, had even saved the prophet's life. This was after Jeremiah had uttered the unpalatable prophesy that if the people did not mend their ways God would make Jerusalem suffer the same fate as Shilo, "and make this city for a curse among all the nations of the earth" (Jeremiah 26:4–6).

The king's advisers had counseled that the prophet should be put to death for fomenting despair, but Achikam used his considerable influence to defuse the situation and save Jeremiah's life. It was certainly on account of Gedaliah's known friendship with Jeremiah and his sympathies for the latter's much-publicized policy of cooperation with the occupying power that prompted his appointment as puppet governor of Judaea, responsible to the Babylonians for ensuring the total submission of the remnant population.

658. What were the events that led up to Gedaliah's appointment?

The Jewish king, Zedekiah, fled from Jerusalem in the night as the Babylonians breached the walls. He made for the Jordan, hoping to seek safety and asylum in Ammon, but he was pursued and overtaken near Jericho by the forces of Nebuchadnezzar and brought back to Jerusalem. There, he was made to witness the execution of his sons; he was blinded and taken in chains to Babylon, where he died soon after.[1] A month later, Nebuchadnezzar dispatched Nebuzaradan, his commander-in-chief, to Jerusalem with commands to destroy its walls and put the Temple to the torch.

A large proportion of the religious, military, and civic leaders were executed, and the rest were deported to Babylon, leaving behind, under the authority of Gedaliah,

---

1. II Kings 25:6ff; Jeremiah 52:9–11.

the lower classes who, it was thought, would be docile and cause no problems for the Babylonian conquerors. With the land and its economy in ruins, the poor peasants who remained were highly unlikely to have the talent, resources, or spirit to mount any revolt, harness any latent nationalistic feeling, or exploit the bitter antipathy felt toward the heartless invaders.

659. So why do we observe a fast day for Gedaliah?

We observe a fast day because of the tragic events that unfolded soon after he assumed his position of governor, with the avowed intention of being a unifying force, of restoring order and some self-respect to the hapless remnant of his people, and of improving their desperate economic plight.

Inevitably, there were many Judaeans who viewed Gedaliah as a collaborator with the hated invader and as a traitor to his people. A plot to kill him was initiated by one Ishmael, a member of the royal house of Zedekiah, who, on that score, would have deeply resented a commoner's assumption of the leadership that rightfully belonged exclusively to one of royal lineage. Ishmael had the backing of the king of Ammon, an erstwhile supporter of Zedekiah, who, fearing Babylonian expansionism, allowed his country to be used as a base for rebellious forces loyal to the Judaean monarchy.

Gedaliah was warned by friends and informants of the personal danger he was in, but, naively, he never dreamed that he could be in danger from his own Jewish compatriots. He paid the supreme price for his naivete, and he was assassinated by Ishmael and his fellow conspirators, who subsequently succeeded in fleeing to Ammon.

Gedaliah's friends and supporters, though totally innocent, feared the violent recriminations that Nebuchadnezzar would inflict on them and on the country, and, disregarding the protestations of the aged prophet Jeremiah, they forced him to flee with them to Egypt. This brought about the final end of the first Jewish Commonwealth, and it is for that reason that a fast day was instituted into the Jewish calendar.

660. For how long did Gedaliah exercise his position of governor of Judaea before he was slain?

We have absolutely no idea, since neither of the two biblical passages that describe the events make this clear. From the chronology, it may have been as short as 2 or 3 months, or, at the very longest, a couple of years.

661. Presumably, Gedaliah was slain on the third of Tishri, the date we observe the commemorative fast day?

One would be right in jumping to that conclusion. However, the Bible is a trifle vague, stating merely that "It was in the seventh month that Ishmael came . . . and slew Gedaliah" (Jeremiah 41:1–2). The classical commentator R. David Kimchi (*Radak*) believes that when the Bible only mentions the month and does not see fit to disclose the precise day of the month, we must assume that it refers to the first day, Rosh Chodesh. Accordingly, Kimchi is of the opinion that Gedaliah was slain on the first day of the seventh month, namely Rosh Hashanah, but because that and the following day were festival days, the commemorative fast was deferred until the day afterward.

THE RELIGIOUS SIGNIFICANCE OF GEDALIAH'S DEATH

662. But why was it so important to mark the death of that fairly insignificant puppet ruler with a solemn fast day?

If it was the case, as Kimchi and other authorities assert, that he was assassinated on Rosh Hashanah itself, it might also explain why his death was regarded as such a tragedy and invested with such religious significance.

The fact that influential Jews of royal lineage chose Rosh Hashanah of all days—the day when we are under the closest divine scrutiny, and the day when we pray, above all, for life—to perpetrate such a dastardly crime, meant that they were, at the same time, undermining the very foundation of that festival and denying its primary significance. They were not only assassinating Gedaliah, therefore, but were also snuffing out the very life and vitality from a hitherto most solemn and sacred festival. The fast may well have been introduced as a collective act of *teshuvah* for a most high profile denial of Rosh Hashanah and "the King who delighteth in life."

663. But is not the fast of Gedaliah the odd one out, in that the other historical fasts commemorate aspects of the siege and destruction of the Temple, whereas it laments the death of a human being?

Rabbi Akivah rationalizes this by saying that "it teaches that the death of the righteous ranks equal to the destruction of the Temple."[2] This may strike one as an audacious statement, one that only an Akivah could articulate. He seems to be telling us that holiness does not reside in the fabric of any material building, but rather within the spiritual Temple that righteous men construct out of their souls. Hence, the death of Gedaliah, perceived as a most righteous man, may justly be categorized among the fast days commemorating the loss of our Temples.

664. But, bearing in mind that Gedaliah is such an obscure biblical personality and that much greater tragedies have befallen our people in subsequent centuries and millenia, for which no fast days have been instituted, is there any modern day relevance, therefore, in observing such a fast day only a week before the great fast of Yom Kippur?

Murder has always been regarded by Jews as the most heinous of crimes, tantamount to diminishing the very image of God. We are not masters of our own

2. *Rosh Hashanah* 18b.

bodies, therefore we have no right to disfigure it in any way. It goes without saying, therefore, that assault upon the body of another can in no way be countenanced. Against this background it will be obvious that the slaying of another human being—especially of a brother Jew—is the most unpardonable crime. Cain's slaying of his brother establishes, at the very beginning of the Bible, a paradigm for the seriousness of such an act.

The Gedaliah episode was the first time in the Jewish national experience that Jews had assassinated one of their own national leaders. It was clearly felt by the sages who instituted the fast of Gedaliah that if such an act went uncondemned and unrecalled, and if a collective national penance was not demanded to bring home to Jews the most heinous nature of that uncharacteristic crime, there was a danger that Jewish political factions might latch onto that method of ridding themselves of leaders whom they opposed. The seeds of anarchy and national dissolution could then so easily have been sown. Hence, the historical justification of this fast.

As regards the fact that the fast day of Yom Kippur is only one week later, this is not a consideration, because, in any case, as we have observed (See Question 163), there were pietists who used to observe the entire ten days of penitence as fast days! It was no extra hardship, therefore, to superimpose the significance of the Gedaliah episode upon its basic spirit as a day of fasting and petition for divine pardon.

Is the fast of Gedaliah still relevant? In the light of the assassination of Premier Yitzchak Rabin, I should have thought that its historical relevance has been hauntingly and fully corroborated. Once again, after a space of 2,500 years, the identical scenario is repeated and a democratically elected Jewish leader—not the puppet of a foreign invader—is cruelly killed by a fellow Jew. How little we have learned from history! How much more do we Jews have to learn about how to govern ourselves peaceably, using speech and persuasion—traditionally the most potent weapons in the Jewish armory—to win over the majority to our view, rather than resorting to the bloodshed from which we have suffered more than any other nation in history?

665. Do we have any external corroboration of the story of Gedaliah?

We do. A seal was discovered at the garrison town of Lachish (about 20 miles due west of Hebron) referring unequivocally to Gedaliah, bearing the words *Ligedaliah [a]sher al ha-bayi[t]*,"To Gedaliah, overseer of the (royal) house." Many other letters were discovered there referring to military and political aspects of this period, leading up to the fall of the first commonwealth at the hands of the Babylonians. The wording of this seal indicates that, before his appointment as governor by Nebuchadnezzar, Gedaliah had occupied the post of chief minister in Zedekiah's cabinet.

That Gedaliah did not suffer the fate of his fellow ministers is indicative that his policy of appeasement of the Babylonians was widely known, even to the Babylonian intelligence. This would explain his obvious choice as governor after the exile of his king.

Since Jerusalem was in ruins, it has been suggested[3] that Gedaliah's seat of government was probably at Mitzpah, about 13 km north of Jerusalem, where he was subsequently assassinated.[4]

THE FAST DAY OBSERVANCES

666. Who is obligated to observe the fast day, and are any exempt?

A girl of 12 and a boy of 13 years are obligated to fast. It is not necessary, as on Yom Kippur, to train them a year or more before to fast part of the day;[5] they should, nevertheless, eat only simple fare on this day, and only as much as needed, in order to empathize with the emotions of the adult community.[6]

In the case of pregnant or nursing mothers, if fasting is particularly painful for them or they feel weak as a result of the fasting, they need not continue to fast.[7]

667. From what stage in pregnancy does this exemption apply?

According to the Mishnah Berurah, it takes effect "from when the fetus is detectable." He adds that "it is possible to apply this [exemption for pregnant women] even from forty days after conception, if she feels distress."[8]

668. Beside fasting, are there any other abstentions?

Abstention from food and drink from dawn to nightfall is the only requirement. Unlike the fasts of Yom Kippur and the ninth of *Av*, there is no prohibition of leather footwear, applying cosmetics, or washing, though there is a view that washing has become prohibited by custom.[9] Again, unlike the latter two fasts, there is no need to abstain from marital relations on the night before the fast.

669. What are the main themes of the *Selichot* (the special petitionary hymns and confessions) prescribed for the fast of Gedaliah?

The *Selichot* for this day include hymns supercharged with nostalgia for the Temple; acknowledgment of our sins and our desperate desire to be cleansed and restored to divine grace; a chronicle of Israel's numerous and murderous enemies, and her incomparable suffering at their hands, coupled with the plea to gather in our dispersed and bring an end to that long, dark night of exile and to Israel's position as a pariah among the nations.

---

3. Bright, J. (1964). *A History of Israel*. London: SCM Press, p. 310.
4. II Kings 25:22ff.
5. *Biur Halakhah* on *Mishnah Berurah* 550:1.
6. *Mishnah Berurah* 550:1 (5).
7. *Mishnah Berurah* 550:1
8. *Mishnah Berurah* 550:1 (3).
9. See *Bayit Chadash* on *Tur Orach Chayyim* 554 (*D.H. Vekatav Ha-Ramban*).

Surprisingly, there is only one composition—*Avlah nafshi*—that makes a passing reference to Gedaliah:

My soul mourns and my face is gloomy. When the lion (Nebuchadnezzar) penetrated my beautiful Temple, even the remnants that had been left alive (by the conquering tyrant) were crushed on the third day of Tishri. . . . The elders of the remnant who escaped the day of vengeance were then laid low on the day when we fast over the death of Gedaliah, son of Achikam.

One particularly urgent plea—in the hymn *Elokim ein biltekha*—almost steps over the bounds of propriety when addressing God: "O Rock, Thy hand is not shortened; thine is strength and might. Why then dost thou sleep? Rouse Thyself, attend to our fervent supplication, behold our feeble state, and rebuke us not in thy anger."

The *Pizmon* (hymn with refrain), *Horeita derekh teshuvah,* poetically reminds God of biblical precedents for His having extended forgiveness and life to those who repented from the most heinous of crimes - notably, Adam, Cain, Reuben, Ahab, and the inhabitants of *Nineveh*—and it calls upon Him to extend that merciful indulgence to us. This plea is reinforced, in the composition *Im afas rova ha-ken*, where the merit of Abraham's great *Akedah* trial is invoked in order to secure such mercy for his children.

670. What is the order of service for the morning of the Fast of Gedaliah?

Since the fast does not commence until dawn, there is obviously no adjustment in the *Ma'ariv* service preceding the fast. However, in the Yemenite tradition, they have the curious practice of reciting *Aneinu* (see below) in *Ma'ariv*, even though they continue to eat and drink throughout that evening until retiring to bed!

The basic format of the morning service is unchanged, though the service will commence at an earlier time in the morning to accommodate the recitation of the *Selichot*. The *tallit* and *tefillin* are not put on until after the recitation of the *Selichot*, unless these are inserted into the Amida.

Following the seventh blessing of the regular morning *Amidah Re'ey ve'anyeinu* ("Look upon our affliction"), the *Chazan* recites the special fast day *Aneinu* ("Answer us") petition, which constitutes an independent, and additional, blessing to the *Amidah*. The congregation defers its recitation until *Minchah*, as one cannot be sure at *Shachrit* that one will feel well enough by later in the day to complete the fast.

After the repetition of the *Amidah*, *Avinu Malkeinu* is said, followed by *Tachanun*, recited leaning on one's right arm. The Torah scroll is then taken out, and three people are called to the usual fast day reading of *Va-yechal* (Exodus 32:11–14; 34:1–10). One who is not fasting should not be called to, nor would it be appropriate for him, to read from the Torah or to serve as *Chazan*. The rest of the service follows the usual order, with the addition of *LeDavid Ha-Shem Oriy*.

671. What is the order of service for the afternoon service on the fast of Gedaliah?

It begins, as usual, with *Ashrei*, followed by half-*kaddish*, after which the Torah is taken out and the same section is read as at *Shachrit*. This time, however, the third person called up recites the fast day *Haftarah* from Isaiah 55:6–56:8, and ends the concluding blessings with *Barukh . . . Magen David.*

In the silent *Amidah*, the private worshiper recites *Aneinu* as an insertion into the *Shema Koleinu* blessing, so as not to alter the standard number of *Amidah* blessings, whereas the reader repeats it in the same position as he did at *Shachrit.*

In places such as Israel, where the priests bless the people every day, this is also performed on the fast of Gedaliah, though only when *Minchah* is recited in the late afternoon (that is, after *pelag ha-Minchah*, or about an hour and a quarter before sundown).

Sim shalom, rather than the usual *Shalom rav*, is recited. The reason is that the former is more appropriate to the priestly blessing in that it contains the phrase *be'or panekhah* ("in the shining of Your face"), which corresponds to the phrase *Ya'eir [Ha-Shem] panav* ("[May the Lord] cause His face to shine [upon you]"). The service concludes with *Avinu Malkeinu, Tachanun* (leaning on left arm), and *Aleinu.* Sephardim add Psalm 102 (*Tefillah le'ani kiy ya'atof*).

SHABBAT SHUVAH

672. When is *Shabbat Shuvah*, and how did it get its name?

Shabbat Shuvah ("The Sabbath of Repentance") is the name given to the Shabbat between Rosh Hashanah and Yom Kippur. It got its name from the opening word, *Shuvah (yisrael),* of the specially prescribed *Haftarah* from Hoseah 14:2. It is the prerogative of the rabbi to recite this particular *Haftarah*, in order to lend greater urgency to its message.

673. What exactly is the message of this *Haftarah*?

It is probably one of the most urgent and poetically and emotionally appealing calls to repentance in the whole of the Hebrew Bible. Hoseah was possessed of a deeply passionate soul, and he believed that God's love for Israel was of the same quality. "I will heal their backsliding; I will love them freely" (verse 5). He asserts that, with that love showered upon her, was destined to flourish and impress all the surrounding nations:

> I will be as dew unto Israel;
> He shall blossom as the lily,
> And cast forth his roots as Lebanon.
> His branches shall spread,
> And his beauty shall be as the olive tree . . .
> They that dwell under his shadow shall again
> Make corn to grow,
> And shall blossom as the vine.
> [verses 6–8]

674. What does Hoseah mean by saying "Take with you words and return unto the Lord" (verse 3)?

The sages understood this to mean that the customary offering of sin-offerings as a token of repentance was not what God was looking for. He wanted not the gifts of our hands, but the sounds of our hearts as reflected in "words" of spontaneous confession. This is made clear in the continuation of this verse: "So we will render for bullocks the offering of our lips." This latter phrase undergirds the whole rabbinic concept of prayer, by which it and the synagogue were viewed as a fully acceptable replacement and natural successor for sacrifices and the Temple, once the latter was destroyed.

But it went even further than that and inspired the wholesale patterning of the early synagogue—its administration, architecture, the direction the synagogue had to face, the number of the daily prayers, the times of the services, the content of the liturgy, the priestly blessings administered and privileges enjoyed, and the choral traditions—upon the precedents established in the Temple.[10] In so many ways, "the offering of our lips"—that is the synagogue and its liturgy—developed and refined the bullock-orientated Temple ritual.

675. Normally, the *Haftarah* confines itself to one single book or prophet. Why does the *Shabbat Shuvah Haftarah* borrow from three different prophetic books?

It borrows from three books for two reasons. First, the *Haftarah*, wherever possible, should contain a minimum of twenty-one verses. This is patterned on the law governing the reading of the Torah on Shabbat, where we read a minimum of three verses for each of the seven people called up—thus making a minimum of twenty-one verses. Now, the first, and foremost, section of our *Haftarah* contains only ten verses, so that the sages were constrained to add another prophetic section dealing with the theme of repentance.

However, instead of selecting but one other source, they chose to include just three verses from Micah (7:18–20), an arrangement that meant that they were still well short of the required twenty-one verses, so that they had to add a third passage (Joel 2:15–27).

Their choice of the three Micah verses seems to have been motivated by the fact that they begin with a rhetorical question *Miy El kamokha* ("Who is a God like unto Thee?"), which made it a stylistically appropriate continuation of the preceding final verse from Hoseah, which contains a similar rhetorical question: *Miy chakham veyaven eileh* ("Who is wise enough to understand these things?").

The final passage is most appropriate to this period, which spans Rosh Hashanah and Yom Kippur, as its opening words, "Sound the shofar in Zion, sanctify a fast, call a solemn assembly" (Joel 2:15), highlight the main features of both festivals.

10. Cohen, J. M. (1993). *Blessed Are You.* Northvale, New Jersey: Jason Aronson Inc., pp. 9–13.

676. Are there any other changes in the synagogue services on *Shabbat Shuvah*?

In the Friday evening service, we insert into the *Amidah* the usual extra lines (*Zokhreinu lachayim, Miy chamokha, Ha-melech ha-kadosh, Ukhetov lechayim*, and *Beseifer chayim berakhah*, etc.) for the Ten Days of Penitence. The only other change that is made is in the *Magen Avot* composition, recited after the *Amidah*, where, instead of the formula *ha-El ha-kadosh*, we substitute *ha-melekh ha-kadosh* (as in the *Amidah*). Being Shabbat, we do not recite *Avinu Malkeinu* after the *Shachrit* and *Minchah Amidah*s.

677. So, apart from the *Haftarah* and the latter minor substitutions, is *Shabbat Shuvah* no different from any other Sabbath?

Its spirit is far more rarified than that of most other Sabbaths, with a pervasive sense of anticipation of the great Day of Atonement a few days ahead. But, in addition to that, *Shabbat Shuvah* is also the occasion for the rabbi to deliver a special public discourse on a theme associated with repentance.

This is popularly referred to as the *Shabbat Shuvah derashah* and attracts a far larger attendance than the usual Shabbat afternoon *shiur*, between *Minchah* and *Ma'ariv*. The rabbi will inevitably invest far more time and greater care in its preparation, to ensure maximum effectiveness, to inspire his audience, and to arouse them spiritually for the great day ahead. In the State of Israel, it is common to see street posters announcing the theme of the *derashah* and the distinguished rabbinic authority who will be appearing as the guest speaker. In America and Britain, the Jewish press will also carry such advertisements.

TEN DAYS OF PENITENCE PRACTICES

678. Are there any other religious prescriptions governing the days between Rosh Hashanah and Yom Kippur?

The *Shulchan Arukh* has only two prescriptions in this regard, which are curiously allocated to two separate, numbered *simanim* (sections), instead of being incorporated into a single section relating to this period. It states, simply, "During all the days between Rosh Hashanah and Yom Kippur we should increase our prayers and petitions."[11]

In the following section, it states that "Even one who, throughout the year, is not particular about eating bread (containing only acceptable ingredients, but) baked by a non-Jewish baker, yet, during this period he should avoid doing so."[12]

---

11. *Shulchan Arukh Orach Chayyim* 602:1.
12. *Op. cit.* 603:1.

679. Do any other authorities expand on these prescriptions?

Indeed. R. Moses Isserles, in his gloss on the *Shulchan Arukh*,[13] quotes the *Maharil*, that "We do not impose a *cherem* (ban of excommunication), nor do we impose a court oath upon anyone until after Yom Kippur." The *Magen Avraham* states that some pietists would adopt greater stringencies and more exacting standards of purity during this period. They would eat only dry cereal that could not be rendered impure (in the absence of any liquid ingredient) and would bend over and drink pure water from a running stream that no impure person could have handled.[14]

680. Are there any other prohibitions that the general community is expected to conform to during this period?

In many communities, they did not solemnize marriages during this period. The Talmud, in its midrashic homily on the verse "Sound the shofar on the new moon when it is concealed (*bakeseh*) for our festive day" (Psalm 81:4), states that "During the month of Tishri the moon is concealed."[15] The kabbalists understood this to mean that Satan envelops the moon with his baneful influences, so that its days are inauspicious for a celebratory event until after Yom Kippur. Where there is no alternative but to fix the wedding for this period, it is permitted to do so.

For the same reason we do not perform the ceremony of *kiddush levanah*, "blessing the new moon," until after Yom Kippur. To express enthusiasm and acclaim for the beauty of the moon and its auspicious symbolism at a time when it is described as being in gloomy concealment is hardly appropriate.

---

13. *Remah ad loc.*
14. *Magen Avraham* on *Orach Chayyim* 603.
15. *Rosh Hashanah* 8b.

II

YOM KIPPUR

XX

Preparations for the Festival

681. What religious preparations are required for the festival of Yom Kippur?

The primary preparation is, of course, the spiritual one, of determining to utilize this unique opportunity for expressing heartfelt remorse for one's moral and ethical and religious shortcomings, and of making sincere resolve not to repeat them. It is also the time to ensure that there are no outstanding debts that we have not settled, especially if these involve charitable pledges. It would make a mockery of Yom Kippur to recite the solemn *Kol Nidre* prayer, highlighting the importance that we place upon vows, and at the same time to leave unpaid pledges we know we have made.

We have already referred to Maimonides' denunciation of insincere repentance, or the outward recitation of confessions in synagogue without any corresponding thoughts in one's heart (See Question 40). We have also quoted the statement in the Mishnah that "Sins committed by man against God are atoned for through the Day of Atonement; sins committed by man against his fellow cannot be atoned for through the Day of Atonement unless he first intercedes for his neighbour's pardon" (See Question 33). The *Shulchan Arukh* regards it, therefore, as an essential preparation for this day, to take practical steps to patch up any outstanding quarrels by approaching the other party, irrespective of who is the guilty party.[1]

In the days before Yom Kippur, it would be appropriate to spend one's leisure time in a more spiritually productive manner. Instead of watching television, one might devote those few evenings to reading a religious book or studying the laws of repentance and of Yom Kippur. Since the festival of Sukkot—with its manifold laws regarding the building of the *sukkah* and aspects of the four species—follows on only four days after Yom Kippur, the opportunity is also presented at this time to study the sections of the *Kitzur Shulchan Arukh,* for a general digest of these laws, or the more standard and detailed codes of law for those who are able to study these in the original Hebrew.

---

1. *Shulchan Arukh Orach Chayyim* 606:1–2.

THE *KAPPAROT* RITUAL

682. What is the *Kapparot* ritual prescribed for the day before Yom Kippur?

It was an ancient practice to take a white rooster for each male member of the family, a white hen for each female, and both for a pregnant woman (in order to cover either eventuality), and to use them in a ceremony of transposition, whereby the sins of the bearers are transferred to these fowl. It has all the hallmarks of the biblical Yom Kippur *Azazel* ritual whereby the goat, laden with the sins of Israel, is sent away to its doom in the desert.

The feet of the fowl are taken in the right hand, and some have the custom at that point to recite the phrase *nefesh tachat nefesh* ("A life for a life"). Then, while swinging the fowl three times around the head, they recite the formula beginning *Zeh chalifati*: This is my exchange, this is my substitute, this is my atonement. This cock/hen will go to its death while I shall enter and proceed to a good long life, and to peace."

This ceremony, with its *Zeh chalifati* formula, is very similar to that of the *Pidyon Ha-Ben*, the redemption of the first born son, whereby the sanctity that attaches to the latter is redeemed and transferred to the purchase price of five *shekalim*. Here, it is the very opposite; it is the iniquity, attaching itself to Israel, that is transferred to the fowl. Either way, the underlying principle is the same.

After the recitations, the fowl is slaughtered and either given to the poor, or redeemed by money that is, in turn, given to the poor.

683. Is this a universally accepted ceremony, and if so, why has it been largely abandoned?

It is not universally acceptable. No less an authority than Joseph Karo devotes a section of his *Shulchan Arukh* to the ritual and contents himself with but one observation: "That custom of performing *Kapparot* on the eve of Yom Kippur . . . should not be permitted"![2]

Support for this is forthcoming from the *Taz* who quotes his teacher's view that this whole ritual "smacks of gross superstition." He goes on to state that although upholders of the ritual point to the *Maharil* as having recommended it, "it seems that he did not research its origin properly"![3]

684. Are there any other aspects of the ritual that might betray such a superstitious basis?

Tur and other early sources[4] mention that, after slaughtering the fowl, "its inwards are thrown onto the roofs of houses or any other place from where the birds can remove them." This reference to hurling food onto roofs immediately alerts

---

2. *Shulchan Arukh* 605:1.
3. *Taz ad loc.*
4. *Remah* on *Shulchan Arukh* 605:1 (end).

students of folklore and superstition to the ancient practice of leaving food as a propitiatory gift to the demons, to neutralize the harm they might otherwise intend to do. The demons were believed to lurk on the roofs of houses (See Questions 582–584).

685. So if authorities like Karo vehemently opposed the ritual, why do some communities still practice it?

Very simply because, while Karo's views were binding upon Sephardim, Ashkenazim defer to the view of the Ashkenazi authority Moses Isserles whenever he records a variant Ashkenazi tradition. In his gloss on Karo's condemnation of the practice in the *Shulchan Arukh*,[5] Isserles states an opposing view: 'It is some of the Geonim who have promoted this *kapparot* ritual, as well as many of the more recent authorities. And it is practised in all our communities, and should not be changed since it is an ancient ritual.'[6]

686. So is it simply a case of Sephardim opposing the practice and Ashkenazim observing it?

Strangely, we answer "yes" and "no" on both counts. While the official Sephardi view is negative, as recorded by Karo, the fulsome endorsement of the practice given by the great mystic R. Isaac Luria and by the illustrious R. Isaiah Horowitz prompted many Sephardim to continue its practice. Conversely, while Isserles greatly recommended its continued observance, many Ashkenazim felt most uncomfortable with it and either abandoned it altogether or dispensed with the use of roosters and, instead, performed the ceremony exclusively with money, which they also swung around their head. This is still widely performed, and the money is donated to charity.

687. Are there any modern day authorities that have come out against the *Kapparot* ritual?

The former Sephardi Chief Rabbi of Tel Aviv, Rabbi Chaim David Halevi, offers two reasons for abandoning the practice. The first reason takes account of the real danger that, with vast crowds, in Israel, queuing up to have their roosters slaughtered on the eve of Yom Kippur (a very short day), the pressure on the slaughterer is enormous. He has to dispatch the fowl so quickly and is frequently so exhausted with the burden of work that there is every reason to fear that he will be negligent of some detail and might unwittingly render the fowl *treifa* (unacceptable to be eaten).

His second objection is based upon the biblical prohibition of cruelty to animals. While, as a concession to human appetite, the Torah gave us permission to take an animal's life, unnecessary slaughter, when not directly required for food, cannot be

---

5. *Remah* on *Shulchan Arukh* 605:1 (beginning).
6. *Ibid.*

condoned. Rabbi Halevi condemns the practice in the strongest of terms: "Why should we, of all times on the eve of this holy day, display unnecessary cruelty to animals by slaughtering them without mercy at the very time when we come to seek life for ourselves from the living God?"[7]

688. Are there any other approaches to the *Kapparot* ritual?

R. Solomon Ganzfried, author of the *Kitzur Shulchan Arukh*, makes a bold attempt to neutralize the superstitious basis of the practice. He states that,

A person should not imagine that this fowl is a tangible medium of atonement, but he should, instead, consider that, on account of his sin, whatever is being done to this rooster should really have been done to him. He should therefore lament his iniquity, and the Holy One, in His mercy, will pardon him.[8]

689. Are there any other specific preparations that are required as a prelude to Yom Kippur?

It is forbidden on Yom Kippur to wear leather shoes (See Questions 733 and 734); therefore one should ensure that one has sneakers or (non-leather) trainers available, and ready cleaned, to put on before going to synagogue on *Kol Nidre* night. It is also the custom to light *Yahrzeit* lights for departed relatives before lighting the festival lights. One should ensure, therefore, in good time, that one has a sufficient number of such candles.

It is the custom in Hasidic and some more observant circles to visit the *mikveh* (ritual bath) on the morning of Yom Kippur, to immerse oneself in its purifying waters. Our sources make the *mikveh* and Yom Kippur analogous in this respect, on the basis of a homiletical interpretation of the verse *Mikveh Yisrael Ha-Shem* ("The Lord is the hope of Israel"). The rabbis observed that "Just as the *mikveh* (ritual bath) purifies the impure, so God purifies Israel (of their iniquity)."[9]

By eating an ample meal, one is also enabled to fast more easily throughout the following day. So one should prepare that meal in good time, in the same way as one does for a Friday night dinner.

Although it is not obligatory to eat bread at this special pre-fast meal (See Question 699), some had the custom to bake special oval-shaped *challot* (loaves). This shape is intended to resemble wings, since on Yom Kippur Israel attains the spiritual level of sinless angels, described by Ezekiel as possessing "six wings" (Ezekiel 1:6).

---

7. Halevi, C. D. (1978). *Asei Lekha Rav.* Tel Aviv: Committee for the Publication of Ha-Gaon Rabbi Chaim David Halevi, III:20, p. 62.

8. Ganzfried, S. *Kitzur Shulchan Arukh*, 131:1.

9. *Berakhot* 7b.

EREV YOM KIPPUR SERVICES

690. Why do we omit Psalm 100 during the morning service of the day before Yom Kippur?

Already in the morning service before Yom Kippur we anticipate the festival by making some adjustments to the usual service. Thus, we omit the recitation of Psalm 100 (*Mizmor Letodah*), the "psalm of thanksgiving." The reason for this is that this psalm corresponds to the thanksgiving sacrifice offered in the Temple each day. This particular sacrifice had to be consumed during the day it was offered and up until midnight, after which time it was disqualified as *notar*, sacrificial meat "left over" beyond the prescribed time limit for its consumption.

Normally, this time frame was sufficient for the meat of the sacrifice to be consumed. On the day before Yom Kippur, however, when eating had to cease before sundown, this sacrifice could not be offered, since there would frequently be insufficient time for its meat to be wholly eaten during that shortened period, so as to avoid infringing the prohibition of *notar*. Since the thanksgiving sacrifice was not offered on the day before Yom Kippur, we do not recite the corresponding thanksgiving psalm.

691. Why do we omit Psalm 20 in the morning service on the day before Yom Kippur?

We omit Psalm 20 (*Ya'ankha Ha-Shem beyom tzarah*), "Answer us, O Lord, in the day of trouble," because the latter sentiment was regarded as inappropriate for Yom Kippur, which is the very antithesis of "a day of trouble." It is a veritable festival, when we achieve a unique proximity with God and when we glory in shedding the burden of our sins.

692. Why do we omit *Tachanun* on the morning before Yom Kippur?

For a similar reason, we omit the recitation of the *Tachanun* supplications, following the *Amidah*. These contain sentiments that refer to our abject plight and the great burden of sin that envelops us. We are supposed to enter Yom Kippur in an optimistic frame of mind, not weighed down by apprehension that we have no merit. Furthermore, Psalm 6, with which the *Tachanun* concludes, commences with a reference to God's anger: "Lord, rebuke me not in thine anger, and chasten me not in thy hot displeasure." This was felt to be inconsistent with the God who is moved to mercy and forgiveness by His children's repentance at this time.

693. Do we recite *Avinu Malkeinu* on the morning before Yom Kippur?

Moses Isserles states that "this is a matter of dispute among latter-day authorities; but the custom of my city is to omit it unless Yom Kippur falls on a Shabbat, when

Avinu Malkeinu is not said. To compensate for this, we recite it at *Shachrit* on the morning before Yom Kippur."[10]

694. Are there any other adjustments to the morning service?

It is our custom that on the morning before Yom Kippur we reduce the number of *Selichot* that we have previously been reciting in the lead-in to Rosh Hashanah and during the subsequent days of repentance. This was clearly not the universal practice, since Moses Isserles refers to communities where they actually expanded on the number of *Selichot* usually recited. He concludes that "it all depends upon one's custom."[11]

We have already referred (See Questions 209–221) to the practice of reciting *Hatarat nedarim*, the absolution of vows formula, on the morning before Rosh Hashanah. Some delay this until the morning before Yom Kippur, regarding it as a most appropriate prelude to *Kol Nidre*, which deals, of course, with that very theme. Those who recite it before Rosh Hashanah presumably felt that, since Yom Kippur was introduced by its own plea for absolution, it was preferable to attach the *Hatarat nedarim* to Rosh Hashanah.

695. Are there any similar adjustments to the afternoon service before Yom Kippur?

The *Minchah* service on the afternoon before *Kol Nidre* constitutes a silent and brief moment of preparatory introspection and repentance before the great collective spiritual drama of the evening. To that end, instead of the recitation of the usual silent *Amidah*, the congregation adds (after the final blessing) the *Ashamnu* and *Al Chet* confessionals, which are recited later, at the end of the *Kol Nidre* and Yom Kippur *Shachrit Amidah*s. There is also a view that these confessions were introduced into the *Minchah* service in case one is unable to recite them later, in the evening service, with the requisite concentration, as a result of having drunk too much at the eve of the festival meal!

MALKOT—SYMBOLIC FLAGELLATION

696. Is there any specific ritual prescribed for after *Minchah*?

The custom developed for people who knew they were guilty of specific sins for which the Talmudic punishment was *malkot* (forty lashes [less one]) to submit to a symbolic flagellation with a strap made of calf's leather. Its purpose was to enable them to feel that they had served their full penance and to induce a spirit of shame and humility to prevent them repeating the sin.

It was customary for the person receiving the token stripes to kneel, facing north,

---

10. Gloss of *Remah* on *Shulchan Arukh Orach Chayyim* 604:2.
11. *Ibid.*

the direction of evil, and to recite the *Viddui* confession while they were being administered. The person administering the stripes would recite three times the *Vehu rachum* line, up to the words, *velo ya'iyr kol chamato* ("And He, being merciful, will forgive iniquity . . ."). As this line has thirteen words, its recitation three times would add up to a total of thirty-nine words, corresponding to the number of lashes being administered.

This is not a ritual that is widely practiced these days, but is reserved for pietistic circles.

SE'UDAH HA-MAFSEKET—THE FINAL PRE-FAST MEAL

697. There is a popular belief that it is not merely a practical necessity to eat a good meal prior to the fast, but that it is actually a *mitzvah*. Is this true?

It is, indeed; so that the meal that is eaten prior to commencing one's fast is regarded, from a halakhic point of view, as a most important festival ritual. The sages state that "whomsoever eats and drinks on the ninth of Tishri is regarded by the Torah as if he had fasted on both the ninth and the tenth."[12]

698. But what is the rationale of this strange statement?

It was actually employed in order to resolve a difficulty in the biblical text, which states, "And you shall afflict your souls on the ninth of the month [of Tishri]" (Leviticus 23:32). Now, we do not afflict our souls on the ninth, but on the tenth of Tishri! Hence, the idea that eating on *Erev* Yom Kippur (the ninth of Tishri), in preparation for the fast, is tantamount to observing the fast on that day also.

699. Are we required to eat bread at the pre-fast meal?

The *Minchat Chinukh* states that, unlike at the Shabbat and festival meals, bread is not required at this meal, since, although it is a *mitzvah* "to eat", the Talmud does not refer to this meal as a *se'udah* (religious banquet), at which bread is obligatory.[13]

700. Are there any regulations regarding what one may or may not eat at this meal?

It is the custom not to eat fish, nor to drink intoxicating drinks or eat heavily spiced foods.

701. What time should this meal be taken?

There is no fixed time, but it should be taken early enough to eat leisurely, so that one has no ill effects or indigestion once the fast has commenced and to complete

---

12. *Yoma* 81b; *Berakhot* 8b.
13. *Minchat Chinukh* (1988). Jerusalem: *Makhon Yerushalayim*, II, p. 487.

the meal leaving time to clear away the table, light the festival candles, and get to synagogue in good time for the commencement of the service.

YOM KIPPUR LIGHTS

702. Is there a custom to light other lights in addition to the normal festival candles?

There is, indeed, a custom to light candles that will stay burning throughout the 25 hours of the festival. The tradition is for married people to light one candle for themselves and an extra candle, where required, for departed parents and relatives. Some have the custom to light a special light for each departed relative.

The personal candle is explained on the basis that it was on Yom Kippur that Moses descended from Mount Sinai with the second set of tablets on which were engraved the Ten Commandments, the kernel of the Torah. The Torah, in our tradition, is symbolized by a light ("For the *mitzvah* is a lamp and the Torah a light"). Hence, to display our loyalty to God's Torah, we light a special Torah light on the eve of Yom Kippur.

Oriental Sephardic Jews have the custom of lighting their memorial candles in the lobby of the synagogue. While the practice is also recommended by Ashkenazi authorities, many communities, familiar with the Catholic practice of lighting such candles in church, were reticent to follow a custom that appeared to contravene the prohibition of *chukkat ha-goy*, aping gentile practices.

The Mishnah also refers to the practice of leaving a light in the bedroom in order to remind the couple that marital relations are forbidden. It leaves this as optional, however, since there was also a contrary tradition, to specifically leave no light on so that one should not see one's wife and have his passions aroused![14]

The light for *havdalah*, at the termination of Yom Kippur, should be taken from that light that has burned throughout the festival, referred to in our sources as *Ner she-shavat*, "a light that has observed the day of rest."

703. What blessings are recited over the Yom Kippur candles?

Two blessings are prescribed, as for every *Yom Tov*. The first is *Barukh . . . asher kidshanu bemitzvotav vetzivanu lehadlik ner shel yom ha-kippurim.* (If Yom Kippur coincides with Shabbat, the formula is *lehadlik ner shel shabbat veyom ha-kippurim.*) The second is the *Shehecheyanu*.

However, where the homemaker will be going to synagogue and reciting the *Shehecheyanu* together with the entire congregation, after the *Kol Nidre* composition, it should be omitted at home. We do not repeat blessings unnecessarily.

---

14. Mishnah *Pesachim* 4:3.

A SECOND DAY OF YOM KIPPUR?

704. Why do we not observe Yom Kippur for 2 days as with other biblical festivals?

It may come as a surprise, but the answer is that a significant proportion of German Jewry, in the twelfth and thirteenth centuries, followed the lead of the pietistic groups among them—called, variously, *Hasidei Ashkenaz, Dorshei reshimot, Hasidim rishonim, Ba'alei ha-Kabbalah, Perushim,* etc.[15]—and observed 2 days.[16]

We learn from the *Tur* (R. Jacob ben Asher) that "Frequently ten men would assemble together and pray the entire order of the Yom Kippur liturgy on the following day." He goes on to report that his father, the *Rosh* (R. Asher ben Yechiel), "reprimanded them for this particular aspect of their observance, though in all other respects they kept the prohibitions and abstention from any work."[17] Two suggestions are offered as to why the *Rosh* took the strong step of reprimanding them: either that he construed it as communally divisive or that it offended against the principle of *yuhara,* religious exhibitionism.[18]

705. But why did it not become standard practice to observe 2 days in order to obviate the usual doubt (See Question 21) as to exactly which day was the tenth of the month?

Joseph Karo, in his *Bet Yoseph* commentary on the *Tur,* quotes a tradition of the Palestinian Talmud[19] that Rav Chisda warned the Babylonian authorities who wished to sanction the practice of observing 2 days Yom Kippur that they were introducing something that could lead to great danger to life. The same passage goes on to record an actual occurrence, whereby the ailing father of the great Babylonian authority, Shemuel, proceeded to fast 2 days, from which he died.

There is a Talmudic principle that "we do not impose upon the community burdens which we know they cannot bear."[20] This was certainly in the minds of those authorities—clearly the majority—who were unhappy with such a practice that the majority would inevitably honor in the breach. It was only in the context of the rigors of medieval Hasidic asceticism that such a practice won wider approbation.

Karo goes on to state his own reason why there is absolutely no necessity any longer in the Diaspora to observe 2 days. In the period of Rav Chisda, he states, it was different, because the new moon was determined in Israel by means of the visual testimony of witnesses. Hence, the Babylonians were unsure as to which day had been fixed in Israel as Rosh Chodesh Tishri, and, consequently, as Yom Kippur.

15. Zimmmels, H. J. *Ashkenazim and Sephardim,* pp. 189–190.
16. *Op. cit.,* p. 192.
17. *Tur Shulchan Arukh Orach Chayyim,* sec. 624.
18. *Loc. cit. (D. H. V'adoni avi).*
19. *Yerushalmi, Challah* Chapter 1.
20. *Bava Kamma* 79b.

Hence, they felt the need to observe 2 days of Yom Kippur. Since the fourth century, however, and the publication of a fixed calendar, "we are experts at determining the date of the new moon, and do not, therefore, observe any of the Biblical festivals for two days. Hence we may not countenance the practice of observing two days of Yom Kippur."[21]

---

21. *Bet Yoseph* on *Tur Orach Chayyim,* sec. 624 (*D. H. Vachasidim*).

XXI

The Letter and the Spirit of Yom Kippur:
The Five Abstentions

706. Does the observance of Yom Kippur itself carry with it atonement, irrespective of the person's ability to express personal remorse?

This is an interesting question, especially bearing in mind that there are many people who simply cannot feel the proximity or reality of God to the extent that they feel comfortable addressing Him and expressing their inner thoughts.

The great Rabbi Judah Ha-nasi, compiler of the Mishnah, states categorically that "for all transgressions mentioned in the Torah—whether or not the sinner has repented—Yom Kippur effects atonement."[1] This is a remarkable concept, according to which a person may have violated, and intends to continue violating, some of Judaism's most cherished and fundamental institutions, and yet the cleansing and benevolent spirit of Yom Kippur wafts over him or her, willy-nilly, and cancels out the past!

Rabbi Akivah has a biblical warrant, however, for such a view. In the section dealing with Yom Kippur, the Torah states: "For on this day shall atonement be made for you, to cleanse you; *from all your sins* shall ye be clean before the Lord" (Leviticus 16:30). It does not state "You shall make atonement," but "atonement shall be made for you." In other words, the effect and spiritually cleansing power of this day will automatically secure atonement. Perhaps Rabbi Akivah's understanding of this verse was that it has to be understood psychologically, namely that, whatever the state of mind of the Jew, if he already observes this day he will not remain totally immune from its influences. And even if it is merely what the sages call a *hirhur teshuvah* ("a murmur of repentance"), it is a spiritual plus. It is an exercise in spirituality, within which lies the seed for further growth and development.

707. So is this the official Jewish line?

No, it is not so straightforward. The *Tosafot Yeshanim*[2] already pointed out the paradox that such an approach would create. For we recite in our prayers the

---

1. *Yoma* 85b; *Shavuot* 13a.
2. *Tosafot Yeshanim* on *Yoma* 85b.

acknowledgment: "On account of our sins we were exiled from our land." Now, if R. Judah is correct that the arrival of Yom Kippur automatically brings in its wake atonement, then why was that atonement powerless to prevent our exile?

Tosafot explains that R. Judah did not mean that Yom Kippur affords total acquittal, of its own accord and without accompanying repentance, but that it secures partial acquittal.

708. What is the nature of the partial acquittal that Yom Kippur confers?

Rav Joseph B. Soloveitchik[3] offers clarification of this. He believes that R. Judah distinguished between two types of atonement: individual and communal. The power and spiritual energy of Yom Kippur infuses the community and grants it a collective expiation that will ultimately affect and condition its fate and destiny. The individual, on the other hand, cannot achieve atonement in the absence of sincere repentance.

We stand before God as both an individual and as a member of the community. R. Judah's view would be, therefore, that if one does not repent, he remains in a state of personal alienation from God, but some of the community's collective merit will nevertheless attach to him and help grant him "partial acquittal."

709. Is this, then, the official Jewish line?

Again, no. Talmudic dialectic and theological speculation rarely provide cut-and-dried answers. They point the way to possible solutions of some of the many multidimensional dilemmas that attend our relationship with God. Very rarely do "the people that walk in darkness see a great light." More often than not, we see only twinkling stars. And even they can be most deceptive, mere refractions of light that come from other sources.

The strength of Judaism has been that we have never pursued "the official Jewish line," but have gloried in a flexible, multidimensional tradition that can be, and was, applied, in all ages, to meet the varying emotional, spiritual, and social concerns of individual Jews, as well as the broader national aspirations and changing perceptions.

So, to answer the question, R. Judah's view was actually contested by the sages. They took the view that, in the context of Yom Kippur, one could not separate individual and communal acquittal. It is a day of repentance and atonement for all. In the words of Soloveitchik:

Since individual acquittal is contingent upon repentance, a person who appears as part of the community without having repented will not benefit from the communal atonement afforded by the essence of the day. That acquittal, which covers both the community and the individual, is indivisible. On the Day of Atonement, either a person enjoys dual acquittal . . . or he receives no acquittal at all. . . . Thus, the Sages ruled, in contrast to

---

3. Peli, P. H. (1980). *On Repentance*. Jerusalem: Oroth Publishing House, pp. 121ff.

R. Judah, that the essence of the Day of Atonement does not[4] afford acquittal unless repentance has taken place.[5]

A DAY LIKE PURIM!

710. Is it true that there is an explanation of the biblical name Yom Kippurim that understands it as Yom ("a day") *KePurim* ("like Purim")? What is the point of such an analogy?

Yes, it is true that the medieval kabbalists made this play on words, based on some fascinating conceptual points of contact between the two festivals.

It was only at the eleventh hour that the Jews of Persia escaped their doom. It was only after 3 days of fasting, prayer, and petition, after tense and dangerous maneuvering and negotiation on the part of Queen Esther, with her husband, the king of the Medes and Persians, "whose laws cannot be revoked," and only after great national introspection and apprehension, that the hangman's noose was finally prized off the Jewish neck. Thus, the historical Purim was, for all who lived through it, a paradigm of Yom Kippur. They also experienced "days of awe," of uncertainty as to their fate, pangs of self-doubt, and the deep and desperate need for faith and reliance upon the mercy and grace of God.

By that analogy, the kabbalists were suggesting that on this most sacred day we should also feel a sense of spiritual anxiety, as if the forces of sin were poised to destroy us personally, culturally, spiritually, and nationally—as was the situation for the Jews of ancient Persia in the Purim story.[6]

711. Are there any other points of contact between Purim and Yom Kippurim?

There are. Purim and Yom Kippur both join a feast day to the fast day. On the day before Purim, we have the fast of Esther. On the day before the fast day of Yom Kippur, we have the *mitzvah* to eat a celebratory meal.

Another point of contact is that in the case of both festivals the drawing of lots features prominently. Purim gets its name from the lots that Haman drew to determine the most auspicious day for the destruction of the Jews, and, in biblical and Temple times, one of the highlights of the Yom Kippur ritual was the drawing of lots to determine which of the two goats selected was to be offered as a sacrifice to God, and which was to be sent to Azazel as a scapegoat for the iniquity of Israel (See Questions 855–856). In addition, there are also the lots that the mariners drew, in the story of Jonah, read to *Minchah* on Yom Kippur, in order to determine who was the cause of the great storm that threatened to destroy them. So here, again, we have the double link between these two festivals, which prompted those sages to declare *Yom Kippur* as *Yom KePurim*, a day like Purim.

---

4. I have here corrected Peli's text, which mistakenly reads "affords acquittal."
5. Pinchas H. Peli, *op. cit.*, pp. 123–124.
6. Cohen, J. M. (1994). *Prayer and Penitence.* Northvale, NJ: Jason Aronson Inc., pp. 135–137.

712. Is there anything particularly unique about the Jewish doctrine of atonement?

It is, indeed, a remarkable idea. The basic meaning of the Hebrew verb "to atone," *kapar*, is "to wipe out" or "efface." This suggests that every single trace of sin can be wiped away without trace. When we consider that God is omniscient, that He knows everything and forgets nothing, we may well wonder what sort of dramatic exercise He, Himself, has to perform on Himself in order to efface all trace of man's sin from His unique mind. It seems that God has to perform an act that is even more heroic than man's repentance!

Dr. Jonathan Sacks, Chief Rabbi of Great Britain, contrasts this concept of *kaparah*, "wiping away all trace," with the Greek notion that

> human destiny was governed by an inexorable fate which, try as we might, we could not avoid. There was a decree that could not be averted. Even today, in secular society, when a figure in public life falls from grace, there tends to be no way back. We say that such a person has a past—meaning that because of their past they have no future. But in Judaism we believe that by sincere remorse and restitution a person can overcome the past. We can begin again.[7]

THE FIVE ABSTENTIONS

713. What are the five biblical abstentions for this day, and what is their biblical basis?

The Torah states "On the tenth day of the seventh month . . . you shall afflict your souls" (Leviticus 23:27). This is universally understood to refer to abstaining from food (*akhilah*) and drink (*shetiyah*). Many authorities attribute only that abstention directly to Torah law and regard the other four abstentions—from washing (*rechitzah*), annointing (*sichah*, that is, applying cosmetics), marital relations (*tashmish ha-mitah*), and wearing leather shoes (*neilat ha-sandal*)[8]—as only rabbinically mandated. The Talmud quotes verses from the Bible to prove that each of these abstentions was regarded as an established method of demonstrating asceticism.[9]

714. Why do we refer to them as the "five abstentions" when there are in fact six?

The Talmud already raised that problem and answered that "drinking is included under the category of eating."[10] It proves this from the biblical verse "And thou shalt eat before the Lord thy God . . . the tithe of thy corn, of thy wine, and of thine oil"

---

7. Sacks, J. (1994). "Yom Kippur: Beginning Again." September 15, 1994, p. 2.
8. *Yoma* 74b.
9. *Yoma* 76b–77b.
10. *Yoma* 76a.

(Deuteronomy 14:23). Thus, the drinking of wine is governed by the verb "to eat," for which reason we regard eating and drinking as but one abstention.

Eating and Drinking

715. How do we infer the prohibitions of eating and drinking from the biblical reference to *iynui nefesh* ("afflicting your soul")?

First, we must be clear that the Bible uses the term *nefesh* in the sense of "self," "body," rather than in any spiritual sense. Indeed, it is the very opposite of "affliction" that we are meant to do with our "souls"! Now, the *Sifra* explains "afflicting" the body in this context as "destroying" it. So the Torah is prescribing that we abstain specifically from providing the body with what is absolutely necessary for its survival, and without which it would be "destroyed."

This only refers to eating and drinking. The other four abstentions are in no way vital for survival, for which reason authorities such as *Tosafot,*[11] *Rosh,*[12] and other *Rishonim*[13] do not regard them as prohibited under biblical, but only rabbinic, law.

716. While we accept the *Sifra*'s identification of "afflicting one's soul" with the exercise of fasting, surely that is merely a Midrashic rationalization of the existing tradition. Is there any explicit biblical evidence for interpreting the biblical reference in that way?

There is, indeed. The prophet Isaiah, no less, provides us with the evidence we seek. He states: "Wherefore have we fasted (*tzamnu*) and Thou dost not see it? Why afflict our souls (*inniynu nafsheinu*) and thou payest no heed?" (Isaiah 58:3).

And then again, two verses later, we have another example that proves conclusively that this is how the Bible understands "affliction of soul": "Is this the sort of fast (*tzom*) that I have required, the day for a man to afflict his soul (*annot . . . nafsho*)?"

We also have the very clearest example in a succinct phrase in the book of Psalms: "I afflicted my soul with fasting" (*inneyti batzom nafshi*).

717. So if "afflicting the soul" only really refers to abstention from eating and drinking, why was the biblical parameter expanded to include the other four abstentions?

They are inferred by the sages[14] from the employment of a double reference — *shabbat shabbaton* (Leviticus 23:35) — as a description of the day. *Shabbat*, in this

---

11. *Tosafot* on *Yoma* 71a (*D. H. Ditnan*).

12. *Rosh* on *Yoma* Chapter 8[1].

13. *Rishonim* ("earlier authorities") is the name given to the halakhists whose works *preceded* the codification of the *Shulchan Arukh* (sixteenth century).

14. *Sifra* 8:3.

context, means "resting, or desisting from," and the double reference comes to cover abstention from wider pleasures, in addition to food and drink.

The *Sefer Ha-Chinukh* explains the objective of these further abstentions:

> Food and drink and the other physical and tactile pleasures arouse the desire to embrace lust and sin, and neutralize the intelligent soul's inclination towards the true way, which is the service of God which provides refinement and satisfaction to all who are possessed of understanding.
>
> It is improper for a slave, on the day he is summoned to be assessed by his master, to appear slothful and bloated with food and drink. For a person is judged only as he appears at that moment; and for that reason it is fitting, on this awesome day, to enable our spiritual qualities to come into prominence, and to subdue our physical appetite before them. In that way we will be considered worthy to receive pardon.[15]

718. Are there any other prohibitions that apply to Yom Kippur?

There are, indeed. Yom Kippur is the "Sabbath of Sabbaths," which means that all the other thirty-nine categories of "work" prohibited on an ordinary Sabbath, and their sub-categories, also apply on Yom Kippur. So one may not kindle fire, cook, ride, carry, etc.

719. What amount of food constitutes "eating," to cause one to be liable for infringing the biblical prohibition?

The sages defined the minimum amount for such liability as the volume of a large date, common in ancient Israel and referred to as a *kotevet*. The *Nodah Bi-Yehudah* defines it as a little less than a medium-sized egg without its shell.[16]

720. But is this not a departure from the usual volume of food — a *kezayit* (size of an olive)[17] — that is used as the normal criterion for the definition of "eating"?

It is, indeed. The reason for this departure is that in the case of Yom Kippur the Torah does not give a blanket prohibition of the very exercise of "eating," which would render prohibited as little as an olive. Instead, it gives a qualitative definition of what constitutes the abstention, namely the stage of "afflicting oneself." The sages believed that until one had eaten as much as a large date one was still, technically, afflicting oneself, since "a person's appetite is not satisfied in any way by less than that volume."

This is not to say that one may go ahead and eat a little less than that volume and

15. Babadr, J. (1962). See Mosad Ha-Rav Kuk edition. Jerusalem. *Sefer Ha-Chinukh, Mitzrah 313*.

16. Landaur, E. (Jerusalem, 1969). *Nodah Bi-Yehudah* on *Orach Chayyim* 38 (*D. H. Vehinneh od ashiv*).

17. Cohen, J. M. (1996). *1001 Questions and Answers on Pesach*. Northvale, NJ: Jason Aronson Inc., pp. 48, 74–75, 150.

regard oneself as still fasting. We are simply defining the prohibition in the case of someone who inadvertently ate, forgetting that it was Yom Kippur. This definition is important, however, when it comes to defining the maximum that a sick person, on doctor's orders, should eat at any one time to sustain him throughout the fast (See Questions 722–728).

721. What is the minimum one may drink before violating the biblical prohibition?

The minimum definition of "drink" is the amount that one can hold in one cheek (*melo lugmav*). This is equivalent to the displacement of about one egg.

Fasting by the sick

722. So how do we apply these definitions in the case of sick people who have to eat and drink?

These, indeed, are the criteria that we apply. It is the doctor who must make the decision as to whether or not a patient has to eat or drink on Yom Kippur, and his decision is final.

Where a person has to eat or drink, he should immediately consult his rabbi for guidance. The principle is that he has to ensure that he takes in, at any one time, less than the basic volume we have already outlined. Also, in order that the food and drink that he takes in at intervals should not combine to exceed the basic definition, the sick person has to space himself, leaving a sufficient interval between each mouthful to constitute a separate act of ingesting, unconnected with the previous one. By leaving such intervals, the sick person may take in up to the amount prescribed by the doctor.

The following procedure is recommended: One should eat, each time, less than the volume of a medium-sized egg (minus its shell). Aim for about two-thirds of an egg, to be on the safe side. Wait for about 8 or 9 minutes before eating the same amount again, and repeat to the required amount. In the case of fluids, drink less than one cheek-full at a time, and leave an interval of about 7 minutes between each drink.

This method may be used even if the doctors state that the patient's life is not actually in immediate danger, but that there would be considerable concern that he or she might weaken through fasting and that this could cause a deterioration in the condition.[18] Where there is a real fear for the patient's life, however, any amount of food or fluid may be administered in whatever way required.

723. Does taking in fluid by intravenous means constitute a violation of the prohibition?

No, it does not. Since on Yom Kippur the criterion is to ensure "affliction," namely that we have no "enjoyment," it is only food or drink that is taken in, and

---

18. *Sefer Ha-Chinukh, ad loc.*

savored, by way of our mouth and throat, that passes the definition of eating and drinking. According to the *Achiezer*[19] and other authorities,[20] even a sick person whose life is not in danger may receive fluids in that way.

724. If the doctor advises the patient that his life will be endangered if he does not eat or drink, may the patient disregard the doctor's advice on religious grounds?

Decidedly not. It makes no difference whether the doctor is Jewish or gentile in this regard. The halakah looks to the doctor's expertise, irrespective of religion. The *Arukh Ha-Shulchan* declares[21] that, in the absence of a doctor, if those around the sick person all concur in their apprehension for his life on account of his great weakness—and especially if the person cannot get out of his sickbed—then he is to be categorized as truly in danger and should be made to eat and drink, by the method indicated.

725. What if a dangerously ill patient is advised by the doctor that fasting will not really aggravate the condition further, but the patient differs and feels that he or she has to eat or drink in order to sustain himself or herself?

Then we listen to the patient, on the basis that no one can determine such needs better than the patient himself. This approach is quite in conformity with present-day medical opinion.

726. Does a sick person recite a blessing over the food he eats?

He does, indeed. He does not recite *kiddush*, as on other festivals, but he must wash (if he is eating bread), recite his usual blessing over bread, and include *Ya'aleh veyavo* in the grace after meals.

727. Do pregnant and nursing women have to fast?

Under normal circumstances, there is no reason why they should not fast. If a pregnant woman is seized with a desperate craving for food and we fear for her if it is withheld, then we should first remind her that it is Yom Kippur, and that she should not be eating. If this does not calm her down, she should be given a minute taste, "as often this is sufficient to calm a craving pregnant woman down."[22] If she still demands it, or her pallor has changed so that it seems she has been affected by her craving, then she should be fed as much as she demands. If, however, she feels that she can take it in the prescribed small quantities, and at intervals, then she should do so.

---

19. Grodzinski, C. O. (1922). *She'eilot U-teshuvot Achiezer*. Vilna, vol. III, Responsum No. 61.
20. Schwadron, S. (1974). *She'eilot U-teshuvot Maharsham*. Jerusalem: Makhon Chatam Sofer, vol. I.
21. Epstein, M. Y. (undated). *Arukh Ha-Shulchan*. Tel Aviv: Yetzu Sifrei Kodesh, 618:12.
22. *Magen Avraham* on *Orach Chayyim* 617:2.

The same applies to any other person—male or female—who is seized by an irrational craving, particularly if his or her face has gone ashen and his or her eyesight has failed.

728. Does a woman who has recently given birth have to fast?

If there were complications and the mother's condition gives some cause for concern and the doctor states that she needs to eat, then there is no question that she must do so.

In the case of a woman who has had a straightforward delivery, it is of the greatest significance that nowhere does the Talmud even discuss whether or not she should be absolved from fasting. Neither does the great codifier, Maimonides, who covers every law of consequence, make any reference to this situation. From this, we may assume that their view is that she is to be regarded as a perfectly healthy person in respect of fasting.

Other codifiers, such as *Tur* and *Shulchan Arukh*, state that "for three days [after childbirth] a woman should not fast at all; from the third to the seventh day, if she says 'I need to eat,' we give it to her. From then on, she is as any other person."[23]

Now, a present day halakhist, R. Chaim David Halevi, advises caution in applying this decision of the *Tur* and *Shulchan Arukh* without qualification. He stresses that the Talmud does not give such a concession, and the incremental scale referred to here (the 3- and 7-day periods) is only mentioned by the Talmud in the context of breaking the Sabbath for her by making a fire and providing necessary hot water. It is not a principle to be applied to Yom Kippur.

Furthermore, that Shabbat situation has nothing to do with her "feelings" about whether or not she requires it. Hot water is a necessity and is provided for all women. They are not qualified to say whether it is necessary or otherwise. Therefore, writes Rabbi Halevi, we cannot just apply that Sabbath incremental scale, or the criterion of whether or not she feels it necessary to eat, from the context of the Sabbath to that of Yom Kippur.

Basing himself on a principle of Nachmanides, R. Halevi asserts that the *Tur* and *Shulchan Arukh* can only be relied upon in a situation where there are no qualified doctors to consult. In that situation, if she says she feels very weak and needs to eat, she may do so during the first 3 days after childbirth, since for that period a woman is halakhically categorized as a sick person. However, if there is a doctor to consult, and he advises that there is no problem with her fasting, and the woman feels equally up to it, then she must fast.

R. Halevi adds that he has consulted three specialists who confirmed that "they can find no reason why a healthy woman who gives birth without complications should not fast during the first three days."[24]

He concludes that this reasoning is based purely on his halakhic analysis. As

23. *Tur Orach Chayyim* 617; *Shulchan Arukh* 617:4.
24. Halevi, C. D. (1981). Committee for the Publication of Ha-Goen Rabbi Chaim David Halevi. *Asei Lekha Rav*, vol. VI, pp. 158–163.

regards applying this opinion in practice, he awaits the concurrence of the distinguished halakhists of his day. My readers must refer to their own halakhic authority for specific guidance on this issue.

729. From what age do young people have to fast?

The biblical obligation takes effect when boys have attained their bar Mitzvah (13 years) and girls their bat Mitzvah (12 years). However, there is a rabbinic duty to prepare them gradually for this marathon fast. Thus, from the age of nine, they should attempt to fast for some of the day, building up to the entire day by one year or two before their bar and batmitzvah. The *Magen Avraham* records, however, that "these days we are not too demanding in this regard."[25] It is forbidden for a child under nine to attempt to fast.

Washing

730. How do we define the prohibition of washing on Yom Kippur?

We are not permitted to bathe, or even immerse our hands in either hot or cold water where this is done for pleasure. Where it is a necessity, however, such as the washing of one's hands and moistening one's eyes on awaking in the morning, or after using the rest room, or if they become dirty, then this is permissible, using the minimum water required. On awaking from sleep, one should wash only up to the joint of the fingers with the hand. Where washing is a prescribed therapy, it is permitted.[26]

The Sephardi codifier, Joseph Karo, is more lenient than his Ashkenazi glossator, Moses Isserles, in permitting someone who is fastidious to wash his face in the morning if he will feel very uncomfortable at not having done so.[27]

731. Are the priests permitted to wash their hands in the usual manner before blessing the people?

For this ritual, the washing of the entire hands, up to the wrist, is prescribed, and the blessing *Al netilat yadayim* is made.

Cosmetics

732. Are there any exceptions to the prohibitions of applying cosmetics on Yom Kippur?

The Hebrew term for this prohibition is *sichah*, which actually means "applying oil or ointments." Perfumes, cosmetics, and after-shaves are certainly prohibited on this day as being totally at variance with its spirit, as is the rubbing in of oils or

25. *Magen Avraham* on *Orach Chayyim* 616:2.
26. *Magen Avraham* on *Orach Chayyim* 613:4.
27. *Shulchan Arukh Orach Chayyim* 613:4.

moisturizers. A sick person, even if he is in no danger, as well as someone who has sores on his head, may apply an emollient.

Leather Shoes

733. What is the point of abstaining from wearing leather shoes?

In earlier times, leather shoes were a luxury that only the wealthy could afford and would wear at important social gatherings. We still use the term "well-heeled" to describe someone of comfortable financial means.

In the ceremony of *chalitzah*, where a man refuses to do his duty and marry his late brother's childless widow, the Torah prescribes that "she shall remove his shoe (*na'al*)." This is a leather shoe and is symbolic of the financial comfort and protection that she had hitherto enjoyed from the family and that her late husband's brother is now withdrawing from her.

Some authorities point out that the definition of the type of shoe that is prohibited on Yom Kippur is the one that is suitable for use in the *chalitzah* ceremony, namely of leather; and those that may not be used in that ceremony, namely, shoes made of rubber, cork, palm leaves, or other vegetable matter, may be worn on Yom Kippur.[28]

This underscores the analogy between *chalitzah* and Yom Kippur. The former symbolizes the breaking of bonds, the severing of relationships, and the removal of protection. Yom Kippur, on the other hand, is the day of "at-one-ment," of coming together, making up and renewing relationships that were strained by disloyalty and sin. Hence, the leather shoe that may be used for *chalitzah*, for breaking relationships, may not be used for Yom Kippur.

734. Are there any exceptions to the prohibition of wearing leather shoes?

The *Kitzur Shulchan Arukh* states that "a sick person, even if he is in no danger, or someone who has a problem with his feet, or a woman for thirty days after childbirth, may don leather shoes."[29]

Marital Relations

735. How does the halakah define this prohibition?

The *Shulchan Arukh* states that "On Yom Kippur it is forbidden to have marital relations, and it is even forbidden to touch one's wife, regarding her as if she was a *niddah* (menstrually unclean)." It is, therefore, forbidden to sleep with her in the same bed."

---

28. *Sefer Ha-Chinukh, Mitzvah* 313 [9].
29. *Kitzur Shulchan Arukh* 133:10.

THE RATIONALE OF THE ABSTENTIONS

736. What is the overall rationale of these five abstentions?

On Yom Kippur, we stand totally alone before the bar of justice, without spouses or others to protect us or to cover or plead for us. This isolation is translated into the rejection of anything that betokens sociability or joyful interaction. We eat and drink for pleasure; and the table is perhaps the greatest symbol of sociability. We bathe and apply cosmetics in order to appear fresh and appealing to others. Leather shoes, as we have said, make a statement regarding our status "in society," and marital relations are the deepest, most intimate, and pleasurable expression of a mutual interaction and need.

On Yom Kippur, we affirm that ultimately we must give account "for ourselves," that however much we may surround ourselves with family, friends, and acquaintances, and think to escape from confronting ourselves through flight into the bosom of the social collective, there is a day in the year that partakes of the nature of the great day of judgement, when we have to detach ourselves, stand alone, and give an account of our "selves" and what we have achieved and contributed, not merely what we have taken and enjoyed. In the words of the psalmist, "Not even a man's brother may redeem him; he cannot pay to God a ransom for him" (Psalm 49:7). Throughout the year, we turn our sights sideward, looking toward our fellow man, giving or taking instructions, seeking support, and hoping for approbation. On Yom Kippur, we turn our sights upward, echoing the psalmist's sentiments: "Whom have I in heaven [but Thee]? And, having Thee, there is none that I desire on earth" (Psalm 73:25).

XXII

The Evolution of Yom Kippur

IN BIBLICAL TIMES

737. How is Yom Kippur described in the Torah?

For the Torah, Yom Kippur is nothing less than a day of private, public, and national atonement, with the emphasis on "afflicting one's souls" and desisting from work.[1] There are also references to meal offerings and special fire offerings[2] and to the shofar, which is sounded on the Yom Kippur of the Jubilee year to serve as its moment of inauguration.[3] The Torah also refers to the ritual of atonement to be led by Aaron, and after him, by the hereditary High Priest, who, dressed in simple linen garments, shall make atonement on behalf of the entire community.[4] There is also a description of the High Priest's entry into the innermost sanctum, the Holy of Holies, once a year, on this special day,[5] and to the scapegoat ritual over which he presides.

738. How was the High Priest to effect his entry into the Holy of Holies on Yom Kippur?

The Torah states that he must first offer a personal sacrifice to atone for himself and his family before he can presume to petition on behalf of the community. He must then dress himself in the special attire: "He shall put on a holy linen tunic, and he shall have linen breeches on his flesh. He shall be girdled with a linen girdle, and with a linen mitre he shall be attired. And he shall bathe his flesh in water before putting them on."[6]

739. In what way did these garments differ from the ones he usually wore?

The normal garments worn by the High Priest, as described in the book of Exodus (chapter 28), were glorious robes, adorned with gold bells and pomegran-

---

1. Leviticus 23:26–27.
2. Leviticus 23:27; Numbers 29:7–11.
3. Leviticus 25:9.
4. Numbers 16:32–34.
5. Leviticus 16:1–34.
6. Leviticus 16:4.

ates. Hence, their description as being "for splendour and for beauty" (verse 2), and the employment of the most skilled craftsmen, who are "wise-hearted, and whom I have filled with the spirit of wisdom, that they may make Aaron's garments to sanctify him" (verse 3). On Yom Kippur, however, there was no place for human glory, for even the fate of the High Priest lay in the balance. And for that reason, he was to wear simple garments of white linen.

To some extent, he was even more concerned for his fate than most. This was because the unintentional manslayer was banished to the cities of refuge "until the death of the high priest" (Numbers 35:25, 28, 32). We are told that the mothers of the High Priests would go and provide the manslayers with food and garments, begging them not to pray for the death of their sons so that they might be released from confinement.[7] Since the manslayers would be praying fervently for their release on Yom Kippur, the High Priests must have felt particularly apprehensive and vulnerable, and would certainly not have relished the wearing of their usual splendid robes.

740. So what did the High Priest do after he had immersed himself, made his sacrifice, and dressed himself in the white linen robes?

The Torah tells us that he had to slaughter a bullock as a sin-offering "for himself and his household" (Leviticus 16:11). This last word was understood by tradition to refer to his priestly fraternity, for whose sins of omission or commission in regard to their sacred ministrations the High Priest also had to atone for. Following that, he had to enter the Holy of Holies for the most dramatic and awesome task of seeking atonement, through meditation, prayer, and ritual, for the entire community.

On his return to the Temple court, he would set about organizing the scapegoat ritual. This involved presenting two goats at the door of the Tent of Meeting and casting lots to determine which shall be "for God" and which subsequently shall be sent out "to Azazel," that is to be regarded as symbolically laden with the sins of all Israel and banished to the desert where it was hurled over a precipice (See Questions 855 and 856).

Before the Azazel goat was sent away, the High Priest was to place both his hands on its head, to make a confession of the sins of Israel that would be symbolically transferred thereby to the goat. A special courier, normally a priest, was deputed to take the Azazel to the desert.

741. Are we told exactly how the High Priest was to make his entry into the Holy of Holies?

This is also described in Leviticus chapter 16, where it is also made clear that entry to the Holy of Holies on any other occasion would bring instant death to the person, whether he be High Priest or commoner (verse 2).

We are told here that, in order to obscure the interior of the Holy of Holies from

---

7. Mishnah *Makkot* 2:6.

the gaze of the High Priest, he had to take a censer full of coals of fire from off the altar and also two handfuls of incense, "and bring it within the veil" (verse 12). The veil was the floor-to-ceiling curtain that totally separated the innermost Holy of Holies from its slightly less holy anteroom. The burning incense would thus create the desired smoke screen.

The Torah continues:

"And he shall place the incense upon the fire [pan] *before the Lord,* that the cloud of incense might cover the ark-cover that is upon the testimony that he die not" (verse 13).

742. But is there not an ambiguity here, for the biblical verses (12 and 13) just quoted, seem to suggest that the High Priest takes in the coals and the incense and only combines them to create the smoke screen when he is already "before the Lord," that is inside the Holy of Holies? But surely by then he would have snatched a view of its interior.

There is, indeed, an ambiguity; and this gave rise to a major difference of opinion in antiquity between the Pharisees and the Sadducees. The latter believed that within the Holy of Holies there actually existed a physical manifestation of God and that it was in order to obscure that divine Presence from the gaze of man that the Torah precribed this precautionary ritual. Accordingly, for it to be effective, the Torah must have meant the High Priest to add the incense to the coals and create the smoke screen, before he entered the inner sanctum.

The Pharisees (early custodians of our oral traditions who handed them down to rabbinic Judaism), on the other hand, hotly contested and regarded as blasphemous any such gross conception of a corporeal God. Their tradition was, indubitably, that Aaron and the future High Priests were to first enter the Holy of Holies and only then—"before the Lord"—create the smoke screen. This indeed seems to be the import of the chronological order of verses 12 and 13. Having performed that ritual, he retired to the anteroom to offer prayers for the coming year.

743. Did the High Priest have any other rituals to perform at that time?

We have already referred to the sin offering that he had to slaughter at the outset, as atonement for himself, his household, and the entire priestly fraternity. The Torah prescribes that he now perform three other activities. First, he had to return to the Holy of Holies in order to sprinkle seven times the blood of that sin offering on the front of the Ark curtain, before again withdrawing to the anteroom.

The goat that had been selected by lot as "for the Lord" was then brought in for him to slaughter. This was to petition for expiation on behalf of the nation as a whole; and once again he had to take its blood with him, in a basin, into the Holy of Holies and sprinkle it seven times against the curtain. He then made a formal confession, while inside the Holy of Holies, and petitioned most fervently on behalf of all Israel.

On emerging from the Holy of Holies, he would place the bowl on a golden stand

and again sprinkles the curtain from the outside, first with the blood of his sin offering and then with the blood of "the Lord's goat." He then mingles the blood of both together and sprinkles it on the golden incense altar in the anteroom. The remainder is poured on the cornerstone of the main altar outside.

IN TEMPLE TIMES

744. Has there been much change in the nature and spirit of Yom Kippur since biblical times?

Indeed, there has. Yom Kippur has undergone a dramatic evolutionary development over the millenia. Each stage of its development—from its celebration in the desert Sanctuary and the Temple; from Temple to early synagogue, and from then to the liturgical embellishments of the medieval period—would have rendered it almost unrecognizable to those who observed it during the previous respective stage.

This is proved beyond doubt by a remarkable Talmudic tradition regarding one particular observance of Yom Kippur, as practiced most probably during the period of the first Temple (ninth through sixth centuries B.C.E.):

> Said Rabban Shimon ben Gamaliel: There were no more festive days in Israel than the fifteenth of Av and the Day of Atonement. On those days the [eligible] girls . . . would go out in borrowed white dresses, in order not to embarrass those who possessed none of their own . . . . The girls of Jerusalem would go and dance in the vineyards. What did they used to say: Young man raise your eyes and make your considered choice [of wife].
>
> The less attractive would say: "Do not focus on beauty; look for family breeding; as it says, 'Grace is false and beauty is vanity; the woman that fears the Lord, she is to be praised'" (Proverbs 31:30).
>
> The beautiful girls would say: 'Consider well our beauty, for that is the very attraction of woman.' And the unprepossessing girls would plead: 'Make your choice in the name of heaven (in other words, do not choose a woman for physical or social reasons, but rather to fulfil the divine *mitzvah* of procreation).'[8]

745. But how do we explain the incongruity of devoting part of the holiest day of the year to the purpose of arranging marriages?

According to tradition, Yom Kippur was the day when Moses descended from Mount Sinai with the replacement two tablets for those he had smashed on his first descent, when he witnessed the Israelites worshiping the Golden Calf. This was the day when God forgave Israel for her previous gross disloyalty; and it accordingly

---

8. Mishnah *Ta'anit* 4:8; Talmud *Ta'anit* 31a.

became a symbol of reconciliation and "coming together" and a day to hail the power of love that "covers all transgressions" (Proverbs 10:12). Hence, its emergence into a day for fostering love and marriage.

The choice of Yom Kippur for such an event presents difficulties only for those who cannot synthesize deep inner joy with a feeling of spiritual awe and who confuse the former with "having a good time" in the purely physical sense.

Religious brides and grooms, to this day, observe the first part of their wedding day, until after the *chupah*, as a fast day, a mini Yom Kippur; and the groom actually recites the Yom Kippur *Vidduy* (confessional) in his silent *Amidah* at *Minchah*. Such couples, who, amid their excitement and joy are also acutely aware of the profound spiritual dimension of their relationship, will feel no contradiction in perceiving of their joyful wedding day as partaking also of the spirit of a Yom Kippur, a day for introspection, prayer, intercession, and mutual resolve. Hence, it is that a precedence for this may be found in the period of the first Temple, when, on the evidence of the Mishnah, Yom Kippur was also the day for arranging marriages.

It should be remembered that, while there was a rich ceremonial and a full order of service at the Temple on this day, yet it was not a pilgrim festival. At that early period, there was also no liturgy for the ordinary folk to occupy themselves with, so there was plenty of time on Yom Kippur for other, spiritually significant, pursuits, such as matchmaking.

A MORE DEMANDING LEVEL OF OBSERVANCE

746. Is a higher level of observance required in relation to Yom Kippur than as regards the other major festivals?

The Torah does not compromise on levels of observance. Where a law is prescribed, total commitment is expected. However, in respect of the basic prohibition of work, the punishment for working on Yom Kippur is far more stringent than for working on any of the other festivals. The Torah states, "Whomsoever doeth any manner of work in that day, that soul will I destroy from among his people" (Leviticus 23:30); yet the biblical punishment for working on any of the other festivals only involved thirty-nine lashes, the usual punishment for infringing a negative precept.

747. Why is infringing the prohibition of work on Yom Kippur so much more serious than on the other festivals?

Rav Ben-Zion Firrer explains this on the basis of the way the prohibition of work on Yom Kippur is formulated and the way the prohibition on all the other festivals is presented.[9]

---

9. Firrer, B. Z. *Leyom Chageinu*. Jerusalem: Author's publication, undated, pp. 42–43.

In connection with all the other festivals (outlined in Leviticus chapter 23), the Torah states the prohibition of work but without giving any rationale other than to describe the day as a *mikra kodesh*, "a holy convocation" (verses 7, 8, 21, 24, 25, 35, 36). In connection with Yom Kippur, however, the Torah does not content itself merely with the description *mikra kodesh* to explain the prohibition of work, but adds the additional explanation "And no manner of work shall you do on that selfsame day, for it is a day of atonement, to make atonement for you before the Lord. For whatsoever soul it shall be that is not afflicted on that day, he shall be cut off from his people" (verses 28 and 29).

We see from the juxtaposition of these two verses here that the prohibition of work is intrinsically associated with that of fasting, or "afflicting one's soul," to provide the identical punishment on both counts.

Rav Firrer explains that there is a vast difference between a fast day whereon one desists from any work, and one where one is preoccupied with work. Alluding to the phrase, "the day is short and the work is great,"[10] he points out that where one is preoccupied with work, "the day is short"; time passes quickly and the fast is much easier. Where one desists from work, however, the fast is doubly onerous.

And this is why the punishment for not desisting from work on Yom Kippur is so dire, because that act of desisting is an essential element of the "afflicting of one's soul." Not working is inextricably interconnected with the rigor of fasting. And hence, one who does not desist from work is liable to the identical punishment as one who neglected to fast.

748. What Temple procedures were followed in preparation for Yom Kippur?

The Mishnah[11] provides details of procedures that were necessary to ensure that there was a High Priest in place for this most solemn day, because his person was vital in the ritual of obtaining pardon on behalf of the nation. He also had to prepare himself spiritually and emotionally for the awesome experience of penetrating the inner sanctum of the residence of the divine Spirit, where the unqualified and unworthy feared to tread on pain of death by divine censure.

We are told that 7 days before Yom Kippur, the High Priest was taken from his residence to the *Lishkat Parhedrin*, "Assessors' Apartment," in the Temple, in order to prepare himself. They would also designate a replacement High Priest in case some disqualification, such as impurity, prevented the High Priest from fulfilling his duties. The replacement was not required to separate from his home, however, in the same way as the incumbent High Priest.

There was also a tradition, recorded in the Mishnah by Rabbi Judah,[12] that they would also designate another wife for the High Priest, so that, if, God forbid, his

---

10. *Pirkei Avot* 2:15.
11. Mishnah *Yoma* 1:1.
12. *Ibid.*

wife died before Yom Kippur, he would not remain without a wife, because a High Priest in that situation could not perform the Temple service on that day.

749. Why did the High Priest have to have a wife?

This was derived from the verse "And he shall atone for himself and for [*beito*] his home" (Leviticus 16:6), and the rabbis understood "his home" as a metaphor for one's wife.

750. Why was the apartment to which the High Priest was taken called by that strange name: *Lishkat Parhedrin* ("Assessors' Apartment")?

It was, indeed, a strange name. *Parhedrin*, or, according to another reading, *Palhedrin*, is from the Greek, *parhedroi*, meaning an assessor, commissioner, or counselor. It was clearly an administrative office, off the Temple Court, which was vacated for the High Priest during the week preceding Yom Kippur.

The Talmud[13] states, however, that originally it was called by a far more grandiloquent Greek name: *Lishkat Boleute*, the "Senators' Apartment," but, in the Roman period, when the status of the High Priesthood was severely undermined, as the Romans replaced the incumbent every year, offering the position to the highest bidder, it was designated *Lishkat Parhedrin* (the "Assessors' Apartment), to indicate the transitory nature of the High Priestly office, just like that of a mere assessor or counselor.

751. So what did the High Priest do during those 7 days of preparation?

The Mishnah[14] tells us that, whereas throughout the year the High Priest could please himself regarding what ritual functions he involved himself with, and whether or not he wished to join in with, or take over from, the priests who were ministering in the Temple as part of their twice-a-year rota, during this pre-Yom Kippur week of preparation, on the other hand, he was not permitted to be idle. He had to busy himself with a host of ministrations: Sprinkling the blood of the morning and afternoon continual offerings; offering the incense on the Golden Altar, morning and afternoon; replacing and trimming the wicks and cleaning out and replenishing the oil of the Menorah; and, in general, attending to the offering of the sacrificial parts of the daily sacrifices.

752. But if, as in the Roman period, the office of High Priest changed every year, did he not require instruction in the special procedures to be followed on Yom Kippur?

He did, indeed. The Mishnah[15] proceeds to describe the method employed to prepare the High Priest for this day:

---

13. *Yoma* 8b.
14. Mishnah *Yoma* 1:2.
15. Mishnah *Yoma* 1:3.

They would delegate some elders of the High Court to instruct him, and they would read before him [each day] the order of the [Yom Kippur] day's proceedings. They would say, 'My lord, High Priest, please read aloud [the Biblical prescriptions], just in case you have forgotten them, or perhaps you might not have learnt them.' On the morning preceeding Yom Kippur they would station the High Priest at the Eastern Gate and cause the various bullocks, rams and he-lambs to pass before him, so that he might familiarize himself with the order of their sacrifice.

753. But how could they possibly impute to someone of the religious standing and background of the High Priest ignorance of the requirements of the day?

We have already referred to the sale of the office by the Romans to the highest bidder. Inevitably, it was a most coveted office, and the Romans, who betrayed a cold indifference to the religious sensibilities of the Jews, would offer the position in the first instance to those assimilated Jews who ingratiated themselves with, and worked for, the Roman administration. For them, previous knowledge or religious observance was no precondition, for the High Priesthood was perceived as a political honor, and the duties that went with it merely as colorful but empty rituals. Hence, because of the total ignorance of so many of the incumbents, the Temple administrators could take nothing for granted.

754. Were there any last-minute instructions to the High Priests?

The Mishnah[16] tells us that for the last meal before the fast the Temple authorities would see that the High Priest only ate lightly since he had to stay awake the whole night of Yom Kippur. The reason was to ensure that he did not have a wet dream. For the same reason, they would not serve him highly spiced foods that warm the body.

On the eve of Yom Kippur, he would be taken to the upper chamber of the family of Abtinas that was responsible for preparing the incense. To collect just the required amount of incense within one's hand and to hold it so that none spilled out before spreading it over the altar was a skill that required practice; and the Abtinas family would instruct the High Priest to ensure that he could do it in the required manner.

755. Were not the Temple authorities apprehensive about entrusting the sacred Yom Kippur ritual to such uneducated priests?

Of course they were; but they had no choice in the matter. We must assume that they first satisfied themselves as to the priestly credentials of the incumbent and then worked on the assumption that once he had "atoned for himself and his household" he was as free of sin as the most worthy of High Priests and as capable thereby of securing atonement for "the whole house of Israel." As to his lack of knowledge, that also did not disqualify him for his tasks on this day. The important thing was

16. Mishnah *Yoma* 1:4–5.

that he perform each of the several duties exactly as instructed and practiced over his 7 days of training.

756. Did the authorities have any guarantee that the High Priest would perform every detail as required?

The Mishnah tells us that they would impose a solemn oath upon the High Priests, "by the One who causes His Name to attach to this place," that he would not change a single detail of the ritual. The fear of breaking such an oath would have been sufficient guarantee that the Pharisaic traditions would be preserved.

The authorities were especially apprehensive in case the High Priest was a Sadducee sympathizer who might alter the order of placing the incense on the fire pan in accordance with their view on this matter and interpretation of the biblical verses relating to that ritual (See Questions 741–742). And it was with this particular aspect of the ritual in mind that they imposed that oath upon the High Priest. The Mishnah goes on to record that invariably both the authorities and the High Priest would burst into tears at that point: the High Priest, because they suspected that he might be a Sadducee; and the authorities, because they were most probably falsely suspecting a worthy man of being a religious renegade.

757. How was that night of Yom Kippur spent?

The Mishnah relates that

If the High Priest was a scholar, he would deliver his own [halakhic] exposition [of the Yom Kippur ritual throughout the night]. If he was not, some sages would be deputed to expound before him. If he was accustomed to read the Scriptures, he would do so; and if not, they would read for him. What Scriptural passages would they read before him? From Job, Ezra and the book of Chronicles. One Zekhariah ben Kevutal related that he had several times read the book of Daniel before the High Priest.[17]

758. Is there any significance in the statement of Zekhariah ben Kevutal?

His statement needs to be read against the background of illiteracy that we have already referred to and the sale of the office of High Priest by the Romans to the highest bidder or as an honor or reward bestowed upon some Jewish collaborator for services rendered. Such assimilated Jews only spoke Aramaic, the *lingua franca* throughout the Middle East; they did not speak Hebrew, the language preserved by the educated classes of loyal Jews. Hence, Zekhariah tells us that he chose to read the book of Daniel for the ignorant High Priests because the first seven chapters of that book are written in Aramaic, which they were able to understand.[18]

---

17. Mishnah *Yoma* 1:6–7.
18. This explanation is quoted by R. Pinchas Kehati, in his commentary on *Yoma* 1:6, in the name of the late Chief Rabbi Isser Yehudah Unterman.

759. What happened if, as was inevitable, the High Priest nodded off?

It was forbidden for him to sleep, and "perchance to dream" (See Question 754). Hence the Mishnah states that

If he drifted off into a snooze, some priestly youngsters would snap their fingers to arouse him, and would say, 'My lord, High Priest, please stand up and walk [with your bare feet] on the cold marble floor.' They would then keep him attentive [with songs and psalms] until the time for the dawn daily sacrifice arrived.[19]

---

19. Mishnah *Yoma* 1:7.

XXIII

Kol Nidre

760. What is so special about *Kol Nidre* night that it has continued to exercise such a hold over our co-religionists?

People have been asking this question for centuries! It has to be acknowledged that this night possesses a mystique of its own—a tension, an excitement, a unique capacity to create a real sense of communal and national bonding. If we are ever able to sense God's eminent Spirit and to believe that His will and Israel's destiny are inexorably interconnected, it will be on that night.

Ne'ilah is another occasion when this ought to be attainable, but *Kol Nidre* preempts it. At this time, there is also a festive overtone, making the service an affirmation of joy in our faith, pride in our solidarity and our unity of purpose, and, above all, confidence in our ability to secure divine grace and atonement. By *Ne'ilah* time, we are left with the awe and spiritual tension, but, because of our weakness and hunger, with little of the festive emotion.

EXTENDING THE FAST

761. Why do we commence the fast an hour before nightfall, thereby extending an already lengthy fast by more than 1 hour?

The Talmud explains the reason for this:

[The Torah states] 'And you shall afflict your souls on the ninth of the month [of Tishri], in the evening' (Leviticus 23:32). I might have thought that the Torah intends here to tell us that we should commence fasting during the day on the ninth. Therefore it states 'in the evening.' If in the evening, then I might have assumed that this refers to when it is dark. Therefore the Torah states, 'on the ninth.' How is this achieved? By commencing fasting on the ninth while it can still be termed daytime.[1]

---

1. *Yoma* 81b. See also *Shulchan Arukh Orach Chayyim* 604:1.

345

762. Is there any other reason offered for the Torah having told us to "afflict our souls" on the ninth, rather than on the tenth, as expected?

R. Chiyya bar Rav offers the following explanation:

The Torah states, 'And you shall afflict your souls on the ninth of the month.' But do we fast on the ninth? Surely it is on the tenth that we do so! But the Torah comes to teach you that he who eats and drinks on the ninth of Tishri is regarded by the Torah as if he had fasted on the ninth and the tenth.[2]

763. But why should that be construed as a particular merit, when the Torah does not require us to fast 2 days? Would that not be an example of the prohibition of *bal tosif*—not adding to the *mitzvot* or requirements of the Torah?

It is a good question. R. Chiyya's statement can perhaps be understood in the light of the question that we have already posed (See Question 704), as to why we do not observe Yom Kippur for 2 days, as with the other biblical festivals, to account for the calendrical uncertainty in ancient times as to which day had been designated by the Sanhedrin, on the basis of witnesses' testimony, as the first day of the month.

R. Chiyya might be inferring here that, indeed, we should be fasting on the ninth and the tenth for that reason. However, because it is a burden that people could not bear, the Torah only imposed 1 day of fasting upon us. The eating on the ninth—by way of preparation, to give us strength, for the tenth day of fasting—gains for us the same merit, states R. Chiyya, as if we had actually fasted 2 days, as strictly required.

764. But is there any philosophical rationale as to why we should commence the fast, and, indeed, Yom Kippur, while it is still only the ninth of Tishri?

Rav Ben-Zion Firrer[3] provides a penetrating explanation, that this was prescribed in order to disabuse us of the erroneous belief that repentance is restricted by the Torah to Yom Kippur. He refers to the dictum of R. Eliezer: "Repent one day before your death."[4] On being questioned by his disciples as to how one could possibly know when he would die, he replied that for that very reason a person had to repent each and every day so that when he died, all his days would have been lived in grace and repentance.[5]

Now, according to Rav Firrer, the whole point of commencing the fast on the ninth of Tishri—technically the day before Yom Kippur—is to reinforce this very teaching.

2. *Yoma ad loc.*
3. Firrer, B. Z. *Leyom Chageinu.* Jerusalem: Author's publication, undated, pp. 44–47.
4. *Pirkei Avot* 2:10.
5. *Shabbat* 153a.

765. Since there is always very little time to get to synagogue after lighting the Yom Kippur candles, is it permitted to ride there after having already lit the candles and made the blessings over them?

This is a gray area in Jewish law. It has to be understood that, for the woman, the lighting of the candles constitutes the acceptance upon herself of the sanctity of the Sabbath or a festival. This is not the case with the men in the family, who will be attending synagogue, because their specific intention is that, on an ordinary Sabbath, they will first pray the afternoon service, followed by *Kabbalat Shabbat*, and that they will not be accepting upon themselves the sanctity of Shabbat until the moment they recite the Sabbath psalm: *Mizmor shir leyom ha-Shabbat*.

Now, where it is at all possible, women should not ride to synagogue once they have lit their Yom Kippur candles. However, in an emergency, such as on *Kol Nidre* night and where they live a very long distance from synagogue, then they may utilize the same principle used by men to delay the acceptance of Shabbat after their wives have lit the candles, namely, to make a mental reservation while lighting them, that it is not their intention to accept upon themselves the sanctity of Yom Kippur until they arrive at synagogue. One should, of course, first consult one's rabbi before adopting such a halakhic solution.

BLESSING OF THE CHILDREN

766. Do we bless our children on the eve of Yom Kippur with the same formula of blessing as prescribed for Friday nights?

We give them the usual, biblical Priestly Blessing, but this is followed by a special blessing prescribed for the eve of Yom Kippur:

May it be the will of our Father in heaven to implant within your heart the love and fear of Him, so that His reverence will be before you all your life. May your desire be to study Torah and fulfill His *mitzvot*. May your mouth ever utter wise words; may your heart frame appropriate plans, and your hands do worthy acts; and may your feet run to fulfill the will of your Father in heaven. May your future partner be a source of blessing, and may God bestow upon you righteous sons and daughters who will occupy themselves with Torah and good deeds all their days. May He enable you to secure your livelihood in a noble way, with ease and in abundance, from His bountiful Hand, and may you have no need of the gifts of flesh and blood. May your livelihood enable you to be free to devote yourself to the service of God; and may you be inscribed and sealed for a long and good life, among all the righteous of Israel. Amen.

TEFILLAH ZAKKAH

767. There is a very lengthy meditation, entitled *Tefillah Zakkah*, which is printed in several editions of the *machzor*, and omitted in others. Who was the author of this meditation?

This meditation was composed by R. Abraham Danzig (1748–1820), the author of the *Chayyei Adam* and *Chokhmat Adam* halakhic compendia, and he recommended it for recitation before *Kol Nidre*. It is, indeed, a most lengthy composition, and the imprimator of the *Chafetz Chaim* for this prayer was undoubtedly responsible for its great popularity in mainstream Ashkenazi circles. The meditation was not without its detractors, however, on account of its sexually explicit subject matter, which many regarded as indelicate and inconsistent with the holy frame of mind that should accompany the prayers on this special night of the year.

768. What is the import of the *Tefillah Zakkah*?

It is essentially a plea for those "who have followed the counsel of the Evil Inclination," to stare lustfully at women and to become ensnared thereby, either by the practice of masturbation or by involuntary emissions as a result of "evil fantasies and foreign thoughts." These emissions are described as the generators of corrupting and destructive forces that will range themselves against the person's good angels, created by his holy thoughts and good deeds, and that will neutralize them. It goes on to catalogue and acknowledge many other serious crimes, including "contaminating the mouth with obscenities, gossip, lies, derision, tale-bearing, bickering, shaming and cursing others, and glorifying oneself at their expense," and offers a moving and desperate plea for mercy, help, and cleansing, coupled with the optimistic anticipation that God will receive us in a spirit of reconciliation and love.

769. What other themes are included in the *Tefillah Zakkah*?

The author proceeds to take Yom Kippur's five abstentions and to petition God that he treat them, respectively, as symbolic atonements for five categories of sin. The abstention from eating and drinking is offered as an atonement for having eaten forbidden food and drink. The abstention from washing and annointing is offered as atonement for having indulged the body in forbidden, as well as excessive, bodily pleasures. The abstention from wearing leather shoes comes to atone for the sin of "running with our feet in pursuit of evil," as well as for those sins of antisocial behavior for which the Jewish court would have imposed a ban that involved the offender having to walk about barefoot. The abstention from marital intercourse is offered as an atonement for the sexual sins of "improper arousal and seminal emission."

770. Who in particular opposed the recitation of this meditation?

The communities of Central Europe, the Progressives, and those under the influence of the Enlightenment movement viewed such a meditation with considerable embarrassment. It was not included in the *machzorim* they produced, such as the once popular and standard Anglo-Jewish *Routledge Machzor*. They joined forces in this respect with a number of Hasidic traditions who objected to its recitation, chief among which were the Chabad, Belz, Vizhnitz, and Karlin Hasidim.

DONNING A *TALLIT*

771. Why do we wear a *tallit* to the *Kol Nidre* evening service while there is no obligation to wear it at any other evening service throughout the year?

The duty of wearing *tzitzit* indeed applies only during the day, as suggested by the phrase *ure'iytem oto* ("And you shall see them") mentioned in the portion of the Law dealing with *tzitzit* (Numbers 15:39), and interpreted to mean that only when one could see them, in the natural daylight, is it necessary to wear them.

The great Rabbi Meir of Rothenberg made *Kol Nidre* night an exception, however, and, when he officiated as reader on this night, he would don a *tallit*, a practice followed by his and other congregations. As the duty of wearing them only applies during daytime, we commence the *Kol Nidre* service before sundown.

A further reason offered for this early start is that *Kol Nidre* constitutes a ceremony of absolution of vows, and Jewish law prohibits the petition for, and the granting of absolution of, vows on Sabbaths and festivals.[6]

Rabbi Meir's innovation was based on the fact that we recite the thirteen divine attributes at this service. Rabbinic tradition has it that God enwrapped Himself in a *tallit*, like a *Chazan*, to disclose these attributes to Moses, saying "When Israel recites these attributes before Me, their pleas will never go unanswered."[7] Because God, as it were, donned a *tallit*, Rabbi Meir felt it appropriate to do likewise at this service when we recite those same thirteen divine attributes.

THE *KITTEL*

772. Why do some wear the white *kittel* robe on Yom Kippur?

There are several reasons offered for its use on Yom Kippur. The first is that, being essentially a shroud, it induces a feeling of contrition, humility, and an acute

---

6. *Magen Avraham* on *Shulchan Arukh Orach Chayyim* 619:5.
7. *Rosh Hashanah* 17b.

awareness of the transience of human life. Because the wedding day is regarded as a Yom Kippur, when all the sins of the past are wiped away, it is customary in Hasidic and other Right Wing Orthodox communities for bridegrooms to don the *kittel* when standing under the *chupah* on their wedding day.

Another reason is that the *kittel* was perceived as approximating the garb of the pure angels, and it was intended to make us appear like the angels in order to wrest divine pardon and indulgence. There is an interesting difference of opinion among Hasidic authorities regarding whether or not a bridegroom should don the *kittel* on his first Yom Kippur after marriage, because his new preoccupation with the physical side of life makes it "difficult for him to emulate the angels"![8]

A third reason is responsible for the practice in the majority of Modern-Orthodox communities for only the *Chazan* wearing the *kittel* on Yom Kippur, because his recitation of the prayers makes him the counterpart of the ancient priests in the Temple, who performed the *Avodah*-ritual in simple white robes.

WOMEN'S YOM KIPPUR ATTIRE

773. Are there any halakhic prescriptions governing appropriate women's attire?

It is a recommended practice for women to wear white dresses on Yom Kippur, as a symbol of purity and also in the same spirit as that connoted by the *kittel* worn by the men. They are also discouraged from adorning themselves in jewelry, as this was regarded as inconsistent with the overriding feeling of fear and awe before the bar of Divine justice.

TAKING OUT THE SCROLLS

774. Why do we take out scrolls of the Torah for the recitation of this formula?

The most common practice is to take out two scrolls. The honor of doing so is given to the most worthy members of the community who position themselves on either side of the *Chazan*. The scrolls are taken out in order to heighten the awe of the *Biyeshivah shel ma'alah* declaration, which, as we have explained, formally suspends the ban of excommunication for the duration of Yom Kippur. Also, since the ban was always imposed in the presence of a scroll of the Torah, it is appropriate that a scroll be brought out in order to lend weight to the temporary lifting of that ban.

8. Mondschein, J. ed. (1995). *Otzar Minhagei Chabad: Elul-Tishri*. Jerusalem: Heikhal Menachem, p. 198.

775. Were there any other practices regarding the taking out of the two scrolls?

Some Ashkenazi communities satisfied themselves with merely opening the Ark for this declaration and not taking out any scrolls. Their authorities believed that it demeaned the honor of a scroll to take it out and not to read from it. There was considerable leeway however in this regard, especially within Hasidic practice. The tradition of *Gur* was to take out but one scroll; others took out three, and some took out as many as seven, and more.

The *Matteh Ephraim*[9] states that the scrolls should be returned to the Ark before the recitation of *Kol Nidre*, a view already expressed by the *Rosh*. This was because, unlike the *Biyeshivah shel ma'alah*, for which recitation there is a sound reason (See Question 745), there is no reason, however, for the taking out of a scroll for *Kol Nidre*, which is merely a plea for indulgence in the matter of future vows.

In many communities, it was the practice to auction the honors of taking out the scrolls, the highest price being paid for the honor of holding the first scroll and leading the procession of scrolls around the *bimah*.

THE *OHR ZARU'A* VERSE

776. Why is the verse *Ohr zaru'a latzaddik uleyishrei lev simchah* (Psalm 97:11) recited while carrying the scrolls to the *bimah*?

Because we are carrying the Torah in procession, this verse—"Light is sown for the righteous"—is particularly apposite, as light is the traditional biblical metaphor for the Torah, as in the verse, "For the *mitzvah* is a lamp and the Torah is a light" (Proverbs 6:23). The image of the Torah light being "sown" is one with which we are familiar from the blessing after the reading from the Torah: "He has given us a Torah of truth, and eternal life He has *implanted* within us."

It is interesting that some traditions, especially Hasidic, recite not just this verse, but the entire Psalm (97). This is especially significant, since this is one of the six *Kabbalat Shabbat* Psalms (95–100) recited on every eve of the Sabbath. Yom Kippur is, of course, described in the Torah as "Sabbath of Sabbaths." Hence, instead of reciting all the usual six psalms, just one of those special *Kabbalat Shabbat* psalms was selected to preserve the Sabbath spirit. In those rites that did not recite the entire Psalm 97, the selection of the single *Ohr zaru'a* verse served the identical purpose.

777. Granted then, that the *Ohr zaru'a* verse has an association with the Torah and with Shabbat, but does it have any association with Yom Kippur?

Viewed as a metonymic verse, representing the entire psalm, it will be seen that Psalm 97 contains a number of phrases that are specifically related to the major

---

9. *Matteh Ephraim* on *Orach Chayyim* 619:10.

themes of Yom Kippur, hence: "The Lord is king" (verse 1); "*righteousness and justice* are the foundation of His throne" (verse 2); "The daughters of Judah are glad because of your judgments, O Lord" (verse 8). In this latter verse, we have an echo of the ancient practice, referred to in the Mishnah, of the daughters of Jerusalem (Judah) rejoicing in the vineyards in anticipation of the marriages that were arranged for them on this sacred day (See Questions 744 and 745).

Other points of contact between this psalm and Yom Kippur may be found in the reference to God as "exalted over the entire earth" (verse 9). Again, His "delivering His loved ones from the hand of the wicked" (verse 10) is suggestive of Israel being exonerated in judgment and escaping the condemnation of Satan and the effects of the evil decree.

There are various customs regarding the number of times the *Ohr zaru'a* verse should be recited. Some traditions prescribe that it be recited but once, others that it be said three times, and others that insist that it be said seven times. In some rites the *Chazan* recites the verse and the congregation repeats it. In the *Chabad* tradition in Israel, the verse is recited aloud by the highest bidder in the auction to take the first scroll to the reading desk, and the congregation repeats it after him.

BIYESHIVAH SHEL MA'ALAH

778. What is the meaning of the introduction: *Biyeshivah shel ma'alah*?

This formula states that "With the permission of the heavenly court and with the permission of the earthly court, with the approval of the Omnipresent and with the approval of the community, we permit prayer with the transgressors."

The entire formula (until the last phrase, "we permit . . .") was the standard introduction to the *cherem*, or ban of excommunication, imposed upon those who refused to be bound by any of the collective regulations of the Jewish community, or whose actions brought the community into disrepute, or who jeopardized its religious and social well-being or financial and political security.

Such people were ostracized from the community, which meant that, in addition to commercial and social ostracism, they were also forbidden to pray with the congregation. On Yom Kippur, however, the ban was relaxed, as the community felt that it had no right to prevent any Jew making his peace with God. Hence, because the ostracism had been initiated with the recitation of that awesome formula, emphasizing that it was "with the permission of the earthly court and the heavenly court" that such extreme action had been imposed, the identical formula had to be used, and the same authority invoked, in order to suspend the ban for the duration of this day.

779. Who introduced the formula of *Biyeshivah shel ma'alah*?

It is attributed to the distinguished thirteenth century halakhist, Rabbi Meir ben Barukh of Rothenburg, whose decisions were regarded as definitive for Ashkenazi Jewry of his day, and for centuries after. Born around 1220 in Worms, he went to

Paris to study under the great Rabbi Yechiel, and, while there, witnessed the burning of the twenty-four cartloads of Talmudic manuscripts, about which he composed a moving *kinah* (elegy).

In 1286, Rabbi Meir was brought back to Germany and incarcerated by the Archbishop of Mayence in the fortress of Ensisheim. Many Jewish communities contributed a vast sum to pay as his ransom, but R. Meir refused to allow them to proceed on the grounds that this would open the floodgates for anti-Semitic authorities to bleed the Jewish community dry by arresting leading rabbis and demanding ransoms. He died after 7 years in confinement. The tragic irony was that the authorities did not release the body for some 14 years—until a vast ransom was paid!

THE MESSAGE OF *KOL NIDRE*

780. What is the overall message of the *Kol Nidre* composition?

Although it appears to deal with fairly abstruse categories of vows, its message is deceptively relevant to man's moral and ethical interaction with his fellow, in that it addresses the main cause of misunderstanding, friction, and violence—namely, the human lips. It seeks to remind us of the vows we make, and break; the words that we offer as our bond, and then either deny or twist out of all recognition; the undertakings we give, and the agreements we enter into—with spouses, partners, employees, suppliers, clients, and colleagues—and then renege upon without a pang of conscience.

Yes, of course *Kol Nidre* is directed primarily at vows between man and God, which only He can waive. But it is clearly also meant as a stimulus for us to consider the nature and quality of all our vows and undertakings.

Elie Wiesel, writing of his initial decision to defer for some 10 years putting into words his experiences and recollections of the Holocaust, refers to his mistrust of words on account of their being "too impoverished, too transparent to express the event." He quotes the Hebrew poet, Chaim Nachman Bialik, who observed that "words are whores. Decked out in their finery, they offer themselves to the first passerby."[10] Viewed in this context, there is a touch of irony underlying the catalogue of all the various types of vow (*nidre, esarei, shevuei, charamei, konamei, kinussei,* and *kinnuyei*) that trip so lightly and unthinkingly off our tongues throughout the year.

Words are cheap, and because of their grace and leanness they so easily out-distance our intentions, commitments, and actions. On the one hand, they are the source of all human woes, while at the same time possessing the capacity to arouse the most intense feelings, soothe the greatest hurt, and serve as balm to the most scarred emotions. *Kol Nidre* is a timely reminder each year of the potency of the fruit of our lips. It cautions us to employ our words with care and with wisdom, and in full knowledge of the profound consequences of rash and intemperate speech.

---

10. Wiesel, E. (1994). *All Rivers Run to the Sea.* London: Harper Collins Publishers, p. 151.

Max Arzt,[11] referring to the final sentence of the *Kol Nidre* composition—
Nidrana la nidrei, ve' esarana la issarei, ushevu'atana la shevu'ot ("Our vows shall
not be vows; our bonds shall not be bonds; and our oaths shall not be oaths") quotes
R. Moshe Mordechai Epstein (1863–1933), head of Slabodka yeshiva, who stated
that we should regard this verse not as a plea but as a confession of our lack of moral
constancy, hence his rendering of the verse as "Our vows *are* not vows; our bonds
are not bonds and our oaths *are* not oaths."

781. How can we possibly declare that God should regard all the vows we take as of no effect? What signal does this send to our gentile friends, and particularly our enemies, regarding the trustworthiness of Jewish promises?

Such a question betrays an unpardonable ignorance of the overarching concept of
the sacredness of the spoken word that underpins Jewish law and ethics. Beginning
with the Torah's insistence that "The utterance of thy lips thou must observe and
fulfill" (Deuteronomy 23:24), that we must "keep far from any false matter"
(Exodus 23:7), as well as the various other references to not telling lies (Leviticus
19:11) or uttering a false oath (Leviticus 19:12) or the prohibition of denying the
truth or giving a false report (Exodus 23:1), the whole of Judaism is rooted in the
principle of unswerving ethical conduct toward the neighbor that we are bidden to
"love as ourselves."

Whereas Christian ethics presented this in the negative form: "Do not unto your
neighbor as you would not have him do to you," which makes ethical conduct a
matter of expediency, to ensure that one does not suffer similar hurt at one's
neighbor's hands at some future time, Judaism converted this into a positive ethical
imperative that we accept as second nature and that should flow naturally and
abundantly from the feelings of love and shared destiny that we cultivate at all times
and that should bind us to our fellow man. So it should not surprise us, therefore,
that there is not a single reference in the entire Talmudic literature to it being
permitted for a Jew to renege on any oral or written promise he has made to his
fellow man.

The vows we seek to annul on *Kol Nidre* night are exclusively mental or verbal
expressions of *religious intent*, expressed in the context of our relationship to God
and our tradition, as, for example, one who vowed to submit himself to an exercise
of nazaritehood or other forms of abstinence, or to refrain from a certain mode of
conduct, or one who had determined or made a commitment to support a poor
person or a charity, but who had inadvertently forgotten about it.

782. Was there ever any sensitivity expressed on the part of those who felt that *Kol Nidre*'s sentiments might be misconstrued?

Jews have long been sensitive to the dangers inherent in this composition.
Already in 1240, in the disputation of Paris between the apostate Jew, Nicholas

---

11. Arzt, M. (1963). *Justice and Mercy*. New York: Holt, Rinehart and Winston, p. 202.

Donin, and the *Tosafist*, Rabbi Yechiel of Paris, the charge was made by the former that the *Kol Nidre* furnished clear evidence that the word of the Jew could not be relied on. Rabbi Yechiel strenuously pointed out that this plea is for absolution from vows that one made unwittingly, but nothing could cancel out vows that one took in full knowledge of their consequences. In his *Sefer Ha-Pardes, Rashi* already stated that *Kol Nidre* can only absolve one from vows that he may have taken, but can no longer remember. Vows that one recalls still have to be fulfilled.[12]

Notwithstanding the victory of Rabbi Yechiel in that disputation, it did not stop another apostate, Pablo Christiani, from raising the same calumny in his disputation with Nachmanides in 1263. And again in the sixteenth century, another apostate and arch anti-Jewish agitator, Johannes Pfefferkorn, published the identical calumny in his rabidly anti-Jewish tract *Judenspiegel.*

Especially from the period of Jewish emancipation, there were many Jews who were uncomfortable with this composition, because of the fact that a superficial, literal reading of it might well lead people, especially gentiles, to that same erroneous conclusion that Jews believed that they could break their word with impunity. In the hands of malicious anti-Semites, it could well prove a most dangerous propaganda weapon.

It was the Reform rabbinate that felt particularly sensitive about this, and one Mendel Hess, the Reform district rabbi of Saxe-Weimar, attempted, unsuccessfully, to persuade the Grand Duke of that Duchy to prohibit its recitation in 1823. It was a subject that remained high up on the agenda of synods of Reform rabbis for generations.

Orthodox support for the growing opposition to *Kol Nidre* came from the distinguished Rabbi Samson Raphael Hirsch, the chief rabbi of the Grand Duchy of Oldenburg in northwest Germany. Around the year 1839, Hirsch abolished its recitation, together with some other rituals, such as *Kapparot, Tashlikh,* and the beating of the willow. Such actions were clearly motivated by his "enlightened background and aesthetic sensibilities,"[13] though they aroused much suspicion regarding his piety on the part of colleagues and members of the Orthodox communities of Germany. This may well have emboldened a synod of the Reform movement in Germany to expunge *Kol Nidre* from their liturgy in 1844.

783. What is the origin of the *Kol Nidre* composition?

I have dealt fully with this in my book, *Prayer and Penitence,* which is a commentary to the High Holy Day *machzor.*[14] I would refer the interested reader to that work.

Suffice it to say that the theory that has gained the widest popularity in the past

---

12. *Likkutei Pardes LeRashi.* Quoted in Ariel, Z. (1967). *Sefer Ha-Chag Veha-Moed.* Tel Aviv: Am Oved Publishers, p. 47.
13. Rosenbloom, N. H. (1976). *Tradition in an Age of Reform.* Philadelphia: The Jewish Publication Society of America, pp. 69–70.
14. Cohen, J. M. (1994). *Prayer and Penitence.* Northvale, NJ: Jason Aronson Inc., pp. 140–144.

is that of Joseph S. Bloch, who suggested in 1917 that its origins go back to the Visigoth persecutions of the Jews of Spain—and their forced conversion to Christianity—in the seventh century c.e.[15] Their conversion vows were made under the most fearful oaths and adjurations. They had solemnly to profess their belief in the new faith and to renounce Jewish practices under penalty of death. They remained secretly faithful, however, to their ancestral beliefs, and on the holiest night of the year those proto-*Marranos* made an effort to celebrate it with their fellow Jews by sneaking into synagogue. (Once the persecution and forced conversions were over, although the rest of Jewry were allowed to practice their faith, there was no going back for those who had already converted. Indeed, they were closely observed, and any disloyalty to Christianity was punishable by death.)

Those courageous *Marranos* nevertheless felt very uneasy praying as Jews on *Kol Nidre* night, because, after all, it still involved breaking the solemn vows they had taken at their baptism. Bloch asserts that the *Kol Nidre* was introduced for their benefit, to enable them first to crave absolution.

Another theory, suggested by Samuel Krauss, is that the rabbis of the eighth century introduced the *Kol Nidre* absolution of vows for polemical reasons, in order to refute the Karaite denunciation of that practice as being totally without basis in Jewish tradition. By prescribing it for the holiest night of the year, those rabbis were emphasizing their conviction that such absolution was rooted in the firm and authentic foundation of Jewish tradition.

MIYYOM KIPPURIM ZEH

784. Does it not seem strange to be seeking prospective annulment for vows that have not yet been made?

It does. The Torah speaks of a husband being able to annul the rash vow of his wife, because, inevitably, he, and possibly also their children, might be affected if she overextends herself over and above the time, care, and attention she had to give to their needs. And if it was a monetary vow, then, again, in earlier times when few women had an independent income, it would be the husband who would have to pick up the tab. For similar reasons, a father could annul the rash vows of his minor daughter.[16] But there was no suggestion that the husband or father could make a prospective annulment *in case* such vows were made.

It is clear from all our sources, from the eighth century onward, that the original version was not the one incorporated into our Ashkenazi rite ("from this Yom Kippur until the next Yom Kippur"), but rather the version found in the Italian and Rumanian rites, seeking absolution for vows committed "from last Yom Kippur until this Yom Kippur," which removes our difficulty. In Spain, they introduced a fusion of both versions.

---

15. Bloch, J. S. (1927). *Israel and the Nations.* Berlin: Hartz, p. 278.
16. See Numbers 30:2–17.

785. But why did the Ashkenazim alter the retrospective formula to a prospective one?

The change was made in the eleventh century by Rabbi Meir ben Samuel, son-in-law of *Rashi* and father of the great *Rabbeinu Tam*. The latter supported his father's objections to the retrospective formula on the grounds that (i) annulment of past vows has to be performed by an experienced *dayyan* (judge) or by three laymen acting as a court of law, whereas, according to the prevailing custom, the reader alone recites the declaration of annulment; (ii) according to Jewish law, the actual vow has to be specified; (iii) a prerequisite for annulment is the expression of *charatah* (regret) at having made the vow, whereas our congregation merely sings along with the *Kol Nidre*; and (iv) there is no one to annul the vows of the reader, which should be done before he presumes to plead for the annulment of those of his congregation.

To overcome these objections, the current Ashkenazi prospective version was introduced, which converts *Kol Nidre* from a ritual of annulment into more of a plea that God should preserve us from making unfulfilled vows, and, in the event of their being made, that He should regard them as merely pious intentions, rather than binding commitments.

786. Is there any telltale evidence of that change from the original retrospective to our prospective version?

There is clear evidence of this in the anomaly of the fact that the past tense, employed in the original retrospective version ("All vows . . . that we have sworn, consecrated or prohibited upon ourselves [from last Yom Kippur until this Yom Kippur]"), was retained in the text even after they had made it refer to vows uttered "from this Yom Kippur to the next Yom Kippur"! The translations faced a major problem rendering this hybrid form and most simply render the past tense verbs (*dindarna, ude'ishtabana ude'acharimna ude'asarna*) as if they were future tense!

787. Why is *Kol Nidre* repeated three times?

At first it was only customary to recite it once. Because some worshipers arrived late and missed its recitation, it became customary to repeat it. The three times recitation was probably introduced as a defensive measure against those who objected to its recitation for the reasons we have explained. This is a typical rabbinic form of dealing with critiques of practices: to go on the offensive and invest those practices with even greater significance by overexaggerating them.

The *Ohr zaru'a* preferred to explain its thrice recitation in the light of the ritual of *hatarat nedarim* (annulment of vows), which also prescribes that the declarations made by the petitioner and the court be repeated three times. (*Ohr zaru'a* might be begging the question here, since it is likely that those threefold repetitions of that ceremony were themselves introduced to overexaggerate and bolster the ritual of annulment in the face of its many detractors.)

BARUKH . . . SHEHECHEYANU

788. Why do we recite *Shehecheyanu* on its own at this point in the service?

It does appear rather detached here from any context. However, it should be borne in mind that the proper place for the *Shehecheyanu* blessing is in the *kiddush*. Because on a fast day no *kiddush* is recited, as we cannot drink from the wine, the blessing was transferred, therefore, to an honorable position just before *Borkhu*.

ASHAMNU

789. How old is this custom of making a formal confession?

This short *Ashamnu* confessional, and the lengthy *Al Chet* that follows it, are referred to by the term *Vidduy*, "confession." It goes back to Temple times when the High Priest invoked the *Tetragrammaton*, the four-letter personal name of God, ten times while making his confession on behalf of Israel. For this reason, the Talmud prescribed that, in our liturgy, we should recite the *Vidduy*-confessional a corresponding number of times: in the silent version of the *Amidah* of the five statutory services of Yom Kippur, and again during the reader's repetition.

790. So does our *Ashamnu* version go back to Temple times?

No, it does not. After the destruction of the Temple (70 c.e.), the precise formula used by the High Priest was forgotten. The sages of the Mishnah, during the century following the destruction, created their own variant formulae, as did the succeeding generations of Talmudists; and several of their confessionals have been incorporated into our own Yom Kippur liturgy.

Thus, the composition *Anna Ha-Shem aviytiy pashatiy chatatiy lefanekha aniy uveitiy* ("I beg of You, Lord, I have committed iniquity, I have trespassed, I have sinned against Thee, I and my household . . ."), recited as part of the *Avodah* (description of the Temple service) in the Yom Kippur *Musaph*, is already mentioned in the Mishnah.[17] Later, in the third century, the great Talmudist, Rav, popularized his own *Vidduy* version, commencing *Attah yode'a razei olam* ("You know the secrets of the universe"),[18] while his colleague, Shemuel, also composed a personal *Vidduy: Mah anu meh chayyeinu* ("What are we? What is our life?"). These all won their place in the standard Yom Kippur liturgy as basic elements of this confessional section of the service, and it was only in the twelfth and thirteenth centuries that the Geonim of Babylon composed the *Ashamnu* and *Al Chet* confessionals as supplement to those of the Talmudic period.[19]

17. Mishnah *Yoma* 4:2.
18. *Yoma* 87b.
19. For a fuller treatment of the *Vidduy*, See Cohen, J. M. (1994). *Prayer and Penitence*, Northvale, NJ: Jason Aronson Inc., pp. 155–163.

791. Is *Ashamnu* merely an exercise in confession, or are there other things to be learned from it?

There are a number of very salient lessons to be learned from it. The first thing to note is that, throughout this confessional, there is not one reference to sins of neglect or omission in the performance of specific ritual practices. The catalogue of sins is restricted to the domain of ethics and morals, as if to emphasize that no Jew who strives after piety may ignore his responsibilities to his fellow man.

Dr. Meir Tamari, the expert in the field of Jewish Business Ethics, has demonstrated how each of the twenty-four statements of the *Ashamnu* can be applied to a different aspect of our dereliction in that particular ethical sphere. We shall quote a few of his examples:

Ashamnu ('We have done wrong') refers to our abuse of the trust placed in us by others, by, for example, denying that we owe a debt, using trust or clients' funds for personal needs, or using employees' pension funds to improve the financial situation of a company.

Bagadnu ('We have betrayed')—through shoddy workmanship or the callous redundancy of longstanding employees.

Gazalnu ('We have robbed') can be more widely applied to withholding wages or using financial clout to force others to agree to a transaction which is to their disadvantage.

Vehirshanu ('We have encouraged lawlessness')—by buying goods or services from firms that evade taxes, or by investing in firms that pollute the environment.

Ya'atznu ra ('We have counselled evil')—by giving advice to clients without disclosing conflicts of interest.

Kizavnu ('We have been deceitful')—by hiding assets from a creditor after a plea of bankruptcy, or by presenting someone else's ideas as our own.

Latznu ('We have scoffed')—by denigrating goods or services sold in order to pay less for them.

Sararnu ('We have turned away'). In our obsessive preoccupation with, and pride in, our own career achievements, we have turned away haughtily from family and friends whom we now deem to be much beneath us, socially, materially and professionally.

Pashanu ('We have oppressed')—in taking advantage of powerless tenants by providing sub-standard housing, or by exploiting another person's lack of knowledge of market conditions or prices.

Shichatnu ('We have corrupted'). False insurance and welfare claims are common examples of corruption, as is lavish business entertaining designed to unduly influence the recipient. Bribery corrupts both the recipient and the giver.[20]

---

20. Passage selected from "*Ashamnu*," a leaflet written by Dr. Meir Tamari and published by the London-based Jewish Association for Business Ethics (1995). Reproduced here with permission.

AL CHET

792. Who is the author of the *Al Chet* confessional?

There is no single author; it is a composite of several hands and versions. It seems to have begun as a mere six-line confessional, composed, it is believed, by the very first known liturgical poet, Yosi ben Yosi (*circa* fourth century). In that form, it confessed sins committed (i) *be'ones* (forcibly), (ii) *beratzon* (willingly), (iii) *bishgagah* (in error), (iv) *be-zadon* (brazenly), (v) *ba-seiter* (in secret), and (vi) *ba-galuy* (openly).

By the period of Maimonides (twelfth century), there was already in vogue a single alphabetical version of twenty-four lines, and our Ashkenazi version expanded that into a double alphabetical acrostic composition of forty-four lines.

793. Why is there considerable duplication of a number of the lines of this very lengthy *Al Chet* confession?

It has to be admitted that there is much duplication. Thus, we have separate lines confessing *bittuy sefatayim* ("the utterance of the lips"), *dibbur peh* ("the words of the mouth"), *si'ach siftoteinu* ("the chatter of our lips"), and *tifshut peh* ("foolish speech").

It can easily be explained in the context of the evolution of the *Al Chet* that we have just described. If our Ashkenazi version came about as a result of a conflation of two independent, single alphabetical, acrostic compositions, this would fully explain how the duplication arose.

794. Why do we need to recite two confessionals: the *Ashamnu* and the *Al Chet*?

The reason for this hinges on a major dispute in the Talmud[21] on the issue of whether or not one requires to detail each sin that he has perpetrated in the course of his confession, or whether an expression of remorse in general terms is sufficient to secure repentance for every sin.

The view of R. Judah ben Bava is that a full and specific confession of each sin is necessary. He derives his view from the biblical precedent of Moses' confession on behalf of wayward Israel: "This people have sinned a great sin, *and have made for themselves a god of gold*" (Exodus 32:31). God certainly knew what was Israel's guilt, but as Moses was formally confessing on their behalf, he clearly felt obliged to specify the particular sin.

Rabbi Akivah, on the other hand, maintained that this was not required. He based himself on the verse: "Happy is he whose transgression is pardoned, whose sin is *covered up*" (Psalm 32:1). The last phrase, according to R. Akivah, is clearly recommending the concealment of the precise nature of the sin, in the context of confession, leaving it to the All-Knowing God to deal with. (As regards the example

---

21. *Yoma* 86b.

of Moses specifying the sin, R. Akivah maintained that this was included in order to offer a special plea of extenuating circumstances. Moses was implying that it was the silver and gold that God Himself made them seize before they left Egypt that was the cause of their succumbing to the sin of the Golden Calf.)

Now we are in a position to answer our original question. For the *Ashamnu* and the *Al Chet* are both recited in order to satisfy both of those respective views. The *Ashamnu* confession, couched in general terms, and without specifying any particular sin, comes to satisfy the view of R. Akivah that such things should be concealed, whereas the lengthy catalogue of specific sins is there to cover R. Judah ben Bava's concept of the proper definition of confession.[22]

795. Are there any customs governing what should be done on returning home after the *Kol Nidre* service?

There is a custom recorded in the *Shulchan Arukh*,[23] and preserved in some old Jewish paintings and woodcuts, of staying behind in the synagogue the whole of the night of Yom Kippur, to recite psalms and prayers, and, at a late hour, laying down one's head to sleep as far away from the Ark as possible. *Chazanim* are advised, however, not to stay awake, because this could cause them to lose their voice!

[On the *Shema*, see Questions 339–345. On the Evening Service *Amidah*, see Questions 248–256; 352–365. On *Avinu Malkeinu*, see Questions 367–370. On the *Selichot*, see Questions 160–176. On *Aleinu*, see Questions 540–547. On *LeDavid Ha-Shem Oriy*, see Questions 145–146. For commentary on the rest of the *Kol Nidre* service, see Jeffrey M. Cohen, *Prayer and Penitence*, pp. 144–165.]

---

22. On the reasons for the respective views of R. Judah and R. Akivah, as propounded by the *Rishonim*, See *Entziklopedia Talmudit* (Jerusalem, 1965), vol. 11, p. 440.
23. See *Shulchan Arukh Orach Chayyim* 619:6.

XXIV

Yom Kippur Day Services: *Shachrit* and the Reading of the Law

[For commentary on the *Shachrit* service, See Questions 258–370.]

THE READING OF THE LAW

796. Why do we call up just six people for the reading of the law on Yom Kippur?

The number of people called up to each reading is commensurate with the religious importance of the day. Thus, on those days when work is permitted—Mondays, Thursdays, Chanukah, Purim, and fast days—we call up only three people. We also call only three on Shabbat afternoons, since we have already fulfilled the *mitzvah* of reading from the Torah in the morning. On Rosh Chodesh, which was originally a minor holy day, with its own special additional offering, and, in synagogue, an additional (*Musaph*) *Amidah*, we call up four people, as we do on the semi-holydays of *Chol Ha-Moed*. We denote the greater sanctity of the full festivals by calling up five people.

On Yom Kippur, we express its status as a "Sabbath of Sabbath" by calling up six; whereas on Shabbat, the ultimate in joyful spiritual expression, we call up seven. Another reason why the ordinary Sabbath is invested with greater importance in this respect than Yom Kippur, the "Sabbath of Sabbaths," is because infringement of the Sabbath laws brings with it the ultimate capital punishment by the hand of man, whereas infringement of Yom Kippur's laws (*karet*) is a delegated and deferred law, left for divine visitation in His good time.

797. What is the origin of the special melody that we employ on both Rosh Hashanah and Yom Kippur for the reading of the Torah?

The melody we employ is, indeed, a variation of the usual one used for every other reading of the Torah throughout the year. It can be traced back to medieval Germany where the practice of using the *Stubentrop* for the High Holy Days was first introduced. *Stubentrop* means "classroom chant," and, as its name implies, it was the melody to which children recited the translation of their sacred texts.

The fifteenth century authority, Rabbi Jacob Molin (*Maharil*), is credited with having been the one to first borrow this melody for use on the High Holy Days.[1] It was also the traditional way of reading the Passover Haggadah, and its characteristic has been described as "not sad, but leisurely and solemn."[2]

EIN KAMOKHA . . . AV HARACHAMIM . . . VAYEHIY BINSO'A

798. Why are these sections employed for recitation before taking out the scrolls?

The key to the relevance of this entire section lies in an appreciation of the Midrashic interpretation of the verse *Hashem oz le'ammo yitein . . .* , "The Lord gives *strength* to His people" (Psalm 29:11). The rabbis regard *oz* (strength) as a metaphor for the Torah about to be read. Its strength resides in its timelessness, an attribute derived from its Creator, who "*is* king, *was* king and *will be* king for ever and ever (*Ha-shem melekh Ha-shem malakh Ha-shem yimlokh le'olam va'ed*)."

By association with the verse "For out of Zion the Torah will come forth and the word of the Lord from Jerusalem" (Isaiah 2:3), which appears in the *Vayehiy binso'a ha'aron* paragraph, we introduce here a timely prayer (*Av Ha-rachamim*) for God to "deal well with Zion and rebuild the walls of Jerusalem."

The *Vayehiy binso'a* verses are taken from Numbers 10:35. They depict the formula that Moses would utter when the Ark of the Testimony was about to be moved from its place, as the Israelites moved camp during their 40 years of wandering in the desert. Reciting it prior to taking the scrolls around the *bimah* suggests that that circuit comes to symbolize those journeyings of the Israelites.

HA-SHEM HA-SHEM KEIL RACHUM VECHANUN

799. Why do we recite the formula *Ha-Shem Ha-Shem* when taking out the scrolls of the Torah?

This formula, known as *Shelosh Esrei Middot [Ha-rachamim]*, "The Thirteen Attributes of Mercy," was taught to Moses by God after He agreed to pardon the Israelites for their sin in worshiping the Golden Calf (Exodus 34:6–7). Moses had smashed the first set of tablets when, on his way down from Mount Sinai, he was confronted by that terrible act of apostasy. But God's merciful attributes, as described in this verse, prompted Him to grant a replacement set of tablets to Israel.

Thus, having spurned the first offer of a Torah (in the form of its kernel, the Ten Commandments), the Torah Israel ultimately received was bestowed as a demonstration of unique divine indulgence and mercy. Hence, as we take out the Torah, we

1. Zimmels, H. J. (1958). *Ashkenazim and Sephardim*. London: Jews' College Publications (New Series No. 2), p. 142.

2. Tobias, A. (1996). "The Trope." *Jewish Bible Quarterly*, vol. xxiv, No. 1 (93), p. 24.

remind ourselves of those divine attributes and petition God to extend His mercies and forgiveness to us in our hour of need.

It was the circle of sixteenth-century mystics, disciples of the *Ari*, R. Isaac Luria, who introduced the recitation of the *Shelosh Esrei Middot* into the prayers at this point. They instituted it at first exclusively for recitation during the month of Elul and the High Holy Day period. Once entrenched, its recitation was expanded, so that it came to be recited on all festivals.[3]

RIBBONO SHEL OLAM

800. Why is the *Ribbono shel olam* introduced at this point?

It is introduced for the reason we have just given. Having just reminded God of His past indulgence to our people, we immediately recite a fervent plea asking for that to be repeated on our behalf, and for Him to extend "a pardon through lovingkindness and a pardon through mercy."

801. Why is *Ribbono shel olam* not recited when Yom Kippur occurs on a Sabbath?

It is not recited because it petitions for specific needs, such as sustenance, clothing, wealth, honor, recovery from sickness, and beneficent treatment at the hands of one's host government. However, on the Sabbath, we are meant to focus on, and rejoice in, the blessings that we possess rather than those we are in need of, for which reason we do not recite on the Sabbath the middle thirteen blessings of the weekday *Amidah*, which are all petitionary blessings.

Some traditions do, however, recite the *Ribbono shel olam* petition even when Yom Kippur occurs on a Sabbath, on the basis that Yom Kippur is, in any case, described as a "Sabbath of Sabbaths," so that it is immaterial whether or not it falls on the actual Sabbath itself. Furthermore, Yom Kippur is, by its nature, a day given over to petitionary prayer, so that there should be no objection to the recitation of these specific petitions even when this day coincides with the Sabbath.[4]

BERIKH SHEMEIH

802. What is the purpose behind the recitation of *Berikh shemeih* before taking out the scrolls of the Torah?

It serves three basic purposes. First, being a passage from the *Zohar*, the central work of Jewish mysticism, it serves to remind us that the written Torah, which we

---

3. Elbogen, I. M. (1988). *Ha-tefillah Beyisrael.* Tel Aviv: Oviv, p. 149.
4. *Mattei Ephraim* on *Shulchan Arukh Orach Chayyim* 619:45.

are about to read, cannot be fully understood without the oral explanatory tradition that accompanied it and that Moses first received during his 40 days and nights on Sinai. This oral tradition was subsequently handed down within the priestly circles, from teacher to disciple, and was ultimately preserved within the Talmudic literature, the commentaries, and the various codes of law.

Secondly, the choice of a prayer from the *Zohar* at this point also served to bolster the claim of the mystical literature to be regarded as an authoritative source of oral tradition, in the face of those many mainstream authorities who were highly suspicious of mystical influences on the gullible masses.

Thirdly, the choice of this particular prayer, culled from the *Zohar*'s commentary on Exodus chapter 26, as a prelude to the reading from the Torah and the *Haftarah* (prophetic literature), was on account of its pertinent reference to God's Torah being true and His prophets being true, and for the worshiper to be granted the privilege of "prostrating himself before the glory of God's Torah," and its closing, fervent plea for God to "open his heart to the Torah."

803. Do we know when the *Berikh shemeih* first entered our prayer book?

According to Abraham Berliner,[5] it was first prescribed in Italy around the year 1540, and from there it was quickly adopted by other prayer rites. At first, it was recited on Sabbath only, but, on account of its great popularity, it was soon regarded as an essential accompaniment to the taking out of the scrolls from the Ark.

The Turkish communities, comprising mainly exiles from Spain in 1492, used to recite *Berikh shemeih* in Spanish, so eager were they that the uneducated masses, who did not understand the Aramaic in which the prayer is couched, should appreciate the directness, beauty, and fervor of its petition.

SHEMA YISRAEL

804. Why is the first verse of *Shema* recited at this point?

Rabbi Jacob Emden suggests[6] that it was introduced here for the sake of latecomers who may have missed the recitation of *Shema* together with the congregation. They are given a further opportunity, therefore, at this point. He adds that there was no need to introduce here the responsive *Borakhu*—again for the sake of those who might have missed it earlier—because the congregation is about to hear it recited by each of the six people who are called up to the reading of the Torah, as well as by the one called to the *Maftir* portion.

---

5. Berliner, A. *Randbemerkungen zum taglichen Gebetbuch.*
6. Emden, J. (1904). *Siddur Bet Ya'akov.* Lemberg, p. 83.

ECHAD ELOKEINU

805. Why is this verse introduced here?

It seems to have been introduced here in order to create a stairlike progression or liturgical bridge between identical words that recur both in the previous line as well as in the line that follows. Thus, its first word, *Echad (hu elokeinu)*, links up to the last word of the previous line *(Ha-shem echad)*, and the occurrence of the word *gadol (adoneinu)* links up to the first word of the following line *(gadlu)*.

GADLU . . . LEKHA HA-SHEM HA-GEDULAH

806. Why is the *Gadlu* verse introduced here?

This verse represents a summons by the *Chazan* to the congregation to join him in declaring God's greatness: "Declare *(Gadlu)* the greatness of God *with me*, and let us exalt *(unerommemah)* His name together" (Psalm 34:4).

Again, the words *Gadlu* and *unerommemah* in this verse link up in the same way to the words *ha-gedulah* and *rommemu* in the passage *(Lekha Ha-Shem ha-gedulah)*, which follows.

So we see how the liturgists, in the context of a section that sets out to hail the greatness and splendor of God, made the most judicious choice of those particular verses that specifically lent themselves to juxtaposition by means of the appropriate interconnecting link-words with which they were endowed.

VEYA'AZOR . . . KOHEIN KERAV YA'AMOD

807. In this special formula for calling up the priest to the first *aliyah*, are not the words *kerav ya'amod* ("let him approach and stand up") in the wrong order, for surely one first "stands up" before "approaching" the *bimah*?

We cannot fault the logic of this question, but neither may we assume that our liturgists missed such an obvious point! In fact, from the "Addenda and Variant formulae" section of our earliest *siddur* of Rav Amram Gaon, we learn of another, and earlier reading. Instead of *kohein kerav,* it has *kohein kera'* ("let the priest read"), reflecting the early period when whoever was called up read his portion himself.

Thus, our problem is now resolved, and the words will be seen to be in their appropriate order, because the formula commences with a general statement that someone from the priestly fraternity will now step forward to read first *(kohein kera')*, and it immediately proceeds to summon the particular priest chosen: *Ya'amod reb . . .* ("let Mr. so-and-so *stand up*").

BLESSINGS OVER THE TORAH

808. What is the origin of the *Borakhu* summons to the congregation ("Bless ye the Lord . . ."), issued by the person being called up to the Torah?

The Talmud[7] traces it back to Moses' instruction to Israel: "When I invoke the name of God, you ascribe greatness to His name" (Deuteronomy 32:3). This verse follows on immediately after a reference to the Torah: "My doctrine shall drop as the rain; my speech shall distil as the dew" (verse 2). Hence, the origin of the one being called to read in the Torah invoking God's name, by reciting a blessing, while the rest of the congregation utters a response: *Barukh Ha-Shem ha-mevorakh* ("Blessed be the Lord, who is to be blessed").

809. Does not the reference, in the blessing before the reading of the Torah, to God having "chosen us from all other peoples," smack of arrogant pre-eminence?

I have already dealt at length with this question in my book *Blessed are You,*[8] where I state that the concept of Israel having been "chosen" by God is one of the most misunderstood ideas of any religion.

We do not regard ourselves as having been chosen for privileges, but for service. And this is clearly implied in this blessing over the Torah; for, immediately after the "offending" reference to God having "chosen us from all other peoples," it continues: "to give us His Torah." In other words, we were chosen (or "volunteered") to accept the yoke of the Torah and to be the embodiment and transmitters of God's spirit and word. We were given a code of moral discipline, ethical rectitude, and spiritual sensitivity, to live by and to pass on to a world largely unwilling to be its recipients. That is an awesome mission, one for which Israel has suffered unspeakable oppression throughout its history. It was no sinecure!

[For the contents of the Torah reading, See Questions 737–743.]

THE *HAFTARAH*

810. What themes are dealt with in the Yom Kippur *Haftarah*?

The passage chosen as *Haftarah* (Isaiah 57:14–58:14) encapsulates some of the most sublime and timely insights into the authentic message of Yom Kippur. Isaiah has much to say to a community that, particularly on Yom Kippur, is so preoccupied with scaling the heavenly gates that it frequently overlooks the fact that the keys to those gates are kept here on earth. And the keys are constructed not only out of

---

7. *Berakhot* 41a.
8. Cohen, J. M. (1993). *Blessed Are You.* Northvale, NJ: Jason Aronson Inc., pp. 184–186.

prayer and ritual, but also out of integrity in one's dealings, charity, and concern for the welfare of one's fellow and one's society.

Chapter 58 opens with an ironic denunciation of those whose religious commitment is rooted in externals, and who naively believe that mechanical observance is a substitute for inner charitableness: "Yet they seek Me out daily, and delight to know My ways, [parading] as a nation that performs righteousness and forsakes not the just laws of their God."

Such externalism prompts its adherents to ask in naive amazement how it can be that "we fast but You do not see it; we mortify ourselves, but You pay no heed?" Isaiah echoes God's disgust at such a sham: "On such a day you are keeping no fast that will carry your cry to heaven. Is it a fast like this that I require, a day of mortification such as this: where a man bows down his head like a bulrush and makes his bed on sackcloth and ashes?"

811. To which particular community was Isaiah addressing these harshly penetrating sentiments?

He was addressing the Jews that had returned to Israel from exile in Babylon in the year 538 B.C.E. Only about 45,000 Jews had taken advantage of Cyrus the Persian's permission for the Jews to return to their land; and those settlers regarded themselves as the elite of Israel. In their preoccupation with the rebuilding of the second Temple (around 520 B.C.E.), the intensity of their nationalistic feelings and religious exhibitionism knew no bounds, and Isaiah's mission was to focus their zeal on the real objectives and values of Judaism:

Is not this what I require of you as a fast: to loose the fetters of injustice . . . to snap every yoke and set free those who have been crushed? Is it not to share your food with the hungry, taking the homeless poor into your house, clothing the naked when you meet them, and never evading a duty to your kinsfolk? . . . Only then, if you call, will the Lord answer; if you cry to Him, He will say, 'Here I am.'

812. Does the *Haftarah* deal with any other theme relevant to our modern-day observance of Judaism?

Indeed, Isaiah ends with a theme that will strike a chord in the hearts of many Jews who are guilty of religious tokenism. He proceeds to castigate those who call upon God only in times of personal crisis or who identify religiously only on occasions (such as the High Holy Days) when they are shamed into doing so by the fact that everyone else is making that symbolic identification. It is the regular communion with God every Sabbath, not the occasional visit, that God seeks:

If you cease to tread the Sabbath underfoot, and keep My holy days free from your own affairs; if you call the Sabbath a day of joy, and the Lord's holy day a day to be honored; if you honor it by not plying your trade, nor seeking your own interests or attending to your own affairs, then you shall find joy in the Lord, and I shall set you riding on the heights of the earth.

YEKUM PURKAN

813. What is the purpose of the *Yekum Purkan* prayer, recited at this point where Yom Kippur falls on a Sabbath?

It was composed as a tribute to the heads of the Babylonian academies, which served, from the eighth to the eleventh centuries, as the repositories of Talmudic and halakhic authority and as a powerhouse of spirituality that energized the entire Jewish world.[9] Indeed, the heads of the two main Babylonian academies, Sura and Pumbedita, known as *Geonim*, "excellencies," were regarded as the supreme religious authorities in the Jewish world, to whom the emerging Diaspora communities, such as Spain and North Africa, would turn for guidance on religious and communal issues.

Although Palestine was in decline at that period and its academies of learning could not boast the appeal or the leadership that Babylon enjoyed, the author of *Yekum Purkan* still included those Palestinian academies and their sages in prayer for the welfare of those engaged in the study of Torah.

814. What is the significance of the title *Reishei khalei*, highlighted in the *Yekum Purkan*?

Reishei khalei, the first of several officials named in this composition, means "heads of the *kallahs*." The *kallah* was a unique, month-long festival of learning staged by the academies of Sura and Pumbedita twice a year, in Elul and Adar. Primarily for laymen, the attendance of the scholars of the academies was also required. It attracted thousands of people, and the organizers and heads of this great adult education program were referred to as *Reishei khalei*.

815. What is the significance of the next-mentioned officials: *Reishei galvata*?

Reishi galvata means "heads of the exile." In addition to the medieval *Geonim*, the religious and academic regius professors of the two great academies in Babylon, there had also been in existence, already from the second century c.e., the office of civic and communal leader of the entire Babylonian Jewry, referred to as *Reish Geluta*, "head of the exile." He enjoyed monarchic authority and prestige, derived internally from the fact that the holder always traced his line to the royal house of David and externally from the recognition of his representative office by successive rulers of Babylonia, and especially during the caliphate of the Arab period.

816. What is the significance of the next-mentioned officials: *Reishei metivata*?

The word *metivata* is the Aramaic equivalent of the Hebrew *yeshiva* (The Aramaic root *yetav* equals the Hebrew *yeshav*.). Thus, the *Reishei metivata* were

9. Reif, S. C. (1993). *Judaism and Hebrew Prayer*. Cambridge: Cambridge University Press, p. 217.

"the heads of the schools," and refers to the great *Geonim*, the heads of the two great academies of Sura and Pumbedita.

817. What is the significance of the next-mentioned official: *Dayyanei di bava?*

These were the "judges of the gates." They were the next in line after the heads of the two academies, though it is unclear what their precise function was. The name suggests that they were the chief justices, since courts of law in ancient times traditionally held their sessions at the city gates. Rav Hai ministered in this capacity for many years before his elevation to the Gaonate of Pumbedita after it had moved to Baghdad.[10] (For more on *Yekum Purkan*, See Questions 450–454.)

[On *Yizkor*, See my companion volume, *1001 Questions and Answers on Pesach*, Questions 567–580.]

[On the prayer for the government, See Questions 455–464.]

AV HA-RACHAMIM

818. What is the purpose of the *Av ha-rachamim* composition?

It belongs to the *Yizkor* genre, being a prayer of remembrance for the Jewish communities that were decimated in the Crusades, and for the countless pious Jews who were martyred *al kiddush Ha-Shem*, in sanctification of the Name of God, and for their loyalty to their faith. It is for this reason that, even in those communities that do not recite *Av ha-rachamim* every Sabbath, it is included as a fitting climax to the *Yizkor* memorial prayers.

819. Why do some communities not recite it every Sabbath?

Opposition to its too frequent recitation arose for two distinct reasons. Some felt that its martyrological sentiments were not in keeping with the joyful Shabbat spirit that we are meant to muster. Those who did recite *Av ha-rachamim* every Sabbath justified it, however, on the grounds that it is no more than an extension of the ordinary *El malei rachamim* memorial prayers, recited on most Sabbaths by people who have *Yahrzeit*.

Other communities, sensitive to the reaction of their Christian neighbors, objected to it on account of its uncompromising demand for vengeance:

"May our God . . . avenge the blood of his servants . . . . He will wreak vengeance on His foes, and make atonement for His land and His people . . . . Let it be known among the nations in our sight that You avenge the spilled blood of your servants . . . . He will execute judgment among the nations, heaping up the dead, crushing the rulers far and wide."

---

10. Asaf, S. (1955). *Tekufat ha-geonim vesifruta*. Jerusalem: Mosad Ha-Rav Kuk, p. 15.

Communities that were worried by Christian reaction to such sentiments made an exception, however, on just two Sabbaths of the year: the one preceding *Shavuot* and the one before the fast of *Av*.

820. But, are not its calls for vengeance truly uncharacteristic and unworthy?

There are two diametrically opposite ways of dealing with this issue. The first is the apologetic approach of S. R. Hirsch who goes to great pains to point out that vengeance is not a Jewish characteristic and that "Israel has borne the most outrageous atrocities . . . without ever attempting to work retribution upon the peoples and rulers who had unleashed their excesses of fanatical inhumanity." Hirsch waxes even more lyrical and draws our attention to the fact that the defiant biblical references chosen for inclusion in this *Av ha-rachamim* refer exclusively to *God* seeing Israel's unremitting suffering and reserving for Himself the exacting of retribution. This fact, states Hirsch, "has kept us free of the lust for vengeance . . . [enabling us] to bear strangling without ever becoming hangmen ourselves, and to tolerate robbery at the hands of our foes without ever robbing in return."[11]

Many observers of the history of the Israel Defense Forces in the twentieth century will find it difficult to sympathize with Hirsch's pacifism and idealization of our people and will rightly construe it as a reflection of a past age when we were simply powerless to exact a justified retribution on those who shed our blood.

This is, in essence, the second approach to the violent sentiments of the *Av ha-rachamim*, and is espoused by such theologians as Eliezer Berkovits. He inveighs against Christianity's misappropriation of Isaiah's doctrine of the "suffering servant" and its inordinate preoccupation with the Crucifixion:

'What is the weight of one sacrifice,' he appositely asks, 'compared to the myriads of sacrifices of Israel? What is one crucifixion beside a whole people crucified through centuries? . . . To torture and to kill one innocent child is a crime infinitely more abominable than the killing of any god. Had Christianity, instead of being preoccupied with what it believed to have been a deicide, concentrated its educative attention on the human crime of homicide, mankind would have been spared much horror and tragedy.'[12]

In the light of the modern Jewish experience, it is a sad reality that we truly have no problem with the rather harsh sentiments of the *Av ha-rachamim*. Hirsch seems to be making a virtue out of the fact that, perforce, we had to "turn the other cheek." For Christianity, that was an ideal to which it paid lip-service but never translated into action. For Judaism, that was never an ideal, but a recipe for the proliferation of yet more and more violence.

11. Hirsch, S. R. quoted in Munk, E. (1963). *The World of Prayer*. New York: Philipp Feldheim, vol. II, p. 151.
12. Berkovits, E. (1973). *Faith after the Holocaust*. New York: Ktav, p. 127.

821. Why is the Sabbath before *Shavuot* an exception to the rule for those communities that do not recite *Av ha-rachamim* throughout the year?

Because, by some quirk of history, the worst massacres of the Crusades were recorded as having taken place in the period between *Pesach* and *Shavuot*. This was because the Crusading knights chose the spring season—when the conditions were neither wintery nor too hot—to undertake their campaigns to rescue Palestine from the Muslim infidel. After *Shavuot*, encased in their armor, they would have sweltered and fainted in the heat of Palestine. Thus, passing through the Rhinelands on their way to the Holy Land, they began their Crusade by destroying the infidel on their doorsteps, the Jewish communities.

822. Why is the Sabbath before the Fast of *Av* the other exception for the recitation of *Av ha-rachamim?*

This is because this fast is not only a commemoration of the destruction of the two Temples in Jerusalem, but was also regarded more broadly as a national commemoration for all the tragedies that have befallen Jewish communities throughout our tear-stained history.

823. Do we know when *Av ha-rachamim* was first introduced into our liturgy?

Samuel Glick has dated it as some time before 1331, when the Nuremberg *Machzor* made its appearance. This was the first prayer book to include the *Av ha-rachamim* for recitation before *Musaf* each Sabbath.[13]

ASHREI YOSHVEI VEITEKHA

824. Why do we recite *Ashrei* (Psalm 145) at this point?

The *Ashrei* psalm was invested with great significance in talmudic times and enjoyed great popularity, perhaps on account of the fact that even the illiterate masses were able to commit it to memory and recite it daily. This was aided by the fact that it followed a simple alphabetical acrostic construction with short lines of equal length.

Its message of absolute trust in God's mercies and its recounting of the constancy of Israel's generational covenant with Him and His reciprocal bounty rendered it a veritable liturgy in its own right. Hence the Talmudic appraisal: "Whosoever recites *Tehillah le-David* three times daily is assured of a place in the World to Come."[14] It is for this reason that we recite it three times a day in our prayers: Among the morning psalms (*Pesukei de-zimra*), at this stage at the end of *Shachrit*, and, finally, at the beginning of *Minchah*.

13. Glick, S. (1991). *Or La-eivel*. Jerusalem: Pardes Publ., p. 138, n. 39.
14. *Berakhot* 4b.

HAVU LA-SHEM

825. Why do we recite *Havu La-Shem* (Psalm 29) at this point?

This psalm was prescribed as an accompaniment to the returning of the scrolls of the Torah to the Ark. It makes seven references to *kol Ha-Shem*, "the voice of God," which is precisely what the Torah embodies in written form. This particular image also evokes the concept of the oral law, the "voice of God" providing Moses with the full elucidation of all the laws stated in mere outline in the Torah.

The psalm also contains two occurrences of the word *oz*, "strength," which, in rabbinic parlance, is a synonym for the Torah, currently being carried to the Ark; as well as a reference to God's Temple (*uveheikhalo*), which the Ark symbolizes.

The Talmud[15] explains that the seven references to "the voice of God" in this psalm made it an appropriate introduction to the (Sabbath and festival) *Amidah*, which, unlike the nineteen blessing weekday *Amidah*, has seven blessings.

LEDAVID MIZMOR

826. Why do we recite *LeDavid mizmor* (Psalm 24), instead of *Havu*, when Yom Kippur (or any other *Yom Tov*) occurs on a weekday?

This psalm is actually more textually relevant as an accompaniment to the return of the scrolls to the Ark, especially with its reference to the psalmist petitioning the gates to open to welcome the King of Glory. The Talmud[16] sees in this a reference to King Solomon's final consecration of the Temple. The gates would not open on his merit—even though he cried fervently "Raise your heads, O gates"—until he invoked the merit of his father, David, who had been the actual architect of the Temple design.

Because of its more specific allusion to the residence of the "King of Glory"— that is the Holy of Holies wherein the two tablets of the law were housed—this psalm was prescribed for daily recitation. It was only on account of its sevenfold reference to the "voice of God" that Psalm 29 is substituted on Sabbaths.

UVENUCHOH YO'MAR

827. What is the significance of this composition, recited as the Torah scroll is returned to the Ark?

The first verse (*Uvenuchoh yo'mar*) is a quotation from Numbers 10:36, and it relates the petitionary formula that Moses would offer as the Israelites, traveling through the desert, encamped in a new place.

---

15. *Berakhot* 29a.
16. *Shabbat* 30a.

We recall that when the Torah was taken out of the Ark we recited the *Vayehiy binso'a ha'aron* verse (Numbers 10:35), which relates the formula Moses used as the Ark was about to commence its travels, whenever the Israelites left each of their encampments. Thus, we may see that the taking out of the Torah and its return after having been read are construed symbolically as reenacting the experiences of our ancestors as they traveled under the divine guidance and the moral discipline of the Torah.

828. What is the relevance of the next three verses: *Kumah Ha-Shem, Kohanekha,* and *Ba'avur david?*

These three verses are taken from Psalm 132:8–10 and were recited (with some slight variation) by King Solomon when he dedicated the Temple.[17] The phrase *va'aron uzekha* (literally, "the Ark of Your strength") employs the noun *oz* ("strength") as a popular metaphor for the Torah (See Question 825). The reference to the priests being "clothed in righteousness" (*Kohanekha yilbeshu tzedek*) is elucidated by the prophet Malachi's description of the priests as repositories of Torah and oracles of instruction to the nation.[18] The reference to King David (*Ba'avur david avdekha*) is in tribute to his having identified the threshing-floor of *Aravna* as the holy site of the future Temple. The phrase "Turn not away the face of your annointed" (*al tasheiv penei meshichekha*) was Solomon's plea to God never to remove His Spirit from that place.

829. What is the relevance of the last four verses: *Kiy lekach tov, Eitz chayyim hiy, Derakheha,* and *Hashiveinu?*

These refer more directly to the Torah that we have just read and are returning to the Ark. The first verse (Proverbs 4:2) calls upon Israel not to forsake its "goodly teaching." The second verse (Proverbs 3:18) describes the Torah as a "tree of life"; and it is for that reason that we provide the Torah scroll with two wooden staves (symbolic of "trees"), to which we apply the name *Eitz chayyim* (plural: *Atzei chayyim*), "tree(s) of life." The third verse (Proverbs 3:17) describes the Torah's ways as "pleasantness" and its paths as "peaceful." And the final verse (Lamentations 5:21) asks God to bring us back into a relationship of proximity and love with Him.

830. What is the meaning of the phrase *chadesh yameinu kekedem?*

Most translations render it as "renew our days *as of old* (*kekedem*)," though it is difficult to determine the precise nuance of the word *kedem* that is being employed here, for, at what stage "in olden times" did Israel experience that sense of "renewal"?

We must assume that the reference is to the time of the giving of the Torah, which

---

17. II Chronicles 6:41–42.
18. Malachi 2:7.

would account for its reference in this particular context. We are essentially asking God to give us that same sense of enthusiasm for Torah that prompted our ancestors at Sinai to respond with the promise that "Whatever the Lord has said we will do" (Exodus 19:8).

There are, however, at least another two ways of interpreting this phrase. The first takes account of a second meaning of the word *kedem*, namely "east." The east is, of course, where the sun rises each day and is thus the scene of the daily dawning of a new day, bringing with it an unprecedented sense of "renewal." We are asking God, therefore, to renew our days "like the east," and to make the words of Torah new to us each day as on the day they were first given on Sinai. This act of daily renewal is, of course, referred to in our daily prayers where we praise God "Who renews in His goodness, each day continually, the work of Creation." In relation to the words of the Torah, the rabbis throw out that very challenge of renewal, saying that "they should be to us as new each day as the day they were first given at Sinai."[19]

Another meaning to *kekedem* is revealed against the backcloth of the renewal of the world after the flood in the time of Noah. We are told that the progenitors of mankind were confined at that time to the east:

And their dwelling was from Mesha, as thou goest toward Sephar, unto the mountain of the east (*har ha-kedem*) . . . . And from these [families] were the nations divided in the earth after the flood . . . . And the whole earth was of one language and one speech; and it came to pass, when they journeyed *from the east* (*mi-kedem*).[20]

Thus, *chadesh yameinu kekedem* might well be a plea to God to "renew our days—*kekedem*—as when [we all lived] in the east." Just as He displayed unique mercy and indulgence to mankind, to renew the world and give it a second chance, so—we pray—may He do to us and prolong "our days" even if our past actions have not justified such mercy.

19. Midrash *Tanna DeBei Eliyahu Rabbah*, Chapter 18.
20. Genesis 10:30–11:2.

XXV

The Yom Kippur *Musaf* Service

MUSAF TIMING

831. Is there any particular time by which *Musaf* should be commenced?

The *Shulchan Arukh* states that "it is commendable to abbreviate the number of *piyyutim* (poetic compositions) and *Selichot* contained in the *Shachrit* service in order to ensure that *Musaf* is begun before the seventh hour (i.e., 13:00 hrs)."[1] The reason for this is given elsewhere,[2] because already at that time the obligation to pray the *Minchah* (afternoon service) has become operative.

A CIRCUMCISION ON YOM KIPPUR

832. If there is a circumcision to be performed in synagogue on Yom Kippur, at what stage in the service is it performed?

It is performed after *Shachrit* and the reading from the Torah, and before *Ashrei*. Some wine from the cup over which the blessing has been recited is given to the baby to drink. It is not given to other minors present (as, for example, after *kiddush* in synagogue on Friday nights and festivals), who could drink the amount of wine usually required in order to justify a blessing, so as not to send the wrong signals to them that one may drink on Yom Kippur in the context of a *mitzvah*.

REPETITION OF THE *AMIDAH*

Shoshan emek . . . Yom miyyamim huchas . . . Tzefeih bevat temutah . . . Esa dei'iy lemeirachok

833. What is the significance of these four compositions?

They were all written by Eleazar Kallir, one of our earliest and most prolific liturgical poets (early seventh century).[3] They form one poetic unit, as is clear from

---

1. *Shulchan Arukh Orach Chayyim* 620:1
2. *Op. cit.* 286:1,4.
3. On Kallir, see the many Index references in Cohen, J. M. (1994). *Prayer and Penitence*, Northvale, NJ: Jason Aronson Inc., p. 297.

their metric and acrostic structure. The first composition, *Shoshan emek*, forms the acrostic *Shabbat Shabbaton* ("Sabbath of Sabbaths"), which is the biblical description of Yom Kippur (Leviticus 16:31). The second, *Yom miyyamim huchas*, is created out of the acrostic *Yom Kippurim*; and the third, *Tzefeih bevat temutah*, forms the acrostic *Tzom He-Asor* ("fast of the tenth day"). The employment of this type of allusion to the various names of the festival is a departure from the usual acrostic pattern wherein either the name of the author or the letters of the alphabet are highlighted acrostically.

In the fourth composition, *Esa dei'iy*, Kallir employs the name acrostic: *Eleazar biribbi Kallir*. Not having enough letters in his name to cover the number of lines he required, he is constrained to repeat some of the letters. Thus, the first and second lines of each stanza commence with the same letter.

IMRU LE-ELOKIM

834. What is the theme and poetic structure of this hymn?

This popular composition, written by R. Meshullam ben Kalonymos (10th-11th century), calls upon Israel to praise the wonders of the Creator: "So say to God (*Imru Le-Elokim*) how wondrous are Your works." It is infused with a happy confidence, affirming God as the One who "hastens the redemption of His people . . . speeds forgiveness to His community and fulfils for us all His promises."

The hymn conforms to the alphabetical acrostic pattern, proceeding all the way through the alphabet. However, the Polish rite, which is followed by most of our editions, has omitted all the eleven stanzas commencing with the letters between *kaf* and *shin*. The stanza commencing with the letter *tav* (*Takif*) has been retained, however, to constitute a logical conclusion. Indeed, a variant version of this hymn, though bearing the identical title, refrain and structure, is recited during the repetition of the *Shachrit Amidah*.

UVEKHEIN GEDOLIM MA'ASEI ELOKEINU

835. What is the theme and poetic structure of this hymn?

This alphabetical acrostic hymn is much tighter in plan than the foregoing hymn, with each succeeding phrase, rather than each stanza, commencing with a succeeding letter. It continues the theme of the previous hymn in praising the deeds of the Creator, who, notwithstanding His transcendence ("He has made His habitation in heaven so high") is, at the same time, capable of manifesting Himself eminently and personally ("He hastens to heed the humble prayers of His people"). Again, a variant of it is recited during the repetition of the *Shachrit Amidah*.

The composition interrupts the alphabetic progression after the letter *reish*, to introduce a contrasting stanza—*Ma'aseh enosh* ("the deeds of man")—which catalogues the deceitfulness, unreliability, and transience of mortal man in whom most of us mistakenly put our trust. This stanza is made up of four lines that follow a reverse alphabetic-acrostic pattern (going back through the letters *tav, shin, reish,* and *kuf*). This contrasting pattern also helps to heighten the contrast between God's and man's deeds. When describing God's works, the acrostic moves forward to convey the idea of constructiveness and creativity; when describing man, on the other hand, the reverse acrostic is employed, to convey man's backsliding and contrariness. (For more on the fascinating evolution of this composition, See Cohen, J. M. (1994) *Prayer and Penitence,* Northvale, NJ: Jason Aronson Inc., pp. 180–182.)

UVEKHEIN LENORA ALEIHEM BE'EIMAH YA'ARITZU

836. What is the theme and poetic structure of this hymn?

The authorship of this double-acrostic poem is uncertain, though it is generally attributed to Yannai, one of our earliest liturgical poets (sixth and seventh century C.E.), many of whose poems were only brought to light this century, after their discovery in the Cairo *Genizah.*

The hymn describes the supreme and omnipotent God, enthroned upon the adoration of the angels, yet still desirous of the praise of worthless man. The superior appeal of the latter is explained in the refrains. Man has been granted freedom of choice. When he exercises it in favor of his Maker's will, that constitutes true praise—*vehiy tehillatekha* ("In truth, this is Your praise"). The angel's praise, on the other hand, is simply a concomitant of the fact that—*umorakha aleihem*—"Your awe is imposed upon them." (For more on this hymn, see Cohen, J. M. (1994) *Prayer and Penitence,* Northvale, NJ: Jason Aronson Inc., pp. 204–205.)

[On *Unetanneh tokef,* See Questions 528–530; on *Kedushah,* See Questions 531–532; on *Vekhol ma'aminim,* See Questions 533–534; on *Uvekhein tein pachdekha,* See Question 535; on *Veye'etayu,* See Question 536; on *Attah vechartanu,* See Questions 355–356; on *Kadosh attah,* See Question 537; on *Umipnei chata'einu,* See Question 538; on *Aleinu,* See Questions 540–547.]

ELOKEINU VE'ELOKEI AVOTEINU HEYEI IM PIFIYYOT

837. What is the purpose of this plea?

This is a plea for divine inspiration to rest on the *Chazan* of the congregation as he frames the next section of the prayers: the *Avodah,* the account of the High Priest's ministrations in the Temple and his entry into the Holy of Holies to petition for forgiveness on behalf of all Israel. It was not composed specifically as an introduction to the *Avodah,* however, and is found again in the repetition of the Rosh Hashanah *Musaf Amidah* where it serves as an introduction to the *Al kein nekaveh* composition. It serves, therefore, to demarcate a new and major section of the *Amidah.*

We have already encountered this genre, designated as a *reshut*, (literally, "permission") at the very outset of the *Chazan*'s repetiton of the *Amidah*, in the *Mi-sod chakhamim unevonim* composition (See Question 346), which is followed by a composition giving expression to the *Chazan*'s sense of unworthiness to represent his congregation in prayer. The present plea is rather more confident, however, and, although prescribed for recitation by the *Chazan*, its sentiments seem more suited to recitation by the congregation, as a plea on behalf of their representatives:

Inspire the mouths of the representatives of Your people . . . . Teach them what they should say; give them discretion in what they express. Fulfil their petitions; make them know the appropriate way of glorifying [You] . . . . May their lips secure blessing for Your people; and may they all be blessed with the blessings of Your mouth . . . . They approach the holy Ark in awe, to turn away anger and wrath, and may You, from heaven, survey them all mercifully . . . that they may not become tongue-tied or indistinct, and shame the multitudes who rely on them. Neither let them utter anything that is unacceptable to You . . . .

One may speculate that it was originally composed for congregations to recite on behalf of their *Chazanim*, but, because it was a plea that would naturally have been near to the hearts of the *Chazanim*, it was probably recited by them also with special fervor, to the extent that it was subsequently construed as primarily a *Chazan*'s composition.

OCHILAH LA'EL

838. What is the purpose of this plea?

This serves the identical purpose of the previous composition, with strong points of contact with it. It is a plea for the *Chazan*, wherein he affirms that he will also request for himself eloquent speech to sing praises to God. We may wonder why two such compositions were necessary. However, a glance at this plea reveals that, unlike the foregoing, this one is phrased in the first person. This further supports our view that the previous composition was originally prescribed for the congregation to recite, and *Ochilah La'El* was intended as the *Chazan*'s response, associating himself with the sentiments expressed by his congregation.

839. What are the main poetic features of this plea?

Its kernel comprises one four-lined stanza, with four words to each line, and the opening word of each line commencing with an *alef*, to emphasize the personal nature of the plea (*alef* standing for the initial letter of *ani*, "I"). There is an added section comprising three biblical verses (Psalms 16:1, 51:17, and 19:15), though the usual introductory formulae (*kakatuv, vene'emar*, etc.) have been omitted before each verse.

THE *AVODAH* (TEMPLE SERVICE): *AMITZ KOACH*

840. What is the subject matter of the *Amitz koach* composition?

It is essentially one long alphabetical poem, descriptive of the Yom Kippur Temple service and the various tasks and rituals performed by the High Priest. The first half of the poem—until the line commencing with the letter *nun* (*Nilvim eilav*)—constitutes an introduction that does no more than trace, chronologically, the early biblical personages, pious and wicked, and God's reaction to their various doings.

It commences with a beautiful description of Creation, moving on to chronicle the sins of Adam and Eve and their punishment, Cain and his retribution, the generation of the flood, and the generation of the dispersion. It then describes the faith of the patriarchs, culminating in Jacob, "from whose loins you drew worthy and beautiful offspring." From those tribes of Israel, God selected Levi to minister to him as priests; and from that holy fraternity "to designate one from his stock to enter the Holy of Holies." Having set the scene, the poem is now ready to deal specifically with the tasks of that chosen High Priest on this special day.

841. Who wrote the *Amitz koach*?

It was written by Meshullam ben Kalonymos (tenth and eleventh century) who is generally regarded as having been an Italian scholar who was brought to Germany by Charlemagne and who laid the foundations of religious life in that country. He is credited with having been one of Rashi's teachers. He was buried in Mainz, where his tombstone was discovered.

His name is interwoven to form the acrostic of the final twenty lines of the poem, which reads *Meshullam Biribbi Kalonymos Chazak*. He is the author of at least eight of the compositions found in our Ashkenazi High Holy Day Prayer Book. Other authors tried their hands at poetic descriptions of the Yom Kippur *Avodah*. The first of these was the early Hebrew poet, Yosi ben Yosi; but it was Meshullam's that won universal acclaim to become the centerpiece of the Yom Kippur *Musaf* service. The Yemenites recite Yosi's *Avodah*.

842. What is the poetic structural design of this poem?

In order that this inordinately long poem should retain its interest, the poet varies his alphabetical structure. Until the letter *samekh* he utilizes quatrains—four-line stanzas—each line of which commences with the same letter of the *alef bet*. For the *samekh* and *ayin* letters, he provides stanzas of eight lines; from *pey* to *shin*, he increases this to twelve-line stanzas, and for *tav*, he provides no fewer than twenty-four lines.

The number of words per line is also varied, commencing with lines of five words, and then, in a most unexpected place, near the very end of the poem and in the middle of his concluding name-acrostic, he changes to lines of four words. To further break the poem up, it is interrupted three times for prostrations and confessions.

ORDER OF THE HIGH PRIEST'S YOM KIPPUR DUTIES

843. What does the second half of *Amitz koach* deal with?

The second half of the poem, beginning with the letter *nun* of the line *Nilvim eilav nevonim*, provides a description of the manifold duties and rituals that the High Priest had to perform on this day in the Temple. This part of the poem is, in turn, divided up into three separate sections by the insertion of the three confession formulae—for the High Priest and his household, for all the offspring of Aaron, and, finally, for the entire house of Israel. The final word of each confession was the Divine Name; and a description is given of the full prostrations made by all present in the Temple when that Name was uttered.

The second half commences with a reference to the elders who guided the High Priest and kept him company during his wakeful vigil on the night of Yom Kippur, familiarizing him with the various types of sacrifices he had to offer and of the importance of only adding the incense to the burning coals once he was inside the Holy of Holies (See Questions 741–742). The poem alludes to the High Priest "quaking and weeping that they should suspect him [of being a Sadducee]," also to his exposition of the laws of Yom Kippur that night, or, if he was not a scholar, to the exposition delivered in his presence by the elders (See Questions 784 and 785). It then refers to the lots that were drawn to determine which priests should have the privilege of removing the previous day's ashes from the altar and the menorah, preparing the incense ritual and the sacrificial parts for burning.

It proceeds to describe the activities that took place as soon as the first light of Yom Kippur day had dawned. They would spread a screen around the High Priest, and he would remove his clothes, immerse himself, and put on his golden vestments (See Question 739). He would then perform a ritual washing of his hands and feet before commencing the slaughtering of the *tamid*, the regular morning continual offering. This was completed by another priest while the High Priest held a basin to receive the blood that flowed from the sacrifice, which he then proceeded to sprinkle on the corners of the altar.

The High Priest would then burn the incense, prepare the menorah, place the sacrificial parts on the altar, and pour wine over it. After that had been completed, he would proceed to the *Parvah* chamber of the Temple, accompanied by the elders. There, they would spread out a white sheet to conceal him while he washed his hands and feet, removed his golden robes, immersed himself, and put on white linen robes, of the finest quality, made in *Pelusium* in Egypt. The bull was then brought to him, and the High Priest placed his hands upon its head and made a wholehearted confession of his own and his household's sins.

VEHA-KOHANIM VEHA-AM

844. This passage refers to the "glorious, awesome and explicit (*meforash*) Name, proceeding from the mouth of the High Priest." To what does this refer?

The *tetragrammaton*, or four-letter (Y-H-V-H) name of God that we are familiar with, was originally pronounced with vowels that have not been preserved. It was originally employed, together with its authentic vowels, each day in the Temple during the priestly blessing of the people.[4] It became known as the *Shem Ha-meforash*, "the explicit Name."

For various reasons, its employment was phased out[5] on a daily basis and preserved only for the High Priest's recitations on Yom Kippur. Even he would recite it inaudibly so that no one else could overhear. Rabbi Tarfon, a priest in whose youth the Temple was destroyed, later related that while giving the priestly blessing on Yom Kippur he inclined his ear to try to catch the pronunciation of the *tetragrammaton* on the lips of the High Priest behind him, but to no avail.[6]

845. How many times did the High Priest employ the authentic Name of God on Yom Kippur?

In all, ten times. Three times during the course of each of the three acts of confession (*Viddui*), and finally, when administering the lots to determine which of the two he-goats shall be *L'Hashem*, "for God." And the Temple congregation would prostrate themselves on each of those ten occasions.

HAYU KOR'IM UMISHTACHAVIM

846. What form did the prostrations in the Temple take?

The precise form of the daily Temple prostrations is a matter of uncertainty. Some authorities believe that it involved bending the knees, followed by *pishut yadayim veraglayim*, the stretching out of the hands and legs, as a token of absolute submission, while others take the view that it was a more simple bending of the knees and bowing, rather than a full prostration. Certainly on Yom Kippur, the communal prostration that accompanied the High Priest's confession involved "bending the knee, prostrating and falling on one's face," with hands and legs fully outstretched.[7]

Outside the Temple, in the houses of prayer, prostrations were practiced in the daily prayers and were an especially prominent feature of the fast day services. At

---

4. Mishnah *Yoma* 3:8.

5. For an account of the history of the employment of the authentic Divine Name in the Temple, see Cohen, J. M. (1993). *Blessed Are You*. Northvale, NJ: Jason Aronson Inc., pp. 7–8.

6. Palestinian *Yoma* 3:7.

7. Mishnah *Yoma* 6:2.

first, there was no regulation governing the number of prostrations or the particular prayers for which they were required. Hence, Rabbi Akivah was famous for the numerous prostrations he made, especially when praying privately.[8]

The rabbis had a tradition that a miracle occurred in the Temple, to the effect that, although while they all stood in the Temple, witnessing the spectacle, they were all pressed tightly together, yet, when they performed their prostrations, there was ample space for all to spread themselves on the ground, to the extent that no one could overhear the other's confession at that time.[9]

BARUKH SHEM KEVOD MALKHUTO LE'OLAM VA'ED

847. Why was this formula used in the Temple as the congregational response to a blessing, whereas the synagogue used, and continues to use, the simple word, Amen?

The Temple authorities preferred this formula ("Blessed be the Name of His glorious kingdom forever and ever" Psalm 72:19) for two main reasons: First and foremost because it is a biblical verse that refers specifically to the *Name* of God and is therefore more appropriate as a response to God's Name in the context of a blessing; secondly, because *Amen* ("It is so") may have been regarded as too absolute an affirmation.

It should be borne in mind that many of the High Priests appointed to the second Temple were adherents of Sadduceanism, which embraced, in many fundamental respects, a variant theology to that of the Pharisees. To recite *Amen* to the blessings or prayers of such a High Priest meant offering blanket confirmation of whatever theological sentiments underpinned his recitations. This the Pharisees were loathe to do. And hence, they pushed through legislation that *Amen* should not be used as a response in the Temple, and, instead, that straightforward biblical verse (*Barukh shem* . . .) be employed.[10]

848. But if we look at Psalm 72:19, we find that the Temple version has added two extra words—*malkhuto* and *va'ed*—to the biblical verse! Why was the word *malkhuto* added?

Indeed, the biblical verse is, simply, *Uvarukh shem kevodo le'olam*. The added word *malkhuto* was introduced by the Pharisaic authorities as part of their nationalistic struggle against the Roman occupation. The word *malkhut* is the one universally employed by the Talmudic sages to describe the detested Roman "kingdom." By introducing that word into their formula of divine praise, the sages

---

8. *Berakhot* 31a.
9. Mishnah *Avot* 5:8.
10. For more on the employment of Amen and *Barukh shem* . . . in the Temple, See Cohen, J. M., *op. cit.*, p. 217.

were implying that it is *God*'s kingdom alone that is to be blessed, and the other Roman kingdom that is execrated.

849. Why was the word *va'ed* added?

This was also added for polemical reasons, this time to constitute a broadside against the Sadducean rejection of the doctrine of the World to Come. *Va'ed* is an elyptical construction that stands for *ve'ad [ha'olam]*, "and until the World [to Come]." The Pharisees were concerned that some may interpret *le'olam* here, not in its sense of "forever," but as meaning "in the world." They wished, therefore, to emphasize that God's Name is not only blessed in this world, but also in the World to Come, hence, the addition of the word *va'ed*.

850. Why are two people deputed to help the *Chazan* rise to his feet after prostrating himself on the ground, whereas they do not assist the rabbi?

The reason is that the *Chazan* is prohibited from moving from his place, or even moving his feet, in the middle of the *Amidah*, even for the sake of making such a prostration. Technically, therefore, he would have to remain standing in his place while the congregation performs the prostrations. However, this was regarded as even more inappropriate, as it gives the impression that he is dissociating himself from this communal token of obeisance. The practice, therefore, developed for the *Chazan* to make the prostration, but in such a way that he still keeps his legs together. This is done by his standing a little back from his reading desk at the commencement of the repetition of the *Amidah* to give himself room to prostrate in this way. While he has little difficulty in making the prostration to the ground, it is not at all easy for him to lever himself up again into a standing position without moving his legs unless he is supported and raised by two people, one on either side. The rabbi, on the other hand, may move his legs freely during the repetition of the *Amidah*, and, unless he is elderly or frail, does not require such support.

VE'AF HU HAYAH MITKAVEIN

851. What was the purpose of the High Priest "intending to complete the Name simultaneously with those reciting the blessing (*Barukh shem . . . le'olam va'ed*)?"

It had a twofold purpose. First, it ensured that the High Priest was able to conceal the proper pronunciation of the Divine Name, which had to be kept secret from anyone outside his fraternity (See Question 844). The sound of the entire congregation uttering the blessing would have muffled the sound of the holy Name. Secondly, it meant that, at the precise moment when the High Priest finished uttering the divine Name, in the biblical verse *Ki ba-yom ha-zeh yekhapper aleikhem . . . lifnei Ha-Shem [titharu]* ("For on this day he shall atone for you . . . before the Lord [you shall be cleansed]"), the congregation were also completing their *Barukh shem* response to its recitation. This meant that the voice of the High Priest could then be heard by all, confidently proclaiming the final word, *titharu*, assuring the assembled masses that "you shall be cleansed."

TZA'AD LEILEKH LO LEMIZRACH AZARAH

852. We have already referred to the contents of the second part of *Amitz koach* (See Question 843), until where it is interrupted by the High Priest's first confession (*Vekhakh hayah omeir*), followed by the communal prostration in the Temple. What does the next section of this long composition deal with?

The next section is very brief by comparison and comprises merely the fourteen phrases commencing with the letter *tzadi*. It continues the account of the High Priest's ministrations at the point where it left off. He would "stride to the east of the Temple courtyard," where he found a pair of he-goats that were to serve as sin-offerings for the nation, for which reason they were purchased from community funds. These were of similar size and appearance. The High Priest then drew the golden lots to determine which would be dispatched ignominiously to *Azazel* and which would be ceremoniously offered as a sacrifice to the Most High (See Questions 743 and 856).

It proceeds to describe how the High Priest would first tie some red-dyed wool to the head of the *Azazel* goat before pointing it in the direction it was to be driven. He would then go back to the bull and would confess over it the iniquity of his priestly tribe.

KACH MA'AKHELET CHADAH

853. The poem is interrupted again at this point for a further confession, this time to include not only him and his household, but also his priestly tribe, as well as for a further prostration. What High Priestly ministrations are described in the section that follows this?

This section, commencing with the line *Kach ma'akhelet chadah*, comprises twenty-four phrases, each commencing with the letter *kuf*, that continue the description of the High Priest's duties. It tells of the slaughtering of the bull "with a sharp knife according to the proper procedure" (See Question 854) and the collecting of its blood in a basin. This would be passed to another priest whose task was to keep stirring it to avoid it becoming congealed before having been sprinkled on the altar. This was because atonement was effected by the commingling of the blood with the altar, to symbolize the sinner's preparedness to surrender his very life if God deemed his sin so heinous as to require it.

The poem then describes how the High Priest would take a long-handled, three-walled shovel, with which he would scoop up some burning coals from the altar. He then took two handfuls of fine incense from a container they brought him, and placed it into a special ladle, which he transferred to his left hand, and, picking up the shovel of hot coals with his right, he quickly passed between the two curtains that separated the Holy of Holies from the rest of the Temple, making his way round to where the staves of the Ark protruded through the inner curtain that concealed the Holy of Holies. He would then place the incense on the coals to create the smoke screen (See Questions 741 and 742), before retracing his steps to outside the outer curtain. Waiting for him there was the priest who had been stirring the blood. The High Priest took it from him and immediately reentered the Holy of Holies, placing himself between the two protruding staves of the Ark, and readying himself to perform the sprinkling of the blood.

854. What is the special significance of being told that the bull was dispatched "with a sharp knife, according to the proper procedure"?

In our contemporary age, when the Jewish method of *Shechitah* is regularly impugned, and in some countries outlawed, it is highly significant to note that Jewish law has always insisted on the most humane and painless method of dispatch. The "sharp knife," slicing through the carotid artery and jugular vein in an instant, causes an immediate drop in blood pressure that renders the animal senseless and immune to pain. Cruelty to animals is a cardinal crime in Judaism, and the sacrificial system was not only no exception, but, indeed, a prime demonstration of this principle in action.

VEKHAKH HAYAH MONEH

855. What is the meaning of the statement, "And so he would count: One, one plus one; one plus two; one plus three," etc.?

This describes how the High Priest performed the sprinkling of the blood. He began by dipping his finger into the bowl, and, with an upward flicking action, he would direct some blood toward the cover of the Ark, counting, "*achat*" (one). He would then repeat that action and accompany it with another flick of blood downward, toward the side of the Ark, reciting *achat ve'achat* ("one plus one"). He would then continue, with one upward flick (*achat*) and two downward flicks (*ushtayim*), and so on, with but one upward flick (*achat*), but increasing each time the number of downward flicks until he reached a total of seven (*achat vasheva*).

He then left that holy place quickly, placing the basin of blood on a stand as he left to go and slaughter the he-goat that had been designated "For God" (See Question 845). Having collected its blood, he would return to the place of the previous sprinkling of the bull's blood and repeat the sprinkling with the blood of the he-goat, counting in the identical way: *achat, achat ve'achat*, etc.

The High Priest would then run (to avoid the blood of the bull congealing) to the stand where he had previously put down the basin of bull's blood and would pick up the latter and replace it with the basin of he-goat's blood. He would then race back to the embroidered curtain that separated the Holy of Holies from the sanctuary, and he would repeat the sevenfold sprinkling ritual against that curtain, taking care to call out the precise number (*achat, achat ve'achat, achat ushtayim,* etc.) each time. He would then rush out and repeat the entire procedure in order to sprinkle the blood of the he-goat against that embroidered curtain. Finally, he would mix the bloods and sprinkle them upon the golden altar, situated inside the sanctuary, on which the incense was burned each day. He would then approach the remaining he-goat, designated for *Azazel*, and he would recite over it the confession of the entire community (*Vekhakh hayah omeir* . . .). Once again, at the mention of the divine Name, the entire Temple congregation would prostrate itself fully (*Veha-kohanim veha'am* . . .).

SHIGRO BEYAD ISH ITTIY

856. What procedures are described in the final section of the poem, covering the letters *shin* and *tav*?

The final section covers the letters *shin* and *tav* of the alphabetical acrostic that comprises this lengthy poetic description of the Temple *Avodah*. There are eight phrases (four lines) commencing with the letter *shin*, and twenty-four phrases commencing with the letter *tav*.

This final part describes the sending away of the *Seir Ha-mishtale'ach*, the he-goat designated by lot for *Azazel*, to meet a violent death and carry into oblivion the sins of Israel.

The courier chosen from before Yom Kippur to guide this goat to its destination in the desert and to direct it over a precipice is called, simply, the *ish ittiy*, "the appointed man," though no details are given of how the appointment is to be made or the criteria for appointment. It is almost as if tradition wanted him to remain anonymous, like some executioner with his face concealed. This was not, in practice, the case, however, since he was accompanied on his trek into the desert by the notables of Jerusalem and provided with refreshment at each of the ten service stations along the way. His task was indubitably an honorable one, but, in order not to detract from the High Priest—the central figure in the day's dramatic events— scant importance is accorded to his appointment.

Our poem also devotes scant attention to this task, other than to state that he took the goat to an isolated place in the harsh desert, where he would push it off a rocky cliff, "its bones disintegrating like crushed earthenware." The poet then immediately returns to what is going on center stage, with the High Priest engaged in tearing open the carcass of the bull and the he-goat, "with a sharpened knife" (See Question 854), in order to remove the parts to be offered on the altar. The remainder of the carcasses of both the bull and the he-goat were intertwined and carried out of Jerusalem to be deposited on the tip where the residue of the altar ashes were placed.

The High Priest then read aloud the day's Torah readings, after which he washed his hands and feet in the special Temple laver. Next, he removed his linen robes and made a further ritual immersion before putting on, once again, his golden vestments.

He then washed his hands and feet again before proceeding to offer his own ram, to atone for the sins of himself, his family, and the priestly fraternity, and the ram that was to atone for the sins of the nation. Once again, he washed his hands and feet before removing the golden vestments. He immersed himself fully before donning, once again, a new set of linen garments to reenter the sanctuary in order to collect the shovel of coals and the incense ladle that he had previously left in the Holy of Holies. On returning, he would wash his hands and feet before removing his white linen garments and storing them away in that special chamber, never to be used again.

He then immersed himself fully once more, before donning his splendid golden robes to complete the service, which involved offering up the late afternoon continual offering (*tamid shel bein ha-arbayim*) and kindling the Temple menorah. The poem then reminds us that, in all, the High Priest completed five full immersions and ten "sanctifications," that is the washing of hands and feet. It goes on to describe the beauty and spiritual glow that illuminated the face of the High Priest as he completed his awesome and physically grueling ministrations and how, after he had put on his own clothing, he would be joyously escorted home by an excited throng of his friends and well-wishers, for whom he would make a great celebration to express his relief at having returned safely from his hazardous entry into the Holy of Holies. He was also buoyed up by the goodwill and blessing of an entire people, confident of having received forgiveness and grace through the worthiness of their pious representative.

857. You mentioned that this courier was offered refreshment as he guided the he-goat to its doom in the desert. But how could he accept food and drink on Yom Kippur?

His ministrations were an extension of the Temple ritual, and just as in the Temple some holy day prohibitions may be set aside in the service of the higher ritual, such as the offering of sacrifices on the Sabbath and festivals, so could the law of fasting be set aside by this courier, given that he was walking along hilly and rough terrain under the hot desert sun. Without such refreshment, he could not have survived; and the Torah itself states, "You shall live through them [the performance of *mitzvot*]," but you may not perform any *mitzvah* that endangers your life.[11]

VEYOM TOV HAYAH OSEH

858. Are there any significant poetic or other features of this "Prayer of the High Priest when he left the Holy of Holies in peace without injury"?

The version of it found in our *machzorim* is a poetic expansion of that found in the Babylonian and Palestinian Talmud. Here it is cast into an alphabetical acrostic,

---

11. The exception to this principle is the act of martyrdom for the Sanctification of the name of God.

and it may be more than coincidental that the word *shanah* ("year") occurs twenty-four times—a multiple of the number of months in the year. The number twenty-four may reflect the fact that the High Priest was praying for twelve months of happiness both for his own family and, in addition, for the whole community.

The version that we have is clearly a composite, with individual pleas that have been inserted at different times, and that reflect the critical situations that inspired them. Thus, the plea for "a year in which we may enter our Temple" is rather anachronistic in the context of a prayer that purports to be that of a High Priest in Temple times! We must assume, then, that it infiltrated this High Priest's prayer from another context. It may have arisen as a congregational petition composed during the difficult Maccabean period (67–65 b.c.e.) when the Greeks overran and polluted the Temple, and Jews were prevented from entering it.

Similarly anachronistic in the context of a High Priest's prayer is the insertion of a plea for "a year wherein You will lead us straight to our land." This plea was clearly created by Jews who had been taken into captivity, probably after the destruction of the Temple (70 c.e.). They obviously saw no difficulty in superimposing their own nationalistic sentiments upon the original version of the High Priest's prayer, which they employed for nostalgic reasons during their Yom Kippur prayers in the lands of their dispersal.

VE'AL ANSHEI HA-SHARON HAYAH OMEIR

859. What is the meaning of this particular plea for the men of the Sharon plain, "that their homes should not become their graves"?

This is popularly explained as having been necessitated by the fact that the heavy rains made the clay soil in that area unsuitable for building upon. The water would collect upon the roofs of the houses and eventually seep through the walls, rotting them and causing the roofs to collapse inwards upon the heads of the inhabitants.

Some scholars suggest, however, that the fear being expressed here was not rain, for which preventive action could be taken by the regular monitoring and strengthening of the roofs and walls, but rather the fear of the sudden and devastating earthquakes that were not unknown in that Sharon area. Josephus records a quake, unprecedented in violence, as having occurred in 31 b.c.e., during which 3,000 people were buried under the debris of their houses.[12] Another such quake was recorded in the area of Lydda and Emmaus, around the year 130 c.e.[13] Such a peremptory and violent visitation would seem to accord more with the sentiment of the prayer: "that their homes should not become their graves."

---

12. Josephus, F. (1926–1963). *Antiquities of the Jews.* London: The Loeb Classical Library, vol. 15, p. 121.

13. Luria, B. Z. (1966). *"Tefillat Kohen Ha-gadol Beyom Ha-kippurim."* Sinai, p. 208, n. 16.

860. What is the relevance of reciting all those details of the sacrificial order of Temple times?

This question is frequently asked, especially in the light of the fact that our daily prayers contain a number of references to the sacrificial system. It has to be said that there are those—albeit a minority—who look forward to the restoration of animal sacrifices in the rebuilt third Temple. For such people, these references are, naturally, most relevant, as preserving the precise details and regulations of the system.

Indeed, the Talmudic sages encouraged the recitation of those Scriptural and rabbinic passages relating to the sacrifices, in the belief that, just as synagogue prayer replaced Temple sacrifices, so synagogue recitations relating to specific sacrifices (*Korbanot*) are as effective in securing atonement as the actual offering of those sacrifices.

Viewed in this light, even the more sophisticated, who are not looking forward to the reintroduction of the sacrificial system, may yet view those references as helpful toward generating that same repentant spirit that infused the donors of sacrifices in Temple times.

There is also another way of approaching this problem, and that is to view the Temple references as part of the essential Jewish charter that reinforces our historical claim to Jerusalem and the site of the Temple. This may seem unnecessary in the context of modern Israel; but it is a fact that, for 1,900 years, the recitation of such *Korbanot* helped to keep the flame of Zionism burning within the Jewish emotion. Reciting those passages transported the Jew back in time, rooting him to the homeland from which he was banished, and investing him with emotional and spiritual citizenship of Jerusalem in the absence of any such temporal identity and reality. They thus helped to inspire and give impetus to the modern-day movement of political Zionism.

861. So, in what way is the recitation of this *Avodah* so different from that of the other sacrificial passages in our prayer book?

On Yom Kippur, we do not merely read the account of the Temple ritual, but we actually recite it, word-for-word, together with the *Chazan*, as if we were ourselves performing the *Avodah*. We even echo the words of the High Priest as he daubed the blood—*Achat, achat ve'achat*. And we prostrate ourselves in the same way as did the Temple congregation as they heard the divine Name pronounced. At this moment, we do not read, as mere passive spectators. We minister. We relive the experience. We atone—as at no other moment—for ourselves and our families; for our friends and community; and for the whole house of Israel.

EMET MAH NEHDAR HAYAH KOHEIN GADOL

862. What is the purpose of this composition, extolling the High Priest in the most exaggerated of terms?

It is true that the author's poetic spirit soars aloft unfettered in this description of the majesty of the High Priest as he emerged safely from the Holy of Holies:

Like the heavenly canopy stretched over those who dwell on high—was the appearance of the High Priest. Like lightning bolts proceeding forth from the splendour of God's *Chayyot*—was the appearance of the High Priest. Like the image of the rainbow amid the clouds. . . . Like a crown that is placed on a king's forehead. . . . Like the morning star on the eastern border. . . . Like a chamber hung with blue and purple tapestries. . . .

The hyperbole was introduced here for very special contextual reasons. Having dealt at length with Yom Kippur past, namely with the High Priestly rituals in the Temple, the liturgy is about to change its mood and focus upon Yom Kippur present, namely all that has been lost since the destruction of the Temple and the cessation of its rich ritual. The latter theme will lead naturally into a series of compositions that chronicle the generational tragedies that have befallen our people since the end of that glorious period of Temple Judaism and Jewish independence and sovereignty. The climax of these compositions is the *Eileh ezkerah* dirge, recounting the execution of the Ten Martyrs.

We can thus see very clearly the literary design of these compositions, with the hyperbolic description of the High Priest serving as the idyllic and radiant backcloth against which the dark swathes of the contrasting later martyrology are drawn.

EILEH EZKERAH: THE TEN MARTYRS

863. Is not this dirge, lamenting the cruel execution of ten of the most illustrious luminaries of the Mishnaic age (first and second centuries c.e.), more appropriate for a fast day than for this festival when atonement, not persecution, is our primary concern?

The point is well taken, especially by Sephardic rites, which recite *Eileh ezkerah* on the Fast of Tisha-b'Ab, when we commemorate the destruction of the Temple. However, there is a justification for its place here, at the point where we have highlighted the sad contrast between the glorious Temple era, on the one hand, and its tragic aftermath, on the other.

The sages had no doubt that the loss of Jewish statehood was to be attributed directly to Israel's sinfulness, as clearly expressed in the prayer *Umipnei chata'einu galinu me'artzeinu*, "And because of our sins we were exiled from our land." Thus, on this day, when we confront sin head-on, it is appropriate to highlight the most obvious and painful example of its catastrophic effects.

864. What is the historical background of the events described in this dirge?

It is set in the period of the Hadrianic persecutions that followed the abortive Bar Kochba revolt (132–135 c.e.). The emperor Hadrian imposed unacceptable edicts outlawing the study of Torah, the practice of circumcision, and other basic observances, on pain of death. Many great rabbis and teachers suffered martyrdom as a result of their heroic defiance of the edicts, though it has to be said that there are no ancient sources—rabbinic or external—that refer to these particular ten leaders as having been tried and executed at one and the same time. Nor is the term *Asarah harugei malkhut* ("Ten Martyrs") found anywhere in the Talmudic literature.

It is only in a minor work of the Talmudic period, the *Midrash of Lamentations*, that a list of martyrs of the period is given. Although the list contains ten names, the term "Ten Martyrs" is not applied to them. It is only in the little known *Midrash Eileh ezkerah* that the term is used, together with the rationale of their plight, namely as an expiation of the sin of the brothers of Joseph.

865. Is it not strange that the Talmud should nowhere have referred to such an unprecedented demonstration of martyrdom?

It is, in fact, not only uncharacteristic but absolutely inconceivable that the Talmudic sages would have omitted a reference to the execution of ten of their colleagues on one day! We must doubt, therefore, its historicity, and conclude that the author of our *Eileh ezkerah*, in his wish to heighten the dramatic effect of his elegy, decided to condense martyrological traditions about various sages who lived and perished during the turbulent period of the great rebellion (66–70 C.E.), the uprising against Trajan (117 C.E.), and the Hadrianic persecutions.

The ten sages enumerated here were not, in fact, all contemporaneous. One of the sages referred to is "Rabbi Ishmael the High Priest, who, purified himself and uttered the Name." He clearly ministered before the destruction of the Temple in the year 70 C.E., as did Rabban Shimon ben Gamliel, neither of whom could have been a colleague of the other martyrs of that group who perished during the Hadrianic persecutions some 70 years later!

866. So where would our poet have gotten his notion of the ten martyrs from?

It is likely that the inspiration for the idea of the number ten came from a circle of mystics of the Talmudic period who, in their attempt to link cause and effect, sin and its expiation, depicted the martyrdom of the ten great sages as an effect of the sin of Jacob's ten sons in selling their brother Joseph into slavery, which episode is referred to in the opening section of the *Eileh ezkerah.*

Solomon Zeitlin[14] traces the origin of this legend to the author of the extra-Canonical Book of Jubilees, written around 150 B.C.E. In this book, it is stated that the Day of Atonement was fixed on the tenth day of the seventh month because that was the day when the children of Jacob dipped their brother Joseph's coat into the blood of the kid they had slaughtered. That sin, he states, was never forgiven, for which reason it was ordained that their offspring, the Children of Israel, should afflict themselves on that day that their ancestors brought to their father the news and made him grieve. For the same reason they must atone for themselves with a young goat.

It is now easy to see how this explanation of the significance of the Day of

14. Zeitlin, S. (1945). "The Legend of the Ten Martyrs and its Apocalyptic Origins." *Jewish Quarterly Review* 36:1–16.

Atonement gave birth to the legend of ten martyrs suffering in expiation for the sins of Joseph's ten brothers, and how our *Eileh ezkerah* came to be written under the influence of that book of Jubilees.[15]

For biographical details of each of the ten martyrs referred to, See my *Prayer and Penitence*, pp. 229–239. On *Ashamnu* and *Al Chet*, See Questions 762–768. On the priestly blessing of the congregation, See Questions 557–565.

WHY NO *EIN KELOHEINU*?

867. Why does the *Musaf* service conclude with kaddish and omit the usual Sabbath and *Yom Tov* recitation of *Ein Keloheinu*?

Two explanations are offered. The first takes account of the *Kol Bo*'s suggestion that one of the objectives of *Ein Keloheinu* is to serve as a supplement to the number of blessings recited during the course of the Sabbaths and festival services, which do not quite reach the required 100 blessings. The concise blessings of God contained in this hymn are therefore construed as blessings in their own right (See Question 573). On Yom Kippur, when the entire day is spent in blessings, petitions, and praises of God, the question of a requisite number of blessings is not a consideration.

The *Kol Bo*'s rationale is suspect, however, as we have explained (See Question 574), and a more likely explanation for the non-recitation of *Ein Keloheinu* on Yom Kippur takes account of its final phrase—*Attah hu shehiktiru avoteinu lefanekha et ketoret ha-samim*—"You are the One before Whom our fathers offered their fragrant incense." This phrase links the hymn with the succeeding Mishnah, *Pittum Ha-ketoret*, dealing with the preparation of the individual spices that went into the incense offering on the Temple altar.

It would constitute unnecessary repetition, therefore, to refer to the incense offering at this point in the service, since we have not long before recited the lengthy *Avodah* service, with its comprehensive description of all the sacrifices offered on this day, including the incense offering. So, because *Ein Keloheinu* and the Mishnah *Pittum Ha-ketoret* constitute one thematic unit, the exclusion of the Mishnah meant that *Ein Keloheinu* was jettisoned with it.

WHY NO *ALEINU*?

868. All synagogue services conclude with *Aleinu*. Why is *Musaf* on Yom Kippur an exception?

It is not an exception, as the *Minchah* service also omits the *Aleinu*. The reason for both omissions is the same and takes account of the fact that *Aleinu* is invested

---

15. For a fuller treatment of *Eileh ezkerah*, See Cohen, J. M., *op.cit.*, pp. 226–229.

with the status of marking the effective conclusion of every act of worship. Now, as regards the *Musaf* and *Minchah* services, we are not, in effect, concluding an act of worship, since we proceed immmediately into the following services, *Minchah* and *Neilah* respectively. (For the same reason, we do not recite *Aleinu* after the Sabbath morning *Shachrit* service, because we are leading straight into *Musaf*.)

XXVI

Minchah and the Book of Jonah

NO *ASHREI* AND *UVAH LETZIYYON?*

869. Why do we omit *Ashrei* and *Uva letziyyon*, which constitute the usual introduction to the Sabbath and festival *Minchah* service?

There are two reasons for this. Because by the time we finish *Musaf*, we are well into the prescribed time for the recitation of *Minchah*, coupled with the fact that there is a lengthy reading from the Torah and an even lengthier *Haftarah* (the book of Jonah) before we get to the *Amidah*. It was felt therefore, that we should proceed to the *Minchah Amidah* with as little delay as possible by curtailing the *Ashrei* and *Uva letziyyon*, and moving them, instead, to the *Neilah* service. The reading of the Torah is regarded, in this instance, as constituting a worthy replacement introduction to the *Amidah*.

The second reason may well be to maintain the literality of the Talmudic assurance that "Whoever recites *Tehillah le-David (Ashrei) three times* daily is assured of a place in the World to Come"[1] (See Question 824).

NO *VA'ANIY TEFILATIY?*

870. Why do we omit the usual verse that is introduced at *Minchah* as a prelude to *Vayehi binso'a ha-aron*, namely, *Va'aniy tefilatiy lekha Ha-Shem eit ratzon* . . . ?

We omit this verse because the sentiments are not appropriate to the occasion. The verse says: "And, as for me, my prayer comes to Thee at a time of good will." *Minchah* has always been regarded as a time of special grace, when God is most amenable to receive our petitions. This is derived from the fact that Elijah's sacrifice was accepted and his superiority over the prophets of Baal vindicated, at *Minchah* time.[2] Yom Kippur, however, is the exception, because we cannot have the temerity, when our fate hangs in the balance and we are suffering a solemn fast day, to be so self-assured as to express such a certainty that it will be for "a time of good will."[3]

---

1. *Berakhot* 4b.
2. I Kings 18:36–38.
3. *Tur Orach Chayyim*, sec. 622.

THE READING OF THE LAW: *PARASHAT ARAYOT*

871. Why do we read the portion (Leviticus, chapter 18) dealing with *Arayot* (forbidden sexual relations) on Yom Kippur, of all days?

It should, indeed, be taken for granted that sex and especially incestuous and adulterous relations are the last things on people's minds at such a time. Apart from the awe of the day, the long fast, of itself, generally induces a physical languor that should leave the emotions immune to such thoughts.

Several explanations have been offered to account for this strange choice of reading. The first is that, notwithstanding what we have assumed, the sex urge is so powerful that, even on such a holy day, people can be distracted by the sight of the opposite sex, all dressed in their best clothes. Freud would agree!

Tosafot[4] quotes an interesting Midrashic explanation, which views it as a ploy to induce God to be merciful to Israel. By reading the lengthy catalog of those "whose nakedness we may not uncover," we are sending a subliminal message to God that He, likewise, should not uncover our spiritual nakedness and expose our moral vulnerability.

A further reason relates to the tradition that at an early period in our history, Yom Kippur was a day when a romantic match-making ritual would be staged. The young women of marriageable age would dress up in white and dance in the vineyards, inviting the young men to select their life's partner (See Questions 744 and 745). A portion of the law that draws attention to the prohibited categories of marriage partners (*arayot*) was considered, therefore, as most timely and relevant.

872. Is there any other, less speculative, explanation of this strange choice of reading?

I have suggested elsewhere[5] that the identical rationale underlies the choice of both the *Arayot* Torah reading and also the book of Jonah as *Haftarah*. The motivation of both readings is to draw attention to the moral and spiritual exclusiveness of Israel and the dangers of her fraternization with the surrounding nations. On Yom Kippur, the special relationship and historical covenant that exists between God and Israel is a central argument in our plea for mercy. The need to stress our superior moral stature over those nations would certainly have been felt in that context. Hence, the choice of *Parashat Arayot*, with its ringing warning to Israel to remain aloof from, and "not to walk in the statutes of," the land of Egypt and the land of Canaan. It goes on to describe the "defilement" and "abominations" wrought by the inhabitants of those lands.

This doctrine of *exclusivity*, we suggest, is at the core of the choice of the reading for this special day. And this is reinforced by the *Haftarah*, which describes a prophet who was uncompromising in his efforts to leave the *goyim* to their own

4. *Tosafot* on *Megilah* 31a.
5. Cohen, J. M. (1994). *Prayer and Penitence*. Northvale, NJ: Jason Aronson Inc., pp. 244–245.

devices and their own doom. His philosophy was that Israel has no interest at all in their spiritual welfare. She has to keep aloof and regard them as a historic and contemporary source of defilement. And the first-century rabbis who not only included Jonah in the Canon of Holy Scriptures, but also prescribed its reading— together with *Parashat Arayot*—for the holiest day of the year, were sending that strong, clear, and uncompromising message to their communities (See also Question 906).

This battening down of the hatch was just one of the many preparations they made at that time for the violent clash with Rome, and also with internal sectarian dissidents, that they saw looming on the horizon. It was also an understandable emotional response to the religious, moral, and national hurt that they were suffering at the hands of a callous heathen invader.

THE BOOK OF JONAH

Chapter I

873. What are the contents of the first chapter of Jonah?

It opens with God appearing to the prophet and commanding him to go to Nineveh, the capital city of Assyria, and to "proclaim against her" on account of her evildoing. In order to escape his mission, Jonah makes his way to Joppa (Jaffa) and boards a ship leaving for Tarshish. God stirs up a violent storm that threatens to overturn the vessel, and, after jettisoning the cargo, the mariners turn to prayer— each to his own god—as a last resort. Jonah is chastized by the captain for sleeping, instead of praying to his God.

They all cast lots in order to determine the identity of the one who is displeasing his god, and the lot falls on Jonah, who discloses to them his Jewish identity and why his God is angry with him. Jonah advises them that they have no alternative but to tip him overboard if they wish to be saved.

The mariners vainly attempt to row to the safety of the shore, after which they then turn in earnest petition to the God of Israel, saying: "O Lord, let us not perish at the price of this man's life; do not charge us with the death of an innocent man" (verse 14). They then reluctantly throw Jonah overboard, and the sea ceases its raging. The mariners, burdened with guilt and fear at what they have done, propitiate the God of Jonah and "offer sacrifices and make vows."

874. Are there any messages to be taken from this opening chapter?

The first and foremost message is that there is no fleeing from before God. The Jews of Jonah's day may well have espoused the fairly universal concept of a deity's influence being confined to the geographical parameter of its adherents; and one of the book's purposes is to disabuse them of such a notion in relation to the God of Israel.

The second message is the universalistic one that is central to the entire book.

Already a certain positive image of the idolatrous mariners is presented, whereby, although they are patently in error, their warm piety and instinctive appeal to the power of prayer stands in stark contrast to Jonah's overt indifference.

The mariners' concern for the fate of Jonah is particularly enigmatic. Mariners have never been known for putting much of a premium on the lives of strangers, especially those who threaten their own safety. In ancient folklore, they are portrayed as rough and violent scoundrels, out to get their hands on the money and belongings of their passengers. Yet here we have a picture of a crew that is overflowing with the milk of human kindness! They row hard to reach the shore in order to save the life of Jonah—a total stranger and foreigner, traveling without any protector or companion—and they do all in their power to avoid having to offer him as a sacrifice to his vengeful God. Furthermore, their conscience burdens them to such an extent that they beg God not to charge them with having shed innocent blood, because clearly they had had no choice.

This latter episode is clearly intended to be used as a backcloth against which to measure, adversely, Jonah's total indifference to the shedding of the blood of the "one hundred and twenty thousand Ninevites who cannot tell their right hand from their left" (4:11). This is reinforced by the last verse of the chapter, which describes the mariners' "great fear of the Lord." Jonah, on the other hand, has no such "fear." He is only concerned for his own reputation. If he is to convey God's threat, then it has to be carried out, unconditionally.

875. But how could the prophet of God presume to flee from the presence of the God of whose existence and omniscience he had had personal confirmation?

This is, of course, the first and foremost problem of the book, one which has exercised the minds of commentators, students, and readers from time immemorial. Some writers, such as the fourteenth-century commentator, Joseph ibn Caspi,[6] regard the first two chapters of the book as nothing more than a prophetic dream or nightmare, induced by fear and apprehension at having to undertake this dangerous mission to a land of violent idolators.

Eliakim Ben-Menachem[7] claims that this is also the view of Maimonides, who, in his *Guide for the Perplexed*, refers to prophetic allegories wherein

> certain objects are seen by the prophet, acts are performed (if the style of the allegory demands it), things are done, the intervals between one act and another, as well as a series of journeys undertaken, are presented as true happenings, whereas they are, in fact, only processes of a prophetic vision. Some of the accounts simply relate these incidents [without indicating that they are part of a vision] because it is obvious. . . .[8]

---

6. Joseph ibn Caspi, Adnei Ha-Kasef (ed. I. H. Last, London, 1911), Introduction.

7. Eliakim Ben-Menachem, *Da'at Mikra on Jonah*, Mosad Ha-Rav Kuk (1973). Introduction.

8. Maimonides, M. (1965). *Guide to the Perplexed*, trans. M. Friedlander. New York: Hebrew Publishing Company, p. 215.

The correctness of this theory cannot be doubted, and only those do not comprehend it who do not know to distinguish between that which is possible and that which is impossible. The instances quoted may serve as an illustration of other similar Scriptural passages not quoted by me.[9]

Thus, by postulating that Jonah only dreamt that he had fled from his mission, but did not actually do so in the cold light of reality, our problem is resolved.

876. What is the meaning of the name Nineveh?

It comes from an Assyrian name *Ninua* and is probably named after a god with an association with a fish. According to Genesis 10:10–12, it was founded in the days of Nimrod, immediately after the flood. We may conjecture, therefore, that it was so named because of the large swarms of fish that the flood deposited on the banks of the Tigris at that point.

877. Where is Nineveh?

It is situated about 1.5 kilometers east of the River Tigris, opposite the city of *Mosul* and about 10 kilometers north of where the Upper Zob tributary branches off the Tigris, wending its way eastward. That Assyrian city fell to the Babylonians in 612 B.C.E., and was totally destroyed.

878. Is there any local tradition that associates the locality of Nineveh with Jonah?

There is. West of the site of the city there is an ancient fortress within which are the remains of royal palaces and holy sites. To the south of the fortress is a small *tel*, which is still called *Nabi Yonis* ("Prophet Jonah"). This is regarded as the traditional burial place of the prophet and is revered by the Muslims who have built a large mosque over it.

879. What is the meaning of the name Jonah?

The Hebrew name, *Yonah*, means "dove" or "pigeon," though it is difficult to link any symbolic significance regarding his name to any events described in the book. By the same token, there is no apparent significance in the name of Moses' wife, Tzipporah, meaning, "little bird, birdie." It would seem to be merely a term of endearment. In the Song of Songs, the shepherdess sings of her beloved and describes him as *"Yonati* ("my dove") in the clefts of the rock" (2:14). The dove is, of course, the bird of peace, which is somewhat ironic when applied to the prophet Jonah, who preferred the path of zealotry to that of pacifism!

---

9. *Op. cit.*, p. 218.

880. So can we not even offer a speculative theory as to the relevance of Jonah's name to the events described in the book that bears his name?

You asked for it! Perhaps we are meant to view Jonah by name-association with the dove (*yonah*) that was sent out by Noah to ascertain whether the waters had subsided after the terrible flood that wiped out mankind. Both Noah's dove and the prophet who bore its name were saved from a watery grave by being enclosed within a sealed capsule: the dove within Noah's Ark; the prophet within the belly of the fish.

Secondly, both of them fled from the one who was their refuge and protector: Jonah from God; the dove from Noah, once the waters had dried up (Genesis 8:12).

Thirdly, in both contexts, the unit of 40 days is significant: the waters of the flood continued incessantly for 40 days, and the Ninevites were given that precise period in which to repent or suffer the consequences.

Rejecting a divine instruction

881. Was Jonah unique in rejecting a divine instruction of this kind?

No, he was not. Jonah was following in the footsteps of other giants of the spirit who challenged the justice of, and mustered powerful and fearless opposition to, a divine decree.

To mention but two examples, Abraham challenged repeatedly God's decree to destroy Sodom and Gemorah: "Shall the judge of the whole world not execute justice?" (Genesis 18:25) he daringly cried. And from him Moses took his cue when he called into question, on several occasions, not only God's condonement of Israel's harsh treatment at the hands of the Egyptians,[10] but God's own considered judgment of doom on a backsliding Israel.[11]

882. But were there any other prophets who, like Jonah, actually sought to escape from the divine summons that they don the mantle of prophecy?

There were, indeed. Moses was the first to do so on receiving, at the Divine revelation to him at the Burning Bush, the instruction to go and "bring out My people, the children of Israel from Egypt" (Exodus 3:10). His immediate reply was, "Who am I that I should go to Pharaoh and that I should bring forth the children of Israel out of Egypt?" (verse 11). Moses followed that attempt at escaping his mission with an outright rejection: "Oh Lord, I am not a man of words . . . for I am hesitant of speech and slow of tongue" (Exodus 4:11).

Isaiah was another great prophet who, at the very outset, was overawed by his unworthiness to don the mantle of prophecy: "Woe is me! I am lost, for I am a man

---

10. Exodus 5:22–23.
11. Exodus 32:11–13, 32.

of unclean lips, and I dwell among a people of unclean lips; yet with these eyes have I seen the King, the Lord of Hosts" (6:5).

And even the courageous Jeremiah's response to his "call" was to attempt to escape it all costs: "Ah! Lord God, I answered, I do not know how to speak; I am only a child" (1:6).

God, of course, knows in advance that His great leaders will question, and even reject on occasions, His decrees. It is His way of rewarding those prophets by seemingly changing His mind at their behest—though, in truth, He had never framed any such irrevocable decree. He was merely awaiting, and utilizing, their intercession, their prayer, and the merit of their concern for their people, as an excuse for allowing the exercise of His mercy to vanquish that of His strict justice. At other times, He stands His ground and allows their criticisms, frustration, and anger to be ventilated before disclosing to them the mystery and the justice of His decision.

883. But surely no other prophet expressed such feelings of deepest depression as vehemently as did Jonah, to the extent of enunciating it as a death wish (Jonah 4:8)?

Wrong! Surprising as it may seem, even Moses gave open expression to his deepest despair in terms that could only be construed as critical of God's judgment. Like Jonah, very shortly after his "call," Moses deeply regrets having been chosen: "Wherefore hast Thou dealt ill with this people? Why is it that Thou hast sent me?" (Exodus 5:22). And later on, Moses expresses a desire to be "wiped out of the book that You [God] have written!" (Exodus 32:32), which would have had the effect of totally negating Moses' entire life and mission.

On another occasion of divine censure, in the episode of "the murmurers" (Numbers chapter 11), Moses expresses a death wish in even more explicit terms: "And if thou wouldst deal thus with me, kill me, I pray thee" (verse 15).

The prophet Elijah, no less, also expresses a death wish, in terms very similar to that of Jonah, in the face of Queen Jezebel's vow to destroy him: "And he went a day's journey into the desert, and came and sat down under a broom-tree; and he requested for himself that he might die, saying, 'It is enough, now, O Lord. Take away my life, for I am not better than my fathers' " (I Kings 19:4).

884. If that is the case, then why is Jonah censured for his attempt to escape his mission?

Very simply, he is censured because Moses was only issuing those demands, making those threats and attempting to escape his mission, for two selfless motives: first, because he truly believed that he was not up to the awesome responsibility of persuading Pharaoh to let Israel go free, and he preferred a more fluent and persuasive ambassador to be appointed. Secondly, he acted exclusively in order to secure mercy for his people. Jonah, on the other hand, spoke only out of pique and for selfish objectives. Moses harbored only love for those to whom God wished to send him; Jonah, on the other hand, harbored only ill-will toward the people to whom he was sent (for more on Jonah's rejection of his mission, see Questions 68–72).

Chapter II

885. What are the contents of the second chapter of Jonah?

God ordains a great fish that swallows Jonah, and he remains for 3 days inside its cavernous stomach. The rest of the chapter is taken up with the prayer that Jonah offers up from within the belly of the fish; and the final verse tells us that, at God's command, the fish vomits Jonah up and spews him onto dry land.

886. Now, if, as has been suggested, the events of the first two chapters came to Jonah as a vision, why would such a vision have taken the form that it did, of Jonah being swallowed by a fish?

According to Ben-Menachem, this is easily explained on the basis of the fact that the city that induced that apprehension—Nineveh—had as its symbol a fish! Indeed, its very name, *nun-naveh*, means "home of the fish," and the Akkadian symbol for the city was a fish inside a house.[12] Thus, from a psychological point of view, it would make sense that his nightmare would have taken the form of a fixation on that predominant characteristic of the city.

887. Is there any message to be derived from Jonah's prayer from the belly of the great fish?

Never was any prayer offered in such a strange place! It provides a novel dimension to the biblical statement that "In every place that you make mention of My name, there will I come and bless thee" (Exodus 20:24).

The message of the prayer is clearly that no place is unsuitable for prayer and that the impetus for prayer comes more spontaneously when we are *in extremis* than when we are comfortable. Our challenge, therefore, is to be constantly aware of our vulnerability and mortality, and to pray to God each day from *extremis*, as if that were our last.

888. Why do you keep referring to it as "a great fish" when it is universally described as a whale?

This is done for two reasons. First, because the book of Jonah consistently refers to it as, simply, "a large fish." It was clearly a unique creation, unrelated to any other recognizable species of fish; and for that reason the Bible does not categorize or name it.

Secondly, to call it a "whale" does not further our capacity to identify it one iota.

---

12. *Entziklopedia Mikra'it* (1968). Jerusalem: Mosad Bialik, p. 831.

We have it on the best authority that "the term 'whale' is more an indication of large size than of zoological classificatory significance."[13]

889. Are there any difficulties presented by Jonah's prayer?

The prayer itself is fairly predictable, though scholars have pointed out some problems, notably that it is written from the perspective of one who has *already* been saved from the danger that encompassed him: "But Thou didst bring me up alive from the pit, O Lord my God. As my senses failed me I remembered the Lord, and my prayer reached Thee in Thy holy temple . . ." (2:7–8).

This is not, however, an insuperable difficulty, as commentators and grammarians have long identified a phenomenon described as the "prophetic perfect," whereby the prophets employ the perfect, or past, tense when they are referring to the future. Their prophetic imagination, or the divine disclosure to them of future events, is so vivid that, to them, it is as if the events have already taken place.

890. Is there any other significant point that emerges from Jonah's prayer?

There is a psychological point of particular significance. Jonah cries out: "In my distress I called upon the Lord, and He answered me; from the depths of Sheol I cried, and You heard my voice" (2:3). He continues: "I had said, 'I am banished from before Your eyes; yet once again I am able to behold Your holy temple' " (2:5).

The supreme irony here is that Jonah sees clearly at this stage that God's mercy and grace are readily restored to those whose wickedness had hitherto caused them to be "banished from before Your eyes," and yet it was inconceivable to him that this principle could possibly be applied comprehensively to include the people of Nineveh! God is ready, as Jonah perceives it, to forgive a prophet who rejects God's word, but He remains deaf to the repentance of those "who cannot tell the difference between their right hand and their left"!

Chapter III

891. What are the contents of the third chapter of Jonah?

God addresses the chastened Jonah and tells him to get going to Nineveh and proclaim there the message that God will shortly disclose to him. We are told that Nineveh was so large that it took 3 days to traverse, but that after but 1 day God discloses the terrible message of doom that Jonah was to deliver: "Within forty days Nineveh will be overthrown" (3:4).

The chapter goes on to relate the immediate and dramatic effects of the prophet's words. The Ninevites—from the king down–proclaim a fast and don sackcloth and ashes. That spontaneous repentance is then reinforced by royal edict and is extended also to the animals who had to be dressed in the same way and who also had to

---

13. Article on "Whale" in *Encyclopaedia Britannica* (1970). Chicago: Encyclopaedia Britannica Inc., p. 451.

refrain from eating and drinking. God saw their earnest resolve, accepted their penitence, and canceled His sentence of doom upon the city.

892. What is the primary message to be learned from this chapter?

It seems to be that God can use man for His own purpose, whether or not man wishes to cooperate. For all his grudge against God for selecting him, and for all his depressive feelings on that score and his determination not to invest any energy into bringing the Ninevites to repentance, Jonah only has to utter a mere five Hebrew words and the heathens are galvanized into remorse and repentance!

893. What was the purpose of forcing the animals to conform to the same tokens of penitence?

This was probably because the heinous sin of the Ninevites, that prompted such a decree of doom, involved bestiality with their animals. Thus, in order to reinforce their terrible guilt and to draw their attention to its primary cause, their animals were made to submit to the same tokens of penance.

894. Can Jonah's naive flight from God be justified in ways other than those suggested, namely that it was a mere allegory, or that it occurred as part of the prophet's nightmare?

Yehezkel Kaufmann[14] suggests that Jonah, although believing in the cosmic dominion of God, was nevertheless committed to the concept of God's "presence" and "revelation" as being restricted to the holy land of Israel. His flight was not, therefore, from God. Indeed, we do the prophet a gross injustice to credit him with such naiveté. His wish to escape his mission was predicated on the view that God would not, on principle, reveal Himself to him with any mission in the lands of the idolators.

895. Does this concept occur anywhere else in the Bible?

Indeed, it is quite a common motif. It is built into the notion of God having separated Israel from all the nations to be "His" alone, and having given them a special land wherein He Himself may dwell among them and reveal His Spirit to them.[15]

King David assumes this concept when he chides the followers of his rebellious son, Absalom. Having to flee the land of Israel, he blames them for "having driven me out this day from my share in the Lord's inheritance, saying, 'Go serve other gods'" (I Samuel 26:19). The rebels certainly said no such thing, but David automatically associates dialogue with, and revelation of, God exclusively with the

---

14. Kaufmann, Y. (1961). *The Religion of Israel*. London: George Allen & Unwin, pp. 128–129.
15. Leviticus 20:24, 26.

land of Israel. Outside of it is the domain of "other gods." On principle, the God of Israel will never reveal Himself in the proximity of those gods.

In the well-known Psalm 137, "By the rivers of Babylon," we see this very idea reflected in the refusal of the Jewish exiles in Babylonia to "sing the Lord's song in a foreign land." It is inconceivable for them to worship Him outside His holy sphere of influence. And hence Jonah's master plan to escape to *Tarshish* in order to avoid the divine revelation of an unpalatable and dangerous mission.

896. But was it justifiable for Jonah to have so demonized, mentally, the inhabitants of Nineveh in that way?

The answer to this must be an unquestionable affirmative. The moral corruption of Nineveh was so endemic—a fact substantiated by other prophets speaking in the name of God—that Jonah must have been totally convinced that they had long since gone beyond the point of redemption.

Hear what the prophet Nahum (*circa* 612 B.C.E.) has to say about the city:

> Woe to the bloody city!
> It is all full of lies and rapine;
> The prey never leaves it . . . [Nahum 3:1]

> I will cast detestable things
> upon thee, and make thee vile,
> And will make thee as dung.
> And it shall come to pass, that all
> they that look upon thee
> Shall flee from thee,
> And say: 'Nineveh is laid waste;
> Who will bemoan her?' [3:6–7]

The same assessment is made by the prophet Zephaniah:

> And He shall stretch out His hand
> against the north,
> And destroy Assyria;
> And will make Nineveh a desolation . . . [Zephaniah 3:13]

> This is the carefree city
> That dwelt unperturbed,
> That said in her heart:
> I am, and there is none else beside me. [3:15]

Assyria maintained an iron grip on her conquests, unleashing unremitting force and cruelty on those who did not fall into line. It is thus not surprising that Jonah, like his other contempraries, should have viewed her downfall as irrevocably sealed. The divine call to him to preach mercy to Nineveh would have been inexplicable in the circumstances. Jonah would indeed have doubted whether or not he was truly receiving an authentic message from God—or whether he was rather being hoodwinked by Satan and his cohorts.

897. Does not the subject matter of Jonah appear to fall more in the realm of legend than historical fact?

We may indeed be forgiven for thinking that such occurrences as a prophet's flight from God, the lot drawn by the mariners just falling on him, his being swallowed by a fish and then being spewed out to safety, a gourd miraculously growing to offer him shade and then withering to teach him a lesson, must all derive exclusively from the folkloristic imagination.

Nevertheless, it has to be said that the Talmudic sages did not take that line, at least not overtly. Strangely, although in relation to the biblical personality of Job, they were prepared to go on record that "there never was any such a created being as Job; the book is a mere allegory,"[16] as regards Jonah, no such rationalization is offered.

898. Why should such a distinction have been made between Job and Jonah?

Possibly because it is nowhere suggested in the book of Job that its hapless subject is even Jewish. He is introduced merely as "a man that once lived in the land of Uz" (Job 1:1). Job's identity and religion are clearly a matter of no consequence. He remains a symbol, a personification of the attributes of courage and faith, and their power to vanquish self-pity and despair. And the book that bears his name is easily interpreted, therefore, as an allegory.

Jonah, on the other hand, is not only a Jew, but a prophet to boot. He stands, therefore, in the closest spiritual relationship and affinity to Israel, on the one hand, and to God on the other. It would be to devalue the concept of the prophet to associate that calling with some fictional character in a biblical drama. Prophets are either true or false; they are not fact or fiction.

899. Are there any other reasons why such a distinction may have been made?

It is conceivably because of the fact that Job appears in the third, and least sacred, section of the Hebrew Bible: the *Ketuvim* ("Writings"). The early synagogue chose only the Five Scrolls (*Megillot*) from that section for use in the synagogue as readings on specific festivals and ignored all the other books, whereas it elevated the prophetic literature, in which Jonah is found, and utilized it freely for the weekly and fast day *Haftarot*.

Having invested it with such significance, it was inconceivable to relegate it to the level of mere allegory, for that could well have sparked off a widespread and dangerous trend to regard other personages and episodes as mere devotional fiction.

---

16. *Bava Batra* 15a.

900. Are we able to date the book of Jonah?

The historical Jonah is only known from the single reference to him in quite another context. In II Kings 14:25, we are told of a prophet, Jonah ben-Amittai from Gath-hepher, who was a contemporary of King Jeroboam II (*circa* 783–743 B.C.E.).

Critical scholarship, on the other hand, distinguishes between the historical Jonah and the book that bears his name. The latter would seem to bear the hallmark of a later, post-exilic (586 B.C.E.) period. This is because of the fact that "in the pre-exilic period such far-reaching universalism and unconditional tolerance [of an alien people and of the inhabitants of the Assyrian city so hated by Israel] are difficult to imagine."[17]

901. Are there no other reasons for such a late dating?

There are other reasons, as for example the fact that the very name of Assyria is nowhere mentioned—not even the fact that Nineveh was the capital city of that great influence on the politics of the entire region. In the pre-exilic period, Assyria was so fearfully intrusive into international affairs and so uncompromising in its relations with Israel, that it would have been inconceivable for a prophet to go and restore them to repentance. Had such a thing happened, references to it would have been emblazoned across the biblical historical books and referred to in the contemporary and later prophetic literature. In the book of Jonah, "the Assyrian empire and its capital are clearly far away in the past."[18]

Another factor supporting a later date for the book itself is the employment of such Aramaisms as *beshelmiy*, "on whose account?" (1:7) and the late form *keri'ah*, "proclamation" (3:2).

Great play is also made of the motivation of the author, which seems to have been to counter the exclusivism and particularism of Ezra and Nehemiah (fifth and fourth century B.C.E.), and the measures they took to divorce Jewry from the contaminating influences of the heathen world (See Ezra chapters 9–10; Nehemiah 13:23–31).

For these reasons, scholars prefer to place Jonah in the post-exilic period and assume a third century B.C.E. date for its composition.

902. Does Nineveh figure at all in modern archaeology?

It most certainly does. In 1845, Henry Layard's spade unearthed the walls of one of the great palaces of Nineveh. The many cuneiform tablets that were unearthed in the region around that period were now able to be deciphered; translations were made, and the correct understanding of the Assyrian script was now ascertained. "The mounds of old Nineveh provided the new world with its most extensive collection of information about ancient times,"[19] and the Assyrian documents were

---

17. Eissfeldt, O. (1965). *The Old Testament.* Oxford: Basil Blackwell, p. 405.

18. *Ibid.*

19. Keller, W. (1963). *The Bible as History.* London: Hodder and Stoughton, p. 248.

found to contain "a wealth of interesting and informative details which corroborate the historical truth of the Bible."[20]

Chapter IV

903. What are the contents of the fourth chapter of Jonah?

This chapter deals with Jonah's response to God's decision to rescind His decree of doom upon the city of Nineveh. He expresses his great distress to God in no uncertain terms: "That is what I feared when I was in my own country, and to forestall it I tried to escape to Tarshish." He then prays to God to take his life, after which he walks to the east side of the city to observe what would happen.

The sun beats down, and God makes a climbing gourd spring up miraculously to provide the prophet with shade. Jonah's distress is relieved somewhat by the comfort of the gourd. But at dawn next morning, God brings a worm to attack the gourd so that it withers; and at sunrise, God ordains that a scorching wind should blow up. The sun beats down on Jonah's head, and he grows faint and prays again for death.

God then points out to Jonah how misguided he is in his anger at the loss of a gourd that he did not have to plant or nurture, but that came up in a night and perished in a night, and yet he cannot bring himself to feel concern for the great city of Nineveh with its vast citizenry of people who have not had the benefit of spiritual influence, and who "cannot tell their right hand from their left."

904. So what picture of Jonah's personality emerges from the text?

Jonah is not presented as a particularly engaging or sympathetic personality. It is true that at times of personal crisis he is quite capable of great passion, sensitivity, and grace of language, as is clear from his majestic plea to God from the belly of the fish (chapter II), but he generally disregards sentiment and speaks in a brusque, concise, and inelegant style. This comes over clearly in his dealings with the mariners (1:9) and when expressing his frustrations to God (4:2–3, 8, 9). Significantly, he totally disregards God's question, "Do you do well to be so angry?" (4:4), and when a similar question is asked later, "Do you do well to be so angry over the gourd?" (4:9), Jonah does not feel that God is owed even the courtesy of a proper explanation. Instead, he gives vent to a self-vindicatory outburst: "I do well to be angry, even to death" (*Ibid.*). Perhaps Jonah's character is best illuminated by the fact that he does not see the need to offer any thanksgiving to God for his miraculous rescue from the fish—even though he had solemnly promised to offer such sacrifices if delivered (See 2:10)!

905. Why does the book of Jonah end so abruptly?

It does indeed end abruptly, with God asking Jonah a rhetorical question that constitutes God's final and incontrovertible argument for saving the Ninevites: "You

---

20. *Op. cit.*, p. 249.

are sorry for the gourd, though you did not have the trouble of growing it, a plant that came up in a night and withered in a night. And should not I be sorry then for the great city of Nineveh, with its hundred and twenty thousand . . . ?" (4:11).

In this situation—where Jonah, as much as the Ninevites, is on trial—surely even God's rhetorical questions call for a response! Would we not have expected Jonah at this point to acknowledge that he had been wrong all along and that man must always pursue mercy, in the same way as does God? That, surely, is the expected denouement of the story, which began with the prophet scorning a mission of mercy and which should have ended with his having embraced it!

The abrupt end of the book indeed corroborates our assessment of Jonah's character. True to form, he does not even have the grace to acknowledge the error of his ways. There is, of course, an alternative explanation, and that is that he did answer God, but his answer was totally inappropriate and too offensive to be recorded!

906. Surely, then, this begs the question of why Jonah was included within the Canon of the Hebrew Bible?

Indeed, it is a problem. However, it all falls into place when we take account of the fact that it was the Patriarch Rabban Gamaliel II who exerted the primary influence over which books were to be accorded Canonical status, to become *Kitvei ha-kodesh* ("Holy Writ") and which excluded. His purpose in fixing the Canon, around the year 90 c.e., was to prevent the infiltration of sectarian, particularly Christian, ideas and to avoid the sowing of confusion among the ignorant Jewish masses who would not have been able to distinguish which books were "traditional" and which "heretical." It was, undoubtedly, for the same reason that Gamaliel instituted (or revised) the prayer against heretics (*Velamalshinim*) in the *Amidah*, to ensure that such sectarians could not pray with the faithful community and have to recite, and listen to, severe condemnation of their own fraternity.[21]

We may now appreciate why Rabban Gamaliel should have elevated the book of Jonah to biblical status. For Jonah's philosophy of exclusivism and his wish to exclude the "*goyim*" from divine grace and forgiveness struck a sympathetic cord with a Patriarch who was bedeviled by gentiles, heretics, Christians, and sectarians all his life.

907. Why is the book of Jonah read on Yom Kippur?

It is read because its theme is repentance and because it teaches that God is concerned for, and awaits the penitence of, all His creatures, irrespective of race and nationality. This is, of course, the central, universalistic teaching of the *Unetanneh tokef* composition, that God reviews at this time "all who enter the world," not merely his own people. That was a teaching that had clearly not won common acceptance in Jonah's day.

---

21. Cohen, J. M. (1993). *Blessed Are You.* Northvale, NJ: Jason Aronson Inc., pp. 29–42.

The second reason we read Jonah is because his pathetic attempt at flight from God is an accurate reflection of what most of us do before the memory of Yom Kippur has had time to fade from our minds. And like Jonah, most of us are more interested in our own comfort than in what is happening to our less fortunate fellow human beings. Like Jonah, in time of crisis we plead, pray, and make firm resolve. Once deliverance comes, however, we conveniently forget God—at least until the next Yom Kippur.

JONAH IN MIDRASHIC LITERATURE

908. Are we given any midrashic information regarding any preparation that Jonah had for his future calling as a prophet?

The Midrash[22] states that Jonah was the most prominent of all the thousands of disciples of the prophet Elisha. While his master was still alive, Jonah was charged with the important mission of annointing Jehu as king over Israel (See II Kings 9:1–10). This was an act of revolution by the prophet, because it signaled the overthrow of Jehoram, son of Ahab, and resulted in the bloody extermination of the latter's entire line (See II Kings chapter 10). Jehu reigned from *circa* 842–814 B.C.E.

909. Does the Midrash fill us in on any detail regarding the ministry of Jonah?

The Midrash places a novel interpretation on the only other biblical reference to Jonah outside the book that bears his name. In that biblical passage, part of which we have already quoted (See Question 27), there is a reference to the King of Israel at that period, Jeroboam II: "He restored (*Hu heishiv*) the borders of Israel, from the approach to Hamath to the sea of the Arabah, according to the word of the Lord, God of Israel, which He spoke by the hand of His servant Jonah, son of Amittai, the prophet, who was from Gath-Hepher."

Now the Midrash,[23] in a conscious attempt to link this solitary reference to Jonah with the events of the prophetic book that bears his name, unconvincingly interprets the phrase "he restored" as referring not to the king, but to Jonah! *Hu heishiv*, in the eyes of the Midrash, now means that "he (Jonah) brought (those who lived within) the borders of Israel to repentance (*teshuvah*)." Thus, we have the picture of a most persuasive and effective prophet who had already had considerable success in his prophetic ministry before being summoned to Nineveh. This explains, of course, why this prophet, whose prophecies are nowhere preserved in the Bible, was chosen once again by God for such a sensitive and dangerous mission.

---

22. Ginzberg, L. (1947). *Legends of the Jews*. Philadelphia: The Jewish Publication Society of America, vol. IV, p. 246.

23. Eisenstein, J. D. (1915). *Otzar Midrashim*. New York: J. D. Eisenstein Publications, pp. 217–222.

910. So why did Jonah get cold feet on this occasion?

According to the Midrash, this was because, after his first successful mission in the northern kingdom of Israel, there had been a second mission—this time to the Jerusalemites—when he had been told to announce the destruction of the city. On this second occasion, the Jews had repented, and God had reversed His harsh sentence. When the people saw that their city was not destroyed, they called Jonah a false prophet, and he was still smarting from their insults when God summoned him to prophesy doom to the Ninevites.

Fearing (correctly) that the same thing would happen again and petrified that he would receive more than mere insults from the Ninevites if his prophecy was not fulfilled because of their repentance, he fled from his mission.

911. How is it that none of Jonah's prophecies have been preserved?

Bearing in mind that, to have brought so many to repentance on three occasions, he clearly must have been a most persuasive and impassioned orator, it is, indeed, mystifying that none of his great public appeals were not preserved to become part of the Hebrew Bible. However, the Midrash we have just cited provides the clue to the solution of this problem. For, if Jonah was an unpopular personality, to whom the name of "false prophet" attached, then it is not surprising that no one was particular to preserve a written record of his speeches.

He certainly comes over as a recluse. There is no record of his having had any social dealings with his fellow countrymen, like Samuel; nor of having had disciples, like Elijah; nor a secretary, like Jeremiah; nor a wife, like Hoseah; nor children, like Isaiah; nor even a job, like Amos. He lived for himself and by himself; and, not surprisingly, therefore, he left no literary legacy to be prized and preserved for posterity.

912. Was it coincidental that such a large fish happened to be passing just when Jonah needed its refuge?

For the Midrashic sages, nothing is coincidental if it affects a divinely ordained mission. That fish, they assert,[24] was especially created at the dawn of Creation for that purpose and programmed to be in the right place at the right time.

913. But does that not mean that God had already predetermined the events, and, if so, that poor Jonah was deprived of his free will?

I thought I'd escaped that hardy annual! No, it does not have to mean that at all. It implies, merely, that God had foreknowledge of how Jonah would behave according to the exercise of his free will; and, foreseeing the consequences of his actions, God merely adjusted His program for Creation to include the creation of

---

24. *Zohar, Sidra Va-yakhel*, sec. 199.

that enormous fish, capable of ingesting Jonah without devouring him, and with a cavernous belly capable of accommodating him without him suffering suffocation.

Jonah's free will was still intact. At any time, he could have abandoned his flight from his mission, and God's unique fish would never have been invented.

914. Why is the fish at first referred to as *dag* (2:1), and later as *dagah* (2:2)?

Dag is a masculine noun, whereas *dagah* is feminine. At first, God sent a male fish, which took Jonah into its much larger belly for 3 days. Because Jonah did not pray all that time, God transferred him to a female fish, pregnant with scores of little fish, so that Jonah was cramped and uncomfortable, and that prompted him to pray.[25]

915. What was it like for Jonah inside the fish?

The Midrash states that he entered like a man entering a large synagogue. Its two eyes were like clear windows, giving him light and enabling him to see all the wonders of the ocean's depths.[26]

916. What prompted Jonah's great fish to spew him out onto dry land?

Gratitude. The Midrash tells us that when their time has come, all fish must swim to the great monster Leviathan, to be devoured by him. Jonah's fish was on his last journey to Leviathan at that moment. When it approached Leviathan, Jonah called out, "I have been sent by God to you, O Leviathan, on a mission to capture you so that you may be slaughtered for the banquet of the righteous in the time to come." Leviathan immediately turned and fled, and Jonah and his fish were saved. In gratitude, the fish carried Jonah to the nearest shore and spewed him out to safety.[27]

There is a clear parallel here, wherein Jonah and the Leviathan are both depicted as fleeing from their God-determined fate.

917. Did the fish show Jonah any other token of gratitude?

It did. Before spewing him out, it took Jonah on a guided tour of all the mysteries of the deep and revealed to him the sites of some of the key installations of Creation. These included the sources of the waters of the great oceans, the spot at which the Israelites crossed the Red Sea, the foundations and pillars of the earth, hell and the depths of Sheol, and the foundation-stone undergirding the Temple.[28]

---

25. Friedlander, G. ed. (1965). *Midrash Pirkei DeRabbi Eliezer*. New York: Hermon Press, chap. 10; See Louis Ginzberg, *op. cit.*, p. 249.

26. Friedlander, *op. cit.*, p. 69.

27. Friedlander, p. 70.

28. *Ibid.*

918. What prompted the rebellious Jonah, who subsequently expressed a wish to die, suddenly to turn to prayer from the belly of the fish?

It was while being shown the point beneath the foundation of the Temple that he came upon the sons of Korach praying there. "Pray at this spot, and you will be answered," they told Jonah, whereupon Jonah felt impelled to follow their earnest instruction.

919. Why should Jonah have been persuaded just by the sons of Korach?

Perhaps on account of their father who, like Jonah, was a rebel against God. Seeing Korach's righteous children offering praise to God might well have moved Jonah, albeit momentarily, to appreciate the power of repentance. For, although reared in an atmosphere of wickedness and rebellion, Korach's sons were not influenced by their father, but chose the path of repentance that led them to being the recipients of God's most generous grace.

920. What ultimately became of the mariners?

On witnessing the miraculous deliverance of Jonah, they were overwhelmed by the power and mercy of the God of Israel. They therefore threw away their idols and returned to Jaffa. From there they went to Jerusalem where they underwent circumcision and conversion.[29] They studied Torah, and became great sages.[30]

921. Was Jonah not entitled to be annoyed that God actually rescinded His decree without informing him?

God measures His words very precisely; and any prophet sensitive to the nuances of the divine communication should have sensed the possibility of that decree being "overturned." After all, God did not tell Jonah to decree that "in forty days Nineveh will be *destroyed (nishmedet)*." He advisedly used the vague word *nehepakhet*, which means, simply, "overturned," "changed." This may imply either a heightened spiritual perception (that is, Nineveh's present wickedness will be "overturned" for good) or it may connote to be "overthrown" and destroyed. The Talmud tells us that Jonah was insensitive to the possibility of it having the former, positive connotation.[31]

922. Was the repentance of the Ninevites wholehearted and permanent?

It was wholehearted at the time, but, alas, it was far from permanent. Had it been so, they would certainly not have gone on to inflict such violence upon the Jewish people, carrying away some ten tribes into captivity and oblivion in Assyria.

---

29. Friedlander, p. 72.
30. Zohar *Vayakhel*, sec. 231.
31. *Sanhedrin* 89b.

Their repentance lasted a mere 40 days, after which they reverted to their previous ways, and even intensified their evil doing. The result was that Jonah's threatened punishment was carried out, and they were swallowed up into the earth.

923. Is it not surprising that God was prepared to impose such traumas upon Jonah just to secure a mere 40 days of repentance on the part of the Ninevites?

We must not lose sight of the fact that we are dealing here with Midrashic, folkloristic ideas, about which the sages had a principle that *Ein moshivin al ha-derash*, "We do not raise counter arguments to such midrashic expositions."

Nevertheless, if pressed, we might answer that we cannot possibly appreciate the significance, in the divine scheme of things, of those 40 days spent in repentance and righteousness. Perhaps, as in the case of the sons of Korach, they were consequential for the offspring of the Ninevites, some of whom might have been influenced to dissociate themselves from the lifestyle of their parents.

924. Does the Midrash supply us with any information concerning the future fate of Jonah?

There are a few traditions on this matter. One has it that, as compensation for Jonah's suffering, God exempted him from death and allowed him to enter Paradise alive. "This is very likely to be understood in the sense that he awaits there the end of time to start on his Messianic mission."[32]

Now there is a widespread Midrashic view that Jonah was the son of the widow of Zarephat whom Elijah resuscitated. Since that child is identified in Jewish folklore with the future Messiah son of Joseph, the forerunner of the true Messiah, son of David, we may understand why Jonah is credited with having entered Paradise alive.

NO *AL HA-TORAH*?

925. Why do we omit the usual final blessing of the *Haftarah*: *Al Ha-Torah ve'al ha-avodah*?

We omit it also in the *Minchah Haftarah* of all other fast days. The reason is because it is a thanksgiving blessing for, among other holy institutions, the *Avodah*, the special Sabbath and festival sacrificial rituals. Because there were no special sacrificial rituals prescribed for this time of the day on Yom Kippur or the other fast days, the blessing was omitted.[33]

---

32. Ginzberg, L. *Ad loc.*
33. *Matteh Mosheh* on *Orach Chayyim* 621:19.

NO PRIESTLY BLESSING?

926. Why do the priests not bless the people at the repetition of the *Minchah* service, as they do during *Musaf*?

The question is even more acute when we consider that, in Israel, the Priestly Blessing is administered on Yom Kippur during *Shachrit* also (as throughout the year), and, in some rites, also at *Ne'ilah*.

So the question should be rephrased as, why, even in Israel, where they have the Priestly Blessing each day, do they not have it during the *Minchah* service? (We would not expect it at *Ma'ariv*, because that was always merely an optional service, not corresponding to any of the two communal daily sacrifices offered in the Temple.) The answer is that there was a fear, throughout the year, that the priests might be inebriated late in the afternoon, which would prohibit their participation in that ritual. We must not forget that people used to eat a large lunch on returning home from work, and this meal continued until *Minchah* time in the late afternoon. Because it was customary to drink wine with their meal, there was a strong chance that the priest might be light-headed and unable to concentrate properly on his solemn duty of blessing the people.

Now, although it was inconceivable for anyone to have drunk anything on Yom Kippur afternoon, our tradition has always promoted consistency. The rabbinic principle is *lo plug*, "not to introduce exceptions" to general modes of practice. Thus, since the Priestly Blessing was omitted every day at the *Minchah* service, for the reason stated, it was similarly omitted on Yom Kippur *Minchah*.

NO *TZIDKATKHA TZEDEK*?

927. Why do we omit the *Tzidkatkha tzedek* verses, which are usually recited after the repetition of the *Minchah Amidah* on Sabbaths and when festivals occur on a Sabbath?

Bearing in mind that Yom Kippur is a "Sabbath of Sabbaths," we would indeed have expected the *Tzidkatkha* verses to be said. They are not recited, however, because their sentiments were not regarded as appropriate. This is because the third verse expresses the concept that God's *judgments* are like a vast deep, whereas on Yom Kippur it is not "judgment" but "mercy" that we desire of God.

XXVII

Ne'ilah and the Conclusion of the Fast

928. What is the precise meaning of Ne'ilah?

Its literal meaning is "closing," though in what precise sense this is to be understood was unclear already in Talmudic times. Hence, a dispute arose between Rav and Rabbi Yochanan. Rav understood it as referring to the service recited at the time of the closing of the heavenly gates to our day's petitions, whereas R. Yochanan applied it, in its literal sense, to the service recited at the time of the closing of the gates of the Temple.

These differing attributions would have ramifications regarding the particular time until which Ne'ilah may be recited (See next question). According to Rav, because the precise time of the closing of the heavenly gates remains unknown, and could continue until nightfall, Ne'ilah itself may be extended until that time. According to R. Yochanan, however, since the Temple gates were closed immediately after the kindling of the Temple menorah, while it was yet still daylight, Ne'ilah likewise would have to be completed by that time.

929. Is there a proper time for the recitation of Ne'ilah?

The Shulchan Arukh states that "the time for the Ne'ilah service is when the sun is over the tops of the trees, so that one will complete it close to sundown." The later codifiers had difficulty in understanding how Ne'ilah could be concluded within such a short period,[1] and they consequently interpreted the Shulchan Arukh to mean, therefore, that it should be commenced while it is still clearly daylight and should be concluded at the end of the sundown period, that is just before nightfall.

The concern that it should be completed before nightfall was in order not to make nonsense of the sentiments of the beautiful composition recited at this service: "The day will fade away; the sun will set and depart—let us enter Your gates." This clearly presupposes that the sun has not yet set. Indeed, we are told that should the service be prolonged and still be in progress after sundown, the words of that line should be altered from the future to the past: "The day has faded (ha-yom panah); the sun has set and departed (ha-shemesh ba' ufanah)."

---

1. Taz on Shulchan Arukh Orach Chayyim 623:2; also R. Tzvi Pesach Frank, Mikra'ei Kodesh (Jerusalem: Makhon HaRav Frank, 1979), p. 175.

NE'ILAH COMPOSITIONS

Mah anu meh chayyenu

930. What is the most important of the *Ne'ilah* compositions?

It was the view of the Talmudic sage Shemuel,[2] that the composition *Mah anu meh chayyenu* was the crux of this service:

> What are we? What is our life, our piety, our righteousness? What is our salvation, our strength, our might? What shall we say before You, O Lord our God and God of our fathers? Are not all the mighty men as nought before You, men of renown as if they had never lived, wise men as if bereft of knowledge, and men of understanding as if devoid of discretion? For most of their achievements are valueless, and the days of their life vanity in Your sight. Truly, the preeminence of man over the beast is a mere illusion, for all is vanity.

The significance of this composition lies clearly in its affirmation of the total eclipse of the human ego, which is precisely what Yom Kippur should have achieved by this time. And so worthy a sentiment was this that it was chosen not just for the Yom Kippur *Ne'ilah,* but was transferred to become an essential part of the daily service throughout the year.

Shema and *Barukh shem kevod malkhuto*

931. Why do we recite the *Shema* verse once and *Barukh shem kevod* three times at this juncture?

We have spoken of God throughout the day, in numerous prayers, hymns, praises, and confessions. We have described Him by an abundance of attributes, as penned by many of our famous and inspired sacred poets. But there comes a moment when God wants to hear—and we wish to express—our own, unadorned but profoundly heartfelt, love of God, the God of our people, the One with Whom we have had a reciprocal covenant of love and loyalty that has stood the test of time and the innumerable trials of faith.

And there is only one line that says it all—the *Shema*. It is the spiritual password of the Jew, which he rehearses thrice daily to keep open the channel of communication and the sense of proximity with His God. There is no other single line that is so saturated with both the pure faith of the young innocents who are taught it as their earliest Hebrew affirmation, as well as with the haunting memories of countless martyrs who recited it with their dying breath, to make sense of their fate, to acknowledge their certainty of God's existence and justice and to commend to Him their bodies in a bond of peace, love, and sanctity.

---

2. *Yoma* 87b.

So, at this moment, when we are saturated with the words we have offered throughout the day, we offer something infinitely more beautiful—a simple emotion: "Hear O Israel, the Lord our God, the Lord is One." He is One, and we are at one with Him. And that has been achieved solely as a result of our at-one-ment.

We only recite that once. That is enough. In any case, the rabbis of the first centuries were most sensitive to any repetition of this affirmation of faith in the one God in case its repetition was misconstrued as recognition of the heretical concepts of duality or trinity, so popular at that period.

The traditional response to the mention of God's Name in the Temple was *Barukh shem kevod malkhuto le'olam va'ed* (See Question 847). Having reenacted the entire Temple *Avodah* during the course of the day, we conclude the day with this response, which affirms that God's kingdom will last forever, with the implication that it is Israel's sacred mission to ensure that it does. This we recite three times, corresponding to God's sole sovereignty in the past, the present, and the future.

932. What is the meaning of the enigmatic shout: *Ha-shem hu ha-Elokim?*

Literally, it means "The Lord He is God." The first, four-letter divine Name, pronounced *Ha-Shem*, is understood in rabbinic tradition to denote the God of mercy, while *Elokim* denotes the God of strict justice. Thus, at this climactic moment of Yom Kippur, we affirm that "it is the merciful God (*Ha-Shem*) who dons the mantle of a God of justice (*Elokim*)"—not the reverse. His essential quality is mercy; his strict justice is merely ephemeral. From this moment on, we can go forward with confidence in the light of *Ha-Shem*, the dispenser of mercy and blessing. There is also the unspoken acceptance that, whatever lies in store for us during this coming year—whether blessing or suffering—proceeds from a righteous God who has decided our fate through the most delicate equipoise of those two attributes.

It is recited seven times, as a mystical farewell to the *Shekhinah* (Divine Presence) that had descended from the seventh, and highest, heaven in order to be accessible to Israel. Just as the sevenfold repetition of Psalm 47 on Rosh Hashanah escorted the *Shekhinah* down to the throne of mercy, so, in the same way, we now escort her on her return.

A Priestly Blessing?

933. We mentioned above that some have the custom for the priests to bless the people (*dukhan*) during *Ne'ilah*. What is the origin of this custom, and why is it not observed in most communities?

If we consult the *Shulchan Arukh*, we find that Joseph Karo states categorically: "We have the priestly blessing to *Ne'ilah*."[3] This goes back to a prescription in the

---

3. *Shulchan Arukh Orach Chayyim* 623:5.

Mishnah,[4] which records that on Yom Kippur (and other public fast days), when an extra prayer—*Ne'ilah*—was added, in order to heighten the urgency of their petitions.

The Ashkenazi glossator, Moses Isserles, states, however, that "the custom in our communities is not to have the priestly blessing."[5] R. Mordechai Jaffe provides the rationale for this, namely, that *Ne'ilah* is frequently drawn out until nightfall, and, because the Priestly Blessing derives its origin directly from the Temple service and there was no service there after nightfall, it is inappropriate to perform it at such a late hour. There were some authorities, however, who followed Karo's view. Thus, the distinguished *Maharil* states that, "even if *Ne'ilah* is protracted until after nightfall, the priests should still perform their blessing."[6] The weight of the later Ashkenazi authorities combined, however, to abolish its recitation.

The Final Shofar

934. Why do we blow the shofar at the end of *Ne'ilah*?

There are several reasons offered, among which is that it is to accompany the Divine Presence on its withdrawal from our midst to its heavenly heights, in accordance with the verse: "God ascends with the trumpet sound" (Psalm 47:6).

Another explanation has it that it commemorates the shofar that was sounded in biblical times on the Yom Kippur that inaugurated the Jubilee year.[7] It remains problematic, though, why, according to this reason, we blow it every year and not just every Jubilee year! R. David Abudraham suggests that it is simply because, since the destruction of the Temple and the suspension of the Jubilee cycle, we are unsure as to which year is, in fact, the Jubilee. Hence it is blown every year.[8]

It will be recalled that, at the Jubilee, slaves had to be granted their freedom. We are also servants of God (*im ka'avadim*), and the Jubilee shofar announces that we have also won our freedom, by way of reprieve from the sentence that until now has been hanging over our head.

935. Why do some synagogues delay the sounding of the shofar until the end of *Ma'ariv*?

This is probably done to ensure that the tired and hungry members of the congregation stay on until the very end of the service, so that it finishes with an

---

4. Mishnah *Ta'anit* 4:1.
5. *Remah* on *Orach Chayyim* 623:5.
6. *Magen Avraham* on *Orach Chayyim* 623:3.
7. Numbers 25:9.
8. Abudraham, D. (1963). *Abudraham Ha-Shalem*. Jerusalem: Usha Publishers, p. 290.

appropriately decorous spirit, rather with a stampede to leave the synagogue, especially by those unaccustomed to reciting the weekday *Ma'ariv* service.

936. But how can the shofar be blown when we have not yet recited the *havdalah* in the *Ma'ariv Amidah*, so that, technically, it is still Yom Kippur?

There is no fear on that score, first, since night has already fallen. Secondly, *Rav* takes the view that, since *Ne'ilah* may be extended until nightfall, it partakes of the nature of an evening service and consequently frees one of the requirement to recite the *Ma'ariv* service.[9] Although we do not follow that view, it is sufficient to invest *Ne'ilah* with that status for the purpose of enabling the final shofar to be blown at this time. And finally, even discounting the last point, one really infringes no halakah in blowing the shofar at such a late twilight hour on Yom Kippur itself, since that act is regarded as a *chokhmah* (skill), rather than a *melakhah* (manual act, prohibited under one of the thirty-nine categories of forbidden Sabbath activities).[10]

937. How many notes should we blow on the shofar at the conclusion of *Ne'ilah*?

The Sephardi codifier, Joseph Karo, states that we should blow a *teki'ah shevarim teru'ah teki'ah,* as on Rosh Hashanah, whereas the Ashkenazi glossator, Moses Isserles states: "But some say that one should blow but one *teki'ah*; and this is the practice in our communities. And we blow after the conclusion of the *Kaddish* at the end of *Ne'ilah*, though there are some places where the practice is to blow before *Kaddish*."[11]

It has also become the practice in many communities to blow, not a single *teki'ah*, but a *teki'ah gedolah*, in order to bring Yom Kippur to a rousing climax.

[For a full commentary on the *Ne'ilah* service, See Cohen, J. M. (1994) *Prayer and Penitence*. Northvale, NJ: Jason Aronson Inc.]

THE *MA'ARIV* SERVICE

938. Should we keep our *tallit* on for the recitation of the *Ma'ariv* service?

While, with the exception of *Kol Nidre* (See Question 771), we do not wear a *tallit* to *Ma'ariv*, it is one thing not having to put it on, but quite another to ceremoniously remove it before another service. This might well be categorized as an unworthy diminution of the status of a religious article; and for this reason it is preferable to keep it on until the conclusion of *Ma'ariv*.

---

9. *Yoma* 87b. See application of this principle in *Bet Yosef* on *Tur Shulchan Arukh Orach Chayyim* 623.
10. *Mishnah Berurah* 623 (18).
11. *Shulchan Arukh Orach Chayyim* 623:6.

939. Are there any halakhic recommendations governing the recital of *Ma'ariv*?

The *Kitzur Shulchan Arukh* states that:

One should depute a worthy person to lead this service, and he should do so slowly and with proper *kavvanah* (religious concentration). Those who rush it should be reproved. We recite *Attah chonantanu* in the (*Attah chonen* blessing of the) *Amidah*; and, if the Yom Kippur day has coincided with Shabbat, we recite *Veyitein lekha*, though we do not recite the usual (*Motzei Shabbat*) *Viyhiy noam/Ve'attah kadosh* composition. After the service, we sanctify the new moon (*Kiddush levanah*), and greet one another joyfully and wholeheartedly as on a festival.[12]

940. Why do we not recite *Viyhiy noam* as on every other *Motzei Shabbat*?

Whenever a festival occurs during the coming week, we omit the *Viyhiy noam* from the *Motzei Shabbat Ma'ariv* service. The reason for this is because the opening verse of *Viyhiy noam* includes the phrase "Establish for us the work of our hands," which invokes divine blessing throughout the coming working week, whereas, when a festival occurs during the course of it, then, naturally, we shall be refraining from "the work of our hands." We thus express our joyful anticipation of the coming festival—in this case, the festival of Sukkot, some 4 days after Yom Kippur—by omitting this composition.

HAVDALAH

941. As regards women who are at home when the fast goes out, do they have to wait until they have heard *havdalah* before breaking their fast?

No, they do not. However, before doing any work or eating they should recite a brief *havdalah* of their own, consisting of the words *Barukh ha-mavdil bein kodesh lechol*. (This formula should be recited throughout the year when Shabbat goes out, if they have to do any work forbidden on Shabbat before they are able to hear *havdalah*.)

942. Why do we not recite the usual blessing over spices in the Yom Kippur *havdalah*, even when it coincides with *Motzei Shabbat*?

The reason for this is that the spices were introduced in order to revive our spirits, every *Motzei Shabbat,* after the sudden withdrawal from within us of the *neshamah yeteirah* ("Additional Soul")—which takes the form of a pep of spiritual adrenalin that gives us an especially good feeling. On Yom Kippur, however, because of the

12. Ganzfried, S., *Kitzur Shulchan Arukh* 132:27.

fasting, it was believed that we are not capable of experiencing that "additional Soul."[13]

To this may be added the fact that spices may actually be inhaled on Yom Kippur, and, indeed, some regard it as meritorious to "*shmeck tabbak*" on this day, in order to make up the shortfall of 3 blessings from the 100 blessings we are meant to recite each day.[14] Thus, because there is nothing unique about inhaling spices when the fast goes out, there is another reason for not including it in the *havdalah* service.

It has to be said, however, that some authorities take the view that, when Yom Kippur coincides with Shabbat, the blessing over the spices should be recited; though they recommend that this should only be done at the home *havdalah* service, not in synagogue.

943. Is there any recommendation regarding the type of candle that one should use for Yom Kippur *havdalah*?

There is. It is recommended that we do not use a light that has been newly created, for example by striking a match, but rather a *ner sheshavat*, a light that has itself been burning over the entire fast day.[15]

The reason for this is that the light that we bless on Yom Kippur is not for the same reason as the light we bless every *Motzei Shabbat*. The reason for the latter is because tradition has it that it was on the first *Motzei Shabbat* of his creation that Adam, quite by accident, struck two flints, one against the other, and made the discovery of how to create sparks, flame, and heat.

On *Motzei Yom Kippur*—which most years does not occur on *Motzei Shabbat*—we light them for quite another reason: to demonstrate that for the whole of Yom Kippur we have been prohibited from creating and using fire, but that now we may enjoy that benefit. This point is underscored far more forcefully by utilizing a light that was kept burning throughout the holy day and that we had refrained from touching by reason of the prohibition, than by creating a new light at this moment.

It is recommended that, after breaking one's fast, we should demonstrate our love of God's *mitzvot* by immediately doing some work on the *sukkah*, even if it is merely a token gesture, such as knocking in a nail.

---

13. *Mishnah Berurah* 624:3.
14. Talmud *Menachok* 43b.
15. *Shulchan Arukh Orach Chayyim* 624:4.

XXVIII

Bereavement on Yom Kippur

The reader is referred to Questions 594–611 for wider treatment and supplementary details of the laws of bereavement during the High Holy Day period.

944. Does one continue to observe Yom Kippur if a close relative passes away on that day?

Because one cannot attend to burial arrangements on Yom Kippur, one does not become an *Onen* (See Questions 598 and 599). Therefore, all the obligations of Yom Kippur remain binding.

945. Should the mourner change his seat in synagogue in that situation?

No, he does not. He has not yet started his official mourning period, and to move his seat would be a premature and public expression of mourning.

946. What is the rationale of the mourner changing his seat in synagogue?

It is to enable the mourner to give token expression to his grief and the inevitable feeling of having come under divine displeasure, detached from God's mercy. This is symbolized by his moving from his regular seat to a few rows further back (about 6 feet) from the Ark. Other authorities understand the move as a symbolic exile, namely a penance for unintentionally having contributed to the death of one's loved one, either through not having helped enough to lighten their physical burdens, or by having caused him or her anxiety or pain, or, simply, by not possessing sufficient merit for God to have spared the deceased for an extra period of life.

947. Does this practice apply on Sabbaths, as well as weekdays?

There are varying customs in this regard. Some authorities rule that this applies even on Sabbaths and festivals, while others take the view that one does not change one's seat on those holy days, because this would constitute a conspicuous public demonstration of mourning. This is not permitted, because it impairs the community's pleasure in its sacred celebration.

Moses Isserles states that "some rule that the mourner should change his seat even on the Sabbath. This is the prevalent custom, and it should not be changed."[1] A popular compromise is that one changes one's seat on weekdays and during the Sabbath of the *shivah*, but on subsequent Sabbaths one sits in one's normal seat. One should always follow the practice of one's own congregation.

948. For how long is the practice of changing one's seat observed?

It is observed for 30 days for relatives other than parents, and for the full 12 months, until the first *Yahrzeit*, for parents. Moses Isserles admits that "this custom has no real basis, but it should, nevertheless, not be changed"![2]

949. Are there any restrictions governing the delivering of a *hesped* (eulogy) before or after Yom Kippur?

It is customary not to deliver a *hesped* on the day before Yom Kippur. This day has a festive character, because it is regarded as meritorious to eat and drink on that day in order to strengthen oneself for the fast. It is similarly inappropriate to deliver a *hesped* on the days between Yom Kippur and Sukkot, which also partake of a festive spirit that pervades the preparation for, and anticipation of, the festival described as "season of our rejoicing."

There are those who draw a distinction between the Talmudic, tear-jerking *hesped* and our more sober "appreciation" of the life of the deceased. Those who make such a distinction would view the latter type of address as in order at all times.

950. What about the *El malei rachamim* memorial prayer?

It is likewise not recited on the day before Yom Kippur and on the days between Yom Kippur and Sukkot.

951. May a mourner lead the services in synagogue during the period between Rosh Hashanah and Yom Kippur?

We have already dealt with the question of a mourner serving as an officiant on Rosh Hashanah and Yom Kippur itself (See Questions 610–611). During the intermediate days of penitence, a mourner may lead the service, as he may on the eve of Rosh Hashanah and the eve of Yom Kippur.

952. When does the mourner get up from sitting *shivah* on the eve of Yom Kippur?

The arrival of Yom Kippur terminates the *shivah*. The mourner may rise a few hours before the onset of the fast, leaving himself or herself enough time to do all the necessary preparations for the festival.

---

1. *Remah* on *Shulchan Arukh Yoreh De'ah* 393:2.
2. *Remah* on *Shulchan Arukh Yoreh De'ah* 393:4.

The mourner is permitted to take a bath or, if it is his custom, to immerse in the *mikveh*, in the late afternoon. He may also attend the *Minchah* service in synagogue and sit on a normal chair to eat the final meal (*Se'udah ha-mafseket*) before the fast.

953. Some have the custom of fasting on the *yahrzeit* of parents. What should they do if this occurs on the day before Yom Kippur?

They do not observe it as a fast day, for the reason mentioned in Question 949.

954. Does a mourner wear the *kittel* on Yom Kippur?

This is a debated issue among authorities. Moses Isserles[3] gives two reasons for wearing the *kittel*: (i) That the white robe is to make us appear as pure as the Ministering Angels, and (ii) it is the shroud that the dead are wrapped in, and hence it induces a mood of contrition.

Taz observes that, according to the first rationale, a mourner should not wear it because his spirits could never induce such confidence; whereas according to the second explanation he certainly should wear it. He permits the wearing of the *kittel* to those who wish to rely on the second interpretation. One should be guided by the custom of one's community.

955. We have already referred to the situation of a burial taking place a few days before Yom Kippur (See Question 604). Where burial takes place after Yom Kippur, how is *sheloshim* calculated?

Shivah is observed until a few hours before the onset of the festival of Sukkot (as long as the mourners require much time to prepare themselves for the festival); and however many days they have sat counts as a full *shivah*, that is 7 days. The 7-day biblical festival itself adds another 7 days. The eighth day, *Sheminiy Atzeret* (being an independent biblical festival), counts, for *sheloshim* purposes, as equal to another 7 days. Add to these the (Diaspora) final day of *Simchat Torah*, and we have a total of 22 days of *sheloshim* already observed. This means that only 8 further days of *sheloshim* require to be observed following the termination of the festival.

956. What is the principle regarding the prohibition of haircutting during *shivah* and *sheloshim*?

Mourners express their sense of social withdrawal by disregarding their appearance and leaving their hair unkempt and uncut. For relatives other than parents, haircuts are not permitted until the end of the *sheloshim*, that is the morning of the thirtieth day after the burial. Mourners for parents are expected to wait a little longer, until such time as they receive *ge'arah* ("social reproach"), that is that their

---

3. *Remah* on *Shulchan Arukh Orach Chayyim* 610:4.

appearance is such that a friend is (or would be) tempted to comment adversely on their appearance. Some authorities[4] permit haircutting on the thirtieth day itself if friends comment adversely.

957. Does this prohibition apply equally to women mourners?

No, it does not. The rabbis were sensitive to a woman's desire to maintain her appearance, and especially to remain attractive to her husband. They therefore allowed women to attend the hairdresser after *shivah*, and to have their hair washed and set, and, where absolutely necessary, to have it cut *after shivah*.

958. What is the situation regarding shaving?

Basically, shaving is governed by the same principle as haircutting regarding the criterion of social reproach (See Question 956). However, some authorities are more lenient in the case of shaving for those who are accustomed to shaving each day throughout the year. To insist—as in the case of haircutting—on an extended period of social reproach, after the *sheloshim*, would involve the mourner in excessive discomfort, which the halakhah is keen to avoid. In any case, unlike the slow growth of hair on one's head, the unkempt appearance is created after only a few days of non-shaving. Hence, one fulfills the duty of manifesting that token of mourning after a much shorter period. One should be guided by one's rabbi.

959. So what is the situation at this Yom Kippur and Sukkot season regarding haircutting and shaving in honor of the festival, when it curtails *shivah* or *sheloshim*?

The onset of the festival during *shivah* only curtails *shivah* and does not therefore bring with it any permission to have a haircut or shave, because there is still the *sheloshim* to be observed.

The onset of the festival after the completion of a full *shivah* enables mourners for relatives other than parents to have a haircut or shave just before evening in time for the festival.

Mourners for parents, however, whose mourning continues for a year, cannot avail themselves of that permissibility to get into the spirit of the festival joy by cutting their hair in honor of a festival that curtails the *sheloshim*. However, if the festival occurs shortly after *sheloshim*, then it curtails the "social reproach" period, and the mourner may have a haircut or shave.

960. What if one's hair growth causes skin irritation?

If absolutely necessary because of one's condition, then one may shave.

---

4. *Chiddushei Rav Akivah Eger* on *Yoreh De'ah* 390:4.

961. What if one has to represent the Jewish community at an official level to the state authorities, or appear at court, or meet with highly placed business associates, and one's unkempt appearance could jeopardize one's situation?

One should consult with one's rabbi who, given the appropriate circumstances, would probably be able to give a lenient ruling.

962. Is there any restriction on mourners trimming their nails?

Women mourners who need to do so in preparation for a post-*shivah mikveh* visit, or if their nails have grown inordinately long, may do so. Male mourners should not do so until after *sheloshim*. However, if absolutely necessary, they may do so even during *shivah*, but preferably with an implement they do not usually use.

963. A man whose wife has died, God forbid, is forbidden to remarry until three festivals have elapsed. Do Rosh Hashanah, Yom Kippur, and Sukkot—all of which occur within a period of three weeks—count for this purpose?

Rosh Hashanah and Yom Kippur do not, as they are not, strictly speaking, religious "festivities," the waiting period of which is to remind him of his first wife and her role in creating the joyful home spirit of the festival celebration. Only Sukkot counts in this context, and (unlike for the counting of the *sheloshim* period) *Sheminiy Atzeret* is not regarded as a festival on its own.[5]

Where the widower is left with small children to look after, the waiting period may be dispensed with.

---

5. *Shulchan Arukh Yoreh De'ah* 392:2.

XXIX

Yom Kippur Customs in Other Countries

ENGLISH SEPHARDI CUSTOMS

964. Are there any distinctive prayers recited by the English Sephardim?

There are, indeed. On the eve of Yom Kippur, their *Arbit* (evening) service includes the "Prayer for the Sovereign and Royal Family," which the Anglo-Jewish Ashkenazim never recite at evening services. This is followed by a "Prayer for the Congregation," which includes the petition that God should "implant within you brotherly love, peace and friendship, and remove from among you all manner of causeless enmity, and break the yoke of the nations from your neck." This was also the practice of some other Oriental communities.

They then proceed to recite a series of *Miy Sheberakh* petitions that are of particular interest. These include special prayers for those elected to the honor of serving as *Chatan Torah* (Bridegroom of the Law) and *Chatan Bereishit* (Bridegroom of the First Portion of the Torah) for the forthcoming *Simchat Torah* festivities. They then recite a *Miy Sheberakh* "For our brethren imprisoned by the Inquisition," followed by one for the safety of those traveling by sea or over land. Finally, they recite memorial prayers for those members of the congregation who have passed away during the past year. In some communities, they also offer prayers for the happiness of the brides and grooms who have married during the past year.

A TUNISIAN CUSTOM

965. Do we know of any distinctly Tunisian pre-Yom Kippur practice?

We have already referred to the practice of undergoing symbolic flagellation in order to purge one's sins for which the traditional penalty is forty lashes (See Question 696). Pious Tunisian Jews would repair to the headquarters of the *Chevra Kadisha* (The "Holy Brotherhood" who prepare the dead for burial), and the lashes would be administered in the special room where they store the shrouds. These surroundings would serve to reinforce the transience of life and the importance of repenting before it is too late.

SYRIAN CUSTOMS

966. Do we know of any distinctly Syrian pre-Yom Kippur practice?

Although they donned the *tefillin* for the morning service on the day before Yom Kippur, they would put them on again for the *Minchah* (afternoon) service. They invested this act with special significance, viewing it as a gesture of atonement for any laxity they may have exhibited when it came to wearing the *tefillin* every day during the past year.

967. Does the Syrian tradition prescribe any variation in the recitation of *Kol Nidre*?

We have already referred to two versions of this petition: a prospective version, petitioning for the rescinding of vows "from this Yom Kippur until next Yom Kippur, may it come to us for good," and a retrospective version, petitioning for the rescinding of vows uttered "from last Yom Kippur until this Yom Kippur" (See Questions 784–786). In the Syrian tradition, the entire congregation chants the *Kol Nidre* for themselves twice in unison, employing the retrospective version. This is then followed by the *Chazan*'s recitation, employing the prospective version. An interesting compromise!

968. Does Syrian tradition have any unique liturgical variation?

Instead of commencing the *Arbit* service with *Borkhu*, as on all festivals, they begin, on *Kol Nidre* night alone, with the ordinary weekday introduction: *Vehu rachum*. This was introduced because its sentiments have special relevance to the theme of repentance and divine forgiveness: "And He, being merciful, will forgive iniquity, and will not destroy. . . ."

969. Are there any major variations or adaptations of standard prayers?

The most distinctive and ambitious variation is in their treatment of the *Ashamnu* Confessional. Following the successive alphabetical terms of confession (*Ashamnu Bagadnu Gazalnu*, etc.), the Syrian *machzor* lists all the 365 negative commandments in the Torah and links them alphabetically to the corresponding word of the *Ashamnu*. Thus, all those negative commandments commencing with the letter *aleph* are introduced by the word *Ashamnu*; those beginning with *bet* under *Bagadnu*, and so on through the entire alphabet. There then follows a further confessional following the identical arrangement, but this time with the 248 positive commandments.[1]

---

1. Dobrinsky, H. C. (1985). *A Treasury of Sephardic Laws and Customs.* New York: Ktav Publishing House, Inc., pp. 335–336. I am greatly indebted to Dobrinsky's work for much of the information contained in this chapter.

970. Are the services led by a *Chazan* in the Syrian tradition, in the same way as in the Ashkenazi tradition?

They not only have one *Chazan*, but two assistant *Chazanim* to help him out. Thus, the *Selichot* and other parts of the services are recited by all three on a rotation basis.

971. Do they have any innovations in the Yom Kippur *Musaf* service?

During the recitation of the *Avodah*, which provides a full and graphic description of the High Priest's duties on this day, as he entered the Holy of Holies, the Syrians would open the Ark and take out and display to the congregation the place in the Torah scroll, at the *sidrah Acharei mot*, which deals with those ritual prescriptions of the *Avodah*.

972. Are there any other innovative Yom Kippur practices?

H. C. Dobrinsky records a past practice that occasioned much controversy within the Syrian community, which was for people to be encouraged to approach the Ark, which was left open for this purpose throughout the *Ne'ilah* service, in order to kiss the scrolls and beg forgiveness for any of its laws that they may have infringed or neglected during the year.

According to Dobrinsky,[2] this occasioned a breakdown in decorum during the service as people thronged forward in a long queue to perform this act. A decision was subsequently taken to allow time for this in the break between *Minchah* and *Ne'ilah*, rather than have the effect of the awesome *Ne'ilah* service marred.

A SICILIAN CUSTOM

973. Do we hear of that practice of kissing the scrolls on Yom Kippur from any other historical source?

Indeed, we hear of it from the diary of the distinguished Italian rabbinic scholar, author of the classic commentary to the Mishnah, Rabbi Obadiah da Bertinoro (1450–1520).

He describes the Jewish community of Palermo, the chief town in Sicily, with a Jewish community of some 850 families. Obadiah spent Yom Kippur and Sukkot at Palermo on his travels to the holy land and records a practice that would send shivers down the spines of some present-day Orthodox rabbis:

> I have noticed the following customs: On the evening of Yom Kippur and Hoshanah Rabbah, at the conclusion of the evening service, the wardens open the doors of the Ark, and remain on duty by them throughout the night. Women then arrive, in family groups, to prostrate themselves and to kiss the

---

2. Dobrinsky, *op. cit.*, p. 339.

Scrolls. Entering by one door and leaving by the opposite door, this ritual continues throughout the entire night.[3]

AFGHANISTANI CUSTOMS

974. We have referred above to the *mitzvah* of eating on the day before Yom Kippur. How seriously did the Jews of Afghanistan take this tradition?

For Afghanistani traditions, I have the benefit of a first-hand report from my congregant, Mr. David Moradoff, who lived in Herat, one of the larger cities of Afghanistan, from 1931 until 1957.

He states that this *mitzvah* was taken very seriously and that some families took as many as seven meals, duly spaced out, throughout that day. It was traditional to eat fish in the morning.

975. Did the Afghanistani tradition observe the ceremony of *Kapparot* on the day before Yom Kippur?

They did, indeed. Their preference was for white chickens: a hen for each female member of the family and a cock for the males. After waving the chickens around the head of each person, and reciting the *Zeh chalifati* formula ("This is instead of me; this is in place of me; this is my atonement, etc."), they would take the chickens to the *shochet* to be slaughtered. They were then cleaned and given to the poor, but the intestines were first thrown on the roofs of the houses for the birds to eat, in the belief that, just as they were merciful in providing food for the birds, so would God have mercy upon them.

976. Did Afghan Jewry observe the custom of *malkot* (symbolic flagellation) that we have already referred to (See Question 696)?

They certainly did. It was not restricted, as in other places, to the specially pious, but was an established eve of Yom Kippur practice. The person receiving the lashes would strip to the waist. He would bend over a pole, facing toward the north, and place his head between his arms. His hands would be tied to the pole, and the rabbi of the community would administer the lashes to the man's back, one lash for each word of the verse *Vehu rachum,* which the rabbi would recite aloud. The verse contains thirteen words, so that its thrice recitation would provide the required thirty-nine lashes.

The strap was made from the hides of a cow and an ass, to recall the verse: "The ox knoweth its owner, and the ass its master's crib; But Israel doth not know, my people doth not consider" (Isaiah 1:2).

The man's hands were then released from the pole, after which the rabbi would pronounce: "Thy sin is pardoned, and thy iniquity atoned." The man would then kiss

3. Eisenstein, J. D. (1926). *Otzar Ha-Masa'ot.* New York: J. D. Eisenstein, p. 108.

the hands of the rabbi, who would respond by blessing him to be inscribed in the book of life. Before leaving, the man would give the rabbi a donation for charitable disbursement. Having completed that ritual, the man would hasten to immerse himself in the *mikveh* (ritual bath), situated in the courtyard of the synagogue.

977. Did the Jews of Afghanistan have any superstitions in relation to Yom Kippur?

They were very superstitious with regard to the special Yom Kippur lights. In the words of Mr. Moradoff:

Each family would kindle a few lights in the synagogue, in addition to those kindled at home. One light was a memorial for departed relatives; and the others were for the living.

The lights comprised a wick fueled by sufficient paraffin to burn until the end of Yom Kippur. Now, if the lights burned brightly and cleanly until the end of the fast, it was taken as an augury for a happy year ahead. If, God forbid, they smoked or the flame was feeble or spluttering or went out prematurely, then it was taken as a bad omen for the coming year, and the family would be deeply anxious. However, if the family had lit two or three lights, and only one went out, then they were not too perturbed!

978. Did they have any other "beliefs" of this kind, associated with a Yom Kippur ritual?

They believed that any rose water in which the priests had washed their hands was efficacious in curing barrenness and heart ailment. Mr. Moradoff recalls that the husbands of such barren women would bring a china bowl of rose water and ask the priests to wash their hands with it a second time, after the official ritual washing. At the termination of the fast, the women would drink the rose water from the bowl.

979. Was the honor of holding the *Kol Nidre* scrolls invested with any particular significance by that community?

It certainly was; and Mr. Moradoff has good reason to remember, nostalgically, his late father's eagerness to acquire that honor—and the community's reciprocal desire that he should do so!

Seven Scrolls were brought out of the Ark for *Kol Nidre*, and the honor of bringing each of them out was sold by auction. The first scroll out was the most expensive of all, and my father used to endeavor to purchase it on most years. Being a Cohen and a leader of the community, people were happy for him to do so, providing he paid a worthy price for it.

I remember that the highest price to pay for that honor was to donate a large barrel of paraffin to light the synagogue lamps. In those days, oil was in short supply, so everyone was happy once they had my father's guarantee. Father had an import-export business. He exported Karakul sheepskins and wool to

Russia and imported sugar and oil from there, hence his ability to provide "the lamps for lighting the synagogue," which is regarded as a great merit.

After the auction, the seven scrolls were brought out of the Ark and carried to the *Bimah*. The first scroll was termed the *Sefer Kol Nidre* (the *Kol Nidre* scroll), and the one who acquired the honor of carrying that one would stand on the *Chazan*'s right for the recitation of that composition. Before returning the scrolls, at the end of *Kol Nidre*, a special *Miy Shebeirakh* was recited by the rabbi in honor of those who had been elected to be the *Chatanim* on *Simchat Torah*.

On arriving home after the *Kol Nidre* service, they would read the entire book of Psalms and the eight chapters of Mishnah *Yoma*. Some people stayed all night in synagogue, reading the Psalms. In the early hours, they would sing Solomon ibn Gabirol's famous philosophical poem, *Keter Malkhut,* which narrates the attributes and the great power and glory of the Creator.

980. Did Afghani Jewry have any other special Yom Kippur customs and unusual "beliefs"?

Each year, in time for Yom Kippur, a special collection was made for lamps for illuminating the synagogues. With the money collected, a large piece of pure wax was purchased. This was melted in a large pot of copper, and the boiling wax was then poured over a thick wick about 1 meter or more in length, especially made for this particular *mitzvah*. It was poured many times, layer upon layer, until it became a very thick and long candle.

On the eve of Yom Kippur, this special candle was lit in the synagogue and would burn for the duration of the fast. At the conclusion of Yom Kippur, it was brought ceremoniously onto the *bimah* to be used for *havdalah*. Everyone tried to retrieve a piece of the wax that dripped from this candle to take home. Not only did it have a pleasant aroma, but, more significantly, it was regarded as a *segulah*, a protection against mishap and a good omen for prosperity. It was regarded as particularly effective in protecting against miscarriage and in securing an easy birth.

MOROCCAN CUSTOMS

981. Do Moroccan traditions have much in common with the above Afghanistani practices?

They have a great deal in common. Among the customs that they share are (i) the observance of the *Kapparot* ceremony, (ii) the *Hatarat nedarim* ("Annulment of vows") ritual, (iii) the eating of much food on the eve of the fast (the Moroccans would, of course, devour a great deal of couscous), (iv) the remaining behind in synagogue all night and the recitation of psalms, Mishnah *Yoma* and Gabirol's *Keter Malkhut,* (v) the absence of any tradition requiring full prostration during *Aleinu* and the *Musaf Avodah* section.

982. Did the womenfolk observe the Yom Kippur in synagogue as a day of prayer?

They did not. However, towards evening, they would suddenly crowd into the synagogues to hear the sounding of the shofar, "which, to them, constitutes the essential feature of the day."[4]

983. Are there any unique Moroccan practices associated with Yom Kippur?

The *Yom Simchat Kohen* ("Day of the Priest's celebration") is unique to Moroccan Jewry. This is based on the tradition, related in the Mishnah[5] and recorded in the *Avodah* composition, that the High Priest would make a party for all his friends after he had emerged safe from his hazardous entry into the Holy of Holies on Yom Kippur. It is celebrated on the following day.

A TURKISH TRADITION

984. Were there any special traditions practiced by Turkish Jewry on the eve of Yom Kippur?

They were particular to invite poor people to their pre-fast banquet, and strangers who were visiting the synagogue for Yom Kippur were singled out for especially warm hospitality. This was because of their apprehension that the visitor might be some great *tzaddik*, or even Elijah himself, in disguise. They would not want to invite heavenly censure by being remiss in the great *mitzvah* of hospitality on this night of all nights!

985. Are there any other unusual Turkish customs?

During the course of Yom Kippur, the *shamash* goes around the synagogue pouring out rose water or tobacco into their hands. It is for the same reason that in small Ashkenazi *shtibls* it used to be the practice for members to swap brands of snuff. This is in order to make up the 100 blessings that we are required to make each day. Throughout the year, we do this comfortably through the meals and drinks that we have throughout the day, and in the 19 blessings recited at each service, and repeated at *Shachrit* and *Minchah*. On Yom Kippur, notwithstanding all the prayers, we are still a few blessings short of the 100. And these were traditionally made up by inhaling aromatic spices or plants and reciting the prescribed blessings: For spices, *Borei miynei besamim*; for plants, *Borei isbei besamim*.

---

4. Dobrinsky, *op. cit.*, p. 341.

5. Mishnah *Yoma* 7:4.

A BULGARIAN PIETISTIC PRACTICE

986. Did Bulgarian Jewry introduce any unique pre-Yom Kippur gesture?

Dobrinsky reports that "in Bulgaria, some of the extremely pious merchants would give the keys to their shops to non-Jewish acquaintances in order to rid themselves on Yom Kippur day of everything which could remind them of everyday anxiety or material interests."[6] There is clearly a parallel here with the practice of handing over the keys of *chametz* stores sold to gentiles before Pesach.

THE *BENE ISRAEL* OF INDIA

987. How did the *Bene Israel*, with their distinctive Jewish rites, come to India in the first place?

The *Bene Israel* have a tradition that their ancestors reached the coast of India as survivors of a shipwreck. They are unclear as to which country the survivors came from, but are certain that they hailed from Jewish stock and possibly from the Ten Lost Tribes of northern Israel. They were the original tribes of Israel that were taken into captivity to Assyria where they assimilated and were "lost." It is still a matter of scholarly dispute when and how they actually came to India.

988. In what way are they distinct from the mainstream Jewish community of India?

Mainstream Indian Jewry is actually a misnomer, because it suggests an indigenous Jewry, as opposed to the more recent incomers. The very opposite is the case. Mainstream Jewry—in the sense of those who hailed from outside countries that inherited the normative halakhic traditions—first arrived in India toward the end of the eighteenth and beginning of the nineteenth centuries when immigrants from Iraq began arriving in Bombay and Calcutta. They achieved maximum numbers, of about 6,500, in the 1940's.[7] On arrival, they discovered two other distinct "Jewish" groups: the so-called Cochin Jews, who inhabited the Indian state of *Kerala*, and the *Bene Israel* of the Konkan area of the *Maharashtra* region. These two separate groups had lived in India, in peace and tranquillity, highly respected and immune from anti-Semitism for centuries, possibly millenia.

The Cochin community possesses a charter, written in the ancient Tamil language, granted by a Hindu ruler of *Malabar*, and inscribed on two copper plates, kept under guard in the Paradesi synagogue. Thought to date back to antiquity, it is now regarded as no earlier than the middle of the tenth century. Unlike the *Bene Israel*, Cochin Jewry maintained close contact with Jewish communities outside

6. Dobrinsky, *op. cit.*, p. 343.
7. Isenberg, S. B. (1988). *India's Bene Israel*. Bombay: Popular Prakashan, p. viii.

India, developed their own liturgical traditions and preserved, copied, and studied halakhic treatises relating especially to Sabbath, festivals, and dietary laws.

The *Bene Israel*, on the other hand, possessed no books or scrolls of the Torah, neither did they have any tradition of Hebrew liturgy. They nevertheless observed Shabbat and would kindle no lights on that day. They circumcised their sons on the eighth day after birth and ate only fish with fins and scales.

989. So which festivals do the *Bene Israel* observe?

Throughout the ages, they observed only those that were in vogue in Palestine during the time of the Second Temple.[8] However, a certain David Rahabi, an Egyptian charismatic and persuasive missionary for Rabbinic Judaism, visited the community at a time that is variously placed at the beginning of the eleventh century, the fifteenth century, or the seventeenth century, and he initiated a religious revival and persuaded them to take on board the remaining Jewish festivals and observances.

Before his arrival they kept only six festivals: (i) *Naviacha San* (the New Year), (ii) *Darfalnicha San* (the Day of Atonement), (iii) *Shila San* (the High Priest's celebration. See Question 992), (iv) *Khiriacha San* (Feast of the Ingathering), (v) *Holicha San* (Feast of Esther), and (vi) *Anashi Dhakacha San* (Passover).

990. What was the significance of *Naviacha San*, the New Year, for the *Bene Israel*?

Interestingly, they observed it as a day when man is judged by God for his deeds over the past year. Whether the *Bene Israel* originated from the period of the Assyrian captivity (721 B.C.E.), or even much later, from the period of Second Commonwealth, their explanation of the New Year—for which no reason is given in the Torah—nevertheless provides corroboration of the antiquity of Judaism's oral tradition, which has always explained Rosh Hashanah in that way.[9]

991. What was the significance of *Darfalnicha San*, the Day of Atonement, for the *Bene Israel*?

The name *Darfalnicha San*, in Marathi, means "holiday of the closing of the doors," and was so called because on this day the community stayed in their homes, with the doors closed and locked, and observed the fast, dressed in white robes. They viewed it in the traditional manner as the final day of judgment or acquittal.

The association with our *Ne'ilah* (literally, "closing") is quite compelling, for the full name of this service is *Ne'ilat She'arim*, "closing of the gates." The precise sense of this term was a matter of dispute and is variously explained in the Talmud as referring either to the service recited at sundown, at the time of the closing of the gates of the Temple, or to the closing of the heavenly gates.

---

8. Isenberg, *op. cit.*, p. 4.
9. *Ta'anit* 26b.

It is tempting, however, to think that the *Bene Israel* borrowed that term, and, after translating it into Marathi, gave it their own interpretation, applying it to the entire Day of Atonement. Indeed, the very origin of their custom of staying indoors may have arisen only as a result of the explanation they read into the name *Ne'ilah*.

992. What is the significance of their *Shila San* (High Priest's celebration)?

This is a day of festivity, almsgiving, and entertaining, observed on the day after the Day of Atonement. Its association with the High Priest is probably on account of the tradition that the High Priest would throw a party for his family and friends after emerging safely from his awesome ordeal of having to enter the Holy of Holies on the Day of Atonement. The *Bene Israel* may have preserved for us here a relic of a more widespread holiday and celebration in ancient Judaea than we have information about (See Question 983).

993. What is the precise meaning of *Shila San*?

Shila means "stale" in Marathi and refers to the foods eaten on this day. No cooking or baking was permitted on the Day of Atonement itself, so that on this third day after its preparation it hardly tasted very appetizing. This clearly did not impair their spirit of celebration on this day.

994. Did they celebrate any other holy days associated with this period of the year?

They did, indeed. The *Khiriacha San*, Festival of the Ingathering, sounds very much as if it corresponds with our Sukkot festival, 2 weeks after the New Year. But this is not the case. The *Bene Israel* did not, in fact, observe the Sukkot (or the *Shavuot*) festival. This agriculturally significant festival, to express thanksgiving for the ingathering of the harvest, was actually observed by them on the day immediately after the New Year, which corresponds with the Jewish fast day of *Tzom Gedaliah*.

995. How was *Khiriacha San* observed?

"Their observance consisted of burning incense and reciting the *Shema* over an offering made of *khir* (basic ingredients: rice or wheat, milk or coconut milk, sugar, cardamom), and then partaking of the concoction."[10]

996. Did they have any tradition of reciting *Selichot* in the period preceding Rosh Hashanah?

Not only did they recite *Selichot*, but they commenced their recitation at the beginning of the month of Elul, and continued to recite them each day before dawn for the entire month prior to Rosh Hashanah. They invested this period with such

---

10. Kehimkar, H. S. Quoted in Isenberg, *op. cit.*, p. 5.

importance, as a spiritual preparation for the High Holy Days, that they even observed the *Selichot* period as a month of semi-fasting, eating only an evening meal after nightfall. This was clearly not part of their native heritage and dates back only to the nineteenth-century religious revival that was initiated through the influence of the Iraqi immigrants. Some writers have suggested that this month of fasting was as a result of the influence of their neighboring Indian Muslims' observance of the month-long fast of Ramadan.[11] This practice has now largely died out. During this month, new clothes were made for all members of the family to wear on Rosh Hashanah, and the houses were given a fresh coating of whitewash.[12]

997. Have we any information regarding how their *Selichot* (propitiatory prayers) were performed?

H. S. Kehimkar reports that while uttering their *Selichot* each day, they would sound the shofar three times. They also adopted the rabbinic practice of not sounding the ram's horn on the morning preceding Rosh Hashanah. On that day, they recited the *Hatarat nedarim* (absolution of vows) ritual, in a manner identical with that practiced by mainstream Judaism. At the conclusion of that ritual, they kiss one another's hands before returning home. There, the kissing of hands is continued by the other members of the family.[13]

998. Are there any other unique *Bene-Israel* practices?

While, in addition to *Selichot*, they absorbed some other mainstream Jewish practices, such as *Tashlikh* and *Kapparot*, there are also some native traditions that are of interest, particularly their avoidance of any contact with gentiles throughout Yom Kippur. Although their native tradition was to stay at home, praying and fasting, for the entire day of Yom Kippur (See Question 991), yet, as a result of Iraqi influence, synagogue attendance gradually became the norm for most. Now, if they had to ride to the synagogue, they would rather pay a high price for a private car to take them than use public transport, which might cause them to brush inadvertently against a gentile.

Another of their ancient pre-Yom Kippur practices was to annoint their bodies with homemade coconut oil, which was then removed with a certain kind of flour before bathing it away, first with hot, then with cold, water. They would then dress in white robes and repair to the synagogue in the afternoon for a special *Hashkavah* (memorial service) and a *Malidah* (food-offering ceremony), which invoked the spirits of three generations of departed relatives to join them for the duration of the fast. Their proximity, it was believed, would prompt them to intercede on behalf of their family for a good year ahead.[14]

---

11. Isenberg, *op. cit.*, p. 118.
12. Kehimkar, H. S. (1937). *The History of the Bene-Israel of India.* Tel Aviv: Dayag Press Ltd., p. 119.
13. Kehimkar, *loc. cit.*
14. Kehimkar, *op. cit.*, pp. 18–19.

They tried to avoid speaking any unnecessary words on Yom Kippur, especially anything unworthy. They did no manual work on that day, and they had a long-standing arrangement with their Hindu neighbors in their villages that the latter would come and milk their cows for them.[15]

THE IRAQI JEWS OF INDIA

999. Did the mainstream Jews of India, who hailed originally from Iraq, have any special Yom Kippur practices?

I am indebted, once again, to my congregant, Mr. Edward Ezra, for his reminiscences:

On the eve of Yom Kippur, my father would come home from market with several live hens and cockerels, and proceed to perform the *kapparot* ritual (See Questions 682–688). He would twirl the squawking birds around our heads—hens for females and cockerels for males. What a commotion! They would then be given as gifts to the poor Jews of Bycallah, a suburb of Bombay.

The meal before the fast was usually light, and a typical dish would be *dal* (lentils) and rice. From the age of 8 to 11, my sisters and I were encouraged to fast half the day, that is until 2:00 P.M.

I remember quite vividly, at the end of the fast, some of the congregants would refresh themselves by splashing their faces with fragrant rose water dispensed from a long silver container with perforations at its top end.

We would break our fast with a kind of almond milk shake, made of ground almonds, sugar, cardamom, and milk.[16]

THE JEWS OF THE SUDAN

1000. Do we have any traditions regarding how the Jews of the Sudan celebrated Yom Kippur?

I am grateful to Mr. Zaki Dweck for his personal reminiscences:

He informs me that preparations for the day began as soon as the slaughterer arrived, usually around 3:00 A.M., in the night preceeding Yom Kippur, to slaughter the chickens for *kapparot*. This would be followed by *Selichot* in synagogue, which commenced around 4:00 A.M. They would auction the *mitzvot* of taking out the scrolls for *Kol Nidre*, which went to the highest bidder.

---

15. Isenberg, *op. cit.*, p. 221.
16. Written communication of Mr. Edward Ezra (October 31, 1996).

Although the Jews of the Sudan were not particularly observant, no one would have had the temerity to drive the long distances from the towns and villages to the only existing synagogue, which was in *Khartoum.* They would arrive, therefore, in good time for the festival, bringing their beds with them, and would camp out overnight in the grounds of the synagogue, it being always warm at that time of the year.

Indeed, the heat during the day was so intense that most people suffered badly from the effects of not being able to drink. At the end of the fast, a buffet was provided, with people quaffing as much liquid as their bladders could absorb![17]

A PERSONAL POSTSCRIPT

1001. What are your feelings on completing 1001 Questions on the subject of the High Holy Days?

Great relief! But more, a sense of wonderment that, for all the long nights of study and research—burning the midnight oil in order to complete this work in 10 months and immersing myself in the letter and spirit of this festival—yet, none of that total intellectual absorption produced anything like the spiritual elation that surges through me during, and as a result of, the authentic and potent experience that those unique days provide.

How accurate is the adage that "Judaism has to be caught, not taught." There is no substitute for that awesome, fervent, and profoundly optimistic spirit that is generated by the collective urgency of Israel at prayer for 25 hours with absolutely nothing else to distract or preoccupy. That spirit cannot be recreated or meaningfully described, even amid the tranquillity of one's study at midnight or in the early hours. It is generated by, and reserved exclusively for, the special time, the special place, and the special people. It is created by the mystic harmonies of the music of their souls.

It is not surprising that the great Rudolph Otto happened upon his concept of the *numinous* only after a visit to a synagogue on Yom Kippur, where he felt overwhelmed by the specially sacred character of this day and its ability to vouchsafe a sense of other-worldliness and divine reality to those caught up in its spirit. And it is not surprising that such a Yom Kippur visit—paid reluctantly by the disaffected Franz Rosenzweig, in 1913, as he was about to embrace Christianity—changed the entire course of his life and his philosophy.

In that synagogue, he discovered his Jewish soul. He found himself aroused, purified, and spiritually elevated by the compelling spirit of Yom Kippur and its capacity to talk to the soul of the Jew. He awoke there to the limited power of reason, and to the place of God in human history and destiny. He knew then that the synagogue alone was truly God's house and that without prayer—without the

---

17. Oral communication of Mr. Zaki Dweck (November 4, 1996).

"I-Thou" relationship, as brilliantly expounded by his friend and collaborator, Martin Buber—there was nothing of any lasting significance, indeed no reality in life.

These are my feelings on completing this humble offering. At best, this book may inform and excite interest. But it is, ultimately, merely "the vestibule which leads into the great banqueting hall."[18] One cannot be satisfied remaining in the vestibule. Go forth now, and make your presence felt in the banqueting hall. And enjoy the great spiritual banquet!

---

18. Mishnah *Avot* 4:16.

Index

About the Author

Rabbi Jeffrey M. Cohen has distinguished himself in the field of religious affairs as a broadcaster, lecturer, writer, and reviewer. A graduate of Jews' College, London, and the Yeshivot of Manchester and Gateshead, Rabbi Cohen gained a first class honors degree and a master's degree in philosophy from London University and a Ph.D. from Glasgow University. He is the author of eleven books, the most recent being *Prayer and Penitence: A Commentary on the High Holy Day Machzor, Following the Synagogue Service*, and *1,001 Questions and Answers on Pesach*, as well as over 300 articles. Rabbi Cohen currently serves as rabbi of the Stanmore Synagogue in London, England, one of the largest congregations in Europe, and is a member of the Chief Rabbi's cabinet. He and his wife, Gloria, have four children and six grandchildren.